FRESH TRADITIONS

FRESH TRADITIONS

Classic Dishes for a Contemporary Lifestyle

JORJ MORGAN

Cumberland House Publishing
Nashville, Tennessee

Published by
Cumberland House Publishing, Inc.
431 Harding Industrial Drive
Nashville, TN 37211

Cover design by Karen Phillips
Text design by Julie Pitkin
Illustrations by JulesRulesDesign

Library of Congress Cataloging-in-Publication Data

Morgan, Jorj
  Fresh traditions : classic dishes for a contemporary lifestyle / Jorj Morgan.-- 1st ed.
      p. cm.
  Includes index.
  ISBN 1-58182-400-9
  1. Cookery. I. Title.
  TX714.M677 2004
  641.5--dc22

                           2004015564

Printed in the United States of America
1 2 3 4 5 6 7 — 10 09 08 07 06 05 04

Dedication

For My Boys

To Morgo, together we continue to build loving, fresh traditions.

To Treyzers, Chris and Jon Boy,
when it's your turn to share traditions and create loving families of your own,
we'll be here.

Table of Contents

Acknowledgements   9

Introduction   11

CHAPTER 1: Food Traditions Made Simple   13

CHAPTER 2: Bacon, Eggs and More   19

CHAPTER 3: Muffins, Breads and Bakery Goodies   43

CHAPTER 4: Soups and Veggie Salads   71

CHAPTER 5: Topless, Grilled and Panini Sandwiches   103

CHAPTER 6: Skewers and Tostada Lite Meals   129

CHAPTER 7: Appys, Snacks and Nibbles   147

CHAPTER 8: Pasta, Rice, and Polenta Bowls   175

CHAPTER 9: It's all about the Veggies   195

CHAPTER 10: Shellfish and Fish Prepared Swimmingly   227

CHAPTER 11: Chicken, Turkey and the Occasional Duck   255

CHAPTER 12: Beef, Pork, Lamb and Veal Meals   279

CHAPTER 13: Dastardly Desserts   313

CHAPTER 14: Recipes for Livin' the Good Life   353

Index   367

Acknowledgements

This book is a labor of love—not just mine, but of so many fellow foodies and culinary cohorts, all eager to share their secrets for living a blissfully satiated life.

First and foremost, I must thank Nancy Roe and Emily Smith of Green Cay Produce in Boynton Beach, Florida. My experience in joining their community-supported farm is the inspiration for this book. I implore you to learn all you can about community-supported agriculture and the professionals who make it happen. For more information check out http://www.nal.usda.gov/afsic/csa.

To Ron Pitkin, who continues to believe in me, thank you for your confidence and the support of your fine, fine Cumberland team, especially Julie Pitkin, the best editor in the world, and Stacie and Chris Bauerle, a dynamic public relations and marketing duo, as well as the proud parents of son Joshua.

To my gal pals, who are infinitely forgiving of my missed dates and tardiness at meetings; our friendship continues to provide me with the most FUN times both in and out of town. Thanks to Doreen Koenig, Sharon Stiles, and Cindy Greenberg. Best pals make the world a better place.

Now on to my recipe testers—what a group! You are diverse, creative, generous and devoted! I can just about guarantee the readers success with every recipe attempted in this book because at least one member of this terrific group has tested and perfected each one. Most of my recipe testers evaluated recipes for my previous two books and, as old hats at the process, are getting really, really good at it! Many went above and beyond the call of duty, testing at least two, if not three and four recipes a week.

A very special "thank-you" to Sharon Murrah, a longtime resident of Fort Lauderdale, who obviously enjoys cooking and entertaining friends and family enough to single-handedly test the majority of the recipes in every chapter. Her sense of tradition adds a special insight, which brought about many savory enhancements to the recipes she perfected.

Thanks to Theresa Shultz of Chicago, Illinois, an event planner and freelance food writer, who has a passion to learn all there is to know about food. She writes a newsletter, aptly named "Love a Fare." A new tester, Theresa, set the bar by braving subzero weather to test out the grilled corn recipes. Now, that's dedication!

Thanks to Amy Kendall of Franklin, Tennessee. A biochemist and mom to $1\frac{2}{3}$ children, she managed to modify all of the recipes she tested for a pregnant palate and an extremely picky three-year old.

Thanks to Diana Shelton, an avid golfer and triumphant hostess, who is also a resident of Fort Lauderdale. Sweet and sly, Diana made a habit of serving tested recipes to her hubby, Steve, and their dinner guests by night, and then by day whipped their butts on the golf course.

Thanks to my dear pal Linda O'Bryon, a national television news executive who lives in South Florida. She modified her recipe choices to suit her hubby, Mike (who then purchased her more and more kitchen appliances, in the hope she would keep on cooking!).

Thanks to Adrienne Lee of Las Cruces, New Mexico, who kept me on schedule with her Saturday shopping days. She e-mailed me every Friday, reminding me that she needed her new recipes before heading off to the grocery store. She also prepared about a million variations of one recipe in order to get it just right—you guess which one!

Thanks to another new member of our testing team, Liz Bray, of Leave It To Liz in

Benton, Arkansas. A former kindergarten teacher (for 21 years), she switched careers and became a certified personal chef. As a tester, she not only experimented with new recipes but solicited opinions from her vast number of clients with their diverse requirements.

Thanks to Gail Jordan of Raleigh, North Carolina, a writer and freelance special events coordinator. She and her sports marketing husband, Dean, are the supremely happy parents of future Oscar/Tony/Grammy winner Carly (12) and future baseball hall-of-famer Adam (5). If the kids gave the dish a thumbs up—trust me, you will too!

To Janet Jordan, supermom to three great kids, super volunteer to a dozen or so organizations in Broward County, Florida, and recent supercook, utilizing all her newly discovered culinary skills.

Thanks to longtime pals, Sherry and co-chef, Jon Hine of Oakland, Florida, who sent digital pictures to beautifully demonstrate their test results, while providing suggestions for over-the-top dish presentation.

Thanks to Terry Maly of Olathe, Kansas, who is a part-time employee and a full-time cooking enthusiast and recipe collector.

Thanks to Veronica Boyd of Glen Allen, Virginia, a full-time mom of an active six-year-old boy, and a full-time human resources consultant. Her hobbies include cooking, reading, ebaying and tap dancing.

Thanks to Kim Churches of Boca Raton, Florida, who works in the non-profit fundraising field and loves cooking and entertaining as a way to relax after a long day.

Thanks to Sharron Jackson, a good pal who recently transplanted her beautiful family to Georgia and subsequently felt the need to test every remotely Southern recipe.

Thanks to Sandra Shu and Margaret Donkerbrook (both friends of Trey's), of Alexandria, Virginia and to Mary Ellen Lemm (another of Trey's friends) from Plano, Texas. Thanks to Teresa Loney of Alexandria, Virginia, Tery Wysocki, a research scientist and mother of three from Flemington, New Jersey, Slee Arnold (daughter of good pal Jan Crocker) of Raleigh, North Carolina, and Dick Bigelow, who also hails from Plano, Texas.

A special thanks to the rest of the Fort Lauderdale contingent of testers, including restaurant owner and tennis partner Louise Proffer, Rose Dreyfus, Mary Beth Mahan, longtime pal Mary Dwors, Susan Holden, and successful hostess and realtor Lucy Weber.

Thanks to the BEST website designer and marketing consultant, my pal Rachael Bender. She helps me keep in touch with my readers.

Thanks and more thanks to my assistants, Gela Garcia, the wheel that keeps our family rolling, and to Jennifer Russon, who painstakingly read and re-read every word in this book.

The cover photo art comes from Robert and Sheila Hurth of Tiffany Photography in Fort Lauderdale, Florida. These guys are really, really good!

Finally, to the most important people in my life, a gigantic THANK YOU to my family for allowing me to host so many of our special occasions and for being the true inspiration for all of our fresh traditions. Thanks to exceptional hubby, Morgo, and the loves of my life: sons Trey, Chris and Jon. Thanks to grandparents George and Mary Jane Morgan; my always-there-for-me brother, Rich, and kids Richi III, Lindsay and Patrick; sister Beth with her special daughter, niecey Meggie-Mo and nephew John; Morgan family members Jimmy and Susie with their kids, Kimberly, Peter and little Laura;, and to those who have meant so much to all of us and inspired most of the classic dishes in this book, Irene Seeley, George and Marie Cohen, John and Mary Magner and Dick and Re Re Magner.

Introduction

We are bombarded with advertising images that promise if you purchase specific products, you will be rewarded with the comforting bliss of the traditional family experience. One television commercial in particular captures the perfect Ozzie and Harriet 50's-style family gathering around the kitchen table for a calm, quiet breakfast. Dad's nose is buried in the paper. Junior is sitting in his impeccably clean high chair, spooning oatmeal into his mouth. Apron-clad Mom is flipping pancakes with one hand, offering pre-teen daughter Jane, a glass of orange juice with the other, and turning the bacon strips with her toes. Cue Jane who smiles, almost curtseys and says, "Good morning, Mother." Then, in the blink of an eye, we flash-forward to the same set of characters ala Ozzy Osbourne and gang. Loud music blares, while Dad is still reading the paper. But now he is also packing up his laptop and talking on his cell phone. While a flat screen blazes in the background, Junior is running around pretending to be a super hero, spewing oatmeal as his weapon of choice. Pierced and tattooed Jane disdainfully demands her glass of juice, while Mom looks to the heavens for assistance. Well, ain't this the truth—at least in advertising!

As a society, we yearn for the simpler life, the shelter and calm of the family kitchen, the black and whiteness of the backsplash and countertops, a Sunday night roasted chicken with mashed potatoes and silky gravy made from strained pan drippings. Yet, we find it tough to blend the soothing traditions of yesterday into the chaotic contemporary life we lead today. There just never seems to be enough time.

Fresh Traditions: Classic Dishes for a Contemporary Lifestyle is designed to blend the traditions of the simpler life we hunger for with the fast-paced schedule of today's family (picture Ozzie cooking supper with Ozzy!). Here you will find thorough, well written, and simple-to-follow recipes for classic dishes in tandem with their contemporary counterparts. A double dose of comfort, and the safety of mom's kitchen, can be yours whether you cling to her recipes or prefer a more modern approach to cooking.

Each classic recipe contains anecdotal information about the roots of the dish as well as reminiscences of simpler days and less hectic lives. Traditional preparation is explained, yet modern cooking techniques are applied. For example, Osso Buco, an Italian dish made of veal shanks braised with olive oil, wine, beef stock and vegetables is prepared using the convenience of a slow cooker in place of a stove-top pot, allowing the cook to take leave while the dish simmers to completion.

Each updated recipe is mindful of new ingredients, healthy choices, and quick food preparation, while upholding its roots within the classic dish.

Both the traditional and the contemporary recipes are modernized using the latest in culinary innovation. For example, bread-making time is shortened by the use of a bread machine. Braised stews are done in a slow cooker rather than a Dutch oven. Vegetables are sliced with a mandoline, grated with a microplane zester, or pulsed in a food processor to save chopping time. A blender is used to emulsify salad dressings rather than whisking; an emersion blender is used in place of a food mill. Pre-packaged fresh ingredients are used to cut down on food preparation, allowing the exhausted cook to buy a fresh-from-the-deli rotisserie chicken for use in a traditional chicken a la king casserole in just minutes.

Making use of simple ingredient substitutions, like olive oil in place of butter, produces a lighter, healthier contemporary recipe. However, taste is prioritized ahead of calorie reduction. Portions and balanced meal plans are offered in place of extreme ingredient replacement, like using fruit paste in place of butter in a cake recipe. Rather than reduce the calorie content (and the pleasure) of a great tasting cake, I suggest making portion-controlled cupcakes with a crumble topping in place of cream cheese frosting.

The recipes in the book are paired—the classic and the contemporary, allowing you to prepare the dish of your choice—traditional or updated. You will find traditional fare like Incredibly Easy Eggs Benedict updated to Eggs Benedict with Smoked Salmon , Cajun Hollandaise, and Fried Oyster Garnish, as well as Quiche Lorraine modernized to a savory Inspired Onion and Bacon Tart, or a second choice of Sausage and Mushroom Strata. The bread machine transforms Irish Soda Bread to glazed Bimini Bread with minimal preparation time. Classic Banana Nut Bread is transformed into mini loaves of Orange Coconut Glazed Banana Bread offering smaller portions and a tropical flavor twist.

Comfort food favorites, like Cream of Roasted Tomato Soup with Grilled Cheese Croutons, morph into the updated Chilled Roasted Tomato Soup with Cream Cheese Pesto Swirl and Pine Nut Garnish. Classic Caesar Salad made tableside is updated to Romaine Salad with Ten Cloves of Garlic Dressing. Spicy Potato Salad gets a new twist in the Grilled Potato Salad preparation. The recipe for traditional Mexican inspired Beef and Bean Nacho Casserole served with fresh salsa and guacamole is placed side by side with Seared Tuna Nachos with Wasabi Cream Sauce and Hot Mango Ketchup. And there are so many more to choose from!

Fresh Traditions is a timely cookbook written for you, the foodie who wants more out of life through boundless food experiences. It is a book that is a celebration of a lifestyle satiated with excellent meals, balanced with a good dose of dietary common sense, and filled with solutions for today's cook. It is a smart, conversational guide to living a contented and rewarding life through stress-free food preparation.

Fresh Traditions meets the needs of passionate, health-minded cooks by offering over 300 well-tested recipes, which are heavily interspersed with relevant ingredient information. Learning that all shrimp are flash frozen is an excellent invitation for you, the cook in the trenches, to buy frozen rather than cooked shrimp, to store for an everyday quick dish. Learning how to handle, cut and roast spaghetti squash allows you, the home chef, to easily substitute this nutritious veggie for pasta, perhaps fooling your household's picky eater. Learning the difference between imported Australian lamb and larger domestic lamb allows you to take advantage of special pricing at the grocer. The recipes in this book are generously peppered with sidebars offering cooking variations, nutritional tips and relevant expert purveyor advice, allowing the art of cooking to become less stressful, more pleasurable, and a respite in our time-constrained existence.

I invite you to peruse the book and find your favorite classic or contemporary recipe. When you are making the dish, remember the good times associated with food preparation and setting the table. As the dish cooks, smell the memories. With the first taste of the dish, surround yourself with family and friends and tell the stories of earlier days. Enjoy the pleasure of food while creating your own fresh traditions.

Chapter I

Food Traditions Made Simple

It's funny how traditions handed down by grandmothers to mothers, from fathers to sons, get reinvented by the demands of a hectic schedule, yet maintain the integrity of the custom. My mother-in-law, Mary Jane, proved just this point to me.

Years ago, in the midst of a full work week, while raising her two boys, my mother-in-law had a Friday shopping tradition. Her first stop was the bakery to purchase fresh bread, sugary glazed doughnuts and must-have gooey butter coffee cake from "The Hill" district in Saint Louis. The next stop was the butcher for specially cut, thick rib eye steaks or veal shanks, depending on his weekly special. Next she was off to the farmer's market where she looked for the ripest tomatoes, most perfect eggplant and armloads of leafy lettuces. Finally, she visited the fishmonger to choose his most recent catch for Friday's supper and shrimp or lobster (if the guests were special) for her Saturday night dinner party. Arriving home, she watched her two sons crash over each other, struggling to see which one could help unload the most parcels. The reason why? Because the winner got the first pick of gooey treats from the white cardboard bakery boxes, affirming the adage, "the way to a boy's heart is through his sugar gene!"

Hearing my husband recount this story, I inwardly scoffed at the whole idea of a weekly multiple errands run. Although I admired her dedication to shop for the ultimate ingredients, I wondered what motivated her to make all of these stops, when one trip to the grocery store would accomplish the same thing.

Jump forward to today. Cooking and grocery shopping have changed dramatically. Butchers and bakers are a hard-to-find luxury, having been replaced with super marts and discount food warehouses. Roadside stands sell hothouse flowers in place of home grown tomatoes. So why is it that NOW I decide to crave fresh, wholesome ingredients? Suddenly, I want to smell the melons, taste the smoked turkey, and run my finger along the scales of the fish that I will stuff with an eggplant, painstakingly chosen and personally squeezed. This is a "Ta Dah" moment; a food shopping tradition just snuck up and pushed my time-choked schedule into chaos.

While still in the thralls of my "Ta Dah" moment, I joined a local community supported farm and drove there weekly to pick up the absolute best produce I have ever tasted. A CSA farm is one that takes in members every season. The members pay a fee and receive a portion of the farm's weekly harvest. You take home what is ready to be picked, depending on the weather conditions, the pests, and the season.

The first week, I took home three types of heirloom tomatoes with exotic names like "Pruden's Purple," "Yellow Sweet Tangerine," and "Super Tasty." I received a head of purple cauliflower, baby broccoli stalks, orange beets, string beans, bell peppers and huge-leafed "Ruby Red" Swiss chard. A plastic bag full of tender young lettuce greens might easily cost over five dollars in the supermarket, and probably ten dollars in a restaurant salad.

I was overwhelmed with all of the yummy veggies and vowed, then and there, not to waste even a leaf of lettuce. Consequently, you will see that the veggie chapter in this book is packed full of traditional and traditionally inspired dishes. From Baked Stuffed Heirloom Tomatoes with Goat Cheese to Pretty Pickles with Ginger, all of these yummy recipe ideas are a direct result of my community supported farm experiment, and the first step in my journey toward the tradition of choosing quality ingredients.

The joy of getting in touch with the produce that found its way to our dinner table was overwhelming. I was hooked on the freshness, the growers, and the most diverse produce that I had ever tasted. It took me only a couple of weeks to understand, all these years later, why my mother-in-law had her Friday shopping tradition. It took me only a couple of days after that to seek out the best bakery in town—then it was the butcher—then the fishmonger, and before I could blink my eyes, my shopping tradition had taken shape.

In less hectic days, our ancestors directly interacted with the food that they ate. Whether growing the produce themselves, or purchasing ingredients from a local market, only the freshest, most brilliant ingredients were selected for family meals. Our time-constrained lifestyle has limited our ability to choose ingredients in this way. Consequently, we may be suffering for it. Frozen, pre-made foods and meats, pumped with chemical, are offered for our convenience. Preservatives extend the shelf-life, and dyes add color to boxed cereals and cake mixes. We microwave entire meals and eat them while watching two television stations at once. We compromise on our ingredients and the food that we eat, possibly affecting our health and the quality of our lives.

Getting in Touch with Your Food

By experimenting with food, I have come to realize that seeking out the freshest, most flavorful ingredients makes all of the difference in the final dish that I serve. Granted, new and improved supermarkets offer everything one could possible want or need to purchase for a weekly meal plan, however, there are irreplaceable interactions when visiting the farmer who grew your tomatoes from seedlings, such as by chatting with the butcher about the difference between imported and domestically produced lamb. The fishmonger is the only one willing to offer new varieties of farm-raised, or caught-in-the-wild fish. And, what about that bakery? When was the last time you stopped and took a whiff of freshly baking bread or sipped a cup of Mexican chocolate coffee while waiting for your panini sandwich to come off the grill? These are experiences at the root of home cooking that we've abandoned in favor of saving time. Think about it, what are we saving the time for?

I believe that there are ways to incorporate the traditions of our ancestors into our contemporary lifestyles. Let's assume that quality food interaction will positively impact our daily lives. This simply means that if you choose the best ingredients that you can find, your finished result will be the best tasting, best quality, dish that you have ever prepared. Best ingredients need less cooking cover up, and only simple enhancements, so that your cooking time is diminished. A gorgeous beef tenderloin filet needs only a dash of salt and pepper and a drizzle of excellent olive oil in order to be grilled to perfection; a luscious red wine sauce enhances the steak and is effortlessly reduced to the essence of the best grown grapes that created the wine.

If we start with the premise that the integrity of the ingredient significantly affects the final dish, we find that when cooking with the best ingredients, we need only complement their flavors, not overpower them.

The search for the best ingredients is part of the FUN of cooking; an outing to the local farmer's market is a relaxing activity to take pleasure in. As you stroll, taste the fruit, sniff the herbs, and pinch the eggplant. Use all of your senses to choose the best ingredients. Enjoy the freedom to incorporate flexibility in your meal plan. If the ingredient you are searching for is not as perky as its next door neighbor, choose the neighbor. There are plenty of ways to prepare whatever ingredient you choose.

Organize Kitchen Tasks to Save Time

To further enjoy quality food interaction, you must find ways to create the free time you'll need to leisurely shop for food ingredients. Begin by organizing your kitchen, which is easier than you think. You can accomplish this in a single afternoon.

Begin with your pantry. Whether you store staple items in a walk-in closet or on two shelves in a cupboard, if you group them by category they will be easier to find. Sorting ingredients also makes purchasing and storing grocery items easier and faster. For example, if the shelf has a vacant space once occupied by a can of diced tomatoes, the vacancy is apparent when you prepare your grocery shopping list. Likewise, when you remove the now-purchased can of tomatoes from your grocery bag, it goes back to the spot that was previously vacated. Now isn't this easier than taking the shopping cart up and down each isle and trying to remember what you need to buy?

Store your staple items in groups (kinda like sorting Legos with the kids!) Use a basket to group together baking items like all-purpose flour, whole wheat flour, corn meal, matzo meal, etc. Another basket on the same shelf (or nearby) holds other items that you use when baking, like baking soda, baking powder, corn starch, honey, cans of puréed pumpkin, and bags of coconut and chocolate pieces. Sort items that you cook with into cans and boxes for easy stacking, like canned black beans, canned corn, diced tomatoes and chicken broth in one area, and rice, pasta, and couscous in another.

Place the jars and tins of spices that you use when cooking into a basket next to your stovetop or in a drawer nearby. Place spices that you bake with on the shelf next to the flour basket. Of course there are crossovers. I love cinnamon on my chicken and in my nut bread. But, if you separate the spices, you need only look through a few tins to find the exact one that you are looking for. Another useful trick is to use bowls to hold kosher salt, flavored salts, and table salt, and place them onto your counter near your food prep area. If you do this, the salt is always nearby when you are cooking, and you get that satisfying "bam" as you liberally sprinkle while you cook. This is also a great way to utilize all of those vessels made by little hands at summer camp!

Once you have your staples organized, employ the same techniques to simplify your kitchen cabinet layout. Place the pots and pans you use daily at your fingertips. Store less used items in the back of cabinets or on a top shelf. Store the utensils that you cook with in the drawers that are close to the stovetop to eliminate extra minutes spent hunting for these tools. Spoons, ladles, and spatulas should be stored in a container on the counter top near the stove for easy grabbing. Place knives in a holder near your cutting board. Place electric mixers and blenders on a shelf out of the way, and pull them out only when you need to use them. This will increase counter space and offer you more room to create a great meal. An organized kitchen yields extra time to spend cooking favorite dishes.

Creating Balanced Meal Plans

Making health conscious choices comes from balancing nutrition requirements within meal planning, further supporting the proposition that quality food interaction will enhance your daily life. My motto is that you needn't deprive yourself of mashed potatoes as long as you don't eat them three times a week. Likewise, sneaking a few veggies into a warm Open Face Meatloaf Sandwich might just fool your picky eater into discovering zucchini!

I use portion control to incorporate all of my favorite foods into a balanced meal plan. I cook big family meals on Sundays, and reinvent leftovers into quick meals during the week. I have salad nights for the days after mashed potatoes, and cook fish at least once a week. Veggies play and important part in every meal that I serve. I grew up thinking that a balanced meal offered meat, a starch and a veggie. Over the years, I've altered my beliefs and now build a menu based on two or more large servings of veggies and a small amount of meat, poultry, or fish into everyday meals. I add a starch like pasta or potatoes every once in a while. By organizing your meal plan in this way, you can indulge in great food and still maintain a healthy meal plan. Naturally, what works for you and your family is the balance that you need to achieve. We ate a lot more potatoes when my three boys were living at home. Now, I experiment with baby bok choy and butternut squash.

Experiment with Cooking Techniques

My Grandma use to say, "There is more than one way to skin a cat!" Rather than take this too literally, I adapted the philosophy and incorporated it into my cooking. There are many cooking techniques and various preparations that will obtain similar results. For example, braising lamb in wine can be done on the stovetop, in the oven, or in a slow cooker. Poaching eggs is done in a pot with boiling water and a swirl of vinegar, or by making use of an egg poacher pan on the top of the stove. Flexible cooking allows you to choose the method that works best with your schedule.

I encourage you to take advantage of all the new advances in cooking equipment designed to simplify your life. A rice cooker cooks perfect rice and keeps it warm and unstuck for hours. A bread machine makes warm loaves as well as the dough for your sticky buns. A waffle iron works well for your panini sandwiches. Melt chocolate in a microwave, use a mandoline to slice veggies paper thin, and use a food processor to cut butter into pastry dough. Wherever you find a shortcut that does not impact the integrity of the ingredient, take it!

Speaking of ingredients, feel free to incorporate your favorite ingredients into the recipes in this book and others. For example, the majority of recipes call for you to season with salt and freshly ground pepper. It's up to you to decide if you prefer table salt, sea salt, coarse salt or kosher salt in your cooking. There is no right or wrong answer. Likewise you choose the blend of peppercorns that you prefer. I like a mix, but you may prefer black or red or white.

In most cases you can substitute vegetable broth for chicken broth, whole milk or fat free milk when milk is the named ingredient, and unsalted or salted butter interchangeably. Substitution is less forgiving in dessert recipes, but doable. In order to take full advantage of this book, I encourage you to experiment with the ingredients that you find most convenient or a unique ingredient that you have not utilized before.

Share Traditions with Family and Friends

Now that you have shopped for the best ingredients available, streamlined your kitchen so that meal preparation is shortened, and identified a balanced meal plan that works for you, what else is needed to ensure quality food interaction in your daily life? The answer is people. The traditions of food include families and friends cooking and eating together. Sharing a story, learning a lesson, recounting a joke, it all adds to the pleasure of lingering over a wonderful meal. Whether you are cooking for your family or yourself, food is meant to be shared. Invite neighbors, coworkers, friends and extended family members to share the meals that you prepare. Before you know it, they will invite you to share one with them.

Encourage your guests to help with food preparation and presentation, thus fostering quality socialization before, during, and after meals. By involving family members and friends in kitchen tasks, you create time with each other for conversation and bonding. The positive side effect is that you pass on cooking traditions to another generation. Likewise, when a dinner guest asks, "What can I do to help?" the door is opened for interaction that immediately sets the tone for a relaxed, stress free, contemporary evening with friends, family, or coworkers.

Science is flirting with the notion that living well truly does the body good. What better way to get maximum enjoyment out of life than to establish your own special food traditions? The blending of a bountiful table with friends and family sharing the bounty is a prescription for a long life. As you create your fresh traditions, expect to have a few "Ta Dah" moments of your own along the way. When you do, remember to pass them on to others.

Chapter 2

Bacon, Eggs, and More

Good morning sunshine! A brisk walk, a nourishing meal, an invitation for what the day has to offer; breakfast time is the beginning of your day. It's up to you to make it count!

And count it will, when you choose any of the mouthwatering recipes found in this chapter. Whether you're looking to grab a meal and dash out the door, or you and your pals want to luxuriate over a decadent brunch, you'll find information, incredible tastes, and inspiration for experiments of your own.

The traditional breakfast fare in this section includes no-fail omelet preparation, crispy fried hash browns, creamy quiche, light-as-air waffles, fluffy pancakes, French toast and more. Updated specialties include on-the-run omelet wraps, a delicate bacon tart, flavorful griddle cakes with fruit garnishes, and even a recipe for your own signature breakfast sausage.

Experts suggest that a healthy meal plan should include breakfast, in order to get our bodies' engines running and our metabolism on track. I have developed the habit of combining breakfast with exercise to get my day happening. A brisk walk allows me to build up some steam, while giving me the time to think through the day's activities. On weekends I coax hubby and kids to come along. The reward for joining in the walk is a leisurely breakfast when we return.

Use the recipes in this chapter to create your own daily smart start—one filled with good tastes, great flavors and your own fresh traditions.

Three Egg Omelet with Ham and Cheese

MAKING AN OMELET IS AS SIMPLE AS 1-2-3. FIRST, YOU NEED THE RIGHT EQUIPMENT, A NON-STICK PAN AND SPATULA. SECOND, YOU NEED TO WHISK THE EGGS WITH A LIQUID. FOR A LIGHT, FLUFFY OMELET, USE MILK OR WATER. FOR A CREAMIER OMELET, USE HALF AND HALF OR CREAM. THIRDLY, YOU NEED TO LEARN TO FOLD THE OMELET IN HALF OR IN THIRDS. YOU CHOOSE. THE BEST NEWS IS THAT IT WILL TASTE TERRIFIC NO MATTER HOW CLEVER YOUR OMELET ORIGAMI SKILLS ARE!

3 large eggs
2 tablespoons half and half
2 tablespoons chopped fresh chives
Salt and freshly ground pepper

2 tablespoons butter
2 ounces diced ham steak
1 ounce grated Swiss cheese (about ¼ cup)
1 ounce grated Cheddar cheese (about ¼ cup)

I. Whisk together the eggs and half and half in a medium bowl until fluffy. Stir in the chives and season with salt and pepper.
2. Melt I tablespoon of butter in a medium non-stick skillet over medium heat. Cook the diced ham in the butter until warmed through, about 3 minutes. Remove the ham to a platter.
3. Melt the remaining I tablespoon of butter in the skillet.
4. Pour in the eggs as soon as the butter begins to bubble (not when it begins to brown).
5. Use a spatula to pull the eggs from the outer edge to the center. Allow the uncooked eggs to travel from the center to the outer edge of the pan. When the eggs are set (still wet but not runny), sprinkle the front half with the ham and cheeses.
6. Fold the back half over the filling. Slide the spatula underneath the omelet to loosen it from the pan. Gently slide the omelet from the skillet to the plate.

SERVINGS: 1 • PREPARATION TIME: 15 MINUTES

ANOTHER WAY TO FOLD AN OMELET IS IN THIRDS, LIKE YOU WOULD A BUSINESS LETTER. FOLLOW THE DIRECTIONS THROUGH STEP 4. CONTINUE WITH STEP 5, BUT SPRINKLE THE FILLING INGREDIENTS ALL OVER THE EGGS. ALLOW TO COOK FOR 30 SECONDS. FOLD ⅓ OF THE OMELET OVER THE CENTER. USE A SPATULA TO LOOSEN THE BOTTOM EGGS FROM THE PAN. TILT THE PAN ONTO A PLATE SO THAT THE UNFOLDED ⅓ OF THE EGGS SLIDES OVER THE PAN'S EDGE. INVERT THE PAN TO ALLOW THE OMELET TO FLIP NEATLY ONTO ITSELF.

DON'T STOP WITH HAM AND CHEESE. THERE ARE NUMEROUS OMELET FILLINGS THAT WORK WELL WITH THIS EASY METHOD. EXPERIMENT WITH BELL PEPPERS, MUSHROOMS, BRIE CHEESE, BLANCHED ASPARAGUS TIPS, SCALLIONS, COOKED SHRIMP, PROSCIUTTO, COOKED BACON, FONTINA CHEESE, BOILED POTATOES AND ALL OF THE FRESH HERBS YOU CAN FIND.

Southwestern Tortilla Omelet Wrap

FOR THE TRULY-ON-THE-GO FAMILY, THIS COMBINATION OMELET AND
SANDWICH WRAP WILL PLEASE ADULTS AND KIDS ALIKE. USE ANY COMBINA-
TIONS OF FILLINGS, AND IF THE PACE SLOWS DOWN ENOUGH TO USE A
FORK, ADD A SALSA GARNISH AND A SIDE OF SHREDDED HASH BROWNS FOR
AN UPDATE ON AN OLD FAVORITE.

3 large eggs
2 tablespoons milk
Salt

1 10-inch flour tortilla
1 tablespoon olive oil
2 ounces grated Monterey Jack cheese (about ½ cup)
¼ medium red bell pepper, seeded and finely diced (about 2 tablespoons)
2 green onions, thinly sliced (about 2 tablespoons)
¼ medium plum tomato, seeded and diced (about 2 tablespoons)
2 ounces smoked turkey breast, cut into strips
⅛ teaspoon red pepper flakes

SALSA IS THE PERFECT
ACCOMPANIMENT FOR A
SOUTHWESTERN EGG DISH.
TRY AVOCADO SALSA (PAGE
142) OR GRILLED PEACH
AND PEPPER SALSA (PAGE
156) TO SEE WHAT I MEAN.

1. Whisk the eggs with the milk until fluffy. Season with salt.
2. Warm the tortilla in a toaster oven over low heat.
3. Heat the olive oil in a small (less than 10-inch) skillet
over medium heat. Pour the eggs into the pan.
4. Use a spatula to pull the eggs from the outer edge to
the center. Allow the uncooked eggs to travel from the
center to the outer edge of the pan. When the eggs are
set (still wet but not runny), sprinkle the cheese, red
pepper, onions, tomato and turkey strips over top.
Season with red pepper flakes.
5. Do not fold the omelet. Slide the spatula underneath
the omelet to loosen it from the pan. Gently slide the
omelet from the skillet onto the warm tortilla.
6. Fold the tortilla, burrito style by folding the side
edges in. Then fold the bottom edge in and roll up both the
omelet and the tortilla. Cut the tortilla wrap on an angle in the
center.

SERVINGS: 1 TO 2 • PREPARATION TIME: 15 MINUTES

Open Face Egg White Omelet with Goat Cheese and Caramelized Veggies

PICTURE A FLUFFY CLOUD SURROUNDING SAVORY VEGGIES AND YOU HAVE THE MAKINGS OF AN "EGGSELLENT" BREAKFAST OR BRUNCH DISH. EGG WHITES ARE FULL OF PROTEIN, AND WHEN ENHANCED WITH VITAMIN-FILLED VEGGIES AND A TOUCH OF GOOD-FOR-YOU OLIVE OIL, THERE ARE JUST A BUNCH OF REASONS TO MAKE THIS MEAL AGAIN AND AGAIN.

YOU CAN ADAPT THIS RECIPE BY CHANGING THE OMELET TOPPINGS TO INCLUDE YOUR FAVORITES. YOU CAN CREATE A MORE TRADITIONAL OMELET BY ADDING 1 EGG YOLK TO THE EGG WHITES.

2 tablespoons olive oil
1 large green bell pepper, seeded and thinly sliced (about 1 cup)
1 large red onion, thinly sliced (about 1 cup)
1 teaspoon balsamic vinegar
Salt and freshly ground pepper
4 large egg whites
2 ounces goat cheese
2 tablespoons chopped fresh basil

1. Heat 1 tablespoon of olive oil in a skillet over medium high heat.
2. Add the pepper and onion slices to the pan. Cook, stirring often, until soft and beginning to brown, about 20 minutes.
3. Pour in the balsamic vinegar. Cook until the veggies are brown and syrupy, about 5 more minutes. Season with salt and pepper. Remove the pan from the heat.
4. Season the egg whites with salt and pepper. Whisk until frothy.
5. Heat the remaining tablespoon of olive oil in a small skillet over medium heat.
6. Pour in the eggs. Cook until the center is just set, lifting the cooked egg whites with a spatula to allow the uncooked parts to reach the edge of the pan.
7. Crumble the goat cheese over the top of the omelet. Place the veggies on top of the goat cheese.
8. Use a spatula to loosen the omelet from the pan. Slide it onto a serving plate. Garnish with fresh basil.

SERVINGS: 1 • PREPARATION TIME 30 MINUTES

Corned Beef Hash with Poached Eggs

THIS IS MY ABSOLUTE FAVORITE SUNDAY BRUNCH BREAKFAST. IF I'M REALLY
FEELING DECADENT, I ADD A LADLEFUL OF HOLLANDAISE SAUCE (SEE
RECIPE PAGE 28) ON TOP OF THE EGGS. I ALSO USE THIS BASIC RECIPE WITH
ANY LEFT OVER MEAT THAT I HAVE ON HAND. ROAST BEEF AND TURKEY
HASH ARE FAVORITES.

2 tablespoons olive oil
1 medium white onion, cut into ¼-inch dice (about ⅔ cup)
1 medium green bell pepper, seeded and cut into ¼-inch dice (about ⅔ cup)
2 medium celery ribs, sliced (about 1 cup)
2 medium cloves garlic, minced (about 1 teaspoon)
2 medium potatoes, peeled and boiled, cut into ¼-inch dice (about 2 cups)
16 ounces cooked corned beef, cut into ¼-inch dice (about 2 cups)
1 teaspoon Worcestershire sauce
2 tablespoons chopped fresh rosemary
Salt and freshly ground pepper
1 tablespoon distilled white vinegar
8 large eggs

1. Heat the olive oil in a skillet over medium high heat.
2. Cook the onions, pepper and celery in the olive oil until soft
and just beginning to brown, about 5 minutes.
3. Add the garlic and cook for 2 minutes more.
4. Add the potatoes and corned beef to the pan.
5. Stir in the Worcestershire sauce and fresh rosemary. Season
with salt and pepper. Cook over medium heat until the hash is
warmed through. Keep the hash warm while you prepare the eggs.
6. Heat 1 quart or mor of water in a large pot to boiling. Add the
vinegar. Break one egg into a small bowl. Swirl the water in the
pan with a spoon. Gently pour the egg from the bowl into the
swirling water. Continue gently swirling. (This will produce a
rounded egg perhaps with a tail or two.) Repeat this process with
as many eggs as will fit into the pot without crowding. Reduce the
heat to low. Simmer the eggs for 4 to 5 minutes or until the egg
white is firm. Use a long-handled basket strainer to gently
remove and drain each egg.
7. Serve the poached eggs on top of the warm corn beef hash.

SERVINGS: 4 • PREPARATION TIME 30 MINUTES

WHEN MAKING A LARGE QUAN-
TITY OF POACHED EGGS, IT IS
POSSIBLE TO COOK THEM AND
HOLD THEM UNTIL YOU ARE
READY TO SERVE. THIS ELIMI-
NATES THE NEED FOR SHORT-
ORDER COOKING WHEN HOST-
ING A CROWD. POACH THE
EGGS ACCORDING TO THE
DIRECTIONS IN STEP 7.
REMOVE THE EGGS TO A
BOWL OF ICE WATER. REPEAT
UNTIL ALL OF THE EGGS HAVE
BEEN COOKED AND SUB-
MERGED IN ICE WATER. YOU
CAN PLACE THIS BOWL INTO
THE REFRIGERATOR FOR UP
TO 24 HOURS. REHEAT THE
EGGS IN A POT OF WARM (NOT
BOILING) WATER FOR JUST A
FEW SECONDS. OR, IF SERV-
ING POACHED EGGS WITH
WARM TOAST AND SAUCE AS IN
INCREDIBLY EASY EGGS
BENEDICT (SEE RECIPE PAGE
28), YOU CAN ELIMINATE
WARMING THE EGGS, AS THE
HOT SAUCE WILL DO THE
TRICK.

CORNED BEEF IS REALLY A
BEEF BRISKET THAT HAS BEEN
BRINED. THE NAME COMES
FROM THE CORN KERNEL-SIZE
OF THE SALT CRYSTAL ORIGI-
NALLY USED TO CURE THE
MEAT. YOU CAN PURCHASE
CORNED BEEF ALREADY PRE-
PARED IN THE MEAT SECTION
OF THE MARKET OR CANNED
ON THE GROCERY SHELF.

Smoked Trout Hash with Fried Eggs

HERE IS AN INTERESTING TWIST ON TRADITIONAL HASH. USING SMOKED TROUT UPDATES THE CLASSIC AND OPENS THE DOOR TO INVENTIVE INGREDIENT SUBSTITUTION. AFTER YOU HAVE MASTERED THIS RECIPE, WHY NOT TRY SMOKED SALMON OR PERHAPS SMOKED OYSTERS IN YOUR HASH. YUMM!

SMOKED TROUT ARE READILY AVAILABLE IN THE MARKET. HOWEVER, IF YOU ARE LOOKING TO TRY OUT YOUR BRAND NEW "HOT SMOKER," FRESH TROUT MAKE FOR GREAT RESULTS BECAUSE OF THEIR RELATIVELY SMALL SIZE, EVEN TEXTURE AND GREAT FLAVOR. TROUT ARE A PERFECT FISH TO HOT SMOKE BECAUSE THE PROCESS COOKS THE TROUT WHILE ADDING THAT GREAT SMOKY FLAVOR.

2 tablespoons olive oil
1 small red onion, cut into ¼-inch dice (about ½ cup)
6 red creamer potatoes, boiled and cut into ¼-inch dice (about 2 cups)
2 ears of fresh corn, cooked, kernels sliced from cob (about 1 cup)
16 ounces smoked trout, skinned and flaked (about 2 cups)
1 bunch (6 to 8) green onions, chopped (about ½ cup)
Salt and freshly ground pepper
2 tablespoons chopped fresh chives

2 tablespoons butter
8 large eggs
Caviar for garnish (optional)

1. Heat the olive oil in a skillet over medium high heat.
2. Cook the red onion and potatoes in the pan until just beginning to brown, about 8 to 10 minutes.
3. Add the corn to the pan and cook for 2 minutes more.
4. Toss in the smoked trout and green onions and cook for 2 minutes more.
5. Season the hash with salt and pepper. Toss in 1 tablespoon of fresh chives. Keep the hash warm while you prepare the eggs.
6. Heat the butter in a large non-stick skillet over medium-low heat. Break one egg into a bowl. Gently slide the egg into skillet. Repeat this process with as many eggs as will fit into the skillet without crowding. Cook the eggs until firm. (You may turn them once during cooking when the egg white becomes solid).
7. Use a spatula to carefully remove each egg from the skillet. Serve the eggs on top of the hash. Garnish each egg with a dab of caviar and a sprinkling of fresh chives.

SERVINGS: 4 • PREPARATION TIME 30 MINUTES

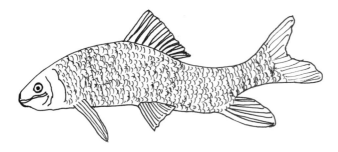

Cinnamon Sugared Bacon

SLOW COOKED BACON CARAMELIZES WITH BROWN SUGAR TO BECOME
CRUNCHY, SWEET AND YUMMY IN THIS SIMPLE RECIPE.

½ cup brown sugar
1 teaspoon ground cinnamon
12 ounces thick bacon (about 8 to 12 strips)

Preheat the oven to 250°.
1. Whisk together the brown sugar and the cinnamon in a shallow bowl.
2. Dredge each strip of bacon in the sugar mixture.
3. Place the bacon onto a baking sheet lined with a Silpat liner or with parchment paper.
4. Slow cook the bacon for 2 or more hours or until it is dark brown and crunchy-chewy. Serve warm or at room temperature.

SERVINGS: 2 TO 3 • PREPARATION TIME 5 MINUTES PLUS 2 HOURS BAKING.

THICK SLICED PORK BACON
WORKS THE BEST IN THIS
RECIPE. TURKEY BACON IS A
LITTLE TOO LEAN TO SLOW
COOK. MAKE A POUND OR
TWO FOR YOUR NEXT BUFFET
PARTY AND SEE HOW MANY
STRIPS ARE LEFT OVER ...
NONE!

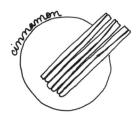

Sautéed Canadian Bacon with Maple Glaze

CANADIAN BACON IS A LEANER ALTERNATIVE TO REGULAR BACON, YET IT
OFFERS THE SAME FLAVOR. ADDING A LITTLE SYRUP SWEETENS THE DISH
AND MAKES IT A GREAT ACCOMPANIMENT FOR PANCAKES AND FRENCH
TOAST.

2 tablespoons butter
4 slices Canadian bacon
2 tablespoons maple syrup

1. Heat the butter in a non-stick pan over medium heat.
2. Place the bacon into the pan. Cook for 1 minute. Turn and cook until both sides are just beginning to brown, about 1 minute more.
3. Pour the maple syrup over the bacon. Turn and coat both sides.

SERVINGS: 2 • PREPARATION TIME 5 MINUTES

CANADIAN BACON IS KNOWN
AS "PEAMEAL BACON" IN
CANADA. COMPANIES SHIP
THE "REAL THING" TO CUS-
TOMERS CRAVING THIS
HEALTHY ALTERNATIVE TO TRA-
DITIONAL AMERICAN BACON.
CANADIAN BACON IS MADE
FROM BONELESS PORK LOINS,
SHORT CUT FROM THE LEAN-
ER PORTIONS OF THE LOIN.
THE EXTERNAL FAT IS TRIMMED
TO WITHIN ⅛-INCH. SMOKE-
LESS AND TENDER, THIS
BACON IS SWEET PICKLE-
CURED AND ROLLED IN A TRA-
DITIONAL GOLDEN CORNMEAL
COATING.

Biscuits N' Gravy with Country Sausage

FRESHLY BAKED BISCUITS ARE A MUST FOR THIS DISH. YOU CAN MAKE
YOUR OWN IN MINUTES, BUT IF TIME IS REALLY SHORT, A FRESHLY BAKED
REFRIGERATED BISCUIT WILL DO NICELY.

8 country-style pork sausage patties (see recipe page 27)
½ cup butter (1 stick)
¼ cup all-purpose flour
2 cups milk
Salt and freshly ground pepper
4 freshly baked biscuits, split in half

1. Cook the patties in a skillet over medium high heat, about 4 to
6 minutes per side. Remove from the pan and keep warm.
2. Melt the butter in the skillet. Use a wooden spoon to scrape
the brown bits from the bottom of the pan.
3. Reduce the heat to medium. Stir in the flour until the mixture
begins to turn golden.
4. Whisk in the milk, stirring constantly until the gravy thickens.
Season with salt and pepper.
5. Serve the biscuits with the sausage and ladle the gravy over top.

SERVINGS: 4 • PREPARATION TIME 20 MINUTES

THIS BREAKFAST FAVORITE TAKES ADVANTAGE OF PRE-PARED SAUSAGE PATTIES. IF NONE ARE HANDY, YOU CAN EASILY PURCHASE GROUND SAUSAGE. CRUMBLE THE SAUSAGE IN THE SKILLET AND COOK IT UNTIL IT BROWNS. REMOVE THE SAUSAGE AND CONTINUE WITH THE RECIPE. IF THE SAUSAGE PRODUCES TOO MUCH FAT, YOU CAN ELIMINATE THE BUTTER. USING TURKEY SAUSAGE WILL LIGHT-EN THE DISH AS WILL USING CHICKEN STOCK IN PLACE OF MILK. HOWEVER, DON'T TRY TO FOOL A SOUTHERNER—WE KNOW OUR SAUSAGE GRAVY!

Buttermilk Biscuits

For terrific buttermilk biscuits whisk together 3 cups all-purpose flour, 2 table-spoons baking powder, 1 tablespoon granulated sugar, ½ teaspoon baking soda, and ½ teaspoon salt in a bowl. Use your hands to add ½ cup room temperature short-ening (like Crisco). Combine until the mixture resembles coarse crumbs. Make a well in the center of this mixture and pour in ½ cup buttermilk. Use a fork to stir quickly until a firm, but sticky dough is formed. (You may have to add a bit more buttermilk or flour to get it just right. Make sure not to overwork the dough. Place the dough onto a floured surface. Pat into a ¾-inch thick round. Use a biscuit cut-ter to cut out rounds. Place the rounds onto a baking sheet lined with a Silpat liner or parchment paper. Bake at 425° for 12 to 15 minutes or until the tops are gold-en brown.

Breakfast Sausage Patties

ONCE YOU LEARN HOW TO SPICE YOUR FRESHLY MADE SAUSAGE, YOU OPEN
THE DOOR TO ALL KINDS OF CREATIONS. THINK TURKEY SAUSAGE WITH
DICED APPLE AND SAGE, OR CHORIZO CHICKEN SAUSAGE. THE SKY'S THE
LIMIT!

2 pounds fresh pork shoulder
2 teaspoons paprika
2 teaspoons garlic powder
2 teaspoons ground cumin
2 teaspoons salt
1 teaspoon dried chili flakes
1 teaspoon dried thyme
1 teaspoon fennel seeds

1. Cut the pork into 2-inch cubes. You can trim some of the fat,
but not all. You want a good ratio of fat to lean meat to flavor the
sausage.
2. Place the pork cubes into a bowl. Sprinkle with all of the seasonings. Toss the pork with the spices with your hands. Cover
and refrigerate for at least 6 hours or as much as 2 days.
3. Use the meat grinder attachment to your mixer, a manual meat
grinder or a food processor to grind the seasoned pork cubes.
For best results, chill the blades on the meat grinder and process
the cubes directly from the refrigerator. If the blade clogs with
strands of fat, clean the blades and chill both the blades and the
pork cubes for several minutes before continuing.
4. Form the sausage into 3-inch round patties about ½-inch
thick. Refrigerate until ready to cook.
5. Cook the patties in a non-stick skillet, turning once, until
cooked through, about 4 to 6 minutes per side.

YIELD: 8 3-INCH PATTIES • PREPARATION TIME 30 MINUTES

USE THE SPICES LISTED AS A
GUIDELINE TO CREATE YOUR
OWN SPECIAL SAUSAGE. YOU
CANNOT TASTE-AS-YOU-GO IN
THIS RECIPE. BUT, YOU CAN
TAKE A SPOONFUL OF THE
GROUND, SEASONED MEAT
AND COOK IT QUICKLY IN A
SMALL PAN. TASTE THE
COOKED MEAT AND ADJUST
THE SEASONINGS AS YOU
WISH. IF YOU DO NOT HAVE A
MEAT GRINDER ATTACHMENT
OR MANUAL MEAT GRINDER,
YOU CAN USE A FOOD
PROCESSOR. MAKE SURE TO
PULSE THE MEAT IN BATCHES.
BETTER YET, ASK YOUR
BUTCHER TO GRIND THE MEAT
FOR YOU, AND ADD THE SEA-
SONINGS WHEN YOU GET
HOME.

Incredibly Easy Eggs Benedict

UNTIL RECENTLY, I NEVER MADE EGGS BENEDICT AT HOME. THE HOLLANDAISE SAUCE RECIPE WAS TOO DAUNTING. THEN, MY PAL SHOWED ME HOW TO MAKE THE SAUCE, USING A MICROWAVE OVEN TO WARM THE MELTED BUTTER, AND A BLENDER TO DO THE REST OF THE WORK. SUCCESS EVERY TIME. NOW, I MAKE THEM FOR EVERY OCCASION—AND SOMETIMES FOR A MIDNIGHT SNACK.

3 large egg yolks
Juice of 1 medium lemon (about 2 tablespoons)
⅛ teaspoon cayenne pepper
¼ teaspoon salt
½ cup butter, melted (1 stick)

4 large eggs, poached
4 slices Canadian bacon
2 English muffins, halved
1 tablespoon chopped fresh parsley
Slivered black olives
Paprika

1. Place 3 egg yolks, lemon juice, cayenne pepper and salt into a blender.
2. Melt the butter in the microwave oven until very hot, just beginning to bubble.
3. Pulse the egg yolk mixture for 3 to 5 seconds.
4. With the machine running on low speed, slowly pour in the hot butter. This should take about 30 to 40 seconds. By the time the butter is incorporated into the egg yolk mixture, the sauce is done. Keep the sauce warm by pouring it into a small bowl and placing that bowl over a pan of warm (not hot) water.
5. Poach the eggs (see tip on page 23). Toast the English muffin halves. Warm the Canadian bacon in a skillet over medium heat, turning once.
6. Assemble the dish by placing an English muffin half onto a plate. Place a slice of Canadian bacon on top of the muffin. Gently slide one poached egg on top of the bacon. Generously ladle warm Hollandaise sauce over the egg. Garnish with chopped fresh parsley, slivered black olives, and a sprinkle of paprika.

SERVINGS: 4 • PREPARATION TIME 30 MINUTES

CLASSIC HOLLANDAISE SAUCE IS MADE WITH A TARRAGON REDUCTION AND COOKED IN A DOUBLE BOILER OVER SIMMERING WATER. THIS IS NOT A DIFFICULT PROCESS, BUT IT DOES DEMAND CONSTANT ATTENTION. IF YOU WANT TO GIVE IT A GO, TRY THIS RECIPE.

Hollandaise Sauce

Melt ½ cup butter in a microwave oven. Keep warm, but not hot. Reduce 2 tablespoons of tarragon vinegar to 1 teaspoon (alternatively, you may use dry sherry). Place 3 egg yolks in a double boiler over simmering (not boiling) water. Whisk until the eggs are pale. Add the reduced vinegar and continue whisking until the egg mixture is pale and thick. Remove the egg yolk mixture from the heat. Slowly whisk in the warm butter. Season with salt and cayenne pepper. Continue whisking until the sauce is thick.

Eggs Benedict with Smoked Salmon, Cajun Hollandaise and Fried Oyster Garnish

PUT A LITTLE SPICE INTO YOU NEXT BRUNCH BY "BAMMING" UP TRADI-
TIONAL HOLLANDAISE AND FRYING UP A LOUISIANA TREAT FOR A STUNNING
TOPPER.

4 large egg yolks
Juice of 1 medium lemon (about 2 tablespoons)
1 tablespoon Cajun spice mix (see recipe)
1 cup butter, melted (2 sticks)

4 ¾-inch slices egg bread, toasted
8 ounces thinly sliced smoked salmon
4 large eggs, poached
2 tablespoons chopped fresh cilantro
4 fried oysters (see recipe, below)

1. Place 4 egg yolks, lemon juice, and Cajun spice mix into a
blender.
2. Melt the butter in the microwave oven until very hot, just
beginning to bubble.
3. Pulse the egg yolk mixture for 3 to 5 seconds. With the
machine running on low speed, slowly pour in the hot butter.
This should take about 30 to 40 seconds. By the time the butter
is incorporated into the egg yolk mixture, the sauce is done.
Keep the sauce warm by pouring it into a small bowl and placing
that bowl over a pan of warm (not hot) water.
4. Assemble the dish by placing a slice of toasted egg bread onto a
plate. Top with strips of smoked salmon. Gently place a poached
egg on top of the salmon. Generously ladle the sauce over and
around the stack. Sprinkle with cilantro and top with a fried oyster.

SERVINGS: 4 • PREPARATION TIME 30 MINUTES

I MAKE THIS SPICE MIX AND
KEEP IT IN A SEALED JAR TO
USE WHENEVER I'M IN THE
MOOD FOR AN OOMPH OF FLA-
VOR:

Cajun Spice Mix
Whisk together in a small bowl
¼ cup of Kosher salt, ¼ cup of
hot paprika, ¼ cup of garlic
powder, 2 tablespoons of
cayenne pepper, 2 tablespoon of
ground black pepper, 2 table-
spoons of dried minced onion, 2
tablespoons of dried oregano,
and 2 tablespoons of dried
thyme.

FOR TIPS ON POACHING AND
HOLDING EGGS SEE PAGE
23. ANOTHER WAY TO PRE-
PARE POACHED EGG IS IN A
PAN THAT IS DESIGNED
SPECIFICALLY FOR THIS USE.
EGG POACHING SETS ARE
PANS THAT SIMMER UP TO 8
EGGS IN NON-STICK CUPS AT
ONE TIME. THE SECRET TO
SUCCESS WITH THIS PAN IS TO
MAKE SURE THAT THE WATER
SIMMERS—NOT BOILS—AND
ALSO TO USE A BIT OF VEG-
ETABLE OIL SPRAY IN EACH
CUP FOR EASY EGG
REMOVAL.

Fried Oysters

*Fried oysters are a great Cajun tradition and a FUN garnish for this dish. An easy
method to prepare this garnish is to pat dry 4 fresh oysters. Mix together 1 large egg
and 1 teaspoon water in a small bowl. Mix together ½ cup plain prepared breadcrumbs with 2 teaspoons Cajun spice mix in another bowl. Place one oyster onto a
fork. Dip it into the egg wash, then the breadcrumb mixture, and then again into the
egg wash and again into the breadcrumb mixture. Repeat with all of the oysters.
Place them onto a rack to dry for 15 minutes. Heat 2 inches of canola oil in a small,
deep pot to 375°. Fry the oysters in the hot oil for 3 to 5 minutes or until golden.
Drain on a paper towel.*

Crispy Hash Brown Potatoes

A STARCHY BAKING POTATO, LIKE A RUSSET, IS THE PERFECT CHOICE FOR THIS DISH. AFTER BAKING, THE POTATO IS THEN CHILLED FOR EASY HANDLING AND A FURTHER CONDENSING OF STARCHINESS. LIBERALLY SEASON THE POTATO AS IT COOKS IN THE HOT OIL RATHER THAN WAIT FOR THE FINISHED DISH.

I LIKE THE ADDITION OF DICED RED AND GREEN BELL PEPPER WITH THIS DISH. SIMPLY ADD THE PEPPER TO THE POTATO ONION MIXTURE AND COOK AS DIRECTED. ANOTHER WAY TO PREPARE THE DISH IS TO PEEL THE POTATOES AND USE A GRATER TO SHRED THEM INTO VERY THIN STRIPS. USE THE SAME TOOL TO PRODUCE GRATED ONION. PLAN AHEAD AND USE EXTRA BAKED POTATOES FROM SATURDAY NIGHT'S DINNER FOR SUNDAY MORNING'S CRISPY HASH BROWNS.

2 large baking potatoes
2 tablespoons olive oil
2 tablespoons butter
1 medium white onion, diced (about ⅔ cup)
Salt and freshly ground pepper

Preheat the oven to 400°.

1. Wash and dry the potatoes. Use a fork to poke several holes in each one. Bake until the potatoes are soft, about 1 hour. Cool to room temperature. Refrigerate until cold, at least 1 hour or overnight.

2. Peel the potatoes and cut into ½-inch dice.

3. Heat the olive oil and butter in a skillet over medium high heat.

4. Cook the potatoes and onions in the skillet until crispy brown. Use a spatula to turn over crisp pieces. Season with salt and pepper.

SERVINGS: 4 • PREPARATION TIME 15 MINUTES PLUS 1 HOUR BAKING AND AT LEAST 1 HOUR TO CHILL POTATOES

Golden Potato Cakes with Ham

THE USE OF BOTH GOLDEN YUKON POTATOES AND BRIGHT ORANGE SWEET POTATOES MAKE THESE POTATO CAKES AS BEAUTIFUL TO PLATE AS THEY ARE TO EAT. LEFT OVER POTATOES WILL WORK JUST FINE IN THIS RECIPE, AS WILL THE ADDITION OF DICED LEFT OVER ROAST BEEF OR TURKEY.

2 large Yukon gold potatoes
1 medium sweet potato
1 bunch (6 to 8) green onions, chopped (about ½ cup)
¼ pound baked ham, cut into ¼-inch dice
½ teaspoon dried thyme
1 large egg, beaten
Salt and freshly ground pepper
2 tablespoons butter
2 tablespoons olive oil

YUKON GOLD POTATOES WERE INTRODUCED IN THE 80S AND RAPIDLY BECAME POPULAR BECAUSE OF THEIR GOLDEN, BUTTERY COLOR AND SWEET-TASTING FLAVOR. ONCE ONLY FOUND IN RESTAURANTS, MOST GROCERY STORES NOW HAVE THEM READILY AVAILABLE.

Preheat the oven to 400°
1. Wash and dry the potatoes. Use a fork to poke several holes in each one. Bake until the potatoes are just soft, about 30 to 40 minutes. Cool to room temperature. Refrigerate until cold, at least 1 hour or overnight.
2. Peel the potatoes. Grate the potatoes into a large bowl.
3. Add the green onion, ham, thyme and egg to the bowl. Season with salt and pepper.
4. Use your hands to combine the mixture and form into 4 patties.
5. Heat the butter and the olive oil in a skillet over medium high heat.
6. Cook the patties in the skillet until golden, about 4 to 6 minutes. Turn the patties and cook until golden on both sides, about 4 to 6 minutes more.

SERVINGS: 4 • PREPARATION TIME 15 MINUTES PLUS 30 MINUTES POTATO BAKING AND AT LEAST 1 HOUR TO CHILL POTATOES

Original Quiche Lorraine

QUICHE ORIGINATED IN THE ALSACE-LORRAINE REGION OF NORTHEASTERN
FRANCE. CLASSICALLY, THE DISH IS COMPOSED OF A TART SHELL FILLED
WITH SAVORY CUSTARD MADE FROM EGGS AND CREAM. FROM THERE THE
INGREDIENTS CAN DIFFER FROM HAM, TO MUSHROOMS, TO LEEKS, AND
INCLUDE VARIOUS CHEESES. TRADITIONAL QUICHE LORRAINE, NAMED FOR
ITS ORIGINS, OFFERS CUSTARD EMBELLISHED WITH CRISP BACON, A BIT OF
FRESH HERBS AND GRUYERE CHEESE.

YOU CAN EASILY CUT IN HALF
THE PREPARATION TIME FOR
THIS DISH BY PURCHASING A
FROZEN PASTRY SHELL.
SIMPLY FOLLOW THE DIREC-
TIONS TO PRE-BAKE (ALSO
CALLED BLIND BAKE) THE
SHELL.

1¼ cups all-purpose flour
¼ teaspoon salt
1 teaspoon salt
½ cup butter, chilled and cut into pieces (1 stick)
3 to 4 tablespoons ice water
1 large egg white

¼ pound bacon, cut into 1-inch pieces
2 cups half and half
3 large eggs
⅛ teaspoon nutmeg
1 tablespoon chopped fresh chives
Salt and freshly ground pepper
4 ounces grated Gruyere cheese

Preheat the oven to 400°

1. Place the flour, salt and chilled butter in the bowl of a food
processor. Pulse until the mixture resembles coarse crumbs. Add
1 tablespoon ice water and pulse again. Continue adding water
and pulsing until the mixture forms a ball. Transfer the dough to
a lightly floured surface and shape into a flat disc. Refrigerate for
at least 1 hour or overnight.
2. Remove the dough from the refrigerator. Transfer to a lightly
floured surface. Roll out the dough to ¼-inch thickness. Place
the dough into a tart shell. Refrigerate for 30 minutes. Place a
sheet of aluminum foil or parchment paper over the shell. Fill
the tart shell with pie weights. Bake for 12 to 15 minutes or until
lightly golden. Remove from the oven. Remove the pie weights
and foil. Bake for another 3 to 5 minutes. Remove from the oven
and brush with beaten egg white.
3. Cook the bacon in a skillet over medium high heat until just
beginning to crisp. Drain on paper towels.
4. Warm half and half in a sauce pan over medium high heat just
to the boiling point. Remove from heat and cool slightly.
5. Beat the eggs with nutmeg, salt and pepper.
6. Slowly whisk the eggs into the warm milk. Stir in the chives.
7. Sprinkle the cheese and bacon into the bottom of the pre-
baked tart shell.
8. Pour the custard into the tart shell.

9. Reduce the oven temperature to 375°. Bake for 35 to 40 minutes or until the top of the quiche is golden brown.

BACON, EGGS, | 33
AND MORE

SERVINGS: 6 • PREPARATION TIME 60 MINUTES PLUS 1 HOUR TO CHILL DOUGH

Inspired Onion and Bacon Tart

ALSACE IS KNOWN FOR ITS GERMAN AND FRENCH INSPIRED CUISINE. POTATOES AND PORK PLAY AN IMPORTANT ROLE. THIS BACON AND POTATO TART TAKES THE TRADITION OF ALSACE AND MERGES IT WITH THE CONVENIENCE OF TODAY'S SHORTCUTS.

1 sheet frozen puff pasty, thawed
1 large egg, beaten
2 ounces finely grated Parmesan cheese (about ¼ cup)

6 ounces bacon, cut into ½-inch pieces
1 medium white onion, thinly sliced (about ⅔ cup)
1 medium potato, peeled and shredded
1 tablespoon balsamic vinegar
2 teaspoons fresh chopped chives
1 tablespoon fresh chopped sage
Salt and freshly ground pepper
½ cup sour cream

PRE-BAKING THE PASTRY DOUGH WILL INSURE A CRISP BOTTOM. YOU CAN BAKE THE TART SHELL UP TO 24 HOURS IN ADVANCE. COOL TO ROOM TEMPERATURE AND WRAP TIGHTLY WITH PLASTIC WRAP. REFRIGERATE UNTIL YOU ARE READY TO CONTINUE THE RECIPE.

Preheat the oven to 350°

1. Thaw the puff pastry in the refrigerator overnight or on the countertop for several hours. Roll out on a lightly floured surface to form a rectangle about 16 x 10-inches. Transfer the pastry to a baking sheet. Crimp the edges up to form a border. Brush with beaten egg and sprinkle with Parmesan cheese. Use a fork to poke holes in the shell. Bake until golden, about 15 minutes. Remove from the oven. Increase the oven temperature to 475°.

2. Cook the bacon in a skillet over medium high heat until just crisp, about 8 to 12 minutes. Remove the bacon to a paper towel lined bowl and drain.

3. Add the onion to the skillet and cook until soft, about 3 to 5 minutes.

4. Reduce the heat to medium and add the potatoes to the skillet. Cook for 3 to 5 minutes.

5. Stir in the vinegar, chives and sage. Season with salt and pepper. Remove from heat.

6. Spread the sour cream onto the pastry tart.

7. Spread the potato onion mixture over top.

8. Sprinkle the bacon over top.

9. Bake until the tart is golden about 10 to 12 minutes. Serve warm or at room temperature.

SERVINGS: 6 • PREPARATION TIME 1 HOUR

Sausage and Mushroom Strata

A CROSS BETWEEN A BREAD PUDDING AND A SOUFFLÉ, THIS EASY-TO-PRE-PARE DISH TAKES ON THE FLAVORS OF TRADITIONAL QUICHE YET SIMPLI-FIES THE PREPARATION SO THAT YOU CAN PREPARE THE DISH THE DAY BEFORE YOUR CELEBRATION BRUNCH.

TO PREPARE THIS DISH IN ADVANCE, FOLLOW THE DIREC-TIONS THROUGH STEP 9. COVER THE CASSEROLE WITH PLASTIC WRAP AND REFRIGER-ATE. REMOVE THE STRATA FROM THE REFRIGERATOR AND ALLOW TO COME TO ROOM TEMPERATURE (ABOUT 20 MINUTES) BEFORE BAK-ING.

THIS SIMPLE RECIPE CAN LEAD TO ALL KINDS OF WON-DERFUL RESULTS. IN PLACE OF SAUSAGE AND MUSH-ROOMS TRY SPINACH, ASPARA-GUS, DICED HAM, CRUMBLED BACON, SAUTÉED SHRIMP, AND ROASTED TOMATOES.

8 large eggs
2½ cups milk
1 tablespoon Dijon mustard
2 or more drops of hot pepper sauce
Salt and freshly ground pepper

1 pound ground sausage
1 medium white onion, diced (about ⅔ cup)
8 ounces button mushrooms, sliced
2 tablespoons chopped fresh parsley

1 loaf Italian bread, cut into 1-inch cubes, about 8 cups
8 ounces grated Gruyere cheese (about 2 cups)
2 ounces grated Parmesan cheese (about ¼ cup)

Preheat the oven to 350°
1. Whisk together the eggs, milk, and mustard in a bowl. Season with hot pepper sauce, salt and pepper. Set aside.
2. Cook the sausage in a skillet over medium high heat until browned. Remove the sausage to a paper-towel-lined bowl and drain. Drain all but 2 tablespoons of drippings from the pan.
3. Add the onion to the pan and cook until golden.
4. Stir in the mushrooms and cook until just brown. Remove the mixture from the heat and stir in the parsley.
5. Toss the bread cubes with Gruyere and Parmesan cheese.
6. Place half of the bread cubes and cheese mixture into a deep casserole dish sprayed with vegetable oil spray.
7. Top the bread cubes with the sausage and mushroom mixture.
8. Add the remaining bread and cheese.
9. Pour the egg mixture over top. Make sure that all of the bread cubes are submerged in the egg mixture. Let the strata stand for 30 minutes.
10. Bake for 40 to 50 minutes or until the strata is golden, puffed and set in the center. Let stand for 5 to 10 minutes before serving.

SERVINGS: 6 TO 8 • PREPARATION TIME 30 MINUTES PLUS 40 TO 50 MINUTES BAKING

Homemade Cinnamon Waffles

BETTER THAN THE FROZEN TOASTER VARIETY, THESE WAFFLES ARE SERVED
HOT FROM THE WAFFLE IRON WITH YOUR FAVORITE GARNISH.

2 cups cake flour
2 teaspoons baking powder
1 teaspoon ground cinnamon
½ teaspoon ground nutmeg
½ teaspoon salt
4 large eggs, separated
1 tablespoon honey
¼ cup butter, melted (½ stick)
1 teaspoon vanilla
2 cups milk

YOU CAN USE THIS BASIC WAF
FLE RECIPE TO INCORPORATE
YOUR FAVORITE TREATS LIKE
BERRIES, CHOCOLATE CHIPS,
NUTS, COCONUT, AND DICED
APPLES. FOR SAVORY WAF
FLES, REPLACE THE HONEY,
CINNAMON, NUTMEG, AND
VANILLA. FLAVOR WITH DICED
BACON, SOUR CREAM,
CHEDDAR CHEESE, OR GREEN
ONION.

1. Heat a waffle iron that has been sprayed with vegetable oil
spray.
2. Whisk together the flour, baking powder, cinnamon, nutmeg
and salt in a large bowl.
3. Stir in 4 egg yolks (reserving the egg whites in another bowl),
honey, melted butter, vanilla and milk.
4. Use an electric mixer to whip the egg whites until soft peaks
form. (You can do this by hand if you are in the mood for a good
workout!)
5. Fold the egg whites into the batter. Pour in enough batter to
cover about three-fourths of the griddle's surface. Cook until the
indicator light shows that the steam has escaped and the waffle is
cooked. Keep the waffles warm on the middle rack of an oven set
on low heat.
6. Serve the waffles with fresh sliced fruit and warm maple syrup.

SERVINGS: 4 • PREPARATION TIME 30 MINUTES

Cornmeal Waffles with Pecan Honey Butter

THESE WAFFLES ARE A LITTLE DENSER THAN TRADITIONAL ONES BECAUSE OF THE CORNMEAL. YOU CAN LIGHTEN THE BATTER BY SEPARATING THE EGGS. ADD THE EGG YOLKS TO THE BATTER. BEAT THE EGG WHITES AND THEN GENTLY FOLD THEM INTO THE BATTER. IT'S UP TO YOU TO DECIDE WHICH TECHNIQUE PRODUCES THE FAMILY FAVORITE WAFFLE.

NATIVE AMERICAN INDIANS TAKE CREDIT FOR DISCOVERING THE SWEET SAP OF MAPLE TREES, USING IT TO FLAVOR THEIR FOOD LONG BEFORE EUROPEAN SETTLERS DISCOVERED IT. TODAY, MICHIGAN ALONE PRODUCES ALMOST 90,000 GALLONS OF SYRUP A YEAR, ALLOWING CONSUMERS TO ENJOY A DRIZZLE OVER PANCAKES AND WAFFLES, AND USE IT IN SAUCES AND FOR GLAZING.

½ cup butter (1 stick)
2 tablespoons honey
½ teaspoon ground cinnamon
⅓ cup pecans, toasted and finely chopped

1 cup all-purpose flour
¾ cup yellow cornmeal
2 teaspoons baking powder
½ teaspoon salt
½ teaspoon ground cinnamon
1½ cups buttermilk
½ cup honey
2 tablespoons butter, melted
2 large eggs, beaten

Maple syrup

Spray a waffle iron with vegetable oil spray and heat.
1. Use an electric mixer to combine the butter, honey and cinnamon until fluffy. Gently stir in the pecans. Set the pecan honey butter mixture aside, or chill until ready to serve.
2. Whisk together the flour, cornmeal, baking powder, salt and cinnamon in a bowl.
3. Use an electric mixer to combine the buttermilk, honey, and butter until smooth.
4. Add the eggs one at a time.
5. Stir in the flour/cornmeal mixture. Pour in enough batter to cover about three-fourths of the griddle's surface. Cook until the indicator light shows that the steam has escaped and the waffle is cooked. Keep the waffles warm on the middle rack of an oven set on low heat.
6. Serve the waffles with pecan honey butter and a drizzle of maple syrup.

SERVINGS: 4 • PREPARATION TIME 20 MINUTES

Sour Cream Oatmeal Waffles
with Grilled Pear Slices

USING CANOLA OIL IN PLACE OF BUTTER LIGHTENS THE BATTER FOR THESE
YUMMY WAFFLES AS DOES COMBINING SOUR CREAM WITH EQUAL PARTS OF
MILK. THE OATMEAL ADDS A NICE CRUNCH.

1½ cups all-purpose flour
½ cup old fashioned rolled oats
2 teaspoons baking powder
1 teaspoon baking soda
½ teaspoon salt
1 cup sour cream
1 cup milk
2 large eggs
1 teaspoon vanilla extract
4 tablespoons canola oil
2 large egg whites, whipped

2 large, ripe pears
Honey
Fresh mint sprigs

THE SECRET TO A SUCCESS-
FUL WAFFLE IS REALLY VERY
EASY ONCE YOU KNOW THE
BASICS. BAKING POWDER
AND-OR BAKING SODA ADDED
TO THE BATTER IS USED TO
LEAVEN THE WAFFLE, MAKING
IT RISE. FOLDING IN BEATEN
EGG WHITES MAKES THE WAF-
FLE AIRY AND LIGHT. THE
GRIDS IN THE WAFFLE MADE
FROM THE WAFFLE IRON ARE
DESIGNED TO "CATCH" AS
MUCH SYRUP AS YOU CAN
POUR ON TOP. BELGIAN WAF-
FLES ARE THICKER THAN NOR-
MAL AND HAVE DEEPER
DEPRESSIONS.

1. Heat a waffle iron that has been sprayed with vegetable oil
spray.
2. Whisk together the flour, oats, baking powder, baking soda
and salt in a large bowl.
3. Stir together the sour cream, milk, eggs, vanilla, and canola
oil in a bowl.
4. Stir the wet ingredients into the dry ingredients.
5. Fold in the egg whites. Pour in enough batter to cover about
three-fourths of the griddle's surface. Cook until the indicator
light shows that the steam has escaped and the waffle is cooked.
Hold waffles in a low oven on the middle of a
rack.
6. Peel and core the pears. Cut into thick
slices. Heat a grill pan over medium high heat.
Spray the pan with vegetable oil spray. Cook
the pear slices in the pan until just beginning
to soften, about 4 minutes. Turn and cook for
2 to 4 minutes more.
7. Serve the waffles with grilled pear slices and
a drizzle of fresh honey. Garnish with fresh
mint sprigs.

SERVINGS: 4 • PREPARATION TIME 30 MINUTES

Double Blueberry Buttermilk Pancakes
with Blueberry Syrup

BLUEBERRIES ARE FULL OF ANTIOXIDANTS, THE GOOD STUFF THAT FIGHTS
HEAT DISEASE, CANCER AND AGING. THESE DELICIOUS PANCAKES OFFER A
DOUBLE DOSE OF BLUEBERRY POWER.

USE THIS BASIC RECIPE TO
ADD YOUR FAVORITE FLAVORS
TO EVERYDAY PANCAKES. OUR
SUNDAY FAVORITE INCLUDES
SEMI SWEET CHOCOLATE
CHIPS AND REDUCED COLA
SYRUP. SPRINKLE THE CHIPS
ON THE PANCAKES AS THEY
COOK. MEANWHILE SIMMER A
CAN OF COLA UNTIL IT IS
REDUCED TO A GLAZE. WHISK
IN 2 TABLESPOONS OF BUT-
TER AND YOU HAVE A SUGARY
COMBINATION THAT IS PER-
FECT FOR A BRUNCH OR BET-
TER YET, FOR A MIDNIGHT
OCCASION!

2 pints fresh blueberries (about 4 cups)
1¼ cups water
2 cups granulated sugar
Zest of ½ medium lemon, peeled in long strips
Juice of ½ medium lemon (about 1 tablespoon)

1½ cups cake flour
1 teaspoon granulated sugar
1 teaspoon baking powder
¾ teaspoon baking soda
½ teaspoon salt
2 large eggs
1 cup buttermilk
¼ cup butter, melted (½ stick)
1 pint fresh blueberries (about 2 cups)

1. Place 2 pints of the blueberries and ¼ cup of water in a saucepan over medium high heat. Cook until the berries are very soft, about 10 to 15 minutes. Cool this mixture to room temperature and then purée in a food processor or with an immersion blender.

2. Place 2 cups sugar, lemon peel and 1 cup water in a sauce pan over medium high heat. Bring to a boil and cook until the sugar is dissolved.

3. Remove the pan from the heat and carefully take out the lemon zest. Add the blueberry mixture to the syrup in the pan. Bring to a boil and cook until thickened, about 5 minutes. Remove from the heat and stir in the lemon juice. Keep the syrup warm while you prepare the pancakes.

4. Whisk together the flour, sugar, baking powder, baking soda, and salt in a large bowl.

5. Stir in the eggs and buttermilk.

6. Stir in the melted butter.

7. Gently fold the remaining 1 pint of blueberries into the batter.

8. Ladle the batter onto a hot griddle that has been coated with vegetable oil spray, or into a skillet over medium high heat. Cook until the top bubbles, about 2 minutes, turn and cook for about 2 minutes more.

9. Serve the blueberry pancakes with warm blueberry syrup.

SERVINGS: 4 • PREPARATION TIME 30 MINUTES

Pumpkin Griddle Cakes with Sautéed Apples

START THE FALL SEASON WITH A BRUNCH THAT FEATURES PUMPKIN PAN-
CAKES. SUGARED APPLES MAKE THE DISH EVEN MORE FESTIVE. IF YOU ARE
NOT COUNTING CALORIES, ADD A BOWLFUL OF WHIPPED CREAM AND A
SPRINKLE OF TOASTED NUTS FOR AN OVER-THE-TOP GARNISH.

4 tablespoons butter
4 medium apples, peeled and thinly sliced (about 4 cups)
3 tablespoons brown sugar
¾ teaspoon cinnamon
Juice of ½ medium lemon (about 1 tablespoon)

2 cups all-purpose flour
½ cup granulated sugar
2 teaspoons pumpkin pie spice
1 teaspoon baking powder
½ teaspoon salt
1 cup canned pumpkin purée
3 large eggs
1 cup milk
2 tablespoons melted butter
2 tablespoons canola oil

USE WHAT EVER YOU CAN
FIND IN THE MARKET TO
ENHANCE THE FLAVOR OF
THESE GRIDDLE CAKES.
GOLDEN DELICIOUS APPLES
WILL WORK FINE. SO WILL
SAUTÉED BANANAS AND
PEARS. TOASTED CHOPPED
WALNUTS, PECANS OR
ALMONDS ARE ALSO A TERRIF-
IC ADDITION TO THIS DISH.

1. Melt 2 tablespoons butter in a skillet over medium heat. Cook
the apples in the butter until soft, about 5 minutes. Reduce heat
to low. Sprinkle the apples with brown sugar and cinnamon and
cook for 2 minutes or until the apples are golden and syrupy. Stir
in the lemon juice. Keep the apples warm.
2. Whisk together the flour, sugar, pumpkin pie spice, salt and
baking soda together in a large bowl.
3. In a separate bowl, whisk together the pumpkin purée, eggs
and milk. Stir this mixture into the flour mixture to form a
smooth batter.
4. Melt the remaining 2 tablespoons of butter and stir into the
batter.
5. Heat the canola oil in a sauté pan or on a griddle over
medium high heat. Pour the batter in ladlefuls into the
pan. Do not overcrowd. Cook until the top begins to bubble, about 2 to 3 minutes. Turn and cook for 2 to 3 minutes more. Serve the griddle cakes with a spoonful of
sautéed apples and warm syrup.

SERVINGS: 4 TO 6 (ABOUT 18 3-INCH PANCAKES) • PREPARATION
TIME 30 MINUTES

Skillet Corn Cakes with Raspberry Basil Jam

PICTURE THE GREAT OUTDOORS: YOU AND YOUR SWEETIE MAKING A PER-
FECT BREAKFAST IN A CAST IRON SKILLET OVER A WELL-BUILT FIRE. BACON
AND EGGS? NOT YOU! SHOW OFF YOUR CAMPSITE CULINARY SKILL BY WHIP-
PING UP A BATCH OF CORN CAKES SERVED WITH RASPBERRY BASIL JAM AND
A DOLLOP OF SOUR CREAM.

CORN IS AT ITS PEAK FRESH-
NESS WHEN IT IS HARVESTED
AND STILL IN THE HUSKS.
PURCHASE CORN FROM THE
FARMER'S MARKET OR ROAD-
SIDE STAND WHEN IT IS AVAIL-
ABLE. THEN HURRY HOME,
SHUCK, AND COOK IT RIGHT
AWAY. COOKED CORN WILL
STAY FRESH IN YOUR REFRIG-
ERATOR FOR SEVERAL DAYS
AND CAN BE USED IN NUMER-
OUS RECIPES.

CORNCAKES ARE A TRADITION
AROUND A CAMPFIRE AND
HAVE VARIATIONS LIKE
FLAPJACKS AND JOHNNY-
CAKES. THE VENEZUELAN
VERSION IS NAMED
CACHAPAS, MEXICAN CORN-
FLOUR PATTIES ARE CALLED
SOPES, AND SOUTHERNERS
ARE FOND OF THEIR HOMINY
CAKES. ALL INCLUDE EITHER
CORN OR CORNMEAL AND ARE
EXCELLENT FOR BREAKFAST,
BRUNCH OR THE GREAT OUT-
DOOR SKILLET SUPPER.

1 pint fresh raspberries (about 2 cups)
1 tablespoon butter
½ cup granulated sugar
¼ cup honey
1 tablespoon chopped fresh basil

6 ears of fresh corn, kernels sliced from cob (about 3 cups) or 3 cups frozen kernels,
    thawed
½ cup cornmeal
½ cup all-purpose flour
1 teaspoon baking powder
½ teaspoon salt
2 tablespoons granulated sugar
2 tablespoons butter, melted
1 egg
½ cup half and half
Canola oil

Sour cream

1. Place the raspberries and 1 tablespoon of butter into a pan
over medium high heat. Cook, stirring often, until just beginning to boil.
2. Add ½ cup granulated sugar and honey. Cook, stirring often
until just beginning to boil.
3. Pour the raspberry mixture into a bowl that sits in a large bowl
filled with ice. Continuously stir the mixture to cool the jam.
When the jam is cool to the touch, stir in the basil.
4. Chill for at least 1 hour. Store in an airtight container.
5. Cook the corn in boiling water for 2 to 3 minutes. Drain well.
6. Place the corn kernels into a blender. Pulse to purée.
7. Add the cornmeal, flour, baking powder, salt, sugar, 2 tablespoons of butter, egg, and half and half. Pulse to combine.
8. Heat 1 tablespoon of canola oil in a griddle (or iron cast skillet) over medium high heat. Ladle the batter onto the griddle to
form pancakes. Cook for about 2 to 3 minutes per side. (Use
additional oil as needed.)
9. Serve the warm cakes with a dollop of sour cream and a spoonful of raspberry basil jam.

YIELD ABOUT 1 CUP OF JAM AND ABOUT 1 DOZEN CORN CAKES. •
PREPARATION TIME 15 MINUTES FOR JAM, 10 MINUTES FOR CORN CAKES

Maple Flavored French Toast

THIS DISH ORIGINATED IN FRANCE AND WAS CREATED AS A WAY TO REVIVE
STALE BREAD. TRADITIONALLY IT IS PREPARED WITH WHITE BREAD, BUT
MULTI GRAIN BREAD COOKS UP JUST FINE.

4 large eggs
½ cup milk
1 tablespoon maple syrup
½ teaspoon ground cinnamon
¼ teaspoon ground nutmeg

2 tablespoons canola oil
2 tablespoons butter
8 slices white bread

Confectioners' sugar
Fresh berries

BAKED FRENCH TOAST IS AN EXCELLENT WAY TO HAVE YOUR FRENCH TOAST, AND MAKE IT IN ADVANCE, TOO! CHOOSE THICK SLICED DAY OLD BREAD. DIP THE SLICES INTO THE BATTER. (EGGNOG IS A GREAT BATTER SUBSTITUTE DURING THE HOLIDAYS.) PLACE THE BATTERED BREAD SLICES INTO A CASSEROLE DISH AND REFRIGERATE OVERNIGHT. PREHEAT THE OVEN TO 375°. BAKE THE FRENCH TOAST UNTIL GOLDEN.

1. Whisk together the eggs, milk, maple syrup, cinnamon and nutmeg.
2. Heat 1 tablespoon canola oil and 1 tablespoon butter in a skillet over medium high heat.
3. Dip each bread slice into the egg batter. Cook in batches in the skillet, turning when golden brown.
4. Continue cooking using additional oil and butter between batches.
5. Serve hot with a sprinkle of confectioners' sugar and fresh fruit.

SERVINGS: 4 • PREPARATION TIME 15 MINUTES

Mocha French Toast Waffles
with Caramelized Bananas

THE FLAVOR OF CHOCOLATE AND COFFEE MIXES WITH CINNAMON TO FLA-
VOR THIS FRENCH TOAST DISH. USING A WAFFLE IRON CREATES A NEW
LOOK, AND SAUTÉED BANANAS LACED WITH RUM TAKE IT OVER THE TOP.

ALCOHOL AND FLAMES CAN BE A TRICKY COMBINATION ESPECIALLY IF YOU ARE USING A GAS STOVETOP. IT IS ALWAYS BEST TO REMOVE THE PAN FROM THE FLAMES BEFORE POURING IN ANY ALCOHOL. AFTER THE LIQUID IS POURED INTO THE PAN, YOU CAN RETURN IT TO THE STOVETOP TO CONTINUE COOKING. THE ALCOHOL CONTENT WILL DIMINISH, BUT THE AROMA AND FLAVOR WILL MARRY THE FRUIT.

4 large eggs
½ cup milk
¼ cup brewed coffee, room temperature
3 tablespoons cocoa powder
1 tablespoon granulated sugar
1 tablespoon vanilla extract
2 teaspoons ground cinnamon
8 ¼-inch slices French bread baguette

4 tablespoons butter (½ stick)
2 tablespoons brown sugar
2 tablespoons dark rum
2 large bananas cut diagonally into 1-inch slices plus extra for garnish

1. Heat a waffle iron that has been sprayed with vegetable oil spray.
2. Whisk together the eggs, milk, coffee, cocoa powder, sugar, vanilla and cinnamon.
3. Dip 4 bread slices into the batter. Place them onto the waffle iron. Close the iron and cook until the French toast is golden, about 3 to 5 minutes. Repeat with the remaining bread slices.
4. Heat the butter in a skillet over medium high heat. Add the sugar and rum. Cook until the mixture bubbles.
5. Add the bananas. Cook for 2 to 3 minutes or until the sauce is reduced and syrupy.
6. Serve the French toast with a spoonful of bananas.

SERVINGS: 4 • PREPARATION TIME 30 MINUTES

Chapter 3

Muffins, Breads, and Bakery Goodies

It's no wonder that doughnut shops and coffee houses are thriving. Who doesn't want to grab for a sugary pick-me-up at some point during a busy day? And why shouldn't we? The truth is, if you balance your favorite sweets with smart veggie and fruit choices in a reasonable meal plan, you can enjoy the occasional muffin, snack cake, and gooey roll without guilt.

My grandmother made fabulous doughnuts on the Tuesday before Ash Wednesday. It was a tradition that we grandchildren loved! We stuffed ourselves with the sugar dusted treats until we could eat no more. Somehow, this splurge helped us better understand the sacrifices and lessons of a spiritual season that began the next day. Good food choices are all about balance—a splurge here—and a sacrifice there.

When it's time to splurge, look no further than the recipes in this chapter. In addition to my grandmother's doughnut tradition, you'll find rich quick breads, scrumptious crumb cakes, and buttery scones. You'll also find savory splurges like cheesy cornbread and freshly baked rolls. Contemporary inspirations include power muffins, citrus flavored sweet rolls, fried apple rings, and bread machine prepared doughs and baked breads.

Use the recipes in this chapter to create foods for bake sales, party favors (offer dinner guests a homemade muffin for the morning-after your party), and coworker fare. I have a philosophy regarding home baked goodies. I believe that if you bake it—they (friends and family) will come… and if you have extras, then it is up to you to share your treasures with those who need a little lift! By adopting the "bake-to-share" philosophy, you get to enjoy the sweet spoils of your labor and avoid the too-much-of-a good thing risk at the same time! Now, isn't this a sweet way to start a fresh baked goody tradition?

The Perfect Cup of Coffee

THE FIRST CUP OF COFFEE IS ALWAYS THE BEST. AFTER THAT, BREWED COFFEE IS A MIXTURE OF MINERAL SALTS, ORGANIC ACIDS AND SUGARS THAT ARE DISSOLVED IN THE WATER. AROMATIC OILS, WHICH DO NOT DISSOLVE IN WATER, ARE A PART OF THE MIX. ALL OF THIS IS BASICALLY UNSTABLE AND CHANGES QUICKLY, EVEN UNDER THE BEST CIRCUMSTANCES. FOR PERFECT COFFEE, THE BEST METHOD IS TO BREW ONLY WHAT YOU PLAN TO POUR. AFTER ABOUT 15 MINUTES, YOU CANNOT EXPECT A CUP TO TASTE THE SAME AS THE FIRST ONE POURED, NO MATTER WHETHER AN INSULATED POT OR ONE WITH A CALIBRATED THERMOSTAT IS USED.

EXPERTS UNITE ON THE TWO SIMPLE FACTS OF COFFEE MAKING. FIRST, FRESHLY GROUND BEANS ARE MOST FLAVORFUL AND SECOND, CHILLED, DISTILLED WATER IS A MUST. THE RATIO OF COFFEE TO WATER DEPENDS ON THE QUALITY OF THE BEAN AND YOUR TASTE PREFERENCE. THE AMOUNT GIVEN BELOW IS A SUGGESTION.

4 ounces freshly ground coffee beans
64 ounces distilled water

1. Scoop the freshly ground coffee beans into the coffee filter. Pour in chilled water and brew according to the manufacturers directions.

SERVINGS: 8 CUPS • PREPARATION TIME 6 TO 8 MINUTES

Mexican Coffee

ONE ORIGINAL RECIPE FOR MEXICAN COFFEE COOKS WHOLE MILK, CINNAMON, AND VANILLA IN A DUTCH OVEN AND THEN ADDS COCOA POWDER AND INSTANT COFFEE. WHATEVER THE METHOD, THIS IS A GREAT TWIST ON TRADITIONAL COFFEE AND GOES WELL WITH GINGER APPLE CRUMB CAKE (RECIPE PAGE 53).

MEXICAN COFFEE IS A RICH COMBINATION OF FLAVORS INCLUDING CINNAMON, CHOCOLATE, AND A GARNISH OF WHIPPED CREAM. SERVED AFTER SUPPER, YOU WOULD BE ENCOURAGED TO SPIKE THE DRINK WITH A TOUCH OF TEQUILA.

8 cups brewed coffee
1 cinnamon stick
2 tablespoons instant cocoa powder
Whipped cream

1. Add the cinnamon stick and cocoa powder to the pot of brewed coffee. Allow the flavors to infuse for 5 minutes. Remove the cinnamon stick and pour the coffee into cups. Garnish with whipped cream.

SERVINGS: 8 CUPS • PREPARATION TIME 10 MINUTES

Irish Coffee

THIS SPECIALTY DRINK WAS MADE FAMOUS IN SAN FRANCISCO'S IRISH PUBS.
THE ORIGINAL VERSION COMBINES A SHOT OF WHISKEY WITH 3 SUGAR
CUBES, HOT COFFEE AND TOPS IT OFF WITH THICKENED CREAM. THIS
RECIPE IS PERFECT FOR HOME ENTERTAINING.

Granulated sugar for dipping
8 cups brewed coffee
1 cup cream
2 tablespoons confectioners' sugar
¾ cup Irish Whiskey
Whipped cream

1. Dip 8 tall glass coffee mugs first into cold water and then into
granulated sugar. Use a cooking torch to carefully brown the
sugar on the glass.
2. Whip the cream with confectioners' sugar.
3. Divide the whiskey among the 8 mugs. Pour in the hot coffee.
Top with whipped cream.

SERVINGS: 8 • PREPARATION TIME 20 MINUTES

Classic Banana Nut Bread

WARM FROM THE OVEN, THIS CLASSIC AMERICAN QUICK LOAF IS A FAVORITE WITH A CUP OF COFFEE OR A GLASS OF CHILLED MILK. THE NEXT DAY'S LEFTOVER SLICES ARE EASILY TOASTED, SLATHERED WITH PEANUT BUTTER, AND STACKED WITH SLICED BANANAS A FOR AN EXCELLENT BREAKFAST STARTER.

A COMBINATION OF FRUIT AND NUTS IS A TERRIFIC WAY TO INCORPORATE HEALTHY SNACKS INTO YOUR DIET. BANANAS ARE A GOOD SOURCE OF FIBER, VITAMIN C, AND POTASSIUM. EXPERTS SUGGEST THAT THAT EATING 1.5 OUNCES PER DAY OF WALNUTS AS PART OF A DIET LOW IN SATURATED FAT AND CHOLESTEROL MAY REDUCE THE RISK OF HEART DISEASE.

2 cups all-purpose flour
1 teaspoon baking soda
1 teaspoon pumpkin pie spice
½ teaspoon salt
1 cup granulated sugar
1 cup canola oil
2 large eggs
3 very ripe bananas, mashed (about 1½ cups)
1 teaspoon vanilla extract
½ cup finely chopped walnuts

Preheat the oven to 350°.
1. Spray a 9 x 5 x 3-inch loaf pan with vegetable oil spray.
2. Whisk together the flour, baking soda, pumpkin pie spice, and salt in bowl.
3. Use an electric mixer to combine the sugar and canola oil.
4. Stir in the eggs, one at a time.
5. Stir in the bananas and vanilla.
6. Add the flour mixture and stir until just combined.
7. Stir in the walnuts until just incorporated.
8. Pour the batter into the loaf pan. Bake for 1 hour, until a toothpick inserted in the center of the loaf comes out clean.

YIELD: 1 LOAF • PREPARATION TIME 20 MINUTES PLUS 1 HOUR BAKING

Orange Coconut Glazed Banana Bread Mini Loaves

GIVE AN EVERY-DAY FAVORITE A TROPICAL UPDATE BY ADDING A HINT OF
CITRUS AND A CRUNCH OF COCONUT. PORTIONS ARE SLEEKER WHEN PRE-
PARED AS MINI LOAVES.

2 cups all-purpose flour
1 teaspoon baking soda
½ teaspoon salt
1 cup granulated sugar
1 cup canola oil
2 large eggs
3 very ripe bananas, mashed (about 1½ cups)
Juice of ½ medium orange (about 2 to 3 tablespoons)
Zest of ½ medium orange (about 1 tablespoon)
½ cup flaked, sweetened coconut

1 tablespoon flaked, sweetened coconut
½ cup confectioners' sugar
Juice of ½ medium orange (about 2 to 3 tablespoons)

Preheat the oven to 350°.
1. Spray four 4½ x 2¾ x 1¼-inch mini loaf pans with vegetable oil
spray.
2. Whisk together the flour, baking soda, and salt in a bowl.
3. Use an electric mixer to combine the sugar and canola oil.
4. Stir in the eggs, one at a time.
5. Stir in the bananas, orange juice and zest.
6. Add the flour mixture and stir until just combined.
7. Stir in ½ cup coconut until just incorporated.
8. Divide the batter into the loaf pans. Bake for 40 minutes or
until a toothpick inserted in the center of the loaf comes out
clean. Cool on a wire rack for 15 minutes.
9. Stir together 1 tablespoon of coconut, the confectioners' sugar
and orange juice to make a glaze.
10. Remove the loaves from the pan and place onto the rack.
Place waxed paper or parchment paper underneath to catch drib-
bles. Drizzle the glaze over the warm loaves.

YIELD: 4 MINI-LOAVES • PREPARATION TIME 20 MINUTES PLUS 40 MINUTES
BAKING

TURN THIS SIMPLE QUICK
BREAD RECIPE INTO AN ELE-
GANT WEEKEND DESSERT BY
SERVING IT AS A TRIFLE. CUT
THE LOAVES INTO BITE-SIZED
CHUNKS. IN A TRIFLE DISH,
OR CLEAR BOWL, PLACE A
LAYER OF THE BANANA BREAD
CHUNKS. TOP WITH DOLLOPS
OF COCONUT CREAM PUDDING
AND THEN ADD LAYERS OF
SLICED FRESH STRAWBERRIES
AND KIWI. FINISH WITH A
LADLEFUL OF RUM FLAVORED
WHIPPED CREAM AND YOU
WILL FEEL LIKE YOU ARE ON A
TROPICAL ISLAND VACATION.
YUMM!

Pumpkin Pie Muffins with Walnut Topping

THE SECRET TO A TERRIFIC MUFFIN IS TO NOT OVERMIX THE INGREDIENTS. STIR THE BATTER ONLY UNTIL ALL OF THE INGREDIENTS COME TOGETHER.

PUMPKIN SEEDS WOULD BE AN EXCELLENT ADDITION TO THE TOPPING FOR THESE MUFFINS. ALSO KNOWN AS PEPITAS, THE SEEDS CAN BE PURCHASED WITH OR WITHOUT THEIR WHITE HULLS, SALTED, ROASTED OR RAW. FOR THIS RECIPE, PURCHASE HULLED, RAW PEPITAS. THEY WILL TOAST AS THE MUFFINS BAKE.

1 cup all-purpose flour
½ cup whole wheat flour
½ cup granulated sugar
¼ cup brown sugar
2 teaspoons baking powder
1½ teaspoon pumpkin pie spice
½ teaspoon salt
1 cup canned pumpkin purée
1 cup milk
2 large eggs
6 tablespoons butter, melted and cooled to room temperature (¾ stick)

2 ounces walnuts (about ½ cup)
2 tablespoons brown sugar
1 tablespoon all-purpose flour
1 teaspoon pumpkin pie spice
1 tablespoon butter

Preheat the oven to 375°.

1. Place paper muffin liners into a muffin pan.

2. Whisk together the flours, granulated sugar, ¼ cup brown sugar, baking powder, 1½ teaspoon pumpkin pie spice, and salt in a bowl.

3. Whisk together the pumpkin purée, milk, eggs and butter in a separate bowl.

4. Stir the liquid ingredients into the dry ingredients until just combined.

5. Spoon the batter into the prepared muffin pan.

6. Place the walnuts, 2 tablespoons brown sugar, flour and 1 teaspoon pumpkin pie spice in the bowl of a food processor. Pulse until the walnuts are coarsely chopped. Add the butter. Pulse until the mixture resembles coarse crumbs.

7. Sprinkle the tops of the muffins with walnut mixture.

8. Bake for 20 to 25 minutes or until the muffins are golden and a toothpick inserted into the center comes out clean.

YIELD ABOUT 12 LARGE OR 18 MEDIUM MUFFINS • PREPARATION TIME 15 MINUTES PLUS 20 MINUTES BAKING.

Banana Orange Muffins

PURÉEING THE BANANAS FOR THIS RECIPE PRODUCES A TENDER MUFFIN. IF YOU'RE FEELING DECADENT, SERVE THESE FOR DESSERT WITH CREAM CHEESE FROSTING AND CALL THEM CUPCAKES. BET YA THE KIDS WILL LOVE 'EM!

1½ cups all-purpose flour
1 cup granulated sugar
1 teaspoon baking powder
½ teaspoon salt
3 very ripe bananas, mashed (about 1½ cups)
Juice of ½ medium orange (about 2 to 3 tablespoons)
4 tablespoons butter, melted and cooled to room temperature (½ stick)
1 large egg
Zest of ½ medium orange (about 1 tablespoon)

Preheat the oven to 375°.

1. Place paper muffin liners into a muffin pan.

2. Whisk together the flour, sugar, baking powder and salt in a bowl.

3. Place the bananas and orange juice in a blender. Pulse to purée.

4. Whisk together the melted butter, egg and orange zest in a separate bowl.

5. Pour the banana purée and butter mixtures into the flour mixture. Fold the ingredients until just combined.

6. Spoon the batter into the prepared pan. Bake for 20 to 25 minutes or until the muffins are golden and a toothpick inserted into the center comes out clean.

YIELD ABOUT 12 LARGE OR 18 MEDIUM MUFFINS • PREPARATION TIME 15 MINUTES PLUS 20 MINUTES BAKING

USE THIS BASIC RECIPE TO EXPERIMENT WITH THE FRUIT THAT YOU HAVE ON HAND. STRAWBERRY PURÉE WILL WORK WELL. SO WILL RASPBERRY AND BLUEBERRY.

Whole Wheat Power Muffins
with Almond Streusel Topping

GIVE YOURSELF AN EXTRA BOOST WITH THESE STURDY, YET DELICIOUS
MUFFINS. YOU CAN MAKE A BATCH, AND FREEZE THEM, PULLING OUT JUST
WHAT YOU NEED. MICROWAVE FROZEN MUFFINS ON HIGH FOR 15 SECONDS
BEFORE SERVING.

NUTRITIONISTS AGREE THAT STARTING THE DAY WITH BREAKFAST GETS YOUR ENGINE RUNNING, MEANING THAT YOUR METABOLISM WILL BURN MORE CALORIES DURING THE DAY IF YOU EAT BREAKFAST THAN IF YOU SKIP IT.

1½ cups all-purpose flour
1 cup whole wheat flour
½ cup old fashioned rolled oats
1 cup granulated sugar
1 tablespoon baking powder
1 teaspoon baking soda
¼ teaspoon salt
2 cups plain yogurt
½ cup milk
¼ cup olive oil
2 teaspoons vanilla extract
1 large egg
1 cup golden raisins

½ cup sliced almonds
1 tablespoon brown sugar
2 tablespoons butter

Preheat the oven to 375°.
1. Place paper muffin liners into a muffin pan.
2. Whisk together the flours, oats and granulated sugar in a bowl.
Measure out ½ cup of this mixture and set aside for the topping.
Whisk in the baking powder, baking soda and salt.
3. Whisk together the yogurt, milk, oil, vanilla and egg together
in a separate bowl.
4. Fold the yogurt mixture into the flour mixture until just combined.
5. Fold in the raisins.
6. Pour the batter into the prepared pan.
7. Combine the reserved flour mixture with the almonds, brown
sugar and butter. Use your hands to form the mixture into coarse
crumbs. Sprinkle this mixture over the top of the muffins.
8. Bake for 20 to 25 minutes or until the tops of the muffins are
golden and a toothpick inserted into the center comes out clean.

YIELD ABOUT 12 LARGE OR 18 MEDIUM MUFFINS • PREPARATION TIME 15
MINUTES PLUS 20 MINUTES BAKING.

Saint Louis Gooey Butter Cake

GROWING UP THIS WAS MY HUBBY'S FAVORITE SATURDAY MORNING TREAT.
RICH AND GOOEY, THIS SUGARY PASTRY IS AS PERFECT ON A BRUNCH TABLE
AS IT IS FOR A MID MORNING SNACK WITH YOUR FAVORITE CUP OF TEA.

1 cup all-purpose flour
3 tablespoons granulated sugar
6 tablespoons butter

1¼ cups granulated sugar
¾ cup butter, room temperature (1½ stick)
1 large egg
1 cup all-purpose flour
⅔ cup evaporated milk
¼ cup light corn syrup
1 teaspoon vanilla extract
¼ cup confectioners' sugar

LEGEND HAS IT THAT THIS CAKE WAS CREATED IN THE EARLY 30S BY A GERMAN BAKER WHEN HE ACCIDENTALLY MIXED THE WRONG PROPORTIONS IN A FAMILY RECIPE. EXTRA BUTTER PRODUCED A GOOEY DELICIOUS MESS, ONE THAT HAS BEEN REPLICATED FOR GENERATIONS!

Preheat the oven to 350°.

1. Spray a 9 x 9 x 1½-inch square baking pan with vegetable oil spray.

2. Place 1 cup of flour, 3 tablespoons of granulated sugar, and 6 tablespoons of butter into the bowl of a food processor. Pulse to form moist crumbs. Press this mixture into the bottom of the baking pan.

3. Use an electric mixer to stir together 1¼ cups granulated sugar and ¾ cup butter until fluffy.

4. Mix in the egg.

5. Stir in the flour alternating with the evaporated milk.

6. Stir in the corn syrup and vanilla extract.

7. Pour this mixture over the crust.

8. Sprinkle the top of the cake with confectioners' sugar.

9. Bake for 25 to 35 minutes or until just set. Remember, the cake is supposed to be gooey!

SERVINGS: 6 • PREPARATION TIME 45 MINUTES

Mango Lemon Snack Cake

THIS FRAGRANT CAKE IS GLAZED WITH HONEY AND TEMPERED BY THE
TROPICAL FLAVORS OF LEMON AND MANGO. LIKE A GOOEY BUTTER CAKE,
IT'S OKAY TO EAT IT RIGHT OUT OF THE PAN!

THE FLESH OF A MANGO IS
PEACH-LIKE AND JUICY. IN
THE CENTER OF THE MANGO,
THERE IS A SINGLE LARGE KID-
NEY-SHAPED SEED. MANGOS
ARE PREVALENT IN THE TROP-
ICS. SLICED PEACHES,
PEARS, OR BANANAS ARE A
GOOD SUBSTITUTE IF MANGOS
ARE UNAVAILABLE.

2 cups all-purpose flour
½ cup granulated sugar
2 teaspoons baking powder
½ teaspoon salt
1 large egg
⅔ cup milk
½ cup butter, melted and cooled to room temperature (1 stick)
Zest of 1 medium lemon (about 1 tablespoon)

¼ cup honey
1 tablespoon butter
Juice of 1 medium lemon (about 2 tablespoons)
1 large mango, peeled and diced

Preheat the oven to 400°.

1. Spray a 9 x 9 x 1½-inch square baking pan with vegetable oil
spray.
2. Whisk together the flour, sugar, baking powder, and salt in a
large bowl.
3. Whisk the egg, milk, melted butter, and lemon zest together in
a separate bowl.
4. Fold the egg mixture into the flour mixture until just combined.
5. Spread the batter into the prepared pan.
6. Bake for 20 to 25 minutes or until a toothpick inserted into
the center comes out clean.
7. Stir together the honey and 1 tablespoon of butter in a pot
over low heat until the butter melts and the mixture is syrupy,
about 5 minutes. Whisk in the lemon juice and stir in the
mango. Cook for 10 minutes more.
8. Remove the cake from the oven. Use a wooden skewer to poke
holes into the baked cake. Spoon the mango syrup over the top of
the cake, so that the syrup drips into the holes and the mango
pieces remain on the top.
9. Return the cake to the oven and bake until the liquid is
absorbed and the top of the cake is golden, about 4 to 5 minutes
more. Cool in the pan. The cake is terrific served warm.

SERVINGS: 9 • PREPARATION TIME 20 MINUTES PLUS 20 MINUTES BAKING.

Ginger Apple Crumb Cake

THIS LIGHT COFFEE CAKE IS REMINISCENT OF HOT-FROM-THE-OVEN APPLE PIE. THE DISH IS BEST WHEN SERVED WARM WITH A PERFECT CUP OF COF-FEE OR ICED COLD GLASS OF MILK.

1 cup all-purpose flour
²/₃ cup granulated sugar
1 teaspoon ground ginger
¹/₂ teaspoon ground cinnamon
¹/₄ teaspoon salt
¹/₈ teaspoon ground cloves
¹/₄ cup butter, chilled, cut into small pieces (¹/₂ stick)
¹/₂ teaspoon baking powder
¹/₂ teaspoon baking soda
¹/₂ cup buttermilk
2 tablespoons dark molasses
1 large egg
2 medium apples, peeled and cut into ¹/₄-inch dice (about 2 cups)

THE FASTEST WAY TO PEEL AND DICE AN APPLE IS TO FIRST CUT IT IN HALF FROM STEM TO BOTTOM. REMOVE THE CORE BY CUTTING A WEDGE INTO THE MIDDLE OF EACH HALF. PEEL THE APPLE HALVES. PLACE THE APPLE CORE SIDE DOWN ONTO A CUTTING BOARD. SLICE THE APPLE HALVES IN HALF AGAIN FORMING DISKS. USE THE TIP OF THE KNIFE TO SLICE DOWN MAKING THIN STRIPS. TURN THE APPLE 90° AND SLICE DOWN TO CREATE A FINE DICE.

Preheat the oven to 350°.

1. Spray a 9 x 2-inch round baking pan with vegetable oil spray and dust with flour.

2. Whisk together the flour, sugar, ginger, cinnamon, salt, and ground cloves in the bowl of an electric mixer.

3. Use the whisk attachment of the mixer to stir in the butter. The mixture will resemble coarse crumbs with a few small balls of butter. (You may also use a pastry cutter to cut in the butter if you prefer.) Remove about ¹/₂ cup of this mixture and set aside for topping.

4. Stir in the baking powder, baking soda, buttermilk, and molasses to the remaining flour mixture.

5. Stir in the egg until just combined.

6. Gently stir in the diced apples.

7. Pour the batter into the pan. Sprinkle the reserved flour mixture over top. Bake for 25 to 30 minutes or until the top of the cake is golden and a toothpick inserted into the center comes out clean.

SERVINGS: 6 • PREPARATION TIME 15 MINUTES PLUS 30 MINUTES BAKING

Sour Cream Coffee Cake
with Pecan and Pear Filling

GROWING UP, WE HAD A SPECIAL COFFEE CAKE THAT WAS FILLED WITH CINNAMON AND GROUND NUTS. THIS ONE IS EVEN BETTER WITH THE ADDITION OF FRESH PEARS AND THE RICHNESS OF SOUR CREAM.

FILL YOUR SOUR CREAM COFFEE CAKE WITH YOUR FAVORITE COMBINATION OF FRUIT, NUTS, AND SPICES. GOOD MIXES INCLUDE ALMONDS AND BLUEBERRIES, APPLES, RAISINS AND CINNAMON, AND OATS AND RASPBERRIES.

6 ounces pecans (about 1½ cups)
⅓ cup dark brown sugar
2 tablespoons all-purpose flour
1 teaspoon ground cinnamon
2 tablespoons butter, chilled and cut into pieces

3 medium pears, peeled and cut into ¼-inch pieces (about 3 cups)
Juice of ½ lemon (about 2 tablespoons)

3 cups all-purpose flour
1 tablespoon baking powder
1 teaspoon baking soda
½ teaspoon salt
1 cup butter, room temperature (2 sticks)
1½ cups granulated sugar
2 large eggs
2 teaspoons vanilla extract
1½ cups sour cream
Confectioners' sugar

Preheat the oven to 350°.
I. Spray a medium to medium large Bundt pan with vegetable oil spray and dust with flour.
2. Place the pecans, brown sugar, 2 tablespoons flour, cinnamon and 2 tablespoons chilled butter into the bowl of a food processor. Pulse until coarse crumbs form. Set aside.
3. Toss the pears with the lemon juice. Set aside.
4. Whisk together the flour, baking powder, baking soda and salt in a bowl.
5. Use an electric mixture to stir together I cup room temperature butter with the granulated sugar until light and fluffy.
6. Mix in the eggs until combined.
7. Stir in the vanilla.
8. Stir in the flour mixture alternating with the sour cream until just combined.
9. Spread half of the batter into the prepared pan. Top with half of the pecan mixture. Top with the diced pears. Sprinkle the remaining nut mixture over top. Spread the remaining batter on top of the pear/nut filling.
10. Bake for 45 to 50 minutes or until the top is browned and a toothpick inserted into the cake comes out clean. Cool in the pan

for 20 minutes. Use a spatula or sharp knife to loosen the cake from the pan. Invert the cake onto a rack to continue cooling. Sprinkle the top of the cake with confectioners' sugar.

SERVINGS: 10 TO 12 • PREPARATION TIME 20 MINUTES PLUS 45 MINUTES BAKING

Simple Cherry Breakfast Cake

YOU CAN MIX TOGETHER THIS SIMPLE CAKE WITH YOUR FIRST SIP OF COFFEE AND BY THE TIME YOU ARE SHOWERED AND DRESSED, THE CAKE WILL BE READY TO EAT. TAKE EXTRA SLICES TO SHARE WITH COWORKERS.

1 12-ounce bag frozen dark sweet cherries, drained and cut in half (about 1½ cups)
2 cups all-purpose flour, plus 2 tablespoons
2 teaspoons baking powder
¼ teaspoon ground nutmeg
¼ teaspoon salt
1½ cups granulated sugar
½ cup butter, room temperature (1 stick)
2 large eggs
1 teaspoon vanilla extract
1 cup buttermilk
Confectioners' sugar

Preheat the oven to 350°.
1. Spray an 11 x 9 x 2-inch baking dish with vegetable oil spray and dust with flour.
2. Toss the thawed cherries with 2 tablespoons flour.
3. Whisk together 2 cups flour, baking powder, nutmeg and salt in a small bowl.
4. Use an electric mixer to combine the sugar and butter until light and fluffy.
5. Mix in the eggs.
6. Stir in the vanilla extract.
7. Stir in the flour mixture alternating with the buttermilk, until just combined.
8. Gently fold the cherries into the batter.
9. Pour the batter into the prepared pan. Bake for 50minutes to 1 hour or until the top of the cake is golden and a toothpick inserted into the center of the cake comes out clean. Cool in the pan. Sprinkle the top of the cake with confectioners' sugar.

SERVINGS: 10 TO 12 • PREPARATION TIME 15 MINUTES PLUS 1 HOUR BAKING

BY TOSSING FRESH OR FROZEN FRUIT WITH A BIT OF FLOUR, YOU PREVENT THE FRUIT FROM BLEEDING INTO THE BATTER. PERSONALLY, I DON'T MIND TINTED BATTER IN THE LEAST, BUT OTHERS MAY PREFER TO SEE MORE INTACT FRUIT. IT'S YOUR CHOICE. USE THIS RECIPE WITH OTHER FROZEN FRUIT LIKE CRANBERRIES, BLUEBERRIES AND RASPBERRIES. DRIED FRUIT LIKE CHERRIES AND APRICOTS WILL ALSO WORK WELL. RECONSTITUTE DRIED FRUIT BY SUBMERGING IN WATER AND THEN MICROWAVING FOR 1 MINUTE ON HIGH. YOU NEED NOT TOSS THIS FRUIT WITH FLOUR. SIMPLY DRAIN THE PLUMPED FRUIT BEFORE MIXING IT INTO THE BATTER. IF YOU CHOOSE TO USE FRESH FRUIT, ADD A BIT OF SUGAR TO SWEETEN.

Old-Fashioned Scottish Scones

TOASTING THE OATS ADDS A DEPTH OF FLAVOR THAT REALLY MAKES THESE SCONES SPECIAL. FEEL FREE TO ADD YOUR FAVORITE SCONE ENHANCER LIKE RAISINS, APRICOTS, OR BLUEBERRIES.

THE SCONE IS SAID TO HAVE BEEN GIVEN ITS NAME FROM THE PLACE THAT SCOTTISH KINGS WERE ONCE CROWNED, THE STONE OF DESTINY. THE ORIGINAL TRIANGULAR-SHAPED SCONE WAS TOTALLY MADE FROM OATS AND BAKED ON A GRIDDLE. TODAY'S SCONES ARE USUALLY MADE WITH FLOUR AND BAKED IN AN OVEN. AMERICAN SCONES ARE PREPARED IN VARIOUS SHAPES, INCLUDING TRIANGLES, SQUARES, DIAMONDS, AND BISCUIT SHAPED ROUNDS.

1½ cups old fashioned rolled oats
½ cup half and half
1 large egg
1½ cups all-purpose flour
⅓ cup granulated sugar
2 teaspoons baking powder
½ teaspoons salt
½ cup butter, chilled, and cut into small pieces (1 stick)

Eggwash (1 egg beaten with 1 tablespoon cold water)
Cinnamon sugar (1 tablespoon granulated sugar mixed with ¼ teaspoon ground cinnamon)

Preheat the oven to 375°.

1. Sprinkle the oats onto a Silpat lined baking sheet, or use parchment paper. Bake in the oven until golden, about 8 to 10 minutes. Remove from the oven and increase the temperature to 450°.

2. Whisk together the half and half and egg into a bowl.

3. Place the flour, sugar, baking powder and salt in the bowl of a food processor. Pulse to combine.

4. Add the butter and pulse until the mixture forms coarse crumbs. Add this mixture into the liquid mixture. Use a wooden spoon (or fork) to combine. Stir in all but 2 tablespoons of the toasted oats.

5. Use your hands to gently bring the dough together on a lightly floured work surface. Form into a 1½-inch thick round. Sprinkle the round with the extra 2 tablespoons of oats. Cut the round into 8 wedges. Place each wedge onto a Silpat lined baking sheet (or use parchment paper). Brush each wedge with egg wash and sprinkle with cinnamon sugar.

6. Bake for 15 to 18 minutes, or until the scones have risen and are golden brown.

SERVINGS: 8 • PREPARATION TIME 45 MINUTES INCLUDING TOASTING AND BAKING

Strawberry Buttermilk Scones

THINK STRAWBERRY SHORTCAKE FOR BREAKFAST AND YOU HAVE AN IDEA
OF HOW MUCH FUN THIS DISH CAN BE. THESE SCONES WOULD BE JUST AS
WONDERFUL WITH FRESH BERRIES OR EVEN CHOCOLATE CHIPS!

2 cups all-purpose flour
2 tablespoons granulated sugar
2 teaspoons baking powder
½ teaspoon baking soda
½ teaspoon salt
½ cup butter, chilled and cut into pieces (1 stick)
1 large egg, slightly beaten
1 cup buttermilk
1 pint fresh strawberries, hulled and chopped in _-inch pieces (about 2 cups)

Eggwash (1 egg beaten with 1 tablespoon cold water)
Granulated sugar

FRESH FRUIT IS A WONDERFUL
ADDITION TO LIGHT AND
FLUFFY SCONES. YOU DON'T
HAVE TO STOP THERE. TRY
INCORPORATING MAPLE
SYRUP, APRICOT JAM, OR A
BIT OF PURÉED PUMPKIN TO
YOUR NEXT BATCH OF BREAK-
FAST SCONES.

Preheat the oven to 450°.
1. Place the flour, sugar, baking powder, baking soda and salt into
the bowl of a food processor. Pulse to combine.
2. Add the butter pieces into the bowl. Pulse until the mixture
resembles coarse crumbs.
3. Pour the flour mixture into a mixing bowl.
4. Whisk the egg into the buttermilk. Stir this mixture into the
flour mixture with a wooden spoon.
5. Gently fold the strawberry pieces into the dough.
6. Use your hands to gently bring the dough together on a lightly
floured work surface. Form into a 1½-inch thick round. Cut the
round into 8 wedges. Place each wedge onto a Silpat lined baking
sheet (or use parchment paper). Brush each wedge with egg wash
and sprinkle with sugar.
7. Bake for 15 to 18 minutes, or until the
scones have risen and are golden brown

SERVINGS: 8 • PREPARATION TIME 20 MINUTES PLUS
BAKING MINUTES

Tuesday's Cake Doughnuts

MY GRANDMOTHER MADE THESE DOUGHNUTS FOR THE FAMILY ON THE TUESDAY BEFORE LENT. WE HAD TO EAT THEM ALL BEFORE THE NEXT MORNING BECAUSE AS A GROUP WE PLEDGED TO GIVE UP SWEETS FOR THE NEXT FORTY DAYS. THESE DOUGHNUTS ARE SOOO GOOD THAT WE EASILY MADE IT THROUGH THE FIRST WEEK WITHOUT LOOKING BACK.

FOR A FUN FALL VARIATION ON THIS RECIPE PREPARE MAPLE FLAVORED DOUGHNUTS BY ADDING ¼ CUP OF MAPLE SYRUP TO THE BATTER. SPRINKLE THE WARM DOUGHNUTS WITH CINNAMON SUGAR.

4 cups all-purpose flour
4 teaspoons baking powder
½ teaspoon ground cinnamon
½ teaspoon salt
¼ teaspoon ground nutmeg
5 tablespoons shortening
1 cup granulated sugar
2 large eggs
1 cup evaporated milk
2 teaspoons vanilla extract
Canola oil for frying
Confectioners' sugar

1. Whisk together the flour, baking powder, cinnamon, salt and nutmeg.
2. Use an electric mixer to combine the shortening, granulated sugar, and eggs.
3. Stir in the evaporated milk and vanilla.
4. Stir in the flour mixture until a loose and sticky dough is formed.
5. Wrap the dough in plastic wrap and chill for at least 2 hours.
6. Flour a rolling pin. Roll out the dough to about ½-inch thickness on a floured surface. The dough will be sticky. If it is too sticky to handle, knead in some more flour.
7. Use a doughnut cutter (dipped in flour) to cut out the doughnuts. Place the cut out doughnuts on paper towels or parchment paper to dry until all of the doughnuts have been cut.
8. Pour canola oil into a deep soup pot about ⅓ full. Heat the oil over medium high heat until the temperature reaches 375°.
9. Fry the doughnuts (and the doughnut holes) in the hot oil, in batches. Do not crowd the pot. The doughnuts will drop to the bottom of the pot and then float to the surface. Use a slotted spoon to gently turn the doughnuts once, to make sure that both sides are golden and puffed, about 1 minute per side. Use the slotted spoon to remove the doughnuts from the pot and place them on a rack over paper toweling to drain.
10. When all of the doughnuts and the holes have been cooked, sprinkle with confectioners' sugar.

YIELD: ABOUT 18 3-INCH DOUGHNUTS AND HOLES • PREPARATION TIME 30 MINUTES PLUS 2 HOURS REFRIGERATION

Coconut Battered Apple Rings

THESE FRUIT FRITTERS ARE A TERRIFIC TREAT FOR BREAKFAST OR FOR
DESSERT. TRY THIS TECHNIQUE WITH BANANA SLICES AND PINEAPPLE
CHUNKS FOR A FUN FRUIT FRITTER.

3 medium apples
1⅓ cups all-purpose flour
2 tablespoons shredded fresh coconut
3 large egg yolks
¼ teaspoon salt
2 tablespoons confectioners' sugar, plus more for sprinkling
1⅓ cups coconut milk
Canola oil for frying

YOU CAN PURCHASE CANNED
COCONUT MILK IN THE GOUR-
MET SECTION OF THE MARKET.
SIMMERING TOGETHER FRESH
COCONUT MEAT WITH WATER
UNTIL FOAMY BEGINS THE
PROCESS. THE MIXTURE IS
THEN STRAINED AND THE
PROCESS IS REPEATED UNTIL
SMOOTH MILK IS PRODUCED.

1. Use a sharp knife to remove the core of the apple first on the
stem end and then on the opposite end. Slice the apples horizontally into ¼-inch rings. (Alternatively, you can cut the apples
into rings and then use a sharp knife to cut out the core from the
center of each ring.)
2. Whisk together the flour, coconut, egg yolks, salt, 2 tablespoons confectioners' sugar and coconut milk until the batter is
smooth,
3. Dip the apple rings into the batter coating well.
4. Pour canola oil into a deep pot about ⅓ full. Heat the oil over
medium high heat until the temperature is about 375°.
5. Use a spoon to remove a coated apple ring from the batter and
carefully place it into the hot oil. Cook the apple in batches. Do
not overcrowd the pan. Turn the rings once so they are golden
on all sides, about 2 to 3 minutes.

YIELD ABOUT 2 DOZEN RINGS • PREPARATION TIME 45 MINUTES

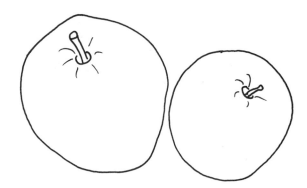

Gooey Maple Pecan Rolls

USING A BREAD MACHINE HELPS TO SHORTEN THE KNEADING AND RISING
PROCESS INVOLVED WITH THESE ROLLS, MAKING THIS AN EASY DISH TO
PREPARE FOR A SPECIAL BREAKFAST.

4 cups all-purpose flour
½ cup old fashioned rolled oats
⅓ cup granulated sugar
4 tablespoons butter, cut into pieces
1 teaspoon salt
1 cup milk
3 large eggs, beaten
2 teaspoons vanilla extract
2½ teaspoons yeast

1 cup pure maple syrup
½ cup butter (1 stick)
1 cup brown sugar

1 cup pecans
½ cup brown sugar
2 teaspoons ground cinnamon
6 tablespoons butter, chilled and cut into pieces (¾ stick)
¼ cup half and half

EVERYONE KNOWS THAT
BREAD MACHINES PRODUCE
AROMATIC LOAVES OF BAKED
BREAD, BUT NOT EVERYONE IS
COMFORTABLE USING THE
DOUGH CYCLE. EACH MACHINE
HAS UNIQUE FEATURES AND
RECIPE REQUIREMENTS. READ
THE MANUFACTURER'S
INSTRUCTIONS BEFORE YOU
BEGIN THE RECIPE. THE
MORE YOU EXPERIMENT, THE
LIGHTER AND MORE DELICATE
YOUR ROLLS WILL BECOME.
DON'T FRET IF IT TAKES YOU A
COUPLE OF BATCHES TO GET
IT RIGHT. I GUARANTEE THAT
THE MISTAKES WILL BE EATEN
UP FASTER THAN YOU CAN
MAKE THE NEXT BUNCH.

1. Place the flour, oats, granulated sugar, butter, salt, milk, eggs,
and vanilla into the bucket of a bread machine. Place the yeast in
the yeast compartment. Set the machine for the dough cycle.
2. Heat the maple syrup, butter and 1 cup brown sugar in a sauce
pan over medium heat until the butter is melted and the sugar is
dissolved. Pour this mixture into a 13 x 9 x 2-inch glass baking
dishes coating the bottom of the dish completely.
3. Place the pecans, ½ cup of brown sugar and cinnamon into the
bowl of a food processor. Pulse until the pecans are finely
chopped. Add the butter and pulse until the mixture resembles
coarse crumbs.

Preheat the oven to 375.
4. After the bread machine cycle is completed, remove the dough
to a floured surface. The dough will be sticky. Coat the dough
with flour and knead several times until the dough is smooth and
elastic. Cover and let rest for 10 minutes. Roll out the dough to
form a 12 x 18-inch rectangle about ¼-inch thick.
5. Sprinkle the pecan filling over the dough leaving about a 1-
inch boarder. Roll up the dough from the long side to form a
log. Cut the log into 12 2-inch thick slices.

6. Place each slice into the syrup in the bottom of the baking dish. Allow the rolls to rise about 1 hour or in the refrigerator overnight.

7. Brush the rolls with half and half. Bake the rolls for 20 to 25 minutes or until the tops are golden and the syrup is bubbling. Remove the pans from the oven. Place a baking sheet over the top of the glass pan. Invert the baking dish so that the rolls fall onto the baking sheet and the syrup drips over top. (Use potholders!) Serve warm.

YIELD: 12 ROLLS • PREPARATION TIME 40 MINUTES PLUS BREAD CYCLE AND 25 MINUTES BAKING.

Citrus Pull-Apart Rolls

WITH THE USE OF A BREAD MACHINE AND AN OPTIONAL OVERNIGHT STAY IN THE REFRIGERATOR BEFORE BAKING, THESE LIGHT AND AIRY ROLLS PRACTICALLY PREPARE THEMSELVES.

4 cups all-purpose flour
1 cup milk
7 tablespoons shortening
3 large eggs, beaten
2 tablespoons granulated sugar
1 teaspoon salt
2½ teaspoon yeast

2 tablespoons butter, melted
¼ cup half and half
Zest of ½ medium orange (about 1 tablespoon)
½ cup granulated sugar
1 cup confectioners' sugar
Juice of 1 medium orange

THE BREAD MACHINE SHORT-CUTS THE DOUGH MAKING PROCESS WITH GREAT RESULTS. FROZEN DOUGH WORKS WELL, TOO. KEEP SOME IN YOUR FREEZER FOR EMERGENCY ROLL MAKING! JUST REMEMBER TO ALLOW ENOUGH TIME FOR THE DOUGH TO THAW BEFORE CONTINUING WITH THE RECIPE.

1. Place the flour, milk, shortening, eggs, 2 tablespoons sugar, and salt into the bucket of a bread machine. Place the yeast in the yeast compartment. Set the machine for the dough cycle.
2. Remove the dough to a lightly floured surface, cover and let rest for 10 minutes. Pat the dough to about ½-inch thickness. Use a pastry cutter (or sharp knife) to divide the dough into 24 equal pieces.
3. Spray a 13 x 9 x 2-inch glass baking dish with vegetable oil spray. Gently shape the dough pieces into balls. Place each ball into the pan. Brush the rolls with butter. Cover and let rise until doubled in size, about 30 minutes. (Or you may refrigerate the rolls overnight and continue with the recipe in the morning.) Preheat the oven to 400°
4. Brush the rolls with half and half.
5. Combine the orange zest and ¼ cup of granulated sugar in a small bowl. Sprinkle over the rolls. Bake the rolls for 15 to 18 minutes or until the tops are golden.
6. Stir together the confectioners' sugar and orange juice. Pour this glaze over the tops of the warm rolls.

YIELD: 2 DOZEN ROLLS • PREPARATION TIME 20 MINUTES PLUS THE DOUGH CYCLE AND TIME TO RISE

Cheddar Corn Bread

THIS EASY-TO-MAKE CORN BREAD IS EQUALLY GOOD WITH A BOWL OF
SPICY CHILI AS IT IS WITH FRIED EGGS. IT IS A PERFECT MAKE-AHEAD DISH
FOR YOUR NEXT OVERNIGHT CAMPING TRIP. IF YOU LIKE, YOU CAN SPICE IT
UP WITH THE ADDITION OF DICED JALAPEÑO PEPPER AND A DASH OF CHILI
POWDER IN THE BATTER. SCALLIONS, COOKED BACON AND MOLASSES ARE
EQUALLY FUN ADDITIONS.

1 cup all-purpose flour
1 cup yellow cornmeal
¼ cup granulated sugar
2 teaspoons baking powder
1 teaspoon baking soda
1 teaspoon salt
1 cup buttermilk
2 large eggs
4 ounces grated Cheddar cheese (about 1 cup)
4 tablespoons butter, melted and cooled to room temperature (½ stick)

Preheat the oven to 400°.

1. Spray a 9 x 2-inch round baking pan with vegetable oil spray.

2. Whisk together the flour, cornmeal, sugar, baking powder,
baking soda and salt in a bowl.

3. Whisk together the buttermilk and eggs in a bowl. Stir in the
cheese and butter.

4. Stir the wet ingredients into the dry ingredients until just
combined.

5. Pour the batter into the pan. Bake until the corn bread is
golden on the top and a toothpick inserted into the center comes
out clean, about 20 to 25 minutes. Cool on a wire rack.

SERVINGS: 4 TO 6 • PREPARATION TIME 30 MINUTES

SOUTHERN STYLE CORN-
BREAD TAKES THIS SAME
BASIC RECIPE AND COOKS IN
A SKILLET. CORNBREAD CAN
BE MADE THICK OR THIN, IN A
SQUARE PAN OR A ROUND
ONE, PREPARED AS A MINI
LOAF OR AS SPOONBREAD.
WHATEVER THE MANNER OF
PRESENTATION, CORNBREAD
IS BASICALLY A QUICK BREAD
THAT COMBINES CORNMEAL
WITH FLOUR. FOR A FESTIVE
FALL PRESENTATION, ADD
PURÉED PUMPKIN, RAISINS
AND PECANS TO YOUR
FAVORITE CORNBREAD
RECIPE. SERVE WARM FROM
THE OVEN WITH A SLATHERING
OF YOUR FAVORITE MAR-
MALADE.

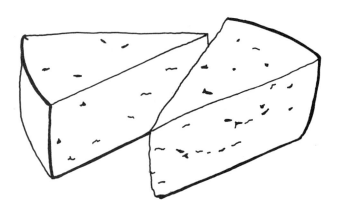

Blue Corn Bread with Red Chile Butter

HERE IS A FUN UPDATE ON A CLASSIC CORN BREAD RECIPE. USING BLUE
CORN MEAL ADDS AN INTERESTING TEXTURE, AND PRODUCES A DENSER
BREAD. SEASONED BUTTER TAKES IT OVER THE TOP.

½ cup butter (1 stick)
2 tablespoons julienned sun-dried tomatoes in oil
1 tablespoon chili sauce
Salt and freshly ground pepper

½ cup butter, room temperature (1 stick)
1 cup ground blue cornmeal
1 cup all-purpose flour
1 tablespoon baking powder
1 teaspoon salt
1 large egg, beaten
1 cup buttermilk

Preheat the oven to 400°.

1. Place ½ cup of butter, sun-dried tomatoes and chili sauce in
the bowl of a food processor. Season with salt and pepper. Pulse
until smooth, about 20 to 30 seconds.

2. Spoon the butter mixture onto a sheet of waxed or parchment
paper. Form a 1-inch log down one end. Roll up the paper to
form a cylinder. Refrigerate at least 1 hour.

3. Spray a 9 x 2-inch round baking pan with vegetable oil spray.

4. Place ½ cup of room temperature butter, cornmeal, flour,
baking powder, salt, and egg into the bowl of a food processor.
Pulse to combine, about 20 to 30 seconds.

5. Pour in the buttermilk. Pulse until just combined, about 20
seconds more. Pour the batter into the prepared pan.

6. Bake for 20 to 25 minutes or until the top is
golden and a toothpick inserted into the center
comes out clean.

7. Serve warm corn bread with a pat of chili butter.

SERVINGS: 4 TO 6 • PREPARATION TIME 30 MINUTES PLUS 1 HOUR TO
CHILL BUTTER

BLUE CORNMEAL IS MADE
FROM BLUE CORN. PUEBLO
TRIBES PLANTED MANY DIF-
FERENT COLORED CORNS,
BUT BLUE CORN BECAME ONE
OF THE MOST IMPORTANT. IT
WAS GENERALLY DRIED ON
ROOFTOPS, STORED AS GRAIN
ON THE COBS, SHELLED, AND
GROUND INTO MEAL AS NEED-
ED. BLUE CORN HAS A
COARSER, SWEETER AND NUT-
TIER TASTE THAN OTHER
TYPES OF FLOUR CORNS. IT IS
THE BASIS FOR MANY TRADI-
TIONAL NATIVE AMERICAN
FOODS. IF GROWING AND
MILLING BLUE CORN IN YOUR
BACKYARD IS OUT OF THE
QUESTION, YOU CAN PUR-
CHASE BLUE CORNMEAL IN
SPECIALTY MARKETS.

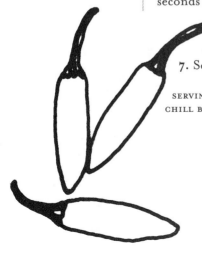

Irish Soda Bread

POPULAR AS A STAPLE IN THEIR NATIVE COUNTRY, IRISH IMMIGRANTS
INTRODUCED THIS DENSE, DELICIOUS SWEET BREAD TO THE UNITED STATES.

3½ cups all-purpose flour
¼ cup granulated sugar
2 teaspoons baking soda
¾ teaspoon salt
1 to 1¼ cups buttermilk
1 large egg
1 cup raisins, soaked in warm water for 15 minutes, then drained

Preheat the oven to 425°.
1. Sift together the flour, sugar, baking soda and salt.
2. Whisk together 1 cup of buttermilk and the egg.
3. Pour the buttermilk mixture into the flour mixture in three
additions mixing the dough with a fork after each addition. The
dough will be moist and sticky. You can do this in a mixer using
the dough hook if you prefer. Use additional buttermilk if the
dough is too dry.
4. Mix the plumped raisins into the dough.
5. Place the dough onto a lightly floured surface.
6. Shape the dough into a round about 2-inches thick. Place the
round onto a Silpat lined baking sheet. Use a sharp knife to cut a
1-inch deep cross into the top of the bread.
7. Bake until golden, about 35 to 40 minutes. The bread will
sound hollow when tapped on the bottom. Cool on a wire rack.

YIELD: 1 LOAF • PREPARATION TIME 15 MINUTES PLUS 30 MINUTES BAKING

THIS TRADITIONAL IRISH
RECIPE HAS MANY VARIATIONS.
ONE OF THE ORIGINAL ONES
IS THE ADDITION OF CARAWAY
SEEDS. OTHER DRIED FRUITS
LIKE CHERRIES OR CURRANTS
ARE ALSO POPULAR ADDI-
TIONS. BROWN SODA BREAD
USES WHOLE WHEAT FLOUR,
OATS AND WHEAT BRAN TO
PRODUCE A VERY HARDY
LOAF.

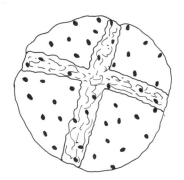

Bimini Bread

THIS RECIPE PRODUCES A LIGHT, WHITE LOAF OF BREAD WITH JUST A HINT OF A SWEET TOPPING. SLICED, IT IS PERFECT AS AN ACCOMPANIMENT FOR SOUPS AND SALADS. SANDWICHED WITH FRESH CAUGHT LOBSTER SALAD, YOU MIGHT THINK YOU'RE IN HEAVEN!

THIS BREAD GETS ITS NAME FROM THE SMALL BAHAMIAN ISLAND JUST OFF THE COAST OF SOUTH FLORIDA, NAMED BIMINI! THE ISLANDERS ARE LAID BACK AND WELCOMING, AS IS THIS LOAF OF BREAD WHEN PREPARED FOR FAMILY AND FRIENDS.

1 cup milk
½ cup water
1 tablespoon shortening
½ teaspoon salt
1 tablespoon granulated sugar
3 cups bread flour
2½ teaspoons yeast

1 tablespoon butter
1 tablespoon honey
2 tablespoons confectioners' sugar

1. Place the milk, water, shortening, salt, granulated sugar, and flour into the bucket of a bread machine.
2. Place the yeast into the yeast compartment.
3. Bake the bread in the machine.
4. Transfer the loaf to a wire rack to cool.
5. Melt the butter in a small pan over medium heat.
6. Stir in the honey.
7. Brush the honey mixture on top of the bread. Sprinkle with confectioners' sugar.

YIELD 1 LOAF • PREPARATION TIME 15 MINUTES PLUS BREAD CYCLE

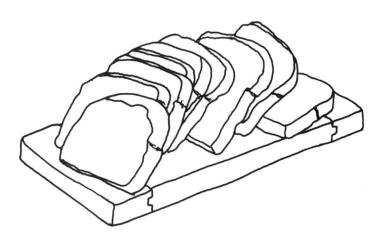

Fresh Baked Garlic Rolls
with Basil Oil for Dipping

THE SMELL OF THESE ROLLS BAKING IN THE OVEN WILL DRAW FRIENDS TO
THE TABLE. SERVE WITH A TOUCH OF BASIL-INFUSED OLIVE OIL FOR DIP-
PING.

3 cups bread flour
1 cup milk
1 tablespoon granulated sugar
2 tablespoons butter, cut into pieces
¾ teaspoon salt
1 large egg, beaten
2½ teaspoons yeast

¼ cup butter (½ stick)
4 medium garlic cloves, minced (about 2 teaspoons)
2 ounces finely grated Parmesan cheese (about ½ cup)

1 cup fresh basil leaves
1 cup olive oil

THIS BASIC ROLL RECIPE WILL
WORK FOR ANY TYPE OF DIN-
NER ROLL THAT YOU WANT TO
MAKE. IN PLACE OF GARLIC
YOU CAN TOP THE ROLLS
WITH POPPY SEEDS, CELERY
SEEDS, CARAWAY SEED,
FRESH HERBS OR GRATED
CHEESE DEPENDING ON WHAT
YOU ARE SERVING FOR SUP-
PER.

1. Place the flour, milk, 1 tablespoon sugar, 2 tablespoons butter,
salt, and egg into the bucket of a bread machine. Place the yeast
in the yeast compartment. Set the machine for the dough cycle.
Preheat the oven to 375°.
2. Remove the dough to a lightly floured surface. Cover and let
rest for 10 minutes.
3. Roll out the dough to a 10 x 8-inch rectangle. Cut the dough
into 20 equal pieces by cutting 3 lengthwise cuts and 4 crosswise
cuts. Gently shape each piece into a ball. Place the balls into a 13
x 9 x 2-inch glass baking dish that has been sprayed with vegetable
oil spray. Cover and let the rolls rise until doubled in size, about
30 minutes.
4. Melt ¼ cup butter in a saucepan over medium heat. Add the
garlic and cook for 30 seconds. Brush the tops of the rolls with
the garlic butter mixture. Bake for 15 to 18 minutes or until the
tops of the rolls are golden.
5. Sprinkle the rolls with the cheese as soon as they come out of
the oven.
6. Place the basil leaves into a blender. With the machine running, slowly pour in the olive oil.

YIELD 20 ROLLS • PREPARATION TIME 20 MINUTES PLUS BREAD MACHINE
AND BAKING

Basil and Parmesan Topped Ricotta Bread

THIS IS MY VERY FAVORITE WHITE BREAD RECIPE. RICOTTA CHEESE ADDS A REAL RICHNESS TO THE LOAF, YET IT IS HIGH AND FLUFFY. THE TOPPING ADDS A FUN DEPTH OF FLAVOR, REMINISCENT OF ITALIAN STYLE GARLIC ROLLS.

3 cups bread flour
6 tablespoons half and half
1 15-ounce tub ricotta cheese
2 tablespoons butter, cut into pieces
1 large egg, beaten
¼ cup granulated sugar
2½ teaspoons yeast

2 tablespoons olive oil
2 tablespoons finely grated Parmesan cheese
2 tablespoons fresh chopped basil

1. Place the flour, half and half, ricotta cheese, butter, egg and granulated sugar into the bucket of a bread machine. Place the yeast in the yeast compartment. Set the machine on the setting for a baked loaf.

2. Combine the olive oil, Parmesan cheese and basil in a small bowl.

3. Place the baked loaf on a serving platter.

4. Brush the top and the sides of the warm loaf with the olive oil mixture. Cut into slices.

YIELD 1 LOAF • PREPARATION TIME 15 MINUTES PLUS BREAD MACHINE CYCLE

THE KEY TO BREAD MAKING SUCCESS IS PROPER DOUGH CONSISTENCY. GENERALLY, DOUGH SHOULD FEEL SOFT, SMOOTH AND NOT TACKY OR MOIST. IT SHOULD NEVER BE DRY OR CRUMBLY, BUT INSTEAD ELASTIC AND RESILIENT, SO THAT WHEN YOU PUSH YOUR HAND INTO IT, THE DOUGH WILL SPRING BACK. TO EXPERIMENT WITH DIFFERENT INGREDIENTS START WITH YOUR FAVORITE RECIPES, AND MAKE ONE SUBSTITUTION AT A TIME. FOR EXAMPLE, RYE FLOUR FOR SOME OF THE WHEAT FLOUR, MAPLE SYRUP FOR HONEY, OR MILK FOR WATER. A GOOD RULE OF THUMB WHEN CREATING YOUR OWN SPECIAL LOAF IS TO SUBSTITUTE DRY FOR DRY AND WET FOR WET. CHEESE SHOULD BE CONSIDERED A WET INGREDIENT; IT MELTS WITH HEAT! YOU CAN ALWAYS THROW IN HERBS, SPICES OR SEEDS FOR A DELICIOUS TWIST OF FLAVOR.

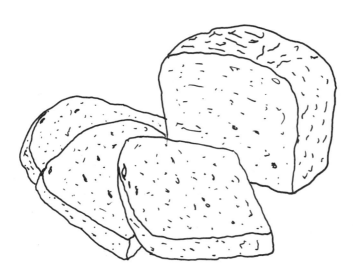

Parmesan Thyme Bread

THE INVITING AROMA OF FRESHLY BAKING BREAD IS EASILY AVAILABLE TO
YOU WITH THE HELP OF A BREAD MACHINE TO DO ALL OF THE WORK.
HOWEVER, IF YOU ARE REALLY FEELING STRESSED-OUT, KNEADING BREAD IS
AN EXCELLENT TENSION REDUCER.

3 cups bread flour
1 cup whole wheat flour
1½ cups water
2 tablespoons olive oil
4 ounces grated Parmesan cheese (about 1 cup)
4 ounces grated Swiss cheese (about 1 cup)
2 tablespoons granulated sugar
1 tablespoon dried thyme
1 teaspoon salt
2½ teaspoons yeast

1. Place the bread flour, whole wheat flour, water, olive oil,
Parmesan cheese, Swiss cheese, sugar, thyme, and salt into the
bucket of a bread machine.
2. Pour the yeast into the yeast compartment (or follow the specific directions for your bread machine).
3. Select the bake cycle and start the bread machine.

YIELD: 1 LOAF • PREPARATION TIME 5 MINUTES PLUS BREAD CYCLE

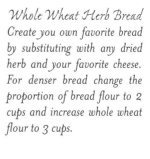

Whole Wheat Herb Bread
Create you own favorite bread
by substituting with any dried
herb and your favorite cheese.
For denser bread change the
proportion of bread flour to 2
cups and increase whole wheat
flour to 3 cups.

*Parmesan Thyme
Bruschetta*
Allow the bread to cool and cut
into ¾-inch slices. Brush 1 side
of the bread with olive oil. Place
the bread onto a hot grill pan
and cook for several minutes.
Use the bruschetta for open face
sandwiches or hors d'ouevres.

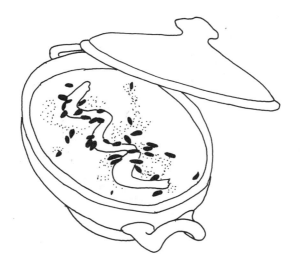

Chapter 4

Soups and Veggie Salads

Fresh veggies are the backbone of a well balanced meal plan. The more vegetables you can pack into your daily fare, the better you will feel and the more satisfied your hunger will be. Adding veggies to your menu is the FUN part! A trip to your local farmer's market on a Saturday morning is an entertaining outing with friends. Just the smell of fresh produce heightens the senses and stimulates your taste buds. Choosing the veggies you will ultimately prepare for your family and friends, is what getting in touch with your food is all about!

Look no further than the recipes in this chapter, when you are trying to find ways to build up your veggie preparation repertoire. Classic soups include Minestrone, black bean, creamy tomato, chowder, and of course—my grandma's chicken soup with matzo balls! Contemporary updates on old-style favorites introduces three onion soup with a tequila chaser, ginger spiced lentil soup, and both an Asian and Colombian twist on my favorite chicken soup that includes tons and tons of yummy veggies.

I find that there are many days during the busy week, when a fresh veggie salad is just what's desired for an easily prepared cold supper. I like to make more than I need to use for tomorrow's lunch, with an extra cup of soup on the side. Classic salad dishes in this section include the real preparation of Caesar salad, wilted spinach and bacon salad, layered and chopped salads, and a chipotle twist in the dressing served over a crisp wedge of iceberg lettuce. Updated fare includes grilled potato salad, garden slaw with jicama, mesclun greens with just about everything, and a lobster Cobb salad to die for.

Use the recipes in this chapter as guidelines when you create your own super salads and savory soups. Both dishes are an excellent way to incorporate those extra veggies that you purchased at the start of the week, and didn't quite get around to serving. For example, thinly sliced fennel is wonderful on top of a chilled salad and, when sautéed, adds an anise flavor to your soup. Extra corn produces excellent corn chowder. Tomatoes, cucumbers, celery, and onions merge into either warm minestrone soup or an easy blender gazpacho.

Simmering soups and chopping fresh veggies is hardly rocket science—but it is a labor of love. Share, share, share your efforts by taking leftover soup to a sniffling friend or extra salad to your cubicle neighbor at the office. My grandma's chicken soup visited every neighbor on her street at one time or another, as did her creamy cucumber salad. Perhaps we should take a page from Grammy's book, and allow old world habits to inspire our soup and salad fresh traditions.

Old World Chicken Soup with Matzo Balls

MY GRANDMA MADE THIS SOUP AT LEAST ONCE A WEEK. IT IS PRETTY ENOUGH TO SERVE RIGHT FROM THE POT. THE LIGHT MATZO BALLS FLOAT TO THE TOP AND FORM AN AIRY CRUST THAT YOU SCOOP THROUGH WHEN YOU LADLE THE SOUP INTO BOWLS. I ADMIT THAT GRAMMY USED A WHOLE CHICKEN, BUT I FIND THAT CHICKEN BREASTS ARE VERY FLAVORFUL AND RENDER LESS FAT, MAKING THIS A LEAN AND MEAN EVERYDAY FAVORITE.

MATZO MEAL IS USED IN A VARIETY OF JEWISH TRADITIONAL HOLIDAY FOODS AND IS READILY AVAILABLE IN THE SUPERMARKET. IT CAN BE FOUND IN A COARSE OR FINE GRIND. YOU CHOOSE YOUR FAVORITE TEXTURE. FOR A GREAT VARIATION, FLAVOR YOUR MATZO BALL WITH CHOPPED FRESH HERBS, ONION OR GARLIC.

5 large chicken breast halves with ribs
3 large carrots, sliced (about 2 cups)
4 medium celery ribs, diced (about 2 cups)
1 large yellow onion, diced into ½-inch squares (about 1 cup)
2 medium turnips, peeled and cut into ½-inch pieces
Salt and freshly ground pepper
4 tablespoons fresh chopped parsley

4 tablespoons olive oil
4 large eggs
1 cup Matzo meal
1 teaspoon salt
¼ cup chicken broth

1. Place the chicken breasts into a deep soup pot. Cover with cold water (about 3 quarts).
2. Toss the vegetables into the pot. Season with salt and pepper. Bring the water to a boil. Reduce heat, cover the pot, and simmer the soup for 2 to 3 hours. Skim any fat that comes to the surface and discard.
3. Remove the chicken from the pot. Cool and remove all of the skin and bones. Shred the chicken and place it back into the soup. Add the parsley to the pot.
4. Whisk the olive oil and eggs together in a bowl.
5. Stir in the matzo meal and salt.
6. Stir in ¼ cup of chicken broth from the soup pot. Refrigerate for 15 minutes.
7. Use 2 spoons to form the matzo mixture into 2-inch balls. Drop each one into the simmering soup. Cover and simmer for at least 30 minutes more.

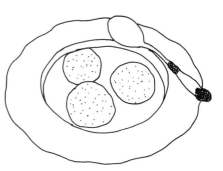

SERVINGS: 6 TO 8 •
PREPARATION TIME: 45 MINUTES PLUS 3 HOURS OR MORE SIMMERING

Asian Inspired Chicken Soup

THIS RECIPE FURTHER DEMONSTRATES THE FLEXIBILITY OF FLAVORINGS IN
TRADITIONAL SOUPS. A SIMPLE MARINADE OF ASIAN INGREDIENTS IS THE
BEGINNING OF A DELICIOUS MEAL.

*2 large (4 to 6-ounce) skinless, boneless chicken breast halves, cut into 1-inch
  pieces (about 3 cups)*
½ cup soy sauce
4 medium garlic cloves, minced (about 2 teaspoons)
1 2-inch piece ginger, grated (about 2 tablespoons)
2 green onions, thinly sliced (about 2 tablespoons)
2 tablespoons peanut oil
1 quart chicken broth
8 to 10 ounces fresh bok choy leaves, cut into 1-inch strips (about 1½ cups)
1 large carrot, grated (about ½ cups)
1 stalk broccoli, shredded (about ½ cup)
1 5-ounce can coconut milk
4 ounces rice noodles
Salt and freshly ground pepper

IN MOST CASES, THE PRU-
DENT THING TO DO IS TO DIS-
REGARD ANY EXTRA MARINADE
THAT HAS BEEN USED TO
INFUSE RAW MEAT OR POUL-
TRY. THE ONLY EXCEPTION TO
THIS RULE IS TO MAKE SURE
THAT YOU COOK THE MARI-
NADE SUFFICIENTLY TO
REMOVE ANY BACTERIA THAT
MAY BE LEFT. MAKE SURE
THAT YOU BRING RESERVED
MARINADE TO A BOIL AND
COOK IT FOR SEVERAL MIN-
UTES BEFORE YOU PROCEED
WITH THE NEXT STEPS OF THE
RECIPE.

1. Place the chicken pieces into a bowl.
2. Whisk together the soy sauce, garlic, ginger, and green onions.
Pour this marinade over the chicken and toss to coat. Cover and
arinate the chicken for 30 minutes or overnight.
3. Heat the peanut oil in a soup pot over medium high heat.
Remove the chicken pieces from the bowl, reserving the marinade.
4. Cook the chicken pieces in the oil, stirring, until just
browned, about 4 to 6 minutes.
5. Pour the reserved marinade into the pot. Simmer until the
marinade boils. Cook for about 3 minutes.
6. Pour the chicken stock into the pot.
7. Stir in the bok choy, carrots, broccoli and coconut milk. Bring
the soup to a boil. Reduce the heat and simmer for 10 minutes.
8. Add the noodles to the soup. Season with salt and pepper.
Simmer for 30 minutes more.

SERVINGS: 4 TO 6 • PREPARATION TIME: 40 MINUTES PLUS MARINATING
THE CHICKEN

Colombian Style Chicken Soup
with Jalapeño Relish

SPICY GARNISHES GIVE CLASSIC CHICKEN SOUP A VERY LATIN FLARE. IF
YOU LIKE THE HEAT, YOU CAN SUBSTITUTE SCOTCH BONNET PEPPERS IN
PLACE OF THE MILDER JALAPEÑO. WHEN WORKING WITH HOT PEPPERS,
REMEMBER TO WEAR GLOVES, OR AT THE VERY LEAST, WATCH YOU HANDS
BEFORE YOU TOUCH YOUR FACE OR EYES.

1 whole (3 to 3½ pound) chicken, cut up into pieces, skin removed
1 large red onion, diced (about 1 cup)
1 large green bell pepper, seeded and cut into 1-inch pieces (about 1 cup)
2 ears of fresh corn, cut into 1-inch pieces
2 medium celery ribs, sliced (about 1 cup)
2 large carrots, sliced (about 1 cup)
2 large potatoes, peeled and cut into 1-inch pieces (about 2 cups)
1 leek, white part only, rinsed well and thinly sliced (about ½ cup)
6 medium cloves garlic, minced
1 tablespoon chicken soup base (or 2 chicken bouillon cubes)
½ teaspoon ground cumin
½ cup fresh cilantro leaves
Salt and freshly ground pepper

2 medium jalapeño peppers, seeded and halved
4 green onions
2 plum tomatoes
1 small white onion, peeled
3 tablespoons white wine vinegar
2 tablespoons fresh cilantro leaves

Diced avocado
Sour cream
Capers
Fried tortilla strips
Cilantro

I. Place the chicken into a large soup pot and cover with water.
Bring the water to a boil. Reduce the heat and simmer for 20
minutes. Skim the top of the water to remove impurities.

2. Add the onion, pepper, corn, celery, carrots, potatoes, leeks
and garlic to the pot. Stir in the soup base, cilantro and cumin.
Cover the pot and simmer until the vegetables are soft and the
chicken is cooked, about 60 to 90 minutes.

3. Place the jalapeño peppers, green onions, tomatoes, white
onion, white vinegar and cilantro into the bowl of a food processor. Pulse to mince the ingredients. Place the relish into a bowl
and set aside.

4. Remove the chicken from the pot and cool to room temperature. Stir in the cilantro, season with salt and pepper, and cook the soup for 5 minutes more.

5. Shred the chicken, removing the bones and cartilage.

6. Place the shredded chicken into shallow soup bowls. Ladle the soup and vegetables over top of the chicken. Place a dollop of jalapeño relish on top of the soup. Garnish with diced avocado, sour cream, capers, fried tortilla strips and additional fresh cilantro leaves.

SERVINGS: 6 TO 8 • PREPARATION TIME: 30 MINUTES PLUS 90 MINUTES SIMMERING

CHRISTOPHER COLUMBUS IS CREDITED WITH BRINGING SPICY CHILI PEPPERS DISCOVERED IN THE NEW WORLD, BACK TO EUROPE. THERE ARE MORE THAN 200 VARIETIES OF SPICY PEPPERS. THEY COME IN ALL SHAPES AND SIZES, VARIOUS COLORS AND, MOST NOTABLY, A WIDE RANGE OF HEAT FROM SPICY TO BLISTERING. THE GENERAL RULE OF THUMB IS THAT THE LARGER THE CHILI, THE LESS HEAT IT CONTAINS. THIS MAKES SENSE BECAUSE THE INTENSE HEAT OF THE CHILI IS IN THE MEMBRANES, SEEDS AND VEINS. A SMALL CHILI HAS MORE SEEDS AND VEINS, PROPORTIONATELY. THE BEST WAY TO EXPERIMENT WITH A HOT CHILI, IS TO REMOVE THE SEEDS AND MEMBRANES AND TASTE A SMALL BITE OF THE PULP. REMEMBER TO HANDLE ALL HOT CHILES CAREFULLY!

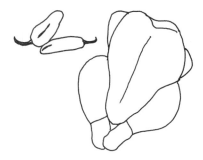

Cream of Roasted Tomato Soup
with Grilled Cheese Croutons

REMINISCENT OF A CHILDHOOD FAVORITE, THIS CREAMY SOUP GETS A MAKE-OVER BY ROASTING THE TOMATOES AND USING MINI FONTINA CHEESE CROUTONS AS A GARNISH.

ROASTING VEGGIES GIVES THEM A DEPTH OF FLAVOR THAT IS WONDERFUL IN SOUPS. THE FLAVORS OF ALL OF THE VEGETABLES IN THE PAN BLEND TOGETHER. THIS IS A GREAT RECIPE TO EXPERIMENT WITH. INSTEAD OF ROASTING TOMATOES, TRY BELL PEPPERS OR CHUNKS OF BUTTERNUT SQUASH. YOU CAN ALSO INFUSE FRESH HERBS INTO THE ROASTING VEGETABLES BY ADDING SPRIGS OF ROSEMARY, THYME, DRIED SAGE, OR BAY LEAVES. THE SKY IS THE LIMIT ON THE WONDERFUL SOUPS THAT YOU CAN CREATE.

6 large beefsteak tomatoes, halved and cored
2 large carrots, diced (about 1 cup)
5 to 6 large shallots, peeled and separated into lobes
6 medium garlic cloves
2 tablespoons olive oil
Salt and freshly ground pepper
1 quart chicken broth
2 tablespoons chopped fresh basil
1 cup half and half

8 ¼-inch thick slices French bread baguette
2 tablespoons butter, softened
4 ounces Fontina cheese, grated (about 1 cup)

Preheat the oven to 425°.

1. Place the tomatoes, carrots, shallots and garlic into a baking pan. Sprinkle with olive oil and season with salt and pepper. Roast until the vegetables are soft, about 45 to 60 minutes. Use a sharp knife to remove the peel from the tomatoes.

2. Place the vegetables with the liquid into a soup pot over medium high heat. Add the chicken stock and basil. Bring the soup to a boil. Reduce the heat and simmer for 30 to 40 minutes.

3. Spread one side of the bread slices with the butter.

4. Place 4 bread slices into a sauté pan, butter side down, over medium high heat. Divide the cheese on top of the bread. Top with the remaining bread slices, butter side up. Cook the sandwiches in the pan until golden, turn and cook until the bread is browned and the cheese is melted. Remove the grilled cheese sandwiches from the pan and set aside for for 1 to 2 minutes. Cut the sandwiches in half.

5. Use an immersion blender (or food processor) to purée the soup. Stir in the half and half.

6. Ladle the soup into bowls, top with grilled cheese croutons.

SERVINGS: 6 TO 8 • PREPARATION TIME: 15 MINUTES PLUS 1 HOUR ROASTING AND 30 MINUTES SIMMERING

Minestrone Soup with Escarole and Shells

THE NAME MINESTRONE MEANS "BIG SOUP" IN ITALIAN. THIS DISH IS
HEARTY ENOUGH TO BE A MEAL IN ITSELF. WITH THE ADDITION OF
SAUSAGE, BROWNED BEEF, OR PANCETTA IT TURNS INTO A MAIN COURSE
STEW.

2 tablespoons olive oil
1 leek, white part only, thinly sliced (about ½ cup)
1 medium white onion, diced (about ⅔ cup)
1 medium fennel bulb, white part only, diced (about 1 cup)
3 medium garlic cloves, minced (about 1½ teaspoons)
1 bay leaf
1 28-ounce can diced tomatoes
1 quart beef broth
1 quart water
Salt and freshly ground pepper
1 16-ounce can cannellini beans
½ pound green beans, cut into 1-inch pieces (about 2 cups)
9 ounces shell pasta
4 cups escarole leaves, washed, dried and chopped
4 ounces shredded Pecorino Romano (about 1 cup)
1 bunch fresh basil, cut into chiffonade

1. Heat the olive oil in a soup pot over medium high heat.
2. Add the leek, onion, fennel and garlic. Cook for 4 to 5 minutes, until soft, stirring often.
3. Place the bay leaf into the pot.
4. Pour in the tomatoes, beef stock and 1 quart of water. Bring to
a boil. Reduce the heat and simmer for 20 to 30 minutes.
Season with salt and pepper.
5. Stir in the cannelloni beans, green beans, shells, and escarole.
Simmer for 15 minutes more.
6. Ladle the soup
into bowls. Sprinkle
with cheese and fresh
basil.

SERVINGS: 6 TO 8 •
PREPARATION TIME: 30
MINUTES

PECORINO ROMANO IS A
SHEEP'S MILK CHEESE. IT
HAS A VERY SHARP FLAVOR,
WHICH GOES PERFECTLY WITH
THIS VEGETABLE SOUP. IT IS A
HARD CHEESE AND IS EASILY
GRATED USING A MICROPLANE
GRATER OR A FOOD PROCES-
SOR. IF THE LATTER IS YOUR
APPLIANCE OF CHOICE,
REMEMBER TO CUT THE
CHEESE INTO SMALL CUBES
BEFORE YOU PULSE.

Slow Cooker Minestrone
This soup recipe is easily adapt-
ed for use in a slow cooker.
Place the leek, onion, fennel
and garlic into the bowl of your
slow cooker. Add the bay leaf
and pour in the diced tomatoes,
beef stock and water. Stir in the
cannelloni beans, green beans,
and escarole. Set the cooker for
medium (or the recommended
temperature for soups) and
walk away. Thirty minutes
before you plan to serve, stir in
the shells and taste for season-
ing. Garnish the soup with
cheese and basil.

Chilled Roasted Tomato Soup
with Cream Cheese Pesto Swirl
and Toasted Pine Nuts

ROASTING THE TOMATOES ADDS AN EXTRA LAYER OF FLAVOR TO THIS DELI-
CIOUSLY SMART SOUP. CHOOSE THE RIPEST TOMATOES FOR A SIMPLE SOUP
THAT WELCOMES THE CREAMY GARNISH.

12 large, ripe plum tomatoes
2 large bell peppers
4 tablespoons olive oil
4 medium garlic cloves, minced (about 2 teaspoons)
1 tablespoon fresh chopped oregano
Salt and freshly ground pepper
1 large yellow onion, diced (about 1 cup)
2 quarts chicken broth
2 tablespoons fresh chopped thyme leaves
Juice of 1 medium lemon (about 2 tablespoons)
½ teaspoon red pepper flakes
2 cups half and half

2 cups fresh basil leaves
1 cup fresh spinach leaves, washed and dried
½ cup pine nuts, toasted (additional for garnish) (see instructions at left)
4 medium garlic cloves, chopped (about 2 teaspoons)
½ teaspoon salt
¼ teaspoon red pepper flakes
Juice of ½ medium lemon (about 2 tablespoons)
4 ounces grated Parmesan cheese (about 1 cup)
½ cup olive oil

6 ounces cream cheese, room temperature
¼ cup half and half
1 cup pine nuts, toasted

HISTORICAL LETTERS FOUND IN THE ARCHIVES OF GENOA MENTION A DRESSING CALLED BATTUTO D'AGLIO, WHICH LIT-ERALLY MEANS "BATTERED GARLIC." THUS THE ORIGINS OF PESTO SAUCE MAY BE ROOTED IN THE EARLY 1600'S. BASIL, THE HEART OF THE PESTO, HAS ITS ROOTS ON THE NORTHERN COAST OF AFRICA, AND IS FAMILIAR TO THE MEDITER-RANEAN SINCE THE EARLY ROMANS. TRADITIONAL-ISTS ARE FOND OF PREPARING PESTO AS IT WAS FIRST INTENDED, GRINDING THE INGREDIENTS WITH A MARBLE MORTAR AND WOODEN PESTO. THE ADVANCES OF FOOD PROCESSORS AND BLENDERS HAVE MADE THE JOB EASIER AND THE INGREDIENTS MORE VARIED.

Toasted Pine Nuts

Toast pine nuts by spreading them in a single layer on a bak-ing sheet. Bake at 350° until the nuts begin to turn golden brown, about 5 minutes. Watch carefully so that you do not burn them.

Preheat the oven to 325°.
1. Cut the tomatoes in half. Core and seed the peppers and cut into quarters. Place the vegetables into a baking pan. Drizzle with 2 tablespoons of the olive oil. Sprinkle with 2 teaspoons garlic and season with fresh oregano, salt, and pepper. Roast for 30 to 40 minutes.
2. Heat the remaining 2 tablespoons olive oil in a large soup pot over medium high heat.
3. Cook the onion in the pot until just soft, about 5 minutes.
4. Add the roasted tomatoes and peppers, chicken broth, thyme, juice of 1 lemon and ½ teaspoon of red pepper flakes. Simmer over medium heat for 10 minutes. Season with salt and pepper.
5. Use an immersion blender (or food processor) to purée the

soup. Chill for at least 3 hours. Just before serving stir in 2 cups of half and half and adjust the seasonings.

6. Place the basil leaves, spinach, ½ cup of pine nuts, 2 teaspoons of garlic, salt, ¼ teaspoon of red pepper flakes, and the remaining lemon juice in a blender. Pulse to combine.

7. Add the Parmesan cheese and pulse again.

8. Pour in the olive oil in a slow drizzle on the slowest blender speed. Set pesto aside.

9. In a small mixing bowl whip together the cream cheese with 2 tablespoons half and half.

10. Stir the cream cheese mixture into the pesto.

11. Ladle the soup into bowls. Swirl in the pesto cream cheese mixture and sprinkle with the remaining toasted pine nuts.

SERVINGS: 8 TO 12 • PREPARATION TIME: 45 MINUTES PLUS ROASTING AND CHILLING

Easy Blender Gazpacho Soup

WHEN TIME IS SHORT AND SIMMERING SOUP IS NOT ON THE SCHEDULE, TRY THIS QUICK AND SPICY CHILLED VEGETABLE SOUP VARIATION.

6 large cucumbers, peeled and seeded
1 large red bell pepper, seeded and cut into quarters
1 small red onion, peeled and cut into pieces
⅓ cup white wine vinegar
2 tablespoons granulated sugar
1 16-ounce can chicken broth
1 16-ounce can diced tomatoes
2 medium cloves garlic, minced (about 1 teaspoon)
2 tablespoons olive oil
Salt and freshly ground pepper

1 cup fresh bread crumbs
Fresh chopped cilantro

CHILLED GAZPACHO SOUP HAS ITS ORIGINS IN SPAIN. IT IS USUALLY UNCOOKED, LIKE THIS BLENDER VERSION, BUT IT CAN BE COOKED AND THEN CHILLED. SOME RECIPES CALL FOR DAY-OLD BREAD TO BE ADDED DIRECTLY TO THE SOUP, WHICH PRODUCES A THICKER RESULT. OTHERS CALL FOR THE SOUP TO BE SERVED OVER ICE CUBES TO MAINTAIN A SLUSHY CONSISTENCY. I LIKE TO SERVE THE CHILLED SOUP FROM CRYSTAL MUGS WITH A SPRIG OF CELERY AND A LIME PINWHEEL ON THE RIM, WHICH I HAVE DIPPED IN SALT.

1. Cut 4 of the cucumbers into chunks and place into a blender. Add the pepper, onion, vinegar, and sugar. Pulse to combine.

2. Pour this mixture into a large bowl. Stir in the chicken broth, tomatoes, garlic and olive oil.

3. Cut the 2 remaining cucumbers into ¼-inch dice. Stir these into the soup. Season with salt and pepper. Cover and chill for at least 1 hour or overnight.

4. Ladle the soup into bowls and garnish with breadcrumbs and fresh cilantro.

SERVINGS: 4 • PREPARATION TIME: 20 MINUTES PLUS CHILLING

Black Bean Soup with Dry Sherry Floater

I FELL IN LOVE WITH BLACK BEAN SOUP IN A LITTLE RESTAURANT IN THE HILLS OF NORTH CAROLINA. BIG BOWLS OF PIPING HOT SOUP WERE SERVED WITH FLUFFY RICE, GARNISHES OF SOUR CREAM, CHOPPED ONION, AND A SHOT OF SHERRY ON THE SIDE. WHEN YOU POUR THE SHERRY FLOATER ON TOP OF THE SOUP AND STIR GENTLY, THE FLAVORS JUMP UP A NOTCH. SERVE THIS DISH TO GUESTS FOR AN UPSCALE PRESENTATION OF A CLASSIC PEASANT SOUP.

BLACK BEANS ARE RICH IN FIBER AND PROTEIN, MAKING THIS SOUP AN EXCELLENT MEATLESS MIDWEEK MEAL. BLACK BEANS ARE ALSO KNOWN AS TURTLE BEANS AND ARE VERY POPULAR IN MEXICAN, SOUTH AMERICAN, AND CARIBBEAN COOKING. I LIKE TO ADD OTHER VEGGIES TO MY BLACK BEAN SOUP, DEPENDING ON WHAT IS AVAILABLE. FRESH CORN, DICED TOMATOES, AND ROASTED BUTTERNUT SQUASH ARE JUST A FEW GOOD ADDITIONS.

1 12-ounce package dried black beans
¼ pound bacon, cut into 1-inch pieces
1 large yellow onion, diced into ½-inch squares (about 1 cup)
1 large green bell pepper, seeded and cut into ¼-inch dice (about 1 cup)
2 large carrots, diced (about 1 cup)
2 medium celery ribs, diced (about 1 cup
4 medium garlic cloves, minced (about 2 teaspoons)
½ cup dry sherry
1 quart chicken broth
1 teaspoon ground cumin
1 teaspoon ground oregano
2 bay leaves
Salt and freshly ground pepper

Cooked white rice
Sour cream
Chopped green onions
Fresh chopped cilantro
Dry sherry

1. Place the beans into a large pot. Cover by 3-inches with cold water. Bring the water to a boil. Cover, reduce the heat to low, and simmer for 1 hour. Remove any foam that comes to the top.
2. Cook the bacon in a soup pot over medium high heat until just crisp. Remove the bacon from the pan and drain on paper towels.
3. Cook the onion, pepper, carrots, celery, and garlic in the pan until the vegetables are soft, about 5 to 10 minutes.
4. Stir in the sherry and cook for 2 minutes.
5. Pour in the chicken broth.
6. Stir the cooked bacon, cumin, oregano, and bay leaves into the soup.
7. Drain the beans through a colander. Reserve 2 cups of the cooked beans. Stir the remaining beans into the soup.
8. Bring the soup to a boil. Cover and reduce the heat to medium low.
9. Place the reserved beans and a ladle full of soup into a blender or food processor. Pulse to emulsify. Pour this mixture back into the soup. Season with salt and pepper.

10. Simmer the soup for 30 to 45 minutes or until the beans are soft.

11. Place a ladle of cooked rice into a soup bowl. Ladle the soup around the rice. Garnish with sour cream and green onion and cilantro. Serve with a shot glass filled with dry sherry on the side.

SERVINGS: 4 TO 6 • PREPARATION TIME: 30 MINUTES PLUS 1 HOUR TO COOK THE BEANS AND 45 MINUTES TO SIMMER THE SOUP.

Red Bean Soup with Barley and Diced Ham

BARLEY IS READILY AVAILABLE AND EASILY STORED IN YOUR PANTRY, WHICH MAKES FOR A QUICK SOUP INGREDIENT. ADD A HAM BONE FROM YOUR FREEZER, SOME EVERYDAY VEGGIES, AND YOU HAVE A FLAVORFUL SOUP READY TO SHARE WITH PALS.

2 tablespoons olive oil
2 medium celery ribs, diced (about 1 cup)
4 large carrots, diced (about 2 cups)
1 large yellow onion, diced (about 1 cup)
1 large ham bone, trimmed of excess fat
2 16-ounce cans red beans, drained
1 gallon water
2 bay leaves
8 ounces quick pearled barley
1 pound baked ham, diced
1 teaspoon Worcestershire sauce
2 or more drops hot pepper sauce
Salt and freshly ground pepper

1. Heat the olive oil in a soup pot over medium high heat.

2. Add the celery, carrots, and onions. Cook until soft, about 10 minutes.

3. Add the ham bone to the pot.

4. Add the canned beans to the pot. Pour in 1 gallon of water. Add the bay leaves.

5. Bring the soup to a boil. Reduce the heat, cover, and simmer for 20 minutes.

6. Stir in the barley and the diced ham. Simmer for 10 minutes more.

7. Remove the ham bone and the bay leaves. Season the soup with Worcestershire sauce, hot pepper sauce, salt, and pepper.

SERVES: 6 TO 8 • PREPARATION TIME: 1 HOUR

Lentil and Barley Soup
In place of canned beans use dried lentils. Add them to the soup with the water. Simmer for 30 to 40 minutes (or until soft) before adding the barley.

Red Bean Soup with Sausage and Orzo
Substitute rice or orzo pasta in place of the barley. Add cooked sausage in place of ham.

New England Style Clam Chowder

OKAY, IF YOU ARE A NEW ENGLAND CLAM CHOWDER PURIST, YOU WILL NOTE THAT THE ORIGINAL SOUP DOES NOT INCLUDE RED BELL PEPPER OR YELLOW CORN. IN FACT, IT IS MOST ALWAYS THICK, WHITE AND RICH. THIS VERSION ADDS A FEW EXTRA VEGGIES AND IS A BIT LESS THICK THAN THE TRADITIONAL. YOU CAN THICKEN THIS CHOWDER WITH THE ADDITION OF A TABLESPOON OR TWO OF FLOUR WHILE SAUTÉING THE ONIONS.

CHOWDER CLAMS ARE EAST COAST HARD SHELL CLAMS, AT LEAST 3-INCHES IN DIAMETER. THEY ARE ALSO KNOWN AS QUAHOG CLAMS. IF YOU WANT TO USE FRESH CLAMS IN YOUR CHOWDER, PURCHASE CHOWDER CLAMS, AND RINSE THEM WELL IN COLD WATER. CUT THE CLAMS INTO SMALL PIECES. ADD THE RAW CLAMS WHEN YOU COOK THE ONION, EXCEPT FOR THE TENDEREST PIECES, WHICH CAN BE ADDED TO THE SOUP AT THE END AND SIMMERED FOR JUST A FEW MINUTES.

¼ pound bacon, cut into 1-inch pieces
1 large yellow onion, diced into ½-inch squares (about 1 cup)
2 baking potatoes, peeled and diced into ½-inch squares (about 2 cups)
1 large red bell pepper, seeded and diced into ½-inch squares (about 1 cup)
2 ears of fresh corn, kernels sliced from cob (about 1 cup)
1 8-ounce bottle clam juice
2 cups half and half
3 10-ounce cans baby clams
2 tablespoons fresh chopped thyme
Salt and freshly ground pepper

1. Cook the bacon in a soup pot over medium high heat until just crisp. Remove the bacon and drain on paper towels. Drain all but 1 tablespoon of the bacon fat from the pot.

2. Add the onion to the pot and cook until soft, about 5 minutes.

3. Add the potatoes, pepper and corn to the onion and cook for 2 minutes.

4. Pour in the clam juice and half and half.

5. Drain the clams, pouring the liquid into the soup. Reduce the heat to medium low, cover, and simmer until the vegetables are soft, about 20 minutes.

6. Stir in the clams, bacon and the thyme. Simmer for 5 to 10 minutes more. Season with salt and pepper.

SERVINGS: 4 TO 6 • PREPARATION TIME: 1 HOUR

Sweet Corn Chowder
with Kielbasa, Peppers and Chives

FOR A QUICK ALTERNATIVE TO LONG SIMMERING SOUPS, CANNED VEGGIES
PROVIDE AN EXCELLENT INGREDIENT CHOICE. IN THIS RECIPE, CANNED
CORN WORKS BEST. FRESH CORN NEEDS TO BE COOKED BEFORE IT IS
PURÉED AND FROZEN CORN WOULD TAKE EXTRA TIME TO THAW.

2 tablespoons butter
1 medium yellow onion, diced (about 1½ cups)
1 large red bell pepper, seeded and diced (about 1 cup)
1 medium jalapeño pepper, seeded and diced (about 2 tablespoons)
2 medium cloves garlic, minced (about 1 teaspoon)
1 tablespoon all-purpose flour
1 quart chicken broth
2 large baking potatoes, peeled and diced into ½-inch squares (about 2 cups)
½ teaspoon ground cumin
Salt and freshly ground pepper

2 15-ounce cans sweet corn kernels, drained
6 ounces cooked Kielbasa sausage, cut into ½-inch slices
1 cup half and half
2 tablespoons fresh chives

KIELBASA IS A SPICY POLISH
SAUSAGE THAT IS MOST OFTEN
SOLD FULLY COOKED, BUT
CAN ALSO BE PURCHASED
PRE-COOKED AND FRESH.
FOR THIS QUICK CHOWDER
RECIPE, THE FULLY COOKED
PRODUCT IS THE ONE TO
CHOOSE. KIELBASA IS ALSO
SOMEWHAT SALTY. TASTE YOUR
SOUP BEFORE YOU ADD THE
FINAL SEASONINGS.

1. Heat the butter in a soup pot over medium high heat.
2. Add the onion, peppers, and garlic and cook for 5 minutes.
3. Sprinkle the veggies with flour and cook for 2 minutes more.
4. Pour in the chicken broth. Stir in the potatoes and season with
cumin, salt and pepper. Bring the soup to a boil. Cover the pot
and reduce the heat. Simmer until the potatoes are soft, about
20 to 30 minutes.
5. Place half of the corn kernels into a food
processor and pulse to purée.
6. Stir in the puréed corn, the remaining
corn, sausage, and half and half. Simmer
the soup uncovered for 20 minutes.
7. Season with salt and pepper and stir in
the fresh chives. Simmer for 5 minutes
more.

SERVINGS: 6 TO 8 • PREPARATION TIME: 1 HOUR

Red Onion Soup with Sun-Dried Tomato and Gruyere Crouton

I LIKE TO USE THE ROBUST RED ONION IN THIS SOUP FOR BOTH THE TASTE AND THE COLOR. FEEL FREE TO EXPERIMENT WITH THE SWEETER, VIDALIA ONION TO COMPARE THE FLAVORS.

YOU CAN ALTER THE CROUTON TOPPING BY SUBSTITUTING CHOPPED OLIVES OR MARINATED ARTICHOKES FOR SUN-DRIED TOMATOES. YOU CAN ALSO SUBSTITUTE WITH YOUR FAVORITE COMBINATION OF CHEESES, PROVIDING YOU PURCHASE A SOFT CHEESE— ONE THAT WILL MELT IN JUST A FEW SECONDS.

2 tablespoons olive oil
2 tablespoons butter
4 large red onions, thinly sliced (about 4 cups)
Salt and freshly ground pepper
1 cup red wine
2 tablespoons tomato paste
1 quart beef broth
1 bay leaf
1 tablespoon chopped fresh rosemary
1 tablespoon chopped fresh thyme

8 ¼-inch slices French bread baguette
4 tablespoons julienned sun-dried tomatoes in oil, drained
4 ounces Gruyere cheese, shredded (about 1 cup)
4 ounces finely grated Parmesan cheese (about 1 cup)

1. Heat the olive oil and butter in a large soup pot over medium high heat.
2. Stir in the onions and season with salt and pepper. Cook until the onions are soft and just beginning to brown, stirring often, about 20 minutes.
3. Pour in the red wine and stir in the tomato paste.
4. Pour in the beef broth. Add the bay leaf. Bring the soup to a boil. Cover, reduce the heat, and simmer for 20 minutes.
5. Stir in the fresh herbs. Simmer for 5 minutes more.
6. Preheat the broiler.
7. Toast the bread slices on one side until golden, about 2 to 3 minutes. Spread a teaspoon of sun-dried tomatoes onto the center of each slice.
8. Ladle the soup into oven proof crocks. Place the crocks into a baking dish or jelly roll pan.
9. Top the soup with a bread slice and generously sprinkle with both cheeses.
10. Broil the soup until bubbly and just beginning to brown, about 3 to 5 minutes.

SERVINGS: 6 TO 8 • PREPARATION TIME: 1 HOUR

Three Onion and Tequila Soup
with Fried Tortellini Crouton

THIS IS NOT YOUR MAMA'S ATTEMPT AT FRENCH ONION SOUP, BUT NEVERTHELESS IS ETHNICALLY INSPIRED! TEQUILA ADDS OOMPH, AS DOES A BIT OF RED WINE, BUT THE FRIED TORTELLINI CROUTON IS WAY OVER THE TOP!

2 tablespoons butter
2 tablespoons olive oil
2 large Spanish onions, sliced (about 3 cups)
2 large Bermuda onions, sliced (about 2 cups)
1 extra large white onion, sliced (about 2 cups)
4 medium garlic cloves, minced (about 2 teaspoons)
1 tablespoon brown sugar
Salt and freshly ground pepper
1 tablespoon Dijon mustard
½ cup tequila
2 tablespoons all-purpose flour
1 cup red wine
1 quart beef broth

12 to 16 fresh cheese filled tortellini, fried (see sidebar at right)
6 ounces grated Monterey Jack cheese (about 1½ cups)
2 tablespoons chopped fresh cilantro

1. Heat the butter and olive oil in a large soup pot over medium high heat.
2. Add the onions and garlic to the pot. Stir in the brown sugar. Season with salt and pepper. Cook until the onions are soft and beginning to brown, stirring often, about 30 minutes.
3. Stir in the mustard, tequila and flour. Cook for 5 minutes.
4. Pour in the wine and the beef broth. Cover, reduce heat and cook until the onions are soft, about 40 minutes.
5. Preheat the broiler
6. Ladle the soup into oven proof crocks. Place the crocks into a baking dish with a lip to catch spills.
7. Top the soup with fried tortellini and grated cheese. Broil for 2 to 3 minutes or until the cheese just melts. Sprinkle with fresh cilantro.

SERVINGS: 6 TO 8 • PREPARATION TIME: 1 HOUR

Fried Tortellini
Choose fresh tortellini from the refrigerated section of the grocery store. I like the cheese filled, but a veggie or meat filling will do just fine. Heat about 2 inches of canola oil in a deep saucepan, over medium high heat to about 350°. Carefully place the tortellini into the hot oil. Cook in batches so that you do not overcrowd the pan. Use a slotted spoon to gently turn the tortellini. Cook until the tortellinis are golden brown and just beginning to crisp. Drain on a wire rack over paper toweling.

BERMUDA ONIONS ARE MILD IN FLAVOR AND ARE EITHER WHITE OR YELLOW SKINNED. SPANISH ONIONS ARE ALSO EITHER WHITE OR YELLOW SKINNED. BOTH VARIETIES ARE AVAILABLE IN THE SPRING. FEEL FREE TO SUBSTITUTE WITH THE FRESHEST, MOST READILY AVAILABLE ONIONS THAT YOU CAN FIND IN THE MARKET. FOR EXAMPLE, VIDALIA ONIONS FROM GEORGIA ARE AVAILABLE FROM MAY THROUGH JUNE AND THE MAUI ONION FROM HAWAII IS ALSO MILD AND JUICY AND IN SEASON FROM APRIL THROUGH JULY.

Lentil Soup with Wild Mushrooms

A COMBINATION OF EARTHY MUSHROOMS AND TENDER LENTILS MAKES A HEARTY DISH THAT YOU CAN PREPARE IN ADVANCE AND SERVE WHEN A SOUP CRAVING SNEAKS UP ON YOU.

LENTILS ARE A GOOD SOURCE OF IRON AND PHOSPHORUS AND CONTAIN VITAMINS A AND B. THERE ARE DIFFERENT TYPES OF LENTILS TO CHOOSE FROM AND ALL WILL WORK WELL IN THIS RECIPE. THE SMALLEST ARE FRENCH LENTILS WHICH HAVE A CREAMY TEXTURE AND ARE GRAYISH-BROWN IN COLOR. YOU CAN ALSO FIND RED AND YELLOW LENTILS IN SPECIALTY SHOPS AND EAST INDIAN MARKETS. THE MOST COMMON LENTILS FOUND IN MOST SUPERMARKETS ARE BROWN AND MEDIUM SIZE. THE SMALLER THE LENTIL, THE FASTER THE LENTIL COOKS. ADJUST YOUR COOKING TIME BASED ON YOUR LENTILS OF CHOICE. IT IS A GOOD IDEA TO RINSE LENTILS IN A COLANDER AND REMOVE ANY FOREIGN PIECES BEFORE USING THEM IN A RECIPE.

2 tablespoons olive oil
1 medium yellow onion, diced (about 1½ cups)
2 large carrots, diced (about 1 cup)
2 medium celery ribs, diced (about 1 cup)
8 ounces button mushrooms, diced (about 2 cups)
4 ounces portobello mushrooms, diced (about 1 cup)
4 ounces shitake mushrooms, diced (about 1 cup)
2 tablespoons chopped fresh thyme leaves
1 14-ounce package dried lentils (about 2 cups uncooked)
1 quart chicken broth
1 quart water
2 to 3 tablespoons balsamic vinegar
Salt and freshly ground pepper
Sour cream
Fresh chopped parsley

1. Heat the olive oil in a soup pot over medium high heat.
2. Stir in the onion, carrots, and celery and cook until the vegetables are soft, about 5 to 8 minutes.
3. Stir in the mushrooms, thyme and lentils.
4. Pour in 1 quart chicken broth and 1 quart water.
5. Bring the soup to a boil. Reduce the heat, cover, and simmer for at least 30 minutes or until the lentils are soft.
6. Stir in the balsamic vinegar and season with salt and pepper.
7. Garnish the soup with a dollop of sour cream and a sprinkle of fresh parsley.

SERVINGS: 6 TO 8 • PREPARATION TIME: 30 MINUTES PLUS SIMMERING

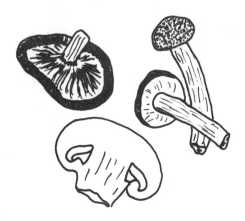

Ginger Lentil Soup

PACKED FULL OF HEALTHY INGREDIENTS, THIS SOUP HAS TONS OF FLAVOR,
AS WELL AS LOTS OF GOOD-FOR-YOU STUFF. USING AN IMMERSION
BLENDER PRODUCES A VELVETY TEXTURE.

2 tablespoons olive oil
1 large yellow onion, diced into ½-inch squares (about 1 cup)
4 medium cloves garlic, minced
1 3-inch piece ginger, grated (about 3 tablespoons)
1 teaspoon ground cumin
¼ teaspoon ground curry
2 medium plum tomatoes, seeded and diced (about ½ cup)
1 14-ounce package dried lentils (about 2 cups uncooked)
1 quart chicken broth
1 quart water
1 dried bay leaf
Salt and freshly ground pepper
½ cup plain yogurt
Salt and freshly ground pepper

Fried ginger slices (see instructions at right)

1. Heat the olive oil over medium high heat in a soup pot.
2. Cook the onion in the oil until soft, about 5 minutes.
3. Stir in the garlic, ginger, cumin, curry, tomatoes and lentils.
4. Pour in 1 quart chicken broth and 1 quart water.
5. Place the bay leaf into the
soup. Bring to a boil. Cover and
reduce the heat to low. Simmer
the soup for 30 to 45 minutes.
6. Remove the cover. Season with
salt and pepper. Use an immersion blender (or food processor)
to coarsely purée the soup.
7. Stir in the plain yogurt and
garnish with fried ginger.

SERVINGS: 6 TO 8 • PREPARATION TIME
30 MINUTES PLUS SIMMERING

Fried Ginger
To make fried ginger, peel a
large piece. Use a mandoline
(or very sharp knife) to cut
paper thin pieces. Heat canola
oil in a small skillet or pot, over
medium high heat. Place the
ginger slices into the hot oil. Use
a slotted spoon or strainer basket to remove the ginger from
the oil, as soon as the pieces turn
golden, about 30 seconds
depending on the thickness of
the ginger. Drain on paper towels. Use this technique to create
other terrific garnishes like fried
parsley, tortilla strips, zucchini
strips and sliced almonds.

Classic Caesar Salad Prepared Tableside

TO THIS DAY, MY FAVORITE ITEM TO ORDER ON ANY RESTAURANT MENU IS
CAESAR SALAD. IN FACT, I PROBABLY BASE MY FIRST IMPRESSIONS ON HOW
THE CHEF PREPARES THIS DISH. THE LETTUCE MUST BE ICE COLD, CRISP
AND JUST DRESSED WITH THE DRESSING, NOT DRENCHED—WHICH SHOULD
BE BARELY EMULSIFIED, BUT NOT CREAMED. ANCHOVIES ARE A MUST, AND
THE CROUTONS SHOULD BE SO FRESHLY BAKED THAT THEY ARE WARM.
OKAY, I'M PICKY, BUT ONCE YOU'VE HAD THE BEST, IT'S HARD TO SETTLE
FOR LESS!

2 medium cloves garlic, minced (about 1 teaspoon)
1 tablespoon Dijon mustard
1 teaspoon Worcestershire sauce
1 2-ounce tin anchovies, packed in oil, drained
1 large egg, coddled
Juice of 1 medium lemon (about 2 tablespoons)
¼ cup balsamic vinegar
½ cup olive oil
1 large head romaine lettuce, washed, dried and torn into strips (about 8 cups)
1 cup homemade croutons
4 ounces grated Parmesan cheese (about 1 cup)
Freshly grated pepper

1. Place the garlic into a large wooden bowl. Use the back of a
wooden spoon to smash the garlic into the bowl.
2. Swirl together the mustard and the Worcestershire sauce into
the bowl.
3. Use the back of the spoon to smash the anchovies into the gar-
lic/mustard mixture.
4. Swirl in the egg and the lemon juice.
5. Whisk in the vinegar.
6. Slowly whisk in the olive oil.
7. Place the lettuce leaves into the bowl
and toss in the dressing.
8. Add the croutons and cheese. Toss to
combine.
9. Season with freshly ground pepper.

SERVINGS: 4 TO 6 • PREPARATION TIME: 15
MINUTES

Croutons

*To prepare your own fresh
baked croutons, cut crusty
bread into 1-inch pieces. In a
plastic bag, combine 2 tablespoons finely grated Parmesan
cheese, salt, pepper and a bit of
garlic powder. Add the bread
cubes to the bag and shake well.
Spray a baking sheet with vegetable oil spray. Toss the croutons onto the baking sheet and
spray again. Bake at 400°
until golden brown, about 3 to
4 minutes.*

Coddled Eggs

*Classic Caesar salad dressing
includes a coddled egg. Prepare
the egg by placing it into boiling
water for 1 to 2 minutes. The
yolk is runny and the white is
still translucent, but the egg is
not raw. If you are concerned
about using an uncooked egg in
your recipe, you can omit it and
still make a wonderful dressing.*

Romaine Salad with Ten Cloves of Garlic Dressing

HERE IS AN UPDATED VERSION OF CLASSIC CAESAR SALAD. THE DRESSING IS
PREPARED WITH A BUNCH OF GARLIC THAT IS SWEETENED WITH AGED
BALSAMIC VINEGAR. USE EXTRA DRESSING TO DRIZZLE ON POACHED FISH
OR AS A DIPPING SAUCE FOR CRUDITÉS. TRUST ME, IF YOU LIKE CAESAR—
YOU'LL LOVE THIS DRESSING!

10 whole garlic cloves
1 tablespoon Dijon mustard
1 teaspoon Worcestershire sauce
1 2-ounce tin anchovies, packed in oil, drained
Juice of 1 medium lemon (about 2 tablespoons)
¼ cup red wine vinegar
½ cup balsamic vinegar
½ cup olive oil
Salt and freshly ground pepper

1 large head romaine lettuce, washed, dried and torn (about 8 cups)
6 medium plum tomatoes, seeded and diced (about 3 cups)
4 ounce Gorgonzola cheese, crumbled (about 1 cup)

1. Place the garlic cloves, mustard, Worcestershire, anchovies,
lemon juice, red wine vinegar and balsamic vinegar into a
blender. Pulse to emulsify.
2. With the machine running, slowly pour in the olive oil.
Season with salt and pepper.
3. Place the romaine leaves into a salad bowl. Toss with enough
dressing to just coat the leaves.
4. Top the salad with diced plum tomatoes and Gorgonzola
cheese. Add another sprinkle of freshly ground pepper.

SERVINGS: 4 TO 6 • PREPARATION TIME: 20 MINUTES

ITALIAN BALSAMIC VINEGAR COMES FROM WHITE TREB-BIANO GRAPE JUICE.
THE JUICE IS AGED IN VARIOUS SIZES AND DIFFERENT TYPES OF WOODEN BAR-
RELS, PRODUCING THE DARK, RICH COLOR AND PUNGENT FLAVOR OF THE
VINEGAR. THE PROCESS IS SIMILAR TO WINEMAKING. IN FACT, YOU CAN PUR-
CHASE BALSAMIC VINEGARS OF VARIOUS VINTAGES. EXPERIMENT WITH THE
MORE EXPENSIVE BOTTLES OF BALSAMIC VINEGAR FOR YOUR BEST SALADS,
AND FOR GLAZES THAT WORK WELL ON DESSERT BERRIES.

Classic Cabbage and Carrot Coleslaw

SHREDDED FRESH VEGGIES AND A CREAMY SWEET SAUCE COMBINE FOR A
WONDERFUL SUMMER SALAD THAT WORKS ALONE, AS A SIDE DISH, OR AS A
TOPPING ON YOUR FAVORITE BARBECUE SANDWICH.

For this recipe you can easily take advantage of the pre-packaged, pre-shredded veggies that are finding their way to your supermarket. Shredded broccoli and purple cabbage are great additions. Others include shredded bell peppers and a touch of sliced onion. For a Mexican spin on traditional coleslaw, add thin strips of seeded jalapeño pepper, a sprinkle of lime juice, and a dash of ground cumin. Garnish with fresh cilantro instead of parsley.

1 2-pound head green cabbage, shredded (about 6 to 8 cups)
2 large carrots, shredded (about 1 cup)
½ cup mayonnaise
2 tablespoons tarragon vinegar
1 tablespoon granulated sugar
1 teaspoon celery seed
Salt and freshly ground pepper
2 tablespoons chopped fresh parsley

1. Place the shredded cabbage and carrots into a large bowl.
2. Stir together the mayonnaise, vinegar, sugar and celery seed. Season with salt and pepper.
3. Pour the sauce over the cabbage and toss to coat. Cover and refrigerate for at least 1 hour.
4. Garnish with chopped fresh parsley.

SERVINGS: 6 TO 8 • PREPARATION TIME: 20 MINUTES PLUS REFRIGERATION

Garden Slaw with Jicama and Green Apples

HERE IS AN UPDATE ON YOUR FAVORITE PICNIC SIDE DISH. JICAMA IS A
CRUNCHY, WHITE ROOT THAT IS SOMETIMES REFERRED TO AS THE MEXICAN
POTATO. ITS TEXTURE IS SIMILAR TO A WATER CHESTNUT. CUTTING THE
VEGGIES INTO THIN MATCH STICK SIZE PIECES PRODUCES A GREAT RESULT.

1 1–pound head green cabbage, shredded (about 3 to 4 cups)
2 large carrots, cut into thin julienne (about 1 cup)
1 small jicama, peeled and cut into thin julienne (about 1 cup)
1 large yellow or orange bell pepper, seeded and cut into thin julienne (about 1 cup)
1 medium green apple, peeled and cut into thin julienne (about 1 cup)
½ small red onion, cut into thin julienne (about ½ cup)

¼ cup buttermilk
¼ cup mayonnaise
Juice of 1 medium lemon (about 2 tablespoons)
1 tablespoon granulated sugar
Salt and freshly ground pepper
2 tablespoons chopped fresh mint

1. Toss the cabbage, carrots, jicama, pepper, apple and red onion
together in a large bowl.
2. Whisk together the buttermilk, mayonnaise, lemon juice and
sugar in another bowl.
3. Pour the sauce into the vegetables and toss to coat. Season with
salt and pepper.
4. Cover and chill for at least 1 hour. Garnish with fresh mint.

SERVINGS: 6 TO 8 • PREPARATION TIME: 20 MINUTES PLUS 1 HOUR TO CHILL

FOR A FUN PRESENTATION OF
YOUR FAVORITE SLAW, SERVE
IN CLEAR GLASS TUMBLERS,
LINED WITH BLANCHED AND
CHILLED ASPARAGUS SPEARS
AND A GARNISH OF CURLED
LEMON PEEL ON THE RIM.

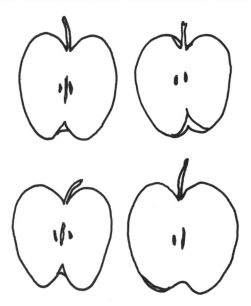

Spicy Potato Salad

POTATO SALAD IS A PICNIC AND COLD SUPPER STAPLE. WHEN SPICED UP
WITH A LITTLE HOT SAUCE, IT BECOMES A DEVILISH ADDITION TO MOST
EVERYDAY MEALS. FEEL FREE TO MAKE THIS A DAY IN ADVANCE TO ALLOW
THE SPICY FLAVORS TO MARRY WITH THE POTATOES.

When boiling veggies in water, the best method is to start with cold water in a cold pan. Fill the pan with water and place it on the stovetop over high heat. Cover the pot to accelerate the heating. When the water boils, add a good amount of salt. Adding the salt at this point, will protect your pan. The salt will cause the water to bubble, so be cautious. Your veggies will absorb a small amount of the salt in the water, which is just what you want!

5 pounds small red creamer potatoes, cut into ¼-inch pieces
1 bunch (6 to 8) green onions, chopped (about ½ cup)
½ cup mayonnaise
¼ cup sour cream
2 tablespoons Dijon mustard
1 teaspoon paprika
4 to 6 drops hot pepper sauce
Salt and freshly ground pepper
2 tablespoons chopped fresh cilantro

1. Boil the potatoes in salted water until just tender, about 10 to 15 minutes. Drain and place into bowl.
2. Add the onions to the bowl.
3. Stir together the mayonnaise, sour cream, mustard, paprika and hot sauce. Pour this mixture over the potatoes.
4. Toss the potatoes with the dressing. Season with salt and pepper and, if you like, with additional hot pepper sauce. Chill the salad for 1 hour or overnight. Sprinkle the salad with fresh cilantro.

SERVINGS: 6 TO 8 • PREPARATION TIME: 30 MINUTES, PLUS CHILLING

Grilled Potato Salad with Dijon Vinaigrette

I USE A GRILL PAN INDOORS TO MAKE EASY WORK OF GRILLING PAR-BOILED
POTATO SLICES, BUT IF YOU'RE IN THE MOOD TO SHOW-OFF, YOU CAN
GRILL THE POTATOES ON THE OUTDOOR BARBIE NEXT TO THE BURGERS. IF
YOU CHOOSE THIS METHOD, MAKE SURE THAT YOUR POTATO SLICES ARE
LARGER THAT THE GRATES ON THE GRILL.

¼ cup sherry vinegar
2 tablespoons Dijon mustard
1 large shallot, minced (about 1 tablespoon)
1 teaspoon honey
¾ cup olive oil
Salt and freshly ground pepper

4 large baking potatoes, sliced into ½-inch rounds
2 tablespoons olive oil
12 ounces mesclun lettuce mix (about 4 cups)
2 tablespoons chopped fresh chives

CLASSIC POTATO SALAD COM-
BINES WARM POTATOES WITH
VINAIGRETTE AND ALLOWS
THEM TO SIT IN THE BOWL,
ABSORBING ALL OF THE FLA-
VORS BEFORE ADDING OTHER
INGREDIENTS. THIS RECIPE
WORKS IN THE SAME WAY, BUT
USES A GRILL PAN TO UPDATE
THE LOOK AND FEEL OF THE
SALAD.

1. Whisk together the vinegar, mustard, shallot and honey in a
bowl.
2. Slowly whisk in the olive oil. Season with salt and pepper.
3. Cook the potatoes in boiling, salted water until just tender,
about 6 to 8 minutes. Drain and pat dry.
4. Brush each side of the potatoes with olive oil and sprinkle with
salt and pepper.
5. Heat a grill pan over medium high heat.
Cook the potato slices in the pan until golden,
about 2 to 3 minutes. Turn and cook until
both sides are golden, about 2 to 3 minutes
more.
6. Place the lettuce mix into a bowl. Drizzle
with 2 tablespoons of the dressing. Place the
potato slices on top of the dressed greens.
7. Pour the remaining salad dressing over the
potatoes. Sprinkle with fresh chives.

SERVINGS: 4 TO 6 • PREPARATION TIME: 30 MINUTES

Wilted Spinach Salad with Warm Cider Dressing

THE SECRET TO SUCCESS IN THIS RECIPE IS TO JUST DRIZZLE THE SALAD WITH THE DRESSING. YOU CAN ALWAYS ADD MORE, BUT YOU CAN'T UNDO AN OVERLY GENEROUS POUR. THE ONIONS ARE BARELY WILTED AND ADD A NICE TOUCH IN PLACE OF TOTALLY RAW ONES. YOU CAN ADD HOMEMADE CROUTONS (SEE PAGE 88) FOR A HEARTIER DISH.

PEOPLE USED TO STAY AWAY FROM SPINACH BECAUSE IT WAS OFTEN GRITTY AND DIFFICULT TO CLEAN. TODAY'S PRODUCE PROVIDERS WASH THE LEAVES FOR US AND, MOST OFTEN, PROVIDE US WITH TENDER BABY LEAVES WITHOUT THE COARSE STEMS. HOWEVER, IF YOU BUY YOUR SPINACH FRESH FROM THE MARKET, YOU ARE IN FOR A REAL TREAT. TO WASH THOROUGHLY, FILL YOUR SINK WITH COLD WATER. LAY THE LEAVES IN THE WATER AND ALLOW ALL OF THE GRIT TO SINK TO THE BOTTOM. USE A SALAD SPINNER TO DRY THE LEAVES THOROUGHLY, AND THEN TEAR THEM INTO BITE SIZE BITES.

¼ pound bacon, cut into 1–inch pieces
1 cup apple cider
2 tablespoon balsamic vinegar
2 medium cloves garlic, minced (about 1 teaspoon)
1 medium white onion, peeled and thinly sliced (about ⅔ cup)
¼ cup olive oil
1 tablespoon Dijon mustard
Salt and fresh ground pepper
1 pound fresh spinach leaves, washed, dried and torn (about 3 cups)
2 hard boiled eggs, peeled and chopped
4 ounces Feta cheese, crumbled (about 1 cup)

1. Cook the bacon in a skillet over medium high heat until crisp. Transfer to paper towels to drain. Remove all but about 2 tablespoons of bacon drippings to the pan.

2. Pour the cider into the pan. Stir in the vinegar and garlic. Bring to a boil and simmer for 5 minutes.

3. Add the onions and cook until just beginning to soften, about 4 minutes more.

4. Stir in the olive oil and mustard, and season with salt and pepper. Reduce the heat to low.

5. Place the spinach leaves into a large bowl. Drizzle enough dressing (including the onions) over the leaves to just wet. The spinach will wilt slightly.

6. Toss the salad with the bacon, eggs and feta cheese.

SERVINGS: 4 TO 6 •
PREPARATION TIME:
20 MINUTES

Mesclun Salad with Brie Cheese, Toasted Almonds, Mandarin Oranges, and Sesame Dressing

IN ALMOST EVERY JUNIOR LEAGUE COOKBOOK YOU WILL FIND A TOSSED
SALAD WITH TOASTED NUTS, BRIE CHEESE, AND A BIT OF FRUIT. IT'S A TINY
BIT OF HEAVEN THAT ENHANCES ANY MEAL. THIS VERSION IS MY FAVORITE,
AND IS EASILY TO PREPARE FOR GUESTS OR FAMILY.

1 tablespoon brown sugar
1 tablespoon butter
1 cup sliced almonds

12 ounces mesclun lettuce mix, about 4 cups
1 8-ounce can mandarin oranges, drained
1 6-ounce wedge Brie cheese, cut into ½-inch cubes

Juice of 1 medium orange (about ⅓ cup)
1 tablespoon soy sauce
1 tablespoon rice wine vinegar
1 tablespoon toasted sesame oil
1 tablespoon Dijon mustard
1 medium clove garlic, minced (about ½ teaspoon)
Zest of 1 medium lemon (about 1 tablespoons)
1 ½-inch piece ginger, grated
1 tablespoon chopped fresh cilantro
¼ cup canola oil
Salt and freshly ground pepper

1. Heat the sugar and butter in a saucepan over medium high
heat. Add the almonds. Cook until golden, about 5 minutes.
Cool.
2. Place the lettuce mix, oranges, and Brie cheese in a large salad
bowl. Chill.
3. Place the orange juice, soy sauce, rice wine vinegar, sesame oil,
mustard, garlic, lemon zest, ginger, and cilantro into a blender.
Pulse to combine.
4. With the machine running, slowly pour in the canola oil.
Season with salt and pepper.
5. Toss the almonds into the salad. Pour in enough dressing just
to moisten the leaves. Toss and season with additional pepper if
needed.

SERVINGS: 4 TO 6 • PREPARATION TIME: 20 MINUTES

Crisp Iceberg Salad
with Chipotle Thousand Island Dressing

CHILLED, CRISP LETTUCE IS THE PERFECT BACKDROP FOR A DECADENTLY RICH SAUCE. THIS TRADITIONAL RECIPE FOR THOUSAND ISLAND DRESSING IS SPICED WITH THE ADDITION OF DICED, RECONSTITUTED CHIPOTLE PEPPER. THE PEPPER IS HOT, HOT. REMOVING THE SEEDS TAKES AWAY SOME OF THE HEAT AND ALLOWS THE SMOKY PEPPER FLAVOR TO INFUSE THE DRESSING.

A CHIPOTLE PEPPER IS A DRIED AND SMOKED JALAPEÑO PEPPER. MOST OFTEN, YOU CAN FIND DRIED PEPPERS IN THE PRODUCE SECTION OF THE MARKET. RECONSTITUTE THEM IN OLIVE OIL OR WARM WATER, OR DICE THEM AS THEY ARE AND ADD THEM TO STEWS OR SOUPS. CHIPOTLE PEPPERS ARE ALSO FOUND ALREADY RECONSTITUTED IN A TOMATO-BASED SAUCE CALLED ADOBO. CANS OF THESE CHILIES ARE USUALLY FOUND IN SPECIALTY MARKETS.

1 large head iceberg lettuce, cut into quarters
6 medium plum tomatoes, seeded and diced, about 3 cups

1 dried chipotle pepper
1½ cups mayonnaise
3 tablespoons chili sauce
1 large shallot, minced (about 1 tablespoon)
2 tablespoons drained sweet pickle relish
1 tablespoon juice from sweet pickle relish
1 large egg, hardboiled, peeled and chopped
Salt and freshly ground pepper

1. Place the lettuce wedges onto a salad plate. Sprinkle each wedge with ¼ of the diced tomatoes. Put the salad plates into the refrigerator to chill for at least 30 minutes.
2. Place the pepper into warm water for 15 minutes. Cut in half and remove the seeds and veins. Dice into small pieces.
3. Mix together the mayonnaise, chili sauce, shallot, pickle relish, pickle juice, and diced pepper. Fold in the hardboiled egg. Season with salt and pepper.
4. Serve the salad with a generous dollop of dressing and sprinkle with additional fresh pepper.

SERVINGS: 4 • PREPARATION TIME: 10 MINUTES PLUS 30 MINUTES TO CHILL

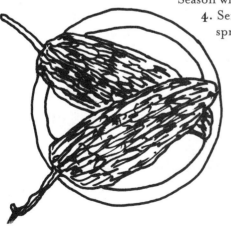

Chilled Green Salad with Warm Goat Cheese and Raspberry Vinaigrette

THE TOSSED SALAD HAS COME A LONG WAY FROM ICEBERG LETTUCE AND ITALIAN SALAD DRESSING. IN JUST MOMENTS, YOU CAN PREPARE A SALAD AT HOME THAT IS EVERY BIT AS UPSCALE AS THE ONES ON THE MENU AT YOUR FAVORITE BISTRO. USE WHOLE FRESH RASPBERRIES AS THE BEGINNING OF THE DRESSING AND AS AN ACCENT TO THE SALAD GREENS. CHILL YOUR SALAD PLATES IN THE FREEZER FOR AT LEAST 15 MINUTES BEFORE PLATING.

14 soda crackers
1 egg
4 ounce log goat cheese, cut into 4 rounds

¼ cup raspberry vinegar
1 tablespoon balsamic vinegar
1 tablespoon chopped fresh thyme
2 teaspoons Dijon mustard
1 large shallot, minced (about 1 tablespoon)
1 cup fresh raspberries, divided
½ cup olive oil
Salt and freshly ground pepper

12 ounces mesclun lettuce mix (about 4 cups)

1. Place the crackers into the bowl of a food processor and pulse to form fine crumbs. Place the crumbs into a shallow bowl.
2. Beat the egg with 1 tablespoon of water in a separate bowl.
3. Place the goat cheese slices, first into the egg mixture, coating both sides. Then dip them into the cracker crumbs, again coating both sides. Place the coated goat cheese onto a baking sheet. Chill for 15 minutes.
4. Place the vinegars, thyme, mustard, shallot and half of the raspberries into blender. Pulse. With the machine running, slowly pour in the olive oil. Season with salt and pepper. Preheat the oven to 475°.
5. Remove the coated cheese from the refrigerator. Bake until warmed through, but not melted, about 3 to 5 minutes.
6. Divide the salad greens among chilled plates. Dot each salad with the remaining fresh raspberries. Place the warm goat cheese on the plate. Drizzle with the raspberry vinaigrette and a sprinkle of freshly ground pepper.

SERVINGS: 4 • PREPARATION TIME: 20 MINUTES PLUS REFRIGERATION

ALSO KNOWN AS CHÈVRE (THE FRENCH WORD FOR GOAT), THIS PURE, WHITE, MILKY CHEESE HAS A UNIQUE, TART TASTE THAT DISTINGUISHES IT FROM OTHER CHEESES. WHILE GOAT CHEESE IS MOSTLY SOLD IN PURE FORM, SOME GOAT CHEESE COMES WITH ADDED COWS' MILK. THE TEXTURE IS MOST OFTEN CREAMY, BUT CAN RANGE FROM MOIST TO ALMOST FIRM. UNLIKE OTHER CHEESE, GOAT CHEESE STORED WELL WILL LAST ONLY UP TO TWO WEEKS IN THE REFRIGERATOR.

Layered Chopped Veggie Salad

USE A CLEAR BOWL, NOT UNLIKE A TRIFLE DISH TO DISPLAY THIS COLORFUL
SALAD. YOU CAN ARRANGE THE LAYERS IN ADVANCE, CHILL, AND DRIZZLE
THE DRESSING BEFORE YOU SERVE THE DISH.

YOU NEEDN'T PREPARE THIS SALAD THE SAME WAY TWICE! THE LAYERS CAN BE ARRANGED IN ANY ORDER. FEEL FREE TO SUBSTITUTE OR ADD OTHER INGREDIENTS LIKE YOUR FAVORITE VEGGIES, OR LAYERS OF INGREDIENTS LIKE CANNED TUNA, BLACK BEANS, OR HOMEMADE CROUTONS.

1 cup sour cream
¼ cup ketchup
Juice of 1 medium lime (about 2 tablespoons)
2 tablespoons capers, drained and rinsed
½ small white onion, chopped (about 2 tablespoons)
½ teaspoon chili powder
½ teaspoon ground cumin
¼ cup olive oil
Salt and freshly ground pepper

1 large head iceberg lettuce, cut into bite size pieces (about 6 cups)
1 cup corn chips, crumbled
4 ounces shredded cheddar cheese (about 1 cup)
1 bunch (6 to 8) green onions, chopped (about ½ cup)
1 pint ripe cherry tomatoes or mixed baby tomatoes
1 large cucumber, seeded and diced (about 1 cup)
1 large carrots, thinly sliced (about 1 cup)
12 whole radishes, sliced (about 1 cup)
1 large yellow bell pepper, seeded and chopped (about 1 cup)
2 tablespoons chopped fresh cilantro

1. Place the sour cream, ketchup, lime juice, capers, onion, chili powder and cumin into a blender. Pulse to purée. With the machine running, slowly drizzle in the olive oil. Season with salt and pepper.
2. Place the lettuce into a bowl. Drizzle with 2 to 3 tablespoons dressing. Toss until lightly coated.
3. Spoon half of the dressed lettuce into the bottom of a large glass bowl.
4. Sprinkle half of the corn chips and half of the cheese on top of the lettuce.
5. Layer half of onions, tomatoes, cucumbers, carrots, radishes and yellow pepper on top. Drizzle with 2 tablespoons of the dressing.
6. Complete the salad by layering the remaining ingredients. Drizzle the remaining salad dressing on top of the layered salad. Garnish with fresh cilantro.

SERVINGS: 4 TO 6 • PREPARATION TIME: 20 MINUTES

Arranged Greek Salad with Grilled Chicken

INSTEAD OF TOSSING YOUR MAIN COURSE SALAD IN A BOWL, ARRANGE IT ON A PLATTER FOR AN EASY-TO-SERVE PRESENTATION.

¼ cup white wine vinegar
Juice of 2 medium lemons (about ¼ cup)
1 tablespoon granulated sugar
2 medium cloves garlic, minced (about 1 teaspoon)
1 tablespoon chopped fresh oregano
1 tablespoon chopped fresh mint
½ cup olive oil
Salt and freshly ground pepper

2 large (4- to 6-ounce) skinless, boneless chicken breasts

1 large medium romaine lettuce, washed, dried and torn (about 6 cups)
½ head iceberg lettuce cut into bite size pieces (about 3 to 4 cups)
6 medium plum tomatoes, seeded and diced (about 3 cups)
1 large cucumber, seeded and diced (about 1 cup)
1 large red bell pepper, seeded and diced (about 1 cup)
1 16-ounce jar Kalamata olives, drained, pitted and chopped
4 ounces Feta cheese, crumbled (about 1 cup)
½ small red onion, cut into very thin (about ¼ cup)
2 tablespoons chopped fresh parsley

1. Whisk together the vinegar, lemon juice, sugar, garlic, oregano, mint and olive oil. Season with salt and pepper.
2. Place the chicken breasts into a shallow dish. Drizzle with 2 tablespoons of the vinaigrette. Turn and drizzle with 2 more tablespoons of the vinaigrette. Chill for 20 minutes.
3. Heat a grill pan over medium high heat. Remove the chicken from the dish and season with salt and pepper. Grill the chicken in the pan, turning once until cooked through (about 4 to 5 minutes per side). Let the chicken rest for 5 to 10 minutes.
4. Place the lettuce in a bowl. Toss with 2 to 3 tablespoons of the vinaigrette. Arrange the lettuce on a large platter.
5. Cut the chicken breasts into very thin slices and arrange, in a row, on top of the dressed lettuce. Continue arranging rows of tomatoes, cucumber, pepper and olives.
6. Drizzle the remaining vinaigrette over the salad. Top with crumbled feta cheese, thinly sliced red onion, chopped parsley and a sprinkle of freshly ground pepper.

SERVINGS: 4 TO 6 • PREPARATION TIME: 20 MINUTES

A CHERRY PITTER IS AN EXCELLENT TOOL TO USE FOR PITTING OLIVES. SIMPLY PLACE AN OLIVE ONTO THE BOWL OF THE PITTER AND SQUEEZE. OUT POPS THE PIT, WHILE A PERFECTLY IN-TACT OLIVE REMAINS. YOU CAN ALSO USE THE FLAT BLADE OF A KNIFE TO REMOVE THE PIT FROM THE OLIVE. PLACE THE OLIVE ON A CUTTING BOARD. PLACE THE FLAT BLADE OF THE KNIFE (SHARP SIDE POINTING AWAY FROM YOU) ON TOP OF THE OLIVE. PRESS DOWN WITH YOUR HAND HARD ENOUGH TO POP OUT THE PIT!

Lobster Cobb Salad
with Tomato Ginger Vinaigrette

THIS RECIPE IS EASY TO INCORPORATE INTO YOUR MEAL PLAN FOR WEEK-
END GUESTS OR A LEISURELY LUNCH. EVERYTHING IS PREPARED IN ADVANCE
AND THEN ASSEMBLED FOR SERVING. TRADITIONAL COBB SALAD FROM THE
BROWN DERBY RESTAURANT FEATURES BROILED CHICKEN, BUT I DON'T
THINK YOU'LL MIND THIS SEAFOOD SUBSTITUTION.

You can easily prepare the lobster for this salad (see page 233), or save some time and buy cooked lobster from your fishmonger. When preparing the ingredients, make sure that you chop the avocado just before assembling to avoid any discoloration. You might also want to substitute using a milder, creamy cheese like Fontina, in place of tart blue cheese.

2 tablespoons sun-dried tomatoes in oil
1 1-inch piece ginger, grated (about 1 tablespoon)
Zest of 2 medium lemons (about 2 tablespoons)
1 teaspoon Dijon mustard
1 teaspoon tomato paste
¼ cup sherry vinegar
¾ cup olive oil
Salt and freshly ground pepper

½ pound bacon, cut into 1-inch pieces
1 large head romaine lettuce, washed, dried and torn (about 8 cups)
1 bunch watercress, washed, dried, stems removed (about 4 cups)
2 pounds cooked lobster meat, chopped into 1-inch pieces
1 pint ripe cherry tomatoes or mixed baby tomatoes
4 large eggs, hardboiled, peeled and cut into quarters
1 large avocado, peeled, pitted and diced (about 1 cup)
4 ounces blue cheese, crumbled (about 1 cup)
2 tablespoons chopped fresh parsley

1. Place the sun-dried tomatoes, ginger, lemon zest, mustard and tomato paste into a blender. Pulse to emulsify.
2. Pour in the sherry vinegar. Pulse to combine.
3. With the machine running, slowly pour in the olive oil. Season with salt and pepper.
4. Cook the bacon in a skillet over medium high heat until crisp, about 6 to 8 minutes. Remove the bacon to paper towels to drain.
5. Place the romaine leaves and watercress into a large bowl. Sprinkle with 5 to 6 tablespoons of vinaigrette. Toss. Lay the leaves onto the bottom of a large platter.
6. Place the lobster chunks into the same bowl. Toss with 2 tablespoons of vinaigrette. Lay the lobster, in a row, on top of the salad greens.
7. Place the tomatoes into the same bowl. Toss with 1 tablespoon of vinaigrette. Lay them alongside the lobster.
8. Arrange the hardboiled eggs alongside the tomatoes, followed by a row of avocado, a row of bacon and a row of cheese.
9. Drizzle with the remaining vinaigrette. Garnish with parsley.

SERVINGS: 6 TO 8 • PREPARATION TIME: 20 MINUTES

Creamy Cucumber and Sweet Onion Salad

MY GRANDMOTHER MADE THIS SALAD FOR ALMOST EVERY SUNDAY NIGHT
DINNER. IT'S LIGHT AND REFRESHING, WHILE CREAMY AND RICH. I THINK
THERE ARE FLAVORS OF HER POLISH HERITAGE IN THE DISH—AT LEAST I
LIKE TO THINK SO. YOU NEEDN'T PEEL THE CUCUMBERS; THE CONTRASTING
COLORS ARE WONDERFUL.

*4 large cucumbers, halved lengthwise, seeded and sliced into ¼-inch slices (about 4
   cups)*
Salt
1 medium white onion, peeled and thinly sliced (about ⅔ cup)
1 cup mayonnaise
1 cup sour cream
⅓ cup white wine vinegar
2 tablespoons granulated sugar
2 tablespoon chopped fresh dill

1. Place the cucumber slices into a colander in the sink. Lightly
sprinkle the cucumber with salt. Let sit for 15 to 20 minutes so
that the excess moisture is released. Rinse with cold water and pat
dry.
2. Place the cucumbers and sliced onion into a bowl.
3. Whisk together the mayonnaise, sour cream, vinegar and sugar
in a small bowl. Pour this mixture over the cucumbers and
onions. Toss and chill for at least 30 minutes.
4. Sprinkle with fresh dill.

SERVINGS: 6 TO 8 • PREPARATION TIME: 20 MINUTES PLUS REFRIGERATION

SALTING THE CUCUMBERS
RELEASES THE MOISTURE SO
THAT THE SAUCE MAINTAINS
ITS CONSISTENCY (AND DOES-
N'T GET WATERY) WHEN
TOSSED WITH THE VEGGIES.
CHOOSE A SWEET ONION FOR
THIS SALAD. FOR A TERRIFIC
PRESENTATION OF THE DISH,
SELECT RIPE HEIRLOOM OR
BEEF STEAK TOMATOES. CUT
THE TOMATOES IN HALF, HOR-
IZONTALLY. GENTLY HOLLOW
OUT THE CENTER OF EACH
TOMATO. MOUND THE CUCUM-
BER SALAD INTO AND OVER
THE TOMATOES. WOW!

Three Bean Salad with Tarragon Vinaigrette

FULL OF PROTEIN, IRON AND CALCIUM, THIS SALAD IS AS GOOD FOR YOU AS
IT IS DELICIOUS. MAKE AN EXTRA BATCH AND STORE IN AN AIRTIGHT CON-
TAINER FOR SEVERAL DAYS IN YOUR REFRIGERATOR.

BEANS ARE ONE OF THE OLD-
EST FOODS KNOWN TO MAN,
DATING BACK AT LEAST
4,000 YEARS. THERE ARE
TWO BASIC TYPES OF BEANS,
THOSE THAT HAVE BEEN DRIED
AND THOSE THAT ARE FRESH.
FRESH BEANS ARE PREPARED
IN THE POD OR SHELLED.
DRIED BEANS MUST BE REHY-
DRATED BEFORE EATING. THE
MOST POPULAR FRESH BEANS
ARE GREEN BEANS, LIMA
BEANS AND FAVA BEANS.
DRIED BEANS ARE FULL OF
PROTEIN, COME IN SEVERAL
VARIETIES, AND ARE OFTEN A
STAPLE FOOD IN MANY
REGIONS OF THE WORLD.

1 tablespoon Dijon mustard
1 tablespoon chopped fresh tarragon
Juice of 1 medium lemon (about 2 tablespoons)
2 tablespoons sherry vinegar
2 teaspoons granulated sugar
½ cup olive oil
Salt and freshly ground pepper

1 pound green beans (about 4 cups)
½ small red onion, cut into very thin slices (about ½ cup)
1 15-ounce can red kidney beans, drained
1 15-ounce can garbanzo beans, drained

1. Whisk together the mustard, tarragon, lemon, vinegar, and
sugar in a bowl. Slowly whisk in the olive oil. Season with salt and
pepper. Set aside.
2. Bring a pot of water to a boil. When the water boils, add a
generous amount of salt. Cook the green beans in the boiling
water until crisp tender, about 5 minutes.
3. Drain the beans and rinse with cold water. Cut the beans into
2-inch pieces.
4. Place the cooled beans into a bowl. Add the onion, kidney and
garbanzo beans.
5. Pour in the vinaigrette and toss to coat.

SERVINGS: 4 TO 6 • PREPARATION TIME: 15 MINUTES

Chapter 5

Topless, Grilled, and Panini Sandwiches

Whether you are scrambling for a fast, mid week supper, or you are planning an upscale picnic with pals, sandwiches are not about peanut butter and jelly anymore! Filled with the freshest ingredients and tweaked with flavorful condiments and sauces, the classic American sandwich is finding its way to upscale bistros and diners. This makes the sandwich a most natural addition to our weekly meal plan.

Sandwiches combine all of the healthy components necessary for a healthy balanced meal. Multi grain breads and crusty rolls, piled high with fillings that include lots of veggies, cheeses, and the protein found in seafood and lean meats produces a perfect combination of good things to eat.

There are so many ways to prepare yummy sandwiches, you can use similar ingredients and come up with several different versions of the same thing. Topless sandwiches can be broiled or grilled. Grilled sandwiches can be cooked in a skillet, on a griddle, in a waffle iron or a sandwich press. Club sandwiches can be built into triple deckers, while hoagies are easily wrapped and passed around to guests. And, we don't stop there—we can batter and fry the sandwich, producing one heck of a French-toasted-grilled-cheese. There's just no stopping us when it comes to creative sandwich building.

Classic sandwiches meet updated counterparts in this chapter without a care as to ingredient substitution or preparation. After all, the sandwich has its roots in ancient England where John Montagu, the 4th Earl of Sandwich, asked that his meat be placed between two slices of bread so that he would not have to interrupt his card game to eat. I bet old John would be proud of us today, especially if he checked out the variety of sandwiches his need for convenience brought to bear.

Use the recipes in this chapter to ease your meal planning while opening the door to your creativity and tailoring your choices to family favorite flavors. For example, the sun-dried vinaigrette drizzled onto the Nicoise Tuna Hoagie can easily be substituted with your favorite sub sauce. You'll find a whole bunch of ideas to create a satisfying open-face pizza sandwich and even more ways to enjoy the good-old grilled cheese "sammich." There is a splash of regional favorites too, like the New England style lobster roll and a California turkey club sandwich. If you have the time, make your own freshly ground beef burgers and then turn the extras into not-so sloppy Joes. Invite friends over and showcase panini sandwiches, either from your panini press or simply smooshed onto a gill.

Whatever your reason, sandwiches are a great way to bring together all of the elements of a well balanced meal plan in minutes. Now isn't this a smart way to begin a fresh tradition or two?

Quick French Bread Pizza Margherita

THE STORY IS THAT THIS DISH WAS NAMED FOR ITALIAN ROYALTY, QUEEN MARGHERITA, AND USES ONLY THOSE INGREDIENTS WITH COLORS FOUND ON THE ITALIAN FLAG. I DON'T THINK THE QUEEN WOULD MIND OUR SUBSTITUTION OF FRESH FRENCH BREAD FOR PIZZA CRUST—NOR WILL YOU!

THIS IS A GREAT DISH FOR A SIMPLE SUPPER, EASY APPY, OR RAINY DAY LUNCH. USE THIS BASIC FRENCH BREAD PIZZA RECIPE TO CREATE YOUR OWN FAMILY FAVORITE. TOP YOUR PIZZA WITH COOKED CRUMBLED SAUSAGE AND MUSHROOMS, ROASTED EGGPLANT AND RED ONION, MINCED CLAMS AND GARLIC, OR A BLEND OF SEVERAL CHEESES LIKE ASIAGO, PARMIGIANO-REGGIANO, PROVOLONE, ROMANO OR GOAT CHEESE.

1 16-ounce loaf French bread, cut in half horizontally
2 tablespoons olive oil, plus more for drizzling
4 medium garlic cloves, minced (about 2 teaspoons)
6 medium plum tomatoes, thinly sliced (about 3 cups)
Salt and freshly ground pepper
4 ounces shredded fresh mozzarella cheese (about 1 cup)
½ cup fresh basil leaves, julienned

Preheat the oven to 400°.

1. Place the bread onto a baking sheet. Brush the bread with olive oil and sprinkle with garlic.

2. Place the tomato slices onto the bread. Season with salt and pepper.

3. Sprinkle the cheese on top of the tomatoes.

4. Bake until the bread is golden brown and the cheese is melted, about 8 to 12 minutes.

5. Sprinkle the basil over the pizza. Drizzle with additional olive oil and sprinkle with pepper. Cut each half into 3 pieces.

SERVINGS: 6 • PREPARATION TIME: 20 MINUTES

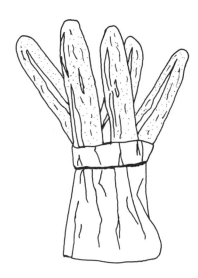

Asparagus, Roasted Pepper, and Fontina Cheese Toasts

THIS YUMMY LUNCH TREAT IS A VARIED TWIST ON FRENCH BREAD PIZZA. DEPENDING ON HOW YOU CUT THE BREAD, YOU CAN ENJOY THIS RECIPE AS LUNCH, AN APPETIZER OR AS CROUTONS IN YOUR FAVORITE SOUP.

6 slices thick bread, toasted
1 pound fresh asparagus spears
2 medium cloves garlic
4 tablespoons butter, room temperature (½ stick)
2 tablespoons Dijon mustard
2 tablespoons fresh parsley
8 ounces Fontina cheese, shredded (about 2 cups)
1 large roasted red bell pepper, cut into thin strips
Freshly ground pepper

Preheat the oven to broil
1. Place the bread slices onto a baking sheet. Toast the bread under the broiler until golden, about 2 to 4 minutes.
2. Remove the tough part of the asparagus stalks. Cut into 1 inch pieces. Blanch the asparagus in boiling salted water until just crisp tender, about 3 to 4 minutes. Drain.
3. Place the garlic, butter, mustard and parsley into the bowl of a food processor. Pulse to combine.
4. Spread the butter mixture onto the bottom of the bread slices.
5. Top with the asparagus pieces.
6. Sprinkle the cheese over top.
7. Lay the roasted red pepper strips on the cheese. Season with fresh pepper.
8. Place the toasts under the broil and cook until the cheese is bubbling and just beginning to brown on the edges, about 5 to 8 minutes.

SERVINGS: 6 • PREPARATION TIME: 20 MINUTES

YOU NEEDN'T LIMIT YOURSELF TO ASPARAGUS AND FONTINA CHEESE FOR THIS YUMMY OPEN FACED SANDWICH. TRY THESE TOAST TOPPERS: BACON AND CHEDDAR CHEESE WITH TOMATOES, HAM AND SWISS CHEESE TOPPED WITH GRILLED ONIONS, OR MOZZARELLA, BASIL AND PEPPERONI.

Roasted Bell Peppers
Jarred roasted peppers will work just fine for this recipe. However, if you want to roast one yourself, simply place the pepper onto a baking sheet. Place it under the broiler and cook until the skin of the pepper turns black and bubbly. Turn the pepper until all of the skin is charred. Place the pepper into a paper bag (or into a bowl and covered with plastic wrap) to steam for 20 minutes. Remove the pepper to a cutting board. Use a sharp knife to scrape off the black skin. Open the pepper and remove the seeds. Cut the pepper into thin strips.

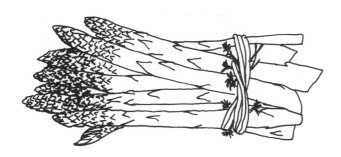

Open Face Rye Toasts with Spinach, Cannellini Beans, and White Cheddar Cheese

LOTS OF GOOD-FOR-YOU STUFF IS PILED HIGH ONTO TOASTED RYE BREAD SLICES IN THIS EASY-TO-MAKE TOPLESS SANDWICH.

USING BUTTER TO GRILL THE BREAD GIVES IT A RICH FLAVOR AND BROWNS QUICKLY AND EVENLY. IF YOU ARE WATCHING CALORIES OR CHOLESTEROL, YOU CAN SUBSTITUTE FOR BUTTER BY BRUSHING ONE SIDE OF THE BREAD WITH OLIVE OIL. BETTER YET, YOU CAN COAT A NONSTICK SKILLET WITH VEGETABLE OIL SPRAY FOR VERY SIMILAR RESULTS!

6 slices thick rye bread
2 tablespoons butter, room temperature
3 tablespoons Dijon mustard
12 ounces fresh spinach leaves, washed, dried and chopped (about 3 cups)
1 16-ounce can cannellini beans, drained
4 medium plum tomatoes, seeded and diced (about 2 cups)
6 ounces shredded white cheddar cheese (about 1½ cups)
1 medium white onion, peeled and thinly sliced (about ⅔ cup)

1. Heat a large skillet or griddle over medium high heat.
2. Spread one side of each slice of bread with butter and the other side with mustard.
3. Place the bread, butter side down, into the skillet.
4. Top the mustard side of the bread with spinach leaves, cannellini beans, tomatoes and cheese.
5. Top with very thin slices of onion.
6. Reduce the heat to medium. Loosely cover the skillet to melt the cheese, making sure that you watch the bread so that it turns golden and does not burn. Use a spatula to transfer the sandwiches to a serving platter.

SERVINGS: 6 • PREPARATION TIME: 20 MINUTES

French Dip Sandwiches with Au Jus

WHETHER YOU USE PRE-COOKED BEEF OR COOK YOUR OWN, THIS SAND-
WICH IS AS FUN TO MAKE AS IT IS TO EAT.

1¹⁄₂ pounds thin sliced cooked roast beef (see sidebar)
Salt and freshly ground pepper
1 tablespoon butter
1 tablespoons olive oil
2 large shallots, minced (about 2 tablespoons)
2 medium cloves garlic, minced (about 1 teaspoon)
2 tablespoons all-purpose flour
1 tablespoon chopped fresh thyme
¹⁄₂ cup sherry
2 cups beef broth
4 small hoagie rolls spit three-fourths down and opened

1. Place the beef onto a cutting board and season with salt and
pepper.
2. Heat the butter and olive oil in a skillet over medium heat.
Add the shallots and garlic and cook until soft, about 2 to 3 minutes.
3. Stir in the flour and thyme. Cook for 1 minute more.
4. Pour in the sherry and beef broth and bring to a boil. Reduce
the heat to medium and simmer until the sauce thickens slightly,
about 5 minutes. Keep warm.
5. Place the beef slices into the au jus until just warm.
6. Use tongs to pile the beef slices on the open hoagie rolls.
Sprinkle with additional pepper and fresh thyme. Serve the sandwiches with any remaining au jus for dipping.

SERVINGS: 4 • PREPARATION TIME: 20 MINUTES

Roast Beef

*This recipe is perfect for left over roast beef or purchased roast beef from the deli.
However, if you want to prepare the beef yourself, start with 1¹⁄₂ pounds cold sirloin. Cut the sirloin into thin slices across the grain. (These results are better if the
meat is very cold and the knife is very sharp). Cook the beef in batches, in a mixture of olive oil and butter, in a skillet over medium high heat. Transfer the meat to
a platter and use the same skillet to continue with the au jus. Return the beef to the
au jus and pour in the remaining drippings from the platter. Pile the beef onto the
rolls and serve the remaining au jus for dipping.*

Grilled Rum Marinated Flank Steak Sandwiches
with Chipotle Lime Aioli

I LIKE TO THINK THE TITLE OF THIS RECIPE SAYS IT ALL! YOUR EVERYDAY BEEF SANDWICH GETS A MAKEOVER WITH A BIG BURST OF FLAVOR. SERVE THIS DISH AT YOUR NEXT BACKYARD BARBECUE OR FOR YOUR FAVORITE SPORTS-WATCHING PARTY!

FLANK STEAK IS A LEAN CUT OF BONELESS BEEF AND THEREFORE, BENEFITS GREATLY BY THE USE OF TENDERIZING BY MEANS OF MARINADE AND RUBS. IF THE FLANK STEAK IS CUT INTO LARGE PIECES AND THEN BROILED, IT IS REFERRED TO AS "LONDON BROIL." IN BOTH CASES, THE MOST TENDER SLICES ARE OBTAINED BY CUTTING ACROSS THE GRAIN OF THE BEEF, DISSECTING THE LONG FIBERS THAT RUN THROUGH IT.

1 1½-pound flank steak
½ cup dark rum
2 tablespoons brown sugar
4 medium garlic cloves, minced (about 2 teaspoons)
Salt and freshly ground pepper

1 cup mayonnaise
1 chipotle pepper in adobo sauce, seeded and finely diced (about 1 tablespoon)
Juice of 1 medium lime (about 1 tablespoon)
2 tablespoons chopped fresh cilantro

2 large red onions, sliced into ¼-inch slices
16 slices Parmesan Thyme Bread (see page 69) or other fresh baked bread
3 large beefsteak tomatoes, sliced into ¼-inch slices
6 ounces mesclun lettuce mix (about 2 cups)

1. Place the flank steak into a shallow dish.
2. Whisk together the rum, sugar and garlic. Season with salt and pepper. Pour this mixture over the flank steak, coating both sides. Marinate the steak in the refrigerator for at least 1 hour or as much as overnight.
3. Whisk together the mayonnaise, chipotle pepper, lime juice and cilantro. Season with salt and pepper.
4. Heat a grill pan over medium high heat. Remove the steak from the marinade. Reserve some marinade for the onions. Grill the flank steak in the pan until medium rare, about 8 to 10 minutes per side. Remove the steak to a cutting board and allow to rest for at least 5 minutes.
5. Place the red onion slices in the pan. Drizzle with a bit of the reserved marinade. Cook until just beginning to brown, about 4 to 6 minutes.
6. Pour off any extra drippings from the pan. Grill the bread slices in batches until just toasted, about 1 to 2 minutes per side.
7. Cut the flank steak diagonally across the grain into thin slices. Spread 1 tablespoon of the chipotle lime aioli onto 8 slices of the toasted bread. Top with slices of flank steak, grilled onions, tomatoes, and lettuce. Top with an extra dollop of aioli and the remaining bread slices.

SERVINGS: 8 • PREPARATION TIME: 30 MINUTES PLUS MARINATING THE STEAK

California Turkey Club with Lemon Mayonnaise and Red Onion Marmalade

CLUB SANDWICHES ARE TRIPLE DECKER AFFAIRS USING TOASTED BREAD AND
TONS OF VEGGIES. I LIKE THE ADDITION OF AVOCADO, BUT FEEL FREE TO
USE YOUR FAVORITE SANDWICH STACKER LIKE CRUMBLED BACON, BEAN
SPROUTS OR SLICED CUCUMBER.

1 cup mayonnaise
Zest of 1 medium lemon (about 1 tablespoon)
Juice of 2 medium lemons (about ¼ cup)
1 tablespoon chopped fresh dill

12 slices thick multigrain bread, toasted
2 large beefsteak tomatoes, sliced into ½-inch slices (about 8 slices)
8 ounces sliced white American cheese
1 pound ounces thin sliced roasted turkey breast
Salt and freshly ground pepper
1 large avocado, peeled, pitted and sliced (about 1 cup)
¼ large head romaine lettuce, washed, dried and torn (about 2 cups)

1. Whisk together the mayonnaise, lemon juice, lemon zest and
dill.
2. Lay 4 slices of toasted bread onto a cutting board or other
work surface. Spread ⅓ of the mayonnaise onto the bread slices.
3. Top each one with the tomato slices and cheese. Layer half of
the turkey breast on top. Season with salt and pepper.
4. Top with another slice of toasted bread. Spread with ⅓ of the
mayonnaise.
5. Place avocado slices on top of the bread. Layer with the
remaining turkey breast and romaine
leaves.
6. Spread mayonnaise onto the last 4
slices of toasted bread. Place the
bread on top of the sandwich, mayonnaise side down.
7. Cut the sandwich into 4 triangles
and serve with red onion marmalade.

SERVINGS: 4 • PREPARATION TIME: 20 MIN-
UTES

Red Onion Marmalade

*Cook 4 large red onions that
have been thinly sliced (about 4
cups) in 2 tablespoons olive oil,
in a skillet over medium high
heat until soft and beginning to
brown, about 5 minutes.
Season with salt and pepper.
Add ¾ cup port, 1 tablespoon
balsamic vinegar and ¼ cup
chopped pitted prunes. Stir
until the liquid is mostly evaporated. Add 1 tablespoon
chopped fresh thyme and stir for
1 minute more. Remove the pan
from the heat. Cool to room
temperature. Place into an airtight container and chill until
ready to serve.*

Jon's Turkey Sub with Pesto and Provolone

MY YOUNGEST SON CREATED THIS SUB, AND PROBABLY EATS MORE OF THESE THAN ANY OTHER DISH I SERVE. IT'S REALLY, REALLY GOOD, ESPECIALLY IF YOU HEAT IT JUST BEFORE SERVING.

1 cup fresh basil leaves
1 tablespoon pine nuts, toasted
2 medium cloves garlic, minced (about 1 teaspoon)
2 ounces grated Parmesan cheese (¼ cup)
1 tablespoon grated Pecorino Romano cheese
⅓ cup olive oil
Salt and freshly ground pepper

4 hoagie rolls
¼ large head romaine lettuce, washed, dried and torn (about 2 cups)
2 large beefsteak tomatoes, sliced into ½-inch slices
1 pound thinly sliced roasted turkey breast
8 ounces sliced Provolone cheese
½ cup dill pickle chips

1. Place the basil leaves, pine nuts, garlic, Parmesan and Pecorino Romano cheese into a blender. Pulse to combine.
2. With the machine running, add the olive oil. Season with salt and pepper.
3. Split the hoagie rolls in half. Spread the pesto over both sides of the hoagie.
4. Layer the hoagie with lettuce, tomatoes, turkey breast, and Provolone cheese.
5. Top with pickle slices, and season with salt and pepper.

SERVINGS: 4 •
PREPARATION TIME: 20
MINUTES

To prepare a large batch of pesto, double the ingredients above and add 2 cups fresh spinach leaves to the blender. Increase the amount of oil to 1 cup. Serve fresh pesto sauce with scrambled eggs, over warm pasta, and as a garnish for creamy soups. Store extra pesto in an airtight container in the refrigerator for several days.

Grilled Ratatouille Vegetable Sandwich with Fontina Cheese

IN A PROVENCE INSPIRED RATATOUILLE DISH, EGGPLANT, SQUASH AND PEP-
PERS SIMMER TOGETHER IN TOMATO SAUCE AND ARE SERVED WITH FRESH
BASIL AND GRATED CHEESE. THIS RATATOUILLE VARIATION USES THE SAME
VEGGIES, BUT SHORTENS THE PROCESS BY GRILLING INSTEAD OF STEWING.
THE VEGGIES ARE THEN PILED ONTO SLICES OF CRUSTY BREAD AND TOPPED
WITH RICH CHEESE, PRODUCING A MODERN-DAY TWIST ON A TRADITIONAL
FAVORITE.

1 medium eggplant, sliced into ½-inch thick lengths
2 medium yellow squash, cut into ½-inch thick lengths
1 medium zucchini, cut into ½-inch thick lengths
1 large green bell pepper, seeded and cut into quarters
4 plum tomatoes, cut in half lengthwise
1 small red onion, cut into ½-inch thick slices
2 tablespoons olive oil
Salt and freshly ground pepper
2 tablespoons fresh chopped basil
6 slices thick crusty white bread
3 tablespoons prepared pesto sauce
4 ounces Fontina cheese, sliced

Preheat the oven to broil
1. Brush the vegetables with olive oil and season with salt and
pepper.
2. Grill the vegetables over a hot grill or in a grill pan until just
beginning to soften, about 3 minutes per side.
3. Cut the grilled vegetables into ½-inch chunks and
place into a bowl.
4. Stir in the basil.
5. Place the bread slices onto a baking sheet. Toast the
bread under the broiler until it begins to turn brown,
about 2 minutes. Turn and toast for 2 minutes more.
Remove the bread from the oven.
6. Brush one side of the toasted bread with pesto sauce.
Mound each slice with ratatouille.
7. Top with slices of Fontina cheese.
8. Place the pan under the broiler until the cheese
begins to melt.

SERVINGS: 4 TO 6 • PREPARATION TIME: 30 MINUTES

Ratatouille Salad

Grill the veggies as instructed in
the recipe. Cut into bite size
pieces. Sprinkle with balsamic
vinegar and olive oil. Garnish
with fresh chopped basil and top
with cubes of feta or goat
cheese.

EXPERTS SUGGEST THAT WE
NEED NOT BE CONCERNED
ABOUT THE POTENTIAL SIDE
EFFECTS OF CARCINOGENS
WHEN GRILLING VEGGIES.
UNLIKE MEAT, VEGGIE DISHES
LIKE, QUESADILLA AND EVEN
VEGGIE BURGERS ARE NOT
SUSEPTIBLE WHEN GRILLED.
YOU CAN CUT DOWN ON THE
RISK OF CARCINOGENS WHEN
GRILLING MEAT AND POULTRY
BY SIMPLY REDUCING THE
FLAME.

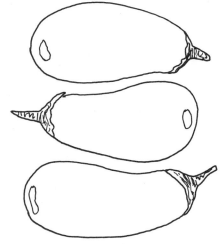

Warm Open Face Meatloaf Sandwich
with Tomato Gravy

THE MEATLOAF CAN BE BAKED SEVERAL DAYS IN ADVANCE FOR THIS COM-
FORTING SANDWICH, REFRIGERATED, AND THEN REHEATED. YOU CAN ALSO
SUBSTITUTE WITH LEFT OVER MOIST AND FLUFFY TURKEY LOAF (RECIPE
PAGE 272), PROVIDING NOBODY GOBBLED IT UP!

Mashed Potatoes

*Of course the perfect side dish
for this yummy meal is mashed
potatoes. Peel 4 large Yukon
potatoes. Cook in salted boiling
water until soft. Drain the
potatoes. Use an electric mixer
to purée the potatoes with olive
oil, butter, milk and a bit of
sour cream. Season with salt
and pepper.*

1½ pounds ground beef
½ pound ground pork
1 cup fresh breadcrumbs
1 large egg
1 tablespoon tomato paste
1 small white onion, finely diced (about ½ cup)
2 medium cloves garlic, minced (about 1 teaspoon)
1 teaspoon dried oregano
¼ teaspoon ground nutmeg
Salt and freshly ground pepper

2 tablespoons olive oil
1 large shallot, minced (about 1 tablespoon)
¼ cup red wine
2 cups beef broth
1 tablespoon tomato paste
1 teaspoon dried oregano

8 slices thick white bread
2 tablespoons chopped fresh oregano

Preheat the oven to 350°.
1. Place the meats, breadcrumbs, egg, tomato paste, onion, garlic, 1 teaspoon ground oregano, nutmeg, salt. and pepper into a
large bowl. Use your hands to combine the mixture and form
into a loaf. Place the loaf into a glass 9 x 5 x 3-inch loaf pan.
2. Bake the loaf until cooked through, 45 minutes to 1 hour.
Remove the meatloaf from the oven. Allow to rest for 15 minutes.
3. Heat the olive oil in a skillet over medium high heat.
4. Cook the shallot in the oil until soft, about 2 minutes.
5. Add the wine and cook for 3 minutes.
6. Add the beef broth, tomato paste and 1 teaspoon dried
oregano. Reduce the heat and simmer until the gravy is reduced
and thickened. (For thicker gravy, stir in a small amount of flour
whisked with cold water.) Season with salt and pepper.
7. Toast the bread slices.
8. Place 1 toasted bread slice onto a plate. Top with sliced meatloaf. Drizzle the sandwich with gravy and garnish with fresh
oregano.

SERVINGS: 8 • PREPARATION TIME: 1 HOUR

Open Faced Sautéed Chicken Liver and Fried Egg Sandwich with Red Onion

SEEKING OUT A BUSY DELI ON A SATURDAY AFTERNOON IS A TRADITION THAT I HAVE WITH MY BROTHER REGARDLESS OF WHETHER WE ARE VISITING NEW YORK OR LAS VEGAS! WE FIGHT OVER WHICH DISH IS THE BEST, BUT I ALWAYS MANAGE TO CHOW DOWN ON MY FAVORITE CHOPPED LIVER SANDWICH, WHICH IS GARNISHED WITH THIN SLICES OF RED ONION AND HARD-BOILED EGG. MY WARM, HOME VERSION USES A BUNCH OF GARLIC AND A DAB OF SHERRY TO PREPARE THE LIVER—PERHAPS NOT AUTHENTIC—BUT DEFINITELY A FAVORITE!

1 tablespoons olive oil
1 tablespoon butter
1 medium yellow onion, thinly sliced (about 2 cups)
6 medium garlic cloves, thinly sliced (about ¼ cup)
1 pound chicken livers
Salt and freshly ground pepper
¼ cup sherry

4 ½-inch thick slices rye bread
1 tablespoon olive oil
4 large eggs
¼ small red onion, cut into very thin slices (about ¼ cup)
2 tablespoons chopped fresh rosemary

RECENTLY, WHILE DINING AT A NEIGHBORHOOD RESTAURANT, I ORDERED A WONDERFUL APPETIZER OF CHICKEN LIVERS SAUTÉED WITH ONION, GARLIC AND WHOLE JALAPEÑO PEPPER. O MY GOODNESS. THIS SPICY DISH WAS SOOO TERRIFIC THAT I RAN HOME AND EXPERIMENTED WITH THE FLAVOR FOR MY NEXT OPEN FACED SANDWICH. IF YOU ARE A FELLOW LIVER LOVER AND HAPPEN TO LIKE SPICY FOOD, THE JALAPEÑO ADDITION IS TERRIFIC. ADD 2 MEDIUM JALAPEÑO PEPPERS THAT HAVE BEEN SLICED WHEN YOU ARE SAUTÉING THE ONIONS AND GARLIC IN THIS RECIPE TO GIVE IT THAT SPICY OOMPH. ALTERNATIVELY, TAKE THE DISH OVER-THE-TOP WITH THE ADDITION OF SEVERAL WHOLE ROASTED JALAPEÑO PEPPERS. YUMM!

1. Heat 1 tablespoon olive oil and 1 tablespoon butter in a skillet over medium high heat.
2. Add the onions and garlic to the skillet and cook until just beginning to brown, about 5 minutes.
3. Add the chicken livers to the pan. Season with salt and pepper. Use a spatula to gently break up the chicken livers while they cook.
4. Pour in the sherry. Cook until the livers are no longer pink in the center and most of the liquid has disappeared, about 10 to 15 minutes.
5. Brush the bread slices on one side with 1 tablespoon olive oil.
6. Place the bread slices, coated side down, onto a grill pan and cook until golden, about 2 minutes.
7. Remove the grilled bread slices to a platter. Top with sautéed chicken livers.
8. Fry the eggs in a pan that has been sprayed with vegetable oil spray, over medium heat, about 3 to 4 minutes. Place the eggs on top of the liver. Sprinkle with red onion slices and fresh rosemary.

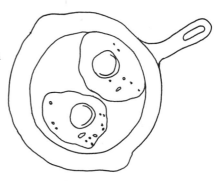

SERVINGS: 4 • PREPARATION TIME: 20 MINUTES

Classic Grilled Cheese Sandwich
with Bacon and Tomato

A GRILLED CHEESE SANDWICH CAN BE THE BEST, MOST COMFORTING SNACK IN THE WORLD, OR A SOGGY, RUBBERY MESS YOU REMEMBER FROM THE GRADE SCHOOL CAFETERIA. BOTH VERSIONS TAKE THE SAME AMOUNT OF TIME, SO YOU MIGHT AS WELL SHUN THE GRADE SCHOOL "BLANDWICH" AND PREPARE THIS REVVED UP VERSION.

THE SECRET TO A SUPERIOR GILLED CHEESE SANDWICH IS TO MAKE SURE THAT THE SKILLET OR GRIDDLE YOU USE IS VERY HOT. YOU WANT THE BREAD TO CRISP UP AND THE CHEESE TO MELT AT THE SAME TIME. USING ROOM TEMPERATURE BUTTER AND SHREDDED CHEESE GETS THE SANDWICH COOKING PROCESS OFF TO A FAST START. COVERING THE SANDWICHES WILL HELP YOU MONITOR THE PROGRESS WHILE THE CHEESE MELTS AND THE BREAD CRISPS. DON'T HESITATE TO USE YOUR FAVORITE CHEESES FOR THIS PERFECT "SAMMICH." GOOD CHOICES ARE GRUYERE, MONTEREY JACK, FONTINA, CAMEMBERT AND SWISS.

¾ pound bacon, 12 strips
8 ¼-inch thick slices country style bread
4 tablespoons butter, room temperature
8 ounces grated Cheddar cheese (about 2 cups)
2 large beefsteak tomatoes, sliced into ¼-inch thick slices (about 8 slices)

1. Cook the bacon in a skillet over medium high heat until crisp. Drain the bacon on paper towels. Use additional paper towels to remove all of the bacon drippings from the skillet.
2. Butter all of the bread slices on one side. Place the bread, butter side down onto a cutting board. Divide the cheese onto the bread.
3. Heat the skillet over medium high heat. Place the cheese topped bread, buttered side down, into the skillet.
4. Top the sandwiches with tomatoes and bacon. Place the remaining bread slices onto the sandwiches, buttered side up. Cover the sandwiches with a lid and cook for 2 minutes.
5. Remove the lid and check the bottom slice of bread to make sure that it has turned golden brown. Use a spatula to turn the sandwiches. Press down on the top of each one. Cook uncovered for 1 to 2 minutes more. Turn the sandwiches one more time and cook for 1 more minute.

SERVINGS: 4 • PREPARATION TIME: 20 MINUTES

Grilled Mozzarella Cheese Sandwich with Tuna, Red Pepper and Basil

HERE'S AN UPDATE ON THE TUNA MELT SANDWICH. USE THE BEST CANNED TUNA YOU CAN FIND; IT MAKES ALL THE DIFFERENCE IN THIS DISH!

8 ¼-inch thick slices Italian bread
4 tablespoons butter, room temperature
8 ounces shredded fresh mozzarella cheese (about 2 cups)
4 tablespoons chopped fresh basil
2 large roasted red bell peppers, cut into thin strips
2 6-ounce cans tuna in olive oil, drained

1. Butter all of the bread slices on one side. Place the bread, buttered side down, onto a cutting board. Divide the cheese onto the bread.
2. Heat the skillet over medium high heat. Place the cheese topped bread, buttered side down, into the skillet.
3. Top the sandwiches with basil, red pepper strips and tuna. Place the remaining bread slices onto the sandwiches, buttered side up. Cover the sandwiches with a lid and cook for 2 minutes.
4. Remove the lid and check the bottom slice of bread to make sure it has turned golden brown. Use a spatula to turn the sandwiches. Press down on the top of each one. Cook uncovered for 1 to 2 minutes more. Turn the sandwiches one more time and cook for 1 more minute.
5. Cut the sandwiches in half and serve.

SERVINGS: 4 • PREPARATION TIME: 20 MINUTES

CANNED TUNA IS SOLD AS WHITE OR LIGHT MEAT ALBACORE; IT IS PRECOOKED AND COMES IN THREE DIFFERENT GRADES. THE BEST GRADE CONSISTS OF LARGE PIECES AND IS OFTEN CALLED "SOLID" OR "FANCY" TUNA. "CHUNK" REFERS TO SMALLER PIECES, AND "FLAKED" OR "GRATED" REFERS TO TUNA MADE UP OF SMALL BITS OR PIECES. TUNA CAN BE PACKED IN OIL OR IN WATER. I PREFER IMPORTED TUNA PACKED IN OIL FOR MOST DISHES; THE FLAVOR GOES ABOVE AND BEYOND EVERYDAY TUNA.

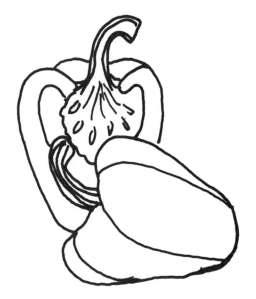

Grilled Brie and Apple Sandwich
with Spicy Apple Chutney

CHUTNEY IS AN EAST INDIAN CONDIMENT THAT PAIRS PERFECTLY WITH CURRIED FOODS; IT IS A BLEND OF HOT AND SWEET AND CAN BE AS SPICY AS YOU LIKE IT. MAKE UP A BIG BATCH, LEAVING PLENTY LEFT OVER TO JAZZ UP A SPUR-OF-THE-MOMENT GRILLED CHEESE SANDWICH, OR PURCHASE THE BEST PREPARED CHUTNEY YOU CAN FIND IN YOUR MARKET.

8 ¼-inch thick diagonally cut French bread slices
4 tablespoons butter (½ stick), room temperature
8 ounces Brie cheese (about 2 cups), rind removed, room temperature
4 tablespoons Spicy Apple Chutney (see sidebar)
2 large apples, peeled, cored and thinly sliced

1. Butter one side of each bread slice. Place the bread, buttered side down, onto a cutting board.
2. Spread (or crumble) the brie cheese over the unbuttered side of 4 of the bread slices.
3. Spread 1 tablespoon of chutney on top of the brie. Distribute the apple slices over top of the chutney.
4. Heat a grill or skillet over medium high heat. Place the brie, chutney and apple topped bread slices, buttered side down, into the skillet. Top with the remaining bread, buttered side up.
5. Cover the sandwiches with a lid and cook for 2 minutes.
6. Remove the lid and check the bottom slice of bread to make sure it has turned golden brown. Use a spatula to turn the sandwiches. Press down on the top of each one. Cook uncovered for 1 to 2 minutes more. Turn the sandwiches one more time and cook for 1 more minute. Cut each sandwich in half and serve.

SERVINGS: 4 • PREPARATION TIME: 15 MINUTES

Spicy Apple Chutney

Heat 2 tablespoons olive oil in a skillet over medium high heat. Cook 1 diced onion and 1 diced red bell pepper in the skillet until soft, about 4 to 5 minutes. Stir in 2 minced garlic cloves, 1 jalapeño pepper, which has been seeded and finely diced, 1 teaspoon ground ginger, 1 teaspoon ground allspice and season with salt and pepper. Cook for 2 minutes. Reduce the heat to medium. Stir in 1 cup brown sugar, ¼ cup raisins, ¾ cups red wine vinegar, 1 cup water and 4 apples that have been peeled, cored and diced. Simmer this mixture until it is completely soft and all of the flavors have come together, about 45 minutes to 1 hour. Cool to room temperature. Store in an airtight container and keep refrigerated.

Freshly Ground Beef Burgers

CURING BEEF CHANGES THE FLAVOR AND TEXTURE OF THE BURGER, WHICH
MAKES THIS RECIPE AN EXCELLENT CHOICE FOR PREPARING AFFORDABLE
CUTS OF MEAT. THE METHOD OF "SALTING EARLY" USED HERE, IS HIGHLY
RECOMMENDED BY FRENCH INSPIRED CHEFS. I RECOMMEND THAT YOU TRY
IT AT HOME FOR THE BEST BURGER YOU'VE EVER TASTED. THE BURGERS SIT
PERFECTLY BETWEEN TWO GRILLED SLICES OF PARMESAN THYME BREAD
(PAGE 69).

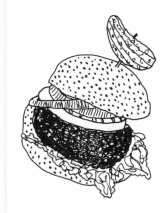

4 pounds beef chuck roast, trimmed of all but 15 to 20% of fat remaining
3 to 4 teaspoons kosher salt

1. Cut the meat into 2-inch strips.
2. Sprinkle both sides of the strips with salt. Seal the meat in a
plastic bag or in a covered dish, and refrigerate for at least 24
hours and up to 3 days.
3. Grind the meat using the fine blade of a food grinder. Repeat
so that the meat is ground 2 times.
4. Form the ground beef into 8 patties.
5. Heat a grill pan or outdoor grill over high heat. Cook the
burgers, turning once, about 8 minutes per side.

SERVINGS: 8 • PREPARATION TIME: 30 MINUTES PLUS CURING

Beef Burgers with Gorgonzola

Place a tablespoon size dollop of Gorgonzola cheese in the center of each patty.
Refrigerate for at least 30 minutes before grilling. You can also use goat, blue, or
cheddar cheese.

Herbed Beef Burgers

Add 2 tablespoons fresh herbs to the meat while grinding. Parsley, cilantro and
thyme will work well.

Freshly Ground Pork, Veal and Turkey Burgers

Use this same process to salt early and grind pork, veal and turkey.

Not So Sloppy Joe Hoagies

KINDA LIKE A CROSS BETWEEN A MEATBALL SUB AND A SLOPPY JOE SANDWICH, THIS SPICY HOAGIE IS GREAT TASTING AND A SUPER MEAL TO PRESENT TO THE GANG WHEN WATCHING YOUR FAVORITE GAME.

CHOOSE A GOOD QUALITY PREPARED TOMATO SAUCE FOR THIS DISH, ONE WITH LITTLE OR NO PRESERVATIVES OR ADDITIVES. OR MAKE YOUR OWN BATCH (SEE RECIPE PAGE 190), AND SAVE EXTRAS FOR RECIPES LIKE THIS. THERE ARE SEVERAL MOUTHWATERING STEAK SEASONING PRODUCTS IN THE MARKETPLACE TO CHOOSE FROM. THE FLAVORS ARE AS DIVERSE AS THE MANUFACTURERS. IF YOU ARE LOOKING FOR A CONSISTENT RESULT, YOU CAN PREPARE YOUR OWN, BRAND OF SEASONING BY COMBINING RED PEPPER FLAKES, DRIED ONION FLAKES, GARLIC POWDER, PAPRIKA AND A DASH OF CORIANDER OR CUMIN. A HINT OF BROWN SUGAR AND A DASH OF DRIED OREGANO ARE GREAT ADDITIONS. DON'T FORGET THE SALT AND PEPPER! STORE THIS MIXTURE IN AN AIRTIGHT CONTAINER AND IT WILL LAST FOR WEEKS. TAKE A LOOK AT MY FAVORITE SEASONING MIX ON PAGE 29.

2 tablespoons olive oil
2½ pounds ground sirloin beef
⅓ cup brown sugar
2 tablespoons prepared steak seasoning
1 large red bell pepper, seeded and chopped (about ½ cup)
1 large yellow onion, diced (about 1 cup)
2 cups prepared marinara sauce
2 tablespoons tomato paste
Salt and freshly ground pepper
8 hoagie rolls, split three-fourths from the top
8 ounces shredded Cheddar cheese (about 2 cups)

1. Heat the olive oil in a skillet over medium high heat.
2. Add the beef and cook until browned, about 6 to 10 minutes.
3. Add the brown sugar, steak seasoning, pepper and onion. Cook for 5 minutes more.
4. Reduce the heat to medium. Stir in marinara sauce and tomato paste. Simmer for 15 minutes. Season with salt and pepper. Preheat the oven to broil.
5. Place the split buns onto a baking sheet. Spoon the sloppy joe mixture onto the buns. Top with cheese. Place the baking sheet in the oven for 2 to 4 minutes or until the cheese has melted.

SERVINGS: 8 • PREPARATION TIME: 25 TO 30 MINUTES

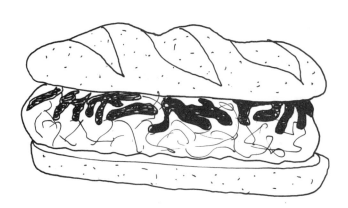

Authentic Cuban Sandwiches

A LONG STANDING TRADITION IN LATIN COMMUNITIES, THIS GRILLED
SANDWICH HAS GAINED POPULARITY WITH THE RISE IN PANINI SANDWICH
OFFERINGS. SLICED TEQUILA MOJO MARINATED PORK TENDERLOIN (SEE
PAGE 292) IS PERFECT HERE, BUT IN A PINCH, YOU CAN PURCHASE COOKED
PORK FROM YOUR NEIGHBORHOOD DELI.

4 7-inch long Cuban bread rolls
4 tablespoons Dijon mustard
1 pound roasted pork, sliced thin
1 pound smoked ham, sliced thin
8 ounces sliced Swiss cheese
4 dill pickles, sliced into thin rounds
4 tablespoons butter, room temperature

Preheat a sandwich grill or waffle iron.
1. Split the rolls in half. Spread the mustard over the cut side of
bread.
2. Layer the bottom halves of the rolls with pork slices, ham slices
and Swiss cheese.
3. Spread the pickle slices over the top half of the roll. Place the
pickle half on top of the meat half.
4. Spread butter on both the top and the bottom of the sandwiches. Place the sandwiches into the grill and close the top to
smash. Cook until the bread is golden brown and the cheese
begins to melt.
5. Remove the sandwiches from the grill and cut diagonally.

SERVINGS: 4 • PREPARATION TIME: 20 MINUTES

A SANDWICH (OR PANINI) PRESS FOR HOME USE IS PATTERNED AFTER THE
LARGE MACHINES FOUND IN THE ITALIAN TRATTORIAS. PERFECT FOR GRILLING
SANDWICHES AND COMPRESSING THEM AT THE SAME TIME, THIS MACHINE IS A
POPULAR ADDITION TO A COOK'S COVETED KITCHEN GADGETS. A WAFFLE IRON
WILL ACCOMPLISH THE SAME RESULTS, HOWEVER NOT QUITE AS EVENLY.
ANOTHER ALTERNATIVE IS TO HEAT A GRILL PAN. PLACE THE SANDWICH INTO
THE PAN AND COVER WITH A GRILL PRESS, WHICH IS A HEAVY LID WITH RAISED
GRILL LINES; IT CAN BE HEATED AND THEN PRESSED ONTO THE SANDWICH. A
HEATED CAST IRON SKILLET, PRESSED HARD ONTO THE SANDWICHES, WILL
AGAIN PRODUCE SIMILAR RESULTS. IF YOU LOVE GRILLED SANDWICHES AS
MUCH AS I DO, A SANDWICH PRESS MAY SOON BE ON YOUR WISH LIST.

Grilled Radicchio, Asparagus, Roasted Pepper, and Mozzarella Panini

PURCHASE FRESHLY BAKED FOCACCIA BREAD ROUNDS TO MAKE THE BEST PANINI SANDWICHES. A GENEROUS SIZE TO ASK FOR IS ABOUT 8-INCHES IN DIAMETER AND ABOUT 3 INCHES HIGH. YOU CAN SUBSTITUTE WITH FRESHLY BAKED HOAGIE ROLLS.

USE THIS SIMPLE RECIPE TO CREATE YOUR MOST FAVORITE PANINI SANDWICHES. FUN COMBINATIONS INCLUDE TOMATO, MOZZARELLA AND BASIL, PROSCIUTTO, PORTOBELLO MUSHROOM, AND GRUYERE, GRILLED VEGGIES AND GOAT CHEESE, AS WELL AS MY PERSONAL FAVORITE: SPINACH, CARAMELIZED ONIONS AND BRIE CHEESE.

½ pound fresh asparagus spears
1 medium head radicchio, cut in half lengthwise
4 tablespoons olive oil, divided
Salt and freshly ground pepper
4 4-ounce focaccia rounds or hoagie rolls
8 ounces pesto sauce (see recipe page 110)
8 ounces shredded fresh mozzarella cheese (about 2 cups)
2 large roasted red bell peppers, cut into strips

Preheat sandwich press

1. Remove the tough stalks from the asparagus spears. Blanch the asparagus in boiling salted water until crisp tender, about 3 minutes. Remove spears from the boiling water and submerge into ice water to stop the cooking process. Drain.

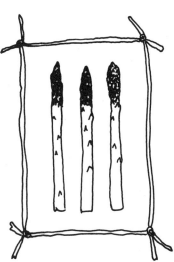

2. Brush the radicchio with olive oil. Season with salt and pepper. Heat a grill pan over high heat. Grill the radicchio in the pan, turning once, until wilted, about 3 minutes per side. Cool and roughly chop.

3. Split the focaccia rounds in half horizontally. Spread the cut side of each half with pesto sauce. Layer one side of each loaf with the cheese.

4. Top the cheese with chopped radicchio, asparagus and roasted peppers. Season with salt and pepper. Place the top half of the bread onto the sandwich.

5. Brush the top and bottom sides of the bread with olive oil.

6. Place the sandwiches into the press and close the top to smash the sandwich together. Cook until the bread is golden and the cheese is melting, about 6 to 8 minutes.

SERVINGS: 4 • PREPARATION TIME: 20 MINUTES

Gruyere, Sun-Dried Tomato and Watercress Panini with Olive Tapenade

THERE ARE SEVERAL GREAT TAPENADE SPREADS AVAILABLE IN THE GOURMET SECTION IN YOUR MARKET, AND THERE'S NO BETTER WAY TO TEST OUT TAPENADE FLAVORS THAN ON A PANINI SANDWICH. IF YOU WANT TO PRE-PARE YOUR OWN, TAKE A LOOK AT THE RECIPE FOR OLIVE TAPENADE IN THE SIDEBAR. THEN EXPERIMENT WITH YOUR OWN FAVORITE FLAVORS.

8 slices (½-inch thick) sour dough bread
1 cup olive tapenade
8 ounces grated Gruyere cheese (about 2 cups)
2 large avocados, peeled, pitted and sliced (about 2 cups)
1 7-ounce jar sun-dried tomatoes in oil, sliced lengthwise into strips
1 bunch watercress, wash, dried, stems removed (about 4 cups)

Preheat sandwich press, waffle iron or griddle.
1. Place the bread slices onto a cutting board. Spread one side of each slice with tapenade.
2. Cover 4 of the bread slices with the cheese. Top with avocado slices, sun-dried tomatoes and watercress. Cover with the remaining bread slices, tapenade side down.
3. Place the sandwiches into the press and close the top to smash the sandwich together. Cook until the bread is golden and the cheese is melting, about 6 to 8 minutes.

SERVINGS: 4 • PREPARATION TIME: 20 MINUTES

TAPENADE IS A CONDIMENT THAT HAS ITS ORIGINS IN THE PROVENCE REGION OF FRANCE; IT MOST OFTEN INCLUDES OLIVES, CAPERS AND ANCHOVIES, BUT CAN BE MADE FROM WHITE BEANS OR SUN-DRIED TOMATOES.

Tapenade

To prepare a flavorful olive tapenade, place 2 medium anchovy fillets, 1 medium clove peeled garlic, the zest of 2 medium lemons (about 2 tablespoons), the juice of 1 medium lemon (about 2 table-spoons), 10 to 12 Nicoise (or other good quality) pitted olives, 1 teaspoon rinsed capers, and 2 tablespoons chopped fresh basil into the bowl of a food processor. Pulse to com-bine. With the machine run-ning, slowly pour in ¼ cup olive oil until smooth. Season with salt and freshly ground pepper. Store tapenade in an airtight container in the refrigerator for up to 2 weeks.

Monte Cristo Sandwich with Mustard Jam

THINK FRENCH TOAST MEETS HAM AND CHEESE, AND YOU HAVE THE PER-
FECT PICTURE OF THIS CLASSIC SANDWICH! IF YOU REALLY WANT TO TAKE
IT OVER THE TOP, ADD A THIRD SLICE OF BREAD AND MAKE IT A TRIPLE
DECKER!

WRAPPING THE SANDWICHES
TIGHTLY IN PLASTIC WRAP WILL
COMPRESS THEM, MAKING IT
DIFFICULT FOR THE EGG TO
SEEP THROUGH. CHILLING
THEM WILL PREVENT THE
CHEESE FROM MELTING
THROUGH THE BATTER. USE
THIS PROCESS TO MAKE THE
SANDWICHES IN THE MORN-
ING, AND THEN COOK RIGHT
BEFORE YOU SIT DOWN TO
LUNCH.

¼ cup red currant jelly
2 tablespoons Dijon mustard
Juice of ½ medium orange (about 2 to 3 tablespoons)

8 ¼-inch slices Italian bread
2 tablespoons mayonnaise
8 ounces cooked turkey breast slices
8 ounces cooked ham slices
8 ounces Swiss cheese slices

4 large eggs, beaten
½ cup milk
Salt and freshly ground pepper

2 tablespoons olive oil
2 tablespoons butter

1. Combine the jelly, mustard and orange juice in a pot over
medium low heat. Whisk until the jelly melts, about 5 minutes.
Remove from the heat. Cool to room temperature.
2. Place 8 slices of bread onto a cutting board. Spread each with
mayonnaise.
3. Top 4 slices of the bread with equal amounts of turkey, ham
and cheese. Top with the remaining bread slices, mayonnaise side
down. Trim the crusts from each sandwich.
4. Wrap each sandwich tightly with plastic wrap. Place the sandwiches into the refrigerator for at least 30 minutes and up to 4
hours.
5. Whisk together the eggs and milk in a shallow bowl. Season
with salt and pepper.
6. Heat the olive oil and butter in a large skillet over medium
heat. (If your skillet is not large enough to hold all 4 sandwiches,
do this step in batches, dividing the oil and butter for each
batch.)
7. Remove the sandwiches from the refrigerator. Dip each one
into the egg mixture coating all sides. Gently place the sandwiches
into the skillet. Cook, turning once, until both sides are golden,
about 3 to 4 minutes per side.
8. Cut the sandwiches in half and serve with mustard jam.

SERVINGS: 4 • PREPARATION TIME: 20 MINUTES PLUS 30 MINUTES OR MORE
REFRIGERATION

Stuffed Eggplant "Sandwiches" with Tomato Relish

THESE FUN "SANDWICHES" ARE STUFFED WITH CREAMY GOAT CHEESE AND
SPUNKY PANCETTA AND THEN SAUTÉED UNTIL THE EGGPLANT IS GOLDEN.
TOPPED WITH SIMPLE RELISH, THIS DISH IS A WINNER ALL AROUND.

3 medium plum tomatoes, seeded and diced (about 2 cups)
2 tablespoons chopped fresh basil
1 tablespoon olive oil
1 tablespoon balsamic vinegar
Salt and freshly ground pepper

4 ⅛-inch thick slices pancetta
1 large eggplant, top and bottom trimmed, peeled and cut into 4 2-inch thick rounds
4 ounces goat cheese, cut into ½-inch thick rounds
4 large fresh basil leaves

2 tablespoons Dijon mustard
½ cup seasoned bread crumbs

2 tablespoons olive oil
2 tablespoons butter

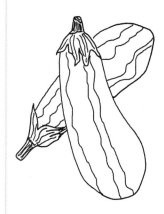

GIVE YOUR EGGPLANT A SPE-
CIAL LOOK BY SLICING STRIPS
INTO THE PEEL. USE A VEG-
ETABLE PEELER TO PEEL A 1-
INCH THICK LENGTH OF PEEL
FROM THE STEM TO THE BOT-
TOM. LEAVE A 1-INCH STRIP
OF SKIN IN PLACE. THEN PEEL
ANOTHER 1-INCH STRIP AWAY.
THE VERTICAL STRIPS OF
PEEL WILL MAKE YOUR "SAND-
WICHES" EVEN MORE FUN TO
PRESENT.

1. Combine the tomatoes, basil, olive oil and vinegar in a small
bowl. Season with salt and freshly ground pepper. Refrigerate
until ready to serve.
2. Place the pancetta slices into a skillet over medium high heat.
Cook, turning once, until just beginning to crisp, about 5 to 8
minutes. Drain on paper towels.
3. Cut each eggplant round in half.
4. Place 1 goat cheese round onto half of the eggplant rounds.
Top the goat cheese with 1 piece pancetta and a basil leaf. Place
the remaining eggplant rounds on top to make sandwiches.
5. Brush both sides of the stuffed eggplant with mustard and dip
into bread crumbs. Season with salt and pepper.
6. Heat the olive oil and butter in a skillet over medium high
heat. Cook the eggplant until golden brown, turning once, about
4 to 6 minutes per side.
7. Place the cooked "sandwiches" onto a serving platter and top
with tomato relish.

SERVINGS: 4 • PREPARATION TIME: 30 MINUTES

New England Style Lobster Roll

THERE ARE SEVERAL VARIATIONS OF THIS TERRIFIC SANDWICH, RANGING
FROM PURE LOBSTER MEAT DRIZZLED ONLY WITH MELTED BUTTER, TO A
MAYONNAISE BASED LOBSTER SALAD PILED HIGH INTO A BUTTERED BUN.
THIS RECIPE IS A COMBINATION OF BOTH—ONE THAT MAKES EVERYONE
HAPPY.

YOU CAN PURCHASE FRESH LOBSTER MEAT FROM THE LOCAL FISHMONGER. MAKE SURE THAT YOU PICK THROUGH THE MEAT TO REMOVE ANY SHELLS, ACCIDENTALLY INCLUDED. AN EXTRAVAGANT ALTERNATIVE IS TO PURCHASE LIVE MAINE LOBSTER, READILY AVAILABLE IN THE SUMMER MONTHS AND A REAL TREAT. TAKE A LOOK AT PAGE 233 FOR TIPS ON LOBSTER COOKING.

2 pounds cooked lobster meat, chopped into 1-inch pieces
2 medium celery ribs, diced (about 1 cup)
¼ cup mayonnaise
Juice of 1 medium lemon (about 2 tablespoons)
Salt and freshly ground pepper
4 split-top rolls (or hot dog buns)
2 tablespoons butter, melted

1. Place the lobster meat, celery, mayonnaise and lemon juice into a bowl. Toss gently to combine. Season with salt and pepper.
2. Brush the outside of the rolls with butter. Heat a skillet over medium heat. Place the rolls into the skillet and cook, turning often, until the outsides are golden.
3. Remove the rolls to a platter. Fill each one with the lobster salad.

SERVINGS: 4 • PREPARATION TIME: 20 MINUTES

Spicy Lobster Rolls
with Orange Sesame Mayonnaise

ALMOST LIKE A CHILLED SEAFOOD PO' BOY, THE FLAVORFUL MAYONNAISE
IN THIS RECIPE ADDS A "POP" TO THE TRADITIONAL LOBSTER ROLL. FOR A
REAL TREAT, MOUND THIS LOBSTER SALAD ON FRESHLY BAKED BIMINI
BREAD (RECIPE PAGE 66).

1 cup mayonnaise
1 tablespoon sesame oil
1 tablespoon rice wine vinegar
Juice of ½ medium orange (about 2 to 3 tablespoons)
Zest of ½ medium orange (about 1 tablespoon)
½ teaspoon red pepper flakes

2 pounds cooked lobster meat, diced
1 medium celery stalk, diced (about 2 tablespoons)
2 green onions, thinly sliced (about 2 tablespoons)
¼ medium yellow or orange bell pepper, seeded and finely diced (about 2 table-
*   spoons)*
2 tablespoons fresh chopped chives
Salt and freshly ground pepper
4 split-top rolls (or hot dog buns)
2 tablespoons butter, melted

1. Whisk together the mayonnaise, sesame oil, rice wine vinegar,
orange juice, orange zest and red pepper flakes in a small bowl.
2. Toss together the lobster meat, celery, onions, yellow pepper
and chopped chives. Season with salt and pepper.
3. Brush the outside of the rolls with butter.
Heat a skillet over medium heat. Place the rolls
into the skillet and cook, turning often, until
the outsides are golden.
4. Transfer the rolls to a platter. Spread mayonnaise on the inside of each one. Top with lobster mixture. Finish with another dollop of
mayonnaise.

SERVINGS: 4 • PREPARATION TIME: 20 MINUTES

ANOTHER MAYO CONDIMENT
TO USE ON YOUR FAVORITE
LOBSTER OR SEAFOOD ROLL
COMBINES 1 CUP MAYON-
NAISE, 2 TABLESPOONS CHILI
SAUCE, 1 TEASPOON (OR
MORE) PREPARED HORSERAD-
ISH, AND 2 TABLESPOONS
CHOPPED FRESH CILANTRO.
USE YOUR FAVORITE FLAVORS
(AND THE OPEN JARS IN YOUR
REFRIGERATOR) TO INVENT
YOUR FAVORITE MAYONNAISE-
BASED CONDIMENTS.

The Best Tuna Salad Sandwich

EVERY ONCE IN A WHILE, I CRAVE A FRESH TASTING TUNA SALAD SANDWICH ON WHOLE WHEAT BREAD WITH RIPE TOMATOES AND CRISP LETTUCE. THE MOST FLAVORFUL TUNA SALAD BEGINS WITH THE BEST TASTING TUNA YOU CAN PURCHASE. I PREFER TUNA PACKED IN OIL, BUT YOU CAN CHOOSE YOUR FAVORITE FOR THIS NO-FAIL SANDWICH.

IF YOU ARE NOT A FAN OF TUNA PACKED IN OIL, YOU CAN SUBSTITUTE WITH TUNA PACKED IN WATER OR TUNA IN A READY-TO-EAT POUCH. IN BOTH INSTANCES, YOU SHOULD ADD MORE MAYONNAISE TO THE TUNA TO COMPENSATE FOR OIL-FREE TUNA.

2 6-ounce cans tuna packed in oil
1/3 cup mayonnaise
Juice of 1 medium lemon (about 2 tablespoons)
1 medium celery stalk, diced (about 2 tablespoons)
2 tablespoons finely chopped fresh parsley
Salt and freshly ground pepper
8 slices multigrain, whole wheat or sour dough bread
2 large beefsteak tomatoes, sliced into 1/4-inch slices (about 8 slices)
1/4 large head romaine lettuce, washed, dried and torn (about 2 cups)

1. Place the tuna with the oil into a small bowl. Use a fork to break up the tuna into fine pieces.
2. Add the mayonnaise and lemon juice and mash, using the fork to combine.
3. Stir in the celery and parsley. (You may add more mayonnaise at this point). Season with salt and pepper.
4. Spread the tuna onto 4 slices of bread. Top with tomatoes and lettuce. Top with remaining bread slices.

SERVINGS: 4 • PREPARATION TIME: 15 MINUTES

The Tuna Melt

Turn this yummy sandwich into another American classic, the Tuna Melt, by broiling the sandwich. Split and toast 4 English muffins. Place each onto a broiling pan. Preheat the oven to broil. Top each one with tuna salad, a tomato slice and shredded Swiss or cheddar cheese. (Shredded cheese melts faster). Broil for 4 to 5 minutes or until the cheese melts. Serve with sweet pickles.

Niçoise Tuna Hoagies
with Sun-Dried Tomato Vinaigrette

IF YOU LOVE NICOISE SALAD, THEN YOU'LL HAPPILY DEVOUR THIS TUNA SANDWICH. THE FLAVORFUL VINAIGRETTE ADDS JUST ENOUGH PIZZAZ TO TAKE THIS HOAGIE FROM THE EVERYDAY TO SOMETHING REALLY SPECIAL.

2 tablespoons chopped sun-dried tomatoes in oil
2 medium anchovy fillets
2 tablespoons chopped fresh parsley
1 tablespoon chopped fresh thyme
2 medium cloves garlic
Juice of 1 medium lemon (about 2 tablespoons)
½ cup olive oil
Salt and freshly ground pepper

4 6-inch long crusty hoagie rolls
2 6-ounce cans tuna packed in oil, drained
4 large eggs, hard boiled and sliced
4 plum tomatoes, cut into quarters
1 small red onion, thinly sliced
10 to 12 Niçoise (or other good quality) olives, pitted and sliced

1. Place the sun-dried tomatoes, anchovies, parsley, thyme, garlic and lemon juice into a blender. Pulse to combine. With the machine running, slowly add the olive oil. Season with salt and pepper.
2. Cut the hoagie rolls in half horizontally three quarters down.
3. Drizzle the cut sides of each roll with 2 to 3 tablespoons of the vinaigrette.
4. Divide the tuna among the rolls. Top with egg, tomatoes, red onion and sliced olives.
5. Drizzle the remaining vinaigrette over top.

SERVINGS: 4 • PREPARATION TIME 20 MINUTES

THIS SANDWICH IS PERFECT FOR A PICNIC BASKET. WRAP THE HOAGIES IN PARCHMENT PAPER. SLICE DIAGONALLY IN HALF. PLACE EACH WRAPPED HALF INTO A FUN CONTAINER—LIKE A CHINESE TAKE-OUT BOX. SERVE WITH GRILLED POTATO SALAD (SEE RECIPE PAGE 93) AND THREE BEAN SALAD (SEE RECIPE PAGE 102) ALSO MOUNDED INTO TAKE-OUT CONTAINERS, AND VOILA, YOU HAVE AN EASY-TO-PREPARE ALFRESCO MEAL!

Creamy Mustard Sauce
To take this sandwich way, way over the top, add a dollop of Creamy Mustard Sauce to the mix. Combine ½ cup mayonnaise, ¼ cup sour cream, 2 tablespoons Dijon mustard, 2 tablespoons chopped fresh tarragon, a squeeze of lemon juice, salt and pepper. Spread this mixture onto the cut sides of the hoagie rolls and then layer with the tuna and toppers. Bon Appetit!

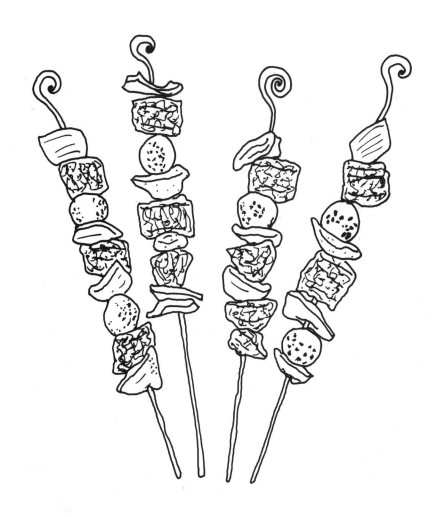

Chapter 6

Skewers and Tostada Lite Meals

Here's an idea! Let's take a giant step away from same-old, ho-hum every night "meat and potatoes" as the hedge stone of our weekly meal plan. Instead, using a little creativity, and by taking advantage of a few good kitchen tools, weekday suppers can be interesting, as well as quick and healthy.

This chapter is all about kebabs and tostadas. Why this combination? Both dishes allow you to work with easy-to-find ingredients, while intermingling favorites with just enough flare to put a smile on your guest's face. Both are quick to prepare. Skewers are grilled either outside on the barbie or inside, using a grill pan. Tostadas are simply toasted tortillas piled high with everything you can imagine.

I remember my mom serving gorgeous beef kabobs, glazed with a red wine sauce and served (skewers and all) on top of white rice pilaf. The beef cubes were huge! You needed a knife and fork to cut into the juicy center. Crisp bell pepper wedges and ripe cherry tomatoes festively lined themselves between pieces of the beef. Yumm....

Mom's "guests-for-dinner" kabob meal inspired many of the dishes in this chapter. I've updated her beef cube skewers by accenting them with a piquant chimichurri sauce. We'll also skewer mahi mahi, shrimp, chicken, pork and veggies, and serve them with everything from banana salsa to avocado, corn and cranberry relish.

Speaking of relishes and sauces, they also play a large part in accenting tostada dishes. With origins in Mexico, tostadas appear on many restaurant menus layered with shredded beef or chicken, topped with guacamole or refried beans, and slathered with melting cheddar cheese. You'll find the basics of tostada preparation in this section. Once armed with all of this new-found information, it won't be long until your imagination runs wild. In no time, you'll discover the tostada is the perfect foundation for pulled pork, barbecue-style chicken, spicy shrimp, roasted butternut squash and much, much more.

Classic kabobs and tostadas are brilliantly updated in this chapter, offering you the incentive you need to invent your own lite suppers. Once you've mastered each of these unique dishes, you might want to work them into your next party plan. For example, why not plan a Tostada Ta Dah party by offering heaping bowls of toasted tortilla toppers, accompanied by your favorite salsas and relishes. On the other hand, perhaps your next neighborhood block party menu features campy kabobs. Easily made in advance, skewers are the perfect dish to serve at your barbecue get-togethers. Imagine each guest being able to choose his favorite combination of meat, veggies and fish, then threading those ingredients onto a skewer. The skewers are grilled to perfection and served with a wild arrangement of salsas, purées, relishes and sauces. The end result is a party filled with giggles. What more could you ask for?

Whether you are looking for a quick and easy mid-week pick-me-up or an easy way to impress your party guests, this chapter offers a new twist on two classic favorites, giving each an easy invitation to become your next lite meal fresh tradition.

Beef, Onions, Pepper, and Tomato Kabobs with Chimichurri Sauce

COOKING KABOBS ON THE GRILL IS A GREAT WAY TO PRESENT A WONDERFUL MEAL. METAL SKEWERS ARE ATTRACTIVE AND FUNCTIONAL. WOOD SKEWERS WORK WELL, BUT YOU MUST SOAK THEM BEFORE EXPOSING THEM TO THE HEAT OR THEY WILL BURN. IF GRILLING IS NOT AN OPTION, TRY BROILING THE SKEWERS—IT'S ALL GOOD...

CHIMICHURRI SAUCE IS AN ARGENTINEAN CONDIMENT, OFTEN SERVED WITH GRILLED MEAT. BECAUSE IT IS MADE WITH FRESH HERBS, THE SAUCE IS THICK IN TEXTURE, LIKE A RELISH. THE GARLIC AND RED PEPPER MAKE THE SAUCE SPICY. SERVE THIS CONDIMENT THE NEXT TIME YOU GRILL FISH OR CHICKEN AND WAKE UP YOUR PALATE WITH A VIVA LA CHIMICHURRI!

1 pound boneless rib-eye roast beef, cut into 2-inch cubes
4 plum tomatoes, cut in half lengthwise
2 large green bell peppers, seeded and cut into quarters
1 large red onion, peeled and cut into 8 wedges

¼ cup olive oil
¼ cup soy sauce
1 tablespoon sesame oil
3 medium garlic cloves, minced (about 1½ teaspoons)
1 tablespoon brown sugar
1 teaspoon ground cumin
¼ teaspoon red pepper flakes
Salt and pepper

1 bunch fresh parsley (about 1 cup)
¼ cup fresh cilantro
4 medium garlic cloves
2 green onions, thinly sliced (about 2 tablespoons)
½ cup olive oil
⅓ cup red wine vinegar
Juice of 1 medium lemon (about 2 tablespoons)
¼ teaspoon red pepper flakes

1. Thread the beef, tomatoes, peppers and onion pieces onto 4 long (12-inch) metal skewers, alternating each ingredient. Place the skewers into a shallow baking dish.
2. Whisk together ¼ cup olive oil, soy sauce, sesame oil, minced garlic, brown sugar, cumin, and ¼ teaspoon red pepper flakes in a bowl. Season with salt. Pour the marinade over the skewers. Place into the refrigerator for at least 1 hour or overnight.
3. To prepare the Chimichurri sauce, place the parsley, cilantro, garlic cloves, green onions, remaining ½ cup olive oil, red wine vinegar, lemon juice, and remaining ¼ teaspoon red pepper flakes into a food processor. Pulse to combine. Taste and season with salt and pepper.
4. Heat a grill pan or outdoor grill on high heat. Grill the skewers, turning once and basting with the marinade, until the beef is medium rare, about 3 to 5 minutes per side.

5. Remove the skewers from the grill. Gently remove the cooked beef and veggies to a platter. Serve with Chimichurri sauce.

SERVINGS: 4 • PREPARATION TIME: 30 MINUTES PLUS MARINATING SKEWERS

Grilled Mahi Mahi Skewers with Banana Salsa

LOOKING FOR A QUICK MIDWEEK MEAL THAT IS BURSTING WITH GOOD STUFF? THIS ONE DEFINITELY FITS THE BILL! THE INTERESTING COMBINATION OF BANANAS AND HOT PEPPERS IN THE SALSA OFFERS A TWANG FOR THE TONGUE.

1½ pounds mahi mahi steaks, cut into 2-inch cubes
1 medium pineapple, peeled, cored and cut into 1-inch dice (about 2 cups)
2 large red bell pepper, seeded and cut into 1-inch pieces
⅓ cup olive oil
Juice of 1 medium lemon (about 2 tablespoons)
2 tablespoons chopped fresh sage
Salt and freshly ground pepper

3 large bananas, peeled and diced into ¼-inch pieces
Juice of 1 medium lime (about 1 tablespoon)
Juice of 1 medium orange (about ⅓ cup)
2 green onions, thinly sliced (about 2 tablespoons)
1 medium jalapeño pepper, seeded and diced (about 2 tablespoons)
1 small red onion, peeled and diced (about ½ cup)
1 medium green bell pepper, seeded and cut into ¼-inch dice (about ⅔ cup)
1 medium red bell pepper, seeded and cut into ¼-inch dice (about ⅔ cup)
1 1-inch piece ginger, grated (about 1 tablespoon)
1 tablespoon fresh chopped mint
1 tablespoon fresh chopped sage

MAHI MAHI IS REALLY DOLPHIN (ALSO KNOWN AS DOLPHIN-FISH). NO, NOT THAT KINDA DOLPHIN! THAT DOLPHIN IS A MAMMAL. THIS ONE IS A FIRM, SOMEWHAT FATTY FISH THAT IS VERY FLAVORFUL. THIS DOLPHIN IS FOUND IN WARM WATERS AND CAN WEIGH AS LITTLE AS 3 POUNDS OR AS MUCH AS 45 POUNDS. THE HAWAIIAN NAMED THIS DOLPHIN MAHI MAHI TO ASSURE CONSUMERS THAT THEY ARE NOT EATING FLIPPER.

1. Thread the mahi mahi chunks, pineapple and pepper onto 4 long (12-inch) metal skewers, alternating each ingredient. Place the skewers into a shallow baking dish. Season with olive oil, lemon juice, sage, salt, and pepper.
2. Combine the bananas, juices, green onion, jalapeño pepper, red onion, bell peppers, ginger, mint and sage in a bowl. Toss and season with salt and pepper.
3. Heat a grill pan or outdoor grill on high heat. Grill the skewers, turning once, about 5 to 8 minutes per side.
4. Remove the skewers from the grill. Gently transfer the cooked fish, pineapple and peppers to a platter. Serve with banana salsa.

SERVINGS: 4 • PREPARATION TIME 45 MINUTES

Baked Butternut Squash Purée with Mint and Cardamom

Cut 2 medium butternut squash in half and take out the seeds. Coat the cut sides of the squash with vegetable oil spray. Place them, (cut side down), into a baking pan and roast at 375° for about 30 minutes, or until the pulp is soft. Scoop out the pulp and place into the bowl of a food processor (or use an immersion blender). Add ¼ cup honey, 2 tablespoons fresh mint, ½ teaspoon cardamom, and season with salt and pepper. Purée until just blended.

Sherry Marinated Shrimp Skewers with Warm Black Bean Relish

THIS DISH COMES TOGETHER IN MINUTES AND IS SHOWY ENOUGH FOR COMPANY. SERVE WITH VEGGIE-STUDDED RICE AND BAKED BUTTERNUT SQUASH PURÉE WITH MINT AND CARDAMOM (SEE SIDEBAR), AND YOU HAVE A FRESH FAST-FOOD FAVORITE.

1½ pounds large uncooked shrimp, peeled and deveined (about 24)
¼ cup dry sherry
¼ cup olive oil
3 medium garlic cloves, minced (about 1½ teaspoons)
2 tablespoons chopped fresh thyme
Salt and freshly ground pepper

1 tablespoon olive oil
1 large green bell pepper, seeded and thinly sliced (about 1 cup)
1 bunch (6 to 8) green onions, chopped (about ½ cup)
1 medium jalapeño pepper, seeded and diced (about 2 tablespoons)
1 teaspoon ground cumin
1 28-ounce can diced tomatoes
1 16-ounce can black beans, drained

2 14-ounce can artichoke hearts, drained and cut into quarters
1 pint ripe cherry tomatoes or mixed baby tomatoes

1. Place the shrimp into a bowl. Add the sherry, ¼ cup olive oil, garlic, and thyme. Season with salt and pepper. Toss together, cover and chill for at least 15 minutes and up to 1 hour.
2. Heat the remaining 1 tablespoon olive oil in a skillet over medium high heat.
3. Cook the green pepper, onions, and jalapeño pepper in the skillet until just beginning to brown, about 3 to 5 minutes.
4. Stir in the cumin, tomatoes and black beans. Cook until just warmed through, about 3 to 5 minute more. Reduce heat and keep warm.
5. Remove the shrimp from the marinade. Thread the shrimp, artichoke hearts, and cherry tomatoes onto 4 long (12-inch) metal skewers, alternating each ingredient.
6. Grill the skewers in a grill pan (or outdoor grill) on medium high heat until the shrimp are opaque, about 3 minutes per side.
7. Serve the shrimp skewers with the warm black bean relish.

SERVINGS: 4 • PREPARATION TIME: 20 MINUTES PLUS MARINATING SHRIMP

Mexican Chili Corn and Tomatillo Skewers with Chipotle Lime Yogurt

THIS IS THE PERFECT VEGGIE SIDE DISH TO SERVE FOR YOUR NEXT GRILL PARTY, OR THE BEGINNING OF A VEGAN DINNER WHEN SERVED WITH BROWN RICE AND RED BEANS.

2 cups plain yogurt
Juice of 1 medium lime (about 1 tablespoon)
Zest of 1 medium lime (about 1 tablespoon)
1 chipotle pepper in adobo sauce, seeded and finely diced (about 1 tablespoon)
2 green onions, chopped (about 2 tablespoons)

4 ears of fresh corn
1 medium zucchini, cut into 2-inch rounds
2 large yellow squash, cut into 2-inch rounds
8 whole tomatillos, papery skin removed
5 to 6 large shallots, peeled
½ cup olive oil
1 tablespoon ground chili powder
1 teaspoon ground cumin
1 teaspoon paprika
¼ teaspoon red pepper flakes
Salt

1. Prepare the sauce by placing the yogurt, lime juice, lime zest, chipotle pepper and green onions into a blender. Pulse to emulsify.
2. Cut the corn into 3-inch rounds. Place the corn, zucchini, squash, tomatillos, and shallots into a bowl.
3. Toss the veggies with olive oil, chili powder, cumin, paprika, and red pepper flakes. Season with salt.
4. Remove the vegetables from the marinade. Thread the veggies onto 4 long (12-inch) metal skewers, alternating each ingredient.
5. Grill the vegetable skewers in a grill pan (or outdoor grill) over medium high heat, turning often, until just beginning to brown.
6. Remove the vegetables from the skewers and serve with the spicy yogurt sauce.

SERVINGS: 4 TO 8 • PREPARATION TIME: 30 MINUTES PLUS GRILLING

Grilled Steak
This veggie combo is ideal served with a perfectly grilled steak. For a 2 to 3-inch thick steak, remove from the refrigerator 30 minutes before grilling. Preheat the grill on high. Just before grilling, season the steak with salt and pepper. (I like to add a drizzle of Worcestershire sauce, too.) Place the steak onto the grill. Reduce the heat to medium high. Don't mess with the steak for 8 minutes. Turn the steak over and cook until desired temperature, about 8 minutes more. Use your finger (carefully) to determine doneness. If the steak is very pliable when touched, it is rare. If the steak bounces back from your touch, it is leaning toward the well done stage.

Barbecued Pork Tenderloin Skewers
with Cranberry, Corn and Avocado Relish

WHAT'S BETTER THAN BARBECUE? SIMPLY PREPARED BARBECUE SKEWERS
ACCENTED WITH CREAMY AVOCADO AND CRANBERRY RELISH—THAT'S WHAT!
SERVE WITH WILD RICE OR POTATO GRATIN (SEE RECIPE PAGE 212) FOR A
MOUTH-WATERING SUPPER.

2 12- to 14-ounce pork tenderloins, cut into 2-inch cubes
1 bunch (6 to 8) green onions, chopped (about ½ cup)
½ cup ketchup
¼ cup dark molasses
⅓ cup soy sauce
1 tablespoon peanut oil
1 tablespoon chili sauce
4 medium garlic cloves, minced (about 2 teaspoons)
2 tablespoons chopped fresh oregano

1 12-ounce bag frozen cranberries, thawed, drained (about 3 cups)
Juice of 1 medium orange (about ⅓ cup)
1 large yellow bell pepper, roasted, skin removed, diced
1 medium jalapeño pepper, seeded and diced (about 2 tablespoons)
Zest of ½ medium orange (about 1 tablespoon)
2 large avocados, peeled, pitted and diced (about 2 cups)
1 16-ounce can corn, drained
1 tablespoon rice wine vinegar
1 tablespoon chopped fresh cilantro
Salt and freshly ground pepper

I. Place the pork cubes into a shallow baking dish.

2. Stir together the green onions, ketchup, molasses, soy sauce,
peanut oil, chili sauce, garlic, and oregano. Pour this mixture
over the pork cubes and toss to coat. Cover and place in the
refrigerator to marinate for at least 30 minutes or overnight.

3. Place the cranberries and orange juice into the bowl of a food
processor. Pulse to coarsely chop. Pour this mixture into a bowl.

4. Stir in the roasted pepper, jalapeño pepper, orange zest, avocados, corn, vinegar, and cilantro. Toss and season with salt and
pepper. Set aside.

5. Remove the pork from the marinade. Thread onto long skewers.

6. Heat a grill pan (or outdoor grill) on high heat. Grill the pork
skewers, basting with the reserved marinade, turning once, until
browned, about 4 to 6 minutes per side. Transfer to a platter.
Serve with cranberry and avocado relish.

SERVINGS: 4 TO 6 • PREPARATION TIME: 30 MINUTES PLUS MARINATING THE
PORK

I GREW UP HATING PORK. IT
WAS DRY, TOUGH AND HARDLY
APPETIZING. NO WONDER,
COOKS IN EARLIER DAYS,
GUARDING AGAINST TRICHI-
NOSIS—A FOOD BORNE DIS-
EASE CAUSED BY A MICRO-
SCOPIC PARASITE—OVER-
COOKED PORK. IN FACT, MANY
OLDER COOKBOOKS SUGGEST
THAT ONE SHOULD ROAST
PORK TO AN INTERNAL TEM-
PERATURE OF 170° TO
185°. TODAY, YOU NEEDN'T
COOK PORK TO THE WELL
DONE STAGE TO KILL THE
TRICHINOSIS PARASITE. MOST
MODERN COOKBOOKS SUG-
GEST COOKING TO AN INTER-
NAL TEMPERATURE OF 150°
TO 165°, ALLOWING YOU TO
ENJOY MEDIUM RARE CUTS
THAT ARE JUICY AND DELI-
CIOUS. PORK IS ALSO LEANER
TODAY THAN IT WAS IN THE
PAST, HAVING ALMOST ⅓
FEWER CALORIES. DUE TO
IMPROVED LIVESTOCK FEED-
ING TECHNIQUES, PORK IS
ALSO HIGHER IN PROTEIN,
SOMETHING WE ALL NEED IN A
HEALTHY, BALANCED DIET.

Mustard-Coated Chicken Skewers with Grilled Veggie Salsa

AN UPDATE ON FAST FOOD CHICKEN FINGERS, THESE FUN SKEWERS ARE
EASY TO PREPARE, AS IS THE GREAT TASTING SALSA. REMEMBER TO SOAK
WOODEN SKEWERS IN WATER FOR AT LEAST AN HOUR BEFORE THREADING.

6 plum tomatoes, cut in half lengthwise (about 1 pound)
1 small eggplant, cut in half lengthwise
1 medium red onion, peeled and cut in half crosswise
2 tablespoons olive oil
1 medium poblano pepper
¼ cup chopped fresh cilantro
Juice of 1 medium lime (about 1 tablespoon)
Salt and freshly ground pepper

6 (4 to 5-ounce) skinless boneless chicken breast cutlets, cut into 1-inch wide strips
2 tablespoons Dijon mustard
1 cup prepared bread crumbs
1 teaspoon dried rosemary

1. Heat a grill pan on high heat or use an outdoor grill. Brush
the cut side of the tomatoes, eggplant, and onion with olive oil.
Place the vegetables into the grill. Place the pepper into the grill.
2. Grill the veggies until they begin to char, but not to the extent
they become mushy. Remove the veggies as they cook. (The tomatoes will take the shortest amount of time, followed by the eggplant, onion and finally the pepper. You want the skin of the
pepper to be quite charred and blackened.)
3. Coarsely chop the tomatoes, onion and eggplant. Peel the skin
from the pepper and chop. Place the veggies into a bowl and toss
with cilantro and lime juice. Season with salt and pepper.
4. Thread the chicken strips, lengthwise onto wooden skewers,
which have been soaked in water. Leave a long enough "handle"
on the skewers so that they overlap the pan.
5. Brush both sides of the chicken with mustard.
6. Combine the breadcrumbs with dried rosemary and season
with salt and pepper. Dredge the chicken strips into the bread
crumb mixture.
7. Heat a grill pan that has been coated with vegetable oil spray,
over medium high heat. Grill the chicken strips, turning once,
until golden brown, about 3 to 4 minutes per side.
8. Serve the chicken skewers with the roasted salsa.

SERVINGS: 4 • PREPARATION TIME: 45 MINUTES

Broiled Veggies
*Broiling the veggies is an
acceptable substitute when
preparing this dish. Set your
oven on the broil setting. Roast
the pepper first, rotating ¼ turn
after each side begins to char
and blister. Place the pepper
into a brown bag or covered
bowl to steam for 10 to 20
minutes. This softens the flesh of
the pepper and makes the skin
easy to peel. Make quick work
of broiling tomatoes, eggplant
and onions by chopping them
into ½-inch pieces and tossing
with olive oil. Place the veggies
onto a baking sheet and broil
for 1 to 3 minutes.*

Shredded Beef Tostadas with Caramelized Onions, Spinach, and Goat Cheese

SLOW COOKING HELPS BREAK DOWN THE BEEF AND ALLOWS THE SEASONING TO CLING TO EVERY SHRED. SAUTÉED SPINACH AND ONIONS ADD ANOTHER DEPTH OF FLAVOR. THINK STEAKHOUSE MENU ALL ON ONE TOASTED TORTILLA!

CARAMELIZING REFERS TO A COOKING TECHNIQUE THAT BREAKS DOWN FOODS, RELEASING THE SUGAR COMPONENTS, THUS SWEETENING A TART VEGGIE, LIKE AN ONION. BROWN SUGAR MAY BE ADDED TO SWEETEN THE END RESULT EVEN MORE. BALSAMIC VINEGAR ALSO HAS A SWEET COMPONENT. THE COMBINATION OF BROWNING AND CARAMELIZING THE ONIONS WITH A TOUCH OF BALSAMIC VINEGAR, CREATES A SWEET TASTING TREAT THAT WORKS WELL AS AN ACCENT FOR ALL TYPES OF TOSTADAS.

1 1½-pound beef chuck roast
2 medium white onions, peeled and cut into 1-inch wedges
4 medium garlic cloves, minced (about 2 teaspoons)
2 cups beef broth
1 bay leaf
1 teaspoon ground oregano
Salt and freshly ground pepper

2 tablespoons olive oil
2 large yellow onions, thinly sliced (about 4½ cups)
1 tablespoon balsamic vinegar
1 pound fresh spinach leaves, washed, dried and torn (about 4 cups)

4 ounces goat cheese, crumbled

8 to 10 6-inch corn tortillas
Vegetable oil for frying

Preheat the oven to 325°.

1. Place the chuck roast into a Dutch oven. Add the white onions and garlic cloves. Pour in the beef broth. Add the bay leaf and oregano. Season with salt and pepper. Cover and roast for 3 hours, or until the meat is easily shredded with two forks. Remove the roast from the pan, cool slightly and shred. Keep the shredded beef warm. (For an extra boost of flavor, you can drizzle the shredded beef with a ladleful of the pan juices.)

2. Place 1 tablespoon olive oil into a skillet over medium high heat. Add the yellow onions. Season with salt and pepper. Cook until the onions are soft and well browned, about 10 minutes. Add the balsamic vinegar. Reduce the heat to medium and cook until the liquid disappears and the onions are syrupy, about 5 minutes more. Transfer the onions to a bowl and keep warm.

3. Place the remaining 1 tablespoon of olive oil in the skillet over medium high heat. Add the spinach leaves. Season with salt and pepper. Cook until the spinach is just wilted. Transfer the spinach to a bowl.

4. Heat enough vegetable oil to coat the bottom of a skillet, over

medium high heat. Place 1 tortilla in the hot oil. Cook for 30 to 60 seconds, or until the tortilla is bubbled and golden. Use tongs to transfer the fried tortilla to a paper towel to drain. Continue until all of the tortillas have been cooked.

5. Assemble the tostadas by layering the ingredients on top of the fried tortillas. Start with the caramelized onions. Top with shredded beef and a spoonful of spinach. Sprinkle goat cheese over top.

SERVINGS: 6 TO 8 • PREPARATION TIME: 30 MINUTES PLUS 2 TO 3 HOURS SLOW ROASTING BEEF

Beef and Sautéed Onion Tostadas
with Avocado and Jack Cheese

YOU CAN PREPARE BEEF TOSTADAS USING LEFT OVER ROAST BEEF OR SLICED
FLANK STEAK, MAKING TOSTADAS A GREAT WAY TO SERVE A FAST, MIDWEEK
SUPPER. FEEL FREE TO SUBSTITUTE WITH YOUR FAVORITE CHEESE (BLUE
CHEESE IS A GREAT CHOICE!) AND ADD VEGGIES LIKE DICED TOMATOES AND
GREEN PEPPERS.

MEXICAN INSPIRED TOSTADAS ARE USUALLY TOPPED WITH SHREDDED BEEF OR CHICKEN AND TOPPED WITH GUACAMOLE, SOUR CREAM, REFRIED BEANS, GRATED CHEESE AND TOMATO SALSA. THINK OF AN OPEN-FACED TACO, AND YOU OPEN A WORLD OF DELECTABLE POSSIBILITIES.

1 pound top sirloin steak, cut into ½-inch cubes
1 teaspoon dried rosemary
Salt and freshly ground pepper
2 tablespoons olive oil
2 medium white onions, peeled and thinly sliced (about 1½ cups)

½ medium romaine lettuce, washed, dried and torn (about 3 cups)
2 tablespoons olive oil
1 tablespoon balsamic vinegar

1 large avocado, peeled, pitted and thinly sliced (about 1 cup)
Juice of 1 medium lime (about 1 tablespoon)

Vegetable oil for frying
8 6-inch corn tortillas
4 ounces grated Monterey Jack cheese (about 1 cup)

1. Season the beef with rosemary, salt and pepper.
2. Heat 1 tablespoon olive oil in a skillet over medium high heat. Cook the beef in the hot oil until brown, about 4 to 5 minutes. Transfer the meat to a bowl.
3. Heat 1 more tablespoon olive oil in the skillet. Cook the onions in the hot oil until soft and browned, about 5 to 8 minutes. Return the beef to the pan. Reduce the heat to low. Keep warm.
4. Combine the lettuce leaves with 2 tablespoons olive oil and vinegar in a bowl. Season with salt and pepper. Toss and set aside.
5. Drizzle the avocado with lime juice. Toss and set aside.
6. Heat enough vegetable oil to coat the bottom of a skillet, over medium high heat. Place 1 tortilla into the hot oil. Cook for 30 to 60 seconds or until the tortilla is bubbled and golden. Use tongs to transfer the fried tortilla to a paper towel to drain. Continue until all of the tortillas have been cooked.
7. Assemble the tostadas by layering the ingredients on top of the fried tortillas. Start with the dressed lettuce leaves. Top with avocado slices and then the beef and onion mixture. Top with shredded cheese.

SERVINGS: 4 TO 6 • PREPARATION TIME 45 MINUTES

Black Bean and Butternut Squash Tostadas with Roasted Jalapeño Garnish

THE SWEETNESS OF ROASTED SQUASH BLENDS WITH THE SPICE OF ROASTED PEPPERS TO TOP TRADITIONAL TOSTADA FARE: MASHED BLACK BEANS.

4 to 6 medium jalapeño peppers

1 medium butternut squash, peeled and diced into 1-inch cubes (about 2 cups)
10 to 12 large shallots, peeled and separated into lobes
2 tablespoons olive oil
1 teaspoon chili powder
½ teaspoons ground cinnamon
Salt and freshly ground pepper

1 tablespoon olive oil
2 medium cloves garlic, minced (about 1 teaspoon)
1 16-ounce can black beans, drained
½ teaspoon ground cumin

8 to 10 6-inch corn tortillas
Vegetable oil for frying

Preheat the oven to broil
1. Place the peppers onto a baking sheet. Broil, turning often, until the skin is blackened and blistered. Place the peppers into a paper bag (or covered bowl) to steam for 15 minutes. Remove the blackened skin and seeds from the peppers. Cut into strips. Set aside.
2. Reduce the oven temperature to 375°. Place the butternut squash cubes and shallots onto a baking sheet. Toss with 2 table-spoons olive oil, chili powder, and cinnamon. Season with salt and pepper. Bake until the veggies are soft and golden, about 20 to 30 minutes.
3. Place 1 tablespoon olive oil in a skillet over medium heat. Cook the garlic in the oil until just soft, about 2 minutes. Add the beans to the skillet. Season with cumin, salt and pepper. Use a potato masher to mash the beans. Keep warm.
4. Heat enough vegetable oil to coat the bottom of a skillet, over medium high heat. Place 1 tortilla into the hot oil. Cook for 30 to 60 seconds or until the tortilla is bubbled and golden. Use tongs to transfer the fried tortilla to a paper towel to drain. Continue until all of the tortillas have been cooked.
5. Assemble the tostadas by layering the ingredients on top of the fried tortillas. Spread a layer of black beans onto the tostadas. Top with roasted squash and shallots. Garnish with strips of roasted pepper.

BLACK BEANS ARE SMALL AND RATHER SQUARE-SHAPED. A MEMBER OF THE KIDNEY BEAN FAMILY, THE BLACK BEAN IS NATIVE TO SOUTH AMERICA, WHICH IS WHY BLACK BEANS SHOW UP SO OFTEN IN LATIN FARE. WHEN COOKED, THE BLACK SKIN OF THE BEAN GIVES OFF A PURPLISH TINT TO THE OTHER INGREDIENTS IN THE DISH. BLACK BEANS ARE ALSO CALLED BLACK TUR-TLE, MEXICAN, OR SPANISH BLACK BEANS. DRIED BLACK BEANS KEEP WELL FOR OVER A YEAR IN AN AIRTIGHT GLASS OR CERAMIC CONTAINER. TO USE DRIED BLACK BEANS FOR THIS DISH, YOU SHOULD FIRST SOAK THE BEANS IN WATER FOR 8 HOURS, THEN PRES-SURE COOK FOR 18 MIN-UTES, OR SIMMER ON THE STOVE FOR 2 HOURS. 1 CUP OF DRIED BLACK BEANS MAKES APPROXIMATELY 2½ CUPS OF COOKED BEANS.

SERVINGS: 6 TO 8 • PREPARATION TIME: 45 MINUTES

Pulled Pork Tostadas Topped with Spicy Slaw

THINK SOUTHERN-STYLE BARBECUE PORK SANDWICHES PILED HIGH WITH
CREAMY SLAW, AND YOU HAVE THE INSPIRATION FOR THIS UNIQUE TOSTADA
DISH.

THE SECRET TO THE MOST FLAVORFUL PULLED PORK DEPENDS ON THREE THINGS: THE RIGHT CUT OF PORK, A FLAVORFUL RUB, AND SLOW COOKING. THE PORK SHOULD HAVE PLENTY OF FAT THAT WILL MELT AWAY AS THE PORK COOKS, THUS FLAVORING THE MEAT, NOT MAKING THE DISH GREASY. PORK SHOULDER (ALSO KNOWN AS PORK BUTT) HAS A GOOD RATIO OF FAT TO MEAT. IF YOU TRY THIS WITH A LEAN CUT OF PORK, THE MEAT WILL BE TOUGH AND UNAPPEALING. THE BEST RUB IS A MIXTURE OF YOUR FAVORITE SPICES. FEEL FREE TO CREATE YOUR OWN SPECIAL BATCH. THERE ARE NO WRONG COMBINATIONS. FINALLY, SLOW ROASTING ALLOWS THE MEAT TO TENDERIZE AND THE SPICES TO FLAVOR EVERY TENDER MORSEL OF PORK.

2 tablespoons garlic powder
2 tablespoons chili powder
2 tablespoons salt
1 tablespoon pepper
1 tablespoons dried oregano
1 tablespoon dried thyme
1 tablespoon paprika
1 4-pound pork shoulder

1 cup ketchup
½ cup chili sauce
⅓ cup white apple cider vinegar
1 tablespoon brown sugar
½ teaspoon paprika
¼ teaspoon ground ginger
Salt and freshly ground pepper

1 1-pound head green cabbage, shredded (about 3 to 4 cups)
½ small red onion, cut into very thin slices (about ½ cup)
1 medium apple, peeled and julienned into very thin matchstick size strips (about 1
    cup; a julienne vegetable peeler works well for this job)
2 tablespoons fresh chopped cilantro
Juice of 2 medium limes (about 2 tablespoons)
1 tablespoon apple cider vinegar
½ teaspoon brown sugar
¼ teaspoon red pepper flakes

8 to 10 6-inch corn tortillas
Vegetable oil for frying

Preheat the oven to 300°.
1. Mix together garlic powder, chili powder, salt, pepper,
oregano, thyme and 1 tablespoon paprika. Rub the pork shoulder
all over with this mixture. Wrap tightly in aluminum foil. Place
into a roasting pan. Roast until the meat is very tender and
falling from the bone, about 8 hours or overnight. Allow the
pork to sit for 30 minutes in the foil. Remove the foil and use 2
forks to shred the pork. Set aside.
2. For barbecue sauce, place the ketchup, chili sauce, ⅓ cup apple
cider vinegar, 1 tablespoon brown sugar, ½ teaspoon paprika, and
ginger in a pot over medium heat. Cook for 5 minutes. Season

with salt and pepper. Reduce the heat to low. Keep warm.

3. Place the cabbage, red onion, apple and cilantro into a bowl. Whisk together the lime juice, I tablespoon apple cider vinegar, $\frac{1}{2}$ teaspoon brown sugar and red pepper flakes. Toss the slaw with the vinaigrette.

4. Heat enough vegetable oil to coat the bottom of a skillet, over medium high heat. Place I tortilla into the hot oil. Cook for 30 to 60 seconds or until the tortilla is bubbled and golden. Use tongs to remove the fried tortilla to a paper towel to drain. Continue until all of the tortillas have been cooked.

5. Assemble the tostadas by layering the ingredients on top of the fried tortillas. Start with shredded pork. Ladle barbecue sauce over the meat. Top with slaw and serve.

SERVINGS: 6 TO 8 • PREPARATION TIME: 1 HOUR PLUS OVERNIGHT SLOW ROASTING THE PORK.

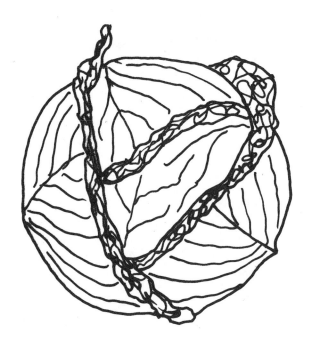

Shrimp Tostadas with Tomatillo Purée and Avocado Salsa

SEASONED SHRIMP TOP A WARM TORTILLA, AND ARE SPICED WITH CONTRASTING TART TOMATILLO AND COOL AVOCADO IN THIS INSPIRED LITE MEAL.

Baking Tostadas

An alternate way to toast a tortilla is to bake it in the oven. This can be tricky. Over-toasted, and the tortilla will crumble into pieces. If under-toasted, the tortilla will have the appeal of wet cardboard. The happy medium is a tostada built on a crispy, yet pliable tortilla. This can be done by placing the tortilla directly onto the rack in the center of a preheated 350° oven. Bake for exactly 7 minutes, testing for pliability after 5 minutes. Once out of the oven, layer your tostada with a wet ingredient first, to keep the tortilla somewhat moist and to help glue on the other toppings.

1 pound medium uncooked shrimp, peeled and deveined (about 30)
¼ cup honey
Juice of 1 medium lemon (about 2 tablespoons)
2 tablespoons olive oil
2 medium cloves garlic, minced (about 1 teaspoon)
½ teaspoon chili powder
1 teaspoon dried oregano
1 teaspoon hot paprika
Salt and freshly ground pepper

1 pound tomatillos, papery skin removed (about 10)
1 tablespoon olive oil
2 tablespoons chopped fresh cilantro

1 large avocado, peeled, pitted and diced (about 1 cup)
1 bunch (6 to 8) green onions, thinly sliced on the diagonal (about ½ cup)
2 medium plum tomatoes, seeded and diced (about 1 cup)
Juice of 1 medium lime (about 1 tablespoon)
1 tablespoon olive oil
8 to 10 6-inch corn tortillas
Vegetable oil for frying

Sour cream

Preheat the oven to the broil setting
1. Place the shrimp into a shallow baking dish. Toss with honey, lemon juice, 2 tablespoons olive oil, garlic, chili powder, oregano, paprika, salt and pepper. Cover and chill for 15 minutes.
2. For purée, remove the stems from the tomatillos. Place into a saucepan and cover with water. Bring the water to a boil. Reduce the heat to low and cook the tomatillos for 5 minutes. Drain the tomatillos and place them into a blender. Add 1 tablespoon olive oil. Pulse to emulsify. Add the cilantro and pulse again. Season with salt and pepper.
3. Place the avocado, green onions and diced tomatoes into a bowl. Toss with lime juice, 1 tablespoon olive oil and season with salt and pepper.

4. Remove the shrimp from the refrigerator. Place the dish under the broiler and cook for 2 minutes. Turn once, and cook for 2 minutes more. The shrimp will be opaque and bubbling.
5. Heat enough vegetable oil to coat the bottom of a skillet, over medium high heat. Place 1 tortilla into the hot oil. Cook for 30 to 60 seconds or until the tortilla is bubbled and golden. Use tongs to remove the fried tortilla to a paper towel to drain. Continue until all of the tortillas have been cooked.
6. Assemble the tostadas by layering the ingredients on top of the fried tortillas. Start with a swirl of tomatillo purée topped with the seasoned shrimp and a spoonful of the diced avocado mixture. Top with sour cream.

SERVINGS: 6 TO 8 • PREPARATION TIME: 30 MINUTES

Chutney Sauced Grilled Chicken
and Mushroom Tostadas

THE SWEET AND SOUR FLAVOR OF TOMATO CHUTNEY SPICES UP EVERYDAY
CHICKEN BREAST FOR A YUMMY AND EASY DISH. SERVE WITH GRILLED CORN
ON THE COB AND A FRESHLY TOSSED SALAD AND YOU HAVE A SAVORY MEAL
WELL WORTH COMING HOME FOR.

6 medium plum tomatoes, seeded and diced (about 3 cups)
¼ cup brown sugar
¼ cup white wine vinegar
3 medium garlic cloves, minced (about 1½ teaspoons)
½ teaspoon hot paprika
½ teaspoon ground ginger
Salt and freshly ground pepper

1 tablespoon olive oil
2 large (4 to 6-ounce) skinless, boneless chicken breast halves
8 ounces button mushrooms, sliced (about 2 cups)

8 to 10 6-inch corn tortillas
Vegetable oil for frying

2 medium plum tomatoes, seeded and diced (about 1 cup)
2 ounces grated white American cheese (about ½ cup)
1 bunch (6 to 8) green onions, thinly sliced on the diagonal (about ½ cup)

1. Prepare the chutney by placing 6 diced plum tomatoes into a
sauce pan over medium heat. Stir in the brown sugar, vinegar,
garlic, paprika and ginger. Simmer for 15 to 20 minutes, until
thickened. Season with salt and pepper.
2. Place the olive oil into a grill pan over medium high heat.
Season the chicken breasts with salt and pepper. Grill the chicken
in the pan, turning once, about 5 to 7 minutes
per side. Let the chicken rest for 5 minutes.
3. Cook the mushrooms in the grill
pan until soft and golden, about 5
minutes. Season with salt and pepper.
4. Slice the chicken across the grain
into thin strips. Place the chicken
into a bowl. Spoon the chutney over
top of the chicken and toss.

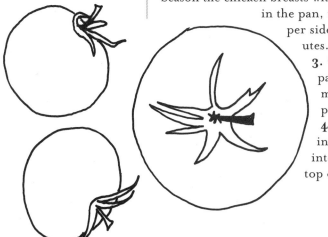

5. Heat enough vegetable oil to coat the bottom of a skillet, over medium high heat. Place 1 tortilla into the hot oil. Cook for 30 to 60 seconds or until the tortilla is bubbled and golden. Use tongs to transfer the fried tortilla to a paper towel to drain. Continue until all of the tortillas have been cooked.

6. Assemble the tostadas by layering the ingredients on top of the fried tortillas. Start with the chutney coated chicken strips. Top with a spoonful of mushrooms, a sprinkle of diced tomatoes and a drizzle of grated cheese. (At this point, you may place the tostadas under a broiler to melt the cheese.) Garnish with slices of green onions.

SERVINGS: 6 TO 8• PREPARATION TIME: 45 MINUTES

CHUTNEY IS AN INDIAN CONDIMENT THAT COMBINES FRUIT AND VINEGAR, SUGAR AND SPICES. THIS VERSION OF TOMATO CHUTNEY IS A COMBINATION OF THE FLAVORS OF THAT CONDIMENT AND THE TEXTURE OF KETCHUP OR CHILI SAUCE. IT'S SPICY ENOUGH TO COAT THE CHICKEN AND THIN ENOUGH TO KEEP THE TOASTED TORTILLA MOIST. IN A PINCH, FEEL FREE TO FLAVOR THE CHICKEN WITH YOUR FAVORITE PREPARED CHUTNEY OR SUBSTITUTE WITH BARBECUE SAUCE.

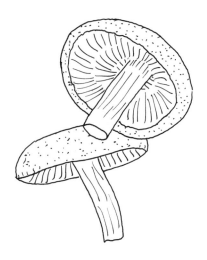

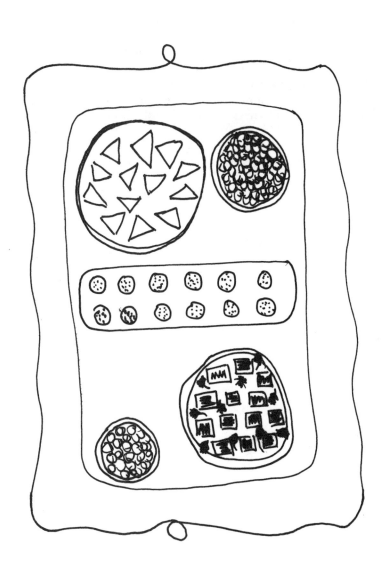

Chapter 7

Appys, Snacks, and Nibbles

The first course, or appetizer, is meant to tempt the palate, to set the stage for the main course. Today, we use appys to ward off starvation. You know the drill; you're invited to a pal's house for dinner. You raced to the house, straight from work. While driving, your tummy rumbles and you suddenly remember that you forgot to eat lunch. Now you are really, really HUNGRY! Your pal opens the door, and gives you an air-kiss on the cheek. You fervently look past the pal, and scour the room for a platter of yummy morsels. Relief, the appys are in sight!

Whether you are planning a first course for your sit down dinner party, bite-size nibbles for your cocktail fete, or bowls of dips for sports-watching-while-grazing, appys are the way to go. In some cases, appys can do double duty as lite meals for midweek fare.

This chapter is filled with great ideas for starter dishes. From traditional bruschetta and shrimp cocktail to tuna nachos and oyster shooters, you will savor a "little bite" of everything in these recipes. My mom's favorite, Swedish meatballs, gets a facelift by adding a dash of chipotle pepper. Skewered rumaki unwinds in sherried chicken livers, and stuffed mushrooms inspire stacks of wildly seasoned eggplant and tomatoes. Have you ever wanted to make your own potato chips? You can—and they will be way better than the ones out of the bag.

You will also find some snacks that include my favorite cocktail enhancers, from spicy nuts to the more nourishing edamame. There are recipes for a couple of granola and popcorn nibbles you can keep in your desk drawer for those times when you just can't get out of the office for lunch.

So shove those chip bags and jars of salsa to the back of the shelf. Choose a few of the freshest ingredients you can find and create your own special starters. For family and for friends—whether traditional or creative—appys, snacks, and nibbles are a great way to begin a fresh tradition.

Classic Bruschetta
with Chopped Tomatoes and Basil

BRUSCHETTA IS SLICED, GRILLED BREAD THAT IS RUBBED WITH WHOLE GARLIC AND THEN TOPPED WITH FLAVORFUL INGREDIENT COMBINATIONS. THE SECRET TO SUCCESSFUL BRUSCHETTA IS TO UTILIZE THE FRESHEST, BEST TASTING TOPPERS YOU CAN FIND AND KEEP THE COMBINATIONS SIMPLE AND EASY TO EAT.

6 medium plum tomatoes, seeded and diced into ¼-inch cubes (about 3 cups)
2 medium cloves garlic, minced (about 1 teaspoon)
Salt and freshly ground pepper
2 tablespoons chopped fresh basil

1 16-ounce loaf French bread, cut into ½-inch thick diagonal slices
½ cup olive oil
2 medium cloves garlic, minced

1. Place the diced tomatoes into a bowl.
2. Use the flat blade of a knife to smash the garlic with ½ teaspoon of salt until the mixture becomes a paste. Add this paste to the tomatoes.
3. Toss the tomatoes with the garlic paste, chopped basil and freshly ground pepper. Let the tomatoes sit for 5 to 10 minutes.
4. Lightly brush both sides of the bread slices with olive oil.
5. Heat a grill pan over medium high heat. Toast the bread (in batches) in the grill pan, until each slice has grill marks and turns golden. Turn and toast the other side, about 4 minutes total.
6. As soon as the bread is toasted, rub one side with fresh garlic.
7. Place a spoonful of chopped tomatoes onto the bread and serve. *Voila!* Bruschetta!

SERVINGS: 8 OR MORE • PREPARATION TIME: 15 MINUTES

Olive Tapenade for Bruschetta

In a food processor place 2 cloves garlic and 1 teaspoon salt. Pulse to emulsify. Add 1 2-ounce tin anchovies, packed in oil, which has been drained with 1 6-ounce jar pimento stuffed green olives that has been drained. Pulse to combine. Add 1 teaspoon drained capers, 2 tablespoons chopped fresh parsley and 1 teaspoon Dijon mustard. Pulse again. Slowly pour in ¼ cup olive oil with the machine running.

Sautéed Succotash Bruschetta
Topped with Grilled Shrimp

HERE'S A SOUTHERN TWIST ON AN ITALIAN DISH. IF YOU ARE SERVING THIS
FUN APPY AS A STARTER AT A COCKTAIL PARTY, CONSIDER ROUGHLY CHOP-
PING THE SHRIMP FOR EASY HANDLING.

1 tablespoon olive oil
1 small white onion, finely diced (about ½ cup)
1 medium green bell pepper, seeded and cut into ¼-inch dice (about ⅔ cup)
2 medium plum tomatoes, seeded and diced (about 1 cup)
1 cup canned corn kernels, drained
1 cup canned baby lima beans, drained
¼ teaspoon hot paprika
2 tablespoons chopped fresh parsley
Salt and freshly ground pepper

1½ pounds large uncooked shrimp, peeled and deveined (about 24)
¼ cup olive oil
2 medium cloves garlic, minced (about 1 teaspoon)
1 teaspoon dried oregano
¼ teaspoon hot paprika

1 16-ounce loaf French bread, cut into ½-inch thick diagonal slices
½ cup olive oil
2 medium cloves garlic

SUCCOTASH IS A SOUTHERN
VEGETABLE TREAT, ALTHOUGH
YOU CAN FIND REGIONAL SUC-
COTASH DISHES FROM ALL
PARTS OF THE COUNTRY. IT IS
COMMONLY PREPARED BY
BOILING TOGETHER CORN,
LIMA BEANS, AND RED OR
GREEN BELL PEPPERS. THE
NAME SUCCOTASH IS DERIVED
FROM THE NARAGANSETT
INDIAN WORD "MSICK-
QUATASH," WHICH MEANS
"BOILED KERNELS OF CORN."

1. Heat 1 tablespoon olive oil in a skillet over medium high heat.
Add the onion and pepper and cook until just soft, about 3 to 4
minutes.
2. Stir in the tomatoes, corn and lima beans. Add the paprika.
Stir in the parsley. Season with salt and pepper. Keep warm.
3. Heat a grill pan over medium high heat. Place the shrimp into
a bowl. Toss with ¼ cup olive oil, garlic, oregano, and paprika.
Grill the shrimp in the pan, turning once, until they are opaque,
about 2 to 3 minutes per side.
4. Lightly brush both sides of the bread slices with the remaining
½ cup olive oil.
5. Heat a grill pan over medium high heat. Toast the bread (in
batches) in the grill pan, until each slice has grill marks and
turns golden. Turn and toast the other side, about 4 minutes
total.
6. As soon as the bread is toasted, rub one side with fresh garlic.
7. Place a spoonful of succotash onto the Bruschetta. Top with
grilled shrimp. Garnish with additional fresh parsley.

SERVINGS: 8 OR MORE • PREPARATION TIME: 30 MINUTES

Cajun Crusted Scallops Served Over Cheddar Grits with Tomato Hot Sauce

CAJUN SPICES BLEND WITH CREAMY SOUTHERN GRITS AND A TOUCH OF ITALIAN-STYLE SAUCE, IN THIS ECLECTIC APPETIZER. THE STAR IS THE SCALLOP, AS IT SHOULD BE.

THERE ARE SEVERAL DIFFERENT VARIETIES OF SCALLOPS. BAY SCALLOPS ARE SMALL, USUALLY ABOUT ½-INCH IN DIAMETER. THEY ARE HARVESTED FROM A SMALL REGION OFF THE EAST COAST OF THE UNITED STATES. EVEN SMALLER SCALLOPS, KNOWN AS CALICO, ARE FOUND OFF THE EAST COAST OF FLORIDA AND IN THE GULF OF MEXICO. BECAUSE OF THEIR TINY SIZE, THEY ARE STEAMED OPEN RATHER THAN SHUCKED; THIS MEANS THESE SMALL SCALLOPS ARE PARTIALLY COOKED WHEN YOU PURCHASE THEM; YOU MUST BE SURE NOT TO OVERCOOK THEM OR THEY WILL BE RUBBERY. SEA SCALLOPS ARE THE MOST POPULAR AND ARE USUALLY ABOUT 1½-INCHES IN DIAMETER. WHEN PURCHASING FRESH SEA SCALLOPS, LOOK FOR ONES THAT ARE CREAMY OR PALE PINK IN COLOR AND NOT BRIGHT WHITE. IN SOME CASES, SCALLOPS CAN BE SOAKED IN A SOLUTION TO PRESERVE THEM. THIS PRODUCES THE WHITENESS. HOWEVER, IT CAN ALSO MEAN THAT THE SCALLOP ABSORBS EXCESS WATER, WHICH IS NOT AS TASTY.

2 tablespoons olive oil
1 medium white onion, diced (about ⅔ cup)
1 large red bell pepper, seeded and diced (about 1 cup)
3 medium garlic cloves, minced (about 1½ teaspoons)
1 28-ounce can diced tomatoes
½ cup white wine
2 to 4 drops hot pepper sauce
2 tablespoons chopped fresh rosemary
Salt and freshly ground pepper

2 cups half and half
1 teaspoon hot paprika
½ cup uncooked grits
1 ounce grated white Cheddar cheese (about ¼ cup)
2 tablespoons butter

2 tablespoons butter
2 tablespoons olive oil
2 tablespoons Cajun Spice Rub (see recipe page)
1 pound sea scallops (about 2 cups)

1. To prepare the sauce, heat 2 tablespoons of olive oil in a sauce pan over medium high heat. Add the onion and pepper and cook until just soft. Stir in the garlic and cook 2 minutes more.

2. Add the tomatoes, wine, hot pepper sauce and rosemary. Reduce the heat and simmer for at least 20 minutes. Remove the sauce from the heat. Use an immersion blender (or food processor) to purée the sauce. Season with salt and pepper. Return the pan to the stovetop and keep warm. (Or, store in an airtight container for up to 3 days. Reheat before serving.)

3. To prepare the grits, heat the half and half in a saucepan over medium high heat. Stir in the paprika. When the half and half begins to boil, carefully stir in the grits. Reduce the heat, cover and simmer the grits, stirring occasionally until thick, about 20 minutes. Stir in the cheese and 2 tablespoons butter. Season with salt and pepper. Keep warm.

4. Heat 2 tablespoons butter and 2 tablespoons olive oil in a skillet over medium high heat. Dip the top and bottom sides of each scallop into the Cajun spice mix. Cook the scallops in the hot oil/butter until golden, about 2 minutes. Turn and cook until the other side is golden, about 2 to 3 minutes more.

5. To serve, place a spoonful of grits in the center of a shallow bowl or dessert size plate. Place the scallops on top of the grits. Pour the sauce around the grits. Garnish with sprigs of fresh rosemary.

SERVINGS: 4 TO 6 • PREPARATION TIME: 45 MINUTES

Shrimp and Scallop Martinis with a Twist

THIS ICE-BREAKING STARTER IS SO VERY EASY TO PREPARE AND SO ORIGI-NAL IN PRESENTATION, YOUR GUESTS WILL BE SURPRISED HOW REFRESHING IT IS. SERVE THE SEAFOOD SALAD IN A MARTINI GLASS, PARTIALLY FILLED WITH SHREDDED LETTUCE LEAVES. GARNISH WITH A "TWIST" OF LEMON.

2 tablespoons olive oil
1½ pounds large uncooked shrimp, peeled and deveined (about 24)
¼ teaspoon dried oregano
Salt and freshly ground pepper
1 pound sea scallops (about 2 cups)
Juice of 3 medium limes (about ¼ cup)
Zest of 1 medium lime (about 1 tablespoon)
4 green onions, thinly sliced (about ¼ cup)
1 medium jalapeño pepper, seeded and thinly sliced (about 2 tablespoons)
2 medium plum tomatoes, seeded and diced (about 1 cup)
1 6-ounce jar pimento stuffed green olives, drained
2 tablespoons chopped fresh cilantro
Shredded lettuce
Lemon curls

1. Heat 1 tablespoon olive oil in a skillet over medium high heat. Add the shrimp. Season with dried oregano, salt and pepper. Stir until the shrimp are just opaque, about 3 to 5 minutes. Remove from the skillet and place into a bowl.
2. Heat 1 more tablespoon of olive oil in the pan. Season the scallops with salt and pepper. Sear the scallops, turning once, about 2 minutes per side. Transfer the scallops to the bowl with the shrimp. (If you are using large scallops, cut them in half or in thirds, horizontally, before adding to the bowl.)
3. Add the lime juice, lime zest, onions, jalapeño pepper, toma-toes, olives and cilantro to the bowl. Stir to toss. Cover and refrigerate for at least 30 minutes and up to two hours.
4. Place shredded lettuce into the bottom of 4 to 6 martini glass-es. Divide the shrimp and scallop salad over top. Garnish with curls of lemon peel.

SERVINGS: 4 TO 6 • PREPARATION TIME: 15 MINUTES PLUS MARINATING

Classic Shrimp Cocktail
Bring a large pot of water to a boil. Stir in 1 or more table-spoons of crab boil. Add 1½ pounds large uncooked shrimp, which have been peeled and deveined (about 24). Simmer the shrimp until they turn opaque, about 5 minutes. Drain the shrimp and plunge them into ice water. Drain again and chill for at least 2 hours or until ready to serve. Stir together 1 cup ketchup with ¼ cup of prepared horseradish and the juice of 1 medium lemon (about 2 tablespoons). Serve the shrimp over shredded lettuce with the cocktail sauce on the side. Garnish with wedges of lemon.

Sausage and Spinach Stuffed Mushrooms

THESE HEARTY STUFFED MUSHROOMS WORK WELL AS A FIRST COURSE APPY.
THEY ARE PERFECT TO SERVE FOR A STAND-AROUND COCKTAIL PARTY. IF
YOU INCREASE THE MUSHROOM SIZE TO THE GIANT PORTABELLA, YOU HAVE
A LITE MIDWEEK MEAL. MAKE DOUBLE THE AMOUNT OF SAUSAGE STUFFING,
AND YOU HAVE THE MAKINGS FOR STUFFED PEPPERS, STUFFED SHELLS OR
STUFFED CHICKEN BREASTS!

THERE ARE SO MANY VARI-
ETIES OF WILD AND CULTIVAT-
ED MUSHROOMS, THAT THE
POSSIBILITY FOR RECIPE
EXPERIMENTATION IS JUST
ABOUT ENDLESS. FOR STUFF-
ING, YOU WANT TO CHOOSE A
MUSHROOM WITH A FULL
BOWL-LIKE CAP TO HOLD THE
FILLING. CREMINI MUSH-
ROOMS ARE BROWN AND THE
MOST COMMON ONES
AROUND. THEY ARE VERY
CLOSELY RELATED TO THE
WHITE MUSHROOM, WHICH IS
ALSO CALLED "BUTTON."
WHEN A CREMINI MUSHROOM
GROWS UP (MATURES) IT
TURNS INTO A PORTOBELLO
MUSHROOM. YOU NEEDN'T BE
CONFUSED. SIMPLY CHOOSE
THE MUSHROOM THAT IS THE
FRESHEST ONE AVAILABLE AND
FITS YOUR MUSHROOM-STUFF-
ING NEEDS!

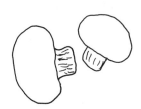

¾ pound hot Italian sausage
1 tablespoons olive oil
1 large white onion, diced (about 1 cup)
1 large yellow bell pepper, seeded and thinly sliced (about 1 cup)
2 medium cloves garlic, minced (about 1 teaspoon)
1 10-ounce bag fresh spinach leaves, washed, dried and chopped (about 3 cups)
4 ounces Gruyere (or Italian Blend cheese) cheese, shredded (about 1 cup)
Salt and freshly ground pepper

1½ pound button mushrooms (about 40)
1 tablespoon olive oil
2 ounces grated Parmesan cheese (about ½ cup)

Preheat the oven to 400°.

1. Brown the sausage in a large skillet over medium high heat.
Drain away the excess fat. Place the cooked sausage into the bowl
of a food processor. Pulse to mince. The mixture will resemble
coarse crumbs. Place the sausage into a bowl.

2. Heat 1 tablespoons olive oil in a skillet over medium high heat.
Add the onion and the pepper and cook until soft.

3. Add the garlic and spinach leaves and cook for 3 to 5 minutes,
or until the spinach is wilted. Cool to room temperature. Place
this mixture into the bowl of the food processor and pulse. Add
this mixture to the sausage.

4. Stir the cheese into the sausage and spinach mixture. Season
with salt and pepper.

5. Scoop out the centers of the mushrooms with a spoon. Fill the
center with a heaping tablespoon of the filling.

6. Place the mushrooms onto a shallow baking sheet, coated with
vegetable oil spray. Sprinkle the mushrooms with remaining 1
tablespoon olive oil and season with salt and pepper. Sprinkle the
tops with grated Parmesan cheese. Bake for 15 minutes to 20
minutes. Serve warm.

YIELD: 40 STUFFED MUSHROOMS • PREPARATION TIME: 45 MINUTES PLUS 15
MINUTES BAKING

Eggplant and Tomato Stacks
with Parmigiano-Reggiano

RATHER THAN STUFFING YOUR FAVORITE VEGGIE, WHY NOT STACK IT! THIS
DISH IS INSPIRED BY EGGPLANT PARMESAN, BUT USES FRESH TOMATOES IN
AN INTERESTING PRESENTATION THAT WORKS WELL FOR A FIRST COURSE.

2 large eggplants
Salt and freshly ground pepper
Canola oil for frying
2 teaspoons dried oregano
4 ounces shredded mozzarella cheese (about 1 cup)
2 large beefsteak tomatoes, sliced into ¼-inch slices (about 12 slices)
2 ounces grated Parmigiano-Reggiano cheese (about ½ cup)
2 tablespoons chopped fresh basil

Preheat the oven to 400°.

1. Cut both ends from the eggplants. Slice horizontally into 16
½-inch rounds. Place the slices into a colander. Sprinkle both
sides of the eggplant rounds with salt and let sit for at least 30
minutes. (Excess moisture from the eggplant is released).

2. Heat about ½-inch of canola oil in a skillet over medium high
heat. Rinse and pat the eggplant slices dry with a paper towel.
Cook the eggplant in the oil, in batches, turning once, until
golden brown, about 2 to 3 minutes per side. Add more oil in
between batches as needed. Make sure the oil is hot before you
add more eggplant slices or the eggplant will be soggy. Transfer
cooked slices to paper towels to drain.

3. Coat a shallow baking sheet (with rim) with vegetable oil spray.
Overlap three slices of eggplant in the baking sheet to make a
stack. (Think Mickey Mouse with big ears!) Continue until you
have 4 stacks of eggplant slices.

4. Season each stack with freshly ground pepper and dried
oregano.

5. Sprinkle the eggplant with half of the mozzarella cheese. Top
the stacks with 2 slices of tomatoes. Season with salt and pepper.

6. Sprinkle the stacks with the remaining mozzarella cheese.
Cover the stacks with 1 more slice of eggplant and 1 more slice of
tomato. Sprinkle the stacks with Parmigiano-Reggiano cheese.

7. Bake until the cheese is bubbly, about 8
to 10 minutes. Serve each stack with a
sprinkle of fresh basil.

SERVINGS: 4 • PREPARATION TIME: 45 MINUTES

WHEN YOU SERVE THIS DISH,
IMPRESS YOUR PALS BY
ADDING A LITTLE TIDBIT OF
INFO. DID YOU KNOW THAT
THE EGGPLANT IS NOT A VEG-
GIE? IN FACT, THE EGGPLANT
IS REALLY A BERRY, WHICH
MAKES IT FRUIT! WHO KNEW??
EGGPLANTS ARE CLOSELY
RELATED TO THE TOMATO AND
THE POTATO, WHICH IS WHY
THE FLAVORS BLEND SO WELL
IN THIS DISH. IN FACT, ADDING
A LAYER OF THINLY SLICED
POTATO WILL JUMP THIS FUN
APPY UP TO A FILLING WEEK-
DAY MEAL.

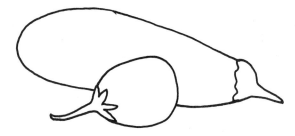

Oven-Baked Seasoned Potato Chips
with Caramelized Onion Dip

INSTEAD OF TEARING OPEN AN ENVELOPE OF ONION SOUP MIX, WHY NOT
TAKE A FEW MINUTES AND GIVE THE REAL THING A TRY? SEASON THE WARM
POTATOES WITH YOUR FAVORITE COMBINATION OF DRY SPICES AND FRESH
HERBS TO CREATE THE UTMOST GOURMET CHIP TREAT.

A MANDOLINE IS A HAND-OPERATED MACHINE THAT USES AN ADJUSTABLE BLADE TO SLICE AND JULIENNE FIRM VEGETABLES AND FRUIT; IT HAS LEGS, ALLOWING IT TO SIT SAFELY ON YOUR COUNTERTOP. THE BEST PART OF THE MANDOLINE IS THE CARRIAGE, PREVENTING THE VEGETABLE SLICER FROM TOUCHING YOUR FINGERTIPS! THE FOOD PROCESSOR'S SLICING BLADE ATTACHMENT IS A GOOD SUBSTITUTION FOR THE MANDOLINE.

2 tablespoons butter
2 tablespoons vegetable oil
2 large yellow onions, thinly sliced (about 4½ cups)
Salt and freshly ground pepper
1 tablespoon balsamic vinegar
4 ounces cream cheese, room temperature
½ cup sour cream
½ cup mayonnaise

2 large baking potatoes
Vegetable oil spray
1 teaspoon coarse salt
1 teaspoon hot paprika

1. Heat the butter and 2 tablespoons of vegetable oil in a skillet over medium high heat. Add the onions and cook until soft and brown. Season with salt and pepper.

2. Stir in the balsamic vinegar and cook until the onions are syrupy. Place the cream cheese, sour cream, and mayonnaise into the bowl of a food processor. Pulse until creamy.

3. Add the caramelized onions to the processor. Pulse to combine. Transfer your finished chip dip to a serving bowl. Preheat the oven to 375°.

4. Use a mandoline to cut the potatoes into paper-thin slices. Place the slices onto 2 baking sheets. Coat both sides of the potato slices with vegetable oil spray.

5. Bake until the chips begin to turn golden, about 20 to 30 minutes, depending on the thickness of each chip.

6. Mix 1 teaspoon of coarse salt with ½ teaspoon of hot paprika. Sprinkle the chips with this mixture.

YIELD ABOUT 2 CUPS
DIP • PREPARATION
TIME: 45 MINUTES

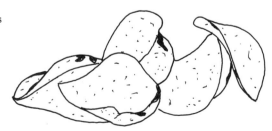

Toasted Pita Chips with Spicy Tuna Dip

HERE'S A FAST AND GREAT TASTING WAY TO SATISFY THE SNACKING URGES
OF AFTER SCHOOL KIDS AND BUDDIES STOPPING BY AFTER WORK.

6 pocketless pita breads
2 tablespoons olive oil
1 ounce grated Parmesan cheese (about ¼ cup)

1 6-ounce can tuna in olive oil, drained
½ cup mayonnaise
½ cup sour cream
Juice of 1 medium lemon (about 2 tablespoons)
2 tablespoons chopped fresh parsley
2 tablespoons Dijon mustard
1 tablespoon capers, drained
4 or more drops hot pepper sauce
Salt and freshly ground pepper

Preheat the oven to 350°.
1. Brush the tops of the pita bread with olive oil and sprinkle with
Parmesan cheese. Place them onto a baking sheet and bake until
golden, about 5 minutes. Cut the pita into wedges.
2. Place the tuna into the bowl of a food processor. Add in the
mayonnaise, sour cream, lemon juice, parsley, mustard, capers,
and as much hot pepper sauce, as you prefer. Pulse to emulsify.
Season with salt and pepper. Place the dip into a bowl, top with
an additional drizzle of olive oil, and add an extra sprinkling of
fresh parsley. Transfer the tuna spread to a serving bowl and serve
with pita chips.

YIELD: ABOUT 2 CUPS DIP • PREPARATION TIME: 15 MINUTES

White Bean Dip
*Place 1 16-ounce can of drained cannellini beans into the bowl of a food proces-
sor. Pulse for 10 to 15 seconds. Add the juice of 1 medium lemon (about 2 tablespoons), 1 minced medium clove garlic, (about ½ teaspoon) and ½ small, roughly chopped carrot (about 1 tablespoon) to the bowl. Pulse to combine. With the
machine running, pour in 2 tablespoons of olive oil. Season with salt and pepper.
Serve in a bowl with a drizzle of olive oil and a sprinkling of lemon zest.*

Grilled Peach and Pepper Salsa

SALSA AND CHIPS IS A STAPLE ON YOUR MUNCHING MENU. HERE'S ONE THAT BLENDS THE SWEETNESS OF FRUIT WITH THE SPICE OF PEPPERS. PERFECT FOR SNACKING, SERVE WITH TOASTED PITA CHIPS (SEE RECIPE PAGE 155) OR GRILLED SHRIMP.

USE THIS RECIPE AS A GUIDELINE TO CREATE YOUR OWN FLAVORFUL SALSA WITH THE BEST INGREDIENTS AVAILABLE. GRILL MANGOS, APPLES, OR WATERMELON FOR A SWEET COMPONENT. ADD RED PEPPER FLAKES, CHIPOTLE OR HABANERA PEPPERS FOR AN ELEMENT OF SPICE. INCORPORATE YOUR FAVORITE FRESH HERBS, AND YOUR SALSA IS DESTINED TO REACH THE SNACKER'S HALL OF FAME!

2 large yellow bell peppers, seeded and thinly sliced (about 2 cups)
2 medium peaches
1 tablespoon olive oil
6 medium plum tomatoes, seeded and diced (about 3 cups)
1 medium jalapeño pepper, seeded and diced (about 2 tablespoons)
1 bunch (6 to 8) green onions, thinly sliced on the diagonal (about ½ cup)
2 tablespoons chopped fresh basil
1 tablespoon chopped fresh mint
2 tablespoons sherry vinegar
Salt and freshly ground pepper

1. Heat a grill pan over medium high heat (or use an outdoor grill). Char the peppers on all sides until the skin is black and blistered. Place the peppers in a brown bag to steam for 15 minutes. Peel the skin from the peppers, remove the seeds and dice into ¼-inch pieces.
2. Cut the peaches in half and remove the pits. Brush the cut side with olive oil and place into the grill pan. Grill the peaches until golden, making sure that you do not burn the flesh. Remove the peaches and cut into ¼-inch pieces.
3. Place the peppers and peaches into a bowl. Add the tomatoes, jalapeño pepper, onions, basil and mint. Drizzle with sherry vinegar and season with salt and pepper.

YIELD: ABOUT 3 CUPS • PREPARATION TIME: 30 MINUTES

Swedish Meatballs

TRADITION INSISTS THAT THESE DELICATE MEATBALLS BE FORMED WITH 2
STERLING SILVER SPOONS. DON'T FRET IF SILVER IS UNAVAILABLE. YOUR
CLEAN FINGERS WILL WORK JUST AS WELL. SERVE THESE FROM A CHAFING
DISH ON A COCKTAIL BUFFET OR OVER NOODLES AS A FIRST COURSE.

2 pounds ground veal
1 large white onion, diced (about 1½ ro 2 cups)
8 slices white bread, crusts removed and cut into cubes
1 tablespoon chopped fresh parsley
Salt and freshly ground pepper

1 tablespoon olive oil
1 tablespoon butter
4 ounces button mushrooms, sliced (about 1 cup)
2 tablespoons all-purpose flour
2 cups beef broth
1 cup cream
2 teaspoons hot paprika
1 cup sour cream

USING A FOOD PROCESSOR
TO DOUBLE GRIND THE VEAL
HELPS TO MAKE THESE MEAT-
BALLS VERY DELICATE. YOU
CAN ALSO USE THE MEAT
GRINDER ATTACHMENT TO
YOUR ELECTRIC MIXER, OR
SAVE TIME BY ASKING YOUR
BUTCHER TO GRIND THE VEAL
TWICE.

Preheat the oven to 350°.
1. Place the veal into the bowl of a food processor. Pulse to finely
grind the meat. Transfer the veal to a bowl.
2. Place the onion into the bowl of the food processor. Pulse to
finely mince. Add the onion to the veal.
3. Place the bread cubes and parsley into the bowl of the food
processor. Pulse to mince. Add this mixture to the veal. Season
with salt and pepper.
4. Form the veal mixture into 1-inch balls and place onto a Silpat
lined baking sheet with a lip. (Alternatively, you can coat the baking sheet with vegetable oil spray or line with parchment paper.)
5. Bake the meatballs until just cooked through, about 10 to 12
minutes.
6. Heat the olive oil and butter in a skillet over medium high
heat.
7. Cook the mushrooms in the oil/butter for 2 minutes.
8. Sprinkle the flour over the mushrooms. Cook for 2 minutes
more.
9. Pour in the beef broth, cream and paprika. Reduce the heat
and simmer for 5 minutes.
10. Stir in the sour cream. Season with salt and pepper.
11. Place the meatballs into a chafing dish or fondue pot. Pour
the sauce over top. Garnish with additional parsley. Serve warm.

YIELD: ABOUT 2 DOZEN MEATBALLS • PREPARATION TIME: 45 MINUTES

Chipotle-Spiced Cocktail Meatballs Simmered in Tomato Sauce and Served with Cilantro Cream

SPICY HOT SMOKED PEPPERS FLAVOR THE MEATBALLS, BUT A SPOONFUL OF SUGAR IN THE TOMATO SAUCE AND THE RICH CREAM REDUCTION, SMOOTHES OUT THE DISH'S FLAVOR, MAKING IT ONE YOUR PALS WILL COME BACK FOR AGAIN AND AGAIN.

CHIPOTLE PEPPERS GIVE THIS DISH REAL ZIP. YOU CAN PURCHASE CANNED CHIPOTLE IN SPECIALTY MARKETS. THESE ARE DRIED AND SMOKED JALAPEÑO PEPPERS, RECONSTITUTED IN A RICH TOMATO SAUCE. USE A LITTLE OF THE SPICY ADOBO SAUCE WITH THE PEPPERS FOR EXTRA FLAVOR. ONE PEPPER (ABOUT THE SIZE OF A SILVER DOLLAR) IS JUST ENOUGH, BUT IF YOU LOVE EXTRA SPICE, GO AHEAD AND INCREASE THE AMOUNT.

1 tablespoon olive oil
1 small white onion, finely diced (about ½ cup)
1 28-ounce can diced tomatoes
2 tablespoons tomato paste
1 teaspoon granulated sugar
2 tablespoons chopped fresh oregano
Salt and freshly ground pepper

1 pound ground beef
1 pound ground pork
1 cup fresh bread crumbs
1 large egg
1 teaspoon ground oregano
1 to 2 chipotle peppers in adobo sauce, seeded and minced (about 1 to 2 tablespoon)

2 large shallots, minced (about 2 tablespoons)
1 tablespoon olive oil
2 cups cream
½ cup chopped fresh cilantro
White ground pepper
Grated Parmesan cheese

1. Prepare the sauce by heating 1 tablespoon olive oil in a sauce pan over medium high heat.

2. Add the onion and cook until soft. Stir in the diced tomatoes, tomato paste, sugar and fresh oregano. Season with salt and pepper. Reduce heat to medium and simmer for 10 minutes.

3. Place the ground beef and pork into a bowl. Add the bread crumbs, egg, oregano and as much chipotle pepper as you like. Season with salt and pepper. Combine this mixture with your hands. Form into bite size (about 1-inch) balls. Place on a baking sheet. Continue until all of the meat has been used.

4. Add the meatballs to the sauce. Simmer for 20 minutes, or until the meatballs are cooked through.

5. Heat a saucepan over medium high heat. Cook the shallots in the remaining 1 tablespoon olive oil until just soft (you do not want them to turn brown). Add the cream to the pan. Stir in the cilantro. Reduce the heat to medium. Simmer the cream until it is reduced by half and thickened (about 20 minutes). Season with salt and white ground pepper.

6. To serve the dish, layer a serving platter or shallow bowl with the cilantro cream sauce. Use a spoon to scoop the meatballs from the sauce. Decoratively arrange the meatballs in the cream. Use extra tomato sauce to drizzle into the white sauce. Keep the dish warm on a heated serving tray, or serve several meatballs as a first course. Garnish with grated cheese and additional fresh cilantro.

YIELD ABOUT 2 TO 3 DOZEN MEATBALLS • PREPARATION TIME: 1 HOUR

Baked Oysters Rockefeller

THIS INCREDIBLY RICH DISH IS APTLY NAMED AFTER JOHN D. ROCKEFELLER. CREATED AT ANTOINE'S NEW YORK RESTAURANT, THIS FIRST COURSE STARTER WITHSTOOD THE TEST OF TIME AND MORPHED INTO AS MANY DELICIOUS VARIATIONS AS ROCKEFELLER HAS DOLLARS!

Rock salt or dried beans for lining baking dish
12 medium oysters, shucked with bottom shells reserved
1 cup creamed spinach (see recipe page 224 or substitute 1 10-ounce package
  frozen, creamed spinach, cooked)
Juice of 1 medium lemon (about 2 tablespoons)
2 tablespoons butter
2 large shallots, minced (about 2 tablespoons)
2 tablespoons all-purpose flour
³/₄ cups milk
1 bay leaf
¼ teaspoon ground nutmeg
Salt and white ground pepper
4 ounces grated Parmesan cheese (about 1 cup)

Preheat the oven to 475°.
1. Pour rock salt or dried beans into a shallow baking dish. Place the oyster shells into the salt or beans to hold them in place.
2. Place a spoonful of creamed spinach into each shell.
3. Place 1 oyster on top of the spinach.
4. Drizzle the oysters with lemon juice.
5. Melt the butter in a saucepan over medium high heat.
6. Cook the shallots in the butter until just soft. Do not brown.
7. Sprinkle the flour over top and whisk to form a bubbling paste.
8. Stir the milk into the paste. Reduce the heat to medium. Add the bay leaf, nutmeg and season with salt and white ground pepper. Stir until the sauce thickens, about 8 to 10 minutes.
9. Place a tablespoon of the white sauce over the oyster.
10. Sprinkle each one with grated Parmesan cheese.
11. Bake until the oysters are plump and cooked through and the cheese has melted, about 8 to 10 minutes.

YIELD: 12 OYSTERS • PREPARATION TIME: 30 MINUTES

TRADITIONALLY, ONE ATE OYSTERS DURING THE MONTHS THAT HAVE AN "R" IN THEIR SPELLING. BUT, LUCKILY, THINGS CHANGE. WITH GREAT REFRIGERATION TECHNIQUES AND INCREASED SHIPPING DISTRIBUTION, OYSTERS ARE AVAILABLE YEAR ROUND. HOWEVER, RAW OYSTER LOVERS KNOW THAT THEY ARE REALLY AT THEIR BEST DURING FALL AND WINTER BECAUSE OYSTERS SPAWN DURING THE SUMMER MONTHS, BECOMING SOFT AND FATTY AS THEY MATURE.

Oyster Shooters

WHAT HAPPENS WHEN YOU COMBINE FRESHLY SHUCKED OYSTERS WITH A PARED DOWN BLOODY MARY? WELL, ALL I CAN SAY IS, "BOTTOMS UP!"

12 shucked oysters with oyster juice
⅓ cup ketchup
1 teaspoon prepared horseradish
Juice of 1 medium lime (about 1 tablespoon)
12 ounces tomato juice
12 ounces cold Vodka
Drops of Hot Pepper sauce

WHEN YOU ARE HOSTING YOUR PALS, FILL A TUB OR LARGE BOWL WITH CRUSHED ICE. PREPARE THE OYSTER SHOOTERS. JUST BEFORE THE GUESTS ARRIVE, PLUNGE THE SHOT GLASSES INTO THE ICE. IF THE GLASSES GET TOO FROSTY, REMIND YOUR EXUBERANT FRIENDS THAT THERE IS AN OYSTER ON THE BOTTOM—WE DON'T WANT TOO MANY SURPRISES!

1. Place each oyster, with its juice, into the bottom of a tall (6-inch) shot glass (or martini glass).
2. Mix together the ketchup, horseradish, and lime juice. Place a dollop of this sauce on top of each oyster.
3. Pour in 1 ounce of tomato juice and 1 ounce of chilled vodka over each oyster. Season with additional hot sauce (if desired). Serve cold.

SERVINGS: 12 (OR 6 IF YOU ARE READY TO PARTY) • PREPARATION TIME: 5 MINUTES

Silver Dollar Potato Pancakes with Smoked Salmon

A CROSS BETWEEN POTATO LATKES AND BITE-SIZE CRAB CAKES, THESE SAVORY BITES ARE PERFECT COCKTAIL PARTY FARE. SERVE WARM OR AT ROOM TEMPERATURE.

6 large baking potatoes, peeled and shredded (about 6 cups)
1 medium white onion, diced (about ⅔ cup)
¼ cup all-purpose flour
Salt and freshly ground pepper
1 large egg, beaten
2 tablespoons chopped fresh parsley
Olive oil for frying

½ cup sour cream
8 ounces smoked salmon, thinly sliced
Chopped fresh dill

TRADITIONAL LATKES ARE USUALLY SERVED DURING HANUKKAH AS A SIDE DISH. INSTEAD OF FLOUR, SOMETIMES MATZO MEAL IS ADDED TO THE MIXTURE. FOR AN UPDATED LATKE, SUBSTITUTE SHREDDED SWEET POTATOES FOR HALF OF THE POTATO MIXTURE AND TOP WITH GRILLED SHRIMP OR SEARED SCALLOPS.

1. Place the shredded potatoes and diced onion into a bowl. Add the flour and stir. Season with salt and pepper.
2. Stir in the egg and parsley. Form mixture into 2-inch (½-inch thick) rounds.
3. Heat 2 tablespoons olive oil in a skillet over medium high heat. Cook the potato pancakes (in batches) until golden, about 3

to 4 minutes. Turn and cook until the other side is golden, about 3 minutes more. Use additional olive oil as needed. Transfer the pancakes to paper towels to drain.

4. Top each potato pancake with a slather of sour cream and a generous slice of smoked salmon. Garnish with chopped fresh dill.

YIELD ABOUT 2 DOZEN • PREPARATION TIME: 45 MINUTES

Sweet Potato and Toasted Corn Pancakes

TOP THESE PANCAKES WITH CAJUN CRUSTED SCALLOPS (RECIPE PAGE 150) OR ALONGSIDE BARBECUED PORK TENDERLOIN SKEWERS (RECIPE PAGE 134) FOR AN UPSCALE SNACK OR FIRST COURSE.

1 medium sweet potato, peeled and diced into 1-inch squares (about 1 cup)
2 ears of fresh corn, kernels sliced from cob (about 1 cup)
3 tablespoons olive oil
Salt and freshly ground pepper
2 cups all-purpose flour
4 teaspoons baking powder
½ teaspoon chili powder
2 large eggs, beaten
2 cups milk

Sour cream
Fresh cilantro

Preheat the oven to 350°.

1. Roast the sweet potato until soft, about 30 minutes. Cool, peel and mash.

2. Toast the corn kernels in 1 tablespoon olive oil in a skillet over medium high heat. Season with salt and pepper.

3. Stir together the flour, baking powder, and chili powder in a mixing bowl.

4. Whisk in the eggs and milk. Stir in the mashed sweet potato and corn kernels.

5. Heat a griddle or large skillet over medium high heat. Pour in a small amount of olive oil to coat the bottom.

6. Drop about ⅓ cup of batter onto the griddle. Continue with as many pancakes that will fit into the pan without overlapping.

7. Cook until brown, puffed and set, about 5 minutes. Turn over and cook about 3 minutes more. Remove the pancakes and keep warm. Continue using all of the remaining batter.

8. Serve warm with a dollop of sour cream and a sprinkle of chopped fresh cilantro.

SERVINGS: 4 TO 6 • PREPARATION TIME: 45 MINUTES

Asparagus and Spinach Pancakes
Substitute cooked asparagus and blanched chopped spinach for corn and sweet potato. Substitute ground nutmeg for chili powder.

Pancakes To Go
Turn your favorite pancake recipe into your next hostess gift or party favor. Use a clean glass jar with lid. Layer the dry ingredients into the jar. Place the jar into a basket or gift bag. Add a sweet potato, 2 ears of corn and the recipe. Now you have pancakes for any occasion!

Beef and Bean Nacho Casserole

THIS IS A SUPER BOWL (NO PUN INTENDED) TO SET OUT DURING INTERMISSION WHILE WATCHING YOUR FAVORITE GAME. ADD AS MUCH SPICE TO THE DISH AS YOU WANT OR GO WAY, WAY OVER THE TOP AND ADD BANANA SALSA (RECIPE PAGE 131) OR ROASTED JALAPEÑO GARNISH (RECIPE PAGE 139). IT'S ALL GOOD...

Ultimate Nachos
Prepare the refried beans and meat as directed above. Spread a teaspoon of beef mixture onto a tortilla chip. Top with a spoonful of meat. Place the chip onto a microwave safe platter. Continue filling chips with the bean and meat mixture until the platter is full. Top each nacho with thinly sliced jalapeño pepper. Top each chip with a spoonful of salsa. Sprinkle the cheese over the chips. Microwave on high until the cheese is melted, about 1 to 2 minutes. Top each chip with guacamole and sour cream.

1 tablespoon olive oil
1 16-ounce can refried beans

1 tablespoon olive oil
1 large yellow onion, diced into ½-inch squares (about 1 cup)
1 pound ground beef
1 teaspoon chili powder
¼ teaspoon red pepper flakes
Salt and freshly ground pepper

6 ounces grated sharp Cheddar cheese (about 1½ cups)

6 medium plum tomatoes, seeded and diced (about 3 cups)
½ small white onion, finely diced (about 2 tablespoons)
2 tablespoons balsamic vinegar
1 tablespoon chopped fresh cilantro

1 large avocado, peeled, pitted and diced (about 1 cup)
Juice of 1 medium lime (about 1 tablespoon)
1 tablespoon cottage cheese
¼ teaspoon chili powder
Sour cream
Tortilla chips

Preheat the oven to 350°.
1. Heat 1 tablespoon of olive oil in a skillet over medium heat. Add the refried beans and cook until soft. Spread the beans into the bottom of a deep casserole dish.
2. Heat 1 more tablespoon of olive oil in a skillet over medium high heat. Add the yellow onion. Cook until soft. Add the beef and cook until brown, about 5 minutes. Season with 1 teaspoon of chili powder, red pepper flakes, and salt. Spoon this mixture on top of the beans.
3. Sprinkle the cheese over top. Bake until the cheese has melted, about 15 minutes.
4. Stir together the tomatoes, white onion, balsamic vinegar, and cilantro in a bowl. Season with salt and pepper. Set aside.

5. For the guacomole, mash together the avocado with the lime juice in a bowl. Stir in the cottage cheese and ¼ teaspoon of chili powder. Season with salt and pepper.

6. Remove the beef and bean casserole from the oven. Cover with the tomato salsa. Garnish with spoonfuls of guacamole and a dollop of sour cream. Serve with tortilla chips.

SERVINGS: 6 TO 8 • PREPARATION TIME: 30 MINUTES

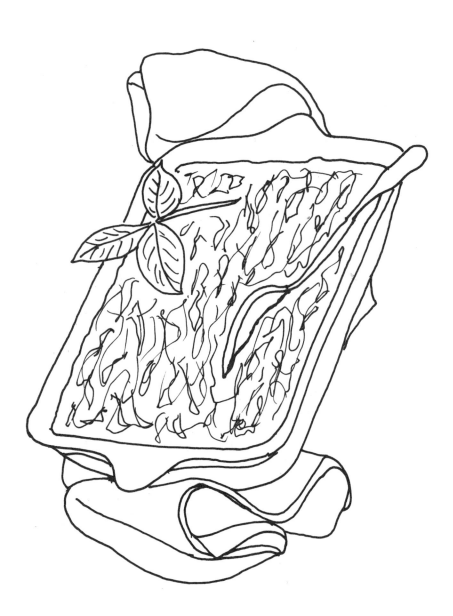

Seared Tuna Nachos
with Wasabi Cream and Hot Mango Ketchup

MY GAL PALS AND I WERE IN THE FLORIDA KEYS FOR A LITTLE R & R WHEN WE STUMBLED ACROSS AN OUTSTANDING RESTAURANT IN KEY LARGO NAMED PIERRE'S. WE INHALED THE APPYS—ESPECIALLY THE SEARED TUNA. THIS IS MY HOME VERSION OF THEIR DISH. IT'S A BIG HIT WITH OR WITHOUT THE PIERRE'S PUNCH WE WERE SLURPING AT THE TIME!

1 8-ounce tuna steak
½ cup rice wine vinegar
4 tablespoons soy sauce
2 tablespoons granulated sugar
1 tablespoon sesame oil
2 medium cloves garlic, minced (about 1 teaspoon)
4 green onions, thinly sliced (about ¼ cup)
1 1–inch piece ginger, grated
1 tablespoon olive oil
4 tablespoons sesame seeds

½ cup sour cream
1 teaspoon wasabi paste
Juice of 1 medium lemon (about 2 tablespoons)

Large, sturdy tortilla chips
2 cups escarole leaves, washed, dried and thinly julienned

Hot Mango Ketchup (see recipe page 165)

WASABI IS A CONDIMENT TRA-DITIONALLY SERVED WITH RAW FISH (SUSHI AND SASHIMI) AND NOODLE (SOBA) DISHES IN JAPAN. IN THE LAST TWENTY YEARS, BECAUSE OF A LOW SUPPLY OF FRESH WASABI RHIZOMES, (THE NAME OF THE ROOT THAT IS GROUND TO MAKE WASABI), SUBSTITUTES MADE FROM MIXTURES OF HORSERADISH, MUSTARD AND FOOD COLORING HAVE TAKEN THE PLACE OF FRESHLY PRE-PARED WASABI. IF YOU ARE BURNING TO GIVE THE REAL THING A TRY, YOU CAN GROW YOUR RHIZOME PLANT OR ORDER FRESH WASABI ONLINE AT HTTP://WWW.FRESH-WASABI.COM.

1. Place the tuna steaks into a shallow dish.

2. Whisk together the rice wine vinegar, soy sauce, sugar, sesame oil, garlic, onion and ginger.

3. Reserve 2 tablespoons of the marinade. Pour the rest of this mixture over the tuna steak. Marinate for at least 30 minutes and up to 2 hours.

4. Heat 1 tablespoon olive oil in a skillet over medium high heat. Remove the tuna from the marinade. Shake off the excess. Coat both sides of the tuna steak with sesame seeds.

5. Sear the tuna in the skillet turning once, about 2 to 3 minutes per side for very rare. For well-done tuna, cook longer, but reduce the heat, so as not to burn the sesame seeds.

6. Remove the tuna to the freezer and chill for 5 to 10 minutes.

7. Stir together the sour cream, wasabi and lemon juice. Place into a squeeze bottle and set aside.

8. Place the tortilla chips on a platter.

9. Toss the escarole with the reserved marinade. Place several shreds of lettuce over the tortilla chips.

10. Remove the tuna from the freezer. Use a very sharp knife to cut very thin slices (across the grain) of seared tuna. Place 1 to 2 slices (depending on how thin you are able to cut) onto each chip. Drizzle with creamy wasabi sauce and hot mango ketchup.

SERVINGS: ENOUGH FOR A CROWD • PREPARATION TIME: 20 MINUTES PLUS MARINATING

Hot Mango Ketchup

TERRIFIC OVER SEARED TUNA, THIS SAUCE IS ALSO WONDERFUL ON POACHED FISH, GRILLED CHICKEN AND BAKED POTATO WEDGES. FOR A FANCIFUL PRESENTATION, POUR THE KETCHUP INTO A PLASTIC SQUEEZE BOTTLE AND DRIZZLE IN ZIG ZAGS OVER YOUR SERVING PLATTER OR IN SWIRLS ONTO THE PLATE.

4 large mangos, pitted, peeled and diced (about 3 cups)
1 28-ounce can diced tomatoes
1 large yellow onion, diced into ½-inch squares (about 1 cup)
1 medium jalapeño pepper, seeded and thinly sliced (about 2 tablespoons
4 medium cloves garlic, minced (about 2 teaspoons)
½ cup cider vinegar
¼ cup dark brown sugar
½ teaspoon ground hot mustard
½ teaspoon ground ginger
⅛ teaspoon ground cloves
1 bay leaf
Salt and freshly ground pepper

1. Place the mangos, tomatoes, onion, jalapeño pepper and garlic into a deep pot. Simmer over medium heat until the vegetables are soft, about 15 to 20 minutes.
2. Remove pot from the heat. Use a hand held blender or food processor to purée the mixture. Return pot to the heat.
3. Stir in the vinegar, brown sugar, mustard, ginger, cloves, and bay leaf to the mixture. Simmer on low heat until the mixture reduces by one third, about 20 to 30 minutes.
4. Remove the bay leaf. Allow the ketchup to cool, slightly. Purée the ketchup in a blender on the highest speed. Season with salt and pepper. Cool to room temperature.

YIELD ABOUT 1 QUART • PREPARATION TIME: 1 HOUR

THIS RECIPE MAKES A LOT OF KETCHUP, WHICH YOU CAN EASILY STORE IN THE REFRIGERATOR FOR SEVERAL DAYS. IF YOU ARE INTO PICKLING AND CANNING, THIS IS THE PERFECT RECIPE TO WHIP UP AND KEEP ON YOUR PANTRY SHELF. OTHER USES INCLUDE BASTING ONTO A FLANK STEAK BEFORE GRILLING, OR BRUSHING ONTO COOKED CORN ON THE COB.

THERE ARE SEVERAL WAYS TO EAT A MANGO. FOR SLICES, TAKE A SHARP KNIFE AND CUT OFF BOTH ENDS OF THE FRUIT. PLACE THE FRUIT ON THE FLAT END AND CUT OFF THE PEEL. CUT SLICES BY CARVING, LENGTHWISE, ALONG THE PIT. TO DICE A MANGO, CUT THE FLESH AWAY FROM THE TOUGH PIT TO FORM TWO "HALVES." USE A KNIFE TO SCORE THE FLESH INTO SQUARES, MAKING SURE THAT YOU DO NOT PUNCTURE THE SKIN. TURN THE MANGO HALF INSIDE OUT. THE SQUARES WILL SEPARATE MAKING THEM EASY TO SLICE OFF.

Rumaki

A perfect bite-size cocktail nibble, this yummy treat can be prepared in advance and then broiled at the last minute. Roasting and grilling will accomplish the same result. Choose the cooking method that works best for your party.

THE ROOTS OF THIS DISH MAY ACTUALLY BE JAPANESE; HOWEVER, MOST CONSIDER RUMAKI TO BE A POLYNESIAN TREAT; THIS IS PROBABLY BECAUSE OF THE WATER CHESTNUT, WHICH IS A STAPLE IN ASIAN CUISINE. I REMEMBER LEARNING TO LOVE THIS BITE-SIZE APPY DURING MY MOTHER'S DINNER PARTIES FOR FRIENDS. I PASSED THE HORS D'OEUVRES TO THE GUESTS—ONE FOR THE GUEST, ONE FOR ME! IF YOU ARE NOT A LOVER OF CHICKEN LIVERS AS I AM, YOU CAN SUBSTITUTE WITH SCALLOPS. MARINATE THE SCALLOPS FOR 15 TO 20 MINUTES AND COOK FOR ONLY 5 TO 8 MINUTES.

6 chicken livers, cut into 24 pieces, about 12 ounces
½ cup soy sauce
2 tablespoons sherry
2 medium cloves garlic, minced (about 1 teaspoon)
1 1-inch piece ginger, grated (about 1 tablespoon)
12 ounces thick bacon, about 8 to 12 strips, cut in half
1 4-ounce can whole water chestnuts, drained and cut into 24 slices
½ cup brown sugar

Preheat the oven to broil.

1. Place the chicken livers into a bowl.

2. Whisk together the soy sauce, sherry, garlic and ginger. Pour this mixture over the chicken livers. Cover and chill to marinate for 2 hours.

3. Soak 24 small (4-inch) bamboo skewers or toothpicks in cold water for at least 1 hour.

4. Drain the livers. Place 1 piece of bacon onto a work surface. Place a piece of liver in the center of the bacon. Top with a slice of water chestnut. Wrap the bacon around both pieces and secure with a skewer. Continue until all of the rumaki have been formed.

5. Dredge each skewer into brown sugar and place onto a shallow roasting pan. Broil, turning once, until the bacon is crisp, about 10 to 15 minutes.

YIELD 24 RUMAKI • PREPARATION TIME: 45 MINUTES
PLUS 2 HOURS MARINATING

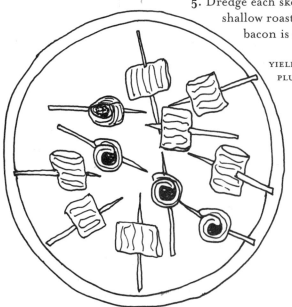

Sherried Chicken Livers on Toast Points

AS RICH AS FOIE GRAS, THIS FLAVORFUL DISH IS EQUALLY TERRIFIC FOR A
COCKTAIL PARTY OR ON A BRUNCH BUFFET TABLE. SET OUT A SILVER SPOON
TO SCOOP OUT THE YUMMY MORSELS ONTO THE DELICATE TOASTS.
CHOPPED FRESH PARSLEY IS A PERFECT GARNISH.

2 tablespoons olive oil
2 tablespoons butter
1 large yellow onion, thinly sliced (about 2 cups)
4 medium cloves garlic, minced (about 2 teaspoons)
1½ pound chicken livers
Salt and freshly ground pepper
⅓ cup sherry
6 slices thin white bread, crusts removed

1. Heat the olive oil and the butter in a skillet over medium high
heat.
2. Add the onion and cook until soft and golden, about 5 to 10
minutes.
3. Add the garlic and cook for 5 minutes more.
4. Add the chicken livers. Season with salt and pepper. Cook the
livers, stirring often, for 5 minutes.
5. Pour the sherry into the skillet. Continue cooking, using a
wooden spoon to gently break up the livers into bite size pieces.
Cook until the chicken livers are no longer pink in the center,
and very little liquid remains in the pan, about 10 to 15 minutes
more.
6. Cut each slice of bread into 4 triangles. Place the triangles on
a baking sheet, coated with vegetable oil spray. Bake for 2 to 3
minutes or until the bread is lightly toasted.
7. Serve the chicken livers from a chafing dish with the toast
points on the side.

SERVINGS: 6 TO 8 • PREPARATION TIME: 30
MINUTES

Chicken Liver Pâté

Prepare the chicken livers as directed above. Use a meat grinder (or food processor) to grind the chicken livers with hard boiled eggs. If you are using a meat grinder, alternate a spoonful of liver with a whole hard boiled egg through the grinder's sleeve. If you are using a food processor, pulse the egg and liver, separately. Pulse briefly, being careful not to over process. Use 3 to 4 eggs per pound of chicken livers. Season with salt and pepper. Fold in 2 to 4 tablespoons of mayonnaise to bind the mixture together. Place the chopped chicken liver mixture into a mold and refrigerate for at least 2 hours. Spread onto crackers or rye rounds for cocktail munchies, or onto rye bread with sliced onion and tomatoes for a great sandwich!

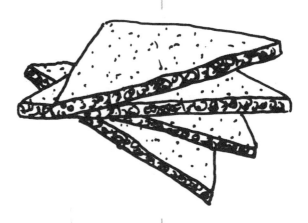

Shrimp Spring Rolls

THIS EASY-TO-MAKE, ASIAN TREAT IS AN INCENTIVE TO GET CREATIVE
USING YOUR FAVORITE INGREDIENTS TO CREATE YOUR OWN UNIQUE SPRING
ROLL. SUBSTITUTE WITH SEARED TUNA OR BARBECUED DUCK IN PLACE OF
SHRIMP, OR ADD SHREDDED CABBAGE AND JULIENNED JICAMA TO THE MIX.
ANY COMBINATION WILL WORK! SERVE A VIBRANT, ORIENTAL DIPPING SAUCE
LIKE THE ONE FOUND ON PAGE 169, TO COMPLETE THE DISH.

A COUPLE OF EXOTIC INGRE-
DIENTS—LIKE FISH SAUCE—
MAKE THE SPRING ROLL A
UNIQUE TREAT. FISH SAUCE IS
A SALTY TASTING CONDIMENT.
THE PRIMARY FLAVOR COMES
FROM FERMENTED FISH, BUT
OTHER INGREDIENTS—LIKE
CHILI PEPPERS—CAN ADD A
KICK. ASIAN MARKETS CARRY
MANY KINDS OF FISH SAUCES
THAT GO BY REGIONAL NAMES
LIKE NAM PLA, WHICH IS
THAI, PATIS FROM THE
PHILIPPINES, AND NUOC
NAM FROM VIETNAM.

RICE FLOUR NOODLES ARE
CHINESE. THE NOODLE IS
EXTREMELY THIN AND ALMOST
TRANSLUCENT. WHEN FRIED,
THEY EXPLODE AND EXPAND
INTO DELIGHTFUL CRUNCHY
TREATS. WHEN BOILED, THEY
ARE SOFT AND SUPPLE AND
WORK WELL IN FILLINGS. RICE
FLOUR NOODLES ARE JUST
ONE TYPE OF ASIAN NOODLE.
OTHERS ARE MADE FROM
INGREDIENTS LIKE MUNG BEAN
STARCH, SOYBEAN, YAM AND
POTATO FLOUR.

2 ounces rice-flour noodles
1 pound medium cooked shrimp, chopped (about 36)
1 large carrot, grated (about ½ cups)
1 bunch (6 to 8) green onions, thinly sliced on the diagonal (about ½ cup)
1 medium yellow bell pepper, seeded and cut into very thin julienne (about ⅔ cup)
½ cup bean sprouts, chopped
1 1-inch piece ginger, grated (about 1 tablespoon)
1 tablespoon fish sauce
Salt and freshly ground pepper
14 egg roll wrappers
1 large egg, beaten
Canola oil for frying

1. Cook the noodles in boiling water until soft, about 2 minutes.
Drain the noodles and rinse with cold water. Chop the noodles
into 2 to 3-inch lengths.
2. Place the noodles into a bowl. Add the shrimp, carrot, onions,
pepper, bean spouts, ginger, and fish sauce. Toss to combine.
Season with salt and pepper.
3. Place 1 egg roll wrapper onto your work surface. Use a pastry
brush to coat the outer edges of the wrapper with the beaten egg.
4. With the narrow end of the wrapper facing you, place about ⅓
cup of filling on the wrapper. Roll up (burrito style) by folding
the bottom of the wrapper over the filling, then the sides and,
finally, roll down the top of the wrapper. Use your finger to press
down the edges to seal. Repeat until all of the spring rolls are
formed.
5. Heat canola oil in a deep pot (no more than ⅓ full) to 350°.
Gently place the wontons into the hot oil in batches, being careful not to over-crowd the pan. The spring rolls will drop to the
bottom and float to the top. Cook until golden, about 4 to 5
minutes. Use a slotted spoon to transfer the wontons to paper
towels to drain.

YIELD: 14 SPRING ROLLS • PREPARATION TIME: 45 MINUTES

Goat Cheese and Pancetta Wontons
with Oriental Dipping Sauce

YOU CAN MAKE THESE IN ADVANCE AND REFRIGERATE UNTIL YOU ARE
READY TO FRY THEM, MAKING THIS A GREAT APPY TO SERVE FOR YOUR
NEXT GET-TOGETHER.

4 ounces pancetta, thinly sliced
8 ounces goat cheese
4 green onions, thinly sliced (about ¼ cup)
2 medium cloves garlic, minced (about 1 teaspoon)
2 tablespoons olive oil
2 tablespoons chopped fresh parsley
Salt and freshly ground pepper
24 wonton wrappers
1 large egg, beaten
Canola oil for frying

¾ cup soy sauce
½ cup honey
2 tablespoons peanut butter
1½-inch piece ginger, grated (about 1 teaspoon)
¼ teaspoon dried red pepper flakes
2 green onions, thinly sliced on the diagonal (about ½ cup)

WONTON WRAPPERS ARE
PAPER THIN SQUARES (OR
ROUNDS) OF DOUGH, MADE
FROM FLOUR, EGGS, WATER
AND SALT. YOU CAN FIND THEM
IN MOST GROCERY STORES
AND ESPECIALLY IN CHINESE
MARKETS. WONTON WRAP-
PERS WORK WELL IN PLACE
OF PASTA DOUGH FOR RAVIO-
LI. LARGER SQUARES OF THIS
SAME DOUGH ARE USED WHEN
MAKING EGG ROLLS.

1. Place the pancetta and goat cheese into the bowl of a food
processor. Pulse to combine.
2. Add the onions, garlic, olive oil, and parsley. Pulse 3 to 4
times or until just mixed together. Season with salt and pepper.
3. Lay 8 wonton wrappers onto your work surface. Use a pastry
brush to coat the outer edges of the wrappers with the beaten egg.
4. Place a spoonful of filling in the center of each wrapper. Fold
the wrappers in half (to form triangles.) Use the back of a fork to
press the edges together and seal well. Twist the corners of the
triangle. Place the wontons onto a baking sheet. Repeat until all
of the wrappers have been filled.
5. Heat canola oil in a deep pot (no more than ⅓ full) to 350°.
Gently place the wontons into the hot oil in batches, being careful not to over-crowd the pan. The wontons will drop to the bottom and then float to the top. Cook until golden, about 1 to 2
minutes. Use a slotted spoon to transfer the wontons to paper
towels to drain.
6. For dipping sauce, whisk together the soy sauce, honey, peanut
butter, ginger and red pepper flakes. Stir in the green onions.
Serve the wontons with dipping sauce on the side.

YIELD: 24 WONTONS • PREPARATION TIME: 30 MINUTES

Lobster Ravioli with Brown Butter Sage Sauce

IF YOU ARE SEEKING A FABULOUS FIRST COURSE, LOOK NO FURTHER. THIS DISH IS ELEGANT, PRESENTS WELL, AND TASTES OUT OF THIS WORLD. IF YOU ARE FEELING REALLY DECADENT, SERVE IT FOR A MAIN COURSE.

2 tablespoons butter
2 large shallots, minced (about 2 tablespoons)
2 medium cloves garlic, minced (about 1 teaspoon)
1 pound cooked lobster meat, diced
Juice of 1 medium lemon (about 2 tablespoons)
Salt and freshly ground pepper
32 wonton wrappers
1 large egg, beaten

³/₄ cup butter (1¹/₂ sticks)
1 tablespoon balsamic vinegar
2 tablespoons chopped fresh sage
1 ounce finely grated Parmesan cheese (about ¹/₄ cup)

1. Melt 2 tablespoons butter in a skillet over medium high heat.
2. Cook the shallots and garlic in the butter until just soft, about 4 to 6 minutes.
3. Add the lobster meat to the skillet. Reduce the heat to low. Sprinkle the lobster mixture with lemon juice. Season with salt and pepper. Cook for 2 minutes. Remove from the heat and cool to room temperature.
4. Lay 8 wonton wrappers onto your work surface. Use a pastry brush to coat the outer edges of the wrappers with the beaten egg.
5. Place a spoonful of filling in the center of each wrapper. Top each one with another wrappers. Use the back of a fork to press the edges together to seal well. (use additional egg if necessary). Place the wontons onto a baking sheet. Repeat until all of the wrappers have been filled.
6. Melt the ³/₄ cup butter in a saucepan over medium heat until it just begins to brown, about 5 minutes. Remove the pan from the heat. Stir in the balsamic vinegar and the chopped sage. Keep the sauce warm.
7. Cook the ravioli in boiling, salted water until tender, about 3 to 5 minutes. Use a slotted spoon to transfer the ravioli to a pasta bowl. Spoon the warm butter sauce over top. Sprinkle with grated cheese

SERVINGS: 6 TO 8 AS A FIRST COURSE • PREPARATION TIME: 30 MINUTES

Pasta for Ravioli

By using wonton wrappers, this dish comes together quickly. For a more traditional approach, use pasta sheets for your ravioli. You can purchase fresh pasta from a gourmet market, and of course, you can prepare your own by combining 2 cups flour with ¹/₂ teaspoon salt. Make a well in the center and pour in 5 large eggs and 1 teaspoon olive oil. Use a fork to combine the flour with the eggs, starting from the inside of the well. Bring the dough together with your hands and knead until the dough is smooth and elastic. (You can add a tablespoon or two of ice water if the dough is too dry.) Allow the dough to rest for 30 minutes. Run the dough through the blades of a pasta machine until it is thin. Cut the dough into squares. Alternatively, lay out one sheet of pasta, and drop tablespoons of filling on top. Cover with another sheet of pasta, and use a ravioli cutter to form the ravioli.

Grilled Grape Leaf Bundles
Stuffed with Brie Cheese and Chutney

GRAPE LEAVES AND GOAT CHEESE GO HAND IN HAND, AS DO THE FLAVORS
OF MILD BRIE CHEESE AND SPICY CHUTNEY. THIS DISH OFFERS A BIT OF
BOTH, AND THE GRILLED BUNDLE MAKES FOR A NICE PRESENTATION. ONCE
YOU MASTER WRAPPING THE LEAVES, WHY NOT STUFF THEM WITH YOUR
FAVORITE THINGS—LIKE FETA CHEESE, POACHED SALMON OR HERB-SPICED
MOZZARELLA?

1 jar grape leaves, in brine, rinsed and stems trimmed
1 8-ounce wedge Brie cheese, cut into 1-inch cubes
¼ cup prepared fruit chutney
Freshly ground pepper
¼ cup olive oil

1. Lay 8 grape leaves, vein side up onto your work surface. (Store
the remaining leaves in the jar, in the refrigerator.)
2. Place a cube of Brie onto 1 grape leaf.
3. Top with a teaspoon of chutney. Season with pepper. Repeat
with the remaining ingredients.
4. Wrap the grape leaf around the Brie to enclose. Place, seam
side down, into a shallow baking dish.
5. Drizzle the olive oil over top. Cover and place into the refrigerator. Marinate the bundles for at least 30 minutes or
overnight.
6. Heat a grill pan over medium high heat. Remove the bundles
from the oil. Grill, seam side down, for 2 minutes, turn and grill
for 2 minutes more. The grape leaves should be lightly browned
and the Brie soft. Don't worry if the Brie
begins to seep out of the leaf.
7. Serve the warm bundles with an extra drizzle of olive oil and sprinkling of fresh pepper.

SERVINGS: 4 • PREPARATION TIME: 20 MINUTES PLUS
MARINATING

GRAPE LEAVES ARE SELDOM
AVAILABLE FRESH, BUT IF YOU
MANAGE TO FIND SOME, COOK
THEM IN SALTED, BOILING
WATER FOR 10 MINUTES OR
SO, UNTIL THEY ARE SOFT AND
PLIABLE. JARRED OR CANNED
GRAPE LEAVES ARE PACKED IN
SALTY BRINE, AND SHOULD BE
RINSED BEFORE CONTINUING
WITH THE RECIPE. IF YOU ARE
A HUGE FAN OF THE GRAPE
LEAF, DON'T HESITATE TO
WRAP THE BRIE IN MORE THAN
ONE; THIS HELPS KEEP THE
BRIE FROM SNEAKING OUT,
WHEN COOKED.

Bar Keeper's Snack

HERE'S A RECIPE FOR THOSE SWEET AND SPICY NUTS YOU LOVE TO NIBBLE, WHILE SIPPING YOUR FAVORITE COCKTAIL. MAKE A BATCH AND STORE IN AN AIRTIGHT CONTAINER FOR SEVERAL WEEKS.

2 cups finely chopped walnuts
2 cups sliced almonds
2 cups cashews
1/3 cup maple syrup
1/3 cup olive oil
1 tablespoon chopped fresh thyme
1 tablespoon chopped fresh rosemary
1 teaspoon garlic powder
1/4 teaspoon dry red pepper flakes
Salt

ADD YOU FAVORITE SNACK INGREDIENTS TO THIS MIXTURE—LIKE CORN AND RICE CEREAL, MINI PRETZELS, AND ALL VARIETIES OF NUTS. YOU CAN ALSO SUBSTITUTE WITH YOUR FAVORITE HERB AND ADD AS MUCH OR AS LITTLE HEAT AS YOU WANT.

Preheat the oven to 350°.
1. Place the nuts into a bowl. Toss with maple syrup, olive oil, thyme, rosemary, garlic powder and red pepper flakes. Transfer mixture to an oven-safe pan.
2. Bake until golden, about 15 minutes.
3. Remove the pan from the oven, season with salt.

YIELD: 6 CUPS • PREPARATION TIME: 20 MINUTES

Easy Granola and Best Trail Mix

MAKE THIS YUMMY MIX WITH YOUR FAVORITE NUTS AND SEEDS ON THE WEEKEND. KEEP A BIG BAG OF GRANOLA IN YOUR OFFICE, TOO!

1/4 cup honey
1/4 cup maple syrup
2 tablespoons butter
1 teaspoon vanilla
4 cups old-fashioned rolled oats
1/2 cup whole almonds
1/2 cup pecans, toasted and finely chopped
1/4 cup roasted unsalted sunflower seeds
1/2 teaspoon ground cinnamon

Best Trail Mix
Combine 2 cups granola with 1/4 cup of several of the following ingredients: Roasted pumpkin seeds (pepitas), cashews, dried cranberries, dried cherries, raisins, dried apricots, whole wheat cereal, dried coconut, pretzel sticks and—if you are really feeling decadent—mini chocolate chips. Place about 1 cup of trail mix into a small cellophane or plastic bag. Seal well and tuck into lunchboxes, backpacks, briefcases and purses.

Preheat the oven to 350°.
1. Heat the honey, maple syrup, and butter in a saucepan until just combined but not boiling, about 4 to 5 minutes. Stir in the vanilla.

2. Place the oats, almonds, pecans, sunflower seeds, and ground cinnamon in a large bowl. Toss to mix.

3. Pour the honey mixture over the oat mixture. Quickly stir the mixture, so that all of the ingredients are well coated. Spread this mixture, in a single layer, onto a Silpat lined rimmed baking sheet.

4. Bake for 6 to 8 minutes. The granola should be crispy, not too brown. After the granola has cooled on the baking sheet, you can place it into an airtight container and store for several days.

YIELD: ABOUT 4 CUPS • PREPARATION TIME: 20 MINUTES

Edamame with Lemon Pepper-Flavored Salt

EDAMAME PODS CONTAIN SOYBEANS. NOT ONLY ARE EDAMAME AT THE ROOT OF EVERYTHING TOFU, THEY ARE NATURALLY GOOD FOR YOU AND MAKE FOR A WONDERFUL SNACK. FROZEN EDAMAME ARE READILY AVAILABLE IN YOUR GROCERY STORE. FRESH EDAMAME ARE HARVESTED IN THE SPRING AND SUMMER MONTHS. IF YOU CHOOSE TO PREPARE THE FRESH VERSION, NOTE THAT THEY WILL REQUIRE 15 TO 20 MINUTES MORE COOKING TIME THAN DIRECTED BELOW. SEASON THE PODS BUT POP THE SOYBEANS IN YOUR MOUTH.

1 1-pound bag frozen soy bean pods
Zest of 2 medium lemons (about 2 tablespoons)
2 tablespoons coarse salt
1 teaspoon black peppercorns

1. Cook the edamame in boiling, salted water until tender and bright green, about 4 to 5 minutes.

2. Immediately transfer to a colander and plunge into a large bowl filled with ice water. Remove the colander and drain the pods.

3. Place the lemon zest, salt and peppercorns into a spice grinder or mini-food processor. Pulse until finely ground. Toss with the edamame.

4. Serve the edamame in a bowl. Sprinkle with the salt and lemon zest spice mix.

SERVINGS: 4 TO 6 AS SNACKS • PREPARATION TIME: 10 MINUTES

Edamame with Wasabi Dipping Sauce
Cook the soybean pods as directed above. Stir together 2 tablespoons soy sauce, 1/4 teaspoon of minced, fresh ginger and 1/2 teaspoon (or more) of wasabi paste. Drizzle the cooked pods with a bit of the sauce. Serve remaining sauce on the side.

YOU CAN FREEZE FRESH EDAMAME SUCCESSFULLY, IF YOU TAKE THE TIME TO BLANCH THEM FIRST. PLACE THE EDAMAME PODS INTO BOILING WATER. COOK FOR 5 MINUTES. REMOVE THE PODS FROM THE WATER AND PLACE INTO A BOWL OF COLD WATER. REMOVE THE CHILLED PODS FROM THE WATER TO A TOWEL-LINED PAN. DRY THE PODS WELL, BEFORE PLACING THEM INTO A PLASTIC BAG. PLACE THE BAG INTO THE FREEZER. WHEN YOU ARE CRAVING A HEALTHY SNACK, SIMPLY PLUCK THE PODS FROM THE BAG. TAKE ONLY AS MANY AS YOU NEED, AND SAVE THE REST FOR ANOTHER DAY.

Over-the-Top Popcorn Balls

THESE YUMMY POPCORN SNACKS ARE FILLED WITH NUTS AND DRIED FRUIT, AND JUST A TOUCH OF CHOCOLATE.

Popcorn Bars
Prepare bars as you would pop-corn balls, but substitute almonds for peanuts, raisins for cherries, and add dried coconut. Pour the mixture into a baking dish, coated with veg-etable oil spray. Cool and cut into bars; wrap each one in plastic wrap.

¾ cup brown sugar
2 tablespoons butter
2 tablespoons corn syrup
2 tablespoons white grape juice
8 cups popped popcorn
¼ cup peanuts
¼ cup dried cherries
¼ cup white chocolate chips

I. Heat the brown sugar, butter, corn syrup and grape juice in a saucepan over medium heat until thickened, about 10 minutes.
2. Coat a large bowl with vegetable oil spray.
3. Place the popcorn, peanuts, cherries and chocolate chips in the bowl. Toss.
4. Pour the syrup mixture over the popcorn mixture. To form the popcorn into balls, coat your fingers with vegetable oil spray, use softened butter or wear plastic gloves. Mound a fist size por-tion of the mixture onto a square of plastic wrap. Twist the wrap together to form a ball. Allow to set for 15 minutes.

YIELD: ABOUT 1 DOZEN BALLS • PREPARATION TIME: 30 MINUTES

Chapter 8

Pasta, Rice, and Polenta Bowls

Pasta side dishes are elevated to a whole new level on today's comfort oriented menus. Therefore, it makes sense that rice, polenta, and bread puddings should rise to the occasion as well. Versatile, and nourishing, these ingredients are an important component of a balanced meal plan. Moreover, if the truth be know, almost everything tastes better with a little bit of pasta on the side.

There are dozens of different shapes of pasta. My rule of thumb when pairing pasta with sauce is the chunkier the sauce, the more shapely the pasta. It is the corners and curls in the pasta shape that hold onto pasta sauce. To absolutely insure that your pasta and sauce grab hold of each other, do not put oil in the pasta water; this will make the pasta slip away from everything that wants to cling. The only chance you have to season the pasta is when it is cooking in the water. I suggest that you add a generous amount of salt to the water after it boils. This will cut down on the wear and tear of your metal pasta pots.

The trick to preparing flakey rice, that does not stick together, is to use just the right amount of cooking liquid. Short or medium grain rice uses 1½ parts liquid to 1 part rice. Long grain rice uses 1¾ parts liquid to 1 part rice. Brown rice uses 2 parts liquid to 1 part rice. Lastly, wild rice uses 3 parts liquid to 1 part rice. (This one also takes about an hour to cook.) A rice cooker is a terrific kitchen gadget, and it keeps rice warm for several hours.

Polenta is an Italian favorite that has made its way onto our everyday menu in a big way. It can be purchased as "instant" polenta, regular polenta, or as cornmeal. The secret to preparing polenta is to bring the cooking liquid to a rapid boil. You then add the polenta slowly, whisking as you pour it into the pan. Stir constantly, as the polenta will immediately thicken. It may bubble and pop like lava, so you must watch it carefully. You can control this by reducing the stovetop temperature and moving the pan to and from the heat.

This chapter takes a few old favorites like mac and cheese, chicken a la king, and creamy grits, and updates them with new ingredient twists and twangs. You will also find a few of my favorite creations, like risotto featuring the combination of mushrooms and butternut squash, a take-along casserole of chicken, sausage and peppers with yellow rice, and a not-at-all pasta dish; roasted spaghetti squash (for those trying to sneak some veggies into the diet)! There are also plenty of upscale pasta dishes, from shellfish cannelloni, to veal and spinach stuffed ravioli, to cioppino with linguini. There are lots and lots of possible combinations that easily come together for scrumptious meals.

It's not about boxes and jars anymore. Pasta, rice, polenta, and bread puddings are easy-to prepare comfort foods that add a special touch to both an elegant dinner and an every night supper.

Experiment with the recipes in this chapter to give you inspiration. Then, create your own fresh pasta sauces, polenta toppers, rice mixers, and bread pudding combos. Before you know it, another new fresh tradition is making its way to your table.

Baked Macaroni and Cheese
with Sausage Crumbles

SPICE UP EVERYDAY MAC AND CHEESE BY ADDING CRUMBLED SAUSAGE AND
CAYENNE PEPPER. SERVE AS A SIDE DISH OR AS A WEEKDAY SUPPER.

FEEL FREE TO USE YOUR
FAVORITE INGREDIENTS TO
MAKE THIS SIMPLY BAKED
PASTA CASSEROLE YOUR OWN.
SUBSTITUTE SAUTÉED MUSH-
ROOMS, SLICED PEPPERONI,
OR COOKED CHICKEN FOR
SAUSAGE. EXPERIMENT WITH
GRUYERE, AMERICAN,
FONTINA AND BRIE CHEESES.

1 pound elbow macaroni
1 pound mild Italian sausage
1 medium white onion, finely diced (about 1 cup)
½ cup butter, melted (1 stick)
½ cup all-purpose flour
2 cups milk
1 cup cream
¼ teaspoon ground nutmeg
¼ teaspoon ground cayenne pepper
Salt
1 pound white Cheddar cheese, grated
4 ounces finely grated Parmesan cheese (about 1 cup)

Preheat the oven to 350°.
1. Cook the macaroni in salted boiling water until "al dente."
Drain and place into a deep casserole dish, coated with vegetable
oil spray.
2. Heat a skillet over medium high heat. Cook the sausage and
the onion in the skillet until the sausage is crumbled and
browned. Transfer this mixture to the pasta and toss.
3. Add the butter to the skillet. Cook until melted.
4. Stir in the flour until it begins to bubble.
5. Pour in the milk and the cream. When the mixture begins to
boil, reduce heat and simmer, stirring often, until thickened,
about 10 minutes.
6. Stir in the ground nutmeg, ground cayenne pepper and season with salt.
7. Stir in the Cheddar cheese until melted.
8. Pour the sauce over the pasta/sausage mixture and toss.
9. Top the casserole with Parmesan cheese.
10. Bake for 30 to 40 minutes or until the casserole is golden on
the top and the casserole is bubbling.

SERVINGS: 4 TO 6 • PREPARATION TIME: 20 MINUTES PLUS BAKING

Veal and Spinach-Filled Ravioli
with Sherry Cream Sauce

THIS IS A VERY RICH AND DECADENT DISH. SERVE WITH A SIMPLE TOSSED
SALAD AND ROASTED ASPARAGUS SPEARS, AND YOU HAVE A MEAL TO DIE
FOR!

1 tablespoon butter
2 large shallots, minced (about 2 tablespoons)
1 pound ground veal
2 tablespoons chopped fresh rosemary
Salt and freshly ground pepper
1 10-ounce package frozen spinach, thawed
2 11 x 14-inch fresh pasta sheet, cut into 18 to 20 squares each

1 tablespoon butter
2 large shallots, minced (about 2 tablespoons)
½ cup sherry
2 cups cream
2 tablespoons chopped fresh tarragon
Parmesan cheese

FRESH PASTA IS AVAILABLE AT
SPECIALTY MARKETS, AND IN
THE FROZEN SECTION OF THE
GROCERY STORE. MANY
TIMES, YOU CAN ORDER
FRESH PASTA FROM YOUR
FAVORITE ITALIAN RESTAU-
RANT. IF YOU ARE UNABLE TO
FIND FRESH PASTA, YOU CAN
PREPARE YOUR OWN, OR TAKE
MY FAVORITE SHORTCUT: SUB-
STITUTE WITH WONTON WRAP-
PERS. IF YOU DO DECIDE TO
USE THIS TRICK, WATCH THE
COOKING TIME, AS WONTON
WRAPPERS ARE SLIGHTLY
MORE DELICATE THAN PASTA
SHEETS.

1. Heat the butter in a skillet over medium high heat. Cook the
shallots in the butter until just soft.
2. Add the veal to the pan. Cook until the veal is browned and
crumbled.
3. Toss in the rosemary. Season with salt and pepper.
4. Add the spinach to the pan. Cook until all of the liquid is
absorbed.
5. Place the veal and spinach mixture into the bowl of a food
processor. Pulse until the mixture is well combined and resembles coarse crumbs.
6. Lay half of the pasta squares onto your work surface. Place a
spoonful of the veal mixture in the middle of each square. Use
your finger to spread ice water around the edge of the square.
Top with another square of pasta. Use a fork, or a ravioli cutter
to seal the filling between the pasta squares.
7. For the sauce, heat 1 tablespoon butter in a pot over medium
high heat. Cook the remaining shallots in the pot until just soft.
Add the sherry and cook until most of the liquid is absorbed.
8. Add the cream and the tarragon to the pot. Bring to a boil.
Reduce the heat and simmer until the liquid has been reduced by
half. Season with salt and pepper.
9. Cook the ravioli in boiling salted water until al dente, about 3
to 5 minutes. Drain.
10. Serve the ravioli with a spoonful of sauce over top. Garnish
with Parmesan cheese.

SERVINGS: 6 TO 8 • PREPARATION TIME: 45 MINUTES

Shellfish Cannelloni

THIS RICH DISH IS WONDERFUL AS AN ELEGANT DINNER PARTY'S FIRST
COURSE, OR ON A SUNDAY BRUNCH BUFFET TABLE. PURCHASING COOKED
SEAFOOD CUTS THE PREPARATION TIME IN HALF.

2 tablespoons butter
2 large shallots, minced (about 2 tablespoons)
2 medium cloves garlic, minced (about 1 teaspoon)
⅓ cup cognac
1 pound cooked lobster meat
8 ounces cooked snow crabmeat
8 ounces cooked shrimp, tails removed, finely diced
2 tablespoons chopped fresh chives
8 ounces ricotta cheese (about 2 cups)
2 ounces shredded fresh mozzarella cheese (about ½ cup)
Salt and freshly ground pepper

1 tablespoon olive oil
1 small white onion, finely diced (about ½ cup)
2 medium cloves garlic, minced (about 1 teaspoon)
1 28-ounce can diced tomatoes
½ cup chopped fresh basil

2 tablespoons butter
1 large shallot, minced (about 1 tablespoon)
2 tablespoons all-purpose flour
1 cup milk
½ cup cream
4 ounces cooked seafood such as lobster, crabmeat and shrimp, finely chopped
    (about ½ cup)
2 tablespoons chopped fresh tarragon

16 4 x 6-inch fresh pasta sheets
Grated Parmesan cheese

TRADITIONAL CANNELLONI IS
MADE WITH A FILLING OF VEAL
AND SPINACH, TOPPED WITH
BÉCHAMEL SAUCE AND MARI-
NARA. ONCE YOU EXPERIMENT
WITH SEAFOOD AS A FILLING,
WHY NOT TRY SOME OTHERS,
LIKE RICOTTA CHEESE MIXED
WITH PROSCIUTTO, OR
SAUTÉED EGGPLANT TOSSED
WITH MOZZARELLA.

Preheat the oven to 350°.

1. For filling, melt 2 tablespoons butter in a skillet over medium
high heat. Add 2 diced shallots and 2 minced garlic cloves and
cook until soft. Pour in the cognac. Return the pan to the stovetop and cook until the liquid is evaporated. Place the cooked lobster, crab and shrimp into the skillet. Remove the pan from the
heat. Toss in the chives to coat. Transfer to a bowl and cool to
room temperature. Stir in the ricotta and mozzarella cheese.
Season with salt and pepper. Set side.

2. For tomato sauce, heat 1 tablespoon olive oil in a pan over
medium high heat. Add the onion and the garlic. Cook until the
vegetables are just beginning to soften. Add the tomatoes and the

basil. Season with salt and pepper. Reduce the heat and allow the sauce to simmer for 15 minutes. Remove from heat. Use an immersion blender to emulsify the sauce. Set aside.

3. For seafood cream sauce, heat 2 tablespoons butter in a pan. Cook 1 large shallot in the butter until just soft, about 2 minutes. Stir in the flour. Pour in the milk and cream. Bring this mixture to a boil. Reduce the heat to medium. Cook, stirring constantly, until thickened. Add the cooked seafood mixture and chopped tarragon. Season with salt and pepper. Set aside.

4. Cook the pasta sheets in salted boiling water until "al dente." Drain and remove to a lightly oiled baking sheet.

5. Assemble the cannelloni by pouring half of the seafood cream sauce into the bottom of a baking dish. Place 2 to 3 tablespoons of the seafood filling into the center of one pasta sheet. Roll the pasta sheet, lengthwise, into a tube. Place the cannelloni, seam side down, into the baking dish. Repeat until all of the pasta sheets are rolled. Cover the cannelloni with the remaining seafood cream sauce. Spoon the tomato sauce over top.

6. Top the casserole with grated Parmesan cheese. Bake for 20 to 30 minutes, or until the casserole is bubbling and the cheese is golden.

SERVINGS: 6 TO 8 AS AN ENTRÉE • PREPARATION TIME: 45 MINUTES

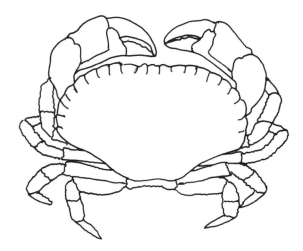

Chicken a la King Served Over Pasta Rags

YOU CAN PURCHASE A DELI ROASTED CHICKEN OR USE LEFTOVERS FROM THE ROASTED CHICKEN WITH HERB BUTTER ON PAGE 258 IN THIS RECIPE TO GET A JUMP START ON THIS HEARTY SUPPER OR SATISFYING FIRST COURSE. YOU CAN SUBSTITUTE WIDE EGG NOODLES FOR THE PASTA RAGS TO PREPARE THE DISH IN MINUTES!

PASTA RAGS REFER TO UNEVENLY SIZED PIECES OF FRESH PASTA. FOR EASY-EATING PURPOSES, CUTTING THE PASTA INTO 2 OR 3-INCH BY 1-INCH LENGTHS WORKS WELL. YOU CAN PURCHASE FRESH PASTA AT MOST SPECIALTY ITALIAN MARKETS OR IN THE FREEZER SECTION OF THE GROCERY STORE. TO COOK THE PASTA, BRING A LARGE POT OF WATER TO A BOIL. ADD A GENEROUS AMOUNT OF SALT. DROP THE PASTA RAGS INTO THE WATER. COOK UNTIL THE PASTA IS AL DENTE, WHICH MEANS: "TO THE TOOTH"—WHEN THE OUTSIDE OF THE PASTA HAS A BIT OF A CRUNCH AND THE INSIDE OF THE PASTA IS TENDER, ABOUT 3 TO 5 MINUTES FOR FRESH PASTA. DRAIN THE RAGS AND PLACE INTO SAUCE. YOU DO NOT NEED TO RINSE THE PASTA OR ADD OLIVE OIL. SERVE IMMEDIATELY.

2 tablespoons olive oil
2 large (4 to 6-ounce) skinless, boneless chicken breast halves, cut into ½-inch pieces (about 3 cups)
Salt and freshly ground pepper
1 tablespoon butter
8 ounces button mushrooms, sliced (about 2 cups)
1 large green bell pepper, seeded and finely diced (about 1 cup)
2 green onions, thinly sliced (about 2 tablespoons)
2 tablespoons all-purpose flour
¼ cup sherry
1½ cups chicken broth
1 cup cream
1 cup frozen peas, thawed
¼ teaspoon ground nutmeg
12 ounces fresh pasta, torn into bite size pieces
½ cup sour cream
1 tablespoon chopped fresh thyme

Parmesan cheese

1. Heat 1 tablespoon olive oil in a skillet over medium high heat. Season the chicken with salt and pepper. Cook the chicken in the skillet until golden brown and tender, about 4 to 6 minutes. Transfer the chicken to a bowl.
2. Heat 1 tablespoon butter in the same skillet over medium high heat. Add the mushrooms, pepper and green onions to the pan. Cook until the veggies begin to soften, about 3 to 5 minutes.
3. Stir the flour into the veggies.
4. Stir in the sherry. Pour in the chicken broth. Bring this mixture to a boil. Stir in the cream. Reduce the heat to medium. Stir in the peas. Season with ground nutmeg, salt and pepper. Add the chicken into the sauce. Simmer until the sauce thickens, about 5 minutes.
5. Cook the pasta in boiling, salted water. Drain.
6. Stir the sour cream and chopped fresh thyme into the sauce. Toss the pasta with the sauce. Sprinkle with Parmesan cheese and fresh pepper.

SERVINGS: 4 • PREPARATION TIME: 20 MINUTES

Cioppino Served Over Linguini

THIS DISH IS NOT ONLY LIGHT, BUT WONDERFULLY SPICY AND FULL OF GREAT SEAFOOD! FEEL FREE TO USE YOUR FAVORITE FISH IN THIS RECIPE. ALASKAN KING CRAB LEGS, LOBSTER TAIL AND PRAWNS ARE GREAT ADDITIONS.

¼ cup olive oil
1 medium yellow onion, diced (about 1½ cups)
4 medium garlic cloves, minced (about 2 teaspoons)
1 28-ounce can diced tomatoes
1 quart chicken broth
2 8-ounce bottles clam juice
1½ cups dry white wine
2 tablespoons tomato paste
2 tablespoons chopped fresh basil
2 tablespoons chopped fresh parsley
1 tablespoon chopped fresh oregano
2 or more drops hot pepper sauce
Salt
1 pound linguini
1 pound clams
1 pound mussels
1 pounds large uncooked fresh shrimp, peeled and deveined (about 20)
1 pound sea scallops
1 pound fresh fish fillet like snapper or cod, cut into 1-inch cubes

FROZEN SHRIMP, CLAMS AND MUSSELS ARE A GREAT CHOICE FOR THIS RECIPE. IN MOST CASES, THE SHELLFISH ARE FROZEN IMMEDIATELY AFTER BEING HARVESTED FROM THE SEA. THAT'S WHY I LIKE THIS RECIPE SO MUCH. IF YOU KEEP BAGS OF FROZEN SHRIMP AND MUSSELS IN YOUR FREEZER, YOU CAN PREPARE THIS DISH WITH JUST A FEW OTHER INGREDIENTS KEPT IN YOUR PANTRY. THIS DISH IS SO EASY AND FESTIVE, IT'S PERFECT TO SHARE WITH FRIENDS!

1. Heat the olive oil in a large pot over medium high heat. Cook the onion and garlic in the pot until just soft, about 8 minutes.
2. Pour in the tomatoes, chicken broth, clam juice and white wine. Bring this mixture to a boil.
3. Stir in the tomato paste, fresh herbs and hot pepper sauce. Reduce the heat to medium. Simmer the sauce for 20 minutes. Season with salt.
4. Cook the linguini in salted, boiling water until just "al dente."
5. Place the clams and mussels into the sauce. Simmer for 3 minutes.
6. Add the shrimp and the scallops to the sauce. Simmer for 3 minutes more.
7. Add the fish to the sauce. Simmer for 3 to 5 minutes more or until the fish is opaque and the mussels and clams have opened.
8. Drain and divide the linguini into 6 pasta bowls.
9. Divide the seafood and the broth over the pasta in the bowls.

SERVINGS: 6 • PREPARATION TIME: 1 HOUR

Pasta Puttanesca

THIS SPICY PASTA DISH COMES TOGETHER IN JUST MINUTES, MAKING IT AN EASY ADDITION TO YOUR WEEKLY MEAL PLAN.

⅓ cup olive oil
1 2-ounce tin anchovies, packed in oil, drained
4 medium garlic cloves, minced (about 2 teaspoons)
½ cup white wine
1 28-ounce can diced tomatoes
2 tablespoons capers, drained and rinsed
1½ cups pitted black olives, chopped
Freshly ground pepper
12 ounces spaghetti or linguini pasta
Parmesan cheese, shaved
2 tablespoons chopped fresh parsley

ALTHOUGH THIS DISH HAS ITS ROOTS IN THE ITALIAN SEAPORT KITCHENS OF WOMEN OF ILL REPUTE (YOU LOOK IT UP), THIS RECIPE IS AN INVITATION TO CREATE PASTA DISHES WITH THE ITEMS YOU KEEP ON HAND IN YOUR PANTRY OR REFRIGERATOR. TRY THESE COMBINATIONS THE NEXT TIME YOU'RE IN SEARCH OF AN EASY MIDWEEK PASTA SUPPER: SUN-DRIED TOMATOES, ARTICHOKE HEARTS AND CANNED TUNA WITH SPAGHETTI, STEAMED BROCCOLI, SLICED GARLIC AND SAUTÉED SAUSAGE WITH PENNE, AND CHOPPED PLUM TOMATOES, FRESH MOZZARELLA CHEESE AND RED PEPPER FLAKES WITH FETTUCCINI.

1. Place the olive oil into a skillet over medium heat. Add the anchovies to the oil. Use the back of a spoon to mash the anchovies into the oil. Add the garlic and cook until soft, about 3 to 4 minutes.
2. Pour in the white wine, tomatoes, capers and black olives. Simmer for 10 to 15 minutes. Season with freshly ground pepper.
3. Cook the pasta in boiling, salted water until "al dente," crunchy on the outside and tender on the inside. Drain.
4. Toss the pasta with the sauce. Garnish with shaved Parmesan cheese and fresh parsley.

SERVINGS: 4 • PREPARATION TIME: 20 MINUTES

Roasted Spaghetti Squash
with Garlic Butter and Parsley

IF YOU AIM TO ADD A FEW VEGGIES TO YOUR EVERYDAY MEAL, TRY SUBSTI-
TUTING PASTA WITH SPAGHETTI SQUASH; IT'S A WINTER SQUASH WITH A
TOUGH OUTER SKIN. CUTTING ONE IN HALF CAN BE A TRICKY PROCESS. I
START BY PLACING THE SQUASH ON A TOWEL ON THE COUNTER TOP; THIS
PREVENTS SLIPPING. USE YOUR SHARPEST KNIFE—AND WATCH YOUR FIN-
GERS! START AT THE TOP STEM PORTION. SLICE DOWN AND INTO THE
SQUASH. CONTINUE MOVING THE KNIFE AROUND THE SQUASH AS YOU
WOULD AN AVOCADO. ONCE YOU HAVE RUN THE KNIFE COMPLETELY
AROUND THE SQUASH, YOU CAN CUT THROUGH THE CENTER, DIVIDING IT
IN HALF.

1 large spaghetti squash, about 2 pounds
4 tablespoons butter (½ stick)
4 medium cloves garlic, minced (about 2 teaspoons)
Salt and freshly ground pepper
2 tablespoons chopped fresh parsley

Preheat the oven to 350°.
1. Carefully cut the squash lengthwise into halves. Remove the
seeds. Place the halves, flesh side down, into a shallow baking
pan. Pour ¼ cup water into the pan. Bake for 30 to 40 minutes
until soft. Remove the squash from the pan to cool slightly.
2. Heat the butter in a small pan over medium high heat until
melted.
3. Add the garlic and cook for 3 to 4 minutes.
4. Use a fork to shred the squash into spaghetti-like strands.
Place into a serving bowl.
5. Pour the garlic butter over the squash. Season with salt and
pepper.
6. Toss and garnish with chopped fresh parsley.

SERVINGS: 4 TO 6 • PREPARATION TIME: 45 MINUTES

Roasted Spaghetti Squash with Cumin Oil

For a less buttery option, try this variation. Combine 1 table-spoon brown sugar with 1 teaspoon cumin, ½ teaspoon of cinnamon, ½ teaspoon of coriander and 1 to 2 minced garlic cloves. Stir in ¼ cup of olive oil. Sprinkle this mixture over the squash.

Spaghetti Squash Puttanesca

If you are trying to fool a pasta lover—use this trick. Prepare a spicy Puttanesca sauce by simmering together 2 minced garlic cloves, 12 sliced black olives, a 2-ounce tin of anchovy fillets packed in oil, and 2 teaspoons of rinsed capers, with 2 cups of marinara sauce. Toss this sauce with the cooked, shredded squash. Season with fresh, chopped basil and Parmigiano Reggiano cheese.

TAKE OUT THOSE GARDENING TOOLS AND PLAN A CROP OF WINTER SQUASH.
GARDENING IS A GREAT DE-STRESSOR AND YOU END UP WITH SOMETHING THAT
IS REALLY GOOD FOR YOU! WINTER SQUASH IS A WARM-SEASON VEGETABLE
THAT CAN BE GROWN IN MOST OF THE COUNTRY. IT DIFFERS FROM SUMMER
SQUASH IN THAT IT IS HARVESTED AND EATEN WHEN THE SEEDS WITHIN HAVE
MATURED FULLY AND THE SKIN HAS HARDENED INTO A TOUGH RIND.

WINTER SQUASH IS A YUMMY SOURCE OF COMPLEX CARBOHYDRATE (NATURAL
SUGAR AND STARCH) AND FIBER. FIBER ABSORBS WATER AND BECOMES BULKY
IN THE STOMACH. GET IT? AFTER YOU EAT A PILE OF SPAGHETTI SQUASH YOU
FEEL LIKE YOU JUST CHUGGED DOWN A PLATE OF PASTA. HOW COOL!

Braised Lamb Risotto

Use extra lamb and sauce from the Braised Lamb with Red Wine Tomato Gravy recipe (see page 302) to top your risotto for a hearty, rustic dish.

Baby Artichoke Risotto

Trim the outer leaves and stems from 10 to 12 baby artichokes. Thinly slice the artichokes. Heat 1 tablespoon olive oil in a skillet over medium high heat. Cook the artichoke until beginning to soften, about 3 to 5 minutes. Set aside. Cook the risotto as directed in the recipe at right. Stir in the cooked artichoke, the juice of 1 lemon and 2 to 3 green onions, cut diagonally into very thin slices. Garnish with chopped fresh parsley.

Seafood Risotto

In a large pot, heat 2 tablespoons olive oil in a skillet over medium high heat. Place 10 medium sea scallops in the skillet. Cook until golden on 1 side, about 4 minutes. Add 10 large uncooked and deveined large shrimp and 1 pound calamari, cut into rings. Cook until the shrimp and the calamari are opaque and the scallops are golden on both sides, about 5 minutes more. Transfer the seafood to a bowl. Cook the risotto in this pan (as directed in the recipe at right), without the addition of the Parmesan cheese. Stir in the seafood and the juices. Serve with an extra drizzle of olive oil, garnish with fresh lemon wedges, and chopped fresh tarragon.

Risotto Primavera

A CLASSIC DISH REMINISCENT OF SPRING, WITH FRESH VEGGIES CHOPPED INTO SMALL PIECES, RISOTTO WORKS WELL AS A LIGHT SUPPER OR A FIRST COURSE AT YOUR NEXT DINNER PARTY.

1 tablespoon olive oil
2 large carrots, cut into ¼-inch dice (about 1 cup)
1 medium zucchini, cut into ½-inch dice (about 1 cup)
2 large yellow squash, cut into ¼-inch dice (about 1 cup)
8 ounces fresh thin asparagus spears, ends trimmed, cut diagonally into ½-inch lengths
Salt and freshly ground pepper

42 ounces chicken broth (5¼ cups)
2 tablespoons olive oil
1 medium white onion, diced into ¼-inch squares (about ⅔ cup)
16 ounces Arborio rice (about 2 cups)
1 cup white wine
1 cup frozen peas, thawed
4 tablespoons butter
4 ounces grated Parmesan cheese (about 1 cup)
½ cup chopped fresh basil

1. Heat 1 tablespoon olive oil in a skillet over medium high heat. Add the carrots, zucchini, squash and asparagus to the pan. Cook until the veggies begin to soften, about 3 to 5 minutes. Season with salt and pepper. Set aside.
2. Warm the chicken broth in a pot over low heat.
3. Heat the remaining 2 tablespoons olive oil in a large pot over medium high heat.
4. Add the onion and cook until soft and just beginning to brown, about 5 minutes.
5. Stir in the rice and cook to toast, about 5 minutes.
6. Stir in the white wine.
7. When the liquid is absorbed, stir in a ladleful of chicken broth. When that liquid is absorbed, add another ladleful of broth. Continue until all of the broth is absorbed. This should take about 20 minutes. The risotto will be wet; not sticky, but chewy on the outside and tender on the inside.
8. Stir in the sautéed veggies, peas, butter and grated Parmesan cheese. Season with salt and pepper. Garnish with chopped fresh basil.

SERVINGS: 6 TO 8 • PREPARATION TIME: 20 MINUTES

Butternut Squash Risotto with Wild Mushrooms

SOME COOKS TEND TO SHY AWAY FROM RISOTTO, THINKING ITS PREPARA-
TION A BURDENSOME AND LENGTHY PROCESS. THE TRUTH IS, THE DISH IS
EASILY COMPLETED IN 20 MINUTES, MAKING RISOTTO AN EVERYDAY FAST
FOOD FAVORITE.

1 medium butternut squash, peeled and diced into ¼-inch squares (about 2 cups)
1 tablespoon brown sugar
1 teaspoon ground cinnamon
1 teaspoon garlic powder
Salt and freshly ground pepper
2 tablespoons olive oil

42 ounces chicken broth (5¼ cups)

2 tablespoons olive oil
1 medium white onion, diced into ¼-inch squares (about ⅔ cup)
8 ounces shitake mushrooms, diced into ¼-inch squares (about 2 cups)
16 ounces Arborio rice (about 2 cups)
1 cup white wine
4 tablespoons butter
4 ounces grated Parmesan cheese (about 1 cup)

Preheat the oven to 400°.

1. Place the diced squash into a shallow baking dish. Toss with
brown sugar, ground cinnamon, garlic powder, and 2 tablespoons of olive oil. Season with salt and pepper. Bake until just
soft, about 15 minutes.

2. Warm the chicken broth in a pot over low heat.

3. Heat the remaining 2 tablespoons olive oil in a large pot over
medium high heat.

4. Add the onion and cook until soft and just beginning to
brown, about 5 minutes.

5. Stir in the mushrooms and cook for 2 minutes more.

6. Stir in the rice and cook until just golden, about 5 minutes.

7. Stir in the white wine.

8. When the liquid is absorbed, stir in a ladleful of chicken
broth. When that liquid is absorbed, add another ladleful of
broth. Continue until all of the broth has been absorbed. This
should take about 20 minutes. The risotto will be wet; not sticky,
but chewy on the outside and tender on the inside.

9. Stir in the butternut squash, butter and Parmesan cheese.
Season with salt and pepper.

SERVINGS: 6 TO 8 • PREPARATION TIME: 20 MINUTES

ARBORIO RICE IS THE INGRE-
DIENT OF CHOICE WHEN MAK-
ING RISOTTO. THE KERNELS
ARE NOT ONLY EXTRA
STARCHY, BUT SHORTER AND
FATTER THAN OTHER SHORT-
GRAINED RICE, WHICH IS THE
REASON THE DISH IS SO
CREAMY. IF YOU ARE CRAVING
RISOTTO AND CAN'T FIND A
SINGLE KERNEL OF ARBORIO
RICE, THEN SUBSTITUTE WITH
ANOTHER TYPE. THE DISH
WON'T BE EXACTLY THE SAME,
BUT HEY—YOU'VE JUST CRE-
ATED A RICE PILAF THAT WILL
TASTE REALLY, REALLY TER-
RIFIC!

Ginger Risotto

RISOTTO IS TRADITIONAL ITALIAN FARE. HOWEVER WITH A HINT OF
CHOPPED SCALLIONS AND A BLAST OF FRESH GINGER, THIS EARTHY DISH
CAN LEND ITSELF TO OTHER LESS TRADITIONAL PREPARATIONS. IF YOU ADD
RED OR BLUSH WINE IN PLACE OF WHITE, THE RISOTTO WILL TAKE ON A
PINKISH-PURPLE CAST. IT STILL TASTES DIVINE—AND THE KIDS THINK PUR-
PLE "RICE" IS COOL!

TAKE THIS SIMPLE RISOTTO
OVER THE TOP WITH SUPER
GARNISHES OF A DRIZZLE OF
TRUFFLE OIL AND A SPRINKLE
OF SLIVERED ALMONDS.

1 quart chicken broth
2 tablespoons olive oil
1 bunch (6 to 8) green onions, thinly sliced on the diagonal (about ½ cup)
1½ cups Arborio rice
½ cup dry white wine
1 1-inch piece ginger cut in half
Salt and freshly ground pepper

1. Warm the chicken broth in a pot over medium heat.
2. Heat the olive oil in a deep pot over medium high heat.
3. Add the onions and cook for 2 minutes.
4. Add the rice, stir and cook for 2 minutes more.
5. Stir in the wine.
6. Bury the ginger pieces in the pot.
7. Place 1 ladle of the broth into the rice mixture. Stir until the
broth is absorbed.
8. Continue ladling the broth into the rice stopping after each
addition until the broth is absorbed, about 20 minutes.
9. Season with salt and pepper. Remove the ginger from the pot
before serving.

SERVINGS: 4 TO 6 • PREPARATION TIME: 30 MINUTES

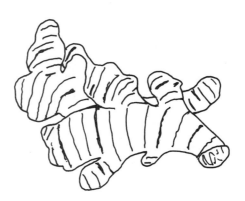

Jambalaya

ORIGINALLY, A CREOLE DISH WITH RICE AND HAM AS ITS MAIN INGREDIENTS, THIS DISH VARIES FROM COOK TO COOK AND FAMILY TO FAMILY. FEEL FREE TO SUBSTITUTE YOUR FAVORITE INGREDIENTS OR KICK UP THE SPICES WITH THE ADDITION OF HOT PEPPERS.

1 tablespoon olive oil
1 pound kielbasa, sliced into ¼-inch thick rounds
1 medium white onion, diced (about ⅔ cup)
1 large bell pepper, seeded and cut into ¼-inch dice (about 1 cup)
2 medium celery ribs, diced (about 1 cup)
2 large carrots, diced (about 1 cup)
1½ cups uncooked long-grain rice
3 cups chicken broth
2 tablespoons chopped fresh cilantro
1 16-ounce can red beans, drained
1½ pounds large uncooked shrimp, peeled and deveined (about 24)
Salt and freshly ground pepper
Green onions, thinly sliced on the diagonal

COOKING RICE IN CHICKEN BROTH ADDS GREAT FLAVOR. HOWEVER, IF YOU ARE WORRIED ABOUT SALT, YOU CAN JUST AS EASILY BOIL THE RICE IN WATER. LIKEWISE, VEGETABLE STOCK MAKES A FINE RICE DISH FOR VEGETARIANS, WHILE IT ADDS AN EXTRA DEPTH OF FLAVOR.

1. Heat the olive oil in a skillet over medium high heat. Add the kielbasa and cook until heated through, about 2 to 4 minutes. Transfer to a bowl.
2. Place the white onion, bell pepper, celery and carrots into the skillet. Cook until the vegetables are just soft and beginning to brown.
3. Add the rice to the skillet. Pour in the chicken broth and stir in the cilantro. Add the red beans and the kielbasa.
4. Bring to a boil. Cover and reduce the heat to medium low. Cook until most of the liquid is absorbed, about 10 minutes.
5. Add the shrimp, cover and cook until the shrimp are opaque and all of the liquid is absorbed, about 8 to 10 minutes more.
6. Season with salt, pepper and garnish with green onions.

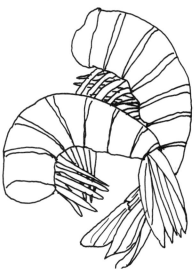

SERVINGS: 6 • PREPARATION TIME: 40 MINUTES

Chorizo Sausage and Spiced Chicken Casserole with Spanish Rice

THIS GENEROUS CASSEROLE TAKES ADVANTAGE OF THE GREAT FLAVORS FOUND IN WELL-MADE SAUSAGE. CHOOSE THE RIPEST BELL PEPPERS—OR A COMBINATION OF YELLOW, ORANGE, RED AND GREEN PEPPERS TO ADD A BURST OF COLOR. GARNISH WITH THE PRETTIEST FRESH TOMATOES AND YOUR BEST QUALITY OLIVE OIL FOR A WONDERFUL PRESENTATION.

YOU CAN EASILY MAKE YOUR OWN LINK SAUSAGE AT HOME. GRINDING AND STUFFING IS EASY WITH THE USE OF A GRINDER ATTACHMENT FOR YOUR ELECTRIC MIXER AND A SAUSAGE STUFFER PACKAGE, WHICH IS LITTLE MORE THAN A FUNNEL SHAPED DEVICE THAT HOLDS THE CASINGS. PURCHASE ONLY NATURAL CASINGS MADE FROM HOGS OR SHEEP. UNNATURAL CASINGS WILL NOT HOLD THE SAUSAGE AND END UP BURSTING WHEN COOKED. BEGIN WITH PORK SHOULDER, CUT INTO CUBES. USE KOSHER SALT TO GENEROUSLY SEASON THE MEAT. PROCESS THE MEAT THROUGH A $\frac{3}{16}$" OR $\frac{1}{4}$" PLATE ON A FOOD GRINDER. MAKE SURE THAT THE PORK IS NOT TOO LEAN, OR THE SAUSAGE WILL BE DRY WHEN COOKED. IF YOU DO NOT HAVE YOUR OWN GRINDER, ASK YOUR BUTCHER TO PROCESS THE PORK FOR YOU. ADD YOUR FAVORITE SPICES TO THE MIX—LIKE FENNEL, GARLIC, ONION AND RED PEPPER. CHILL YOUR MIXTURE BEFORE STUFFING THE CASINGS. IF YOU DO NOT HAVE A GRINDER ATTACHMENT, YOU CAN GET YOUR FEET WET BY STARTING WITH PATTY SAUSAGE (PAGE 27)—A LOT LIKE MAKING HAMBURGERS—ONLY MORE FUN!

1 16-ounce package yellow rice
4 to 5 cups chicken broth
2 to 3 tablespoons olive oil
1 pound chorizo sausage
1 pounds mild Italian sausage
4 pound skinless, boneless chicken breasts
1 teaspoon ground cumin
Salt and freshly ground pepper
1 large red onion, thinly sliced (about 1 cup)
2 large bell pepper, seeded and thinly sliced (about 2 cups)
4 large garlic cloves, thinly sliced (about 2 teaspoons)
1 28-ounce can diced tomatoes
1 large yellow tomato, cored and cut in thin wedges
2 tablespoon chopped fresh cilantro

Preheat the oven to 350°.

1. Prepare the rice according to the directions on the package, substituting chicken broth for water.
2. Heat 1 tablespoon olive oil in a skillet over medium high heat.
3. Cut the sausages into bite-size slices. Cook the sausages in batches and transfer to a bowl.
4. Cut the chicken into bite size pieces. Heat 1 more tablespoon olive oil in the same skillet. Cook in batches. Season with ground cumin, salt and pepper. Transfer cooked chicken pieces to a bowl.
5. Heat 1 more tablespoon of olive oil in the same skillet. Add the onion and peppers, and cook until soft and beginning to brown. Add the garlic and cook until soft. Remove the vegetables from the heat.
6. Add the diced tomatoes to the cooked rice. Season with salt and pepper.
7. Place the rice mixture into 1 large or 2 small baking dishes. Add the sausage, chicken and vegetables. Gently toss the ingredients.
8. Core and cut the yellow tomato into thin wedges. Lay the wedges on top of the casserole. Sprinkle with chopped fresh cilantro. Drizzle the top with additional olive oil.
9. Bake the casserole for 25 to 30 minutes.

SERVINGS: 8 TO 10 • PREPARATION TIME: 30 MINUTES PREPARATION, PLUS BAKING

Orzo Salad with Spring Veggies

WHAT LOOKS LIKE RICE, ACTS LIKE RICE AND TASTES LIKE RICE? ORZO! ORZO ARE TINY RICE SHAPED PASTA, EASILY INTERCHANGED IN MOST RICE DISHES AND ESPECIALLY GOOD IN CRUNCHY, VEGGIE SALADS. SERVE THIS SALAD IN A HOLLOWED-OUT BELL PEPPER OR WITH TOASTED PITA CHIPS (SEE RECIPE PAGE 155).

8 ounces snow peas, trimmed (about 1 cup)
8 ounces fresh thin asparagus spears, ends trimmed, cut diagonally into ½-inch
    lengths (about 1 cup)
1½ pound orzo (about 3 cups)
4 medium plum tomatoes, seeded and diced (about 2 cups)
1 large cucumber, seeded and diced (about 1 cup)
1 bunch (6 to 8) green onions, chopped (about ½ cup)
2 tablespoons chopped fresh parsley
2 tablespoons fresh chopped mint

Juice of 2 medium lemons (about ¼ cup)
Zest of 2 medium lemons (about 2 tablespoons)
2 medium cloves garlic, minced (about 1 teaspoon)
1 tablespoon Dijon mustard
1 cup olive oil
Salt and freshly ground pepper

1. Bring a pot of water to a boil. Add a generous amount of salt. Blanch the snow peas in the water until crisp and tender, about 2 minutes. Transfer to a bowl of ice water. Drain and set aside.
2. Repeat with the asparagus.
3. Cook the orzo in the same water until al dente, about 6 to 8 minutes. Drain and cool to room temperature.
4. Place the orzo into a bowl. Stir in snap peas, asparagus, tomatoes, cucumber, green onions, parsley and mint.
5. For the dressing, whisk together the lemon juice, zest, garlic, and mustard. Slowly whisk in the olive oil. Season with salt and pepper.
6. Pour the dressing over the salad. Toss.

SERVINGS: 4 TO 6 • PREPARATION TIME: 30 MINUTES

BLANCHING VEGGIES, LIKE SUGAR SNAP PEAS AND ASPARAGUS, HELPS MAINTAIN THEIR VIBRANT COLOR AND ENSURE AN EXTRA CRUNCH ON THE OUTSIDE WITH A TENDER CENTER. BLANCH THE VEGGIES FOR JUST A FEW MOMENTS—TOO LONG WILL TURN A GREEN VEGGIE GRAY. COLD WATER WILL IMMEDIATELY STOP THE COOKING PROCESS. BLANCHING ALSO WORKS WELL WHEN USING FRESH VEGGIES, LIKE BROCCOLI AND CAULIFLOWER IN YOUR SALAD.

Soft Goat Cheese Polenta with Tomato Basil Sauce

SOFT POLENTA HAS A CREAMY, PORRIDGE LIKE CONSISTENCY. HERE, GOAT CHEESE ADDS BOTH FLAVOR AND TEXTURE, WHILE THE RICH TOMATO SAUCE SENDS YOUR TASTE BUDS DANCIN'.

1 tablespoon olive oil
1 large yellow onion, diced (about 1 cup)
1 large carrot, diced (about ½ cup)
3 medium garlic cloves, minced (about ¼ teaspoons)
⅓ cup red wine
1 28-ounce can diced tomatoes
1 tablespoon tomato paste
2 tablespoons chopped fresh basil
1 teaspoon granulated sugar
Salt and freshly ground pepper

1 quart milk
1 cup instant polenta
4 ounces goat cheese, crumbled
½ cup cream

Parmesan cheese
Fresh Basil leaves

YOU CAN FIND INSTANT POLENTA IN MOST GROCERY STORES. POLENTA IS CORNMEAL COOKED IN LIQUID: EITHER WATER, STOCK, OR IN THIS CASE, MILK. POLENTA CAN BE YELLOW OR WHITE, MADE FROM EITHER COARSELY GROUND OR FINELY GROUND CORNMEAL. THE CLASSIC ITALIAN VERSION IS MADE FROM COARSELY GROUND YELLOW CORN AND IS SERVED BY POURING THE POLENTA ONTO A WOODEN TABLE AS SOON AS IT IS COOKED, COOLED AND THEN CUT INTO PIECES WITH A STRING.

CREATE YOU OWN SOFT POLENTA DISH BY SUBSTITUTING YOUR FAVORITE CHEESE FOR GOAT CHEESE, OR BY TOPPING WITH YOUR FAVORITE VEGGIES OR SEAFOOD. SUGGESTIONS FOR TOPPINGS INCLUDE SAUTÉED BROCCOLI RABE, SHERRIED MUSHROOMS, AND CARAMELIZED SEA SCALLOPS.

1. Heat the olive oil in a pot over medium high heat. Cook the onion and carrot in the pot until soft, about 4 to 6 minutes. Add the garlic and cook for 2 minutes more.
2. Pour in the wine and cook until most of the liquid is absorbed, about 3 to 5 minutes.
3. Stir in the tomatoes, tomato paste, chopped basil and sugar. Season with salt and pepper. Bring the sauce to a boil. Reduce the heat, cover, and simmer for 15 minutes. Use an immersion blender or food processor to purée the sauce. Keep warm.
4. To cook polenta, heat the milk in a pot over medium high heat, until just beginning to boil. Season with salt.
5. Slowly stir in the polenta and cook until thickened, about 5 minutes.
6. Reduce the heat to low. Stir in the goat cheese until melted. Whisk in the cream until the polenta reaches a porridge consistency.
7. Serve the polenta in bowls with a ladleful of tomato sauce over top. Garnish with shaved Parmesan cheese and fresh basil leaves.

SERVINGS: 6 • PREPARATION TIME: 30 MINUTES

Baked Polenta Squares with Mushroom Ragu

BAKING POLENTA, GIVES THIS DISH AN ENTIRELY DIFFERENT TEXTURE.
CRISPY, BAKED POLENTA GOES WELL WITH STEWS AND BRAISED VEGGIES.
YOU CAN PREPARE THE POLENTA IN ADVANCE AND BAKE AN HOUR BEFORE
SERVING.

2 cups chicken broth
2½ cups water
Salt
1½ cups cornmeal
1 tablespoon olive oil

2 tablespoons olive oil
8 ounces button mushrooms, sliced (about 2 cups)
4 ounces Baby portobello mushrooms, sliced (about 1 cup)
4 ounces shitake mushrooms, chopped (about 1 cup)
1 tablespoon balsamic vinegar
1 tablespoon Dijon mustard
2 tablespoons chopped fresh thyme
Salt and freshly ground pepper
Crumbled blue cheese
Sage leaves

FOR ANOTHER MOUTH-WATER-
ING POLENTA CREATION, PRE-
PARE THE POLENTA AND POUR
INTO A NON-STICK OR VEG-
ETABLE SPRAY COATED SKIL-
LET. USE A SPATULA TO EVEN
OUT THE SURFACE. TOP WITH
YOUR FAVORITE RAGU AND
CHEESE, AND BAKE AT 450°
UNTIL THE POLENTA IS GOLD-
EN, AND THE CHEESE IS MELT-
ED, ABOUT 20 MINUTES.

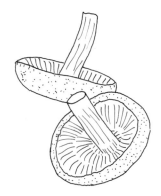

Preheat the oven to 425°.
1. Coat an 11 x 9 x 2-inch baking dish with vegetable oil spray.
2. Heat the chicken broth and water to a boil over medium high
heat. Season with salt. To make the polenta, slowly stir in the
cornmeal and cook until thickened, about 8 to 10 minutes.
3. Pour the polenta into the prepared pan. Brush the top with 1
tablespoon olive oil. Bake until the polenta is firm and the top is
golden, about 60 to 90 minutes.
4. To make the mushroom ragu, heat the remaining 2 tablespoons of olive oil in a skillet over medium high heat. Add all of
the mushrooms and cook until soft and golden, about 8 to 10
minutes.
5. Stir in the vinegar, Dijon mustard and fresh thyme. Season
with salt and pepper.
6. Cut the polenta into squares. Top with a spoonful of mushroom ragu. Garnish with crumbled blue cheese and whole sage
leaves.

SERVINGS: 6 • PREPARATION TIME: 30 MINUTES PLUS 1¼ HOURS BAKING

Creamy Cheese Grits

THIS IS AN UPSCALE, SOUTHERN-STYLE FAST FOOD. SERVE CREAMY GRITS
WITH BRAISED SHORT RIBS, SAUTÉED FISH, AND STEWED VEGGIE COMPOTE
TO ADD A HINT OF SOUL TO YOUR MEAL.

3 cups half and half
¾ cup grits
3 tablespoons butter
Salt and white ground pepper
4 ounces grated Monterey Jack cheese (about 1 cup)

1. Warm the half and half over medium high heat until just
beginning to boil.
2. Slowly stir the grits into the half and half. Reduce heat to low.
3. Simmer the grits until thickened, about 5 to 8 minutes, stirring constantly.
4. Stir in the butter and cheeses until melted.
5. Season with salt and white ground pepper.

SERVINGS: 4 TO 6 • PREPARATION TIME: 10 MINUTES

Southwestern Spice Grits

*Cook the grits in water. Add ¼
teaspoon of red pepper flakes
and sharp Cheddar cheese in
place of Monterey Jack. Top
with cooked, crumbled bacon.*

Breakfast Grits

*Cook the grits in milk. Stir in
butter, 1 teaspoon of sugar and
¼ teaspoon of ground cinnamon.*

HOMINY GRITS, OR JUST
PLAIN GRITS, ARE A TRADITION
IN THE SOUTH, THOUGH THEY
CAN BE FOUND ON RESTAU-
RANT MENUS ACROSS THE
COUNTRY. HOMINY IS MADE
FROM CORN WITH HARD KER-
NELS THAT ARE DRIED ON THE
COB, REMOVED AND SOAKED
IN A SOLUTION OF BAKING
SODA, LIME, OR WOOD ASH.
THIS PROCESS CAUSES THE
HULLS TO SOFTEN AND
SWELL. THE KERNELS ARE
HULLED, CLEANED AND THEN
DRIED. IN THE MARKET, YOU
WILL FIND "REGULAR" GRITS
THAT HAVE LARGE GRANULES,
"QUICK" GRITS THAT BREAK
DOWN THE LARGE GRANULES
INTO SMALLER ONES (ALLOW-
ING THE GRITS TO COOK
FASTER), OR "INSTANT" GRITS
THAT ARE PRE-COOKED AND
THEN DRIED FOR PACKAGING.

Jalapeño Cheese Grit Cakes

YOU CAN TOP THESE MAKE-AHEAD, SKY'S THE LIMIT CAKES WITH EVERY-
THING FROM SIMMERED COLLARD GREENS, (SEE THE RECIPE ON PAGE 196)
TO BRAISED CHICKEN (PAGE 257).

1 cup milk
1 cup chicken broth
¾ cup uncooked quick-cooking grits
1 medium jalapeño pepper, seeded and diced (about 2 tablespoons)
2 ounces grated Cheddar cheese (about ½ cup)
1 tablespoon butter
Salt and freshly ground pepper
2 tablespoons olive oil

1. Bring the milk and chicken broth to a boil in a sauce pan over
medium high heat.
2. Stir in the grits and the jalapeño. Cover the pan, reduce the
heat to medium low and simmer until thick, about 4 to 6 minutes.
3. Stir in the cheese and the butter. Cook until the cheese is
melted. Season with salt and pepper.
4. Spread the grit mixture into an 8-inch round cake pan, coated

with vegetable oil spray. Cover and refrigerate overnight, or until set.

5. Turn the grits onto your work surface. Cut into 6 wedges.

6. Heat 2 tablespoons of olive oil in a skillet over medium high heat. Cook the grit wedges in the oil until golden, about 4 minutes. Turn and cook about 4 minutes more.

SERVINGS: 6 • PREPARATION TIME: 20 MINUTES PLUS REFRIGERATING OVERNIGHT

FLAVOR YOUR GRIT CAKES WITH YOUR FAVORITE INGREDIENTS. SUGGESTIONS INCLUDE CHOPPED CARAMELIZED ONIONS, FROZEN PEAS, CHOPPED FRESH HERBS AND SAUSAGE CRUMBLES. SUBSTITUTE WITH YOUR FAVORITE CHEESES, LIKE GOAT CHEESE, FONTINA, AMERICAN AND MONTEREY JACK.

Caramelized Onion Bread Pudding

THIS HEARTY SIDE DISH IS A GREAT ACCOMPANIMENT TO ROASTED PORK, BEEF OR BRAISED CHICKEN.

2 tablespoons olive oil
2 tablespoons butter
2 large yellow onions, thinly sliced (about 4½ cups)
Salt and freshly ground pepper
1 tablespoon chopped fresh thyme
1 tablespoon chopped fresh rosemary
4 cups milk
4 large eggs, beaten
1 16-ounce loaf French bread, cut into (1-inch thick) cubes
4 ounces Gruyere cheese, shredded (about 1 cup)

Preheat the oven to 425°.

1. Heat the olive oil and butter in a skillet over medium high heat. Add the onions. Cook until the onions are softened and golden, about 10 to 15 minutes. Season with salt and pepper, and stir in fresh thyme and rosemary.

2. Stir together the milk and eggs. Stir in half of the cheese.

3. Place the bread cubes into a bowl. Pour in the milk/cheese mixture. Make sure that all of the cubes are covered with liquid.

4. Coat a deep casserole dish with cooking oil spray. Place half of the bread into the dish. Top with half of the onions and half of the remaining cheese. Continue layering with the remaining bread, onions and cheese.

5. Bake for 25 to 30 minutes or until the pudding is set and the top is golden.

SERVINGS: 6 TO 8 • PREPARATION TIME: 30 MINUTES PLUS 30 MINUTES BAKING

FOR YOUR NEXT DINNER PARTY PRESENTATION, PREPARE THIS DISH IN INDIVIDUAL PORTIONS. TOSS TOGETHER ALL OF THE INGREDIENTS (RESERVING ABOUT 2 TABLESPOONS OF THE CHEESE). COAT A MUFFIN TIN WITH VEGETABLE OIL SPRAY. SPOON THE PUDDING MIXTURE INTO THE TIN. TOP EACH WITH CHEESE. BAKE FOR 10 TO 15 MINUTES. ALLOW THE PUDDING TO COOL SLIGHTLY. USE A RUBBER SPATULA TO TRANSFER THE PUDDINGS FROM THE CUPS TO THE PLATE.

Southern Style Dressing with Sausage and Apples

DRESSING OR STUFFING DIFFERS FROM BREAD PUDDING IN THE AMOUNT OF LIQUID ADDED. BREAD PUDDINGS USE CUSTARD MADE FROM MILK AND EGGS TO BIND THE BREAD TOGETHER. DRESSINGS USE STOCK TO MOISTEN THE CRUMBS. THE FLAVORS ARE INTERCHANGEABLE, AND BOTH ARE WONDERFUL AS A HEARTY SIDE DISH.

SOUTHERNERS LOVE THEIR DRESSINGS AND USE AS MANY DIFFERENT INGREDIENTS WITH THEIR BREADS AS THEY HAVE COOKS. OTHER FAVORITE ADDITIONS INCLUDE, PECANS, OYSTERS, MUSHROOMS, DRIED FRUIT, AND CHESTNUTS. THE BREAD CAN BE SOURDOUGH OR CORNBREAD, AND SOME COOKS PREFER WILD RICE AS THE BASE. WHICHEVER YOUR CHOICE, REMEMBER THAT DRESSING IS A FINE WAY TO SPRUCE UP AN EVERYDAY MEAL. IT'S NOT JUST FOR TURKEYS ANY MORE!

2 16-ounce loaves French bread, or other crusty bread
1 cup butter, 2 sticks
2 large yellow onions, thinly sliced (about 4½ cups)
4 medium celery ribs, diced (about 2 cups)
4 medium Granny Smith apples, cored, peeled and diced
1 pound sausage
2 cups chicken broth
2 large eggs, beaten
¼ cup chopped fresh sage
Salt and freshly ground pepper

Preheat the oven to 250°.
1. Cut the bread into 1-inch cubes. Place onto a rimmed baking dish. Cook until dried, about 5 to 10 minutes. Place the bread cubes into a plastic bag. Use a rolling pin to crush the cubes into coarse crumbs. Place the crumbs into a bowl.
2. Heat the butter in a skillet over medium high heat until melted. Add the onions and celery to the pan and cook until soft, about 15 minutes.
3. Add the apples to the pan and cook for 5 minutes more.
4. Pour this mixture over top of the bread crumbs.
5. Cook the sausage in the skillet until browned and crumbled. Add the sausage to the crumb mixture.
6. Pour the chicken broth over the crumb mixture. Toss.
7. Stir in the eggs and sage.
8. Season with salt and pepper.
9. Place the dressing into a deep baking dish, coated with vegetable oil spray.
10. Increase the oven temperature to 350°. Bake until the top is golden, about 30 to 40 minutes.

SERVINGS: 6 TO 8 • PREPARATION TIME: 30 MINUTES PLUS BAKING

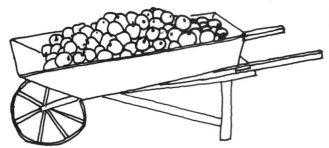

Chapter 9
It's All About the Veggies

There is probably no better example of getting in touch with your food than the experience of actually growing the veggies that you bring to your table. From the quality of the soil, to the task of feeding and watering, to the time spent watching the leaves grow, the entire experience of gardening enriches your meal.

If your schedule does not permit this luxury, you can benefit from the farming experience in other ways. Whether you grow your veggies in your back yard, share in the bounty of a community farm, or just enjoy a weekly visit to the farmer's market, it's about choosing the freshest veggies available, which will, in turn, guarantee you a wonderful dish.

This chapter is packed full of terrific veggie dishes. The idea is to encourage the addition of vegetables into your weekly meal plan in a big, big, way. From their nutritional benefits, to their ease of preparation, you will discover tons of reasons why it is beneficial to include these yummy foods.

Nutrition is not the only important reason to tip the scales of your balanced meal plan with veggies. The real reason to do so is the taste. Freshly picked, well seasoned, smartly cooked veggies are a delicious indulgence. Don't you and your family deserve the best?

The classic vegetable recipes are all here: simmering collard greens, dill pickles, broccoli with brown butter, smashed potatoes, creamed spinach, and many more. Then there are the dishes new to your repertoire—those destined to become future classics, such as asparagus ribbons, celery root purée, baked heirloom tomatoes, and chili roasted corn with lime flavored cream. Yumm!

Take a page or two from this chapter and begin a new, healthy, fresh tradition by seeking out and preparing the freshest, most flavorful veggies that you can find. I guarantee you will enjoy yourself in the process, and your friends and family well beg for more.

Slow-Simmered Collard Greens

THERE'S NOTHING QUITE AS FLAVORFUL AS SLOW COOKED GREENS. MY GAL
PAL, CINDY, MAKES THE WORLD'S BEST COLLARD GREENS. HER SECRET IS
THE ADDITION OF BALSAMIC VINEGAR.

2 bunches collard greens
1 tablespoon olive oil
12 ounces bacon, cut into 1-inch pieces
½ cup balsamic vinegar
2 cups chicken broth
2 cups water
Salt and freshly ground pepper

1. Remove the tough center stem from the center of the collard
leaves. Wash and dry the leaves. Place several leaves on top of each
other. Roll up several leaves into a cylinder. Cut into ½-inch
thick strips. Repeat until all of the leaves are sliced.
2. Heat 1 tablespoon olive oil in a large, deep skillet over medium high heat. Add bacon and cook until just beginning to crisp,
about 5 minutes.
3. Add the collard to the skillet. Toss with the bacon.
4. Stir in the balsamic vinegar. Pour in the chicken broth and the
water. Press down the leaves until all are covered with liquid.
5. Bring the mixture to a boil. Reduce the heat, cover the pan,
and simmer the collards in the liquid until quite soft, about 2 to
3 hours. The liquid will evaporate as the collards cook.
6. Season with salt and pepper.

SERVINGS: 6 TO 8 • PREPARATION
TIME: 20 MINUTES PLUS 2 HOURS
SIMMERING

*Kielbasa and Collard
Greens*
*Slice kielbasa into thinly sliced
rounds. Sauté in olive oil until
just brown. Add chopped collard greens and stir. Add chick-
en broth and water, and bring
to a boil. Reduce the heat and
simmer for at least 1 hour and
up to several hours, adding liquid as needed. Younger collard
greens will cook more quickly
than older ones. If you are using
purchased chicken broth, be
sure to use a low sodium product for this dish. Kielbasa is
plenty salty on its own.*

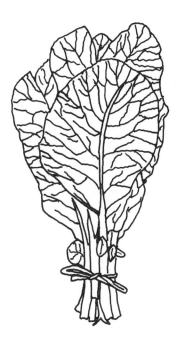

Swiss Chard with Red Beans

"GREENS" MAKE UP AND ENTIRE CATEGORY OF VEGETABLE, DEPENDING ON
THE COOK AND THE REGION. THIS RECIPE WORKS FOR THOSE HEART
HEALTHY DARK GREENS, LIKE KALE, COLLARD GREENS, AND SPINACH. YOU
CAN USE ANY BEAN YOU LIKE. FEEL FREE TO SOAK DRIED BEANS, IF YOU
PREFER. I THINK CANNED BEANS WORK JUST FINE—AFTER ALL, THE STAR OF
THIS DISH IS THE BRILLIANT RED TIPPED SWISS CHARD LEAF.

2 pounds Swiss chard
1 leek, white part only
2 tablespoons olive oil
2 medium cloves garlic, minced (about 1 teaspoon)
1 cup chicken broth
Salt and freshly ground pepper
1 16-ounce can red beans, drained

1. Wash and dry the leaves. Separate the green leaves from the
stem. Cut the stems into match-stick size pieces. Chop the leaves
into 2-inch strips.
2. Blanch the Swiss chard in boiling water for 6 to 8 minutes.
Rinse under cold water and dry, thoroughly. Chop.
3. Split the leek in half and rinse in cold water to remove any
grit. Cut into thin slices.
4. Heat the olive oil in a skillet over medium high heat.
5. Cook the garlic and the leek in olive oil until just soft, about 2
minutes.
6. Add the chopped chard and stir.
7. Pour in the chicken broth and reduce the heat.
8. Simmer until the liquid is absorbed, about 10 minutes.
Season with salt and pepper.
9. Add the beans to the pan. Stir and cook for 5 minutes or until
warmed through.

SERVINGS: 4 TO 6 • PREPARATION TIME: 20 MINUTES

SWISS CHARD, COLLARDS, AND KALE ARE HEARTY GREENS, AND AS SUCH,
REQUIRE COOKING. THEY ALSO CONTAIN LOTS OF VITAMINS C AND E, WHICH
BOLSTER THE IMMUNE SYSTEM AND PROTECT AGAINST RAVISHING DISEASES.
GREENS ARE ALSO A GOOD SOURCE OF CALCIUM, POTASSIUM, IRON AND
FIBER.

SPINACH GROWING IN THE GARDEN IS A WELCOME SIGN OF SPRING, AND A
STRONG SOURCE OF VITAMIN A. SPINACH IS RICH IN IRON, CALCIUM AND PRO-
TEIN, AND GROWS AS A SPRING AND A FALL CROP. CRINKLED LEAVED VARI-
ETIES TEND TO CATCH SOIL DURING RAINFALLS. PLANT A PLAIN LEAVED VARI-
ETY TO AVOID "GRITTY" SPINACH WHEN CHEWED.

*Chopped Kale
with Navy Beans*
Substitute chopped kale for
Swiss chard, and navy beans in
place of red beans. If you choose
a dried bean, soak it in water
overnight. Bring the water to a
boil. Reduce the heat to simmer
and cook until the beans are
soft. Drain. Season and add the
beans to the cooked kale.

Kicked Up Spinach
Substitute spinach leaves for
Swiss chard. In place of garlic,
add 2 medium jalapeño peppers, seeded and diced (about 4
tablespoons). Add canned corn
in place of the beans. Spinach
will cook faster than the other
greens.

Dill Pickles

THESE CLASSIC PICKLES ARE FUN TO MAKE AND WILL KEEP FOR SEVERAL
DAYS IN THE REFRIGERATOR. TRY THEM ON YOUR NEXT BARBEQUE BUFFET
TABLE AND REAP THE COMPLEMENTARY HOOTS AND HOWLS!

YOU CAN CERTAINLY FLAVOR
THE PICKLING BRINE WITH
YOUR FAVORITE INGREDIENTS.
GOOD ADDITIONS TO THIS
RECIPE ARE CUMIN, TURMER-
IC, ONION, CELERY, CLOVES,
AND HOT PEPPERS.

SPICE UP YOUR BLOODY
MARY WITH A SPEAR OR TWO
OF THESE GREAT PICKLES
FOR A SPICY ICE-BREAKING
GARNISH!

4 pounds small cucumbers
3 cups white wine vinegar
2 cups water
1 large head garlic, peeled (10 to 12 whole cloves)
⅓ cup coarse salt
2 tablespoons granulated sugar
1 teaspoon black peppercorns
1 bay leaf
1 bunch fresh dill

1. Bring a pot of water to boil over medium high heat. Plunge the
cucumbers into the water. Remove them immediately, rinse with
cold water and drain.
2. Bring the rest of your ingredients to boil in a large pot over
medium high heat.
3. Once the pickling liquid boils, immediately remove the pot
from the heat and place the cucumbers into the pot. Cover and
place in the refrigerator for no less than 2 days before serving.

YIELD: 8 OR MORE PICKLES • PREPARATION TIME: 45 MINUTES PLUS 2 DAYS
CURING

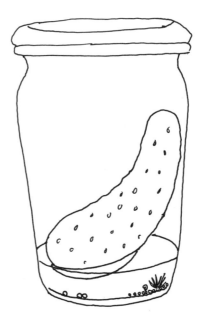

Pretty Pickles with Ginger

THIS IS A REALLY NEAT WAY TO PRESERVE FRESHLY HARVESTED VEGGIES. THE BRINE MIXTURE ALLOWS CRISP VEGETABLES TO LAST IN YOUR FRIDGE FOR AT LEAST SEVERAL DAYS AND UP TO SEVERAL WEEKS. THIS SHOWSTOPPER DISH WORKS WELL ALONGSIDE PANINI SANDWICHES, AS SALAD TOPPERS, OR ALL BY THEMSELVES ON YOUR PICNIC TABLE. ANY VEGGIE AND VEGGIE COMBO WILL WORK IN THIS RECIPE.

2 cups raspberry vinegar
2 cups water
1 cup granulated sugar
2 tablespoons coarse salt
4 medium garlic cloves, minced (about 2 teaspoons)
2 teaspoons pink peppercorns
2 bay leaves
1 teaspoon ground turmeric
1 (1-inch piece) ginger, grated (about 1 tablespoon)
2 tablespoons chopped fresh parsley

2 large yellow squash
2 large zucchini
1 medium red bell pepper

1. To make brining liquid, combine the vinegar, water, sugar, salt, garlic, peppercorns, bay leaves, turmeric, and ginger in a large pot over medium high heat. Bring to a boil. Cook for 2 minutes.
2. Remove the pot from heat. Stir in the parsley. Cool to room temperature.
3. Cut the squash, zucchini and pepper into very thin slices using a mandoline or food processor.
4. Layer the vegetables into glass jars, or plastic containers with lids.
5. Pour the brining liquid, saturating all of the vegetables. Seal the container.
6. Refrigerate for at least 4 hours or up to several days. Drain the pickles from the brine, reserving extra liquid for re-packing leftover pickles.

YIELD: ABOUT 2 QUARTS • PREPARATION TIME: 20 MINUTES PLUS CHILLING

Blanched Veggie Pickles

It's totally A-OK to blanch veggies before placing them in the brine. This process (placing the veggie in boiling water, then refreshing in ice water), brings out the color in green beans and crisp-cooks broccoli and cauliflower. Other nice pickling choices include English cucumbers (which are seedless), boiled beets, pearl onions, patty pan squash, and julienned carrots.

Spiced Pickles

You should always experiment with your favorite herbs, spices and flavors in the brine. Substitute with distilled white wine or apple cider vinegar. Cumin, mustard seeds, white and black peppercorns, whole coriander, cloves and fennel seeds, are just a few of the possible brine flavorings.

WHEN PLANNING YOUR GARDEN, YOU MIGHT CONSIDER INCLUDING SUMMER SQUASH: A TENDER, WARM-SEASON VEGETABLE, GROWN THROUGHOUT THE UNITED STATES ANYTIME DURING THE WARM, FROST-FREE SEASON. A FEW HEALTHY AND WELL-MAINTAINED PLANTS PRODUCE ABUNDANT YIELDS. BECAUSE SUMMER SQUASH DEVELOPS RAPIDLY AFTER POLLINATION, THEY ARE SOMETIMES TOO LARGE AND OVER-MATURE WHEN PICKED; FOR BEST QUALITY, THEY SHOULD BE HARVESTED WHEN SMALL AND TENDER.

Baked Broccoli
with Brown Buttered Bread Crumbs

*Sautéed Broccoli
with Lemon*

Blanch the broccoli and drain.
Heat 2 tablespoons olive oil in a
skillet over medium high heat.
Add 2 minced garlic cloves.
Place the broccoli into the pan.
Sprinkle with the juice of 1
lemon. Season with salt and
freshly ground pepper.

Broccoli with Ginger Sauce

Blanch broccoli and drain.
Heat 2 tablespoons butter in a
skillet over medium high heat.
Add 1 teaspoon freshly minced
ginger. Place the broccoli into
the pan. Pour in 1 tablespoon
soy sauce and sprinkle with 1
tablespoon sesame seeds.
Season with freshly ground
pepper.

THE PERFECT WAY TO ENJOY FRESHLY HARVESTED BROCCOLI IS WITH A
CONDIMENT THAT ENHANCES ITS FLAVOR INSTEAD OF DISGUISING IT;
BROWNED BUTTER AND BREAD CRUMBS DO JUST THAT IN THIS DISH.

1 bunch broccoli, cut into florets, about 2 cups
6 tablespoons butter
Salt and freshly ground pepper
2 medium cloves garlic, minced (about 1 teaspoon)
½ cup fresh bread crumbs
1 large egg, hardboiled and finely chopped
1 tablespoon chopped fresh cilantro

Preheat the oven to 350°.
1. Cut the broccoli into 2-inch pieces. Blanch in boiling water
for 4 to 5 minutes or until bright green. Drain through a colander.
2. Melt 2 tablespoons butter. Place the broccoli into a baking
dish. Toss with melted butter and season with salt and pepper.
Bake for 10 minutes.
3. Melt the remaining butter in a skillet over medium high heat.
4. Cook the garlic in the butter for 2 minutes.
5. Add the bread crumbs and cook until they turn brown and
begin to crisp, about 4 minutes. Season with salt and pepper.
6. Remove the broccoli from the oven. Spoon the bread crumbs
over the top. Sprinkle with chopped hardboiled egg and cilantro.

SERVINGS: 4 • PREPARATION TIME: 15 MINUTES

BROCCOLI GOT A BAD RAP WHEN FORMER PRESIDENT GEORGE BUSH
UTTERED, "I DO NOT LIKE BROCCOLI. AND I HAVEN'T LIKED IT SINCE I WAS A
LITTLE KID AND MY MOTHER MADE ME EAT IT. AND I'M PRESIDENT OF THE
UNITED STATES AND I'M NOT GOING TO EAT ANY MORE BROCCOLI"; THIS
SOUNDED A CALL TO COOKS AROUND THE WORLD, STRIVING TO BRING OUT
THE BEST IN BROCCOLI. NOT WILLING TO PUSH ASIDE A VEGGIE, CHALKED
FULL OF CANCER KILLING ANTIOXIDANTS AND ARTERY CLEANING FIBER, BROC-
COLI RECIPES REMAIN AS WIDE-SPREAD AND DIVERSE AS PASTA DISHES.

Broccoli Rabe Sautéed with Garlic and Red Pepper

BROCCOLI RABE CAN HAVE A BITTER TASTE, BUT WHEN BLANCHED AND BLENDED WITH SAUTÉED GARLIC AND A HINT OF RED PEPPER, THE DISH IS UNBELIEVABLY TASTY AND FILLED WITH GREAT VITAMINS.

2 large bunches broccoli rabe (about 1½ to 2 pounds)
Salt and freshly ground pepper
2 tablespoons olive oil
6 medium garlic cloves, thinly sliced (about ¼ cup)
¼ teaspoon red pepper flakes
Juice of 1 medium lemon (about 2 tablespoons)

1. Bring a pot of water to boil over high heat.
2. Cut the tough stems from the broccoli rabe. Chop the stems into 1-inch pieces. Roughly chop the leaves.
3. Generously salt the water. Add the stems and cook until just tender, about 5 minutes. Add the leaves and cook for 3 to 5 minutes more.
4. Drain the pot into a colander. Plunge the greens into a bowl filled with cold water to stop the cooking process. Drain.
5. Heat the olive oil in a skillet over medium high heat.
6. Add the garlic to the pan and cook until just golden, about 3 minutes.
7. Add the red pepper flakes to the pan and stir.
8. Add the blanched broccoli rabe to the pan and toss.
9. Sprinkle with lemon juice and season with salt and pepper.

SERVINGS: 4 TO 6 • PREPARATION TIME: 20 MINUTES

Pasta with Broccoli Rabe, Sun-Dried Tomatoes, and Fresh Mozzarella

Cook pasta according to package directions. Combine blanched broccoli rabe, sun-dried tomatoes cut into strips, and cubes of fresh mozzarella in a serving bowl. Drain pasta and toss into the bowl. Toss until the mozzarella just begins to melt. Season with salt, pepper and shavings of Parmesan.

Lasagna with Broccoli Rabe

Prepare your favorite lasagna recipe. Mix together ricotta cheese with cooked and chopped broccoli rabe. (I add an egg and Parmesan to this mixture, which binds it together.) Drop generous spoonfuls of the ricotta mixture on top of the lasagna noodles, covered with marinara sauce. Continue layering for a red, white and green treat.

REST ASSURED, ALL YOU BROCCOLI HATERS, BROCCOLI RABE IS NOT BROCCOLI! IN SPITE OF RESEMBLING A BROCCOLI FLORET, BROCCOLI RABE IS ITS DISTANT COUSIN, FILLED WITH THE SAME GOOD ANTITOXINS THAT HELP PREVENT CANCER. BROCCOLI RABE IS A QUICK GROWING, COOL WEATHER PLANT. IF HARVESTED CORRECTLY, YOU WILL GET MORE THAN ONE CUTTING FROM EACH PLANT.

Braised Savoy Cabbage with Apples and Cinnamon

CABBAGE IS AN EXTRAORDINARILY VERSATILE AND NUTRITIOUS VEGGIE; ITS NATURALLY BLAND TASTE SOAKS IN YOUR FAVORITE FLAVORS.

1 2-pound head Savoy cabbage
2 tablespoons butter
2 tablespoons olive oil
1 medium red onion, thinly sliced (about 1½ cups)
Salt and freshly ground pepper
2 medium apples, peeled and thinly sliced (about 2 cups)
1 cup apple cider
2 cups chicken broth
⅓ cup apple cider vinegar
2 tablespoons brown sugar
½ teaspoon ground cardamom
½ teaspoon ground cinnamon

1. Cut the cabbage into thin slices.
2. Melt the butter with the olive oil in a large skillet over medium heat.
3. Add the onion and cook until soft, about 5 minutes.
4. Add the cabbage, season with salt and pepper, and cook for 10 minutes.
5. Stir in the apples.
6. Pour in the cider. Cook until very little liquid remains.
7. Add the chicken broth, apple cider vinegar, brown sugar, cardamom, and cinnamon. Cover and simmer until soft, about 30 minutes.

SERVINGS: 4 TO 6 • PREPARATION TIME: 20 MINUTES PLUS 30 MINUTES TO SIMMER

Cabbage with Caraway Seeds

Cook the cabbage as directed above, but eliminate the apples, cider, cardamom and cinnamon. Pour in 1 cup of white wine, after the cabbage is seasoned. Sprinkle with 2 teaspoons caraway seeds. Simmer.

Cabbage with Pepper and Garlic

Cook as directed above. In place of the apples, add 4 garlic cloves, thinly sliced. In place of cider, stir in 2 tablespoons balsamic vinegar. Eliminate cardamom and cinnamon. Sprinkle freshly ground pepper on the cooked cabbage before serving.

THE WORD CABBAGE IS A DERIVATIVE OF THE FRENCH WORD CABOCHE, A COLLOQUIAL TERM FOR "HEAD." THE CABBAGE FAMILY—INCLUDES BRUSSELS SPROUTS, BROCCOLI, CAULIFLOWER AND KALE. CHOOSE A CABBAGE WITH FRESH, CRISP-LOOKING LEAVES THAT ARE FIRMLY PACKED; THE HEAD SHOULD BE HEAVY FOR ITS SIZE. CABBAGE MAY BE REFRIGERATED AND TIGHTLY WRAPPED, FOR ABOUT A WEEK. CABBAGE CONTAINS A HEALTHY DOSE OF VITAMIN C AND SOME VITAMIN A.

Baby Bok Choy in Ginger Soy Sauce

BOK CHOY IS A MEMBER OF THE CABBAGE FAMILY AND ORIGINATES IN
CHINA, WHERE THE TITLE QUITE LITERALLY TRANSLATES TO "WHITE VEG-
ETABLE." THE HEALTH BENEFITS ARE WELL TOUTED, AND YOU CAN EASILY
INCORPORATE THIS YUMMY VEGGIE INTO YOUR WEEKLY MEAL PLAN.

2 tablespoons peanut oil
3 heads baby bok choy, cut in half lengthwise
2 medium cloves garlic, minced (about 1 teaspoon)
1 1-inch piece ginger, grated
2 tablespoons soy sauce
¼ cup chicken broth
Salt and freshly ground pepper
1 tablespoon cornstarch dissolved in 2 tablespoons cold water
2 tablespoons chopped fresh chives

1. Heat 2 tablespoons peanut oil in a skillet over medium high
heat.
2. Place the bok choy, cut side down, in the pan. Cook for 2
minutes, turn and cook for 2 minutes more.
3. Transfer the bok choy to a platter.
4. Add the garlic to the pan. Stir.
5. Add the ginger to the pan. Stir.
6. Add the soy sauce and chicken broth to the pan.
7. Return the bok choy to the pan and simmer for 3 to 5 minutes.
8. Season with salt and pepper.
9. Add the cornstarch to the pan, and stir until the sauce begins
to thicken, about 3 minutes.
10. Garnish with chopped fresh chives.

SERVINGS: 4 TO 6 • PREPARATION
TIME: 15 MINUTES

*Grilled Baby Bok Choy
with Dijon Vinaigrette*
*Split the Bok Choy in half,
lengthwise. Drizzle with olive oil
and season with salt and pepper. Grill each half in a grill pan
over medium high heat. Serve
the grilled Bok Choy with Dijon
vinaigrette.*

WHEN PLANNING A HOME GAR-
DEN, KEEP IN MIND BABY BOK
CHOY GROWS TO ABOUT 6
INCHES IN HEIGHT, COMPARED
TO REGULAR BOK CHOY THAT
CAN GROW FROM 10 TO 12
INCHES. BABY BOK IS DELI-
CATE AND SOMEWHAT SWEET
TASTING; IT IS BEST GROWN IN
A COOL CLIMATE, NOT FARING
WELL IN HEAT.

Baked Stuffed Heirloom Tomatoes
with Goat Cheese

HEIRLOOM TOMATOES DIFFER IN COLOR AND TEXTURE FROM THE STORE BOUGHT VARIETY. THEIR FLAVOR IS OUTSTANDING AND SHOULD ONLY BE ENHANCED IN PRESENTATION—NOT DISGUISED. IF YOU CANNOT FIND HEIRLOOM TOMATOES, SUBSTITUTE WITH RED, RIPE BEEFSTEAK TOMATOES.

3 large heirloom tomatoes
Salt and freshly ground pepper
6 slices white bread, crusts removed
1 bunch (6 to 8) green onions, chopped (about ½ cup)
2 tablespoons chopped fresh basil
2 tablespoons chopped fresh parsley
3 medium garlic cloves, minced (about 1½ teaspoons)
3 ounces goat cheese, crumbled
2 tablespoons olive oil

Preheat the oven to 400°.
1. Core and halve each tomato. Place onto a baking dish. Use a spoon or your fingers to remove the seeds from the center of each half. Season with salt and pepper.
2. Use a food processor to chop the bread slices into fine crumbs.
3. Combine fresh bread crumbs, onions, basil, parsley, garlic, and ½ teaspoon salt in a small bowl.
4. Fill the tomatoes with the crumb/herb mixture. Bake for 10 to 15 minutes, or until the filling begins to brown.
5. Remove the dish from the oven and sprinkle with crumbled goat cheese. Drizzle with olive oil and return to the oven. Bake for 1 to 2 minutes, or until the cheese begins to melt.

SERVINGS: 4 TO 6 • PREPARATION TIME: 20 MINUTES

HEIRLOOM TOMATOES HAVE FASCINATING NAMES SUCH AS "BLACK PLUM, CARBON, SWEET OLIVE, SUNGOLD, GOLIATH, GREEN ZEBRA, ODORIKO, PAUL ROBESON, GOOSE CREEK, AND BLACK ZEBRA." THERE ARE ALSO FESTIVALS LIKE TOMATOMANIA IN LOS ANGELES, WHEREIN THE ACTIVITIES INCLUDE A TOMATO TASTING TO DECIDE ON THE BEST HEIRLOOM VARIETY OF THE YEAR.

Mustard-Glazed Tomatoes

Prepare a mixture of fresh herbs, Dijon mustard, garlic and olive oil. Cut the tomatoes into 1-inch slices. Spread a spoonful of the herb and mustard mixture on each slice. Place the tomatoes under the broiler for 5 to 7 minutes, or until bubbling.

Tomato Bread Salad

Toast and cut the bread into chunks. Prepare the herb mixture as directed in the recipe at right. Cut the tomatoes into chunks, add 1-inch chunks of cucumber and the bread, and toss with vinaigrette for a terrific tasting bread salad.

Braised Baby Tomatoes, Radishes, and Cucumber with Mint

ENJOY THE FLAVORS OF THE GARDEN BY COMBINING SALAD FAVORITE VEG-GIES IN A WARM BRAISING LIQUID.

2 tablespoons olive oil
1 large cucumber, peeled
1 pint ripe cherry tomatoes or mixed baby tomatoes
12 whole radishes, sliced (about 1 cup)
1 cup chicken broth
¼ teaspoon red pepper flakes
Salt
2 tablespoons chopped fresh mint

1. Heat the olive oil in a skillet over medium high heat.
2. Cut the cucumber into 1½-inch matchstick size pieces.
3. Cut the tomatoes in half.
4. Add the vegetables to the pan and stir.
5. Pour the chicken broth over the vegetables.
6. Stir in the red pepper flakes. Reduce the heat to medium and simmer for 3 to 5 minutes.
7. Season with salt and garnish with chopped fresh mint.

SERVINGS: 4 TO 6 • PREPARATION TIME: 15 MINUTES

AFTER YEARS OF TRYING TO PRODUCE THE PERFECT TASTING TOMATOES, GROWERS IN MEXICO AND FLORIDA CAME UP WITH A FRUIT THAT IS AVAILABLE YEAR ROUND—THE GRAPE TOMATO. SOME FOOD STORES REPORT THAT GRAPE TOMATOES OUTSELL CHERRY TOMATOES 10 TO 1. LOOK FOR MORE AND MORE VARIETIES TO SHOW UP IN YOUR NEIGHBORHOOD STORE, AND GIVE 'EM ALL A TRY!

Slow-Roasted Cherry Tomatoes

Place tomatoe halves into a shallow baking dish. Season with minced garlic, minced shallot, salt and pepper. Pour enough olive oil, so that the sides of the tomatoes are half submerged. Roast in a 250° oven for several hours, or until the tomatoes begin to fall apart. Serve the warm tomatoes with the flavored oil alone, as a pasta or bruschetta topping, or on a melted cheese sandwich.

Steamed Artichokes
with Balsamic Mayonnaise Dipping Sauce

THE BEST WAY TO COOK AN ARTICHOKE IS TO PLACE IT INTO A STEAMER INSERTED INTO (OR JUST ABOVE) SIMMERING WATER, COVERED WITH A LID. ALTERNATIVES INCLUDE MICROWAVING IN A COVERED DISH WITH AN INCH OR MORE OF WATER IN THE BOTTOM, OR IN A COLANDER INSERTED INTO BOILING WATER. NO MATTER YOUR PREFERENCE, ALWAYS REMEMBER TO DOUBLE CHECK THE ARTICHOKES FOR DONENESS BY INSERTING THE TINES OF A FORK INTO THE STEM; WHEN IT INSERTS EASILY, YOUR ARTICHOKES ARE DONE!

4 large artichokes
1 cup mayonnaise
1 tablespoon Dijon mustard
Juice of 1 lemon (about 2 tablespoons)
1 tablespoon balsamic vinegar
1 tablespoon chopped fresh dill
Salt and freshly ground pepper

1. Cut the top ¼ off the artichokes. Remove the thorny tips from the leaves. Cut all but about 1 inch of stem and peel off the stringy outer part. Remove the tough outer leaves.
2. Place the artichokes into a steamer pan and cook until tender, about 30 to 45 minutes. Let them cool slightly.
3. Cut the artichokes in half from stem to top (vertically). Remove the thorny inner leaves, exposing the heart.
4. Stir together the mayonnaise, Dijon mustard, lemon juice, vinegar and fresh dill. Season with salt and pepper.
5. Place a generous spoonful of the sauce into the cavity of the artichoke.

SERVINGS: 4 TO 6 • PREPARATION TIME: 1 HOUR

Grilled Artichokes with Tarragon Sauce

After the artichokes have been steamed and halved, place them onto a hot grill pan. Drizzle with olive oil and cook for 2 minutes per side. Stir together ½ cup of mayonnaise, ½ cup of sour cream, lemon juice, balsamic vinegar and fresh tarragon for a terrific sauce.

Braised Baby Artichokes in Lemon Cream Sauce

ONCE YOU LEARN HOW TO TRIM A BABY ARTICHOKE, YOU WILL FIND MANY
WAYS TO INCORPORATE THIS FUN VEGGIE INTO YOUR MENU. UNLIKE ITS
LARGER COUSIN, YOU DO NOT NEED TO REMOVE THE INSIDE "CHOKE"; BABY
ARTICHOKES ARE DELICATE ENOUGH TO USE SLICED PAPER-THIN IN YOUR
NEXT SALAD.

1 2½-pound bag baby artichokes (about 18)
Lemon wedges
2 tablespoons olive oil
4 medium cloves garlic, minced (about 2 teaspoons)
1 cup white wine
1 teaspoon dried oregano
Juice of 1 medium lemon (about 2 tablespoons)
½ cup sour cream
2 tablespoons chopped fresh parsley
Salt and freshly ground pepper

Preheat the oven to
1. Trim the dark, outer leaves from the artichokes and discard.
Trim the stems and cut off the pointed tips. Cut each one in
half. Place trimmed artichokes in a bowl filled with cold water.
Squeeze lemon wedges into the water to prevent the artichokes
from discoloring.
2. Heat the olive oil in a skillet over medium
high heat. Cook the garlic in the skillet until
soft, about 3 to 4 minutes.
3. Add the artichokes to the pan.
4. Pour in the white wine. Stir in the oregano.
Reduce the heat, cover, and simmer the artichokes until they are soft, about 20 minutes.
5. Remove the lid. Squeeze in 2 tablespoons of
lemon juice. Stir in the sour cream and parsley.
Season with salt and pepper. Cook for 2 minutes more.

SERVINGS: 4 TO 6 • PREPARATION TIME: 30 MINUTES

Fried Baby Artichokes
Trim the artichokes as directed
in the recipe at left. Cut the
artichokes from tip to stem into
⅛-inch slices. A mandolin is a
great tool for this job. Dredge
the slices into flour, beaten eggs
and then into flour again. Place
into very hot canola oil until
golden, about 2 minutes per
side. Drain on paper towels and
season with salt and pepper.

Old-Fashioned Creamed Corn

WHEN YOU DRIVE BY THE CORNER ROADSIDE PRODUCE STAND AND SEE BASKETS OF CORN FOR PENNIES, USE THIS RECIPE TO TAKE ADVANTAGE OF THE BOUNTY. IF THE CRAVING FOR CORN SNEAKS UP ON YOU IN THE WINTERTIME, KNOW THAT YOU CAN EASILY SUBSTITUTE WITH FROZEN CORN IN A PINCH!

8 ears of fresh corn, kernels sliced from cob (about 4 cups) or 4 cups frozen kernels, thawed
2 tablespoons butter
1 medium white onion, diced (about ⅔ cup)
2 medium cloves garlic, minced (about 1 teaspoon)
2 tablespoons all-purpose flour
1 cup chicken broth
1 cup half and half
½ teaspoon ground nutmeg
Salt and freshly ground pepper

Southwestern Style Creamed Corn
Add 1 seeded and diced jalapeño pepper and 1 seeded and diced red bell pepper to the onion-garlic mixture. Substitute 1 teaspoon chili powder for ground nutmeg.

1. Cook the corn kernels in boiling water until tender, about 5 minutes. Drain and set aside.

2. Melt the butter in a pot over medium high heat.

3. Add the onion and garlic to the pan and cook until soft, about 5 minutes.

4. Reduce the heat to medium. Sprinkle the flour over the onion-garlic mixture.

5. Pour the chicken broth into the pan. Cook, whisking constantly, until smooth and beginning to thicken, about 2 to 3 minutes.

6. Slowly pour the half & half into the pan. Stir until smooth and thick, about 2 to 3 minutes more.

7. Add 3 cups of kernels to the mixture and stir. Cook for 5 minutes.

8. Remove the pan from heat. Use an immersion blender (or food processor) to coarsely purée this mixture.

9. Season the mixture with ground nutmeg, salt and pepper.

10. Stir in the remaining 1 cup of kernels.

SERVINGS: 6 TO 8 • PREPARATION TIME: 25 MINUTES

Chili Roasted Corn on the Cob with Lime Cream

SOAKING THE CORN IN THEIR HUSKS WILL PREVENT THE HUSKS FROM
BURNING ON THE GRILL. HOWEVER, YOU MUST WATCH THEM CAREFULLY. IF
THE FIRE IS TOO HOT, SIMPLY MOVE THE CORN AWAY FROM THE DIRECT
HEAT. FOR A MORE SIMPLE PRESENTATION, REMOVE THE HUSKS AND BROIL
THE CORN FOR SEVERAL MINUTES, TURNING OFTEN.

6 ears of fresh corn with husks
2 tablespoons butter, melted
2 tablespoons chili powder
1 teaspoon ground cumin
Salt and freshly ground pepper
½ cup sour cream
¼ cup cream
Juice of 1 medium lime (about 1 tablespoon)

I. Submerge the corn (with the husks) in cold water for at least
30 minutes and up to 1 hour. Gently peel the husks away from
the corn, leaving it connected at the stem. Clean the silk threads
from the corn.

2. Stir together the melted butter, chili powder and cumin.
Brush this mixture onto the corn. Season with salt and pepper.
Loosely rewrap the husks around the corn.

3. Heat an outdoor grill over medium high heat. Grill the corn,
turning often, watching carefully so that the
husks do not burn. Transfer the corn to a platter.

4. For lime cream, whisk together both sour
and regular cream with lime juice.

5. Peel back the corn husks. Drizzle the lime
cream over the corn. Garnish with an additional shake of chili powder.

SERVINGS: 6 • PREPARATION TIME: 45 MINUTES

CORN IS IN SEASON FROM
LATE SPRING THROUGH THE
END OF SUMMER. WHITE, YEL-
LOW AND BICOLOR ARE JUST
A FEW OF THE MANY VARIETIES
OF SWEET CORN AVAILABLE.
PURCHASE THE FRESHEST
CORN YOU CAN FIND. THE
HUSKS SHOULD BE BRIGHT
GREEN. YOU NEED ONLY TO
PULL BACK THE HUSK A TAD,
TO MAKE SURE THAT THE KER-
NELS ARE LINED UP IN TIGHT
ROWS, ALL THE WAY TO THE
TIP OF THE COB. STORE
FRESH CORN, IN THEIR
HUSKS, IN THE REFRIGERATOR
FOR SEVERAL DAYS.

Creamy Smashed Parmesan Potatoes
with Green Onions

POTATOES WITH LESS STARCH WORK PERFECTLY IN THIS RECIPE ALTHOUGH,
IN A PINCH, DON'T BE AFRAID TO USE A GOOD OLD IDAHO SPUD! SMALL, 2-
INCH RED CREAMER POTATOES ARE MY FAVORITE AND LOOK THE BEST.

Golden Mashed Potatoes
For a golden, creamy mashed side dish, cook peeled Yukon gold potatoes in salted, boiling water until tender. Use an electric mixer to blend butter, milk, salt and pepper with the potatoes until the desired consistency is achieved.

2 pounds red creamer potatoes, about 12 to 15
Salt and freshly ground pepper
4 tablespoons butter (½ stick)
½ cup cream
2 ounces finely grated Parmesan cheese (about ½ cup)
½ cup sour cream
1 bunch (6 to 8) green onions, chopped (about ½ cup)

Preheat the oven to 350°.
1. Cook the potatoes in boiling, salted water until tender, about 10 to 15 minutes.
2. Place the cooked potatoes into a large bowl. Add the butter, cream and Parmesan cheese. Use a potato masher to just combine.
3. Fold in the sour cream and onions. Season with salt and pepper.

SERVINGS: 4 TO 6 • PREPARATION TIME: 30 MINUTES

BECAUSE EVERYONE LOVES THE TASTE OF NUTRIENT-RICH POTATOES, IT'S EASY TO PREPARE A HEALTHY DISH BOTH ADULTS AND KIDS WILL EAT. POTATOES ARE FULL OF ENERGY-PROVIDING CARBOHYDRATES, AND THEY DON'T CONTAIN ANY FAT. ONE MEDIUM POTATO (ABOUT 5 TO 6 OUNCES) PROVIDES 45 PERCENT OF THE DAILY VALUE FOR VITAMIN C, 21 PERCENT OF THE DAILY VALUE FOR POTASSIUM, AND THREE GRAMS OF FIBER. AT THE SAME TIME, IT CONTAINS ONLY ABOUT 100 CALORIES. A BRISK 30-MINUTE WALK WILL TAKE CARE OF THOSE CALORIES AND MORE. SO GO AHEAD AND WORK A FEW POTATOES INTO YOUR WEEKLY MEAL PLAN.

Celery Root Purée

A FUN WAY TO LIGHTEN UP TRADITIONAL MASHED POTATOES, THIS SUPER SIDE DISH GOES WELL WITH EVERYTHING FROM TURKEY MEATLOAF TO BRAISED SHORT RIBS.

2 celery roots, peeled and cut into ½-inch pieces (about 3 pounds)
2 medium potatoes, peeled and cut into ½-inch pieces
3 cups chicken broth
1 cup cream
3 tablespoons butter
¼ teaspoon ground nutmeg
Salt and freshly ground pepper

1. Place the celery root and potatoes into a saucepan. Cover with chicken broth. Cook over medium high heat until soft, about 10 minutes.
2. Pour the cream into the pan. Continue cooking until most of the liquid has been absorbed, about 10 minutes more.
3. Remove the pan from the heat.
4. Stir in the butter.
5. Season with nutmeg, salt and pepper.
6. Use an immersion blender to purée the mixture.

SERVINGS: 4 TO 6 • PREPARATION TIME: 30 MINUTES

Roasted Celery Root
Season peeled and diced celery root with salt, pepper and drizzle with olive oil. Place onto a baking sheet and roast for 350°. until golden, about 20 minutes depending on the size of the dice.

Potato Gratin with Caramelized Onions and Goat Cheese

BECAUSE IT IS EASY TO PREPARE, BAKES QUICKLY AND MAKES USE OF YOUR FAVORITE INGREDIENTS, AU GRATIN IS BOTH AN ELEGANT DINNER PARTY DISH AND A WEEKDAY MENU STAPLE. YOU NEEDN'T PEEL THE POTATOES— USING A MANDOLINE WILL ENSURE THE SLICES ARE THIN AND UNIFORM.

Potato Gratin with Fontina Cheese and Roasted Garlic

The basic potato gratin recipe BEGS for your inspiration and personal touch. Use any cheese you have on hand, substituting roasted garlic for caramelized onions just for a start. You can also alternate slices of sweet potatoes with the white ones.

Ways with Potato Gratin for Brunch

Place finished gratin on a brunch buffet and serve with the best caviar, smoked salmon, crème fresh, capers and a smidge of finely diced red onion on the side. Not over-the-top enough for you? Try serving a wedge of warm gratin topped with a sautéed slice of Canadian bacon. Layer with a perfectly poached egg and a ladleful of Hollandaise sauce, and you have Eggs Benedict topped gratin to die for!

1 tablespoon olive oil
2 large yellow onions, thinly sliced (about 4½ cups)
1 tablespoon balsamic vinegar
Salt and freshly ground pepper
6 to 8 large Yukon gold potatoes, thinly sliced
4 medium cloves garlic, minced (about 2 teaspoons)
8 ounces goat cheese, crumbled (about 2 cups)
½ cup butter, melted (1 stick)
2 tablespoons chopped fresh chives
2 cups cream

Preheat the oven to 400°.
1. Heat the olive oil in a skillet over medium high heat.
2. Add the onions and cook until soft and golden, about 10 minutes.
3. Sprinkle the onions with balsamic vinegar and season with salt and pepper. Continue cooking until the onions are quite brown and syrupy. Cool to room temperature.
4. Coat a baking dish with vegetable oil spray. Place an overlapping layer of potatoes in the bottom of the dish.
5. Season the potatoes with salt and pepper. Sprinkle ⅓ of the minced garlic over the potatoes.
6. Sprinkle ⅓ of the goat cheese and onions over the potatoes. Drizzle with 2 tablespoons of the melted butter. Sprinkle with chopped fresh chives.
7. Continue layering the potatoes as stated above, ending with a layer of overlapping potatoes. Reserve some of the melted butter for the top of the last layer.
8. Pour the cream into the baking dish, over and around the potato layers.
9. Bake for 30 to 40 minutes or until the casserole is bubbling and the top layer of potatoes begins to brown. Allow the gratin to rest for 10 minutes before serving.

SERVINGS: 4 TO 6 • PREPARATION TIME: 20 MINUTES PLUS BAKING

Mashed Sweet Potatoes
with Maple Granola Topping

SERVE THIS SWEET AND SAVORY CASSEROLE FOR YOUR NEXT HOLIDAY MENU,
OR TRICK YOUR PICKY EATER AND SERVE IT FOR DESSERT! EITHER WAY THIS
IS A YUMMY WAY TO INCORPORATE A HEALTHY VEGGIE INTO YOUR EVERY-
DAY DIET.

4 large sweet potatoes (about 2 pounds)
¼ cup butter (½ stick)
½ cup half and half
¼ cup maple syrup
1 teaspoon ground cumin
½ teaspoon cinnamon
½ teaspoon ground nutmeg
Salt and freshly ground pepper

½ cup Easy Granola (see page 172)
2 tablespoons butter, cut into small pieces
2 tablespoons maple syrup

Preheat the oven to 375°.

1. Bake the potatoes until soft, about 45 minutes.

2. Remove the potatoes from the oven. Cool slightly, peel, and
place them into the bowl of an electric mixer.

3. Add ¼ cup of butter, half and half, maple syrup, cumin, cinnamon, and nutmeg. Season with salt and pepper. Stir until the
mixture is well mashed.

4. Spread the sweet potatoes into a baking dish that has been
sprayed with vegetable oil spray.

5. Sprinkle the granola over top. Dot the granola with the
remaining butter and drizzle with the remaining 2 tablespoons
maple syrup.

6. Reduce the heat to 350°. Bake until the top is golden, and the
casserole is heated through, about 30 minutes.

SERVINGS: 6 • PREPARATION TIME: 30 MINUTES PLUS BAKING POTATOES

*Mashed Sweet Potatoes
with Rum "Gravy"*
*Bake, peel, and mash sweet
potatoes with butter, cream (or
milk), and your favorite seasoning. In a saucepan, over
medium heat, melt 1 stick butter, ½ cup of brown sugar and
¼ cup of dark rum. Stir together until the sugar has melted.
Cook for 2 to 3 minutes. Pour
the "gravy" over the mashed
sweet potatoes and serve.*

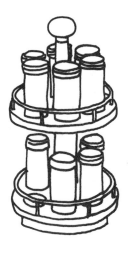

Brussels Sprouts in Horseradish Cream Sauce

THE SHARP FLAVOR OF THE SPROUTS IS ENHANCED BY THE PIQUANCY OF THE HORSERADISH SAUCE AND TAMED BY RICH CREAM. FEEL FREE TO ADD MORE OR LESS HORSERADISH, AS YOU PREFER.

1 pound Brussels sprouts (about 4 cups)
2 tablespoons butter
2 tablespoons all-purpose flour
2 to 3 tablespoons prepared horseradish
1 cup cream
Salt and freshly ground pepper

1. Remove the outer leaves from the sprouts. Cut off the tough stems. Make a cross-wise incision on the bottom of the sprout. Place into a microwave safe dish with about 1-inch of water. Cover and steam the Brussels sprouts in the microwave oven on high heat until soft, about 10 minutes. Place the sprouts into a bowl of ice water to stop the cooking process. Drain the sprouts. (You can store and refrigerate the sprouts at this point for up to 24 hours.)
2. Cook the butter and the flour in a saucepan over medium high heat until bubbling.
3. Stir in the horseradish.
4. Stir in the cream. Cook until the sauce begins to thicken, about 5 minutes. Reduce heat to medium and cook for 5 minutes more.
5. Add the sprouts to the sauce. Season with salt and pepper.

SERVINGS: 4 TO 6 • PREPARATION TIME: 30 MINUTES

THE KEY TO COOKING BRUSSELS SPROUTS IS MAKING SURE YOU DO NOT OVERCOOK THEM. THE LEAVES COOK FASTER THAN THE CORE, SO BY MAKING A SMALL INCISION IN THE BOTTOM OF THE STEM, YOU GUARANTEE EVEN COOKING FOR WHOLE SPROUTS. AS A RULE OF THUMB, WHEN BRUSSELS SPROUTS HAVE LOST THEIR BRIGHT GREEN COLOR, THEY ARE OVERCOOKED AND HAVE ALSO LOST A CONSIDERABLE AMOUNT OF NUTRITIONAL VALUE. DEPENDING ON SIZE, COOKING TIME SHOULD NOT EXCEED 7 TO 10 MINUTES, WHETHER YOU ARE STEAMING, BRAISING OR BOILING.

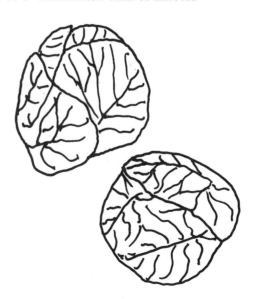

Braised Brussels Sprouts in Wine with Orange Zest

YOU CAN EASILY PREPARE THE SPROUTS IN ADVANCE FOR THIS EASY DISH,
AND THEN COOK THEM IN THE SAUCE JUST BEFORE SERVING.

1 pound Brussels sprouts (about 4 cups)
2 tablespoons olive oil
3 medium garlic cloves, minced (about 1½ teaspoons)
Salt and freshly ground pepper
Zest of ½ medium orange (about 1 tablespoon)
1 cup white wine

1. Remove the outer leaves from the sprouts. Cut off the tough
stems. Make a cross-wise incision on the bottom of the sprout.
Place into a microwave safe dish with about 1-inch of water.
Cover and steam the Brussels sprouts in the microwave oven on
high heat until soft, about 10 minutes. Place the sprouts into a
bowl of ice water to stop the cooking process. Drain the sprouts.
(You can store and refrigerate the sprouts at this point for up to
24 hours.)
2. Heat 2 tablespoons olive oil in a skillet over medium high
heat.
3. Cook the garlic in the pan until soft, about 2 minutes.
4. Add the cooked Brussels sprouts. Season with salt and pepper.
5. Stir in the orange zest and white wine. Cook until the Brussels
sprouts are warmed through and the wine is reduced by half.

SERVINGS: 6 • PREPARATION TIME: 30 MINUTES

*Braised Brussels Sprouts
with Herbs*
Cook sprouts as instructed at
left and cut in half. Place the
sprouts into a skillet. Cover
with chicken broth. Add tarragon or sage leaves, salt and
pepper. Cook until the liquid is
reduced by half and the sprouts
are tender, about 5 minutes.

Golden Stuffed Cauliflower

WITH JUST A HINT OF INDIAN SEASONINGS AND A TOUCH OF GOLDEN
RAISINS, THIS EASY TO MAKE DISH IS A BIG HIT ON AN EVERYDAY TABLE.

*Baked Cauliflower
with Cashews*

Steam the whole cauliflower
using a steamer insert, or by
placing the head into a baking
dish and adding 1 inch water.
Cover and microwave for 6 to
8 minutes. Place the cooked
cauliflower into a baking dish.
Process 1 cup cashews in a food
processor. Toast the nuts in 2
tablespoons butter. Spread this
mixture over the cauliflower.
Roast in the oven for 15 minutes.

1 tablespoon ground turmeric
1 large head cauliflower, outer leaves removed
2 tablespoons olive oil
1 small red onion, diced (about ½ cup)
2 large carrots, diced (about 1 cup)
2 medium celery ribs, diced (about 1 cup)
1 teaspoon ground cumin
½ teaspoon ground coriander
½ cup golden raisins
½ cup chicken broth
Salt and freshly ground pepper
2 tablespoons yellow mustard

Preheat the oven to 450°.

1. Place the turmeric into a large pot of boiling water. Cook the
cauliflower head in the turmeric water until just tender, about 10
to 15 minutes.

2. Heat the olive oil in a skillet over medium high heat.

3. For stuffing, add onion, carrots and celery to the skillet. Cook
until just soft, about 10 minutes.

4. Stir in the cumin and coriander.

5. Add the raisins and chicken broth to the pan. Reduce until
most of the liquid is absorbed, about 5 minutes. Season with salt
and pepper.

6. Carefully remove the cauliflower from the pot. Place it into a
baking dish. Use your fingers to gently pry apart some of the
flowerets.

7. Spoon the stuffing into and underneath the crevices of the
cauliflower.

8. Spread the mustard over the top.

9. Bake until golden brown, about 30 minutes.

SERVINGS: 4 TO 6 • PREPARATION TIME: 1 HOUR

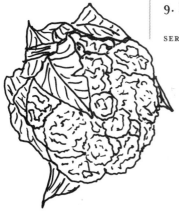

Garlic Roasted Cauliflower

ROASTING GARLIC PRODUCES A SWEET RESULT. ROASTING CAULIFLOWER GIVES IT A TOUCH OF NUTTINESS. TOGETHER, THE COMBINATION IS MOUTHWATERING. THE DISH COMES TOGETHER IN JUST MINUTES, MAKING THIS VEGGIE SIDE, A MUST HAVE IN YOUR WEEKLY MEAL PLAN.

1 large head cauliflower, broken into (1-inch) flowerets
8 to 10 large garlic cloves, peeled
¼ cup olive oil
2 ounces finely grated Parmesan cheese (about ½ cup)
1 teaspoon paprika
Salt and fresh ground pepper

Preheat the oven to 350°.
1. Place the flowerets into a baking dish. Toss in the garlic cloves.
2. Drizzle with olive oil. Sprinkle with Parmesan cheese and paprika. Season with salt and pepper.
3. Cook until the cauliflower is soft, about 20 to 30 minutes.

SERVINGS: 4 TO 6 • PREPARATION TIME: 15 MINUTES PLUS 30 MINUTES BAKING.

WHEN PURCHASING CAULIFLOWER, CHOOSE A TIGHT PACKED HEAD THAT IS FREE OF BRUISES OR BROWN SPOTS. YOU CAN STORE A WHOLE HEAD OF CAULIFLOWER IN A PLASTIC BAG IN THE REFRIGERATOR. (POKE HOLES IN THE BAG TO ALLOW THE AIR TO CIRCULATE.) IT WILL STAY FRESH FOR SEVERAL DAYS AND UP TO 1 WEEK. THE MOST COMMON VARIETY OF CAULIFLOWER IS IVORY WHITE, BUT IF YOU HAVE A CHANCE TO PURCHASE THE PURPLE OR GREEN VARIETY, DON'T HESITATE TO DO SO!

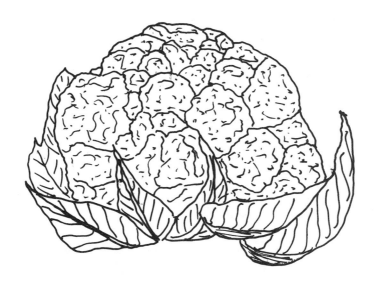

Orange-Laced Green Beans in Wine Sauce

A HINT OF ORANGE ZEST PERKS UP EVERY-DAY GREEN BEANS IN THIS EASY VEGGIE DISH. LEMON AND LIME ARE JUST AS MUCH FUN. WHEN ZESTING CITRUS, REMEMBER TO GRATE JUST THE OUTSIDE PEEL. THE WHITE PITH OF THE FRUIT IS BITTER TASTING.

1 pound fresh green beans, about 4 cups
2 tablespoons olive oil
2 medium cloves garlic, minced (about 1 teaspoon)
½ cup white wine
Juice of ½ medium orange (about 2 to 3 tablespoons)
Zest of ½ medium orange (about 1 tablespoon)
Salt and freshly ground pepper

1. Steam the green beans in a stovetop steamer or microwave oven, until just crisp-tender, about 3 to 4 minutes. Drain.
2. Heat the olive oil in a skillet over medium high heat.
3. Cook the garlic in the olive oil for 2 minutes.
4. Add the drained green beans to the pan.
5. Pour in the wine and cook for 3 to 4 minutes.
6. Stir in the orange juice and zest. Season with salt and pepper.

SERVINGS: 4 TO 6 • PREPARATION TIME: 15 MINUTES

GREEN BEANS ARE A TERRIFIC SOURCE OF VITAMIN A AND POTASSIUM; THEY CONTAIN ABOUT 40 CALORIES PER CUP. WONDERFUL BEAN FLAVOR ENHANCERS INCLUDE DILL, GARLIC, CUMIN AND TARRAGON.

Green Beans with Mushrooms

Cook the green beans with the garlic as described above. Add 1 pound sliced mushrooms, sautéed in butter. Season with salt, pepper, and dried thyme. Eliminate the wine and orange zest. Stir in 2 tablespoons sour cream.

Green Beans with Bacon

Steam the green beans. Cook diced bacon in the skillet. Add the garlic. Transfer the cooked bacon and garlic to a bowl. Pour off all but 1 tablespoon of the bacon drippings. Add the green beans to the pan and cook for 2 minutes. Add the cooked bacon and garlic to the pan and stir to coat. Season with salt and pepper.

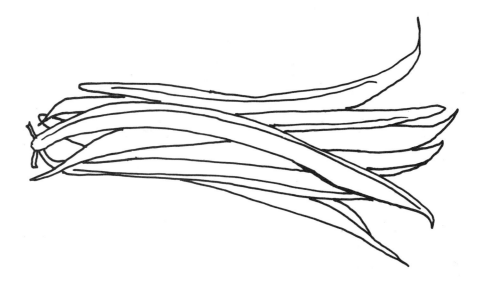

Asparagus Ribbons

THIN RIBBONS OF ASPARAGUS MAKE FOR AN ELEGANT AND FESTIVE VEGGIE PRESENTATION.

1 pound large, fresh asparagus spears
1 tablespoon olive oil
2 tablespoons sesame seeds
Juice of 1 medium lemon (about 2 tablespoons)
1 tablespoon soy sauce
Freshly ground pepper

1. Cut the tough end from the asparagus spears. Use a vegetable peeler to cut the spears, from stem to tops, into very thin slices. (A mandoline is an excellent tool for this job as well.)
2. Heat the olive oil over medium high heat. Toast the sesame seeds in the hot oil until golden, less than 1 minute.
3. Add the asparagus ribbons into the pan.
4. Toss with the lemon juice and soy sauce. Season with pepper. Cook until just warmed through, about 3 to 4 minutes.

SERVINGS: 4 TO 6 • PREPARATION TIME: 30 MINUTES

USE THIS SAME TECHNIQUE TO PREPARE AN OVER-THE-TOP SALAD. SHAVE THE ASPARAGUS AS DIRECTED ABOVE. TOSS WITH ORANGE SECTIONS AND CANDIED WALNUTS. ADD A DRIZZLE OF VINAIGRETTE AND TOP WITH TOASTED COCONUT. YOU CAN ALSO ADD RIBBONS OF ZUCCHINI AND YELLOW SQUASH TO FILL UP THE SALAD BOWL EVEN FURTHER.

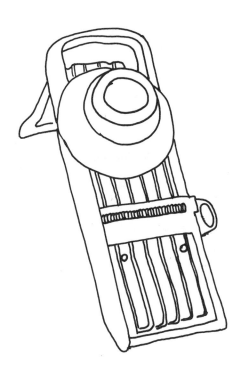

Warm Butternut Squash and Lentil Salad

JUST A SPOONFUL OF SUGAR ADDS SO MUCH FLAVOR TO THIS WARM AND NOURISHING AUTUMN DISH, SUPERB NO MATTER WHAT THE SEASON. SERVED WARM OR AT ROOM TEMPERATURE, THIS SALAD IS A WONDERFUL ADDITION TO ANY SUPPER BUFFET.

Butternut Squash Purée
Roast the squash as instructed in the recipe at right. Place into a food processor. Add 2 tablespoons butter, ½ cup of whipping cream, 2 teaspoons of orange zest and ¼ teaspoon of ground cinnamon. Pulse until smooth.

DRIZZLING GREAT QUALITY OLIVE OIL OVER THE DISH JUST BEFORE SERVING IS A GREAT WAY TO BOOST THE FLAVOR; USE OIL WITH A RICH ESSENCE. EXPERIMENT WITH TRUFFLE OIL, LEMON INFUSED OIL OR OLIVE OIL CONTAINING SPICY PEPPERS.

2 tablespoons butter
2 tablespoons olive oil, plus more for garnish
1 tablespoon brown sugar
1 teaspoon dried thyme
1 teaspoon ground cumin
½ teaspoon garlic powder
1 medium butternut squash, peeled and diced into 1-inch squares (about 2 cups)
1 large yellow onion, diced into ½-inch squares (about 1 cup)
Salt and freshly ground pepper
1 cup dried lentils (about 6 to 7 ounces uncooked)
2 cups chicken broth
2 tablespoons chopped fresh parsley

Preheat the oven to 375°.
1. Heat the butter and olive oil in a skillet over medium high heat.
2. Stir in the brown sugar, dried thyme, ground cumin, and garlic powder. Cook until the sugar dissolves. Remove from heat.
3. Place the vegetables into a baking dish. Pour the butter mixture over the butternut squash and onion. Stir to coat. Season with salt and pepper.
4. Roast until golden and crisp, turning once, about 30 minutes.
5. Cook the lentils in chicken broth until tender, about 20 minutes.
6. Place the lentils into a bowl.
7. Stir in the roasted vegetables and chopped fresh parsley.
8. Drizzle with additional olive oil and season with salt and pepper.

SERVINGS: 4 TO 6 • PREPARATION TIME: 45 MINUTES

Roasted Root Vegetables with Balsamic Glaze

ROASTING IS A WONDERFUL WAY TO PREPARE YOUR FAVORITE VEGGIES; THE PROCESS BRINGS OUT THEIR NATURAL SUGARS, WHICH ARE THEN ENHANCED WITH SUBTLE SEASONINGS. THE SIMPLE GLAZE USED IN THIS RECIPE ADDS SUCH ROBUST FLAVOR, YOU'LL WANT TO MAKE THIS DISH A ONCE-A-WEEK FAVORITE.

2 medium carrots, peeled and cut into 1-inch pieces
1 medium white onion, peeled and cut into 1-inch wedges
2 medium parsnips, peeled and cut into 1-inch pieces
1 medium sweet potato, peeled and cut into 1-inch pieces
4 large shallots, peeled
1 medium turnip, peeled and cut into 1-inch pieces
3 tablespoons olive oil
2 medium cloves garlic, minced about 2 teaspoons
1 teaspoon dried rosemary
1 teaspoon dried thyme
Salt and freshly ground pepper

2 tablespoons balsamic vinegar
1 tablespoon honey
1 teaspoon soy sauce
Zest of ½ medium orange (about 1 tablespoon)
Juice of 1 medium orange (about ⅓ cup)
2 tablespoons chopped fresh cilantro

Preheat the oven to 425°.

1. Place all of the vegetables into a large roasting pan.

2. Combine the olive oil, garlic and dried herbs in a small bowl.

3. Pour the olive oil mixture over the vegetables. Toss to coat. Season with salt and pepper.

4. Roast the veggies until just beginning to brown, turning once, about 30 minutes.

5. Combine the vinegar, honey, soy sauce, orange zest, orange juice and cilantro in a bowl.

6. Pour this mixture over the vegetables. Return the pan to the oven and cook for an additional 10 minutes, or until most of the liquid evaporates.

SERVINGS: 4 TO 6 • PREPARATION TIME: 30 MINUTES PREP PLUS 40 MINUTES ROASTING

More Ways with Roasted Veggies

Use your favorite combination of veggies for another roasted vegetable dish. Great choices include potato wedges, Brussels sprouts, red onions, beets, rutabaga, whole garlic cloves and tomatoes. Toss the veggies with olive oil and add your favorite dried seasonings such as cumin, coriander, cayenne pepper, paprika, and curry powder. Add a spoonful of honey to curb the spice.

Stuffed Poblano Peppers
with Roasted Tomato Sauce

THE FIRE OF THESE SPICY PEPPERS IS MUTED BY THE ROASTING PROCESS, BUT THEY STILL PACK ENOUGH HEAT TO SPICE UP THAT EVERYDAY MEAL.

Roasted Poblano Peppers
To roast poblano peppers, heat an outdoor grill over medium high heat. (Alternatively, you can char the peppers under a broiler or over a gas flame.) Place the peppers onto the grill. Cook the peppers until the skin begins to blister and turn brown. Rotate until all of the skin begins to char. Transfer the peppers and place them on your work surface. Cool until they are easy to handle. Use a paper towel to gently remove the charred skin from the pepper. Be careful to wash your hands each time they are exposed to the fiery seeds and veins.

6 large plum tomatoes, cut in half lengthwise (about 1 pound)
2 tablespoons olive oil
2 medium cloves garlic, minced (about 1 teaspoon)
Salt and freshly ground pepper
1 cup chicken broth

8 large poblano peppers, roasted
1 cup cooked white rice
4 ounces shredded Monterey Jack cheese (about 1 cup)
1 cup canned corn kernels, drained
1 cup canned black beans, drained
1 medium red bell pepper, seeded and finely diced (about ⅔ cup)
2 large shallots, minced (about 2 tablespoons)
2 tablespoons chopped fresh basil
2 tablespoons olive oil

Preheat the oven to 350°.
1. For the sauce, place the tomatoes onto a rimmed baking sheet. Drizzle with the olive oil and garlic. Season with salt and pepper. Roast until soft, about 30 minutes.
2. Transfer the tomatoes and the juices into a blender. Add the chicken stock. Pulse to purée.
3. Cut a slit in one side of each pepper. Carefully open the pepper. Use a sharp knife to remove the seeds and veins.
4. Place the rice into a bowl. Stir in the cheese, corn, black beans, red pepper, shallots, basil, and 2 tablespoons of olive oil. Season with salt and pepper.
5. Place ⅛ of the rice filling into each roasted pepper. Place each pepper into a baking dish that has been sprayed with vegetable oil spray. Cover the peppers with the roasted tomato sauce.
6. Bake until the cheese melts, about 15 minutes.

SERVINGS: 8 • PREPARATION TIME: 45 MINUTES

Roasted Peppers Stuffed with Tuna and Olive Salad

INSPIRED BY THE ARTISTIC FRENCH NICOISE SALAD, THE ADDITION OF ROASTED PEPPERS SERVES AS BOTH A FLAVOR BOOSTER AND AN EDIBLE CONTAINER.

3 large yellow or red bell peppers
1 8-ounce tuna steak
1 tablespoon olive oil
Salt and freshly ground pepper
2 large eggs, hard boiled and sliced
10 to 12 Nicoise (or other good quality) olives, pitted
4 to 6 2-inch red creamer potatoes, boiled until tender, cut in half
8 ounces haricots vert (or other seasonal green bean) blanched
1 2-ounce tin anchovies, packed in oil, drained

1 tablespoon Dijon mustard
1 tablespoon chopped fresh tarragon
1 medium clove garlic, minced about ½ teaspoon
Juice of 1 lemon (about 2 tablespoons)
⅓ cup tarragon vinegar
¾ cup olive oil

The health benefits of incorporating olives and olive oil into your diet were first widely acknowledged by the scientific community in the mid-1950's. The virtues of the Mediterranean diet have been promoted with increasing enthusiasm ever since. While there is no scientific consensus, numerous studies have shown the benefits of substituting monounsaturated fats, as found in olive oil, for the saturated fats found in meat and dairy products; it is now widely accepted that the consumption of excessive saturated fat increases the levels of cholesterol in the blood, which can lead to serious health conditions. So perk up your palate with the addition of a few olives everyday. As mama says, "It couldn't hurt!"

1. Char the outside of the peppers over a hot grill or flame, or underneath the broiler element in the oven. The peppers should be black on all sides. Place the peppers into a bag to steam for at least 15 minutes.
2. Brush the tuna steak with 1 tablespoon olive oil. Season with salt and pepper. Grill over a hot flame until just rare on the inside, about 4 minutes per side for a 1-inch thick steak.
3. Cut the tuna into bite size pieces and place into a bowl. Add the sliced egg, olives, boiled potatoes, green beans and anchovies. Toss with fresh pepper.
4. Whisk together the mustard, tarragon, garlic, lemon juice and vinegar.
5. Slowly whisk in ¾ cup olive oil. Set dressing aside.
6. Peel the charred skin from the peppers. Cut each one in half. Remove the seeds.
7. Place a pepper half on a plate. Place ⅙ of the tuna mixture into each half.
8. Drizzle the dressing over the tuna salad and peppers.

SERVINGS: 6 • PREPARATION TIME: 30 MINUTES

Creamed Spinach with Boursin Cheese

CREAMED SPINACH IS SO RICH AND THICK THAT IT IS ALMOST A MEAL IN ITSELF. THE ADDITION OF TANGY CHEESE, TAKES IT WAY, WAY OVER THE TOP. IF YOU ARE A PURIST, YOU CAN PREPARE THE DISH "NAKED"—AND IF YOU ARE ADVENTURESOME—GO AHEAD AND EXPERIMENT WITH THE CHEESE OF YOUR CHOICE.

LET'S GIVE A BIG WAH HOO TO THE PERSON WHO DECIDED TO PACKAGE PRE-WASHED SPINACH LEAVES IN A CONVENIENT PLASTIC BAG. THAT SAID; DON'T SHY AWAY FROM JUST PICKED SPINACH WHEN YOU ARE STROLLING THE FARMERS MARKET! CHOOSE SPINACH WITH DARK, CRISP AND FRAGRANT LEAVES (AVOID LIMP OR DISCOLORED LEAVES). REFRIGERATE IN A PLASTIC BAG FOR SEVERAL DAYS. POKE HOLES IN THE BAG TO ALLOW THE AIR TO CIRCULATE. BEFORE USING, PLACE THE SPINACH LEAVES IN A SINK FULL OF COLD WATER. THE GRIT WILL FALL TO THE BOTTOM. DRY THE LEAVES BEFORE CONTINUING WITH THE RECIPE.

2 tablespoons butter
2 large shallots, minced (about 2 tablespoons)
2 tablespoons all-purpose flour
1½ cups half and half
¼ teaspoon ground nutmeg
4 ounces Boursin cheese, crumbled (about 1 cup)
2 10-ounce packages fresh spinach leaves, washed, dried and chopped
Salt and freshly ground pepper
Parmesan cheese

1. Heat the butter in a large pot over medium high heat.
2. Add the shallots and cook until soft, about 3 to 4 minutes.
3. Stir in the flour until the mixture is bubbling.
4. Pour in the half and half. Stir until thickened, about 6 to 8 minutes. Season with nutmeg.
5. Add the cheese. Stir until the cheese is melted.
6. Add the spinach in batches, as it wilts down into the sauce. Season with salt and pepper.
7. Use an immersion blender to purée the spinach and the sauce.
8. Serve with a sprinkle of grated Parmesan cheese.

SERVINGS: 4 TO 6 • PREPARATION TIME: 40 MINUTES

Julienne Zucchini with Spinach and Basil Pesto

WHEN YOU TOP WARM, COOKED ZUCCHINI WITH FRAGRANT PESTO, THE
CHEESE MELTS AND THE ENTIRE DISH COMES TOGETHER IN HARMONY.
STORE EXTRA PESTO IN AN AIR TIGHT CONTAINER IN THE REFRIGERATOR
FOR SEVERAL DAYS.

2 cups fresh basil leaves
1 cup fresh spinach leaves, washed and dried
½ cup pine nuts, toasted (additional for garnish)
4 medium garlic cloves, chopped (about 2 teaspoons)
½ teaspoon salt
4 ounces grated Parmesan cheese (about ½ cup)
½ cup olive oil
4 large zucchini
Freshly ground pepper

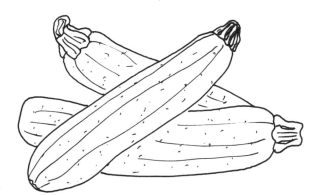

1. For pesto, place the basil, spinach,
pine nuts, garlic, salt and Parmesan
cheese into a blender. Pulse until combined. With the motor running, slowly
pour in the olive oil. Set aside.
2. Peel and julienne the zucchini (cut
into thin match-stick size pieces).
3. Place the zucchini into a colander,
over simmering water. Cover and steam
until just soft, about 2 to 3 minutes.
4. Transfer the zucchini to a bowl. Pour
½ cup of the pesto over top. Toss. Garnish with additional pine
nuts and additional freshly ground pepper.

SERVINGS: 4 • PREPARATION TIME: 30 MINUTES

Pasta with Zucchini, Chicken, and Pesto
Turn this simple side dish into an inspired pasta entrée. Prepare 12 ounces of your
favorite pasta. Grill 2 boneless, skinless chicken breasts and slice into thin strips.
Steam the zucchini. Drain the pasta and place in a large bowl. Add the sliced chick-
en and zucchini. Toss with as much pesto sauce as you prefer. Garnish with strips of
sun-dried tomatoes pack in olive oil and fresh basil leaves.

Marinated Beets

THESE BEETS ARE FRESHLY FLAVORED AND SERVED CRISP, NOT MUSHY.
MARINATING OVERNIGHT ADDS A FUN FLAVOR ZING. SERVE THE BEETS
TOSSED WITH YOUR FAVORITE SALAD GREENS, AND A TABLESPOON, PER-
HAPS, OF DICED RED ONION AND A HANDFUL OF FRESH ORANGE SEGMENTS.
WHEN HANDLING BEETS, USE PLASTIC GLOVES TO PREVENT TURNING YOUR
FINGERS RED!

Best Beets

Roasted beets are delicious and beautiful. Place beets in a baking dish and heat in the oven, set at 375°. Cook until soft, about 1 hour. Trim the leafy top and bottom stem. Peel and cut into wedges. Season the beets by heating olive oil in a skillet over medium high heat. Add your favorite spice combination. (I like a combination of ground cinnamon and nutmeg, brown sugar, cumin and chili powder. Toss the beets and stir to coat. Cook for 5 to 10 minutes until the beets are seasoned and warmed through.

6 2- to 3-inch diameter beets
Juice of ½ medium orange (about 2 to 3 tablespoons)
1 tablespoon red wine vinegar
1 tablespoon olive oil
Zest of ½ medium orange (about 1 tablespoon)
1 tablespoon chopped fresh mint
Salt and freshly ground pepper

Preheat the oven to 375°.

1. Wash the beets. Cut the bottom and top shoots from each beet and discard. Place the bulbs into a casserole dish with lid. Place about ½ inch of water in the bottom of the dish. (Use gloves!)

2. Cook until the beets begin to soften, about 40 to 45 minutes. (The beets will not be as soft as a cooked potato; however, you will be able to insert the tip of a sharp knife.

3. Allow the beets to cool to room temperature.

4. Use a knife to peel the beets and cut into ⅛-inch slices.

5. Place the sliced beets in a bowl. Pour in orange juice, vinegar, olive oil and season with orange zest, chopped fresh mint, salt, and pepper. Toss to coat.

6. Cover the dish and chill the beets overnight.

SERVINGS: 4 TO 6 • PREPARATION TIME: 1 HOUR PLUS MARINATING
OVERNIGHT

CONSIDER GROWING BEETS IN YOUR HOME GARDEN; THEY ARE A POPULAR ADDITION BECAUSE THEY ARE RELATIVELY EASY TO CULTIVATE, AND YOU CAN EAT MOST OF THE PLANT. BEETS CAN BE GROWN IN MANY DIFFERENT COLORS INCLUDING RED, YELLOW OR WHITE. THE TOPS OR "GREENS," ARE BEST WHEN THEY ARE YOUNG AND FRESH; THEY ARE EXCELLENT IN SALADS! WHEN THE PLANT IS OLDER, THE GREENS CAN BE COOKED. THE GREENS ARE EVEN MORE NUTRITIOUS THAN THE ROOTS. BEETS PREFER A COOLER CLIMATE, ALTHOUGH THEY ARE TOLERANT OF HEAT. TEMPERATURES OF 60 TO 65 F AND BRIGHT SUNNY DAYS ARE IDEAL FOR BEET PLANT GROWTH AND DEVELOPMENT. THEY CAN WITHSTAND COLD WEATHER SHORT OF SEVERE FREEZING, MAKING THEM A GOOD LONG-SEASON CROP.

Chapter 10

Shellfish and Fish Prepared Swimmingly

If you are dependent on FAST food to make your life more manageable, then I have a really big secret to share with you. Fast food really means FISH food. Yep, that's right! You can forget all those greasy burgers and soggy fries. In the time it takes for you to drive through your corner fast food joint, you can prepare a delicious, nutritious fish dish in the comfort of your own kitchen. What's better than that?

Due to modern farming and shipping practices, great varieties of fish are readily available in your grocery store or at your neighborhood fishmonger. The shrimp stored in your freezer was flash frozen on the boat that pulled them out of the sea. New breeds of fish are gaining popularity like Arctic char and barramundi, while favorites like sea bass and swordfish are abundant with better conservation management.

In most cases, fish is baked, grilled, poached or fried in minutes. Marinating takes place in twenty minutes or less; any accompanying sauces are prepared in the time it takes to cook the fish. The only thing you have to do to insure a quick, nourishing fish meal is to remember to buy it!

In this chapter, you will find classic shellfish dishes with updated modern counterparts. For example, the baby scallops appearing in the Coquilles St. Jacques recipe are compared with "diver" scallops in a California restaurant inspired dish. Contrast classic fried calamari with today's lighter lemon marinated, charred calamari preparation. Perfect crab cakes are a delicacy, but just wait until you give tuna cakes a try. Classic Sole Meuniere is a French dish prepared at the finest restaurants, and can be easily replicated in your kitchen. When that same sole is poached, a completely new flavor experience comes front and center.

Fish is a wonderful addition to a well balanced meal plan. Incorporating several fish dishes into your weekly menu is bound to start a fresh, fast-food tradition—one that I'm sure you will love.

Seafood Salad in Avocado Boats

SERVE THIS DISH COLD ON CHILLED PLATES FOR MAXIMUM ENJOYMENT. MAKE A DOUBLE BATCH OF DRESSING TO USE FOR CRUDITÉS DIP—IT'S THAT GOOD!

1 pound cooked shrimp, shells and tails removed, chopped
1 pound cooked lobster meat, chopped
2 medium celery ribs, diced (about 1 cup)

1 cup mayonnaise
1½ cup prepared chili sauce
2 tablespoons prepared horseradish
1 tablespoon Worcestershire sauce
1 teaspoon yellow mustard
4 or more drops hot pepper sauce
Salt and freshly ground pepper

3 large ripe avocados, cut in half, pitted
1 pint cherry tomatoes, cut in half
Lemon wedges
Fresh dill sprigs

To HALVE AN AVOCADO, USE A SHARP KNIFE, AND CUT IN HALF LENGTHWISE, CUTTING AROUND THE CENTER PIT. CAREFULLY ROTATE EACH HALF IN OPPOSITE DIREC-TIONS TO SEPARATE. USE THE TIP OF A KNIFE TO STAB THE PIT AND REMOVE. (ALTER-NATIVELY, YOU CAN USE A LARGE SPOON TO SCOOP UNDERNEATH THE PIT AND LIFT IT OUT.) TO PREVENT DISCOL-ORATION, SQUEEZE FRESH LEMON JUICE ON TOP OF THE CUT SIDE OF THE AVOCADO. SOME BELIEVE THAT IF YOU STORE A CUT AVOCADO WITH THE PIT IN PLACE, THAT THIS WILL PREVENT DISCOL-ORATION. NOT SO! THE PIT PREVENTS AIR FROM GETTING TO THE AVOCADO ONLY WHERE IT IS PLACED. OTHER AREAS WILL TURN BROWN WITH OXIDATION.

1. Place the shrimp, lobster and celery into a bowl.
2. Whisk together the mayonnaise, chili sauce, horseradish, Worcestershire, and mustard. Add as much hot pepper sauce as you prefer. Season with salt and pepper.
3. Pour half of the sauce over the seafood. Toss to coat.
4. Place an avocado half onto a chilled plate. Place a scoop of seafood salad into the center. Garnish with tomatoes. Repeat until you have filled all of the avocados. Drizzle the remaining dressing over the filled avocados. Garnish with lemon wedges and fresh dill sprigs.

SERVINGS: 6 • PREPARATION
TIME: 20 MINUTES

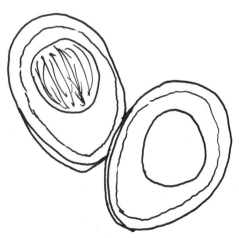

Shrimp Fajitas

READY IN JUST MINUTES, THIS DISH IS PERFECT FOR WEEKDAY SUPPERS AND IMPROMPTU GUESTS. IN PLACE OF TORTILLAS, YOU CAN SERVE THE SHRIMP OVER RICE OR PASTA; OR, IF YOU PREFER, SUBSTITUTE SHRIMP WITH THE FRESH CATCH OF THE DAY, LIKE DOLPHIN OR SNAPPER.

1½ pounds large uncooked shrimp, peeled and deveined (about 24)
4 tablespoons olive oil
2 medium cloves garlic, minced (about 1 teaspoon)
½ teaspoon ground cumin
½ teaspoon chili powder
¼ teaspoon red pepper flakes
Juice of 1 lime (about 2 tablespoons)
Salt and freshly ground pepper

1 medium jalapeño pepper, seeded and thinly sliced (about 2 tablespoons)
1 large red bell pepper, seeded and thinly sliced (about 1 cup)
1 large green bell pepper, seeded and thinly sliced (about 1 cup)
1 large red onion, thinly sliced (about 1 cup)

4 10-inch, or 8 6-inch flour tortillas, warm
Sour cream
Chopped fresh cilantro
Salsa

1. Place the shrimp into a bowl.
2. Whisk together 2 tablespoons olive oil, the garlic, ground cumin, chili powder, red pepper flakes and lime juice. Pour this mixture over the shrimp and toss to coat. Season with salt and pepper.
3. Heat the remaining 2 tablespoons of olive oil in a skillet over medium-high heat.
4. Add the vegetables to the skillet. Cook until the edges begin to turn brown, about 5 minutes. Season with salt and pepper.
5. Add the shrimp to the pan. Stir and cook until the shrimp turn pink and opaque, about 3 minutes.
6. Place a tablespoon or more of the shrimp mixture into the center of a warm tortilla. Roll the tortilla, and garnish with sour cream and chopped fresh cilantro. Serve with a dollop of fresh salsa.

SERVINGS: 4 • PREPARATION TIME: 15 MINUTES

FRESH SHRIMP ARE HIGHLY PERISHABLE. SO, UNLESS YOU ARE ABOARD THE SHRIMPER'S BOAT OR HANGING AROUND THE DOCKS WAITING FOR HIM TO RETURN, YOU CAN BE SURE THE SHRIMP YOU GET FROM YOUR FISHMONGER HAVE BEEN FROZEN. LUCKILY, SHRIMP FREEZE BEAUTIFULLY AND THAW PERFECTLY. IN FACT, THE SHRIMP DISPLAYED ON ICE AT THE GROCER'S HAVE BEEN THAWED AND SHOULD BE MARKED "PREVIOUSLY FROZEN." SHOPPERS ARE BECOMING MORE SAVVY ABOUT THE SHRIMP FRESHNESS ISSUE. FOR THAT REASON, MANY MARKETS OFFER BAGS OF FRESH-FROZEN SHRIMP THAT ARE EASY TO STORE IN YOUR FREEZER. THESE FROZEN SHRIMP COME IN ALL SIZES AND MAY BE PEELED AND DEVEINED, TAIL ON OR TAIL OFF. THAW ONLY THE AMOUNT OF SHRIMP YOU PLAN TO USE, AND DO NOT REFREEZE EXTRAS. TO THAW, YOU NEED ONLY PLACE THE SHRIMP INTO A COLANDER IN THE SINK. RUN COLD WATER OVER TOP FOR 5 MINUTES; OR, YOU CAN PLACE FROZEN SHRIMP IN THE REFRIGERATOR OVERNIGHT. USE RAW SHRIMP IN RECIPES LIKE THIS ONE FOR FAJITAS. HOWEVER, IF YOU ARE SIMPLY LOOKING FOR A GREAT SHRIMP COCKTAIL, YOU CAN BOIL THE SHRIMP IN SALTED WATER FOR 3 MINUTES OR UNTIL THEY TURN PINK. CHILL FOR 30 MINUTES OR MORE AND YOU ARE READY TO EAT!

Fried Calamari with Tuna Caper Dipping Sauce

THE SECRET TO PERFECT CALAMARI IS IN MAKING SURE YOU DON'T OVER-
COOK IT. THE PIQUANT SAUCE ADDS AN INTERESTING TWIST. TOMATO BASIL
SAUCE IS EXCELLENT, TOO. (SEE THE RECIPE ON PAGE 190). DON'T FORGET A
SPRINKLING OF FRESH LEMON JUICE OVER THE TOP!

SQUID IS A MEMBER OF THE
MOLLUSK FAMILY AND A
COUSIN TO THE OCTOPUS.
THE MEAT HAS A FIRM, CHEWY
TEXTURE, YET A MILD, ALMOST
SWEET TASTE. FOR THIS REA-
SON, IT DOES WELL WITH SIM-
PLE PREPARATIONS. YOU CAN
PURCHASE FRESH SQUID AND
CLEAN IT YOURSELF. MORE
OFTEN THAN NOT, CLEANED
SQUID IS AVAILABLE AT YOUR
LOCAL FISH MARKET.

1 cup mayonnaise
1 6-ounce can tuna, packed in oil
2 tablespoons capers, drained and rinsed
Juice of 1 medium lemon (about 2 tablespoons)
2 tablespoons chopped fresh cilantro
½ teaspoon hot paprika
Salt and freshly ground pepper

1 pound uncooked calamari, cleaned
1 cup all-purpose flour
¼ teaspoon cayenne pepper
Salt

Canola oil

1. To make the sauce, place the mayonnaise, tuna, capers, lemon juice, and cilantro into a blender. Pulse to emulsify. Season with paprika, salt and pepper.
2. Cut the bodies of the calamari into thin rings and tentacles.
3. Season the flour with cayenne pepper and salt.
4. Heat canola oil in a deep pot to 365°.
5. Dredge the calamari rings in the flour. Shake off excess. Carefully drop the rings into the hot oil. Fry until golden brown, about 30 seconds. Use a slotted spoon (or Chinese wire basket) to remove the calamari from the oil. Drain on paper towels. Continue with the tentacles.

SERVINGS: 4 TO 6 • PREPARATION TIME: 20 MINUTES

Lemon Charred Calamari

THE HARDEST PART OF THIS RECIPE IS TAKEN CARE OF BY YOUR FISH MON-GER—CLEANING THE SQUID. THE REST IS EASY AND ELEGANT. THIS DISH IS PERFECT ON ITS OWN, BUT IF YOU WANT TO SPARK IT EVEN MORE, TRY ADDING A DIPPING SAUCE LIKE HOT MANGO KETCHUP (SEE THE RECIPE ON PAGE 165) OR ORANGE SESAME MAYONNAISE (SEE PAGE 125).

1 pound uncooked calamari, cleaned
2 tablespoons olive oil
2 medium garlic cloves, minced (about 1 teaspoon)
¼ teaspoon dried red pepper flakes
Salt
Juice of 1 medium lemon (about 2 tablespoons)
2 tablespoons chopped fresh parsley

1. Cut the bodies of the calamari into 2 pieces.
2. Combine the olive oil with garlic, red pepper flakes and season with salt. Brush the calamari with the seasoned oil.
3. Heat a grill pan over medium high heat. Grill the calamari until it just begins to char, about 1 to 2 minutes per side. Transfer to a platter. Drizzle with lemon juice and chopped fresh parsley.

SERVINGS: 4 TO 6 • PREPARATION TIME: 15 MINUTES

THERE IS ONLY ONE SECRET TO COOKING DELICIOUS CALA-MARI, AND THAT IS THE AMOUNT OF COOKING TIME. CALAMARI MUST BE COOKED QUICKLY OVER HIGH HEAT OR SLOWLY IN STEWS OR SOUPS. ANYTHING IN BETWEEN WILL YIELD A CHEWY, GUMMY MESS.

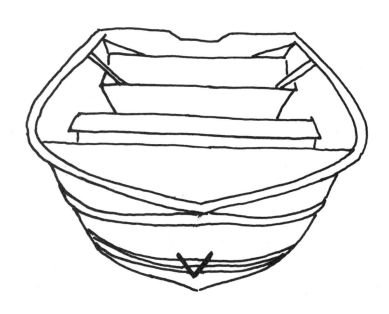

Baked Stuffed Lobster in Mornay Sauce

THIS DISH WORKS WELL AS AN ELEGANT LUNCHEON DISH, OR FABULOUS
FIRST COURSE FOR YOUR SIT-DOWN DINNER PARTY; SINCE IT IS SO VERY
EASY TO PREPARE, IT ALSO MAKES FOR A CASUAL COFFEE TABLE SUPPER
WITH FRIENDS. SERVE THE LOBSTER AND RICH SAUCE IN THE TAIL SHELL
FOR A CLASSY PRESENTATION. YOU CAN ALSO POUR THE LOBSTER AND
SAUCE OVER SIMPLE BRUSCHETTA OR FLUFFY RICE. GARNISH WITH CURLS
OF LEMON PEEL.

4 medium lobster tails, split or 2 whole lobsters (see sidebar, page 233)

4 cups milk
1 bay leaf
1 large shallot, minced (about 1 tablespoon)
½ teaspoon ground white pepper

4 tablespoons butter (½ stick)
4 tablespoons all-purpose flour
2 ounces grated white American cheese (about ½ cup)
½ cup cream
¼ teaspoon ground nutmeg
Salt

2 tablespoons butter, melted
1 cup fresh bread crumbs

Preheat the oven to 350°.

1. Place the split lobster tails onto a baking sheet. Bake for 8 to 10 minutes or until the lobster meat is just cooked. Be careful not to burn the shells. Remove the lobster meat from the shells, reserving the tail shell for presentation. Cut the lobster meat into ½-inch cubes.

2. Increase the oven heat to broil setting.

3. Heat the milk in a saucepan over medium high heat.

4. Add the bay leaf, shallot, and ground white pepper. Cook until the milk begins to boil. Remove the pan from the heat. Let sit for 15 minutes. Strain through a sieve reserving the infused milk.

5. Heat 4 tablespoons butter in a saucepan over medium high heat. Whisk in the flour until smooth. Cook for 2 minutes, whisking constantly.

6. Pour in the infused milk. Whisk over medium heat until the sauce thickens, about 7 to 10 minutes.

7. Remove the sauce from the heat and stir in the cheese and cream. Season with ground nutmeg, salt and ground white pepper.

8. Stir the cooked lobster meat into the sauce.

9. Place remaining 2 tablespoons melted butter into a bowl.

To insure that your lob-
ster dish is the best ever,
follow these tips when
choosing and storing live
lobster. First and last,
do not name your lobster;
this will prevent emotion-
al upheaval when meal
preparation begins! Do
choose an active lobster,
one with his claws held up
(not hanging) and with the
tail curling underneath
the body. Do not be afraid
of the lobster's appear-
ance. Black marks or
holes in the shell are
most often a result in
wear and tear, and may
indicate an older lobster
that has not recently
shed its shell; these are
not harmful in any way.
Likewise, quality live lobsters are often greenish
brown or black, but can
also be blue, yellow,
red, or, very rarely,
white. Color does not
affect flavor or texture.
Do choose live lobsters
that are stored in circu-
lating sea water tanks in
the store or restaurant.
Once you bring your live
lobster home, do store
them in an open container
in the refrigerator, cov-
ered with seaweed, seawa-
ter-dampened towels, or
newspaper to keep the
gills moist. Hard shell
lobsters can be kept alive
for 24—48 hours in this
manner. New shell lob-
sters can be stored for
12—24 hours. Do try to
cook your lobsters as
soon as possible!

10. Add the bread crumbs to the bowl and toss.

11. Place the lobster tail shells into a baking dish. Fill each shell with the lobster cream mixture. Sprinkle with bread crumbs.

12. Place the baking dish under the broiler and cook until the bread crumbs begin to turn golden, and the lobster mixture is heated through and bubbling.

SERVINGS: 4 • PREPARATION TIME: 30 MINUTES

> WHEN YOU'RE READY FOR AN EXCITING CHALLENGE, USE THE ABOVE RECIPE TO STUFF A WHOLE LOBSTER. COOK THE LOBSTER IN BOILING WATER UNTIL IT TURNS BRIGHT PINK, ABOUT 10 TO 20 MINUTES, DEPENDING ON THE SIZE. DRAIN THE LOBSTER AND SPLIT IN HALF. PULL THE MEAT FROM THE TAIL AND CLAWS. RESERVE THE CAVITY OF THE LOBSTER AND FILL AS DESCRIBED ABOVE.

Lobster in Arrabiata Sauce

INFUSING TOMATOES WITH A DICED WHOLE CHILI—SEEDS AND ALL- SPICES UP THIS SAUCE! YOU CAN TONE DOWN THE HEAT BY REMOVING THE VEINS AND SEEDS FROM THE INSIDE OF THE PEPPER, OR BY ADDING A TEASPOON OF SUGAR TO THE SAUCE.

2 tablespoons olive oil
2 medium cloves garlic, minced (about 1 teaspoon)
12 large plum tomatoes, cut into quarters (about 4 cups)
1 medium poblano pepper, finely diced
½ cup fresh basil leaves

4 (1 to 1¼ pounds) whole lobsters, cooked (about 2 pounds cooked lobster meat)
1 pound pasta, cooked

1. Heat the olive oil in a saucepan over medium high heat.

2. Cook the garlic in the olive oil for 3 minutes.

3. Add the tomatoes and poblano pepper to the pan.

4. Reduce the heat. Simmer for 1 hour, uncovered until the sauce thickens.

5. Add the fresh basil leaves and cook for 5 minutes more.

6. Use an immersion blender, food mill or food processor to purée the sauce.

7. Remove the lobster meat from the shell. Cut into ½-inch pieces.

8. Add the lobster meat to the sauce. Cook over medium heat until just warmed through, about 5 minutes.

9. Serve over pasta.

SERVINGS: 4 • PREPARATION TIME: 15 MINUTES PLUS 1 HOUR TO SIMMER

WHEN BUYING WHOLE (COOKED) LOBSTERS, MAKE SURE THEIR TAILS ARE CURLED; THIS IS A GOOD SIGN THEY WERE ALIVE WHEN COOKED. COOKED LOBSTER MEAT SHOULD BE SWEET SMELLING AND SNOW-WHITE. ASK YOUR FISHMONGER WHEN THE LOBSTERS IN HIS TANK WERE CAUGHT. SOME MARKETS KEEP LOBSTERS FOR A WEEK OR MORE, AND THESE WON'T BE AS SUCCULENT AS FRESH-CAUGHT LOBSTER. FOR A SINGLE GOOD-SIZED SERVING, PLAN ON 8 OUNCES OF COOKED LOBSTER MEAT PER PERSON.

Coquilles St. Jacques

FOUND IN THE BEST FRENCH RESTAURANTS, THIS DISH TAKES ADVANTAGE OF TINY BAY SCALLOPS; IT CAN BE SERVED AS AN INDIVIDUAL FIRST COURSE, OR AS AN ENTRÉE DESIGNED FOR TWO.

BAY SCALLOPS ARE HARD TO FIND AND, SUBSEQUENTLY, EXPENSIVE; THEY LIVE ON THE EAST COAST AND ARE QUITE SMALL, MEASURING IN AT ABOUT ½-INCH IN DIAMETER. THERE ARE ABOUT 100 OF THESE TINY MORSELS TO THE POUND; THEIR TINY SIZE IS WHY YOU MUST TAKE EXTREME CARE IN NOT OVERCOOKING THEM, LEST THEY GET TOUGH.

6 tablespoons butter (¾ stick)
2 large shallots, minced (about 2 tablespoons)
½ cup white wine
1 pound bay scallops
8 ounces button mushrooms, thinly sliced (about 2 cups)
Juice of 1 medium lemon (about 2 tablespoons)
¼ cup all-purpose flour
1 cup half and half
½ teaspoon cayenne pepper
Salt
Grated Parmesan cheese
Fresh thyme sprigs

Preheat the oven to the broil setting
1. Heat 1 tablespoon butter in a sauce pan over medium high heat. Cook the shallots until just soft. Add the wine.
2. Place the bay scallops into the sauce pan. Reduce the heat to medium. Simmer the scallops in the wine until just cooked, about 2 to 3 minutes. Use a slotted spoon to transfer the scallops to a bowl. Reduce the remaining liquid to about ⅓ cup. Transfer the reduced scallop liquid to a separate bowl.
3. Heat 2 more tablespoons butter in the same sauce pan over medium high heat. Cook the mushrooms in the butter until soft and just beginning to brown, about 4 to 6 minutes. Transfer the mushrooms to the bowl containing the scallops. Season with lemon juice. Toss.
4. Heat the remaining 3 tablespoons butter in the saucepan over medium high heat. Whisk in the flour and cook until bubbling. Pour in the reserved scallop cooking liquid and whisk until smooth.
5. Pour in the half and half and whisk until thickened, about 6 to 8 minutes. Season with cayenne pepper and salt.
6. Divide the scallops and mushrooms, among 6 individual ramekins or shells, or 2 individual casserole skillets.
7. Cover the scallops and mushrooms with the sauce. Sprinkle with finely grated Parmesan cheese.
8. Place the shells or ramekins onto a baking sheet. Broil, until the cheese begins to brown, about 5 minutes. Garnish with sprigs of fresh thyme.

SERVINGS: 6 AS A FIRST COURSE • PREPARATION TIME: 45 MINUTES

Diver Scallops with Peas, Wild Mushrooms, and Cabernet Sauce

MY INSPIRATION FOR THIS DISH COMES FROM A WONDERFUL RESTAURANT IN SAN DIEGO CALLED PAMPELMOUSSE. WHEN I ASKED WHAT DIVER SCALLOPS WERE, THE CHEF REPLIED, "SCALLOPS THAT THE DIVERS PICK BY HAND!" NO WONDER THEY WERE THE BEST I EVER HAD! FOR A CLOSE TASTING RIVAL, FEEL FREE TO SUBSTITUTE WITH FRESH SEA SCALLOPS.

¾ pound diver scallops
Salt and freshly ground pepper
2 to 4 tablespoons butter
2 to 4 tablespoons olive oil
1 small white onion, finely diced (about ½ cup)
4 ounces Baby portobello mushrooms, sliced (about 1 cup)
4 ounces shitake mushrooms, sliced (about 1 cup)
2 medium cloves garlic, minced (about 1 teaspoon)
1 cup cabernet wine
1 cup frozen peas, thawed
1 tablespoon all-purpose flour mixed with ¼ cup cold water
1 tablespoon chopped fresh thyme, plus extra sprigs for garnish

1. Season the scallops with salt and pepper.

2. Heat 1 tablespoon butter and 1 tablespoon olive oil in a skillet over medium high heat. Sear the scallops, in batches, until browned on both sides and just opaque in the center, about 1 minute per side. Transfer to a platter and keep warm. Repeat until all of the scallops have been seared. You may use additional butter and olive oil in between batches.

3. Heat 1 more tablespoon butter and olive oil in the same skillet over medium high heat. Add the onions and cook until soft, about 2 to 4 minutes.

4. Add the mushrooms and garlic and cook until soft and just beginning to brown, about 4 to 6 minutes.

5. Pour in the wine and stir in the peas. Simmer until the liquid is reduced by half, about 5 minutes.

6. Stir in a small amount of flour mixed with cold water to thicken the sauce. Stir in the thyme and season with salt and pepper.

7. Ladle the sauce onto a serving platter. Place the scallops on top of the sauce. Garnish with fresh thyme sprigs.

SERVINGS: 4 TO 6 • PREPARATION TIME: 30 MINUTES

SEA SCALLOPS ARE MUCH LARGER THAN BAY SCALLOPS, AVERAGING ABOUT 1 ½-INCHS IN DIAMETER. THERE ARE USUALLY ABOUT 30 TO THE POUND, THUS EVEN A HEARTY APPETITE WILL BE SATISFIED WITH 4 BIG SCALLOPS. THE MEAT IS A LITTLE CHEWIER THAN SMALLER SCALLOPS, BUT STILL HAS A SWEET TASTE.

Sautéed Crab Cakes with Three Sauces

DELICATE CRAB CAKES ARE ENHANCED WITH THREE DISTINCTIVE SAUCES.
THE SECRET IS TO GENTLY MIX AND FORM THE CRAB CAKES, THOROUGHLY
CHILLING THEM BEFORE SAUTÉING.

CRABMEAT WILL DIFFER IN
PRICE, BASED ON THE TYPE
OF CRAB AND THE PART
OF THE CRAB THE MEAT COMES
FROM. IN ALL CASES, CARE-
FULLY PICKING THROUGH THE
MEAT BEFORE YOU BEGIN THE
RECIPE, INSURES YOU DON'T
FIND A SMALL PIECE OF
SHELL IN THE FINAL DISH.

1½ pounds lump crabmeat
3 cups Japanese (Panko) bread crumbs
4 green onions, thinly sliced (about ¼ cup)
1 medium jalapeño pepper, seeded and diced (about 2 tablespoons)
2 tablespoons chopped fresh parsley
4 eggs
Juice of 1 lemon (about 2 tablespoons)
1 teaspoon Worcestershire sauce
½ teaspoon Dijon mustard
½ teaspoon cayenne pepper
½ teaspoon salt
2 to 4 tablespoons vegetable oil

Tartar Sauce:
1 cup mayonnaise
2 tablespoons sweet pickle relish
2 green onions, thinly sliced (about 2 tablespoons)
Juice of 1 lemon (about 2 tablespoons)
1 tablespoon capers, rinsed and drained
1 tablespoon chopped fresh parsley
1 tablespoon chopped fresh chives

Remoulade Sauce:
½ cup mayonnaise
½ cup Dijon mustard
½ large red bell pepper, seeded and chopped (about ½ cup)
2 green onions, chopped (about 2 tablespoons)
1 tablespoon ketchup
2 medium anchovy fillets
1 tablespoon chopped fresh dill
1 tablespoon chopped fresh cilantro

Spicy Lemon Aioli:
1 cup mayonnaise
Juice of 2 lemons (about ¼ cup)
4 medium garlic cloves, minced (about 2 teaspoons)
1 tablespoon tomato paste
1 teaspoon hot paprika

Mesclun salad mix
Olive oil
Lemon juice

1. Carefully pick through the crab meat to remove any shells.

2. Place the crabmeat, 1 cup of the bread crumbs, green onions, jalapeño and parsley into a bowl.

3. In a separate bowl, whisk together the eggs, lemon juice, Worcestershire sauce, mustard, pepper and salt.

4. Gently combine the wet ingredients with the crabmeat, making sure to keep the crabmeat pieces in tact.

5. Spread 1 cup of the bread crumbs onto a baking sheet.

6. Form the crab mixture into 8 cakes. Place the cakes onto the bread crumbs. Sprinkle the remaining bread crumbs over top and around the cakes to coat. Refrigerate for at least 1 hour.

7. Heat 2 tablespoons vegetable oil in a skillet over medium high heat. Cook the crab cakes in batches, turning once, until both sides are golden brown, about 3 to 4 minutes per side. Use additional oil as needed. Drain on paper towels.

8. For tartar sauce, combine all of the ingredients in a bowl. Season with salt and pepper. Chill.

9. For Remoulade sauce, combine all of the ingredients in the bowl of a food processor. Pulse to combine. Season with salt and pepper. Chill.

10. For spicy aioli, combine all of the ingredients in a bowl. Season with salt and pepper. Chill.

11. Serve the crab cakes on a bed of mesclun salad, lightly dressed with olive oil and lemon juice. Place a dollop of each sauce on the plate.

SERVINGS: 4 TO 6 • PREPARATION TIME: 30 MINUTES PLUS 1 HOUR TO CHILL

Tuna Cakes with Avocado Mayonnaise

NOT YOUR MOTHER'S FRIDAY NIGHT TUNA CAKES, THESE ARE PREPARED
WITH FRESH TUNA AND DRESSED IN A RICH, AVOCADO MAYONNAISE. MAKE
MINI-CAKES FOR YOUR NEXT DINNER PARTY APPY.

1 large avocado, peeled, pitted and diced (about 1 cup)
½ cup mayonnaise
Zest of 2 medium lemons (about 2 tablespoons)
Juice of 1 medium lemon (about 2 tablespoons)
½ teaspoon ground cumin
Salt and freshly ground pepper

2 8-ounce tuna steaks
1 medium red bell pepper, seeded and finely diced (about ½ cup)
1 bunch (6 to 8) green onions, chopped (about ½ cup)
2 tablespoons chopped fresh mint
2 tablespoons chopped fresh tarragon
¼ cup fresh bread crumbs
Juice of 1 medium lemon (about 2 tablespoons)
1 tablespoon mayonnaise
1 large egg, beaten
1½-inch piece ginger, grated (about 1 teaspoon)

½ cup fresh bread crumbs
2 tablespoons canola oil

FRESH BREAD CRUMBS WORK
WELL IN MOST FISH CAKE
RECIPES. PREPARE BREAD
CRUMBS USING FRESH, WHITE
BREAD. REMOVE THE CRUSTS
FROM THE BREAD. CUT THE
BREAD INTO CUBES. PLACE
THE CUBES INTO THE BOWL
OF A FOOD PROCESSOR.
PULSE UNTIL THE CUBES
FORM COARSE CRUMBS. FIVE
SLICES OF BREAD WILL PRO-
DUCE ABOUT 1 CUP OF
CRUMBS.

1. Place the avocado, mayonnaise, lemon zest, 2 tablespoons
lemon juice, and cumin into a blender. Pulse to combine.
Season with salt and pepper. Chill.
2. Cut the tuna into chunks. Place it into the bowl of a food
processor. Pulse to finely chop the tuna. Transfer to a bowl.
3. Add the red pepper, onions, mint, tarragon, ¼ cup bread
crumbs, 2 remaining tablespoons lemon juice, mayonnaise, egg
and ginger to the bowl. Season with salt and pepper. Use your
hands to gently combine all of the ingredients. Form into 6 patties.
4. Dredge each patty in the remaining bread crumbs.
5. Heat 2 tablespoons canola oil in a skillet over medium high
heat. Cook the tuna cakes in the skillet until golden, about 3
minutes. Turn and cook until browned, about 3 to 4 minutes
more. Serve the tuna cakes with the avocado mayonnaise.

SERVINGS: 4 • PREPARATION TIME: 30 MINUTES

Baked Halibut with Julienne Vegetables and Buttery Dill Sauce

HALIBUT IS A DELICATELY FLAVORED FISH THAT WORKS EXCEPTIONALLY WELL WITH QUITE A FEW MOUTH WATERING COMBINATIONS. IF HALIBUT IS NOT AVAILABLE, SUBSTITUTE WITH ANOTHER FIRM, WHITE FISH SUCH AS SEA BASS. THIS SIMPLE DISH IS ONE OF MY FAVORITES.

4 8-ounce halibut steaks
Salt and pepper
2 tablespoons olive oil

2 tablespoons butter
2 large carrots, cut into julienne (about 1 cup)
2 large zucchini, cut into julienne (about 1 cup)
2 large yellow squash, cut into julienne (about 1 cup)
2 tablespoons chopped fresh tarragon

4 large shallots, minced, about ¼ cup
¼ cup tarragon vinegar
¼ cup white wine
½ cup cream
2 tablespoons chopped fresh dill
4 tablespoons butter, chilled, cut into pieces

Preheat the oven to 400°.

I. Season the halibut with salt and pepper. Drizzle with olive oil. Place in a shallow baking dish. Bake until the fish is cooked and opaque, about 10 to 12 minutes.

2. Heat 2 tablespoons butter in a skillet over medium high heat. Cook the carrots, zucchini and squash in the skillet until soft, about 6 minutes. Stir in the tarragon. Season with salt and pepper. Keep warm.

3. For the sauce, cook the shallots and the vinegar in a sauce pan over medium high heat until the liquid is absorbed, about 3 to 4 minutes. Add the wine and cook until the liquid evaporates, about 3 to 4 minutes more. Stir in the cream and the dill. With the sauce at a slow simmer, whisk in the butter until just melted. Season with salt and pepper.

4. Place a fish fillet onto a dinner plate. Spoon the veggies around the fish. Top with the sauce.

SERVINGS: 4 • PREPARATION TIME: 30 MINUTES

WHEN YOU ARE PURCHASING FRESH FISH, REMEMBER TO USE YOUR SENSE(S). FIRST, LOOK AT THE FISH. THE EYES, SCALES, AND FLESH SHOULD BE BRIGHT, NOT DULL. THE FISH SHOULD BE DISPLAYED ON ICE, NOT IN WATER. SECONDLY, SMELL THE FISH. AVOID ANY FISH WITH STRONG ODORS. THE FISH SHOULD SMELL LIKE THE OCEAN. FINALLY, TOUCH THE FISH TO MAKE SURE THAT IT IS FIRM, NOT STICKY OR SLIMY.

Ginger and Soy Marinated Halibut

THE TANGY MARINADE IN THIS DISH TAKES THE FLAVOR OF HALIBUT FROM MILD TO MOUTH WATERING. SERVE WITH FRESH VEGGIES AND A CITRUS SALAD FOR A GREAT MID-WEEK SUPPER.

HALIBUT MEAT IS FIRM, LOW FAT, WHITE, AND MILD-FLAVORED; IT'S THE PERFECT FOOD TO INCORPORATE INTO A WELL-BALANCED MEAL PLAN. FRESH HALIBUT IS AVAILABLE YEAR ROUND AND ESPECIALLY PREVALENT FROM MARCH TO SEPTEMBER. FROZEN HALIBUT IS A GOOD SUBSTITUTE.

4 6-ounce halibut steaks
2 cups soy sauce
½ cup brown sugar
1 medium jalapeño pepper, seeded and thinly sliced (about 2 tablespoons)
½ cup chopped fresh cilantro
1 2-inch piece ginger, grated (about 2 tablespoons)
Salt and freshly ground sugar
Olive oil

1. Place the halibut steaks into a shallow baking dish.
2. Whisk together the soy sauce, brown sugar, jalapeño pepper, cilantro and ginger. Season with salt and pepper. Pour the marinade over the fish. Turn to coat all sides. Cover with plastic wrap and refrigerate for 20 minutes.
3. Heat a grill pan over medium high heat. Drizzle the pan with olive oil.
4. Remove the fish from the marinade. Shake off excess. Place the filets into the grill pan. Cook until browned, about 6 to 8 minutes. Turn and cook until golden, about 6 to 8 minutes more.

SERVINGS: 4 • PREPARATION TIME: 30 MINUTES

Yogurt-Marinated Chilean Sea Bass
with Coconut and Chutney

THIS TRADITIONAL INDIAN-SPICED PREPARATION WILL WORK WITH OTHER MILD FLAVORED FISH, LIKE HALIBUT OR SOLE. FRESH COCONUT AND CHUTNEY ARE PERFECT ACCOMPANIMENTS FOR THE SPICY MARINADE.

1 cup plain yogurt
1 bunch (6 to 8) green onions, chopped (about ½ cup)
1 2-inch piece ginger, grated (about 2 tablespoons)
2 medium cloves garlic, minced (about 1 teaspoon)
Juice of ½ lime (about 1 tablespoon)
1 medium jalapeño pepper, seeded and diced (about 2 tablespoons)
1 tablespoon brown sugar
1 teaspoon hot paprika
1 teaspoon ground cumin
¼ teaspoon ground cinnamon
Salt and freshly ground pepper
6 4- to 6-ounce sea bass filets
2 tablespoons olive oil
3 tablespoons butter, cut into pieces
2 tablespoons chopped fresh cilantro
2 tablespoons shredded fresh coconut
2 tablespoons prepared fruit chutney

1. Combine the yogurt, green onions, ginger, garlic, lime juice, jalapeño pepper, brown sugar, paprika, cumin, and cinnamon in a bowl. Stir and season with salt and pepper.
2. Brush the filets all over with the marinade. Refrigerate for at least 1 hour and up to 4 hours.
3. Heat 2 tablespoons olive oil in a skillet over medium high heat.
4. Shake off the excess marinade from the fish. Place into the pan. Cook for 5 minutes, turn and cook for 3 to 4 minutes more.
5. Dot the top of the cooked fish with the pieces of butter. Garnish with cilantro, a sprinkle of coconut and chutney.

SERVINGS: 6 • PREPARATION TIME: 20 PLUS MARINATING

CHILEAN SEA BASS IS A LARGE FISH FOUND IN THE COLD, DEEP WATERS OF THE SOUTHERN HEMISPHERE; ITS INTRODUCTION TO THE MARKET PLACE HAS BEEN PHENOMENAL. FIFTEEN YEARS AGO, NO ONE HAD HEARD OF THIS FISH. TODAY YOU CAN HARDLY PICK UP A RESTAURANT MENU THAT DOES NOT INCLUDE IT AS FEATURED FARE. THE REASONS FOR ITS POPULARITY ARE CLEAR. THE FILLETS ARE GOOD SIZED WHITE MEAT WITH A MILD FLAVOR AND FIRM TEXTURE. CHILEAN SEA BASS HAS A HIGH FAT CONTENT, MAKING IT ALMOST IMPOSSIBLE TO OVERCOOK. DESPITE ITS NAME, CHILEAN SEA BASS IS UNRELATED TO THE TRUE SEA BASS (MANY OF WHICH GO BY THE NAME "GROUPER") OR TO OTHER SALTWATER BASS LIKE STRIPED BASS. CALL IT WHAT YOU LIKE, THIS FISH IS HERE TO STAY!

Fresh Sea Bass Provençal

THIS DISH COMES TOGETHER IN JUST MINUTES, AND IS MADE UP OF THOSE EVERYDAY INGREDIENTS IN YOUR PANTRY. THE SECRET IS FINDING THE FRESHEST FISH IN THE MARKETPLACE, AND CHOOSING THE BEST MARINATED INGREDIENTS. SERVE THIS FOR YOUR NEXT DINNER PARTY—OR FOR A SIMPLE WEDNESDAY NIGHT MEAL.

THE MEASUREMENTS ON THE INGREDIENTS LISTED IN THIS RECIPE ARE SUGGESTIONS. IF YOU FIND A 16-OUNCE JAR OF ARTICHOKES, GRAB IT. IF YOUR SUN-DRIED TOMATOES COME IN 7-OUNCE SIZE, THAT'S JUST FINE. IF THE BEST QUALITY OLIVES YOU CAN FIND COME FROM THE SELF-SERVE DELI DEPARTMENT, SCOOP AWAY. THIS IS A RUSTIC DISH, INTENDED TO BE A COMBINATION OF EXCELLENT FLAVORS; IT'S HARDLY STUCK ON SPECIFIC PROPORTIONS. LIKEWISE, IF SEA BASS IS NOT AVAILABLE, DON'T BE AFRAID TO TRY HALIBUT, SNAPPER, OR EVEN BARRAMUNDI FOR THIS DISH!

Juice of 1 medium lemon (about 2 tablespoons)
1½ pounds sea bass fillet
Salt and freshly ground pepper
¼ cups prepared bread crumbs
1 14-ounce can marinated artichoke hearts, drained
1 8.5-ounce jar julienned sun-dried tomatoes in oil
1 7-ounce jar Kalamata olives
1 cup white wine
Olive oil

Preheat the oven to 400°.

1. Pour the lemon juice over the sea bass. Place the fish into a shallow baking dish. Season with salt and pepper.

2. Sprinkle the bread crumbs onto the top of the sea bass.

3. Cut the artichoke hearts into quarters and place into the baking dish.

4. Sprinkle the sun-dried tomatoes over the sea bass and into the dish. Pour the oil from the jar over the top.

5. Pit the olives using a pitter or the flat blade of a knife. Place the olives into the baking dish.

6. Pour white wine around the fish and over the vegetables.

7. Drizzle the top of the fish with a bit more olive oil.

8. Place the dish into the oven. Immediately reduce the heat to 350°. Bake for 20 to 30 minutes, depending on the thickness of the fish. Serve the fish in chunky portions with generous spoonfuls of the Provençal sauce overtop.

SERVINGS: 4 • PREPARATION TIME: 40 MINUTES

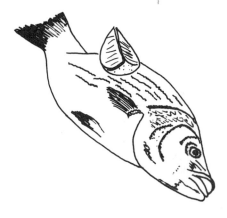

Pan-Sautéed Barramundi
with Dilled Cream and Caper Sauce

A CLOSE COUSIN TO STRIPED BASS, BARRAMUNDI IS SHOWING UP IN
RESTAURANTS AND IN HOME KITCHENS MORE AND MORE OFTEN.
ORIGINATING IN THE AUSTRALIAN WILDS, BARRAMUNDI IS NOW BEING FARM
RAISED AND BECOMING A POPULAR ALTERNATIVE TO CHILEAN SEA BASS.
THE FLESH IS MILD AND MELTS IN YOUR MOUTH.

3 tablespoons olive oil
1 small white onion, finely diced (about ½ cup)
½ cup white wine
1 pint cream
2 tablespoons capers, drained and rinsed
2 tablespoons chopped fresh dill
Salt and ground white pepper

4 6 to 8-ounce fresh Barramundi filets
Juice of 1 lemon (about 2 tablespoons)
½ teaspoon chili powder

1. Heat 1 tablespoon olive oil in a sauce
pan over medium high heat.
2. Add the onion to the pan. Cook until
just soft, about 2 minutes.
3. Add the white wine to the pan. Reduce
for 5 minutes.
4. Pour the cream into the pan. Reduce
heat to medium low, and wait for the
cream to thicken, about 8 to 10 minutes
(ideally, the cream should coat the back of a wooden spoon).
5. Stir in the capers and chopped fresh dill. Season with salt and
ground white pepper. Keep the sauce warm.
6. Season the fish with lemon juice, chili powder, salt and pepper.
7. Heat the remaining 2 tablespoons olive oil in a skillet over
medium high heat.
8. Place the fish, flesh side down, in the pan. Cook for 4 to 6
minutes.
9. Turn the fish and cook for 4 to 6 minutes more. When pushed
with a fingertip, the flesh of the fish should show a slight inden-
tation.
10. Serve the fish with a ladleful of caper sauce.

SERVINGS: 4 • PREPARATION TIME: 30 MINUTES

*Roasted Barramundi
with Banana Salsa*
Season the fish with red pepper
flakes, ground cumin and
minced garlic. Roast on a baking sheet for 8 to 10 minutes
(depending on thickness). Serve
with fresh banana salsa (page
131).

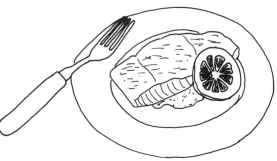

Cumin Crusted Salmon
with Tarragon Caper Sauce

THIS IS BY FAR ONE OF THE MOST POPULAR DISHES THAT I PREPARE. IT'S
FANCY ENOUGH TO SERVE AT YOUR NEXT DINNER PARTY, YET EASY ENOUGH
TO MAKE FOR AN AFTER-WORK SUPPER. SERVE WITH CREAMY CHEESE GRITS
(PAGE 192) AND ROASTED VEGGIES (PAGE 221).

You don't need to use an
entire fillet for this
recipe. For fewer serv-
ings, you can use individual fillets or salmon
steaks. Feel free to cut
the sauce in half—or pre-
pare it as listed, and save
extras for crudité dip-
ping. The salmon is equally terrific served warm
from the oven or at room
temperature on a buffet
table. Use left over
salmon to create a won-
derful salmon salad.

1 2½ pound center-cut whole salmon fillet with skin
Juice of 1 medium lemon (about 2 tablespoons)
¼ cup brown sugar
2 tablespoons chili powder
1 teaspoon garlic powder
1 teaspoon hot paprika
1 teaspoon ground cumin
½ teaspoon ground oregano
Salt and freshly ground pepper
2 tablespoons olive oil

1 cup sour cream
½ cup mayonnaise
¼ cup cream
3 tablespoons capers, drained and rinsed
2 tablespoons tarragon vinegar
2 tablespoons chopped fresh tarragon

Preheat the oven to 400°.
1. Place the whole fillet, skin side down, on a rimmed baking
sheet, coated with vegetable oil spray. Drizzle the lemon juice on
top.
2. Combine the brown sugar, chili powder, garlic powder, paprika, cumin, and oregano in a small bowl. Season with salt and
pepper. Rub this mixture all over the salmon, coating well.
3. Drizzle the top with olive oil.
4. Place the salmon into the oven. Reduce the temperature to
350°. Roast until the salmon is rare in the center, about 8 minutes per inch of thickness, about 15 to 30 minutes.
5. For sauce, stir together the sour cream, mayonnaise, cream,
capers, tarragon vinegar and fresh tarragon. Season with salt and
pepper.
6. Serve the salmon with the sauce on the side.

SERVINGS: 6 TO 8 • PREPARATION TIME: 30 MINUTES

Grilled Salmon with Maple Orange Glaze

SALMON IS A TERRIFIC FISH TO GRILL BECAUSE OF ITS FIRM TEXTURE AND AMOUNT OF FAT. IF GRILLING IS NOT ON YOUR LIST OF THINGS TO DO, GO AHEAD AND ROAST THE SALMON INSTEAD.

1 cup maple syrup
1 2-inch piece ginger, grated (about 2 tablespoons)
Juice of 1 medium orange (about ⅓ cup)
¼ cup soy sauce
3 medium garlic cloves, minced (about 1½ teaspoons)
1 2½ pound center-cut whole salmon fillet with skin

Thinly sliced orange
Green onions, thinly sliced on the diagonal
Sesame seeds

Preheat the oven to 350°.

1. Place the maple syrup, ginger, orange juice, soy sauce, and garlic in a saucepan over medium high heat and bring to a boil. Reduce the heat and simmer until the liquid is reduced to about 1 cup, about 10 to 15 minutes. Pour half of the maple sauce into a bowl. Set aside.

2. Heat an outdoor grill (or grill pan) over high heat. (Coat the grill or grill pan with vegetable oil to prevent sticking.)

3. Brush the flesh side of the salmon with the maple sauce. Place the flesh side down onto the grill. Cook for 5 minutes, turn.

4. Cook until the center of the salmon is rare, about 5 to 8 minutes, basting often.

5. Place the salmon onto a serving platter. Drizzle with the reserved maple sauce. Garnish with thin slices of orange, green onions and sesame seeds.

SERVINGS: 6 TO 8 • PREPARATION TIME: 30 MINUTES

IF YOU REALLY WANT TO SHOW OFF, TRY GRILLING THIS DISH USING A CEDAR PLANK. THE ADVANTAGE IS THE FISH ABSORBS THE FLAVOR OF THE WOOD OVER INDIRECT HEAT, MAKING IT A FOOLPROOF METHOD OF COOKING. PURCHASE A NON TREATED CEDAR PLANK. THESE ARE AVAILABLE AT SPECIALTY GOURMET SHOPS OR AT YOU LOCAL LUMBER YARD! SOAK THE PLANK FOR SEVERAL HOURS. NOT ONLY WILL THIS PREVENT BURNING, BUT ALSO THE DAMP WOOD WILL KEEP THE FISH MOIST. PLACE THE PLANK ONTO THE GRILL AND HEAT FOR 5 MINUTES. CAREFULLY TURN THE PLANK OVER. PLACE THE SALMON, SKIN SIDE DOWN, ONTO THE PLANK. CLOSE THE TOP OF THE GRILL, OR COVER THE FISH WITH FOIL. GRILL FOR 15 MORE MINUTES. BRING THE FISH, PLANK AND ALL, TO THE TABLE. USE POTHOLDERS!

Pan-Seared Arctic Char with Watercress Sauce

ARCTIC CHAR IS POPPING UP ON RESTAURANT MENUS AND FISH MARKETS MORE AND MORE. WITH A TEXTURE AND TASTE THAT IS A CROSS BETWEEN SALMON AND TROUT, IT'S WELL WORTH A TRY!

CHAR THRIVE IN THE ICY WATERS OF NORTH AMERICA AND EUROPE. ARCTIC CHAR IS MORE PREVALENT TODAY BECAUSE IT IS RAISED ON GOVERNMENT SPONSORED FISH FARMS IN ICELAND. BECAUSE OF ITS STURDY TEXTURE AND SALMON/TROUT-LIKE FLAVORING, CHAR IS EASILY SUBSTITUTED IN MOST FISH RECIPES AND CAN BE GRILLED, BAKED, BROILED, FRIED, POACHED AND STEAMED.

4 6 to 8-ounce Arctic char fillets
Salt and freshly ground pepper
Juice of 1 medium lemon (about 2 tablespoons)
2 tablespoons butter
2 tablespoons olive oil
4 large shallots, minced (¼ cup)
½ cup white wine
1 pint ripe cherry tomatoes or mixed baby tomatoes, cut in half
1 cup cream
1 bunch chopped fresh watercress, about 1 cup

I. Season the fish with salt and pepper. Sprinkle with lemon juice.

2. Heat the butter and the olive oil in a skillet over medium high heat. Place the fish, flesh side down, into the skillet. Cook until golden, about 2 to 3 minutes. Turn and cook for about 3 to 4 minutes more. Transfer to a platter. Keep warm.

3. Place the shallots into the pan. Cook until soft, about 2 minutes.

4. Pour in the wine. Add the tomatoes to the pan. Cook until soft, about 3 to 4 minutes.

5. Pour in the cream. Bring the sauce to a boil. Cook until slightly thickened, about 3 to 5 minutes.

6. Stir the watercress into the sauce. Season with salt and pepper.

7. Serve the char with a drizzle of sauce over top.

SERVINGS: 4 • PREPARATION TIME: 30 MINUTES

Pan-Fried Pecan Crusted Trout
with Wilted Arugula Salad

FRESH TROUT IS MILD AND QUICKLY PREPARED. WHOLE TROUT IS AN EASY
FISH TO PREPARE AND ONE THAT GUESTS WILL LOVE. FEEL FREE TO SUBSTI-
TUTE WITH SMALL WHOLE TROUT IN PLACE OF TROUT FILLETS IN THIS
RECIPE.

4 8 to 10 ounce boneless trout fillets
½ cup buttermilk
1 cup ground pecans
Salt and freshly ground pepper
2 tablespoons butter
2 tablespoons corn oil (or more)

1 tablespoon olive oil
3 cups arugula leaves, washed and dried
2 cups fresh spinach leaves, washed and dried
Juice of 1 lemon (about 2 tablespoons)
¼ teaspoon dried red pepper flakes
Lemon wedges

1. Place the trout into a baking dish. Pour the buttermilk over the
fish, turning once to coat.
2. Dredge the trout in the pecans, shaking off excess coating.
Season with salt and pepper.
3. Heat 1 tablespoon butter and 1 tablespoon corn oil in a skillet
over medium high heat.
4. Cook the trout (in batches), flesh side down, until golden,
about 3 to 5 minutes. Use a fish spatula to turn the fish and cook
for 3 to 5 minutes more. Place the fish onto a platter. (Use additional butter and oil as needed between batches.)
5. Heat 1 tablespoon olive oil in the skillet. Add the arugula and
spinach to the pan.
6. Sprinkle with lemon juice. Season with red pepper flakes and
salt.
7. Toss the leaves in the skillet until they just
begin to wilt.
8. Place the barely wilted salad on the top of
the trout. Garnish with additional lemon
wedges.

SERVINGS: 4 • PREPARATION TIME: 20 MINUTES

THE UNITED STATES TROUT
FARMERS ASSOCIATION
OFFERS SOME GREAT TIPS TO
REMEMBER WHEN PURCHAS-
ING AND COOKING TROUT. DO
PURCHASE FRESH TROUT
THAT IS GLISTENING, FLAW-
LESS AND CLEAN SMELLING.
THE FLESH SHOULD BE FIRM
AND SPRING BACK WHEN
PRESSED. WHEN BUYING
WHOLE TROUT, DO LOOK FOR
BRIGHT RED GILLS AND SHINY
SKIN. WHETHER YOU BUY
FISH FRESH OR FROZEN,
MAKE SURE IT'S THE LAST
THING YOU PURCHASE
BEFORE HEADING HOME. IF
YOU HAVE A WAY TO GO, DO
HAVE IT PACKED ON ICE. DO
STORE FRESH TROUT IN THE
COLDEST PART OF YOUR
REFRIGERATOR AND USE IT
QUICKLY; WITHIN TWO DAYS.
YOU DO NOT HAVE TO SCALE
TROUT. DO USE MILD-FLA-
VORED FATS TO COOK THE
TROUT. THE BEST ARE BUT-
TER, HYDROGENATED SHORT-
ENING, PEANUT OR CORN
OILS. DO COOK TROUT QUICK-
LY AND AT HIGH TEMPERA-
TURES. THE FISH WILL GET
SOGGY IF COOKED AT A LOW
TEMPERATURE. DO NOT OVER-
COOK TROUT. IT SHOULD BE
MOIST AND FORK-TENDER.
OVERCOOKING DRIES OUT AND
TOUGHENS THE FISH. IF,
WHEN YOU POKE IT WITH A
FORK, THE SKIN FLAKES OFF,
THE TROUT IS DONE.

Whole Trout Stuffed with Eggplant and Arugula
with Lemon Rosemary Butter Sauce

ONE LARGE TROUT IS PLENTY FOR TWO PEOPLE. SERVE ON A SINGLE BIG
PLATTER AND OFFER TWO FORKS. ALTERNATIVELY, YOU CAN PREPARE THE
DISH WITH SMALLER TROUT AND SERVE ONE PER PERSON.

You can prepare this dish for outdoor grilling. Simply use a fish grill basket and cook over high heat, turning once, for about 15 minutes, depending on the thickness of the fish. You can also lay the stuffed trout on a piece of aluminum foil. Brush with olive oil and lay fresh thyme sprigs and some lemon slices over top. Seal the package and place on the grill to cook for about 20 minutes.

12 ounces bacon, cut into 1-inch pieces
1 large yellow onion, diced into ½-inch squares (about 1 cup)
1 large eggplant, peeled and diced into ½-inch squares (about 2 cups)
Salt and freshly ground pepper
2 tablespoons chopped fresh rosemary
2 cups arugula leaves, washed and dried
2 large (12- to 16-ounce) whole trout, cleaned
Rosemary sprigs
2 tablespoons olive oil

Juice of 8 medium lemons (about 1 cup)
1 cup white wine
6 large shallots, minced (about ½ cup)
¼ cup tarragon vinegar
½ cup cream
½ cup butter, chilled, cut into pieces
Lemon wedges

Preheat the oven to 350°.

1. Cook the bacon in a skillet over medium high heat until crispy. Transfer the bacon to paper towels to drain. Pour off all but 1 tablespoon of the bacon drippings.

2. Add the onion to the pan, cook until soft and beginning to brown, about 4 to 6 minutes.

3. Add the eggplant to the pan, cook until soft, about 4 to 6 minutes more. Season with salt and pepper.

4. Add the chopped fresh rosemary to the pan. Remove the pan from the heat. Toss in the arugula until just wilted. Toss in the bacon. Allow mixture to cool to room temperature.

5. Season the inside of the fish with salt and pepper. Fill the cavity with the eggplant/arugula stuffing. Place the trout into a baking dish, coated with vegetable oil spray. Layer with rosemary sprigs and brush with olive oil. Roast the trout until cooked through, about 22 to 25 minutes.

6. For sauce, place the lemon juice, wine, shallots, and vinegar in saucepan. Add 2 to 4 rosemary sprigs. Bring to a boil over medium high heat. Boil until the liquid is reduced to about ½ cup, about 15 to 20 minutes. Remove the rosemary. Stir in the cream. Cook for 3 minutes more. Remove the sauce from the heat. Whisk in the butter, 1 to 2 pieces at a time, until just melted.

Season with salt and pepper.

7. Serve the trout with the sauce on the side. Garnish with fresh rosemary and lemon wedges.

SERVINGS: 4 • PREPARATION TIME: 60 MINUTES

Sole Meuniere

THIS CLASSIC DISH IS USUALLY FOUND ON FINE FRENCH RESTAURANT MENUS. YOU WILL BE SURPRISED AT HOW EASY IT IS TO PREPARE AT HOME. THE SECRET IS IN USING THE FRESHEST FISH YOU CAN FIND AND KEEPING THE DISH SIMPLE!

1 cup all-purpose flour
Salt and ground white pepper
½ cup cream
½ cup white wine
2 tablespoons olive oil
2 to 6 tablespoons butter
4 6-ounce sole fillets
Juice of 1 medium lemon (about 2 tablespoons)
2 tablespoons capers, drained and rinsed
2 tablespoons chopped fresh parsley

MEUNIERE TRANSLATES TO "MILLER'S WIFE" AND REFERS TO DUSTING THE FLOUR. ALTHOUGH THIS DISH IS A CLASSIC, YOU WILL FIND SEVERAL DIFFERENT NUANCES FROM EACH AND EVERY COOK. CAPERS AND PARSLEY ARE OPTIONAL, WHILE BUTTER AND LEMON JUICE ARE NOT.

1. Place the flour into a shallow bowl. Season with salt and ground white pepper.
2. Whisk together the cream and wine in a second shallow bowl.
3. Heat 1 tablespoon olive oil and 1 tablespoon butter in a skillet over medium heat.
4. Dip 1 sole fillet into the cream mixture and then into the flour. Repeat with another fillet. Cook both fillets in skillet until golden, about 3 minutes. Carefully turn and cook until golden brown on the outside and flaky on the inside, about 2 to 3 minutes more. Carefully transfer to a platter. Keep warm. Repeat with the other two fillets. You may add 1 more tablespoon of butter and remaining tablespoon of olive oil as needed.
5. Reduce the heat to low. Cut the remaining 4 tablespoons of butter into pieces. Whisk the butter in the pan until melted.
6. Remove the pan from the heat. Stir in the lemon juice, capers and parsley. Season with salt and white pepper. Pour the sauce over the fish.

SERVINGS: 4 • PREPARATION TIME: 20 MINUTES

Poached Sole with Ginger, Green Onions, and Carrots

POACHING IS AN EXCELLENT WAY TO INFUSE FLAVOR WITHOUT ADDING EXTRA FAT; THIS MAKES THE DISH AN EXCELLENT ADDITION TO YOUR WELL BALANCED MEAL PLAN.

WHEN POACHING FISH, THE MOST IMPORTANT THING TO REMEMBER IS THAT THE WATER SHOULD SIMMER, NOT BOIL. IF IT BOILS, THE DELICATE FISH MAY BREAK APART. COVERING THE PAN, HELPS STEAM THE FISH IN ADDITION TO POACHING, LESSENING THE COOKING TIME EVEN MORE. CHOOSE YOUR FAVORITE FLAVORS TO INCORPORATE INTO YOUR POACHING LIQUID AND VARY THE LIQUID WITH EVERYTHING FROM BEER TO CHAMPAGNE!

4 6-ounce sole fillets
Salt and freshly ground pepper
¾ cup chicken broth
¾ cup bottled clam juice
1 1-inch piece ginger, grated (about 1 tablespoon)
2 medium cloves garlic, minced (about 1 teaspoon)
1 bunch (6 to 8) green onions, thinly sliced on the diagonal (about ½ cup)
1 large carrot, grated (about ½ cup)
¼ cup soy sauce
2 tablespoons sesame oil
2 tablespoons chopped fresh parsley

1. Season the sole with salt and freshly ground pepper. Place the fillets onto a large piece of parchment paper.
2. Pour the chicken broth and clam juice into a deep skillet with lid.
3. Stir in the ginger and garlic. Simmer this mixture over medium low heat.
4. Gently slide the paper holding the fish into the liquid, sumberging the fish. Cover the fish with onions and shredded carrot. Drizzle the soy sauce and sesame oil over top. Cover the pan and simmer until the sole is just cooked through, about 3 to 5 minutes, depending on thickness.
5. Uncover the pan. Gently lift out the parchment paper and slide the fish onto a platter.
6. Add the parsley to the poaching liquid. Bring this liquid to a boil. Cook for 3 to 5 minutes. Pour the poaching liquid around and over the fillets.

SERVINGS: 4 • PREPARATION TIME: 30 MINUTES

Snapper Vera Cruz

USE YOUR FAVORITE, FRESHEST SNAPPER FOR THIS DISH. I PREFER YELLOW
TAIL, BUT RED SNAPPER WILL WORK JUST FINE. THE FISH COOKS IN HERBED
VEGGIE AND ANCHOVY SAUCE, ABSORBING ALL ITS SAVORY FLAVORS. THE
COOKED FILETS ARE SO TENDER, THEY MAY BREAK APART WHEN YOU
REMOVE THEM FROM THE BAKING DISH. NOT TO WORRY. SERVE THE PIECES
OVER RICE OR PASTA AND GIVE EVERYTHING A QUICK SPRINKLE OF GRATED
CHEESE BEFORE SERVING.

6 6 to 8-ounce snapper filets
Juice of 1 lemon (about 2 tablespoons)
Salt and freshly ground pepper

1 28-ounce can diced tomatoes
1 medium white onion, thinly sliced (about ⅔ cup)
4 medium garlic cloves, thinly sliced (about 2 tablespoons)
2 bay leaves
2 anchovy filets
1 teaspoon dried oregano
1 teaspoon dried basil
½ teaspoon red pepper flakes
8 to 10 ounces fresh spinach leaves, torn

Preheat the oven to 375°.

1. Season both sides of the fish with lemon juice, salt and pepper.

2. To make the sauce, use a large skillet or Dutch oven to combine the diced tomatoes, onion, garlic, bay leaves, anchovy filets,
oregano, basil, and red pepper flakes. Cook over medium high
heat for 5 minutes.

3. Submerge the fish in the sauce.

4. Place the spinach leaves into the sauce.

5. Place the pan into the oven and bake until the fish is done,
about 15 to 20 minutes, depend-
ing on the thickness of the filets.

6. Remove the bay leaves from the
sauce. Serve the fish and sauce
with rice or pasta.

SERVINGS: 6 • PREPARATION TIME: 30
MINUTES

RED SNAPPER ARE FOUND
OFF THE GULF AND ATLANTIC
COASTS FROM NORTH
CAROLINA TO THE "SNAPPER
BANKS" OF FLORIDA, OFF THE
COASTS OF TEXAS AND
LOUISIANA, AND AS FAR
SOUTH AS MEXICO. RED
SNAPPER ARE CONSIDERED A
MOST DESIRED DEEPSEA DEL-
ICACY. YELLOWTAIL SNAPPER
ARE NATIVE TO THE WESTERN
ATLANTIC FROM MASSA-
CHUSETTS TO BRAZIL,
THOUGH THEY ARE SELDOM
FOUND NORTH OF THE
CAROLINAS. THEY ARE MOST
COMMON IN SOUTH FLORIDA,
THE BAHAMAS, THE GULF OF
MEXICO AND THE CARIBBEAN.
YELLOWTAIL SNAPPER ARE
FOUND IN COASTAL WATERS
NEAR CORAL REEFS. UNLIKE
MOST SNAPPER, THE YELLOW-
TAIL SNAPPER IS FOUND
ABOVE THE BOTTOM OF THE
OCEAN AT DEPTHS OF 10 TO
300 FEET; THEY PREFER
WARMER WATER TEMPERA-
TURES.

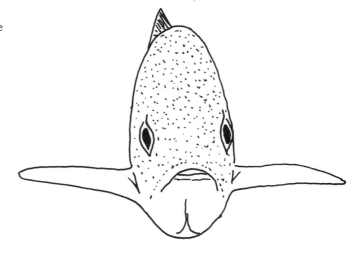

Orange Roughy Oreganato

DRIED OREGANO KICKS UP THE FLAVORFUL CRUMB COATING FOR FISH, WHILE FRESH OREGANO ADDS AN EXTRA DEPTH OF FLAVOR TO THE SAUCE; DRIED OR FRESH, IT ALL ADDS UP TO A SUPERB FISH DISH, WORTHY OF GUESTS ON SATURDAY, OR A CASUAL FRIDAY SUPPER. SERVE EACH FILET ON TOP OF A LIGHTLY DRESSED ARUGULA SALAD FOR A PRETTY PRESENTATION.

ORANGE ROUGHY IS A VERY MILD TASTING FISH THAT COMES FROM THE DEEP WATERS OF NEW ZEALAND AND AUSTRALIA; THEY GROW VERY SLOWLY, TAKING ALMOST 20 YEARS TO REACH SPAWNING AGE. THE GOOD NEWS IS THAT THEY CAN LIVE TO BE 100 YEARS OLD! ORANGE ROUGHY WAS IN DANGER OF BEING FISHED-OUT IN THE MID-80S, BUT DUE TO BETTER MANAGEMENT, IS NOW READILY AVAILABLE FROM YOUR LOCAL FISHMONGER.

½ cup all-purpose flour
2 large eggs
2 cups fresh bread crumbs
1 ounce finely grated Parmesan cheese (about ¼ cup)
1 teaspoon dried oregano
Salt and freshly ground pepper
6 6- to 8-ounce Orange Roughy filets
2 to 4 tablespoons olive oil
4 medium cloves garlic, minced (about 2 teaspoons)
Juice of 2 lemons (about ¼ cup)

½ cup white wine
1 cup clam juice
1 14-ounce can artichoke hearts, drained and chopped
1 16-ounce jar Kalamata olives, drained, pitted and chopped
2 tablespoons chopped fresh oregano

1. Place the flour into a shallow dish.
2. Beat the eggs with 2 tablespoons water in a second shallow dish.
3. Combine the bread crumbs, cheese and dried oregano in a third shallow dish. Season with salt and pepper.
4. Dip the fish, first into the flour, then into the egg, and finally into the breadcrumb mixture. Place the fish onto a platter.
5. Heat 2 tablespoons olive oil in a skillet over medium high heat. Add the garlic and cook until golden, about 2 minutes.
6. Cook the filets in the garlic oil for 5 minutes. Sprinkle each filet with lemon juice. Turn and sprinkle again with additional lemon juice. Cook for 3 to 5 minutes more. The fish filets will be golden brown. If your pan is not large enough to accommodate all of the fillets, cook them in batches using the remaining olive oil. Transfer the fish to a platter and keep warm.
7. Pour the wine into the pan. Cook for 5 minutes, scraping the bottom of the pan.
8. Pour the clam juice into the pan. Cook for 5 minutes more.
9. Add the chopped artichokes and olives to the pan. Cook for 2 minutes. Stir chopped fresh oregano into the sauce.
10. Pour the sauce over the fish and serve.

SERVINGS: 6 • PREPARATION TIME: 20 MINUTES

Grilled Swordfish Steaks
with Warm Sun-Dried Tomato Relish

THE TEXTURE OF SWORDFISH IS FIRM, ALMOST LIKE A CHICKEN BREAST.
IT'S BEST SERVED MEDIUM-RARE IN THE CENTER. ACCOMPLISH THIS BY
SLIGHTLY UNDERCOOKING THE FISH. BY NATURE, THE FISH WILL CONTINUE
TO COOK AFTER IT IS REMOVED FROM THE HEAT.

4 8-ounce swordfish steaks, 1 to 1½-inch thick
¼ cup olive oil
Juice of 1 lemon (about 2 tablespoons)
2 tablespoons balsamic vinegar
1 tablespoon Dijon mustard
1 tablespoon Worcestershire sauce
Salt and freshly ground pepper

1 7-ounce jar sun-dried tomatoes in oil, sliced lengthwise into strips
4 medium cloves garlic, minced (about 2 teaspoons)
1 16-ounce jar Spanish olives, pitted, drained and chopped

2 tablespoons butter
2 tablespoons chopped fresh parsley

SWORDFISH ARE MAKING A COMEBACK IN A BIG WAY. PROGRESSIVE CONSERVATION PRACTICES BROUGHT THIS WONDERFUL GAME FISH BACK FROM THE ROAD TO EXTINCTION. IT'S NOT SURPRISING THAT HUNTING FOR SWORDFISH HAS BECOME A POPULAR OFFSHORE FISHING ACTIVITY.

1. Place the swordfish steaks into a baking dish.
2. Whisk together the ¼ cup olive oil, lemon juice, vinegar, mustard, and Worcestershire sauce. Pour this mixture over the fish, turning once to coat. Season with salt and pepper. Marinate for 15 to 30 minutes.
3. Place the sun-dried tomatoes and the oil from the jar in a skillet over medium high heat.
4. Add the garlic and Spanish olives. Cook for 5 minutes. Reduce heat to lowest setting.
5. Heat a grill pan (or outdoor grill) over medium high heat.
6. Remove the fish from the marinade. Place the fish into the grill pan. Cook for 5 minutes. Turn and cook, 4 to 6 minutes more. The fish should spring back when touched.

7. Place the fish onto a platter. Top each steak with ¼ of the butter.
8. Pour the sun-dried relish over the steaks. Garnish with chopped fresh parsley.

SERVINGS: 4 • PREPARATION TIME: 30 MINUTES

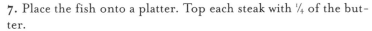

Fried Tilapia Fingers

THESE NIBBLES ARE A GREAT SNACK! PAIRED WITH FRENCH FRIES AND SERVED WITH VINEGAR, GET READY TO ENJOY AN AUTHENTIC ENGLISH FISH AND CHIPS MEAL.

USE THE BATTER IN THIS RECIPE TO COAT THICK SLICES OF SWEET ONION. DEEP-FRY THE COATED ONIONS IN HOT OIL AND DRAIN ON PAPER TOWELS.

HOLD FRIED FISH FINGERS ON A BAKING RACK SET INTO A RIMMED BAKING SHEET. PLACE THE BAKING SHEET INTO A 300° OVEN WHILE YOU FRY ALL OF THE PIECES.

1½ pounds tilapia (or other firm, white fish), cut into 1-inch strips
Salt and freshly ground pepper
2 cups flour
1 tablespoon baking powder
½ teaspoon Old Bay Seasoning
1 12-ounce can beer
Canola oil
Cornstarch

1. Season the fish with salt and pepper.
2. Whisk together the flour, baking powder, and Old Bay Seasoning in a bowl.
3. Whisk in the cold beer until the batter is smooth. Refrigerate the batter for at least 15 minutes and up to 1 hour.
4. In a deep pot, pour canola oil to ⅓ full. Heat to 350°.
5. Dredge the fish pieces into the cornstarch. Shake off excess. Dip into the batter. Carefully drop into the hot oil. Cook until golden brown, turning once, about 2 to 4 minutes. Drain on a rack over paper towels.

SERVINGS: 4 • PREPARATION TIME: 30 MINUTES

Chips

For the "chips" part of fish and chips, peel russet potatoes and cut into thin strips. (You can leave the peel on if you prefer.) Heat canola oil to 325°. Cook the fries in the oil until they are limp, about 2 to 4 minutes. Drain and cool to room temperature. Reheat the oil to 375°. Place the fries in the hot oil in batches and cook until golden brown. Remove, drain and season.

Chapter II

Chicken, Turkey, and the Occasional Duck

FDR's promise of a "chicken in every pot" led to a revolution in Sunday night family suppers; one that led to inventive meal stretching. This concept is one of the things I love about meal planning—creative ways to use leftovers. Not only are meal-stretching cooks budget minded, they are also at the root of creative cooking. Less we think of this as cut-rate, or unappetizing, consider the plight of the hardworking restaurant owning chef. What do you think he does with the whole roasted chickens that do not sell for Tuesday night's special? You got it—here comes Wednesday's individual chicken pot pies. Home cooks can take a lesson from our gourmet counterparts and plan ahead to prepare more than one weekend chicken, making short work of Tuesday night's supper. This chapter will give you plenty of suggestions to show you how it works.

One of the biggest criticisms of leftover turkey and chicken is that the meal is dry; this makes sense because most of the time, the poultry has been cooked perfectly the first time and then cooked again in either an oven or a microwave; this naturally dries out the meal. Therefore, it is important that a creative leftover meal use a well stored ingredient that is suitable for cooking twice. For this reason, if you roast or grill a whole chicken, the best way to re-use it is to bring the chicken to room temperature, and then wrap it tightly in plastic wrap. Refrigerate until you are ready to begin your creative midweek meal. If you leave the meat on the bone, it will remain moist. If you cut the meat from the chicken and then store it, it will begin to dry out.

Chicken and turkey meals are not all about leftovers. In this chapter you will find classic dishes prepared with updated recipes that are easy, quick and delicious. The flavors found in chicken Français, a French inspired dish, are reinvented in Baked Lemon Chicken. Traditional Chicken Cordon Bleu is updated in Pepperoni Stuffed Chicken Breasts. Chicken pieces are battered and "fried," both in a deep fryer and in the oven. Taking a clue from our favorite fast food joint, we will add "fried" chicken fingers to our favorite veggies for a satisfying salad.

You will find foolproof techniques in these pages to guide you in the roasting of a moist and tender turkey, "jointing" a whole chicken, brining and then flawlessly grilling chicken pieces, and last but not least, roasting a duckling to perfection.

FDR promised us a new wave of prosperity that led to a new way of creative cooking, blended with a good dose of thriftiness. This chapter offers a promise of delicious new ways with poultry that are sure to become family fresh traditions.

Chicken Cacciatore

THIS DISH USES A BRAISING TECHNIQUE. THE CHICKEN IS BROWNED IN
ORDER TO SEAL IN THE JUICES; THEN SIMMERED IN A FLAVORFUL SAUCE TO
FINISH COOKING. THE CHICKEN SHOULD BE SO TENDER THAT IT BEGINS TO
FALL AWAY FROM THE BONE. THE ACTUAL AMOUNT OF TIME REQUIRED WILL
DIFFER BASED ON HOW AGGRESSIVELY YOU SIMMER THE SAUCE. LONGER
COOKING TIME IS BETTER THAN SHORTER FOR THIS RECIPE.

1 4-pound chicken, cut into 8 pieces
Salt and freshly ground pepper
1 tablespoon olive oil
3 ounces bacon, cut into 1-inch pieces
1 large yellow onion, diced into ½-inch squares (about 1 cup)
8 ounces button mushrooms, sliced (about 2 cups)
4 medium garlic cloves, minced (about 2 teaspoons)
1 cup red wine
1 cup beef broth
1 28-ounce can diced tomatoes
2 tablespoons chopped fresh oregano
½ teaspoon dried red pepper
Pasta
Fresh parsley

1. Season the chicken with salt and pepper.
2. Heat the olive oil in a deep pot (or Dutch oven) over medium high heat. Cook the bacon until crispy, about 4 to 6 minutes. Remove the bacon from the pot and drain on paper towels.
3. Brown the chicken in the pot in batches until golden on all sides, about 6 to 8 minutes. Remove from heat. Transfer browned chicken to a platter.
4. Add the onion to the pot (or Dutch oven) and cook until soft, about 4 to 6 minutes.
5. Add the mushrooms and garlic to the pot and cook until just beginning to brown, about 4 to 6 minutes.
6. Add the wine, broth and tomatoes to the pot. Stir in the oregano and red pepper. Place the chicken and bacon back into the pot. Bring to a boil. Reduce the heat to medium low, cover, and simmer until the chicken is tender, falling off the bone, about 1 to 2 hours. Season with salt and pepper.
7. Transfer the chicken to a platter. Keep warm. Bring the liquid to a boil. Cook until reduced by half and thickened, about 15 to 20 minutes.
8. Serve the chicken over pasta with the sauce over top. Garnish with chopped fresh parsley.

SERVINGS: 4 • PREPARATION TIME: 30 MINUTES PLUS SIMMERING FOR 1 TO 2 HOURS

PURCHASING A WHOLE CHICKEN AND "DISJOINTING" (CUTTING IT UP) IS ECONOMICAL AND VERY EASY TO ACCOMPLISH. BEGIN BY SITTING THE CHICKEN ONTO YOUR WORK SURFACE, BREAST SIDE UP, WITH THE DRUMSTICKS POINTED TOWARD YOU. ROTATE ONE LEG UNTIL YOU FIND THE JOINT CONNECTING THE THIGH TO THE BODY. CUT THROUGH THE SKIN AND THROUGH THE JOINT TO SEPARATE. REPEAT WITH THE OTHER LEG/THIGH. THEN SEPARATE THE THIGHS FROM THE LEGS BY LOCATING THE JOINT THAT JOINS THEM. CUT THROUGH THE SKIN AND THE JOINT, AND SET THESE 4 PIECES ASIDE. USE THE SAME TECHNIQUE TO FIND THE JOINTS CONNECTING THE WINGS. CUT THROUGH THE SKIN AND THE JOINTS TO REMOVE THE WINGS, AND SET THESE ASIDE. STAND THE CHICKEN ON ITS HAUNCHES. CUT DOWN, FROM THE NECK OPENING, TO REMOVE THE BACKBONE SECTION. (SAVE THIS PART FOR STOCK). LAY THE BREAST SECTION FLAT ONTO THE WORK SURFACE. CUT THE BREAST IN HALF THROUGH THE BREAST BONE. THERE YOU HAVE IT! 8 PIECES OF CHICKEN FOR THE PRICE OF 1!

Braised Chicken Pieces with Chorizo Sausage and Baby Artichokes

WHEN YOU TAKE EVERYDAY BRAISED CHICKEN AND SPICE IT UP WITH
SPANISH SAUSAGE, YOU HAVE AN UPSCALE "PEASANT" DISH, GRAND
ENOUGH FOR ANY OCCASION. THE BABY ARTICHOKES ADD A NICE TOUCH.
YOU CAN SUBSTITUTE WITH CANNED ARTICHOKES, OR FOR A FUN TWIST TRY
TURNIPS.

2 tablespoons olive oil
8 chicken thighs
8 chicken legs
Salt and freshly ground pepper
1 pound Chorizo sausage, thinly sliced
2 large yellow onions, peeled and cut into 2-inch wedges (about 4 cups)
1 large red bell pepper, seeded and thinly sliced (about 1 cup)
1 large yellow bell pepper, seeded and thinly sliced (about 1 cup)
*1 pound baby artichokes, outer leaves removed, stems trimmed, cut in half (about 8
  to 10)*
2 cups Shiraz
1 28-ounce can diced tomatoes
2 tablespoons chopped fresh basil
2 tablespoons chopped fresh oregano
Rice

Preheat the oven to 350°.

1. Heat the olive oil in a large pot (or Dutch oven) over medium
high heat. Season the chicken with salt and pepper. Brown the
chicken pieces in batches until golden on all sides, about 6 to 8
minutes. Transfer the browned chicken to a platter.

2. Cook the sausage until browned, about 4 to 6 minutes.
Transfer to the platter. Remove any excess fat from the pot.
Retain at least 2 tablespoons of the drippings.

3. Cook the onions and the peppers until soft, about 10 minutes.

4. Add the artichokes to the pot.

5. Pour in the Shiraz and diced tomatoes. Stir in the basil,
oregano and season with salt and pepper.

6. Return the chicken and the chorizo to the pot. Bring to a boil.
Cover the pot and carefully place into the oven. Cook for at least
1 hour and up to 2 hours, or until the chicken is tender, falling
from the bone.

7. Remove the pot from the oven and return to the stove top.
Remove the chicken from the pot. Bring the liquid to a boil and
cook until it thickens, about 10 minutes. Serve with rice and garnish with additional chopped fresh basil.

SERVINGS: 6 TO 8 • PREPARATION TIME: 30 MINUTES PLUS BAKING

FOR BEST RESULTS, MAKE
SURE YOU PAT THE CHICKEN
DRY BEFORE PLACING IT INTO
THE OIL. IF THE CHICKEN IS
WET, THE OIL WILL COOL
DOWN AND THE CHICKEN WILL
STEAM—NOT SEAR.

USE CAUTION WHEN HANDLING
RAW CHICKEN. KEEP A CUT-
TING BOARD JUST FOR JOINT-
ING THE CHICKEN. USE A SEP-
ARATE BOARD FOR FRESH
FOODS LIKE HERBS AND
SALAD. WASH YOUR HANDS IN
WARM SUDSY WATER EACH
TIME YOU HANDLE THE CHICK-
EN. MAKE SURE YOU CLEAN
THE CUTTING BOARD AND ALL
OF THE UTENSILS THOROUGH-
LY.

Roasted Chicken with Herb Butter

THIS DISH WILL TAKE YOU DOWN MEMORY LANE TO YOUR GRANDMA'S KITCHEN, WHERE THE AROMA OF ROASTED CHICKEN, LADEN WITH RICH BUTTER, FILLED THE ENTIRE HOUSE. WHAT MAKES THIS EVEN BETTER IS THAT THE RECIPE IS FOOLPROOF—ONE THAT IS JUST AS EASY TO MAKE ON TUESDAY AS IT IS FOR SUNDAY NIGHT'S FAMILY SUPPER.

AN UPRIGHT ROASTER IS A GREAT TOOL TO USE WHEN BAKING CHICKEN. THE CHICKEN SITS UP AND BROWNS EVENLY ON ALL SIDES. STUFF THE CHICKEN WITH ORANGE SEGMENTS (BETWEEN THE ROASTER AND THE CHICKEN CAVITY) TO KEEP THE CHICKEN EXTRA MOIST.

½ cup butter, room temperature (1 stick)
2 tablespoons chopped fresh rosemary
2 tablespoons chopped fresh thyme
2 tablespoons chopped fresh oregano
2 tablespoons chopped fresh sage
1 4-pound chicken
Salt and freshly ground pepper
1 whole orange, cut into sections
½ cup sherry

Preheat the oven to 450°
1. Mix together the softened butter with the herbs.
2. Use you hands to cover the chicken with the herb butter. (Use you fingers to gently loosen the skin and place some of the butter between the skin and the meat.) Season the chicken with salt and pepper.
3. Place the orange sections into the cavities of the chicken.
4. Place the chicken on an upright roaster (or on a rack) in a baking pan. Pour the sherry over the chicken.
5. Place the chicken into the oven. After 10 minutes, reduce the heat to 350°.
6. Bake until the skin is crisp and the juices run clear, about 20 minutes per pound.

SERVINGS: 4 TO 6 • PREPARATION TIME: 15 MINUTES PLUS ROASTING

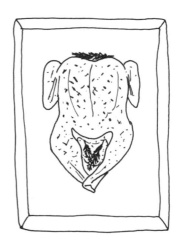

Thyme-Roasted Chicken Salad
with Apples and Almonds

CHICKEN, TURKEY, AND | 259
THE OCCASIONAL DUCK

THIS SALAD IS A PERFECT EXAMPLE OF A RECIPE THAT STRETCHES YOUR
SUNDAY NIGHT ROAST CHICKEN INTO TUESDAY'S EASY SALAD SUPPER. PLAN
AHEAD TO SUBSTITUTE WITH LEFTOVER ROASTED CHICKEN WITH HERB
BUTTER (SEE THE RECIPE ON PAGE 258), INSTEAD OF ROASTING BREASTS
FOR THIS DISH.

2 large (6 to 8-ounce) skinless, boneless chicken breast halves
Salt and freshly ground pepper
1 tablespoon olive oil
Fresh thyme sprigs

2 medium apples, peeled and cut into ½-inch dice (about 2 cups)
2 medium celery ribs, thinly sliced (about 1 cup)
1 4-ounce can sliced water chestnuts, drained
1 cup sour cream
½ cup mayonnaise
Juice of 1 medium lemon (about 2 tablespoons)
1 cup sliced almonds
2 tablespoons chopped fresh thyme

Lettuce
Tomato wedges
Cucumber slices

YOU CAN STRETCH THIS DISH
EVEN FURTHER, BY ADDING 2
CUPS OF COOKED WILD RICE
OR 1 CUP OF COOKED PASTA,
LIKE FUSILLI OR ROTINI.
DICED PINEAPPLE, HALVED
GRAPES, AND THINLY SLICED
RADISHES ALSO ADD A TASTY
KICK.

Preheat the oven to 350°.
1. Place the chicken breasts into a baking dish. Season with salt
and pepper. Drizzle with olive oil. Place thyme springs in and
around chicken. Roast until the chicken is just cooked, about 20
to 30 minutes. Cool to room temperature and cut into ½-inch
cubes.
2. Place the chicken, apples, celery and water chestnuts into a
bowl.
3. For the dressing, whisk together the sour cream, mayonnaise
and lemon juice.
4. Pour the dressing into the bowl with chicken and apple/celery
mixture. Toss to coat.
5. Fold in the sliced almonds and chopped fresh thyme. Season
with salt and pepper.
6. Serve the salad on a bed of lettuce, and garnish with tomato
wedges and cucumber slices.

SERVINGS: 4 • PREPARATION TIME: 20 MINUTES PLUS ROASTING CHICKEN

Buttermilk Fried Chicken

SERVED HOT OR COLD, THIS TENDER CHICKEN IS TERRIFIC ON YOUR SUPPER
TABLE AND EVEN BETTER THE NEXT DAY FOR A DESKTOP PICNIC!

2 4-pound chickens, cut into 16 pieces
Salt and freshly ground pepper
2 cups buttermilk
2 large eggs
1 teaspoon hot paprika
1 teaspoon dried rosemary
1 teaspoon dried oregano
2 teaspoons baking powder
1½ teaspoons baking soda
2 or more drops hot pepper sauce
4 cups all-purpose flour
Canola oil

I LIKE THE TECHNIQUE OF FIRST FRYING THE CHICKEN AND THEN FINISHING IT IN THE OVEN FOR 20 TO 30 MINUTES. ALTERNATELY, YOU CAN SKIP THE OVEN AND COMPLETELY COOK THE CHICKEN IN A FRY PAN. MAKE SURE YOU CHECK THE INTERNAL TEMPERATURE WITH A THERMOMETER; IT SHOULD REGISTER 160° AND THE JUICES SHOULD RUN CLEAR.

1. Season the chicken with salt and pepper.
2. Whisk together the buttermilk, eggs, paprika, rosemary, oregano, baking powder, baking soda and as much hot pepper sauce as you like.
3. Divide the flour into 2 separate, shallow bowls.
4. Dip one piece of chicken into the flour. Shake off excess. Dip it into the buttermilk mixture, allowing the excess to drip off. Finally, dip the chicken into the second bowl of flour. Place the chicken onto a rack. Continue until all of the chicken has been coated.
5. Heat canola oil in a skillet over medium high heat.
6. Cook the chicken pieces in the oil until golden, about 8 to 10 minutes. Turn and fry until browned and cooked through, about 8 minutes more. Transfer the chicken to a rack. Make sure chicken sits on a rimmed baking sheet. Season with salt and pepper. (You can finish the chicken in a low oven, about 300°, for up to 1 hour.)

SERVINGS: 6 TO 8 •
PREPARATION TIME: 1
HOUR

Oven-Fried Chicken

BRINING THE CHICKEN PIECES MAKES THE END RESULT EXTRA JUICY.
BAKING THE CHICKEN IN THE OVEN, PRODUCES A CRUSTY COATING. THE
COMBINATION IS OH SO GOOOD!

½ cup granulated sugar
½ cup kosher salt
4 cups water
2 4-pound chickens, cut into 16 pieces
1 cup low fat yogurt
2 tablespoons Dijon mustard
2 tablespoons chopped fresh thyme
Salt and freshly ground pepper
4 cups corn flake crumbs
2 tablespoons olive oil

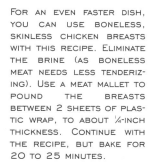

FOR AN EVEN FASTER DISH, YOU CAN USE BONELESS, SKINLESS CHICKEN BREASTS WITH THIS RECIPE. ELIMINATE THE BRINE (AS BONELESS MEAT NEEDS LESS TENDERIZING). USE A MEAT MALLET TO POUND THE BREASTS BETWEEN 2 SHEETS OF PLASTIC WRAP, TO ABOUT ¼-INCH THICKNESS. CONTINUE WITH THE RECIPE, BUT BAKE FOR 20 TO 25 MINUTES.

Preheat the oven to 450°.

1. To make the brine, place sugar, salt and water into a pot over medium high heat. Cook until the salt and sugar are dissolved. Cool to room temperature.

2. Place the chicken pieces into a deep pot. Cover with the brine. Cover the pot and refrigerate for 2 hours.

3. Whisk together the yogurt, mustard and thyme. Season with salt and pepper.

4. Remove the chicken from the brine and pat dry.

5. Brush each piece of chicken with the yogurt/mustard mixture.

6. Place the cornflake crumbs into a shallow bowl. Dip the chicken into the corn flake crumbs. Place into a shallow baking dish, coated with vegetable oil spray. Repeat until all of the chicken is in the pan. Drizzle with olive oil.

7. Bake for 30 minutes or until the chicken is golden and cooked through.

SERVINGS: 6 TO 8 • PREPARATION TIME: 1 HOUR

Chicken Finger Salad
with Roasted Garlic Ranch Dressing

THIS IS A DOUBLY FUN RECIPE. NOT ONLY DOES THE CHICKEN TASTE DIVINE, BUT THE PRESENTATION IS EQUALLY APPEALING.

½ cup butter, melted (1 stick)
½ cup grated Parmesan cheese
2 large (6- to 8-ounce) skinless, boneless chicken breast halves, cut into strips
1 cup seasoned bread crumbs
Salt and freshly ground pepper

1 cup mayonnaise
4 cloves roasted garlic
2 green onions, thinly sliced (about 2 tablespoons)
1 tablespoon chopped fresh parsley
1 tablespoon chopped fresh basil
1 tablespoon chopped fresh chives
⅓ cup buttermilk

2 large heads Boston lettuce, washed, dried and torn (about 6 cups)
6 medium plum tomatoes, seeded and diced (about 3 cups)

Preheat the oven to 350°.
1. Melt the butter in a small bowl. Stir in the Parmesan cheese. Dip the chicken strips into the butter/cheese mixture and then into the bread crumbs. Place into a baking dish. Repeat until all of the chicken is coated. Season with salt and pepper. Bake until the chicken fingers are golden and cooked through, about 20 minutes.
2. To make ranch dressing, place the mayonnaise, roasted garlic, onions, parsley, basil and chives into a blender. Pulse to combine. With the motor running, slowly pour in the buttermilk. Season with salt and pepper.
3. Place the lettuce and tomatoes onto a platter. Top with warm chicken fingers. Drizzle with ranch dressing.

SERVINGS: 4 •
PREPARATION
TIME: 30 MINUTES

ROASTED GARLIC ADDS A NICE FLAVOR TO ORDINARY RANCH DRESSING. TO PREPARE ROASTED GARLIC, REMOVE THE TOP FROM 1 OR 2 GARLIC HEADS. PLACE ONTO A SHEET OF ALUMINUM FOIL. DRIZZLE WITH OLIVE OIL, DRIED OREGANO, SALT AND PEPPER. CLOSE THE FOIL AROUND THE GARLIC, LEAVING A SMALL OPENING. ROAST THE GARLIC AT 350° UNTIL THE CLOVES ARE SOFT AND PEAKING OUT FROM THE HEAD, ABOUT 20 TO 30 MINUTES. SQUEEZE THE VELVETY CLOVES FROM THE HEAD AND USE IN YOUR FAVORITE RECIPE.

Perfectly Grilled Chicken with Maple Rum Glaze

FOR BEST RESULTS, SOAK THE CHICKEN IN BRINE (A COMBINATION OF SALT AND SUGAR DISSOLVED IN WATER—SEE THE BUTTERMILK FRIED CHICKEN RECIPE ON PAGE 261), FOR 2 TO 3 HOURS BEFORE GRILLING. PAT THE CHICKEN DRY, SEASON, AND COAT WITH VEGETABLE OIL SPRAY TO PREVENT STICKING.

⅔ cup fresh orange juice
⅓ cup maple syrup
¼ cup dark rum
2 tablespoons brown sugar
2 tablespoons soy sauce
1 tablespoon Dijon mustard
2 medium cloves garlic, minced (about 1 teaspoon)
1 teaspoon dried thyme

1 4-pound chicken, cut into 8 pieces
Salt and freshly ground pepper

YOU CAN USE THIS SAME TECHNIQUE TO GRILL A WHOLE CHICKEN THAT YOU BUTTERFLY. PLACE THE CHICKEN, BREAST SIDE DOWN, ONTO YOUR WORK SURFACE. USE POULTRY SHEARS OR A VERY SHARP KNIFE TO REMOVE THE BACKBONE BY CUTTING ALONG ONE SIDE AND THEN THE OTHER. USE YOUR HANDS TO OPEN UP THE CHICKEN AND FLATTEN IT. TURN THE CHICKEN OVER AND FLATTEN IT SOME MORE. YOU CAN USE YOUR HANDS TO PRESS DOWN ON THE CHICKEN (IF YOU WORK OUT!), OR YOU CAN USE A MEAT MALLET TO GENTLY BREAK THE STERNUM AND THE RIBS. GRILL THE CHICKEN ACCORDING TO THE METHOD DESCRIBED ABOVE.

1. Whisk together the orange juice, maple syrup, rum, brown sugar, soy sauce, mustard, garlic, and thyme in a bowl. Set aside.
2. Heat an outdoor grill. Arrange the coals so that most of the heat is concentrated over ¾ of the grill area. The remaining ¼ of the grill area should have coals that are cooler and at medium heat.
3. Season the chicken with salt and pepper. Coat both sides with vegetable oil spray.
4. Place the chicken, skin side down, onto the hottest part of the grill. Cook until golden, about 5 minutes. Turn and cook for 5 minutes more. Continue to turn the chicken pieces every 5 minutes, while moving them from the hottest part of the grill to the coolest. Thicker pieces, like the breasts, will take longer to cook than smaller pieces, like the legs. All of the chicken pieces will cook in about 25 to 30 minutes total. The internal temperature should reach 165 to 170°, and the juices should run clear. Do not overcook; the chicken should be moist and juicy.
5. Baste the chicken pieces with the maple rum mixture during the last 10 minutes of cooking.

SERVINGS: 4 • PREPARATION TIME: 45 MINUTES

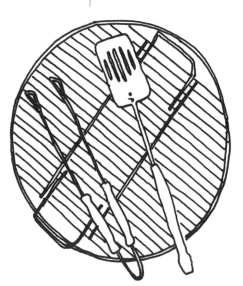

Individual Chicken Pot Pies

YOU CAN GET A JUMPSTART ON MANY CHICKEN RECIPES BY SIMPLY COOK-
ING DOUBLE THE AMOUNT OF CHICKEN YOU NEED FOR ONE MEAL, AND
SAVING THE SURPLUS FOR ANOTHER PREPARATION. BEGINNING WITH LEFT-
OVER PERFECTLY GRILLED CHICKEN (SEE PAGE 263) OR ROASTED CHICKEN
WITH HERB BUTTER (SEE PAGE 258) WILL CUT YOUR PREP TIME IN HALF.

USING FROZEN PUFF PASTRY
MAKES THIS DISH A FAST
CHOICE FOR A MIDWEEK SUP-
PER. ALTERNATIVELY, YOU
CAN TOP YOUR POT PIE WITH
HOME MADE PASTRY, MASHED
POTATOES OR EVEN POLENTA!
YOU CAN ALSO PREPARE THIS
RECIPE, USING 1 LARGE BAK-
ING DISH. POUR THE CHICKEN
MIXTURE INTO THE DISH AND
CROWN WITH ANY OF THE
ABOVE TOPPERS, OR DROP
HOMEMADE (OR FROZEN) BIS-
CUIT DOUGH ONTO THE FILL-
ING. INCREASE THE BAKING
TIME TO 30 TO 40 MINUTES
FOR THIS CASSEROLE.

4 tablespoons butter
1 large yellow onion, diced into ½-inch squares (about 1 cup)
4 tablespoons all-purpose flour
2 cups chicken broth
1 cup cream
1 4-pound chicken, cooked, skin and bones discarded, cut into ½-inch cubes (about
     4 cups)
2 large carrots, diced and blanched (about 1 cup)
1 cup frozen peas, thawed
1 cup frozen pearl onions
1 tablespoon Worcestershire sauce
Salt and freshly ground pepper
2 tablespoons chopped fresh parsley
2 sheets frozen puff pastry, thawed
1 egg, beaten
2 tablespoons grated Parmesan cheese

Preheat the oven to 350°.
1. Heat the butter in a large pot over medium high heat. Cook
the onion in the butter until soft, about 5 to 7 minutes.
2. Sprinkle the flour over the cooked onions. Stir and cook for 2
minutes.
3. Pour in the chicken broth and cream. Cook, stirring constantly until slightly thickened, about 4 to 6 minutes.
4. Stir in the chicken, carrots, peas, and pearl onions.
5. Season with Worcestershire sauce, salt, and pepper. Stir in the
parsley.
6. Pour the chicken mixture into 6 individual ramekins.
7. Cut 6 circles out of the puff pastry. The circles should be
slightly larger than the diameter of the ramekins.
8. Brush the top of each ramekin with beaten egg. Lay the puff
pastry circle on top of the ramekin. Crimp the edges of the pastry
to seal the top. Cut several slits into the top of the pastry to allow
the steam to escape. Brush the top with the remaining egg mixture. Sprinkle with grated Parmesan cheese.
9. Place the ramekins onto a rimmed baking sheet.
10. Bake for 25 to 30 minutes or until the pastry tops are puffed
and golden.

SERVINGS: 6 TO 8 (DEPENDING ON THE SIZE OF YOUR RAMEKINS) •
PREPARATION TIME: 45 MINUTES PLUS 30 MINUTES BAKING

Lemon Caper Chicken Cutlets

TRIMMED BONELESS, SKINLESS BREASTS ARE THE EASIEST WAY TO BEGIN
THIS DISH. HOWEVER, THE MOST ECONOMICAL WAY WOULD BE TO TRIM THE
BREAST FROM THE BONE AND REMOVE THE SKIN YOURSELF. EITHER WAY,
THE BUTTERY SAUCE BRIGHTENS UP EVERYDAY CHICKEN.

6 4 to 5-ounce skinless boneless chicken breast cutlets
2 tablespoons olive oil
4 tablespoons butter (½ stick)
½ cup all-purpose flour
Salt and freshly ground pepper
2 large eggs, beaten
1 large shallot, minced (about 1 tablespoon)
½ cup white wine
1 cup chicken broth
Juice of 1 lemon (about 2 tablespoons)
Zest of 1 medium lemon (about 1 tablespoon)
2 tablespoons capers, drained and rinsed
Fresh parsley

1. Place the chicken pieces between two pieces of waxed paper. Use a meat mallet or rolling pin to pound each piece to about ½-inch thickness.
2. Heat 2 tablespoons of olive oil and 2 tablespoons of butter in a skillet over medium high heat.
3. Dredge the chicken in flour, seasoned with salt and pepper.
4. Dip the chicken into the beaten eggs, allowing the excess to drip off.
5. Cook the chicken in batches in the hot oil/butter mixture until golden, about 3 to 4 minutes per side. Use additional oil and butter as needed.
6. Transfer the chicken to a platter and keep warm.
7. Add the minced shallot to the pan. Drizzle one teaspoon of the seasoned flour over the shallot and stir.
8. Add the wine to the pan and cook for 2 to 3 minutes.
9. Add the broth to the pan and reduce for 2 to 3 minutes.
10. Sprinkle half of the lemon juice and all of the zest into the pan.
11. Stir in the capers. Adjust the seasoning.
12. Pour the sauce over the chicken. Sprinkle the remaining lemon juice over top. Garnish with additional lemon slices and chopped fresh parsley.

SERVINGS: 4 TO 6 • PREPARATION TIME: 20 MINUTES

Traditional Chicken Francese

Prepare the chicken as directed in the recipe at left, and cook in hot oil. To make the sauce, place slices of 1 whole lemon into the pan. Sprinkle with flour. Eliminate the shallot and capers. Add the wine, chicken broth, lemon zest and lemon juice. Place the chicken back into the pan and cook for several more minutes, basting each cutlet with sauce. Serve with garnishes.

Lemon Ginger Chicken

THIS IS A YUMMY DISH, BEST SERVED OVER RICE OR ALONGSIDE SPAGHETTI
SQUASH TO ABSORB ALL OF THE ORIENTAL INSPIRED SAUCE.

1 cup all-purpose flour
1 tablespoon garlic powder
1 tablespoon hot paprika
Salt and frehly ground pepper
2½ pounds skinless, boneless chicken breasts, cut into 1-inch cubes
1 large red bell pepper, seeded and sliced into strips (about 1 cup)
2 tablespoons olive oil

⅓ cup soy sauce
Zest of 1 medium lemon (about 1 tablespoon)
Juice of 1 medium lemon (about 2 tablespoons)
1 tablespoon honey
1 1-inch piece ginger, grated (about 1 tablespoon)
1 bunch (6 to 8) green onions, thinly sliced on the diagonal (about ½ cup)
4 medium garlic cloves, minced (about 2 teaspoons)
½ cup olive oil
Chopped fresh tarragon

Preheat the oven to 425°.
1. Combine the flour, garlic powder and paprika in a plastic bag.
Season with salt and pepper.
2. Place the chicken cubes into a plastic bag in batches. Shake to
coat. Transfer the cubes to a baking pan, sprayed with vegetable
oil spray. Continue until all of the cubes are coated.
3. Lay the pepper strips around the chicken cubes in the pan.
Drizzle with 2 tablespoons of the olive oil.
4. Whisk together the soy sauce, lemon zest, lemon juice, honey,
ginger, onions, garlic and the remaining ½ cup olive oil.
5. Bake the chicken for 10 minutes. Remove the pan from the
oven. Pour the soy mixture over top. Reduce the heat to 350.
Bake for 20 minutes more. Garnish with chopped fresh tarragon.

SERVINGS: 4 • PREPARATION TIME: 30 MINUTES

IT IS IMPORTANT TO USE THE UTMOST CARE IN HANDLING CHICKEN. RAW CHICKEN MAY CONTAIN BACTERIA, LIKE SALMONELLA, WHICH CAUSE ILLNESS. MAKE SURE THAT NO RAW CHICKEN COMES IN CONTACT WITH ANY OTHER FOOD. THIS INCLUDES THE WRAPPER, HOLDING THE CHICKEN AND ANY JUICES. REMEMBER, WHEN PACKING UP YOUR GROCERIES, PLACE CHICKEN PACKAGES IN SEPARATE BAGS. A LEAKY CHICKEN PACKAGE, NEXT TO YOUR HEAD OF LETTUCE, CAN CAUSE REAL TROUBLE! WHEN PREPARING CHICKEN, USE A CUTTING BOARD RESERVED FOR THAT USE—PREFERABLY NOT A WOODEN ONE. WASH THE CUTTING BOARD, UTENSILS, AND YOUR HANDS JUST AS SOON AS YOU ARE FINISHED.

Chicken Cordon Bleu

THIS IS THE PERFECT CHICKEN DISH FOR A TASTY MIDWEEK MEAL; IT
BAKES IN MINUTES, AND CAN BE STUFFED WITH ALL OF YOUR FAVORITE
THINGS!

4 large (4- to 6-ounce) skinless, boneless chicken breast halves
Salt and freshly ground pepper
4 thin slices baked ham
4 thin slices Swiss cheese

½ cup all-purpose flour
2 large eggs
1 cup fresh bread crumbs
2 tablespoons chopped fresh rosemary
1 tablespoon olive oil

THIS IS A SIMPLE RECIPE,
JUST BEGGING FOR INGREDI-
ENT SUBSTITUTION. VARY THE
CHEESE WITH LORRAINE,
GRUYERE, BRIE OR GOAT
CHEESE. IN PLACE OF HAM,
EXPERIMENT WITH COOKED
BACON, PROSCIUTTO, ROAST-
ED ASPARAGUS, SUN-DRIED
TOMATOES AND OLIVE TAPE-
NADE. THERE ARE NO WRONG
CHOICES.

Preheat the oven to 350°.

1. Place the chicken breasts between 2 pieces of plastic wrap. Use
a meat mallet to pound the chicken to ¼-inch thickness. Season
with salt and pepper.

2. Place 1 piece of ham and 1 piece of cheese on each breast.

3. Tuck in the sides of the chicken. Roll up jelly-roll style.
Repeat with all four breasts.

4. Place the flour into a shallow bowl.

5. Beat the eggs with 2 tablespoons water in a shallow bowl.

6. Combine the bread crumbs with the chopped fresh rosemary
and olive oil.

7. Dip each rolled chicken breast first into the flour, then into
the egg, and finally into the seasoned bread crumbs. Place, seam
side down, into a baking dish, coated with vegetable oil spray.

8. Bake for 20 to 30 minutes or until the cheese is melted.

SERVINGS: 4 • PREPARATION TIME: 45 MINUTES

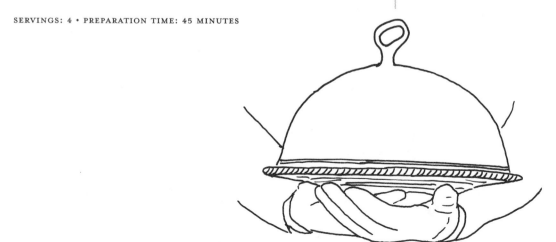

Pepperoni Stuffed Chicken Breasts
with Red Bell Pepper Sauce

IF YOU CAN IMAGINE USING A CHICKEN BREAST AS A CALZONE WRAPPER, THEN YOU GET THE GIST OF THIS EASY DISH. SERVE ON TOP OF FLORENTINE COLORED FETTUCCINI AND DRIZZLE WITH EXTRA SAUCE.

½ cup olive oil (using 2 tablespoons at a time)
1 medium yellow onion, diced (about 1½ cups)
1 large red bell pepper, seeded and diced into ½-inch pieces
4 medium garlic cloves, minced (about 2 teaspoons)
1 28-ounce can diced tomatoes
2 tablespoons tomato paste
1 teaspoon granulated sugar
Salt and freshly ground pepper

6 6- to 8-ounce skinless boneless chicken breast halves
1 10½-ounce log goat cheese
4 ounces pepperoni, chopped
2 ounces grated Parmesan cheese (about ½ cup)
2 tablespoons chopped fresh basil
2 tablespoons chopped fresh oregano
1 cup prepared bread crumbs

Preheat the oven to 350°.

1. Heat 2 tablespoons of olive oil in a saucepan over medium high heat.

2. Add the onion and pepper to the pan and cook until soft, about 5 minutes.

3. Add the garlic to the pan and cook for 2 minutes more.

4. Pour in the canned tomatoes and stir.

5. Stir in the tomato paste and sugar. Season with salt and pepper. Reduce the heat to low and simmer for 20 minutes.

6. Cut a pocket into each chicken breast.

7. Place the goat cheese and pepperoni into the bowl of a food processor. Pulse to combine.

8. Add the Parmesan cheese, basil and oregano. Pulse until just combined.

9. Stuff each chicken breast with the goat cheese filling. Season the stuffed breasts with salt and pepper.

10. Heat 2 more tablespoons of olive oil in the skillet over medium high heat.

11. Dredge each breast in bread crumbs and then place into the hot oil. Cook the breasts, turning once, until golden, about 3 to 4 minutes per side. Use additional oil as needed.

12. Place the breasts into a baking dish. Pour the sauce over the chicken. Place into the oven and cook for 15 to 20 minutes.

SERVINGS: 6 TO 8 • PREPARATION TIME: 30 MINUTES PLUS BAKING

USE AN ENTIRE BONELESS CHICKEN BREAST HALF FOR THIS DISH. CHICKEN TENDERS OR CUTLETS WILL NOT WORK AS WELL. REMOVE ANY EXTRA FAT FROM THE BREAST AND PLACE IT ONTO A CUTTING BOARD. USE A SHARP KNIFE TO SLICE INTO THE BREAST AT THE THICKEST END. CAREFULLY CUT THE POCKET, KEEPING THE KNIFE PARALLEL TO THE BOARD. YOU MAY PLACE YOUR NON-CUTTING HAND ON TOP OF THE BREAST TO KEEP THE KNIFE FLAT. CUT ABOUT A 1-INCH SLIT INTO THE BREAST, SO THAT YOU CAN INSERT ABOUT A TEASPOON OF FILLING AT A TIME. USE YOUR FINGER TO ENLARGE THE POCKET. PLACE A SPOONFUL OF FILLING INTO THE POCKET, AND PRESS IT AS DEEPLY INTO THE BREAST AS YOU CAN. CONTINUE, USING ABOUT 2 TO 3 HEAPING TEASPOONS OF FILLING.

ONCE YOU HAVE LEARNED TO MAKE THE POCKET, FEEL FREE TO FILL IT WITH YOUR FAVORITE THINGS. USE A COMBINATION OF COOKED BACON, SCALLIONS AND CHEDDAR CHEESE FOR A SOUTHWESTERN TASTE, FETA CHEESE, OLIVES AND WHITE ONIONS FOR A MEDITERRANEAN FLAVOR, OR CORNBREAD STUFFING, RAISINS AND SAUSAGE FOR A TRULY SOUTHERN FLARE. USE ANY SAUCE ON TOP OF THE CHICKEN, OR SERVE IT ON ITS OWN WITH ROASTED VEGGIES ON THE SIDE.

Chicken Cutlets Topped with Eggplant, Fontina Cheese, and Sherry Mushrooms

PREPARE THIS DISH FOR AN EASY MID-WEEK MEAL, OR SERVE IT TO YOUR
BUDDIES AT YOUR NEXT UPSCALE DINNER PARTY.

2 baby eggplants, cut lengthwise into ¼-inch slices
Salt and freshly ground pepper
Olive oil for sautéing
6 4- to 5-ounce skinless boneless chicken breast cutlets
¼ cup seasoned bread crumbs
6 ounces Fontina cheese, cut into cubes
4 ounces Baby Portobello mushrooms, chopped (about 1 cup)
4 ounces shitake mushrooms, chopped (about 1 cup)
¼ cup red wine
2 tablespoons chopped fresh parsley

Preheat the oven to 350°.

1. Season the eggplant slices with salt and pepper.

2. Heat 2 tablespoons olive oil in a skillet over medium high
heat.

3. Cook the eggplant in the skillet until golden brown, turning
once, about 4 to 5 minutes per side. Transfer the eggplant to a
paper towel-lined platter.

4. Add 2 more tablespoons of olive oil to the skillet.

5. Sprinkle both sides of the chicken cutlets with salt and pepper
and the bread crumbs.

6. Cook the chicken in the skillet until golden brown, turning
once, about 5 to 7 minutes per side. Place the cutlets into a large
baking dish.

7. Top each cutlet with eggplant slices.

8. Sprinkle the cubed cheese over top.

9. Add 2 more tablespoons of olive oil to the skillet.

10. Cook the mushrooms in the skillet until golden, about 3 to 4
minutes. Season with salt and pepper as they cook.

11. Pour the wine over the mushrooms. Continue cooking until
the liquid disappears, about 2 to 3 minutes more. Spoon the
mushrooms over the cheese.

12. Bake until the chicken is cooked through and the cheese
melts, about 20 minutes. Sprinkle with chopped fresh parsley.

SERVINGS: 6 • PREPARATION TIME: 30 MINUTES

BABY EGGPLANTS (ALSO
REFERRED TO AS ITALIAN EGG-
PLANTS) ARE THE PERFECT
CHOICE FOR THIS DISH;
THEY'RE ALSO IDEAL FOR ANY
QUICK AND EASY MEAL. THE
SKIN OF A BABY EGGPLANT IS
MORE DELICATE THAN ITS
LARGER COUNTERPART, AND,
THEREFORE, DOES NOT NEED
TO BE PEELED.

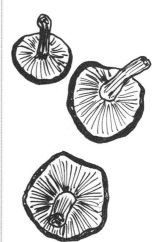

Oven-Roasted Turkey with Brandy Spiked Gravy

Marinating Turkey

If you have the time, you can insure a tender, moist turkey by marinating it overnight; this is a perfect technique to use with a small turkey or a large chicken. Place the turkey in a large soup pot. Combine ½ cup of brown sugar, 4 cups of apple juice, ½ cup of apple cider vinegar, ½ cup of brandy, salt, pepper, 4 bay leaves, fresh rosemary and thyme leaves in a bowl. Stir until the sugar dissolves. Pour this mixture over the turkey. Pour cold water over the turkey until it is completely covered. You can use a weight (heavy tomato can) to keep the turkey submerged in the marinade. Cover and refrigerate for at least 4 hours or overnight. Remove the turkey from the marinade and pat dry to continue with the recipe.

FRESH MARKETS NOW OFFER TURKEYS THAT ARE "FREE RANGE" AND "ORGANIC." DO NOT BE DAUNTED BY THESE TERMS. THESE PRODUCTS ARE A FEASIBLE ALTERNATIVE TO THE OTHERS AT YOUR GROCER. BASICALLY, THE DIFFERENCE IS THAT THE NATURAL TURKEY WILL HAVE NO ADDED FAT OR FLAVORINGS. BECAUSE OF THIS, YOU WANT TO PAY SPECIAL ATTENTION TO THE ROASTING PROCESS. AT THE START, ADD FAT AND FLAVOR IN THE FORM OF OLIVE OIL AND HERBS, OR BUTTER AND SPICES. THE BIRD MAY COOK IN LESS TIME THAN A FAT-INJECTED BIRD, SO WATCH IT CAREFULLY. ONCE YOU GET THE HANG OF IT, A "NATURAL" BIRD IS A MOIST AND HEALTHY CHOICE FOR YOUR NEXT ROASTED TURKEY SUPPER.

STUFFING THE TURKEY CAVITIES WITH FRUIT, KEEPS THE TURKEY MOIST AND TENDER. SOAKING THE FRUIT IN LIQUOR, ADDS A UNIQUE FRAGRANCE.

2 medium apples, cut into fourths
½ cup brandy
1 10-pound turkey, parts removed from cavity, rinsed
¼ cup olive oil
1 tablespoon garlic powder
1 tablespoon dried rosemary
1 tablespoon dried thyme
Salt and freshly ground pepper

1 cup chicken broth
½ cup Brandy
2 tablespoons brown sugar
2 tablespoons Worcestershire sauce
¼ cup all-purpose flour mixed with 4 tablespoons cold water

Preheat the oven 325°.
1. Soak the apples in ½ cup of brandy for 30 minutes.
2. Place the turkey on a rack in a roasting pan, breast side up.
3. Combine the olive oil, garlic powder, rosemary and thyme in a small bowl. Brush this mixture all over the turkey. Season with salt and pepper.
4. Place the brandy-soaked apples into the cavity of the turkey.
5. Roast the turkey until golden and the juices run clear, about 20 minutes per pound. Insert a thermometer to check the temperature, which should reach 175 to 180°. Baste the turkey with pan juice during the last 30 minutes of roasting.
6. Transfer the turkey to your work surface. Discard the apples. Allow the turkey to rest for 15 minutes before carving. Place the roasting pan onto the stove top, over medium high heat.
7. Pour the chicken broth and brandy into the pan. Stir, scraping any loose bits from the bottom of the pan.
8. Whisk in the brown sugar and Worcestershire sauce. Bring to a boil and cook for 5 minutes.
9. Whisk in the flour mixture, a little at a time, until the gravy thickens. Season with salt and pepper. Strain the gravy through a colander.
10. Serve the turkey with the gravy on the side. Garnish with fresh herbs.

SERVINGS: 8 TO 10 • PREPARATION TIME: 30 MINUTES PLUS ROASTING

Moroccan Spiced Cornish Hens
with Forty Cloves of Garlic

THIS RECIPE IS INSPIRED BY A PROVENÇAL DISH THAT INCORPORATES 40 CLOVES OF GARLIC WITH OVEN-ROASTED CHICKEN. (POULET A QUARANTE GOUSSES D'AIL.) THE GARLIC HERE IS TEMPERED WITH SWEET SHALLOTS AND BUTTERNUT SQUASH. CORNISH HENS GIVE THE DISH AN INSPIRED UPDATE.

3 (1 to 1¼ pound) Cornish hens
¼ cup honey
Juice of 2 medium lemons (about ¼ cup)
¼ cup olive oil
2 tablespoons chili powder
1 tablespoon hot paprika
1 teaspoon ground cinnamon
1 teaspoon ground cumin
1 teaspoon salt
½ teaspoon cayenne pepper
2 medium butternut squash, peeled and diced into 1-inch squares (about 4 cups)
6 to 8 large shallots, peeled and separated into lobes
3 large heads garlic, cloves separated and peeled

2 to 4 tablespoons olive oil

Preheat the oven to 425°.
1. Cut the hens in half. Use poultry scissors or a sharp knife to remove the backbone. Turn the hen over and flatten with your hands. Cut through the breastbone.
2. Whisk together the honey, lemon juice, ¼ cup olive oil, chili powder, paprika, cinnamon, cumin, salt and cayenne pepper in a bowl.
3. Place the squash, shallots and garlic into a large baking dish or roasting pan. Toss with half of the spice mixture. Place into the oven and cook for 15 minutes.
4. Brush the hens with the remaining spice mixture.
5. Heat 2 additional tablespoons olive oil in a large skillet over medium high heat.
6. Place the hens (in batches) skin side down, into the skillet. (Use additional oil as needed.) Cook until golden, about 4 to 5 minutes. Turn and cook until golden, about 3 to 5 minutes more.
7. Remove the baking dish from the oven. Reduce the heat to 350°.
8. Place the hens on top of the vegetables. Roast until the hens are cooked through and the juices run clear, about 45 minutes.

SERVINGS: 6 • PREPARATION TIME: 35 MINUTES PLUS 45 MINUTES ROASTING

MAKE EASY WORK OF DICING BUTTERNUT SQUASH. BEGIN BY CUTTING OFF THE STEM END. THIS WILL ALLOW YOU TO STAND THE SQUASH ONTO A CUTTING BOARD. USE A SHARP KNIFE TO CUT DOWN THE CENTER OF THE SQUASH LEAVING 2 HALVES. SCOOP OUT THE SEEDS FROM THE FAT END OF THE SQUASH. USE A VEGETABLE PEELER TO CUT OFF THE OUTSIDE SKIN LEAVING THE BRIGHT ORANGE FLESH. CUT LENGTHWISE 1-INCH STRIPS AND THEN CUT THOSE INTO 1-INCH PIECES. THE WHOLE PROCESS WILL TAKE YOU LESS TIME THAN IT TAKES TO READ THIS TIP!

Moist and Fluffy Turkey Loaf

FOR THE BEST RESULTS, PURCHASE FRESHLY GROUND TURKEY. PROCESS THE TURKEY AGAIN, USING A FOOD GRINDER. USE YOUR HANDS TO MIX THE INGREDIENTS TOGETHER UNTIL JUST COMBINED. FOR A SMOOTH, MOIST AND FLUFFY RESULT, DO NOT OVER-MIX.

2½ pounds ground turkey
8 slices white bread, crusts removed
1 cup cream
1 bunch (6 to 8) green onions, chopped (about ½ cup)
4 medium cloves garlic, minced (about 2 teaspoons)
1 teaspoon fennel seeds
2 large eggs, beaten
Salt and freshly ground pepper
1 cup chili sauce

Preheat the oven to 350°.
1. Place the ground turkey into a large mixing bowl.
2. Place the bread into the bowl of a food processor. Pulse to form crumbs. Place the crumbs into a bowl.
3. Pour the cream over the bread crumbs and allow to soak for 5 minutes.
4. Add the green onions, garlic and fennel seeds to the gro turkey mixture.
5. Add the bread crumbs and eggs to the bowl. Season with salt and pepper. Mix together and form into a loaf.
6. Place the loaf into a baking dish. Pour the chili sauce over the top of the loaf. Bake for 45 minutes to 1 hour. Allow the loaf to rest for at least 10 minutes before serving.

SERVINGS: 6 TO 8 • PREPARATION TIME: 20 MINUTES PLUS 1 HOUR BAKING

Ground Turkey Meatballs and Ground Turkey Mini-loaves

Turn same-old, same-old turkey loaf into creative fun by simply altering the shape of the dish. Form the mixture into individual loaves and reduce the oven time to 20 to 25 minutes for fast baked personalized mini loaves. You can also form the mixture into meatballs, bake for 10 minutes and place into a hoagie bun with an extra drizzle of chili sauce for turkey ball hoagies.

Turkey La Bamba Casserole

LEFTOVERS FROM OVEN ROASTED TURKEY (SEE RECIPE PAGE 270) IS THE PERFECT START FOR THIS EASY DISH. IF THE LEFTOVERS HAVE BEEN GOBBLED UP, YOU CAN START WITH COOKED TURKEY FROM THE DELI OR BROWNED GROUND TURKEY.

1 tablespoon olive oil
1 small red onion, diced (about ½ cup)
2 medium cloves garlic, minced (about 1 teaspoon)
4 cups cooked turkey meat, shredded
1 teaspoon ground cumin
Salt and freshly ground pepper
1 28-ounce can diced tomatoes
4 cups tortilla chips
1 16-ounce can refried beans
2 cups sour cream
1 16-ounce can corn, drained
1 bunch (6 to 8) green onions, chopped (about ½ cup)
2 medium jalapeño peppers, seeded and diced (about ¼ cup)
8 ounces grated Cheddar cheese (about 2 cups)

Preheat the oven to 375°.

1. Heat the olive oil in a skillet over medium high heat. Cook the onion until soft, about 5 to 6 minutes.

2. Add the garlic and cook for 1 minute more.

3. Stir in the turkey. Season with cumin, salt and pepper. Set this mixture aside.

4. Pour half of the canned tomatoes into the bottom of a large baking dish.

5. Top the tomatoes with half of the corn chips.

6. Warm the refried beans in the microwave long enough to make them soft. Spread the beans on top of the chips.

7. Top the beans with half of the chicken mixture.

8. Top the chicken with half of the sour cream.

9. Add a layer of corn chips, followed by the remaining tomatoes, the corn, chicken and sour cream.

10. Top the casserole with green onions, jalapeño peppers and cheese.

11. Bake for 30 minutes, or until the cheese is melted and the casserole is bubbling. Let the casserole rest for 15 minutes before cutting.

SERVINGS: 6 • PREPARATION TIME: 30 MINUTES PLUS 30 MINUTES BAKING

THIS CASSEROLE IS AN INVITATION TO CREATE YOUR OWN BEST DISH. SUBSTITUTE CHICKEN OR GROUND BEEF FOR TURKEY AND ADD SPICES LIKE CHILI POWDER AND CAYENNE TO HEAT UP THE MEAL. SUBSTITUTE COOKED RICE FOR TORTILLA CHIPS OR BLACK BEANS FOR REFRIED. THERE ARE NO RULES HERE. SERVE WITH A TOSSED SALAD AND YOU HAVE A YUMMY DISH IN NO TIME.

Our Grandma's Stuffed Cabbage Rolls

WHEN SHE AND HUBBY ROBERT SHOT THE COVER FOR THIS BOOK, SHEILA
HURTH AND I REMINISCED ABOUT A LABOR-OF-LOVE DISH THAT OUR
GRANDMOTHERS USED TO PREPARE. YES, IT WILL TAKE YOU AWHILE—BUT
THE END RESULT IS WELL WORTH THE EFFORT. MY GRAM MADE FINGER-
SIZED CABBAGE ROLLS AND SIMMERED THEM IN A DEEP POT FOR HOURS.
THIS RECIPE MAKES LARGER BUNDLES, SO THAT YOU CAN SERVE ONE AS A
FIRST COURSE, OR SEVERAL FOR A HEARTY SUPPER.

MY MOTHER USED A SHORT-
CUT TO PREPARE THIS DISH.
SHE PUT THE ENTIRE HEAD
OF CABBAGE INTO THE FREEZ-
ER OVERNIGHT. THE NEXT
DAY, SHE REMOVED THE CAB-
BAGE AND PLACED IT ON THE
COUNTER. AS THE CABBAGE
THAWED, THE LEAVES BECAME
SOFT. IT WORKED FOR HER—
BUT SHE NEVER TOLD MY
GRANDMOTHER!

1 whole cabbage
2 tablespoons olive oil
2 large yellow onions, diced into ½-inch squares (about 2 cups)
4 medium garlic cloves, minced (about 2 teaspoons)
2 pounds ground turkey
Salt and freshly ground pepper
2 cups cooked white rice
1 cup raisins
¼ cup ketchup
1 tablespoon dried minced onions
1 teaspoon hot paprika

1 tablespoon olive oil
1 medium white onion, diced (about ⅔ cup)
2 tablespoons hot paprika
2 tablespoons tomato paste
1 28-ounce can diced tomatoes
1 cup chicken broth
2 tablespoons brown sugar
2 tablespoons balsamic vinegar
1 tablespoon chopped fresh sage

1. Heat a large pot of water to boiling over high heat. Cut the
stem and the core from the cabbage. Plunge the cabbage into the
water. This will loosen some of the outer leaves. Cook the leaves
in the boiling water for 2 minutes. Gently remove the loosened
leaves. Plunge them into a bowl of ice water to stop the cooking
process. Pat the leaves dry. Continue until all of the large leaves
have been blanched.
2. Heat 2 tablespoons olive oil in a skillet over medium high
heat. Cook the yellow onions until soft and just beginning to
turn brown, about 5 to 6 minutes. Add the garlic to the pan and
cook for 2 minutes more.
3. Add the ground turkey to the pan. Cook, breaking up the
turkey with a spatula, until browned, about 8 to 10 minutes.
Season with salt and pepper.

4. Transfer the turkey mixture to a large bowl. Add the cooked rice, raisins and ketchup. Season with salt, pepper, dried minced onions, and 1 teaspoon paprika.

5. Place ⅓ cup turkey mixture on the bottom stem portion of a cabbage leaf, leaving about a 1-inch border. Wrap the leaf, from the stem border, over the filling. Fold in the sides. Continue wrapping until all of the leaves and filling have been used.

6. Prepare the sauce by heating the remaining 1 tablespoon olive oil in a sauce pot over medium high heat. Cook the white onion until soft. Add the remaining 2 tablespoons paprika and tomato paste. Cook for 2 to 3 minutes. Add the diced tomatoes, chicken broth, brown sugar, balsamic vinegar and sage. Simmer for 5 to 10 minutes. Season with salt and pepper.

7. Place the stuffed cabbage in a single layer into a large, deep pot or Dutch oven. Cover the cabbage with the sauce. Cover the pot and simmer for 1 to 2 hours. Serve the cabbage with the sauce drizzled over the top.

SERVINGS: 6 TO 8 (ABOUT 12 TO 14 3-INCH ROLLS) • PREPARATION TIME: 90 MINUTES PLUS 2 HOURS TO SIMMER

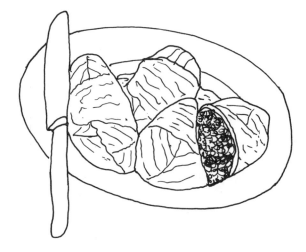

Turkey and White Bean Chili

IF YOU HAVE LEFTOVER COOKED TURKEY, FEEL FREE TO USE IT IN THIS RECIPE. YOU CAN SPICE THE DISH UP BY ADDING AS MUCH CHILI POWDER AS YOU LIKE.

LIKE MOST SOUPS AND STEWS, CHILI OFTEN TASTES BETTER THE DAY AFTER YOU COOK IT. THE FLAVORS HAVE TIME TO MARRY AND BLEND. TO STORE THE CHILI, COOL THE POT TO ROOM TEMPERATURE. IF YOU STORE HOT CHILI, STEAM WILL FORM AND ADD LIQUID TO THE DISH. POUR CHILI INTO A CONTAINER WITH AN AIRTIGHT LID. STORE IN THE REFRIGERATOR FOR SEVERAL DAYS OR IN THE FREEZER FOR UP TO 3 MONTHS. REHEAT REFRIGERATED CHILI BY SIMMERING IN A POT OVER MEDIUM HEAT. IF THE CHILI IS THICK, ADD A SMALL AMOUNT OF CHICKEN STOCK TO REACH THE DESIRED CONSISTENCY. FOR A REAL TREAT, SERVE LEFT OVER CHILI ON BAKED POTATOES, PASTA OR WITH SPAGHETTI SQUASH.

2 tablespoons olive oil
1 large yellow onion, diced into ½-inch squares (about 1 cup)
2 medium jalapeño peppers seeded and diced (about ¼ cup)
2 medium cloves garlic, minced (about 1 teaspoon)
2 pounds ground turkey
Salt and freshly ground pepper
2 tablespoons chili powder (or more)
1 teaspoon ground cumin
1 28-ounce can diced tomatoes
2 tablespoons tomato paste
1 16-ounce can cannellini beans, drained

Chopped fresh cilantro
Plain yogurt
Thinly sliced green onions

1. Heat the olive oil in a large skillet over medium high heat. Cook the onion and peppers until soft and just beginning to brown, about 5 to 6 minutes. Add the garlic and cook for 2 minutes more.

2. Add the ground turkey to the pan. Cook, breaking up the turkey with a spatula, until browned, about 8 to 10 minutes. Season with salt, pepper, chili powder and cumin.

3. Stir in the tomatoes and tomato paste. Bring the chili to a boil. Reduce heat, and simmer for 15 minutes.

4. Add the cannellini beans and simmer for 10 minutes more.

5. Serve the chili in bowls, garnished with cilantro, yogurt, and green onions.

SERVINGS: 6 • PREPARATION TIME: 30 MINUTES

Simply Roasted Duck with Orange Cranberry Glaze

THE HARDEST PART OF THIS DISH IS THAWING THE BIRD. MOST DUCK IS
PURCHASED FROZEN. THE BEST WAY TO THAW THE WHOLE BIRD IS TO PLACE
THE FROZEN DUCK IN YOUR REFRIGERATOR FOR 24 TO 36 HOURS.

1 4- to 5-pound duck, parts removed from cavity, rinsed
Salt and freshly ground pepper
1 orange cut into 4 wedges

1 15-ounce can jellied cranberry sauce or 1 10-ounce bag frozen cranberries
Juice of 3 medium oranges (about 1 cup)
Zest of 1 medium orange (about 2 tablespoons)
2 tablespoons chopped fresh rosemary

Preheat the oven to 425°.
1. Season the duck with salt and pepper. Place the orange wedges
into the cavity of the duck. Use a sharp knife to score (cut small
slits in) the skin of the duck. Place the duck on a rack in a roasting pan, breast side up. Roast for 15 minutes, or until just beginning to turn golden. Reduce the heat to 350°.
2. Combine the cranberry sauce, orange juice, orange zest and
chopped fresh rosemary in a saucepan over medium heat. Cook
until the cranberry sauce melts and the sauce is smooth.
3. Continue roasting until the duck is cooked to medium rare
(about 20 minutes per pound). Baste the duck with the sauce
during the last 15 minutes of roasting.
4. Remove the orange wedges. Allow the duck to rest for 15 minutes before carving. Serve the duck with extra sauce drizzled on
top.

SERVINGS: 6 • PREPARATION TIME: 15 MINUTES PLUS ROASTING

UNLIKE CHICKEN, DUCK CAN
BE SERVED RARE OR MEDIUM
RARE. YOU CAN DETERMINE
THE DONENESS OF A DUCK BY
OBSERVING THE COLOR OF
THE JUICES. THE MORE ROSY
THE JUICE, THE MORE RARE
THE BIRD. FOR MEDIUM RARE
DUCK, PICK THE DUCK UP
FROM THE PAN. NOTE THE
JUICES RUNNING OUT FROM
THE BIRD. IF THE JUICES ARE
PALE AND JUST SLIGHTLY
ROSY, THE DUCK IS MEDIUM
RARE.

Roasted Duck Breasts with Poached Cherry Sauce

SIMMERING FRESH CHERRIES IN PORT WINE MAKES FOR A LUSH ADDITION TO ORDINARY BUTTER SAUCE. ADD PERFECTLY ROASTED DUCK BREAST AND YOU ARE WAY, WAY OVER-THE-TOP!

ONLY FARM RAISED DUCK IS SOLD TO THE CONSUMER. MOST DUCK IS FROZEN, AND LABELED "DUCKLING," AS IT IS MARKETED WHEN THE BIRD IS ONLY A FEW MONTHS OLD. THE MEAT IS MILD, TENDER AND LEAN. CONSIDER COOKING DUCK AS YOU WOULD IN MOST POULTRY RECIPES. THE SIGNIFICANT DIFFERENCE IS THAT DUCK SKIN WILL YIELD MORE FAT THAN CHICKEN OR TURKEY, BUT IT IS EASILY SKIMMED AWAY.

4 6-ounce boned duck breast halves
Salt and freshly ground pepper

1 pound fresh cherries, pitted
2 large shallots, minced (about 2 tablespoons)
1 tablespoon balsamic vinegar
1 cup Port
6 tablespoons butter, chilled, cut into pieces
2 tablespoons chopped fresh thyme
Fresh rosemary sprigs

Preheat the oven to 375°.

1. Season the duck breasts with salt and pepper. Use a knife to gently score the skin.

2. Heat a skillet, coated with vegetable oil spray, over medium high heat. Place the duck, breast side down, into the skillet and cook until golden, about 5 minutes. Turn the duck. Place the skillet into the oven and roast until the duck is medium rare, about 15 minutes. Carefully remove the skillet from the oven. Transfer the duck to a platter. Keep warm.

3. Place the skillet on the stovetop over medium high heat. Add the cherries, shallots, balsamic vinegar and Port. Bring to a boil. Reduce the heat and simmer the sauce until the cherries are soft, about 6 to 8 minutes.

4. Remove the skillet from the heat. Whisk in the butter, in small amounts, until just melted. Swirl in the thyme and season with salt and pepper.

5. Carve the duck breasts into slices. Serve the sauce over top of the duck. Garnish with fresh rosemary sprigs.

SERVINGS: 6 • PREPARATION TIME: 45 MINUTES

Chapter 12

Beef, Pork, Lamb, and Veal Meals

Red meat is either the dark angel or the white knight of dieting, depending on which guru you choose to follow. My philosophy is, as with all foods, red meat has its place in a well balanced meal plan. Our fathers and mothers, as well as their fathers and mothers, were raise on beef, veal, lamb, and pork. What did they know that we do not? I tend to think that the answer has to do with portion control. I remember summer Sunday nights at my grandmother's house. Dad mastered the grill (a la Bobby Flay), while we three kids sang along with Pop Pop as he accompanied himself on the piano. Dad cooked the best porterhouse steaks—two of them—that we then sliced and divided between the seven members of the family. Fast forward to today, and steakhouse menus offer twenty-four ounce porterhouse steaks for ONE person.

Economical cooks of the fifties cooked roasts on Sundays and reinvented left overs into Wednesdays' casseroles. Successful restaurants' most experienced chefs use this cost effective method of meal planning today. Buying in bulk, cooking, and then reinventing, is a method that one can easily adapt into an efficient meal plan.

This is why you will see red meat meals paired with casseroles in this chapter. Sunday night's lamb roast turns into a rich, veggie studded Moussaka casserole. Cooking extra veal shanks produces a Moroccan spiced veal and veggie pot pie. The same cut of beef purchased for tender pot roast slow cooks to create yummy barbecued beef.

There are loads of classic dishes in these pages. Who can resist Steak Diane or my very favorite, and simple to prepare, Beef Wellington? Beef Stroganoff served over buttered egg noodles may have originated in 19th century Russia, while pork spareribs roasted with sauerkraut is a customary New Year's dish.

You will find some fun updates, too. The grilled lamb chops with a ragu of spring veggies dish is inspired by an evening spent in a fabulous West Coast restaurant. More than one Italian restaurant offers butterflied veal chops prepared Milanese style—and now you can cook the same dish at home.

Balancing well made, flavorful, red meat dishes with ample amounts of vegetable, fish and chicken alternatives, produces a reasonable and deprivation-free meal plan. I can't help reflecting back on family supper memories when planning dinner for my group of friends and pals—it's about comfort food—its about reinventing grand meals—it's about the freshness of new traditions.

Beef Wellington

THIS RENOWNED DISH IS EASY TO MAKE AND A SUPER WAY TO SHOW OFF IN FRONT OF YOUR GUESTS. THE GOOD NEWS IS THE BEEF PACKAGES CAN BE PREPARED IN ADVANCE AND BAKED 30 MINUTES BEFORE YOU SEAT YOUR GUESTS. TALK ABOUT "FAST FOOD"!

Red Wine Sauce
Heat 1 tablespoon olive oil in a skillet over medium high heat. Cook 2 large minced shallots until soft. Pour in 1 cup dry red wine. Reduce until ½ cup remains. Pour in 1 cup beef broth. Reduce until 1 cup remains, about 15 minutes. Stir in 2 tablespoons Dijon mustard, 1 tablespoon lemon juice and 1 tablespoon chopped fresh thyme. Season with salt and pepper. Simmer for 5 minutes more, or until the sauce is slightly thickened. Strain before serving.

4 1½- to 2-inch thick beef tournedos (center cut fillet of beef)
1 tablespoon olive oil
Salt and freshly ground pepper

1 tablespoon butter
2 large shallots, minced (about 2 tablespoons)
8 ounces Baby portobello mushrooms, sliced (about 2 cups)
2 tablespoons sherry
⅓ cup cream
1 tablespoon chopped fresh tarragon

1 1-pound package frozen puff pastry, thawed
1 egg, beaten with 1 tablespoon water

4 to 6 ounces pate, preferably duck mousse, cut into 4 slices

1. Brush the beef with olive oil. Season with salt and pepper. Heat a skillet over high heat. Place the steaks into the skillet and sear until well browned, about 3 to 4 minutes. Turn until both sides are golden, about 3 to 4 minutes more. Transfer to a rack and cool to room temperature.
2. Heat the butter in a skillet over medium high heat. Cook the shallots in the pan until soft, about 3 to 4 minutes. Add the mushrooms to the pan and cook until soft, about 5 minutes. Add the sherry, cream and tarragon to the pan. Season with salt and pepper. Cook until most of the liquid is absorbed, about 3 to 5 minutes more. Cool this mixture to room temperature.
3. Roll out the puff pastry sheets to about ¼-inch thickness. Cut into 4 rectangles.
4. Coat a rimmed baking sheet with vegetable oil spray.
5. Place a beef slice onto a pastry rectangle. Brush the edges of the dough with beaten egg.
6. Place a slice of pate on top of the beef. Top with sautéed mushrooms in the tarragon cream sauce. Wrap the layered beef with the pastry. Crimp the top ends together to seal the package. (Form the bundle into a purse, trimming off the excess pastry.) Repeat with all of the filet slices. Place each bundle onto the prepared baking sheet. Cover and chill for at least 1 hour or overnight.
Preheat the oven to 425°.

9. Brush each package with beaten egg. Bake for 10 minutes. Reduce the temperature to 375°. Bake until the pastry is golden, about 20 minutes more. Allow to rest for 10 minutes before serving. Serve with red wine sauce.

SERVINGS: 4 • PREPARATION TIME: 1 HOUR PLUS 30 MINUTES BAKING

Pan-Seared Steaks with Bordelaise Sauce

THE BETTER THE STEAK, THE LESS YOU HAVE TO DO TO IMPROVE ITS TASTE. CHOOSE A STEAK THAT HAS SOME MARBLING (A LITTLE FAT RUNNING THROUGH THE MEAT) TO INSURE GREAT FLAVOR.

1 tablespoon olive oil
2 large shallots, minced (about 2 tablespoons)
1 cup red wine vinegar
1 cup dry red wine
1 cup beef broth
1 tablespoon veal demi-glace
2 tablespoons butter, chilled, cut into pieces
Salt and freshly ground pepper

1 tablespoon olive oil
1 tablespoon butter
4 10- to 12-ounce boneless strip steaks, ¾- to 1-inch thick
2 tablespoons Worcestershire sauce
2 tablespoons chopped fresh parsley

BORDELAISE SAUCE IS TRADITIONALLY PREPARED WITH A BROWN STOCK, WHICH BEGINS BY BROWNING MARROW BONES IN A SKILLET, ADDING STOCK, AND REDUCING TO PRODUCE A RICH, DARK FLAVORFUL LIQUID. A SPOONFUL OF DEMI-GLACE CAN SIMULATE THE SAME RICH RESULTS, WITH MUCH LESS EFFORT. DEMI-GLACE IS AVAILABLE IN BEEF, VEAL, CHICKEN AND EVEN VEGGIE ESSENCES. YOU CAN FIND DEMI-GLACE IN SPECIALTY MARKETS AND ONLINE.

1. Heat the olive oil in a saucepan over medium high heat. Cook the shallots in the pan until soft, about 2 to 3 minutes. Pour in the vinegar and wine. Bring this mixture to a boil. Reduce heat and simmer until the liquid reduces to about ½ cup, about 30 minutes.
2. Add the beef broth. Simmer until the liquid reduces to 1 cup, about 15 minutes more.
3. Stir in demi-glace. Strain the sauce through a sieve over a small pot. Whisk in the butter. Season with salt and pepper. Keep the sauce warm, but do not simmer.
4. Heat 1 tablespoon olive oil and 1 tablespoon butter in a large skillet, over high heat to just smoking. Season the steaks with Worcestershire sauce, salt and pepper. Place the steaks into the skillet. Cook until well browned on one side, about 4 to 5 minutes. Turn and cook until browned, about 3 to 5 minutes more.
5. Serve the steaks with a drizzle of sauce and garnish with fresh parsley.

SERVINGS: 4 • PREPARATION TIME: 1 HOUR

Steak "Diane"

WITH THE RESURGENCE OF TABLESIDE DINING, THIS DISH IS GAINING A NEW AUDIENCE. AS A CHILD, I ORDERED IT EVERY TIME MY FAMILY TOOK ME TO A FANCY RESTAURANT. I STILL LOVE WATCHING THE WAITER FLAME THE BRANDY IN A SAUTÉ PAN! THIS HOME VERSION IS SIMPLE—YET ELEGANT FOR ENTERTAINING. PREPARE THE DISH IN SEPARATE BATCHES TO GET THE FULL FLAVORS FOR THE SAUCE. THE STEAKS WILL KEEP WARM IN A WARMING DRAWER OR ON THE LOWEST SETTING IN YOUR OVEN.

EXPERIENCED CHEFS KNOW HOW TO FLAME LIQUOR COMPONENTS USED IN SAUCES. THIS IS A TERRIFIC PRESENTATION TRICK, BUT ONE THAT CAN BE A LITTLE SCARY. FLAMING THE LIQUOR REMOVES THE ALCOHOL AND ALLOWS THE FLAVOR TO INFUSE INTO THE SAUCE. REDUCING THE LIQUOR OVER MEDIUM HIGH HEAT ACCOMPLISHES THE SAME THING. WHEN USING A GAS STOVE, BE CAREFUL TO REMOVE THE PAN AWAY FROM THE FLAME, BEFORE ADDING THE BRANDY! IF THE SAUCE ACCIDENTALLY IGNITES, SIMPLY ALLOW THE BRANDY TO BURN OFF (IT WILL TAKE JUST A FEW MOMENTS), THEN WINK AT YOUR GUESTS AND PRETEND YOU PLANNED IT ALL ALONG!

2 pounds thin-sliced top sirloin steak
Salt and freshly ground pepper
2 tablespoons butter
2 tablespoons olive oil
2 large shallots, minced (about 2 tablespoons)
8 ounces button mushrooms, sliced (about 2 cups)
2 tablespoons Dijon mustard
¾ cup brandy
¾ cup beef broth
⅓ cup cream
2 tablespoons chopped fresh chives

Preheat the oven to the lowest setting or heat a warming drawer.

1. Season the steaks with salt and pepper. If thin slices are not available, cut 6 portions. Place each portion between 2 pieces of waxed paper or plastic wrap. Use a meat mallet to pound each into ¼-inch thickness.

2. Heat 1 tablespoon butter and 1 tablespoon olive oil in a skillet over medium high heat.

3. Place 2 of the steaks in the butter/oil mixture. Cook until just brown, about 2 minutes. Turn the steaks and cook for 2 minutes more. Transfer the steaks to a platter. Continue until all of the steaks are cooked and transferred to the platter. Use additional oil and butter as needed.

4. To begin the sauce, add the minced shallots to the pan. Stir and cook over medium high heat for 1 minute.

5. Add the mushrooms to the pan. Stir and cook for 2 minutes.

6. Stir the mustard into the sauce.

7. Remove the pan from the heat. Pour in the brandy. Carefully return the pan to the heat. Cook until most of the liquid disappears from the pan, about 5 to 7 minutes.

8. Pour in the beef broth. Cook for 3 to 5 minutes more. The liquid should reduce to about ½ cup.

9. Pour in the cream. Cook for 2 minutes more.

10. Pour the sauce over the steaks. Garnish the dish with chopped fresh chives.

SERVINGS: 6 • PREPARATION TIME: 30 MINUTES

Mustard-Crusted Broiled Skirt Steak

SKIRT STEAK IS A RICHLY MARBLED CUT OF MEAT. BROILING THE STEAK
CARAMELIZES THE TOPPING, ADDING AN EXTRA BOOST OF FLAVOR.

1 1½ pound skirt steak
4 medium garlic cloves
2 tablespoons soy sauce
2 tablespoons Dijon mustard
Juice of 1 medium lime (about 1 tablespoon)
2 tablespoons chopped fresh cilantro
2 tablespoons chopped fresh thyme
¼ cup olive oil
Salt and freshly ground pepper

Preheat the oven to broil setting

1. Cut the skirt steak so that it will fit onto a broiling pan.

2. Place the garlic, soy sauce, Dijon mustard, lime juice,
cilantro, and thyme into a food processor. Pulse to combine.
With the motor running, pour in the olive oil. Season with salt
and pepper.

3. Brush the mixture over the skirt steak. Let the steak sit for 30
minutes.

4. Broil the steak until medium rare, about 6 to 8 minutes.
Allow the steak to rest for 5 minutes before slicing across the
grain.

SERVINGS: 4 • PREPARATION TIME: 20 MINUTES

SKIRT STEAK IS CUT FROM
THE BEEF FLANK; IT IS A LESS
TENDER CUT OF MEAT, AND IS,
THEREFORE, OFTEN MARINAT-
ED BEFORE GRILLING.
HOWEVER, IF YOU CUT THE
MEAT ACROSS THE GRAIN, IT
IS FLAVORFUL AND QUITE
SUPPLE. SKIRT STEAK IS
MOST OFTEN USED FOR FAJI-
TAS, AND IS OFTEN FOUND
GRILLED WITH SPICY
CHIMICHURRI SAUCE.

Classic Beef Stroganoff with Wild Mushrooms

THIS DISH SCREAMS "COMFORT FOOD" AND IS BEST SERVED ON A CHILLY
NIGHT WHEN THE ONLY SCHEDULED, AFTER-SUPPER ACTIVITY IS LIFTING
YOUR FEET ONTO THE OTTOMAN!

THE SECRET TO SUCCESS IN PREPARING THIS DISH IS IN MAKING SURE YOU ADD THE SOUR CREAM AT A TEMPERATURE THAT DOES NOT COMPROMISE THE RICH SAUCE. A SAFE METHOD IS TO PLACE THE SOUR CREAM INTO A BOWL. ADD A LADLEFUL OF HOT SAUCE FROM THE PAN. WHISK THE SAUCE INTO THE SOUR CREAM. REDUCE THE HEAT OF THE SAUCE TO MEDIUM LOW. SLOWLY ADD THE SOUR CREAM MIXTURE TO THE PAN.

2½ pounds beef tenderloin, cut into ½ x 2-inch strips
Salt and freshly ground pepper
½ cup all-purpose flour
2 to 6 tablespoons olive oil
2 to 6 tablespoons butter
4 ounces Baby portobello mushrooms, sliced (about 1 cup)
4 ounces shitake mushrooms, chopped (about 1 cup)
1 large yellow onion, thinly sliced (about 1 cup)
2 tablespoons chopped fresh rosemary
½ cup red wine
2 tablespoons tomato paste
1 tablespoon Dijon mustard
1 tablespoon Worcestershire sauce
3 cups beef broth
1½ cups sour cream

1 pound wide egg noodles, cooked and tossed with butter
2 tablespoons chopped fresh parsley

1. Season the beef with salt and pepper. Dredge each piece in flour. (Place the flour in a plastic bag. Add the beef, in batches. Seal the bag and shake to coat.)

2. Heat 2 tablespoons olive oil and 2 tablespoons of butter in a large skillet over medium high heat. Cook the beef in batches until browned, about 1 to 2 minutes. Transfer the beef to a platter. Add additional oil and butter as needed.

3. Place 2 tablespoons more olive oil and butter into the same skillet. Cook the mushrooms and onion until soft and golden, about 5 to 7 minutes. Season with chopped fresh rosemary, salt and pepper.

4. Pour the wine into the pan, scraping the brown bits from the bottom. Simmer for 5 minutes.

5. Stir in the tomato paste, mustard and Worcestershire sauce. Whisk in the beef broth. Simmer until the sauce thickens, slightly, about 5 to 8 minutes.

6. Add the beef and mushrooms to the pan. Stir in the sour cream. Serve over wide buttered noodles and garnish with chopped fresh parsley.

SERVINGS: 4 TO 6 • PREPARATION TIME: 1 HOUR

Ground Meat and Peas

WE GREW UP EATING THIS EASY-TO-PREPARE DISH. A CROSS BETWEEN CHILI AND SPAGHETTI, IT'S A CHILDHOOD FAVORITE. SERVE IT OVER RICE, PASTA OR ALL BY ITSELF IN A BIG CROCK. YOU CAN GARNISH WITH CHOPPED FRESH HERBS AND ADD YOUR FAVORITE VEGGIES—BUT DON'T DARE TELL ANYONE HOW SIMPLE IT IS—THEY WON'T BELIEVE YOU!

1 tablespoon olive oil
1 large yellow onion, diced into ½-inch squares (about 1 cup)
2 medium cloves garlic, minced (about 1 teaspoon)
2 pounds lean ground beef
1 teaspoon ground cumin
Salt and freshly ground pepper
2 tablespoons Worcestershire sauce
½ cup ketchup
1 16-ounce can baby peas, drained

1. Heat the olive oil in a skillet over medium high heat. Cook the onion in the pan until soft and well browned, about 8 minutes.
2. Stir in the garlic and cook for 5 minutes more.
3. Add the beef to the pan. Cook, breaking up the meat with a spatula, until browned, about 8 to 10 minutes. Season with cumin, salt and pepper.
4. Stir in the Worcestershire sauce, ketchup and peas.

SERVINGS: 6 • PREPARATION TIME: 20 MINUTES

FAMILY FAVORITE RECIPES ARE HANDED DOWN FROM GENERATION TO GENERATION; EACH COOK TAKES THE DISH TO THE NEXT LEVEL. MY GRANDMOTHER MADE THIS DISH WHEN THE KIDS DROPPED BY FOR A SLEEP OVER. MY MOM ADDED PASTA AND CHEESE AND BAKED THE DISH TO MAKE HER FAMILY FAVORITE "GLOP." I ADD MY TWIST BY SERVING THE BEEF MIXTURE IN SAVORY PEPPERS AND THEN ROASTING THE DISH WITH SOME SPICY TOMATO SAUCE. ANY WAY YOU SLICE IT, A FAMILY FAVORITE RECIPE IS ALL ABOUT THE GOOD TIMES SHARED.

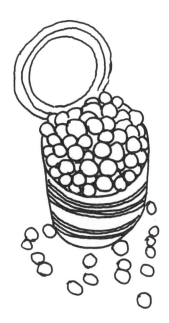

Yankee Pot Roast

A POT ROAST BECOMES A "YANKEE" POT ROAST WITH THE ADDITION OF VEGETABLES. ADD THE VEGGIES TO THE DISH WITH ABOUT 1 TO 1½ HOURS COOKING TIME REMAINING. THE ROAST WILL TAKE A MUCH LONGER TIME TO COOK THAN THE VEGGIES. IF YOU ADD THEM AT THE START OF THE COOKING PROCESS, THEY WILL TURN TO MUSH.

BRAISING THE ROAST IN LIQUID OVER LOW HEAT FOR SEVERAL HOURS, TENDERIZES AN OTHERWISE TOUGH PIECE OF MEAT. YOU CAN PREPARE THIS DISH USING A SLOW COOKER. SIMPLY BROWN THE ROAST IN A SKILLET, AND THEN TRANSFER IT TO YOUR SLOW COOKER. BROWN AND ADD THE VEGGIES. CONTINUE WITH THE WINE, BROTH AND SEASONINGS. COOK ACCORDING TO THE DIRECTIONS ON YOUR MACHINE, BUT COUNT ON ALL-DAY COOKING AT THE VERY LEAST. BECAUSE THIS MACHINE COOKS SO SLOWLY, THE VEGGIES WILL RETAIN THEIR TEXTURE. THICKEN THE SAUCE ON THE STOVETOP BY ADDING THE BEURRE MANIE (FLOUR AND BUTTER PASTE).

1 (3 to 4 pound) chuck roast
Salt and freshly ground pepper
½ cup all-purpose flour
2 tablespoons olive oil
2 large yellow onions, peeled and cut into 2-inch wedges (about 4 cups)
6 large carrots, peeled and cut into 2-inch pieces (about 4 cups)
4 medium celery ribs, cut into 2-inch pieces (about 2 cups)
6 large potatoes, peeled and cut into 2-inch pieces (about 6 cups)
2 cups beef broth
2 cup red wine
Fresh thyme sprigs
2 bay leaves
2 tablespoons butter, room temperature
2 tablespoons all-purpose flour

1. Season the beef with salt and pepper. Dredge in flour.
2. Heat the olive oil in a large pot with lid, or Dutch oven, over medium high heat. Brown the roast in the pot on both sides. Transfer to a platter.
3. Add the vegetables to the pot and cook until just beginning to turn golden, about 10 minutes. Transfer the vegetables to a bowl and set aside.
4. Return the roast to the pot.
5. Pour in the beef broth and wine.
6. Add thyme sprigs and bay leaves. Bring the liquid to a boil. Cook for 5 minutes. Reduce the heat, cover the pot, and simmer for 1 to 1½ hours.
7. Add the vegetables to the pot. Continue cooling until the meat is so tender, it falls away from the bone, and the vegetables are very tender, about 3 to 3½ hours total. (You can place the covered pot in a 325° oven for the same amount of time.
8. Remove the meat and vegetables to a platter. Slice the beef into pieces. Remove the bay leaves and thyme sprigs from the liquid.
9. Use a fork to combine the butter and flour to a smooth paste. Add this to the liquid in the pot. Increase the heat, so that the sauce simmers and thickens. Season with salt and pepper. Cook for about 5 minutes. Serve the sauce as gravy over the meat and veggies. Garnish with additional fresh thyme sprigs.

SERVINGS: 6 • PREPARATION TIME: 40 MINUTES PLUS SIMMERING FOR 3 OR MORE HOURS

Beef Brisket Braised in Beer

IN OUR FILE OF BRAISED BEEF RECIPES, BEEF BRISKET SHOULD NOT BE
OVERLOOKED. THIS RECIPE INFUSES GREAT FLAVORS WITH DARK BEER TO
PRODUCE ONE GREAT TASTING BRISKET. SERVE WITH MASHED POTATOES
AND BRAISED VEGGIES FOR A HEARTY MEAL.

1 3-pound beef brisket
Salt and freshly ground pepper
2 tablespoons olive oil
¼ pound baked ham, cut into ¼-inch dice
2 large yellow onions, diced into ½-inch squares (about 2 cups)
½ cup ketchup
½ cup chili sauce
½ cup honey
⅓ cup Worcestershire sauce
2 tablespoons soy sauce
2 12-ounce bottles dark beer
2 bay leaves

Preheat the oven to 300°.

1. Season the brisket with salt and pepper.
2. Heat the olive oil in a large pot (with lid) or Dutch oven over
medium high heat.
3. Cook the ham until just beginning to crisp. Transfer the ham
to paper toweling to drain.
4. Brown the brisket in the oil on all sides. Remove from the pot
and transfer to a platter.
5. Cook the onions in the oil and drippings until soft and gold-
en, about 6 to 8 minutes.
6. Stir in the ketchup, chili sauce, honey, Worcestershire sauce
and soy sauce.
7. Return the brisket and ham to the pot. Pour in the beer. Add
the bay leaves.
8. Cover and braise the brisket in the oven for 3 to 4 hours.
9. Remove the bay leaves from the pot. Transfer the brisket to a
platter. Slice the meat in strips against the grain.
10. Bring the liquid to a boil. Thicken with beurre manie (2
tablespoons room temperature butter, combined with 2 tablespoons all-purpose flour). Serve the sauce over top of the brisket
slices.

SERVINGS: 6 • PREPARATION TIME: 30 MINUTES PLUS 3 TO 4 HOURS BRAIS-
ING IN THE OVEN

BRISKET IS CUT FROM THE
BREAST SECTION, AND IS USU-
ALLY SOLD WHOLE AND BONE-
LESS. THE "FLAT CUT" IS
LEANER AND MORE EXPENSIVE
THAN THE "POINT CUT,"
WHICH HAS MORE FAT. MOST
COOKS ARE FAMILIAR WITH
THE SAINT PATRICK'S DAY
DISH OF CORNED BEEF AND
BOILED CABBAGE. CORNED
BEEF IS MADE FROM BEEF
BRISKET.

THIS IS A TERRIFIC RECIPE TO
ADAPT FOR YOUR SLOW COOK-
ER. FOLLOW THE RECIPE
THROUGH STEP NUMBER 5.
THEN THROW EVERYTHING
INTO YOUR MACHINE; SET THE
TEMPERATURE TO MEDIUM AND
COME BACK AT THE END OF
THE DAY TO A GREAT MEAL!

Beef Short Ribs in Red Wine Sauce

TOUGHER CUTS OF BEEF BENEFIT FROM A SLOW-COOKING PROCESS THAT BOTH TENDERIZES AND INFUSES THE MEAT WITH YOUR FAVORITE FLAVORS. THE END RESULT IS A SUCCULENT SERVING OF MEAT AND THE MAKINGS OF A FRAGRANT, SAVORY SAUCE.

8 meaty beef short ribs, about 3 pounds
Salt and freshly ground pepper
Flour for dredging
4 tablespoons olive oil
1 large yellow onion, diced (about 1 cup)
2 large carrots, diced (about 1 cup)
2 medium celery ribs, diced (about 1 cup)
6 medium garlic cloves, thinly sliced (about ¼ cup)
2 cups red wine
3 cups beef broth
2 sprigs fresh rosemary
2 tablespoons tomato paste
2 tablespoons chopped fresh parsley

Preheat the oven to 350°.

1. Season the ribs with salt and pepper.
2. Dredge each rib in flour. Shake off excess.
3. Warm the olive oil in a deep Dutch oven (or heavy pot) over medium high heat.
4. Place the ribs in the oil, turning to brown on all sides. Transfer the ribs to a platter.
5. Add the onion, carrots, celery, and garlic to the pan. Cook until the veggies are soft and begin to brown.
6. Return the ribs and any juices from the platter to the pot.
7. Pour in the wine and beef stock and submerge the rosemary sprigs. Cover the pot and bring to a boil.
8. Place the pot into the oven and continue cooking for about 2 hours.
9. Remove the pot from the oven and return to stovetop. Remove the lid. The meat should be tender and falling off the bone. Use tongs to transfer the ribs to a serving platter.
10. Bring the sauce to a boil over medium high heat. Remove the rosemary sprigs. Stir in the tomato paste. Cook for 10 minutes. Use an immersion blender to purée all of the vegetables in the sauce.
11. Pour the sauce over the ribs. Season with parsley, salt, and pepper.

SERVINGS: 4 TO 6 • PREPARATION TIME: 20 MINUTES PREPARATION PLUS 2 HOURS SIMMERING

Italian Braised Beef Short Ribs

For a different twist on this easy recipe, add a 28-ounce can of diced tomatoes to the braising liquid, along with a teaspoon of ground oregano. Finish the sauce with chopped fresh basil in place of parsley.

THIS IS A SUPER RECIPE TO USE IN YOUR SLOW COOKER. THE SECRET IS TO BROWN THE BEEF IN A SKILLET, AND THEN PLACE THE RIBS INTO THE COOKER. ADD THE REST OF THE INGREDIENTS, COVER, AND RETURN SEVERAL HOURS LATER TO FIND A TASTY, WELL-COOKED DISH. YOU CAN EASILY POUR THE EXCESS LIQUID INTO A POT AND BRING TO A BOIL, REDUCING AND THICKENING TO A SAUCE. YUMM!

Slow-Cooked Barbecued Beef

USING A SLOW COOKER MAKES EASY WORK OF THIS DISH. IF YOU'RE IN A HURRY, PREPARE THE BEEF BY SIMMERING THE INGREDIENTS IN A COVERED POT OVER MEDIUM HEAT, ABOUT 45 MINUTES.

2 pounds beef chuck roast, trimmed, cut into 1-inch cubes
Salt
2 large yellow onions, sliced (about 2 cups)
1 cup ketchup
1 cup chili sauce
½ cup white wine vinegar
2 tablespoons brown sugar
1 tablespoon Dijon mustard
1 teaspoon hot paprika
½ teaspoon dried red pepper flakes
1 teaspoon cornstarch mixed with 2 tablespoons cold water

6 large Kaiser rolls, toasted

YOU CAN FLAVOR THIS DISH WITH YOUR FAVORITE BARBE- CUE SAUCE INGREDIENTS— OR TAKE A TOTAL PASS AND DUMP A BOTTLE OF BARBE- CUE SAUCE INTO THE SLOW COOKER, SET THE DIAL, AND HEAD TO YOUR OFFICE; REMEMBER TO KEEP THIS HANDY LITTLE TRICK BETWEEN US!

1. Season the beef with salt.
2. Place the beef and onions into the bottom of a slow cooker.
3. Whisk together the ketchup, chili sauce, vinegar, brown sugar, mustard, paprika, and red pepper flakes. Pour this mixture over top of the beef and onions. Stir.
4. Cook (according to the directions on your machine) until the meat is very tender, about 8 hours.
5. Remove the beef from the slow cooker. Use a fork to shred the meat. Return the shredded beef to the pot.
6. Turn up the heat and simmer the beef mixture. (You may have to transfer the contents of the slow cooker to a pot on the stove.)
7. Stir in the cornstarch mixture and cook to thicken the sauce, about 10 minutes.
8. Serve the barbecue beef on toasted rolls.

SERVINGS: 6 • PREPARATION TIME: 15 MINUTES PLUS SLOW COOKING FOR 8 HOURS

Sausage Stuffed Pork Roast

THIS DISH IS ELEGANT ENOUGH TO SERVE AT A DINNER PARTY, AND EASY ENOUGH TO PREPARE FOR A FAMILY SUPPER.

4 tablespoons olive oil
1 large yellow onion, diced into ½-inch squares (about 1 cup)
1 pound mild Italian sausage
2 medium apples, peeled and cut into ½-inch dice (about 2 cups)
1 pound fresh spinach leaves, washed, dried and torn (about 3 cups)
Salt and freshly ground pepper

1 3- to 4-pound boneless pork roast

Preheat the oven to 350°.

1. Heat 2 tablespoons olive oil in a skillet over medium high heat. Cook the onion until soft, about 3 minutes.

2. Add the sausage to the pan. Cook, breaking up the sausage with a spatula until browned, about 8 to 10 minutes.

3. Add the apples and cook for 3 to 5 minutes. Add the spinach and cook until just wilted, about 4 minutes more. Cool the stuffing to room temperature.

4. Cut a lengthwise slit in the pork roast, forming a pocket. Do not cut all the way through. Season the pork roast on the inside and out with salt and pepper.

5. Pack the stuffing in the pocket. Use butcher's twine to tie the pork roast together.

6. Heat remaining 2 tablespoons olive oil in the skillet, over medium high heat. Place the tied pork roast into the skillet. Brown on all sides. Place the pork roast on a rack in a roasting pan. Bake until a thermometer reaches an internal temperature of 170°, about 25 minutes per pound.

7. Allow the pork roast to rest for 10 minutes. Remove the twine. Cut into 8 to 10 slices.

SERVINGS: 6 TO 8 •
PREPARATION TIME: 30
MINUTES PLUS ROASTING

FEEL FREE TO STUFF THE PORK ROAST WITH YOUR FAVORITE INGREDIENTS. TASTY SUGGESTIONS INCLUDE PINE NUTS, SUN-DRIED TOMATOES, BREAD CRUMBS, SEAFOOD, DRIED FRUIT, MUSHROOMS, HERBS AND SPICES. REMEMBER THAT A STUFFED PORK ROAST WILL TAKE ABOUT 10 MINUTES MORE PER POUND TO ROAST VS. ONE THAT IS NOT STUFFED. IF YOU'RE HANDY AT USING A PASTRY BAG, YOU CAN EMPLOY AN ALTERNATIVE STUFFING METHOD: USE A SHARP KNIFE TO MAKE AN "X" SHAPED INCISION AT ONE END OF THE PORK ROAST. INSERT A LONG METAL PROBE (LIKE A KNIFE SHARPENING BLADE) THROUGH THE INCISION AND INTO THE MIDDLE OF THE ROAST. MOVE THE PROBE AROUND TO CREATE A CENTER POCKET. USE A FOOD PROCESSOR TO EMULSIFY THE STUFFING INGREDIENTS. PLACE THE STUFFING INTO A PASTRY BAG. INSERT THE TIP OF THE BAG INTO THE POCKET. GENTLY SQUEEZE THE STUFFING INTO THE CENTER HOLE THAT YOU HAVE CREATED. THERE IS NO NEED TO TIE THE PORK ROAST TOGETHER, AS THE HOLE IS IN ITS CENTER.

Lemon Baked Pork Chops
with Green Peppercorn Sauce

FRESHLY SQUEEZED LEMON JUICE ADDS A TERRIFIC FLAVOR TO EVERYDAY
PORK CHOPS, WHILE THE SPICY SAUCE TAKES THEM FROM A MIDWEEK SUP-
PER TO SATURDAY NIGHT'S SPECIAL IN JUST MINUTES.

4 8-ounce boneless pork chops, about 1½-inch thick
Salt and freshly ground pepper
Seasoned bread crumbs
Juice of 2 medium lemons (about ¼ cup)
2 tablespoons olive oil

1 tablespoon olive oil
2 tablespoons green peppercorns
1 small white onion, finely diced (about ½ cup)
2 medium cloves garlic, minced (about 1 teaspoon)
½ teaspoon dried red pepper flakes
½ cup balsamic vinegar
½ cup Worcestershire sauce
¾ cup molasses
2 tablespoons tomato paste
3 cups beef broth
2 tablespoons chopped fresh cilantro

Lemon slices
Chopped fresh parsley

Preheat the oven to 350°.

I. Season the pork chops with salt and pepper. Dredge in seasoned bread crumbs. Squeeze half of the lemon juice over both
sides of the chops. Heat 2 tablespoons olive oil in a large skillet,
over medium high heat. Cook the chops until golden, about 4 to
6 minutes. Turn and cook until both sides are golden, about 4 to
5 minutes more. Place the chops in a baking dish. Sprinkle with
the remaining lemon juice. Bake until cooked through, about 25
to 30 minutes.

2. Heat I more tablespoon olive oil in a saucepan over medium
high heat. Cook the peppercorns, onion, garlic, and red pepper
flakes until the onion is soft, about 5 minutes.

3. Pour in the vinegar and Worcestershire. Simmer until this
mixture reduces to about ½ cup. Pour in the molasses, tomato
paste and beef broth. Bring to a boil. Reduce heat and simmer
vigorously until the liquid reduces to about 1½ cups. Stir in the
cilantro. Season with salt and pepper.

4. Swirl a ladleful of sauce onto a serving plate. Top with a pork
chop. Garnish with lemon slices and chopped fresh parsley.

SERVINGS: 4 • PREPARATION TIME: 45 MINUTES

DID YOU KNOW THAT PEPPER
STIMULATES GASTRIC JUICES,
THEREBY AIDING DIGESTION?
NO WONDER THERE IS A PEP-
PERMILL ON EVERY DINING
TABLE IN EVERY RESTAURANT
IN AMERICA! PEPPERCORNS
ARE BERRIES, FOUND IN INDIA
AND INDONESIA. IF THE
BERRIES ARE RIPE, THEY ARE
BLACK AND VERY PUNGENT.
WHITE PEPPERCORNS HAVE
RIPENED, BUT THE SKIN IS
REMOVED TO CREATE A LESS
SPICY BERRY. GREEN PEP-
PERCORNS ARE UNDER RIPE
BERRIES FROM THE PEPPER
PLANT. MOST OFTEN, GREEN
PEPPERCORNS ARE PRE-
SERVED IN BRINE AND ARE
SOFT. A GOOD SUBSTITUTION
FOR GREEN PEPPERCORNS
ARE CAPERS.

Tequila Mojo-Marinated Pork Tenderloins with Black Bean Sauce

THE MARINADE FOR THIS DISH HAILS FROM TRADITIONAL MEXICAN MOJO SAUCE, WHICH IS A BLEND OF CITRUS AND GARLIC. THE TEQUILA ADDS A NICE OOMPH! FOR AN EVEN SPICIER SAUCE, SUBSTITUTE WITH ONE CHIPOTLE PEPPER IN ADOBO SAUCE, SEEDED, IN PLACE OF THE JALAPEÑO.

PORK TENDERLOIN IS A LEAN CUT OF PORK, PERFECT FOR THE GRILL. BECAUSE OF ITS SWEET, MILD TASTE, PORK PAIRS WELL WITH ALL TYPES OF VEGGIES AND FRUIT. A FAST COOKING MEAT, IT HAS AN IMPORTANT PLACE IN A WELL-BALANCED MEAL PLAN. FRESH PORK WILL HAVE A CLEAN SMELL, WHITE FAT AND PINK (NOT GRAY) FLESH. STORE IN THE REFRIGERATOR FOR 2 TO 3 DAYS, OR IN A FREEZER FOR UP TO 3 MONTHS. REMEMBER TO WRAP WELL IN PLASTIC WRAP OR BAGS TO PREVENT FREEZER BURN.

½ cup tequila
½ cup olive oil
Juice of 1 medium grapefruit (about 1 cup)
2 tablespoons chopped fresh cilantro
6 medium garlic cloves, minced (about 3 teaspoons)
Salt and freshly ground pepper
2 14- to 16-ounce pork tenderloins

1 16-ounce can black beans
2 medium cloves garlic, minced (about 1 teaspoon)
2 medium jalapeño peppers, seeded and diced (about ¼ cup)
1 16-ounce can diced tomatoes
1 teaspoon ground cumin
Fresh rosemary sprigs

1. Whisk together the tequila, olive oil, grapefruit juice, cilantro and 3 teaspoons minced garlic. Season with salt and pepper.
2. Place the tenderloin into a baking dish. Pour the mojo over top. Turn the pork to coat. Cover and refrigerate for at least 30 minutes, and up to 4 hours.
3. For sauce, heat the black beans, remaining teaspoon minced garlic, peppers, tomatoes and cumin in a saucepot over medium high heat. Simmer for 5 to 10 minutes. Pour this mixture into a food processor. Pulse to emulsify. Keep the sauce warm.
4. Heat a grill (or grill pan) over medium high heat. Remove the pork from the marinade and disregard the liquid. Grill the tenderloins, turning once, until medium rare, about 8 minutes per side.
5. Allow the tenderloins to rest before carving. Slice into diagonal medallions. Serve with the warm sauce. Garnish with fresh rosemary sprigs.

SERVINGS: 4 TO 6 • PREPARATION TIME: 45 MINUTES PLUS MARINATING

Hoisin and Ginger Spiced Pork with Veggies

IF YOU LOVE STIR-FRY, YOU'RE SURE TO APPLAUD THIS COMBINATION OF TENDER PORK, BRAISED VEGGIES AND GINGER. THE MEAL COOKS QUICKLY, EVEN THOUGH THE RECIPE USES A SLOW COOKING METHOD. TO MAKE THIS DISH USING A SLOW COOKER, SUBSTITUTE PORK SHOULDER FOR PORK TENDERLOIN AND SERVE WITH GINGER RISOTTO (SEE PAGE 186).

2 tablespoons olive oil
2 whole pork tenderloins cut into 1-inch cubes (about 2 pounds)
Salt and freshly ground pepper
3 large carrots, cut into 1-inch pieces (about 2 cups)
2 medium white onions, cut into wedges (about 1⅓ cups)
2 medium red bell peppers, seeded and cut into wedges (about 2 cups)

½ cup red wine
2 cups beef broth
1 2-inch piece ginger cut in half
¼ cup Hoisin sauce
1 teaspoon cornstarch mixed with 2 tablespoons water (optional)

HOISIN SAUCE IS A CHINESE CONDIMENT, ALSO REFERRED TO AS PEKING SAUCE; IT IS THICK, REDDISH-BROWN IN COLOR, AND HAS A SWEET, YET SPICY TASTE. HOISIN SAUCE IS A MIXTURE OF GARLIC, SOYBEANS, CHILIES AND OTHER SPICES AND WORKS WELL TO FLAVOR MEAT, POULTRY AND SHELLFISH DISHES. HOISIN SAUCE IS FOUND IN ASIAN MARKETS AND IN MOST LARGE GROCERY STORES.

1. Heat the olive oil in a large pot over medium high heat.
2. Season the pork cubes with salt and pepper.
3. Cook the pork cubes in the hot oil until browned on all sides. Remove the pork from the pot.
4. Add the vegetables to the pot and cook for 3 to 5 minutes until they just begin to brown.
5. Return the pork to the pot with its juices.
6. Pour in the wine and beef stock.
7. Bury the ginger pieces in the pot.
8. Stir in the Hoisin sauce.
9. Simmer the pork and vegetable, uncovered for 20 to 30 minutes, or until the sauce is reduced and slightly thickened. Remove ginger pieces before serving. For a thicker sauce, add additional Hoisin or a mixture of corn starch and water.

SERVINGS: 4 TO 6 • PREPARATION TIME: 40 MINUTES

Beer-Basted Baby Back Ribs
with Jack Daniels Barbecue Sauce

THIS IS A FOOLPROOF WAY TO PREPARE MOIST, TENDER AND NEVER OVER-COOKED RIBS. BY STEAMING THE RIBS IN A SLOW OVEN, THE MEAT COOKS IN ADVANCE OF GRILLING; THEREFORE, THE TIME SPENT GRILLING IS SIGNIFICANTLY REDUCED.

THIS METHOD WILL WORK BEAUTIFULLY IN YOUR NEXT BARBECUED CHICKEN MEAL! SEASON AND STEAM THE CHICKEN AS DIRECTED. YOU NEED ONLY PLACE THE STEAMED CHICKEN ON THE GRILL FOR 5 TO 10 MINUTES OVER MEDIUM HEAT.

6 pounds baby back ribs
Salt and freshly ground pepper
Garlic powder
1 12-ounce can beer

1 16-ounce can diced tomatoes
1 cup cider vinegar
½ cup dark molasses
¼ cup canola oil
¼ cup Jack Daniels whiskey
2 tablespoons prepared mustard
1 tablespoon chili powder
1 teaspoon ground cinnamon
4 or more drops hot pepper sauce
Salt and freshly ground pepper

Preheat the oven to 300°.

1. Season the ribs with salt, pepper and garlic powder. Place them onto a rack in the bottom of a large roasting pan. Pour the beer into the pan. Cover the pan with aluminum foil. Place the pan into the oven. Steam for at least 1 hour (or longer if desired).

2. For the sauce, bring the tomatoes, vinegar, molasses, canola oil, whiskey, mustard, chili powder, cinnamon and as much hot pepper sauce as you like, to a boil in a saucepan over medium high heat. Reduce the heat and simmer for 20 minutes. Season with salt and pepper.

3. Transfer the ribs to an outdoor grill over medium high heat. Cook, turning often until well browned, about 5 to 10 minutes. Baste the ribs with sauce during the last 5 minutes of cooking.

4. Cut the ribs, and serve with extra sauce on the side.

SERVINGS: 4 TO 6 •
PREPARATION TIME: 30
MINUTES PLUS STEAMING
AND GRILLING THE RIBS

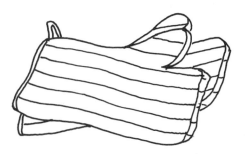

Pork Spare Ribs with Sauerkraut

SLOW COOKING THE RIBS MAKES THEM EXTRA TENDER. THE ADDITION OF
APPLES, ADDS A TOUCH OF SWEETNESS TO THE TART SAUERKRAUT. THE
COMBINATION IS MOUTHWATERING!

1 28-ounce can sauerkraut
½ small head green cabbage, thinly sliced (about 2 to 3 cups)
1 large yellow onion, thinly sliced (about 1 cup)
2 medium apples, peeled and thinly sliced (about 2 cups)
1 cup apple cider
2 tablespoons fennel seeds
Freshly ground pepper

2 2-pound racks meaty spare ribs
Salt
1 tablespoon brown sugar
1 tablespoon garlic powder
1 teaspoon ground cumin

Preheat the oven to 325°.
1. Place the sauerkraut and juices, cabbage, onion and apples in
the bottom of a Dutch oven or large roasting pan.
2. Pour the apple cider over top. Sprinkle with fennel seeds and
freshly ground pepper.
3. Season the spare ribs with salt, pepper, brown sugar, garlic
powder, and cumin.
4. Place the spare ribs on top of the sauerkraut/cabbage mixture.
5. Cover the pan and bake until the meat falls from the bone,
about 3 hours.
6. Cut the racks into ribs. Serve the ribs and sauerkraut over
mashed potatoes.

SERVINGS: 4 TO 6 • PREPARATION TIME: 30 MINUTES PLUS 3 HOURS ROAST-
ING

SAUERKRAUT CAN BE PUR-
CHASED IN BAGS FROM THE
PRODUCE SECTION IN YOUR
MARKET, OR IN CANS ON THE
VEGGIE AISLE. SAUERKRAUT
IS BASICALLY BRINED CAB-
BAGE. YES, YOU CAN PRE-
PARE YOUR OWN, BUT THE
PROCESS WILL TAKE YOU A
WHILE. I LIKE TO START WITH
THE PREPARED PRODUCT AND
THEN ADD SOME MORE INGRE-
DIENTS ALONG THE WAY.

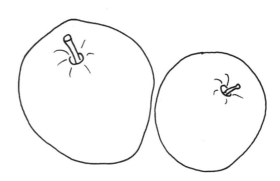

Sunday Night Roasted Leg of Lamb
with Brown Veggies and Dark Gravy

AFTER YEARS OF PRODDING, MY MOTHER FINALLY CONFESSED THE SECRET TO HER DELICIOUS MAHOGANY COLORED LAMB GRAVY AND PERFECTLY BROWNED ROASTED VEGGIES. THE RICH GRAVY COLOR COMES FROM A DELIGHTFUL LITTLE PRODUCT NAMED "KITCHEN BOUQUET," A BLEND OF SEASONINGS, VEGETABLES AND CARAMEL COLORING; IT'S SMALL ENOUGH TO HIDE IN YOUR PANTRY, SO THAT NO ONE EVER DISCOVERS YOUR SECRET! (IF YOU'RE A PURIST, YOU CAN SUBSTITUTE WITH A MORE ELEGANT TEA-SPOON OF VEAL OR BEEF DEMI-GLACE.) SCORING THE VEGGIES BEFORE ROASTING PRODUCES A CRISP OUTSIDE AND A TENDER INSIDE—WELL WORTH THE EFFORT.

BUTCHER'S NOTE:
AUSTRALIAN LEG OF LAMB CUTS ARE SMALLER THAN DOMESTIC CUTS, AND OFTEN MORE ECONOMICAL WHILE MAINTAINING EXCELLENT QUAL-ITY. SINCE EITHER ONE IS PERFECT FOR THIS RECIPE, FEEL FREE TO CHOOSE THE BEST VALUE AVAILABLE IN THE MARKET.

4 medium garlic cloves, minced (about 2 teaspoons)
1 teaspoon dried rosemary
1 teaspoon dried thyme
1 teaspoon salt
1 teaspoon pepper
2 tablespoons Dijon mustard
½ cup olive oil
1 11- to 13-pound bone-in leg of domestic lamb, trimmed or 2 4- to 6-pound Australian bone-in leg of lamb (see Butcher's Note at left)

2 large yellow onions, peeled and cut into 2-inch wedges (about 4 cups)
6 large potatoes, peeled and cut into 2-inch pieces (about 6 cups)
6 large carrots, peeled and cut into 2-inch pieces (about 4 cups)

2 cups dry red wine
2 cups beef broth
2 sprigs fresh rosemary
1 tablespoon cornstarch mixed with 2 to 3 tablespoons cold water
1 to 2 teaspoons "Kitchen Bouquet"

Preheat the oven to 425°.
1. In a small bowl, combine minced garlic, dried herbs, salt, pepper, Dijon mustard and 2 tablespoons olive oil to make a gar-lic paste.
2. Heat 2 teaspoons of the olive oil in a Dutch oven or deep roasting pan over medium high heat.
3. Place the lamb into the hot oil and brown on all sides.
4. Remove the lamb from the pan and brush with garlic paste.
5. Return the lamb to the pan and place it into the preheated oven. Roast for 30 minutes.
6. Score the vegetables with the back of a fork on all sides. Toss with the remaining olive oil. Season with salt and pepper.
7. Reduce the oven temperature to 350°. Add the vegetables to the roasting pan. Continue roasting until the lamb cooks to 130°

(for medium rare) and the vegetables begin to brown, about 1 hour.

8. Transfer the lamb to a platter and let rest while you prepare the gravy. Transfer the vegetables to a bowl and cover to keep warm.

9. Heat the pan on the stovetop over medium high heat. Pour in the wine. Cook, stirring the brown bits from the bottom of the pan until the wine reduces by half, about 10 minutes.

10. Pour in the beef broth. Stir until reduced by half again, about 10 minutes more.

11. Add the rosemary sprigs.

12. Stir in the cornstarch paste in small amounts, stirring to thicken the sauce.

13. Add 1 to 2 tablespoons of "Kitchen Bouquet" to darken the gravy. Remove the rosemary sprigs and season the sauce with salt and pepper.

SERVINGS: 6 TO 8 PLUS EXTRAS FOR THE MAKINGS OF INDIVIDUAL SHEPHERD'S PIES (SEE PAGE 301) • PREPARATION TIME: 45 MINUTES 1½ HOURS PLUS ROASTING

Greek Moussaka Casserole

THINK LASAGNA WITH EGGPLANT INSTEAD OF PASTA, LAMB IN PLACE OF
BEEF, AND YOU HAVE THE ESSENCE OF THIS GREEK INSPIRED DISH. FEEL
FREE TO ADD YOUR FAVORITE VEGGIES TO THE SAUCE. WITH THIS CASSE-
ROLE, ANYTHING GOES.

FEEL FREE TO USE LEFT OVER
LAMB FROM YOUR SUNDAY
NIGHT LAMB ROAST FOR THIS
DISH. SIMPLY SHRED THE
LAMB AND ADD TO THE SKIL-
LET WITH THE COOKED VEG-
GIES. IMMEDIATELY ADD THE
WINE AND TOMATOES, CONTIN-
UING WITH THE RECIPE.

3 large eggplants, peeled and sliced into ½-inch thick lengths
Salt and freshly ground pepper
4 to 6 tablespoons olive oil

1 large yellow onion, diced into ½-inch squares (about 1 cup)
2 large carrots, diced (about 1 cup)
2 medium cloves garlic, minced (about 1 teaspoon)
2 pounds lean ground lamb
1 cup red wine
1 16-ounce can diced tomatoes
2 tablespoons tomato paste
1 teaspoon dried oregano
1 cinnamon stick

3 tablespoons butter
3 tablespoons all-purpose flour
2 cups milk
4 ounces finely grated Parmesan cheese (about 1 cup)
½ teaspoon ground nutmeg

Preheat the oven to 350°.
1. Season the eggplants with salt and freshly ground pepper. Place
into a colander for 30 minutes to release excess moisture. Rinse
and pat the eggplant dry. Heat 2 tablespoons of olive oil in a skillet over medium high heat. Cook the eggplant in batches, turning
once until soft and just beginning to brown, about 2 minutes per
side. (Do not let the eggplant slices get too mushy.) Drain on
paper towels. You may add more olive oil as needed.
2. Heat 2 more tablespoons of olive oil in the skillet. Cook the
onion and carrots until soft and golden, about 5 to 7 minutes.
Add the garlic and cook for 2 minutes more.
3. Add the lamb to the pan. Cook, breaking up the meat with a
spatula until browned, about 8 to 10 minutes.
4. Stir in the wine, tomatoes, tomato paste, oregano and cinnamon stick. Simmer for 15 minutes. Season with salt and pepper.
Remove the cinnamon stick.
5. Heat the butter in a saucepot over medium high heat. Whisk in
the flour. Cook until golden and bubbling, about 2 to 4 minutes.

Pour in the milk. Cook, stirring constantly until the sauce is thickened, about 6 to 8 minutes. Stir in the Parmesan cheese. Season with ground nutmeg, salt and pepper.

6. Assemble the moussaka by placing a layer of eggplant slices in the bottom of a 9 x 13-inch baking dish. Top with half of lamb mixture. Add another layer of eggplant and another layer of lamb. Finish with a layer of eggplant. Top the casserole with béchamel sauce. Bake until the casserole is bubbling and the top is golden, about 30 to 40 minutes. Allow the casserole to sit for 15 minutes before serving.

SERVINGS: 6 TO 8 • PREPARATION TIME: 30 MINUTES PLUS 40 MINUTES BAKING

Grilled Lamb Chops with Ragu
of Roasted Shallots, Fresh Peas, and Mushrooms

IF YOU WANT TO CAPTURE THE FLAVORS OF SUNDAY NIGHT'S LAMB ROAST WITH BROWNED POTATOES, CARAMELIZED ONIONS AND A SIDE DISH OF PEAS MIXED WITH MUSHROOMS, GIVE THIS UPDATED RECIPE THE OLD COLLEGE TRY! BY USING LAMB CHOPS, THE MEAL COOKS IN MINUTES, NOT HOURS, AND THE RAGU COMBINES ALL THE VEGGIES YOU WANT IN A LIGHT MERLOT SAUCE. IT'S SO GOOD, YOU MIGHT JUST HAVE TO INVITE THE NEIGHBORS OVER FOR A BITE.

FOR THE MOST JUICY, TENDER MEAT, SERVED GRILLED OR BROILED LAMB CHOPS WITH A PINK CENTER. IF OVERCOOKED, THE MEAT WILL TAKE ON A GAMEY FLAVOR. SOME PEOPLE ARE PUT-OFF BY THE AROMA OF COOKING LAMB. IT IS THE FAT OF THE LAMB THAT HAS AN ASSERTIVE, UNPLEASANT SMELL. ALLEVIATE THIS ISSUE BY REMOVING AS MUCH FAT AS YOU CAN FROM THE MEAT BEFORE COOKING.

8 4 to 5-ounce loin lamb chops, cut 1½ to 2-inches thick
4 tablespoons olive oil (or more)
1 to 2 teaspoons dried thyme
Salt and freshly ground pepper
5 to 6 large shallots, peeled and separated into lobes
6 small (2- to 3-inch) red potatoes, quartered
4 ounces baby portobello mushrooms, sliced (about 1 cup)
1 cup Merlot wine
4 ounces fresh green peas
1½ cups beef broth

Preheat the oven to 375°.
1. Place the lamb chops in a dish. Sprinkle with 2 tablespoons olive oil and season with 1 teaspoon dried thyme, salt and pepper. Marinate for 30 minutes.
2. Place the shallots and the potatoes in a shallow baking dish. Toss with 1 tablespoon olive oil and season with salt and pepper. Roast for 30 minutes, or until the shallots are soft and the potatoes are browned.
3. Place 1 tablespoon olive oil in a skillet over medium high heat.
4. Cook the mushrooms in the pan until soft. Season with salt, pepper and 1 teaspoon dried thyme.
5. Pour in the red wine. Reduce heat to low.
6. Add the peas to the pan.
7. Pour in the beef broth. Simmer until the sauce reduces by half and the peas are tender, about 25 to 30 minutes.
8. Heat a grill pan over high heat. Cook the lamb chops, turning once, about 4 minutes per side for medium rare. Remove from the pan and keep warm.
9. Add the sautéed shallots and potatoes to the mushroom and pea mixture. Toss to coat all of the veggies with the sauce. Adjust seasonings.
10. Serve 2 lamb chops per dish. Surround the chops with the vegetable ragu. Garnish with fresh thyme.

SERVINGS: 4 • PREPARATION TIME: 45 MINUTES

Individual Shepherd's Pie Skillets

INDIVIDUAL SKILLETS OR MINI CASSEROLE DISHES MAKE PERFECT VESSELS
FOR THE PRESENTATION OF THIS PEASANT STYLE DISH. YOU CAN ALSO PRE-
PARE THE DISH FOR A CROWD, USING A LARGE (13 X 9-INCH) BAKING DISH.

6 large baking potatoes, peeled and cut into chunks
½ cup half and half
4 tablespoons butter
Salt and freshly ground pepper

2 tablespoons olive oil
1 large yellow onion, diced into ½-inch squares (about 1 cup)
1 medium red bell pepper, seeded and cut into ¼-inch dice (about ⅔ cup)
2 large carrots, diced (about 1 cup)
2 pounds lean ground lamb
1 cup red wine
2 cups beef broth
1 tablespoon chopped fresh rosemary
2 tablespoons butter, room temperature
2 tablespoons all-purpose flour
1 16-ounce can baby peas, drained
8 to 10 ounces fresh spinach leaves, washed, dried and torn (about 1½ cups)

Preheat the oven to 350°.

1. Cook the potatoes in boiling water until fork-tender. Drain and place into a bowl. Use an electric mixer to combine the potatoes, half and half and butter. Season with salt and pepper. Set the mashed potatoes aside.

2. Heat the olive oil in a skillet over medium high heat. Cook the onion, pepper, and carrots until soft and beginning to turn golden, about 8 minutes.

3. Add the lamb to the pan. Cook, breaking up the meat with a spatula until browned, about 8 to 10 minutes more. Season with salt and pepper.

4. Add the red wine, beef broth, and chopped fresh rosemary. Simmer for 10 minutes.

5. Use a fork to combine 2 tablespoons room temperature butter and flour to a smooth paste. Whisk this into the lamb mixture. Stir until the sauce thickens, about 3 to 5 minutes.

6. Stir in the peas and spinach. Cook for 5 minutes more. Spoon this mixture into individual skillets, casseroles, ramekins or ovenproof crocks.

7. Cover each one with mashed potatoes. Place the skillets onto a rimmed baking sheet. Bake until the potatoes are brown and the lamb mixture is bubbling, about 20 to 30 minutes. Allow the casserole to rest for 10 minutes before serving.

SERVINGS: 6 TO 8 • PREPARATION TIME: 1 HOUR

THE MEAT AND SAUCE FROM BRAISED LAMB WITH RED WINE TOMATO GRAVY (SEE RECIPE PAGE 302) IS PERFECT FOR THIS DISH. SIMPLY ADD SOME COOKED VEGGIES AND TOP WITH CREAMY SMASHED POTATOES (SEE RECIPE PAGE 210), OR UPDATE THE DISH BY TOPPING WITH MASHED SWEET POTATOES (SEE RECIPE PAGE 213). WHAT AN INVENTIVE WAY TO COOK ONCE AND EAT TWICE!

Braised Lamb with Red Wine Tomato Gravy

THIS RECIPE CONVERTS FOR EASY USE IN A SLOW COOKER. IF THE ROAST IS TOO LARGE FOR THE BOWL, SIMPLY ASK THE BUTCHER TO CUT IT IN HALF. YOU MAY HAVE TO THICKEN THE SAUCE JUST BEFORE SERVING. USE A MIXTURE OF FLOUR, CORNSTARCH OR ARROWROOT, WHISKED INTO COLD WATER. USE THIS MIXTURE SPARINGLY, SIMMERING JUST UNTIL THE SAUCE THICKENS.

1 4- to 5-pound lamb shoulder boned, rolled and tied
Salt and freshly ground pepper
2 tablespoons olive oil
1 large yellow onion, diced (about 1 cup)
2 medium celery ribs, diced (about 1 cup)
2 large carrots, diced (about 1 cup)
4 medium cloves garlic, thinly sliced (about 2 teaspoons)
2 or more sprigs fresh rosemary
2 or more sprigs fresh thyme
½ teaspoon ground nutmeg
¼ teaspoon ground cloves
1 750-millimeter bottle red wine
1 14.5-ounce can diced tomatoes

Preheat the oven to 325°.

1. Generously season the lamb with salt and pepper. Place in a plastic bag, seal, and refrigerate for 24 hours, or up to 3 days.

2. Heat the olive oil in a deep roasting pan with a lid, over medium high heat.

3. Brown the roast on all sides in the hot oil. Remove the roast from the pan.

4. For gravy, add the onion, celery, carrots, and garlic to the pan. Stir the vegetables until just beginning to brown, about 5 minutes.

5. Return the lamb to the pan with the vegetables.

6. Add the rosemary, thyme, nutmeg, and cloves to the pan.

7. Pour in the red wine and diced tomatoes.

8. Bring the liquid to a boil. Cover the pan and place into the oven. Cook for 2½ to 3 hours, or until the meat is very tender.

9. Remove the lamb from the pan and let sit for 10 minutes.

10. Bring the gravy to a boil over medium high heat. Reduce heat and simmer for 10 minutes or until thickened.

11. Remove string from the roast. Cut into ½-inch slices. Pour the sauce over the lamb and serve.

SERVINGS: 6 TO 8 • PREPARATION TIME: 30 MINUTES PREPARATION PLUS 2½ TO 3 HOURS ROASTING

Braised Lamb with Fennel

Add diced parsnips or fennel to the vegetable mixture to give the lamb a distinctive flavor.

Sage Marinated Braised Lamb

Add a few fresh sage leaves to the lamb when salted. Serve the finished roast with fried sage leaves for garnish. Prepare fried sage leaves by brining olive oil to 350°. Dust the sage leaves with flour or cornstarch. Carefully place the leaves into the hot oil. When golden, (within 2 to 3 minutes) remove the leaves with a mesh strainer basket and lay on paper towels to drain. Serve immediately.

Marinated Lamb Shoulder Chops

MARINATING LAMB CHOPS ADDS AN EXCELLENT FLAVOR AND ACTS AS A
TENDERIZER, TOO. YOU CAN PREPARE THE CHOPS AFTER WORK OR SCHOOL
AND HAVE DINNER READY BY 7:00!

4 8-ounce lamb shoulder blade chops
Salt and freshly ground pepper
¼ cup soy sauce
¼ cup balsamic vinegar
¼ cup olive oil
Zest of 1 medium lemon (about 1 tablespoon)
2 medium cloves garlic, minced (about 1 teaspoon)
2 teaspoons dried thyme

1. Place the lamb chops in a baking dish. Season with salt and
pepper.
2. Whisk together the soy sauce, vinegar, olive oil, lemon zest,
garlic, and thyme. Pour this mixture over the lamb chops. Turn
once to coat. Cover and refrigerate for at least 30 minutes or up
to 4 hours.
3. Heat a skillet over medium high heat. Remove the chops from
the marinade. Place into the skillet. Cook until browned, about 5
to 8 minutes. Turn and cook until both sides are browned, about
2 to 3 minutes more.

SERVINGS: 4 • PREPARATION TIME: 15 MINUTES PLUS MARINATING

THE BLADE CHOP CUT OF
LAMB COMES FROM THE
SHOULDER SECTION; IT'S
QUITE MARBLED WITH FAT,
WHICH MAKES IT BOTH FLA-
VORFUL AND A BIT TOUGH.
MARINATING THE CHOP HELPS
TO BREAK DOWN SOME OF
THE FAT. TO SCORE THE FAT,
USE A SHARP KNIFE ON THE
OUTERMOST EDGES TO PRE-
VENT CURING IN THE PAN.

Veal Marsala

MY MOTHER-IN-LAW PREPARED THIS DISH FOR BIG FAMILY SUPPERS ON
SUNDAY NIGHT. SHE SERVED OUR VEAL WITH BAKED POTATOES, BUT FET-
TUCCINI, EGG NOODLES, RICE OR RISOTTO ARE GREAT ADDITIONS, TOO!

IF YOU WANT A WONDERFUL
DISH, YOU MUST CHOOSE A
WONDERFUL MARSALA WINE
TO COOK WITH. MARSALA IS
IMPORTED FROM SICILY AND
MADE FROM LOCAL GRAPES;
IT HAS A RICH, SOMEWHAT
SMOKY FLAVOR, SIMILAR TO
SHERRY. YOU CAN FIND DRY
MARSALA (SECCO), SEMI-
SWEET (SEMISECCO) AND
SWEET (DOLCE). I PREFER
THE DRY VARIETY FOR THIS
DISH. MARSALA COOKING
WINE, FOUND IN THE GRO-
CERY STORE, IS LOADED WITH
EXTRA SALT AND IS NOT AS
FLAVORFUL AS THE REAL
THING!

1½ pounds veal scallops
Salt and freshly ground pepper
2 tablespoons all-purpose flour
2 to 4 tablespoons butter
2 large shallots, minced (about 2 tablespoons)
8 ounces button mushrooms, sliced (about 2 cups)
1 cup Marsala wine
1 cup beef broth
2 tablespoons chopped fresh parsley

1. Place the veal between 2 pieces of plastic wrap. Use a meat
mallet to pound to ⅛-inch thickness. Season with salt and pepper. Dredge in flour.

2. Heat 1 tablespoon butter in a skillet over medium high heat.
In the skillet, cook the veal in batches until golden, about 30 seconds per side. Use additional butter as needed. Transfer to a
platter.

3. Melt 2 more tablespoons butter in the skillet. Cook the shallots until soft, about 2 to 3 minutes.

4. Add the mushrooms and cook until soft. Season with salt and
pepper.

5. Pour in the wine and beef broth. Simmer until the sauce
reduces and is slightly thickened, about 8 to 10 minutes.

6. Add the veal and parsley to the pan. Cook for 3 to 4 minutes
more.

SERVINGS: 4 • PREPARATION
TIME: 30 MINUTES

Veal Rollatini with Mushrooms and Leeks

THIS IS A SIMPLE DISH TO MAKE AND JAMMED WITH GREAT FLAVORS! FEEL FREE TO EXPERIMENT WITH THE FILLING. SAUTÉED SPINACH WITH PINE NUTS OR CRABMEAT WITH CREAM CHEESE ARE JUST A COUPLE OF GREAT SUBSTITUTION IDEAS.

1½ pounds veal cutlets (about 8)
7 ounces shitake mushrooms
1 leek, white part only
2 or more tablespoons olive oil
Salt and freshly ground pepper

1 cup ricotta cheese
2 ounces finely grated Parmesan cheese (about ½ cup)
1 large egg
2 tablespoons chopped fresh parsley

2 cups marinara sauce

Preheat the oven to 350°.

1. Use a mallet to pound the veal cutlets between 2 pieces of plastic wrap to about ⅛-inch thickness.

2. Remove the stems from the mushrooms and dice the caps into ¼-inch cubes.

3. Clean the leek well. Cut into thin slices.

4. Heat 1 tablespoon olive oil in a skillet over medium high heat.

5. Cook the mushrooms and the leeks in the olive oil for 5 minutes. Season with salt and pepper. Cool to room temperature.

6. Place the ricotta cheese, Parmesan cheese and egg into a bowl. Stir in the mushroom mixture. Season with chopped fresh parsley.

7. Spread a thin layer of the ricotta mixture over each of the veal cutlets leaving a ¼-inch border.

8. Roll up the veal, jelly-roll style, and secure the end with a 4-inch skewer. Season with salt and pepper. Refrigerate the rollatini for at least 15 minutes.

9. Heat the remaining tablespoon of olive oil in the same pan over medium high heat. Brown the rollatini in the pan in batches, adding more oil as needed, about 2 to 4 minutes per side.

10. Place 2 tablespoons tomato sauce in the bottom of an 11 x 7 x 2-inch baking dish.

11. Place the browned rollatini, seam side down, in the baking dish. Pour the remaining tomato sauce over top. Bake for 20 minutes, or until the cheese is melted and the sauce is bubbling.

SERVINGS: 4 TO 6 • PREPARATION TIME: 45 MINUTES

TAKE ADVANTAGE OF SOME OF THE DELICIOUS JARRED TOMATO SAUCES FOR THIS RECIPE. CHOOSE ONE THAT USES FRESH INGREDIENTS AND LIMITS PRESERVATIVES AND SUGAR, OR PREPARE YOUR OWN TOMATO SAUCE AND KEEP CONTAINERS IN THE FREEZER FOR EASY THAWING.

Simple Marinara Sauce

1 tablespoon olive oil
1 small onion, diced
1 medium clove garlic, minced (about ½ teaspoon)
1 28-ounce can diced tomatoes
1 tablespoon tomato paste
1 teaspoon sugar (optional)
2 tablespoons chopped fresh basil
Salt and freshly ground pepper

Heat the olive oil in a skillet over medium heat. Cook the onion in the olive oil until soft, about 3 to 5 minutes. Add the garlic and cook for 2 minutes more. Stir in the tomatoes, tomato paste and sugar. Simmer for 10 to 20 minutes. Stir in the basil and season with salt and pepper. Use an immersion blender or food processor to blend the sauce together.

Osso Buco with Gremolata Garnish

ITALIAN OSSO BUCO INCLUDES ANCHOVIES IN ITS RICH, RUSTIC SAUCE. IF YOU ARE AN ANCHOVY LOVER (AS I AM), FEEL FREE TO ADD SEVERAL FILETS TO THE SAUCE, AS IT SIMMERS AWAY IN THE OVEN. THE END RESULT IS A SUBTLE, EXTRA DEPTH OF FLAVOR. SERVE THE DISH WITH CONVENTIONAL RISOTTO OR FASTER RICE, AND SPRINKLE WITH THE TRADITIONAL GREMOLATA GARNISH.

YOU CAN ASK YOUR BUTCHER TO PREPARE THE VEAL SHANKS TO YOUR SPECIFICATIONS. I PREFER 2 SMALLER SHANKS PER SERVING, BUT 1 3-INCH, 16-OUNCE SHANK IS A STANDARD, MOST GENEROUS PORTION.

6 8- to 12-ounce veal shanks
Salt and freshly ground pepper
¼ cup all-purpose flour
2 tablespoons olive oil
1 medium white onion, diced (about ⅔ cup)
2 large carrots, diced (about 1 cup)
2 medium celery ribs, diced (about 1 cup)
4 medium garlic cloves, minced (about 2 teaspoons)
1 28-ounce can diced tomatoes
2 cups red wine
2 cups beef broth
2 tablespoons tomato paste
2 sprigs rosemary
2 sprigs thyme

2 medium cloves garlic, minced (about 1 teaspoon)
4 tablespoons chopped fresh parsley
Zest of 2 medium lemons (about 2 tablespoons)

Preheat the oven to 375°.
1. Season the veal shanks with salt and pepper, and dredge in flour.
2. Heat the olive oil in a large pot (or Dutch oven) over medium high heat.
3. Cook the veal shanks in the pot until brown, about 3 minutes per side.
4. Remove the veal shanks from the pot.
5. Add the onion, carrots, celery, and 2 teaspoons minced garlic to the pot. Cook until the vegetables are soft, stirring often, about 5 minutes.
6. Return the veal shanks to the pot. Add the tomatoes, wine, and beef broth. Stir in the tomato paste. Add the fresh herbs. Bring the mixture to a boil.
7. Cover the pot and place it into the oven. Cook for 2 to 2½ hours, or until the meat falls away from the bone. Return the pot to the stovetop. Remove the shanks and place onto a platter. Simmer the sauce until it is reduced and slightly thickened.

8. For the gremolata, mix together the remaining I teaspoon minced garlic, chopped parsley, and lemon zest.
9. Serve the veal shanks with risotto or rice. Add a generous ladleful (or two!) of sauce and a sprinkling of the Gremolata garnish.

SERVINGS: 6 TO 8 • PREPARATION TIME: 40 MINUTES PLUS 2 HOURS SIMMERING

YOU CAN EASILY PREPARE THIS DISH IN A SLOW COOKER. FOLLOW THE RECIPE THROUGH STEP 5. PLACE THE VEGETABLES AND VEAL SHANKS INTO THE BOTTOM OF A SLOW COOKER. POUR IN THE TOMATOES, WINE AND BROTH. STIR IN THE TOMATO PASTE AND ADD THE FRESH HERBS. SET THE COOKER FOR MEDIUM TO MEDIUM HIGH AND COOK FOR 6 TO 8 HOURS, DEPENDING ON YOUR COOKER. THE MEAT SHOULD FALL AWAY FROM THE BONE. REMOVE THE SHANKS FROM THE COOKER AND KEEP WARM. POUR THE SAUCE INTO A POT. HEAT THE POT OVER MEDIUM HIGH HEAT AND SIMMER THE SAUCE UNTIL REDUCED AND SLIGHTLY THICKENED.

Moroccan Spiced Braised Veal Shanks
with Toasted Orzo

AN EXCELLENT FLAVOR TWIST ON TRADITIONAL ITALIAN STYLE BRAISED
VEAL SHANKS, THIS DISH ALSO ADDS AN ABUNDANT AMOUNT OF NUTRI-
TIOUS VEGGIES TO THE SLOW SIMMERING SAUCE. TO HEAP ON EVEN MORE
HEALTH BENEFITS, ADD A CUP OF DRIED LENTILS WITH THE SQUASH AND
SWEET POTATOES.

6 8 to 12-ounce veal shanks
1 tablespoon chili powder
1 teaspoon ground turmeric
1 teaspoon ground cumin
1 teaspoon salt
1 teaspoon pepper
½ teaspoon ground coriander

1 tablespoon olive oil
1 extra large white onion, diced (about 3 cups)
4 medium celery ribs, diced (about 2 cups)
4 large carrots, diced (about 2 cups)
1 2-inch piece ginger, grated (about 2 tablespoons)
4 medium garlic cloves, minced (about 2 teaspoons)
1 tablespoon hot paprika
1 tablespoon dark brown sugar
1 teaspoon ground turmeric
½ teaspoon ground coriander
Juice of 1 medium lemon (about 2 tablespoons)
1 cup white wine
1 quart chicken broth
1 6-ounce can tomato paste
2 medium butternut squash, peeled and diced into 1-inch squares (about 4 cups)
2 medium sweet potatoes, peeled and diced into 1-inch squares (about 2 cups)

4 tablespoons olive oil
2 cups orzo
3 cups water
Zest of 1 medium lemon (about 1 tablespoon)
Salt
Juice of 1 medium lemon (about 2 tablespoons)
Freshly ground pepper
2 tablespoons chopped fresh parsley

Preheat the oven to 375°.
1. Trim excess fat from veal shanks.
2. Combine the chili powder, turmeric, cumin, salt, pepper and
½ teaspoon ground coriander in a small bowl.

To prepare this dish using a slow cooker, follow steps 1 through 8. Place the vegetables and the veal shanks in the bottom of the slow cooker. Add the chicken broth and stir in the tomato paste. Add the butternut squash and sweet potatoes. Simmer on medium or medium high for 4 to 6 hours, depending on your cooker. To reduce and thicken the sauce before serving, remove the shanks from the cooker and keep warm. Transfer the sauce and vegetables to a pot. Cook over medium high heat until the sauce reduces about 20 minutes.

3. Place the veal shanks into the spice mixture, coating top, bottom and sides.

4. Heat the olive oil in the bottom of a large pot (or Dutch oven) over medium high heat.

5. Place the shanks into the pot. Cook until well browned (about 3 minutes) turn and cook 3 minutes more. Transfer the shanks to a platter.

6. Reduce the heat to medium. Add the onion, celery, carrots, ginger and garlic to the pan. Cover and cook until the veggies are soft, stirring often, about 5 minutes.

7. Stir in the paprika, brown sugar, remaining turmeric and coriander to the vegetables.

8. Stir in the lemon juice and white wine. Cook for 3 minutes.

9. Pour in the chicken broth and tomato paste. Bring to a boil.

10. Place the veal shanks back into the pan. Cover and cook in the oven for 45 minutes.

11. Remove the pan from the oven. Turn the veal shanks and toss in the butternut squash and sweet potatoes. Return to the oven and cook for 45 minutes more.

12. Remove the pan from the oven and place on the stovetop over medium heat. Simmer until the sauce reduces and thickens, about 20 minutes more.

13. Heat 2 tablespoons olive oil in a pot over medium high heat. Add the orzo to the pot and cook until the pasta turns golden, about 5 to 7 minutes.

14. Pour in 3 cups of water, lemon zest and salt. Reduce heat to medium, cover and simmer until the liquid is absorbed, about 10 to 15 minutes. Fluff the orzo with a fork and season with lemon juice, the remaining 2 tablespoons of olive oil, freshly ground pepper, and chopped fresh parsley.

15. Serve the veal shanks next to a helping of toasted orzo. Spoon a generous ladleful (or two) of the fragrant sauce around the dish and over the veal shanks. Garnish with additional chopped fresh parsley and lemon zest.

SERVINGS: 4 TO 6 • PREPARATION TIME: 30 MINUTES PREPARATION PLUS 2 HOURS BRAISING

Veal and Veggie Pot Pie
This dish spawns a leftover family favorite that simply can't be beat: Veal and Veggie Pot Pie. Reserve any extra veggies and sauce. If you have leftover meat, you can shred it and add it to the sauce. If the veal gets devoured, (like at my house), brown ground veal and add it to the sauce and veggies. Place the mixture into a shallow baking dish, or individual ovenproof dishes. Roll out a sheet of puff pastry to ⅛-inch thickness. Cover the top of the baking dish with the pastry. Trim excess and fold over to seal the edges. Cut vents in the pastry. Brush the top of the pastry with egg wash (a whole egg mixed with a small amount of water). Bake in a 350° oven for 15 to 20 minutes (depending on the size of the dish) or until the pastry is golden and the filling is bubbling. Serve hot.

Veal Chops Milanese

SERVE A SALAD OF LIGHTLY DRESSED ARUGULA LEAVES AND HALVED BABY
TOMATOES ON TOP OF YOUR FINISHED VEAL CHOPS FOR AN AUTHENTIC,
RUSTIC SUPPER.

4 10- to 12-ounce veal chops, 1½- to 2-inches thick, butterflied
2 cups half and half
2 large eggs, beaten
2 tablespoons chopped fresh parsley
4 ounces finely grated Parmesan cheese (about 1 cup)
2 cups seasoned bread crumbs
Salt and freshly ground pepper
2 to 4 tablespoons olive oil
2 to 4 tablespoons butter
Juice of 2 medium lemons (about ¼ cup)

TRADITIONAL MILANESE PREP-
ARATION REQUIRES YOU TO
DIP THE MEAT INTO A DRY
INGREDIENT, LIKE FLOUR OR
CORNMEAL, THEN INTO A WET
INGREDIENT, LIKE EGG MIXED
WITH MILK OR CREAM, AND,
FINALLY, INTO A SEASON DRY
MIXTURE OF BREAD CRUMBS
MIXED WITH FLOUR AND
CHEESE. THIS RECIPE'S
METHOD OF SOAKING VEAL,
SHORTCUTS THE PROCEDURE
AND OFFERS A FABULOUSLY
MOIST RESULT.

Preheat the oven to 350
1. Use a meat mallet to pound both sides of the butterflied chops
to ⅛-inch thickness. Place the chops into a baking dish.
2. Whisk together the half and half, eggs, parsley and Parmesan
cheese. Pour this mixture over the chops. Turn to coat. Cover
and refrigerate for at least 30 minutes, and up to 4 hours.
3. Place the bread crumbs in a shallow bowl. Remove the chops
from the cream mixture. Shake off excess. Dredge the chops in
the bread crumbs. Season with salt and pepper.
4. Heat 2 tablespoons olive oil and 2 tablespoons butter in a skillet over medium high heat. Place the chops in the skillet in
batches. Cook until golden, about 4 to 6 minutes. Turn and cook
until both sides are golden, about 4 to 6 minutes more. Use
additional butter and olive oil as needed.
5. Place the chops into a baking dish. Squeeze lemon juice over
the chops. Bake until the veal is tender and moist, about 10 to
15 minutes. Do not overcook.

SERVINGS: 4 • PREPARATION TIME: 45 MINUTES PLUS MARINATING

Broiled Veal Chops with Lime Herb Butter

THE FLAVORS OF THE MARINADE ARE REPLICATED IN THE MELTING OF BUT-
TER ON TOP OF THE CHOPS, MAKING THIS AN UPSCALE, EASY-TO-MAKE,
MIDWEEK SUPPER.

4 10- to 12-ounce veal chops, 1½- to 2-inches thick
½ cup olive oil
Juice of 4 medium limes (about ¼ cup)
4 medium garlic cloves, minced (about 2 teaspoons)
2 tablespoons Dijon mustard
2 tablespoons chopped fresh rosemary
2 tablespoons chopped fresh cilantro

4 tablespoons butter, room temperature
2 tablespoons chopped fresh cilantro
Zest of 1 medium lime (about 1 tablespoon)
2 medium garlic cloves, minced (about 1 teaspoon)
Salt and freshly ground pepper

USING THE BROILER ELEMENT IN YOUR OVEN PRODUCES THE SAME RESULT AS AN OUT DOOR GRILL. YOU ARE COOK-ING DIRECTLY OVER (IN THIS CASE—UNDER) DIRECT HEAT. FOR BEST RESULTS, PREHEAT THE BROILER. PLACE THE RACK ABOUT 4 TO 6 INCHES FROM THE HEAT, AND LEAVE THE OVEN DOOR SLIGHTLY AJAR. TURN ON THE EXHAUST FAN—THERE WILL BE SMOKE. THE FOOD COOKS QUICKLY, SO WATCH IT CAREFULLY. YOU NEED ONLY TURN THE MEAT ONE TIME.

I. Place the veal chops into a baking dish. Whisk together the
olive oil, lime juice, 2 teaspoons of minced garlic, mustard,
rosemary,q and 2 tablespoons cilantro. Spread this marinade
over both sides of the chops. Cover and refrigerate for at least 30
minutes or overnight.
2. Place the butter, remaining 2 tablespoons of cilantro, lime
zest, and remaining 2 garlic cloves in a food processor. Pulse to
combine. Transfer the seasoned butter to a sheet of waxed paper.
Form the butter into a log (about 1-inch in diameter and 4-
inches long). Chill for at least 30 minutes.
Preheat the oven to broil.
3. Transfer the veal chops to a broil pan. Season with salt and
pepper.
4. Broil until the top is golden, about 6 minutes. Turn and broil
until both sides are golden and the
center is pink, about 4 minutes more.
Remove the broiler pan from the
oven.
5. Cut the butter into 4 pieces. Top
each chop with a slice of lemon herb
butter. Place the pan back under the
broiler for 30 seconds, or until the
butter begins to melt.

SERVINGS: 4 • PREPARATION TIME: 30 MIN-
UTES PLUS MARINATING

Chapter 13

Dastardly Desserts

In previous chapters, we got in touch with our food in a big way: purchasing the freshest produce on the market, looking a whole fish in the eye, and exploring the differences in free-range poultry.

Things change a bit when preparing healthy desserts. After all, the words "healthy" and "desserts" are seldom found in the same sentence. Achieving healthy desserts doesn't mean sacrificing quality; on the contrary, *Fresh Traditions* allows you to create splashy desserts by using prepared, pre-packaged and pre-made ingredients. We don't have to create ladyfingers from scratch to prepare a decadent tiramisu. Nor, do we have to bake the bread for bread pudding, or cut the butter into the puff pastry used in a decadent apple strudel.

Creating foolproof desserts is almost a guarantee if we follow a few simple rules. For example, pan size does make a difference. If a recipe suggests baking cake batter in an eight-inch round pan, and you only have a nine by twelve-inch rectangular pan, baking time will differ. Oven temperature calibration also affects baking time, as does altitude and freshness of ingredients. How do you account for all of these factors and still bake a wonderful cake? You simply watch the cake while it's baking. Check the cake several minutes before its baking deadline. If need be, remove the cake early, or keep it in the oven for a few extra minutes.

Ingredients can be tricky. Most baking recipes list "unsalted" butter in the ingredient list, and then ask you to add salt to the dry mixture. In these recipes, it's acceptable to substitute salted butter, refraining from adding the salt listed. I treat cream and milk the same way. There are several different types of cream, all differentiated by the amount of milk fat contained in each one. Similarly, milk can be fat free, low fat, two percent milk fat or whole milk. In these recipes, feel free to use your preference. Your choice will not noticeably affect the outcome of the final product. The possible exception to this rule is apparent when choosing the cream used for whipped cream topping. In this case, "heavy whipping cream" or "whipping cream" is the best choice.

When measuring ingredients for desserts, use a level scoop measure for dry ingredients like flour and sugar. Scoop the measure into the ingredients, using a knife to level off the extra amount. Use a clear measuring cup for liquid ingredients; this will allow you to see the liquid reach the proper line and pour out easily.

Now that we have some kitchen baking basics down pat, it's time to look at the dessert pages! Traditional fare includes a rich dark chocolate cake, pecan pie, cherries jubilee, angel food cake and ice cream sandwiches. Updated confections showcase merlot poached cherries, carob and tofu cupcakes, a trifle made from candy canes, and bread pudding teamed with a banana split!

In these recipes, you will find lots of shortcuts, and heaps of updates. Certainly, when you serve these desserts to family and friends, they will beg for more and more and more! Oops, we just started another fresh tradition!

Just Like Grammy's Apple Strudel

MY GRANDMOTHER'S APPLE STRUDEL WAS A SWEET CONCOCTION OF THINLY SLICED APPLES, A HINT OF RAISINS AND LIGHT, FLAKY DOUGH THAT TOOK HER HOURS AND HOURS TO MAKE; THIS RECIPE IS AS CLOSE TO GRAMMY'S MAGIC AS WE CAN GET. PURCHASED PHYLLO DOUGH ELIMINATES THE NEED FOR HOURS OF DOUGH KNEADING.

PHYLLO IS VERY DELICATE PASTRY DOUGH. PURCHASE IT IN THE FROZEN PASTRY SECTION IN THE GROCERY STORE. DEFROST THE DOUGH OVERNIGHT IN THE REFRIGERATOR OR ON THE COUNTER TOP FOR 3 TO 4 HOURS. WHEN YOU WORK WITH PHYLLO, YOU MUST KEEP IT COVERED WITH A DAMP TOWEL, OR IT WILL QUICKLY DRY, EITHER TEARING OR FLAKING AWAY. BECAUSE THE PASTRY BAKES SO QUICKLY, YOU MUST CUT THE APPLES AS THINLY AS POSSIBLE, SO THAT THEY, TOO, BAKE IN THE CRUST. A MANDOLIN IS THE PERFECT TOOL FOR THIS TASK.

½ cup golden raisins
¼ cup water
½ cup butter, (1 stick)
¼ cup fresh bread crumbs
4 medium Granny Smith apples, quartered, cored, peeled and sliced into very thin slices
Juice of 1 medium lemon (about 2 tablespoons)
½ cup granulated sugar
½ teaspoon ground cinnamon
½ teaspoon salt
10 sheets phyllo dough, defrosted

Preheat the oven to 475°.

1. Place the raisins into a small bowl. Pour in ¼ cup water. Cover the bowl with plastic wrap. Microwave on high for 1 minute. Set aside.

2. Melt 1 tablespoon of the butter in a small skillet over medium heat. When melted, add the bread crumbs. Stir and cook until the bread crumbs are golden, about 1 to 2 minutes. Set aside.

3. Place the apple slices into a bowl. Sprinkle with lemon juice. Stir in ¼ cup of the sugar and ¼ teaspoon of the ground cinnamon.

4. Drain the raisins and add them to the apple mixture. Stir in the bread crumbs.

5. Melt the remaining 7 tablespoons of butter.

6. Combine the remaining ¼ cup sugar with remaining ¼ teaspoon cinnamon. Stir in the ½ teaspoon of salt.

7. Place a piece of parchment paper (larger than a sheet of phyllo) onto your work surface.

8. Place 1 sheet of phyllo onto the parchment paper. Gently brush melted butter over the entire sheet. Lightly sprinkle the phyllo with a small amount of the cinnamon sugar mixture. Place a new piece of phyllo on top of the buttered sheet. Continue buttering, sprinkling with sugar and layering phyllo until 5 sheets have been used.

9. Place half the filling across the wide end of the phyllo sheets, leaving 2 inches from the sides and bottom. Roll the bottom edge over the filling. Fold in the sides. Brush the folded and top edges with butter. Continue rolling until you have a neat package. Place the strudel, seam side down, on a baking sheet, coated with vegetable oil spray. Brush the top with butter, sprinkle with a small amount of cinnamon sugar and cut several 1-inch vents into the top.

10. Repeat with the remaining ingredients. You will have two 12 x 3-inch logs.

11. Bake for 10 to 12 minutes or until the strudels are golden. Allow to cool for 5 minutes. Use 2 spatulas to transfer the strudels to a rack to cool for 20 minutes more. Serve warm with a dollop of whipped cream or a scoop of cinnamon vanilla ice cream.

SERVINGS: 12 (2-INCH SLICES) • PREPARATION TIME: 45 MINUTES

Double Chocolate Phyllo Cups

SPRINKLING COCOA POWDER AND SUGAR BETWEEN LAYERS OF DELICATE PHYLLO ADDS ENOUGH STABILITY TO FORM FANTASTIC EDIBLE VESSELS FOR YOUR FAVORITE FILLING; THIS ONE SHOWCASES DOUBLE CHOCOLATE PUDDING. FEEL FREE, HOWEVER, TO CHOOSE YOUR OWN FAVORITE!

PHYLLO MUFFIN CUPS ARE EASY TO MAKE, WHILE OFFERING A DRAMATIC DESSERT PRESENTATION. DON'T LIMIT YOURSELF TO CHOCOLATE PUDDING AS A FILLING. ICE CREAM, SLICED FRUIT, MOUSSE AND ALMOND CREAM ALL WILL WORK WELL—AND SO WILL MARSHMALLOWS, PEANUT BUTTER CREAM, CHOCOLATE SYRUP. SOUNDS LIKE AN UPDATED VERSION OF S'MORS!

2 cups milk
¼ cup granulated sugar
3 ounces bittersweet chocolate, finely chopped
4 eggs, beaten,
1 teaspoon vanilla extract
1 ounce bittersweet chocolate, roughly chopped

2 tablespoons granulated sugar
1 tablespoon cocoa powder
12 sheets phyllo dough, defrosted
6 tablespoons butter, melted

Whipped cream
Sliced strawberries

Preheat the oven to 475°.
1. Stir the milk, sugar, and 3 ounces of finely chopped chocolate in a small pot over medium high heat, until the chocolate melts.
2. Pour the milk mixture over the eggs, stirring constantly. Return this mixture to the pan.
3. Stir in the vanilla. Continue cooking over medium heat until the pudding thickens. Have an ice-filled bowl standing by.
4. Pour the pudding into a bowl that you then place into the ice-filled bowl. Continue stirring until the pudding is cool.
5. Stir in 1 ounce roughly chopped chocolate. Put the pudding into the refrigerator while you prepare the cups.
6. Coat a 6-cup jumbo muffin tin with vegetable oil spray.
7. Stir 2 tablespoons granulated sugar with 1 tablespoon cocoa powder in a small bowl.
8. Place a piece of parchment paper (larger than a sheet of phyllo) onto your work surface.
9. Place 1 sheet of phyllo onto the parchment paper. Gently brush melted butter over the entire sheet. Lightly sprinkle the phyllo with a small amount of the sugar/cocoa mixture. Place a new piece of phyllo on top of the buttered sheet. Continue buttering, sprinkling with sugar and layering phyllo until 4 sheets have been used.
10. With the wide edge of the layered phyllo facing you, cut it in half from top to bottom.
11. Place one half into a muffin cup forming it into a bowl with jagged edges at the top. Continue with the other half.

12. Repeat the layering process until all 6 cups are formed.

13. Place the muffin tin into the oven. Bake for 5 to 8 minutes or until the cups are golden and crisp. Watch carefully!

14. Remove the muffin tin from the oven. Cool for 5 minutes. Carefully remove the phyllo cups from the tin. Cool completely on a wire rack.

15. Serve each muffin cup with a ladleful of pudding. Top with whipped cream and sliced strawberries.

SERVINGS: 6 • PREPARATION TIME: 45 MINUTES

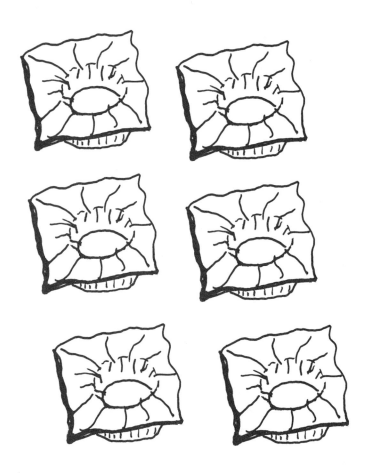

Southern Pecan Pie

THIS TRADITIONAL RECIPE IS A WINNER ON EVERY DESSERT TABLE. IF YOU WANT TO EXPERIMENT, TRY SUBSTITUTING BLACK WALNUTS FOR PECANS AND BOURBON FOR RUM. YUMM!

2 cups all-purpose flour
¼ cup confectioners' sugar
¼ teaspoon salt
½ cup butter, chilled and cut into pieces (1 stick)
1 to 2 tablespoons ice water

¼ cup butter, room temperature (½ stick)
½ cup granulated sugar
3 large eggs
1 tablespoon dark rum
1 cup light corn syrup
1 cup pecan halves

Preheat the oven to 450°.

1. Place the flour, confectioners' sugar, and salt into the bowl of a food processor. Add ½ cup chilled butter pieces. Pulse until the mixture resembles coarse crumbs. With the blade running, pour 1 tablespoon of ice water through the feed tube. Repeat until the mixture comes together around the blade.

2. Transfer the dough onto a sheet of plastic wrap. Gently form into a round disk. Wrap and chill for at least 30 minutes.

3. Roll out a pastry disk to about ⅛-inch thickness. Place the pastry into the bottom of a deep pie dish. Crimp the edges to form a decorative crust.

4. Pierce the bottom of the crust with the tines of a fork. Bake for 5 to 7 minutes. Remove from the oven and reduce the temperature to 375°.

5. Use an electric mixer to combine ¼ cup room temperature butter with the granulated sugar until smooth and fluffy.

6. Stir in the eggs, one at a time.

7. Stir in the rum and corn syrup.

8. Place the pecan halves in the bottom of the pie shell. Pour the filling over the top. Bake for 40 to 50 minutes, or until a knife inserted into the filling comes out clean and the pastry is golden.

9. Serve warm with a scoop of vanilla ice cream or a dollop of freshly whipped cream.

SERVINGS: 6 • PREPARATION TIME: 45 MINUTES PLUS BAKING

BLIND BAKING MEANS PARTIALLY OR FULLY BAKING AN UNFILLED PASTRY SHELL. THERE ARE SEVERAL WAYS TO BLIND BAKE; THIS RECIPE PRICKS THE PASTRY TO PREVENT IT FROM PUFFING UP AS IT BAKES. ALTERNATIVELY, YOU CAN FILL THE PASTRY WITH PIE WEIGHTS OR DRIED BEANS. TO DO THIS, CUT A PIECE OF FOIL TO OVERLAP THE PASTRY SHELL. COAT ONE SIDE WITH VEGETABLE OIL SPRAY TO PREVENT THE FOIL FROM STICKING TO THE PASTRY. PLACE THE COATED SIDE DOWN AND INTO THE SHELL. FILL WITH WEIGHTS OR BEANS. BAKE ACCORDING TO THE TIME REQUIRED IN THE RECIPE. REMOVE THE FOIL A FEW MINUTES BEFORE, ALLOWING THE PASTRY CRUST TO BROWN.

USING PREPARED PIE DOUGH IS AN ACCEPTABLE SHORTCUT WHEN YOU'RE IN A HURRY. SINCE YOU ARE SAVING TIME AND "BREAKING WITH TRADITION," YOU MIGHT AS WELL GO ALL THE WAY. HERE'S A DASTARDLY SUGGESTION: ADD ½ CUP SEMISWEET CHOCOLATE CHIPS TO THE FILLING FOR A CHOCOLATE-PECAN PIE.

Maple Pecan Bars

THESE EASY-TO-BAKE BARS ARE A LITTLE BIT BROWNIE, A LITTLE BIT
COOKIE AND WHOLE LOTTA PECAN AND MAPLE.

1½ cups all-purpose flour
1 teaspoon baking powder
½ teaspoon baking soda
¼ teaspoon salt
½ cup granulated sugar
¼ cup butter, room temperature (½ stick)
1 cup maple syrup
1 large egg
½ cup chopped pecans
¼ cup semisweet chocolate chips

Preheat the oven to 350°.

1. Whisk together the flour, baking powder, baking soda, and salt
in a bowl.

2. Use an electric mixer to combine the sugar and butter until
smooth and fluffy.

3. Stir in the flour mixture and beat until smooth. Do not over
mix.

4. Stir in the maple syrup, egg and pecans.

5. Pour the batter into a 11 x 9 x 2-inch baking dish that has been
coated with vegetable oil spray. Bake for 30 minutes. Cool for 15
minutes.

6. Melt the chocolate chips in a microwave safe bowl in the
microwave oven on medium temperature, stirring often. Drizzle
the chocolate over the cookies. Cut into bars.

SERVINGS: 12 • PREPARATION TIME: 45 MINUTES

WHICH CHOCOLATE TO USE?
WELL, HERE'S THE SKINNY:
UNSWEETENED CHOCOLATE IS
ALSO CALLED BAKING OR BIT-
TER CHOCOLATE. WHEN
SUGAR IS ADDED TO UNSWEET-
ENED CHOCOLATE, IT MORPHS
INTO BITTERSWEET, SEMI-
SWEET OR SWEET CHOCO-
LATE, DEPENDING ON HOW
MUCH SUGAR IS ADDED.
BITTERSWEET HAS THE LEAST
AMOUNT, WHILE SWEET
CHOCOLATE HAS THE MOST
SUGAR. ADDING DRY MILK TO
SWEET CHOCOLATE CREATES
MILK CHOCOLATE. YOU CAN
SUBSTITUTE BITTERSWEET,
SEMISWEET, AND SWEET
CHOCOLATE AT WILL—BUT
REMEMBER THAT BAKING
CHOCOLATE WILL NOT BE THE
SAME, AND MILK CHOCOLATE
IS AN INGREDIENT DIFFERENT
FROM THE REST.

Old-Fashioned Lemon Meringue Pie

YOU CAN ALSO MAKE THIS PIE WITH A GRAHAM CRACKER CRUST, WHICH
ALLOWS YOU TO JUMPSTART THE WHOLE PROCESS WITH A GOOD QUALITY
STORE-BOUGHT INGREDIENT.

2 cups all-purpose flour
2 tablespoons confectioners' sugar
¼ teaspoon salt
½ cup butter, chilled and cut into pieces (1 stick)
1 to 2 tablespoons ice water

Juice of 4 medium lemons (½ cup)
1 tablespoon cornstarch
1 14-ounce can condensed milk
5 large egg yolks

5 large egg whites
1 teaspoon vanilla extract
¾ cup granulated sugar

IN ORDER TO PRODUCE A
SMOOTH AND SHINY SOFT
MERINGUE, IT IS IMPORTANT
THAT YOU WHISK THE SUGAR
INTO THE BEATEN EGG WHITES
A SMALL AMOUNT AT A TIME;
THIS WILL ALLOW THE SUGAR
TO DISSOLVE COMPLETELY.
PERFECTLY COOKED
MERINGUE HAS BROWN TIPS
AND GOLDEN VALLEYS.

Preheat the oven to 375°.
1. Place the flour, confectioners' sugar and salt into the bowl of a
food processor. Add ½ cup chilled butter pieces. Pulse until the
mixture resembles coarse crumbs. With the blade running, pour
1 tablespoon of ice water through the feed tube. Repeat until the
mixture comes together around the blade.
2. Transfer the dough onto a sheet of plastic wrap. Gently form
into a round disk. Wrap and chill for at least 30 minutes.
3. Roll out the pastry disk to about ⅛-inch thickness. Place the
pastry into the bottom of a deep pie dish. Crimp the edges to
form a decorative crust. Cut a piece of foil to overlap the pastry
shell. Coat one side with vegetable oil spray to prevent the foil
from sticking to the pastry. Place the coated side down and into
the shell. Fill with the pie weights or dry beans. Bake for 20 minutes. Remove the foil and bake until golden, about 8 to 10 minutes more. Cool to room temperature.
4. Whisk together the lemon juice and cornstarch in a saucepan
over medium heat.
5. Whisk in the condensed milk and egg yolks. Bring the mixture
to a boil. Stir constantly, until thickened, about 8 to 10 minutes.
Pour the filling into the crust.
6. Use an electric mixer to whip the egg whites until soft peaks
form. Stir in the vanilla. Add the sugar, 1 tablespoon at a time,
whipping after each addition. The meringue will be stiff and
shiny. Spoon the meringue completely over the filling.

7. Raise the oven temperature to 450°. Bake the pie until the meringue is golden and browned on the edges, about 5 to 7 minutes. Refrigerate for at least 4 hours or overnight.

SERVINGS: 6 TO 8 • PREPARATION TIME: 30 MINUTES PLUS 40 MINUTES TOTAL BAKING

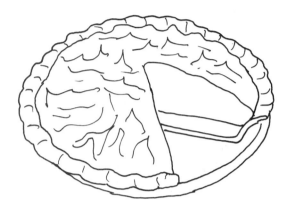

Chocolate Meringue Cookies

WHEN YOU'RE LOOKING FOR A FAST, LOW CAL, SWEET TREAT, LOOK NO FARTHER THAN THESE EASY TO PREPARE CRISPS.

3 large egg whites
¼ teaspoon cream of tartar
¼ teasooon salt
¾ cup sugar
3 tablespoons cocoa powder

Preheat the oven to 300°.
1. Use an electric mixer to whip the egg whites, cream of tartar, and salt, until soft peaks form.
2. Add the sugar, 1 tablespoon at a time, until stiff peaks form.
3. Remove the bowl from the mixer. Sprinkle the cocoa powder over the egg whites. Use a spatula to fold the cocoa powder into the egg whites until blended.
4. Line a baking sheet with parchment paper (or with a Silpat liner). Drop the meringue by level tablespoons onto the baking sheet.
5. Bake until crisp, about 35 to 40 minutes. Cool to room temperature.

YIELD: 4 DOZEN 1-INCH COOKIES • PREPARATION TIME: 1 HOUR

THE RECIPE FOR THESE COOKIES IS MADE FROM A HARD MERINGUE. IT INCLUDES MORE SUGAR THAN A SOFT MERINGUE AND IS BAKED FOR A LONGER AMOUNT OF TIME, THUS DRYING OUT THE MERINGUE, PRODUCING A CRISPY RESULT. FOR BEST MERINGUE RESULTS, REMEMBER THESE TIPS: USE THE FRESHEST EGGS YOU CAN FIND, ALLOW THE EGG WHITES TO COME TO ROOM TEMPERATURE BEFORE YOU WHIP THEM, MAKE SURE THAT NO BIT OF EGG YOLK GETS INTO THE EGG WHITE, AND IF YOU HAVE ONE, USE A COPPER BOWL INSERT, WHICH HELPS TO INCREASE THE VOLUME OF THE WHIPPED EGG WHITES.

Tropical Carrot Cake
with Coconut Cream Cheese Frosting

AN UPDATE ON THE CLASSIC CARROT CAKE, THIS TRIPLE-DECKER USES MACADAMIA NUTS, SWEETENED COCONUT AND CHUNKS OF PINEAPPLE TO SPICE UP THE DESSERT.

A FINE SHRED ATTACHMENT ON YOUR FOOD PROCESSOR IS THE PERFECT TOOL FOR GRATING CARROTS IN THIS RECIPE. YOU CAN ALSO GRATE THE CARROTS ON A BOX GRATER. PURCHASING PRE-SHREDDED PACKAGED CARROTS FROM THE PRODUCE SECTION OF THE MARKET, IS AN ACCEPTABLE WAY TO SHORTCUT THE PROCESS. MAKE SURE THAT THE PRE-PACKAGED CARROTS ARE FRESH, MOIST AND FINELY—NOT COARSELY—GRATED. MINCED CARROTS WILL GIVE THE CAKE A DIFFERENT TEX-TURE, ONE THAT WILL WORK ESPECIALLY WELL IF YOU ARE TRYING TO HIDE VEGGIES FROM YOUR PICKY EATER. MEASURE THE CARROTS AFTER YOU GRATE OR MINCE THEM TO MAKE SURE YOU HAVE TWO CUPS.

2½ cups all-purpose flour
1 cup flaked, sweetened coconut
1 cup macadamia nuts
2½ teaspoons baking powder
1 teaspoon ground ginger
1 teaspoon ground cinnamon
½ teaspoon baking soda
½ teaspoon salt

2 cups granulated sugar
1 cup canola oil
4 large eggs
2 teaspoons vanilla extract
2 cups finely grated carrots
2 8-ounce cans crushed pineapple, drained

3 8-ounce packages cream cheese, room temperature
¾ cup unsalted butter, room temperature (1½ sticks)
2 cups confectioners' sugar
1 teaspoon vanilla extract
Zest of 1 medium lime (about 1 tablespoon)
1 cup flaked, sweetened coconut

Preheat the oven to 350°.

1. Coat 3 9-inch round cake pans with vegetable oil spray. Line the bottom of each pan with parchment paper. Spray the paper with vegetable oil spray.

2. Place ½ cup of the flour, 1 cup sweetened coconut, and the macadamia nuts in the bowl of a food processor. Pulse until the nuts are ground and the mixture resembles coarse crumbs. Pour the nut mixture into a bowl.

3. Use a whisk to add the remaining 2 cups of flour, baking powder, ginger, cinnamon, baking soda and salt to the nut mixture.

4. Use an electric mixer to combine the granulated sugar and canola oil until smooth.

5. Stir in the eggs, one at a time.

6. Stir in the vanilla.

7. Stir in the flour/nut mixture.

8. Stir in the carrots and pineapple.

9. Divide the batter between the 3 pans. Bake for 30 minutes, or until a toothpick inserted in the center of the cake comes out clean. Cool the cakes in the pan for 15 minutes. Run a knife around the edges of the cakes. Invert onto a rack, and cool to room temperature.

10. For frosting, use an electric mixer to combine the cream cheese and butter until smooth. Stir in the confectioners' sugar, vanilla extract and lime zest.

11. Place one cake onto a cake stand. Frost with about ¾ cups of frosting. Repeat with the next layer. Top with the third cake. Frost the sides and top of the cake with the remaining frosting. Sprinkle the top of the cake with the remaining 1 cup unsweetened coconut.

SERVINGS: 10 TO 12 • PREPARATION TIME: 30 MINUTES PLUS BAKING 1 HOUR FOR BAKING AND COOLING CAKES

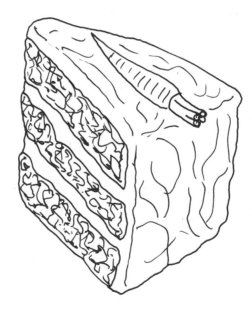

Carob Carrot Cupcakes with Tofu Cream Frosting

THOUGH NOT A TREMENDOUS FAN OF TOFU, I JUST CANNOT RESIST THE ALLURE OF GOOD-FOR-YOU FROSTING. GIVE THESE CUPCAKES A TRY AND ENJOY A GUILTLESS TREAT.

CAROB POWDER IS A CHOCO-LATE-FLAVORED INGREDIENT MILLED FROM THE CAROB-TREE POD. FOUND IN HEALTH FOOD MARKETS, IT IS A POPU-LAR SUBSTITUTE FOR CHOCO-LATE. TREAT IT AS YOU WOULD COCOA POWDER, OR, TO ADD CAROB POWDER TO YOUR FAVORITE RECIPE, SUBSTI-TUTE 1 PART CAROB POWDER AND 3 PARTS FLOUR FOR THE AMOUNT OF FLOUR REQUIRED.

1½ cups all-purpose flour
½ cup carob powder
2 teaspoons baking soda
½ teaspoon salt
1½ cup granulated sugar
½ cup canola oil
¼ cup buttermilk
3 large eggs
2 cups finely grated carrots

3 8-ounce packages soy cream cheese
¼ cup honey
1 tablespoon vanilla extract

Preheat the oven to 350°.
1. Whisk together the flour, carob powder, baking soda and salt in a bowl.
2. Use an electric mixer to combine the granulated sugar with the canola oil until smooth.
3. Stir in the buttermilk and the eggs, one at a time.
4. Stir in the carrots.
5. Stir in the flour mixture.
6. Divide this batter into 18 to 20 muffin cups lined with paper liners.
7. Bake for 20 to 22 minutes or until a toothpick inserted in the center comes out clean. Cool in the pan for 10 minutes. Transfer to a rack and cool to room temperature.
8. For frosting, use an electric mixer to combine the soy cream cheese, honey and vanilla until smooth. Chill for 20 minutes.
9. Spread the cupcakes with the frosting.

SERVINGS: 18 TO 20 CUPCAKES • PREPARATION TIME: 45 MINUTES

Three Milks Cake (Tres Leches)

THIS LATIN INSPIRED DISH GETS ITS NAME FROM THE THREE DIFFERENT
MILKS SOAKING INTO THE RICH CAKE; IT TASTES BETTER THE DAY AFTER,
SO YOU CAN BAKE IT THE NIGHT BEFORE FOR YOUR PARTY DESSERT.

2 cups cake flour
2 teaspoons baking powder
6 large eggs
2 cups granulated sugar
½ cup milk
1 teaspoon vanilla extract

1 14-ounce can sweetened condensed milk
1 14-ounce can evaporated milk
1 cup cream
½ cup dark rum

2 cups cream
½ cup confectioners' sugar
Fresh strawberries

EVAPORATED MILK IS
UNSWEETENED AND HOMOGE-
NIZED MILK. SIXTY PERCENT
OF THE WATER EVAPORATES
BEFORE ADDING VITAMIN D.
EVAPORATED MILK IS CREAMY
IN TEXTURE AND ADDS A VEL-
VETY QUALITY TO CUSTARDS
AND SAUCES. SWEETENED
CONDENSED MILK IS A MIX-
TURE OF MILK AND SUGAR—
ALMOST 50 PERCENT SUGAR!
THE SAME PROCESS REMOVES
THE WATER; THE RESULT IS A
THICK, VERY SWEET MIXTURE.

Preheat the oven to 350°.
1. Whisk together the flour and baking powder in a bowl.
2. Separate the eggs into 6 whites and 6 yolks.
3. Use an electric mixer to whip the egg whites until soft peaks
form. Gradually add the sugar until it dissolves and stiff peaks
form.
4. Stir in the egg yolks, one at a time.
5. Stir in the flour mixture.
6. Stir in the milk and vanilla.
7. Pour the batter into a 9 x 13 x 2 inch baking dish, coated with
vegetable oil spray. Bake until golden, 25 to 30 minutes.
8. Pour the sweetened condensed milk, evaporated milk, 1 cup
cream, and rum into a blender. Pulse for 1 minute to combine.
9. Remove the cake from the oven. Use a wooden skewer to poke
holes in the cake. Pour the milk mixture over the entire cake.
Cool to room temperature. Cover with plastic wrap. Chill for at
least 4 hours or overnight.
10. Whip the remaining 2 cups of cream with the confectioners'
sugar until soft peaks form.
11. Remove the cake from the refrigerator. Spread the whipped
cream over top. Cut into squares. Serve with fresh strawberries.

SERVINGS: 10 TO 12 • PREPARATION TIME: 1 HOUR PLUS CHILLING

Valentine's Day Red Velvet Cake with Walnut Cream Cheese Frosting

THE BEAUTIFUL RED COLOR OF THIS CAKE IS ACHIEVED USING EITHER FOOD COLORING LIQUID OR FOOD COLORING PASTE—THE LATER OF WHICH IS A MORE CONCENTRATED PRODUCT AVAILABLE AT GOURMET STORES. FOR INTIMATE FARE, YOU CAN BAKE THE CAKE IN A HEART-SHAPED PAN, OR BETTER YET, OFFER INDIVIDUAL CUPCAKES OR SMALL CAKES FROM INDIVIDUAL MOLDS; THIS CAKE GLADLY LENDS ITSELF TO CREATIVITY.

FOR A TWIST ON THIS YUMMY CAKE, ADD A LAYER OF SLICED FRESH STRAWBERRIES. TOP EACH FILLING LAYER OF CREAM CHEESE WITH THE STRAWBERRIES. GARNISH THE CAKE WITH A WHOLE STRAWBERRY IN THE CENTER AND A LAYER OF SLICED STRAWBERRIES AROUND THE BASE.

2½ cups cake flour
1 teaspoon baking soda
1 teaspoon salt
1 cup vegetable shortening
1½ cups granulated sugar
2 large eggs
1 teaspoon vanilla extract
1 teaspoon white vinegar
2 tablespoons cocoa powder
2 teaspoons red food coloring paste (or 2 ounces red food coloring)
1 cup buttermilk

3 8-ounce packages cream cheese, room temperature
1 cup unsalted butter, room temperature (2 sticks)
1 teaspoon vanilla extract
4 cups confectioners' sugar
1 cup finely chopped walnuts
2 tablespoons cream (optional)

Preheat the oven to 350°.

1. Prepare three 8-inch round baking pans by lining each one with a circle of parchment paper. Coat the pan with vegetable oil spray and place the parchment paper in the bottom of the pan. Spray the parchment paper.
2. Sift together the cake flour, baking soda, and salt. Set aside.
3. Use an electric mixer to cream together the shortening and granulated sugar until fluffy, about 3 to 5 minutes.
4. Stir in the eggs until just combined.
5. Stir in the vanilla extract, vinegar, and cocoa powder.
6. Stir in the food coloring paste.
7. Stir in the flour mixture in 3 additions, alternating with the buttermilk.
8. Divide the batter into the prepared pans. Bake for 20 to 15 minutes or until a toothpick inserted into the center comes out clean. Cool in the pans. Remove the cakes from the pans and remove the parchment paper. Cool completely.
9. Use an electric mixer to cream together the cream cheese and butter.

10. Stir in the vanilla.

11. Stir in the confectioners' sugar.

12. Fold in the chopped walnuts. If the frosting is too thick, thin with a few drops of cream.

13. Frost the cake between the layers and on the top and sides.

SERVINGS: 10 TO 12 • PREPARATION TIME: 45 MINUTES PREP PLUS 30 MIN-UTES BAKING

LONG BEFORE INTERNET E-MAIL, THERE WAS A WIDELY-TOLD STORY ABOUT A WOMAN WHO ASKED WALDORF ASTORIA FOR ITS RED VELVET CAKE RECIPE. SHE WAS GRANTED HER REQUEST, ALONG WITH A BILL FOR $100! SOUND FAMILIAR? IT SEEMS THAT GUESTS ENJOY A LITTLE LEGEND IN EVERY TRADITION-AL CAKE, AND THIS ONE IS NO EXCEPTION. EXCELLENT ANY DAY OF THE YEAR, THE RICH RED COLOR OF THIS CAKE IS ESPECIALLY IDEAL FOR OCCASIONS LIKE VALENTINE'S DAY AND CHRISTMAS. CREATIVE BAKERS CAN FIND MANY WAYS TO FASHION THIS DISH. LET'S NOT FORGET THE AWFUL GROOM'S CAKE SHOWCASED IN WEDDINGS, LIKE THE ONE IN THE STEEL MAGNOLIAS MOVIE. DID SOMEBODY SAY ARMADILLO?

Dark Chocolate Cake with Rich Chocolate Icing

USING OIL IN THE BATTER MAKES THE CAKE MOIST AND DENSE. THE ICING
IS SMOOTH AND SHINY. THE COMBINATION IS DEADLY!

3 cups all-purpose flour
2 cups granulated sugar
½ cup unsweetened cocoa powder
2 teaspoons baking soda
½ teaspoon salt
2 cups strong, hot, brewed coffee
¾ cup canola oil
2 tablespoons white vinegar
1 teaspoon vanilla

½ cup butter, melted (1 stick), room temperature
2 cups confectioners' sugar
1¼ cups unsweetened cocoa powder
1¼ cups cream
¼ cup sour cream
1 teaspoon instant coffee powder mixed with 1 tablespoon warm water
2 teaspoons vanilla

AN EASY METHOD OF SPLIT-
TING A CAKE LAYER INTO TWO
HALVES IS USING SEWING
THREAD. SIMPLY TAKE A
LENGTH OF THREAD AROUND
THE PERIMETER OF THE
CAKE, OVERLAPPING THE TWO
ENDS. MAKE SURE THE
THREAD IS PLACED HALFWAY
BETWEEN THE TOP AND BOT-
TOM OF THE CAKE. CROSS
THE ENDS AND PULL WITH
STEADY PRESSURE. THE
THREAD WILL SPLIT THE CAKE
IN ONE EVEN DRAG.

Preheat the oven 375
1. For cake, whisk together the flour, granulated sugar, ½ cup
cocoa, baking soda and salt in a bowl.
2. Place the coffee into a bowl. Stir in the canola oil, vinegar and
vanilla.
3. Whisk the wet ingredients into the dry ingredients until just
combined.
4. Divide the batter between 2 8-inch cake pans, coated with vegetable oil spray and lightly dusted with flour. Bake for 30 to 35
minutes, or until a toothpick inserted into the center of the cakes
comes out clean. Transfer to a rack and cool completely.
5. For frosting, use an electric mixer to combine the melted butter with the confectioners' sugar until smooth.
6. Stir in 1¼ cups cocoa.
7. Stir in the cream, sour cream, instant coffee mixture, and
vanilla, until smooth and shiny. If the mixture is too thin, add
more confectioners' sugar, 1 tablespoon at a time, until spread-
able.
8. Use a serrated knife to split each cake layer horizontally.
9. Place one cake layer onto a cake stand. Spread a layer of frosting over top. Continue layering and frosting. Spread the frosting
on the sides and finally, the top of the cake.

SERVINGS: 8 TO 10 • PREPARATION TIME: 45 MINUTES

Classic Angel Food Cake with Lemon Glaze

LIGHT AS AIR, THIS CAKE IS A CLASSIC ON SUMMER MENUS. ONCE YOU GET THE TECHNIQUE DOWN, EXPERIMENT WITH ADDING FLAVORS TO MAKE THIS CAKE YOUR OWN. ADD COCOA POWDER, CITRUS JUICE, APPLESAUCE, AND EVEN MAPLE SYRUP!

1 cup cake flour
¾ cup granulated sugar
¼ teaspoon salt

12 large egg whites, room temperature
1 teaspoon cream of tartar
¾ cup granulated sugar
1 teaspoon vanilla extract
½ teaspoon almond extract

1 cup confectioners' sugar
2 tablespoons cream
Zest of 1 medium lemon (about 1 tablespoon)
Juice of 1 medium lemon (about 2 tablespoons)

Preheat the oven to 325°.

1. Whisk together the flour, ¾ cup sugar and salt in a small bowl.

2. Use an electric mixer to whip the egg whites and cream of tartar until soft peaks form.

3. Add the remaining ¾ cup of sugar into the egg whites, 2 tablespoons at a time until all of the sugar is dissolved and stiff peaks form. Stir in the vanilla and the almond extract.

4. Pour ¼ of the flour/sugar mixture over the egg whites. Use a large spatula to gently fold in the flour. Repeat until all of the flour has been incorporated.

5. Pour the batter into a 10-inch tube pan. Swirl a knife through the batter to break up air pockets. Bake for 55 minutes. The cake will spring back when touched and the top will be golden. Invert the pan to cool completely. Use a dinner knife or spatula to loosen the cake from the sides of the pan. Invert onto a cake stand.

6. Whisk together the confectioners' sugar, cream, lemon zest and juice. Pour the glaze over the top of the angel food cake.

SERVINGS: 8 TO 10 • PREPARATION TIME: 30 MINUTES PLUS BAKING

A TUBE PAN IS A ROUND PAN WITH DEEP SIDES AND A HOLLOW CENTER TUBE. THE TUBE ALLOWS FOR EVEN RISING AND BAKING. ONE TYPE OF TUBE PAN IS AN ANGEL FOOD CAKE PAN; IT MAY HAVE REMOVABLE BOTTOMS AND EXTENDED METAL FEET THAT RISE FROM THE SIDES OF THE PAN, ALLOWING AN INVERTED PAN TO REST ON ITS OWN LEGS. IF YOUR PAN DOES NOT HAVE THESE "LEGS," YOU CAN INVERT THE PAN ON A CAN OR COKE BOTTLE.

THE PROPER TOOL TO SLICE AN ANGEL FOOD CAKE IS AN ANGEL FOOD CAKE SERVER; IT RESEMBLES A LONG-TOOTHED METAL COMB. THE TINES OF THE SERVER ARE DESIGNED TO GENTLY TEAR THE CAKE INTO EVEN WEDGES. IF YOU DO NOT HAVE AN ANGEL FOOD CAKE SERVER, YOU CAN USE 2 FORKS TO SEPARATE THE SLICES.

Macadamia Nut Butter Cookies

OKAY, YOU'VE TASTED PEANUT BUTTER COOKIES AND LOVED THEM. HERE'S AN INTERESTING UPDATE: MACADAMIA NUT BUTTER IN PLACE OF PEANUTS; THESE ARE CRUMBLY AND LACED WITH CHOPPED DRIED CHERRIES.

WHEN YOU GRIND NUTS, THEY RELEASE THEIR NATURAL OIL. A FOOD PROCESSOR IS THE BEST TOOL TO GRIND NUTS INTO A SMOOTH PASTE. YOU DO NOT NEED TO ADD ANY ADDITIONAL OIL OR SEASONINGS. ALL NUTS CAN BE TURNED INTO NUT BUTTER. TRY SUBSTITUTING WITH YOUR FAVORITE NUTS FOR A FUN VARIATION ON PEANUT BUTTER COOKIES.

1 cup all-purpose flour
½ teaspoon baking soda
¼ teaspoon salt
¼ teaspoon ground nutmeg
1 cup macadamia nuts
1 cup granulated sugar
1 large egg
1 teaspoon vanilla extract
½ cup dried cherries, chopped

Preheat the oven to 375°.

1. Whisk together the flour, baking soda, salt and nutmeg in a bowl.
2. Place the nuts into the bowl of a food processor with 1 tablespoon of the sugar. Pulse until the nuts become a smooth butter.
3. Use an electric mixer to combine the macadamia butter and remaining sugar until smooth and fluffy.
4. Stir in the egg and vanilla.
5. Stir in the flour mixture.
6. Stir in the chopped cherries. Chill the dough for 15 minutes.
7. Use a tablespoon to portion out enough dough for 1 cookie. Roll the dough into a ball. Place the balls on a Silpat (or parchment paper) lined baking sheet about 3 inches apart.
8. Use the back of a fork to press down on each cookie forming a crosswise pattern. Sprinkle the cookies with additional granulated sugar.
9. Bake until the cookies are golden, about 8 to 10 minutes. Bake the cookies on a rack.

SERVINGS: 2½ DOZEN COOKIES • PREPARATION TIME: 30 MINUTES PLUS 15 MINUTES CHILLING

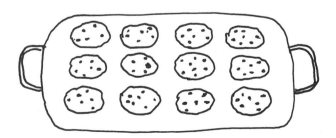

Macadamia and Chocolate Chip Biscotti

USE THIS RECIPE AS A GUIDE TO CREATE YOUR OWN FAVORITE BISCOTTI.
SUBSTITUTE YOUR FAVOR NUT, WHITE OR MILK CHOCOLATE, OR ELIMINATE
BOTH AND ADD A TABLESPOON OF YOUR FAVORITE LIQUOR OR A TOUCH OF
ALMOND EXTRACT. IT'S ALL GOOD!

2 cups all-purpose flour
1½ teaspoon baking powder
¼ teaspoon salt
¾ cup granulated sugar
½ cup butter, room temperature (1 stick)
2 large eggs
1 tablespoon vanilla
1 cup macadamia nuts, coarsely chopped
1 cup semisweet chocolate chips

Preheat the oven to 350°.

1. Whisk together the flour, baking powder and salt

2. Use an electric mixer to combine the sugar and butter until smooth and fluffy.

3. Stir in the eggs, one at a time.

4. Stir in the vanilla.

5. Stir in the flour mixture.

6. Stir in the macadamia nuts and chocolate chips.

7. Divide the dough in half. Wrap each half in plastic wrap and freeze for 20 minutes.

8. Remove the dough from the freezer. Use your hands to form each piece into a log, about 12 inches long and 3 inches wide. Place both logs on a Silpat (or parchment) lined baking sheet. Bake until golden brown, about 20 minutes. Remove from the oven.

9. Reduce the oven temperature to 300°. Cool the logs for 15 minutes. Use a serrated knife to cut each log into diagonal ½-inch slices. Lay the slices onto the baking sheet. Bake until the biscotti is golden and dry to the touch, about 30 more minutes.

YIELD: 3 DOZEN • PREPARATION TIME: 20 MINUTES PLUS REFRIGERATING
THE DOUGH AND 1 HOUR TOTAL BAKING TIME

ITALIAN BISCOTTI IS A TWICE BAKED CRISP BISCUIT, DESIGNED TO BE SERVED FOR DUNKING—IN COFFEE OR YOUR FAVORITE DESSERT WINE. TRADITIONAL BISCOTTI IS FLAVORED WITH ANISE SEEDS AND HAZELNUTS. YOU CAN MAKE YOUR BISCOTTI EVEN MORE EXOTIC BY DIPPING THE ENDS INTO MELTED CHOCO-LATE.

Classic Date Bars

ASSEMBLED AND BAKED IN MINUTES, THERE'S NO REASON NOT TO KEEP THESE YUMMY SNACK BARS AROUND ALL THE TIME.

2 cups pitted dates, chopped
2 cups water
1 teaspoon vanilla extract
2 cups all-purpose flour
1 cup brown sugar
1 cup old-fashioned rolled oats
1 teaspoon ground cinnamon
½ teaspoon allspice
¼ teaspoon ground cloves
½ teaspoon baking soda
1 cup unsalted butter, cut into small pieces, room temperature (2 sticks)

Preheat the oven to 350°.

1. Place the dates into a saucepan. Cover with 2 cups water. Heat the date mixture over medium high heat. Simmer until the dates become soft and thick, about 8 to 10 minutes. Add the vanilla. Cool to room temperature.

2. Place the flour, brown sugar, oats, cinnamon, allspice, cloves and baking soda into the bowl of a food processor. Pulse to combine.

3. Add the butter to the bowl. Pulse to incorporate the butter into the flour mixture.

4. Place half of the dough into the bottom of a 9 x 11 x 2-inch baking dish, coated with vegetable oil spray.

5. Cover the dough with the date mixture.

6. Crumble the remaining dough over top of the filling. Gently press down to adhere.

7. Bake until the top is golden and the center is set, about 30 to 40 minutes. Cool in the dish to room temperature. Use a sharp knife to cut into bars.

SERVINGS: 12 • PREPARATION TIME: 20 MINUTES
PLUS BAKING

DATES ARE NATIVE TO THE MIDDLE EAST AND HAVE A HISTORY OF AT LEAST 5,000 YEARS. THE NAME OF THE FRUIT COMES FROM THE GREEK WORD "DAKTULOS," WHICH TRANSLATES TO "FINGER" FOR THE SHAPE OF A DATE. DATES ARE VERY SWEET, AND, WHEN DRIED, BECOME EVEN SWEETER. DRIED DATES ARE AVAILABLE WHOLE AND CHOPPED, YEAR ROUND IN MOST GROCERY STORES.

Almond Fig Bars

THINK OF YOUR FAVORITE PACKAGED FIG BAR COOKIE AND YOU GET THE BASIC IDEA OF HOW YUMMY THESE BARS ARE. THE COMBINATION OF SWEET FIG FILLING AND FLAKY ALMOND CRUST, MAKE THIS A POPULAR DISH FOR DESSERT OR YOUR NEXT COFFEE BREAK.

¼ cup boiling water
2 tablespoons granulated sugar
2 tablespoons honey
Juice of ½ medium orange (about 2 to 3 tablespoons)
2 cups dried figs (about 12 ounces)
Zest of ½ medium orange (about 1 tablespoon)

1½ cups all-purpose flour
¼ teaspoon salt
¼ teaspoon baking powder
½ cup butter, room temperature (1 stick)
½ cup brown sugar
¼ cup granulated sugar
1 large egg
1 teaspoon vanilla extract
1 cup sliced almonds

ORIGINALLY, FIGS WERE AN EARLY SYMBOL OF PEACE AND PROSPERITY. FIGS CAME TO NORTH AMERICA BY WAY OF THE SPANISH FRANCISCAN MISSIONARIES, INTENT ON SETTING UP CATHOLIC MISSIONS IN SOUTHERN CALIFORNIA. CHANCES ARE, YOU'VE HEARD OF THE POPULAR MISSION FIG. FRESH FIGS ARE EXTREMELY PERISHABLE, BUT WHEN DRIED, ARE READILY AVAILABLE IN THE GROCERY STORE. FIGS ARE A GREAT SOURCE OF CALCIUM AND IRON.

Preheat the oven to 350°.
1. For filling, pour ¼ cup water, 2 tablespoons granulated sugar, honey and orange juice in a saucepan over medium high heat until boiling. Place the figs and orange zest into the bowl of a food processor. Pulse to mince the figs. With the machine running, pour the hot liquid onto the minced figs. Process until well blended.
2. For dough, whisk together the flour, salt and baking powder in a small bowl. Use an electric mixer to combine the butter, brown sugar and remaining granulated sugar until smooth and fluffy. Stir in the egg and vanilla. Stir in the flour mixture and almonds.
3. Coat a 9 x 11 x 2-inch square baking dish with vegetable oil spray. Press half of the dough mixture into the bottom of the pan.
4. Spoon the filling on top of the dough.
5. Crumble the remaining dough over top of the filling. Gently press down to adhere.
6. Bake until the top is golden, about 25 to 30 minutes. Cool in the dish to room temperature. Use a sharp knife to cut into bars.

SERVINGS: 12 TO 16 • PREPARATION TIME: 20 MINUTES PLUS BAKING

Shortbread Cookies

SHAPE THESE RICH COOKIES INTO HEARTS FOR VALENTINE'S DAY,
SNOWFLAKES FOR HOLIDAY PLATTERS, PUMPKINS FOR HALLOWEEN TREATS,
OR DIAMONDS FOR YOUR BRIDGE CLUB DESSERT.

COOKIES HAVE A RICH HISTORY. THE FIRST ONE MAY HAVE ORIGINATED WITH THE ROMAN CHEF, APICIUS WHEN HE BOILED A THICK PASTE OF WHEAT FLOUR AND SPREAD IT ONTO A PLATE. WHEN IT DRIED AND HARDENED, HE CUT IT INTO PIECES, FRIED IT UNTIL THE PIECES WERE CRISP, AND SERVED THEM WITH HONEY AND PEPPER. THE MIDDLE AGES SAW THE BEGINNINGS OF MERINGUE COOKIES. SAVOY COOKIES WITH EGG WHITES, SUGAR AND FLOUR ORIGINATED IN THE 1600S IN FRANCE AND SPAIN, IN THE FORM OF BISCUITS. COOKIES BASED ON CREAMING BUTTER AND SUGAR APPEARED IN THE 18TH CENTURY. THE COOKIE REALLY GAINED SOME GROUND IN THE 19TH CENTURY WHEN THE PRICE OF SUGAR AND FLOUR DROPPED. I SUBMIT THAT IF IT WEREN'T FOR THE GIRL SCOUTS, WE MIGHT BE EATING CAKES AND BISCUITS INSTEAD OF COOKIES!

1½ cup unsalted butter, room temperature (3 sticks)
1 cup granulated sugar
1 teaspoon vanilla extract
¼ teaspoon salt
3½ cups all-purpose flour
Colored sugar for decorating

Preheat the oven to 350°.

1. Use and electric mixer to blend the butter and sugar into cream. Stir in the vanilla.

2. Sift together the salt and flour. Stir into the butter mixture until the dough just comes together.

3. Pour the dough onto a lightly floured surface. Pat together and form into a disk. Place the disk between two pieces of plastic wrap. Use a rolling pin to roll the dough to about ½-inch thickness. Chill for 15 minutes.

4. Cut the dough into shapes. Place the cookies onto a Silpat lined baking sheet. Gather the scraps and place between plastic wrap. Use a rolling pin to roll out the remaining dough to ½-inch thickness and continue.

5. Sprinkle the cookies with colored sugar. Bake for 12 to 15 minutes (depending on cookie size), or until the cookies are set and just beginning to color on the bottom. Transfer to a rack and cool completely.

YIELD: ABOUT 2 DOZEN
2-INCH COOKIES •
PREPARATION TIME: 30
MINUTES

Chocolate Walnut Shortbread Cookies

THE ADDITION OF CHOCOLATE AND WALNUTS TO TRADITIONAL SHORT-
BREAD, UPDATES A SCOTTISH STAPLE. THIS VERSION IS SO DECADENTLY
RICH ONE COOKIE IS SURE TO SATISFY ANY CHOCOLATE CRAVING!

1 cup walnuts
1½ cups all-purpose flour
¼ cup cocoa powder
½ teaspoon salt
¾ cup unsalted butter, cut into small pieces, room temperature (1½ sticks)
½ cup granulated sugar, plus extra for sprinkling
1 large egg yolk
1 teaspoon vanilla extract
1 cup semi-sweet chocolate chips

Preheat the oven to 375°.

1. Place the walnuts in the bowl of a food processor. Pulse to coarsely chop. Pour the walnuts into a bowl.

2. Add the flour, cocoa powder, and salt to the same bowl. Whisk to combine.

3. Place the butter into the bowl of the food processor.

4. With the machine running, add ½ cup sugar, egg yolk and vanilla.

5. Add the walnut/cocoa/flour mixture and pulse until the mixture forms a dough.

6. Pour the dough into a bowl. Use your hands to mix in the chocolate chips. Use a tablespoon to portion the dough. Roll each portion into 2-inch balls. Place each ball onto a Silpat lined baking sheet. Flatten each ball with the bottom of a glass dipped in sugar. Bake for 15 to 18 minutes until the cookies are firm to the touch.

YIELD: ABOUT 2½ DOZEN COOKIES • PREPARATION TIME: 30 MINUTES

USING A FOOD PROCESSOR SPEEDS UP THIS RECIPE'S MIXING PROCESS, IN ALLOWING ONE MACHINE TO DO THE WORK OF TWO. THE SAME TOOL THAT CHOPS THE NUTS, MIXES TOGETHER THE COOKIE DOUGH. THE SECRET IS NOT TO OVER PROCESS WHEN YOU ADD THE WALNUTS AND FLOUR. JUST A FEW PULSES WILL YIELD A TENDER DOUGH.

YOU CAN USE THIS SAME TECHNIQUE AND RECIPE TO CREATE YOUR OWN FAVORITE SHORTBREAD COOKIE. ELIMINATE THE CHOCOLATE, COCOA POWDER AND WALNUTS, AND ADD CHOPPED PECANS AND DRIED CRANBERRIES, OR CHOPPED HAZELNUTS AND RAISINS. SLIVERED ALMONDS AND A TEASPOON OF ALMOND EXTRACT IS ANOTHER GOOD COMBINATION.

Tiramisu

A RICH BLEND OF CUSTARD AND LADYFINGERS SOAKED IN COFFEE MAKES AN ELEGANT DESSERT. THE GOOD NEWS IS, IT'S AN EASY ENTERTAINING DISH, AS YOU MUST PREPARE IT A DAY IN ADVANCE OF SERVING.

6 large egg yolks
4 tablespoons granulated sugar
6 large egg whites
3 tablespoon granulated sugar
2 cups mascarpone cheese
1 teaspon vanilla extract
¼ cup sweet vermouth
4 7-ounce packages plain ladyfingers
1 cup strong coffee, cooled to room temperature
Cocoa powder
Amoretti cookies, finely ground
Fresh berries

Cooked Custard Variation
This recipe comes together quickly because the custard is not cooked. If you are concerned about eating or serving raw eggs, substitute with cooked custard that is chilled and set. Whisk together 1 cup of milk, 1 cup of granulated sugar and 1 teaspoon of vanilla in a saucepan over medium high heat until the sugar dissolves. Whisk together 4 large eggs and ⅓ cup of flour in a bowl until smooth. Pour 1 cup of the hot milk mixture into the egg mixture. Pour the tempered egg mixture back into the saucepan. Simmer the custard, whisking constantly, until thickened. Remove from heat. Stir in 1 cup mascarpone and 1 tablespoon of butter until smooth. Stir in ¼ cup of vermouth. Pour the custard into a bowl. Cover with plastic wrap, pressing it into the custard, to prevent a skin from forming. Chill until cold.

1. Use an electric mixer to beat the egg yolks with 1 tablespoon of sugar until light and frothy. Set aside.
2. Use an electric mixer to beat the egg whites and 3 tablespoons of sugar until stiff, increasing in volume by half.
3. Beat the mascarpone and vanilla into the egg yolks.
4. Stir in the vermouth.
5. Gently fold the egg whites into the egg yolk mixture. Chill.
6. Coat a 9 x 5 x 3-inch loaf pan with vegetable oil spray. Line the pan with plastic wrap, allowing to overlap the edge. Spray again.
7. Stand the ladyfingers, side by side, making a wall around the sides of the loaf pan. Place a layer of ladyfingers on the bottom. Brush the ladyfingers with coffee.
8. Place ⅓ of the custard on top of the ladyfingers. Continue layering with ladyfingers, coffee, and custard, finishing with ladyfingers.
9. Wrap tightly with the overlapping plastic wrap. Refrigerate overnight.
10. Remove the tiramisu by unwrapping the plastic wrap from the top. Invert the loaf pan onto a serving platter. Gently pull the plastic edges, affixing the tiramisu to the platter. Generously dust with cocoa powder and ground amoretti cookies. Serve with fresh berries.

SERVINGS: 6 TO 8 • PREPARATION TIME: 30 MINUTES PLUS REFRIGERATING OVERNIGHT

Candy Cane Trifle

THIS TERRIFIC DISH IS EASY TO ASSEMBLE, USING PREPARED INGREDIENTS.
IF YOU HAVE EXTRA TIME, YOU CAN PREPARE YOUR FAVORITE POUND CAKE
OR ANGEL FOOD CAKE RECIPE, AND MAKE YOUR FAVORITE VANILLA CUS-
TARD A DAY IN ADVANCE OF YOUR PARTY.

2 pints strawberries hulled and quartered (about 2 cups)
¼ cup chambois liqueur (optional)
2 tablespoons granulated sugar
1 5-ounce package instant vanilla pudding
2 cups whipping cream
1 small package candy canes
1 15-ounce angel food cake, cut into large chunks
Fudge sauce

THE ONLY THING BETTER THAN
A TRIFLE FOR DESSERT IS A
TRIFLE TOPPED WITH A DRIZ-
ZLE OF WARM CHOCOLATE
SAUCE. CHECK OUT THE SIM-
PLE RECIPE ON PAGE 343
FOR AN OVER-THE-TOP TREAT.

1. Place the strawberries into a bowl. Pour in the liquor and
sprinkle with sugar. Toss gently, cover and refrigerate for at least
30 minutes or as much as overnight.
2. Prepare the pudding according to the directions on the package.
3. Whip the cream until soft peaks form. Gently fold the whipped
cream into the pudding. Refrigerate until ready to assemble.
4. Place the candy canes into the bowl of a food processor. Pulse
until the mixture resembles coarse crumbs. You need at least 1
cup of candy crumbs.
5. Assemble the trifle in a tall glass or crystal bowl. Place ¼ of the
pudding mixture into the bottom of the bowl.
6. Top the pudding with ⅓ of the cake cubes.
7. Top the cake with ½ of the macerated strawberries, including ½
of the fruit juices.
8. Continue layering with pudding and cake. Sprinkle this cake
layer with half of the candy cane crumbs.
9. Top the candy crumbs with the remaining strawberries and
juices.
10. Finish the trifle with pudding and cake. Reserve some pudding for the top of the trifle.
11. Sprinkle the remaining candy cane crumbs over the pudding.
12. Chill the trifle in the refrigerator until ready to serve (up to
4 hours). Serve with warm fudge sauce.

SERVES: 10 TO 12 • PREPARATION TIME: 20 MINUTES PLUS MARINATING THE
STRAWBERRIES.

Chocolate, Banana, and Walnut Trifle

THE ORIGINAL ENGLISH TRIFLE IS LAYERED WITH LADYFINGERS OR SPONGE CAKE, WHICH HAS BEEN SOAKED IN LIQUOR (USUALLY SHERRY). IT IS THEN LAYERED WITH JAM, CUSTARD AND WHIPPED CREAM. I'VE TAKEN A FEW LIBERTIES HERE—BUT BET YOUR GUESTS WILL LOVE THE RESULT.

YOU CAN MAKE THIS RECIPE EVEN EASIER BY INCORPORATING REFRIGERATED WHIPPED TOPPING AND PACKAGED PUDDING INTO THE RECIPE. TAKE A LOOK AT THE RECIPE FOR CANDY CANE TRIFLE (SEE PAGE 337) TO SEE WHAT I MEAN.

6 tablespoons granulated sugar
3 tablespoons cornstarch
1½ tablespoons cocoa powder
¼ teaspoon salt
1 cup milk
2 cups cream
1 teaspoon vanilla extract
6 ounces milk chocolate, chopped
2 tablespoons butter, cut into pieces

4 ripe bananas, sliced (about 2 cups)
¼ cup Kahlua liquor

2 cups whipping cream
½ cup confectioners' sugar

1 15-ounce angel food cake, cut into large chunks
2 1.4-ounce Heath bars, chopped

2 tablespoons butter
2 tablespoons brown sugar
1 cup walnut pieces

1. Whisk together the sugar, cornstarch, cocoa powder, salt and milk in a saucepan over medium heat until smooth.
2. Stir in 2 cups cream. Cook, stirring constantly, until the mixture thickens, about 5 minutes.
3. Pour in the vanilla, then chocolate, and stir until smooth.
4. Pour the pudding into a bowl. Whisk in the butter. Cover with plastic wrap and chill until set, about 1 hour.
5. Toss the bananas with the Kahlua in a small bowl. Set aside.
6. Use an electric mixer to whisk 2 cups cream with confectioners' sugar until stiff peaks form. Set aside.
7. Toss the angel food cake cubes with the chopped Heath bar in a bowl. Set aside.
8. Heat 2 tablespoons butter with 2 tablespoons brown sugar, in a skillet, over medium high heat. Add the walnut pieces. Toss to coat. Cook for 2 minutes. Remove from heat.

9. Assemble the trifle by placing a layer of the pudding on the bottom of a trifle dish. Add a layer angel food cake and candy. Top with a layer of bananas. Add a layer of whipped cream. Continue layering until all of the ingredients have been used. **10.** Top the trifle with the candied walnuts. Chill for 1 hour or overnight.

SERVINGS: 10 TO 12 • PREPARATION TIME: 1 HOUR

Fresh Baked Cherry and Apple Pie

THIS COMBINATION OF APPLES AND CHERRIES, MAKES FOR A WONDERFUL FRESH FRUIT FILLING IN A DELICATE, YET SWEET PASTRY CRUST. GET YOUR PALS INVOLVED BY HAVING THEM PIT FRESH CHERRIES, WHILE YOU ROLL OUT THE DOUGH.

4 cups all-purpose flour
1 cup confectioners' sugar
½ teaspoon salt
1 cup butter, chilled and cut into pieces (2 sticks)
2 to 4 tablespoons ice water

2 medium apples, peeled and thinly sliced (about 2 cups)
1 pound cherries, stemmed and pitted (about 3 cups)
Zest of ½ medium orange (about 1 tablespoon)
1 cup granulated sugar
¼ cup all-purpose flour

1 egg white, beaten
2 tablespoons butter (melted)
½ cup half and half
2 tablespoons granulated sugar

Preheat the oven to 450°.

1. Place 3¾ cups of flour, confectioners' sugar, and salt into the bowl of a food processor. Add the chilled butter. Pulse until the mixture resembles coarse crumbs. With the blade running, pour 1 tablespoon of ice water through the feed tube. Repeat until the mixture comes together around the blade.
2. Transfer the dough onto a sheet of plastic wrap. Gently form into 2 round disks. Wrap and chill for at least 30 minutes.
3. Place the apples and cherries into a bowl. Stir in the orange zest and 1 cup granulated sugar. Let the fruit sit for 15 minutes.
4. Toss the fruit with the remaining ¼ cup all-purpose flour.
5. Roll out 1 pastry dish to about ⅛-inch thickness. Place the pastry into the bottom of a deep pie dish.
6. Brush the bottom of the pie shell with beaten egg white.
7. Pour the cherry/apple mixture into the pastry. Dot with 2 tablespoons butter that has been cut into small pieces.
8. Roll out the remaining pastry disk. Cover the pie with the second disk. Crimp the bottom and top pastries together to form a decorative crust. Use a knife to cut vents into the top crust.
9. Brush the top with half and half and sprinkle with sugar.
10. Place the pie onto a baking sheet. Bake for 10 minutes. Reduce heat to 350°. Bake until the pie is golden and the filling is bubbling, about 40 to 45 minutes more.

SERVINGS: 6 • PREPARATION TIME: 30 MINUTES PLUS BAKING

PIE CRUST NEED NOT BE DAUNTING. JUST A FEW SIMPLE TIPS WILL GUARANTEE PRODUCTION OF A PERFECT PIE EVERY TIME.

TIP #1—MAKE SURE YOU USE VERY COLD BUTTER, ICE WATER, AND A FOOD PROCESSOR BOWL AND BLADE THAT IS NOT HOT OR RIGHT OUT OF THE DISHWASHER. GREAT CRUST COMES FROM COLD BUTTER. ONCE THE BUTTER BEGINS TO MELT, THE CRUST BECOMES DIFFICULT TO WORK WITH.

TIP #2—USE A FOOD PROCESSOR TO PREPARE THE DOUGH. AFTER THE COLD BUTTER IS INCORPORATED, ADD ICE WATER, A SPOONFUL AT A TIME, AND WAIT TO SEE IF THE DOUGH COMES TOGETHER BEFORE ADDING THE NEXT SPOONFUL. THE FLOUR WILL RISE UP THE SIDES OF THE BOWL AND THEN FALL INWARD, TOWARD THE CENTER; IT WILL THEN CLUMP TOGETHER. DO NOT ADD MORE WATER ONCE THE DOUGH BEGINS TO CLUMP.

TIP #3—ROLL OUT THE DOUGH BETWEEN TWO SHEETS OF PLASTIC WRAP. THE DOUGH WILL NOT STICK TO THE ROLLING PIN OR WORK SURFACE; THUS, TRANSFERRING THE DOUGH TO THE PIE PLATE IS A BREEZE.

Apple Pandowdy

PANDOWDY GOT ITS NAME FROM THE VERY PLAINNESS OF THE DESSERT, ONE THAT UTILIZES FRESH FRUIT AND LEFTOVER BREAD OR BISCUIT DOUGH—HOW DOWDY?! THIS VERSION SPRUCES UP THE DISH WITH THE USE OF PREPARED PUFF PASTRY AND THE ADDITION OF A CHINESE SPICE. ONE SPOONFUL, AND YOU WILL SEE WHAT I MEAN!

8 to 10 medium apples, peeled and thinly sliced (about 8 cups)
Juice of 1 medium lemon (about 2 tablespoons)
1 cup brown sugar
2 tablespoons all-purpose flour
½ teaspoon ground cinnamon
½ teaspoon Chinese five spice
2 tablespoons butter
1 frozen 8-ounce puff pastry sheet, thawed according to package directions
2 tablespoons cream
2 tablespoons granulated sugar

Preheat the oven to 400°.
1. Toss together the apples, lemon juice, brown sugar, flour, cinnamon, and Chinese five spice in the bottom of an 11 x 7 x 2-inch baking dish.
2. Dot the top of the apple mixture with butter.
3. Roll out the pastry sheet to a 12 x 8-inch rectangle on a lightly floured surface.
4. Place the pastry sheet on top of the apple filling, tucking the edges into the dish. Brush the top with cream and use a sharp knife to cut several slits. Sprinkle the pastry with granulated sugar.
5. Bake until golden and bubbly, about 30 to 40 minutes. Serve warm or at room temperature, with ice cream or another drizzle of cream.

SERVINGS: 6 • PREPARATION TIME: 20 MINUTES PLUS 40 MINUTES BAKING

YOU CAN CHOOSE FROM DOZENS OF VARIETIES OF APPLES. WHEN BAKING APPLES, CHOOSE ROME BEAUTY OR GRANNY SMITH; THEY ARE A LITTLE TART, AS OPPOSED TO SWEET, BUT WORK BEST IN THIS RECIPE. A RED DELICIOUS IS GORGEOUS AND GREAT TASTING, TOO, BUT IT WILL NOT WORK AS WELL IN THIS DISH.

MAKE EASY WORK OF PEELING APPLES BY USING ONE OF THOSE NIFTY GADGETS YOU FIND IN THE STORE. AN APPLE/PEELER/CORER/SLICER (YEP, THAT'S THE NAME) MAKES THIS DISH COME TOGETHER IN MINUTES.

S'mores

A LONG-ESTABLISHED, CAMPFIRE TREAT, S'MORES OWE THEIR NAME TO BEING HIGHLY ADDICTIVE. ONCE YOU'VE HAD ONE OF THESE OOEY GOOEY SANDWICHES, YOU JUST HAVE TO HAVE "SOME MORE."

12 whole cinnamon coated graham crackers
6 3.5-ounce chocolate bars, broken into pieces
12 large marshmallows

1. Place 6 whole crackers onto your work surface.
2. Place the chocolate on top of the crackers.
3. Thread the marshmallows onto skewers. Cook the marshmallows over an open flame, outdoor grill, or under a broiler until soft and beginning to brown.
4. Place 2 marshmallows on top of the chocolate. Cover each sandwich with the remaining whole graham crackers.

YIELD: 6 SANDWICHES • PREPARATION TIME: 10 MINUTES

YOU NEED NOT LIMIT YOURSELF TO A CAMPFIRE TO MAKE THIS YUMMY TREAT. A MICROWAVE OVEN WILL MELT BOTH MARSHMALLOWS AND CHOCOLATE IN SECONDS. FEEL FREE TO VARY THE DISH, GIVING IT YOUR OWN SPECIAL TWIST. HERE ARE SOME FUN IDEAS: USE CHOCOLATE WAFER COOKIES IN PLACE OF GRAHAM CRACKERS, MINI MARSHMALLOWS OR MARSHMALLOW CRÈME IN PLACE OF FLAMED LARGER ONES, OR CHOCOLATE ICE CREAM IN PLACE OF CHOCOLATE BARS.

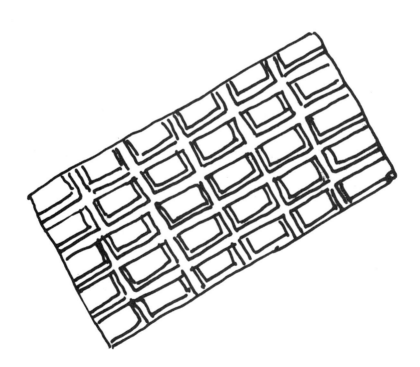

Quesadilla S'mores

A TRUE TROPICAL TWIST ON A CAMPFIRE DESSERT, THESE SIMPLE-TO-MAKE QUESADILLAS ARE FUN AND YUMMY. TRY THESE ON YOUR OUTDOOR GRILL, NEXT TAILGATE PARTY, OR AT HOME FOR A KIDS' SLEEPOVER. WATCH OUT—THESE ARE GOOEY!

4 8-inch flour tortillas
2 tablespoons butter, melted
1 tablespoon sugar combined with ½ teaspoon ground cinnamon
1 cup marshmallow cream
1 12-ounce package semisweet chocolate chips
½ cup graham cracker crumbs

1. Heat a grill pan over medium high heat or prepare an outdoor grill.
2. Brush 2 tortillas with butter. Sprinkle with ¼ of the cinnamon sugar.
3. Place one tortilla buttered-side down into the grill pan. Spread with ½ of the marshmallow cream.
4. Sprinkle ½ of the chocolate chips over top.
5. Sprinkle ½ of the graham cracker crumbs on top of the chocolate chips.
6. Top with the other tortilla, buttered-side up.
7. Grill the quesadilla until the chocolate begins to melt, about 2 to 4 minutes. Use 2 spatulas to flip the quesadilla. Cook for 2 to 4 minutes more. The quesadillas should be golden and the chocolate melted.
8. Transfer the quesadillas to a platter and cut into fourths. Continue with the remaining ingredients.
9. Serve with melted chocolate and whipped cream for dipping.

YIELD: 8 SLICES • PREPARATION TIME: 20 MINUTES

Warm Chocolate Sauce
I like to drizzle the quesadillas with warm chocolate sauce. Melt 1 tablespoon of butter, ½ cup of unsweetened cocoa, ¼ cup of confectioners' sugar and 1 cup of dark corn syrup, in a saucepan over medium high heat. Stir until smooth (watch carefully to prevent the sauce from burning). Stir in 1 tablespoon of whipping cream to produce a velvety, smooth chocolate sauce. Remove from the heat and keep warm. Store extra chocolate sauce (in an airtight container) in the refrigerator. Warm up the sauce over medium heat, in a saucepan, or in a moderately set microwave oven.

Cherries Jubilee

ALTHOUGH PERFECTLY PITTED, SWEET AND DARK CHERRIES ARE ESSENTIAL FOR THE QUALITY OF THIS SIMPLE DISH; IT'S ALL ABOUT PRESENTATION! THE SAUCE IS COOKED AND THEN FLAMED. IF YOU CAN ARRANGE FOR TABLESIDE PRESENTATION, THEN BY ALL MEANS, SERVE THIS DESSERT WITH A FLARE. IF YOU JUST WANT TO HAVE SOME FUN, INVITE YOUR PALS AND CONGREGATE IN THE KITCHEN WHILE YOU PREPARE THE DISH. (A LITTLE PRACTICE ON THE IGNITING PART COULDN'T HURT!)

½ cup butter (1 stick)
1 cup granulated sugar
1 pound fresh cherries, pitted (about 2½ to 3 cups)
Juice of 2 medium lemons (about ¼ cup)
Zest of 1 medium lemon (about 1 tablespoons)
1 tablespoon cornstarch mixed with 2 tablespoons cold water
1 cup brandy

Vanilla ice cream
Fresh mint leaves

1. Melt the butter and granulated sugar, in a skillet, over medium high heat until the sugar dissolves.
2. Stir in the cherries, lemon juice and lemon zest. Simmer for 3 to 4 minutes.
3. Stir in the cornstarch mixture. Cook for 2 minutes more.
4. Place a scoop of ice cream into a chilled dessert dish.
5. Remove the skillet from the heat. Pour in the brandy. Return the skillet to the heat. Carefully ignite the brandy. (See sidebar).
6. Spoon the cherries and the sauce over the ice cream. Garnish with fresh mint leaves.

SERVINGS: 4 • PREPARATION TIME: 20 MINUTES

IF YOU ARE USING A GAS STOVETOP WITH A FLAME, YOU CAN IGNITE THE BRANDY BY GENTLY TIPPING THE SKILLET AND ALLOWING THE FLAME TO JUMP INTO THE SAUCE. IF YOU HAVE AN ELECTRIC STOVETOP, LIGHT A LONG-HANDLED BUTANE LIGHTER AWAY FROM THE SKILLET. CAREFULLY BRING THE FLAME TO THE SAUCE, CLOSE ENOUGH TO IGNITE THE LIQUOR. AS YOU SPOON THE IGNITED SAUCE, THE FLAME WILL GO OUT.

Orange Butter Cake with Merlot Poached Cherries

THIS FESTIVE DESSERT TAKES ADVANTAGE OF THE FRESH FRUIT FLAVORS OF ORANGE AND CHERRY. YOU CAN MAKE THE CAKE A DAY IN ADVANCE, PREPARING AND STORING THE CHERRIES FOR SEVERAL DAYS (IN AN AIR-TIGHT CONTAINER) IN YOUR REFRIGERATOR. THIS IS A DELICIOUS MAKE-AHEAD DESSERT—A MUST FOR YOUR NEXT PARTY!

1½ cups all-purpose flour
2 teaspoon baking powder
½ teaspoon salt
1 cup unsalted butter, room temperature (2 sticks)
1½ cups granulated sugar

3 eggs
1 cup half and half
1 teaspoon orange oil
Zest of ½ medium orange (about 1 tablespoon)

1 pound fresh cherries, pitted (about 2½ to 3 cups)
1 750 ml bottle merlot
⅓ cup honey
Zest of ½ medium orange (about 1 tablespoon)

Confectioners' sugar
Whipped cream
Fresh mint leaves

Preheat the oven to 350°.

1. Coat a Bundt pan with vegetable oil spray and dust with flour.
2. Whisk together the flour, baking powder, and salt in a bowl. Set aside.
3. Use an electric mixer to combine the butter and sugar until fluffy.
4. Add the eggs, one at a time, until just combined.
5. Stir together the half and half, orange oil and 1 tablespoon orange zest.
6. Stir in the flour mixture in 3 additions, alternating with the half and half mixture until just combined.
7. Pour the batter into the prepared pan and bake for 45 to 50 minutes or until a toothpick, inserted into the center, comes out clean.
8. Place the cherries into a sauce pan. Cover with 1 bottle of merlot. Stir in ⅓ cup honey and the remaining orange zest. Bring this mixture to a boil over medium high heat. Reduce the heat and simmer until the cherries are soft, about 20 minutes. Transfer the cherries to a bowl and continue to simmer the liquid until it is reduced to about 1 cup and is thick and syrupy, about 1 hour altogether. Add the cherries back to the syrup and refrigerate until ready to serve.
9. Present the cake on a cake platter and dust with confectioners' sugar. Spoon the cherries into the center of the cake, serving the remaining cherries from a bowl. Top each slice with whipped cream and garnish with fresh mint leaves.

SERVINGS: 12 TO 16 • PREPARATION TIME: 30 MINUTES PLUS BAKING AND SIMMERING

POACHING FRUIT IN LIQUOR IS AN EXCELLENT WAY TO MARRY FLAVORS. AS YOU SIMMER THE WINE, THE LIQUID REDUCES, AS DOES THE ALCOHOL CONTENT. WHAT REMAINS IS THE ESSENCE OF THE WINE; THIS IS WHY CHOOSING A GOOD QUALITY WINE FOR THIS AND ALL RECIPES THAT CALL FOR IT, IS PARAMOUNT.

ORANGE OIL IS A VERY CON-CENTRATED ESSENCE OF ORANGE. IT IS STRONGER THAN ORANGE FLAVORING. YOU CAN FIND IT AT GOURMET MARKETS OR ONLINE AT GOURMET FOOD WEB SITES. A LITTLE BIT GOES A LONG WAY, SO EXPERIMENT WITH LESS THAN YOU NEED—YOU CAN ALWAYS ADD MORE!

Pumpkin Crème Caramel

THIS WONDERFULLY RICH CUSTARD IS SERVED CHILLED, WITH THE SYRUPY
TOPPING DRIPPING OVER THE TOP. YOU CAN USE INDIVIDUAL RAMEKINS, OR
SCOOP THE CRÈME CARAMEL FROM ONE LARGE DISH.

IN ITALY, THIS DISH IS CALLED
CREMA CARAMELLS, IN SPAIN
IT'S KNOWN AS FLAN, AND IN
FRANCE, THE NAME IS CRÈME
RENVERSEE. THE CUSTARD
CAN BE FLAVORED WITH YOUR
FAVORITE ESSENCE. THE
SECRET IS TO COAT THE DISH
WITH THE CARAMEL, SO THAT
IT ENDS UP DRIZZLING OVER
THE TOP.

½ cup granulated sugar
¼ cup water

⅓ cup brown sugar
2 tablespoons honey
3 large eggs
½ cup canned pumpkin purée
½ cup cream
1 teaspoon vanilla extract
¼ teaspoon nutmeg
¼ teaspoon salt
1 12-ounce can evaporated milk

Preheat the oven to 325°.

1. Coat 6 6-ounce ramekins with vegetable oil spray (or use a 9 x
11 x 2-inch glass baking dish).

2. To make the caramel, place granulated sugar into a saucepan
over medium heat. Cover the sugar with ¼ cup water. Stir until
the sugar dissolves. Cook, without stirring, until the sugar mixture begins to turn golden, about 2 minutes. Continue cooking
until the caramel is deep golden brown, about 2 to 3 minutes
more. Carefully pour the caramel into the bottom of the
ramekins. Turn the ramekins around, in order to fully coat the
bottom of each one. Place the ramekins into a baking dish.

3. Use an electric mixer to combine the brown sugar, honey, and
eggs until smooth.

4. Stir in the pumpkin, cream, vanilla, nutmeg, salt, and evaporated milk until well blended. Divide this mixture between the
ramekins.

5. Pour hot water into the baking dish until it comes half way to
the top of the ramekins. Bake for 60 to 70 minutes, or until the
caramel is set and a knife, inserted into the center, comes out
clean. Remove the ramekins from the pan, cover and chill for at
least 4 hours.

6. Loosen the edges of the custard with a dinner knife or rubber
spatula. Place a dessert plate, upside down, on top of a ramekin.
Invert the ramekins onto a dessert plate, allowing the custard to
slip out and the caramel syrup to drizzle over the top.

SERVINGS: 6 • PREPARATION TIME: 30 MINUTES PLUS BAKING AND CHILLING

Pumpkin Tofu Cheesecake
with Chocolate Cookie Crumb Crust

YOU WON'T MISS THE CREAM CHEESE IN THIS WONDERFULLY TAILORED
DESSERT RECIPE. ADAPTED BY PERSONAL CHEF, LIZ BRAY FROM BENTON,
ARKANSAS, IT SATISFIES VEGAN AND CARNIVORE SWEET TOOTH'S ALIKE.

1 pound silken tofu

1 9-ounce package chocolate wafer cookies (about 40 cookies)
¼ cup canola oil

2 16-ounce cans pumpkin purée
⅓ cup honey
⅓ cup brown sugar
2 large eggs
1 teaspoon vanilla
1 tablespoon pumpkin pie spice

WHAT IS TOFU, EXACTLY?
BEAN CURD. YEP, THAT'S THE
LONG AND SHORT OF IT. TOFU
IS MADE FROM SOY BEANS. IN
ITS TOFU FORM, IT IS AN
ACCEPTABLE SUBSTITUTE FOR
EVERYTHING FROM CREAM
CHEESE TO CHICKEN! TOFU IS
FULL OF PROTEIN AND HAS A
MILD TASTE, MAKING SEASON-
ING IMPERATIVE.

Preheat the oven to 325°.
1. Remove excess moisture from tofu. Cut the tofu into slices.
Lie the tofu on paper towels or place into a colander. Use a
weight (heavy cans) to press the tofu.
2. Place the cookies in the bowl of a food processor. Pulse until
medium-size crumbs form. Add the canola oil and pulse again.
3. Press the cookie crust into the bottom, and up the sides of a
9-inch spring form pan, coated with vegetable oil spray. Bake for
8 minutes. Remove from the oven. Increase oven temperature to
350°.
4. Place the tofu into the bowl of a food processor. Add the
pumpkin, honey, brown sugar, eggs, vanilla and pumpkin pie
spice. Pulse until smooth and creamy.
5. Pour the filling into the cookie shell. Bake until the center is
set, about 50 to 60 minutes. Cool to room temperature. Chill
for at least 4 hours.

SERVINGS: 10 TO 12 • PREPARATION TIME: 30 MINUTES PLUS BAKING, AND
CHILLING

Neighborhood Ice Cream Sandwiches

DO YOU REMEMBER THE ICE CREAM TRUCK, ROLLING DOWN THE NEIGH-
BORHOOD STREETS ON A HOT AFTERNOON? NOTHING WAS AS GOOD AS THAT
TWENTY-CENT ICE CREAM SANDWICH—JUST SOFT ENOUGH TO MELT IN YOUR
MOUTH, AND CHILLY ENOUGH TO STAVE OFF THE HEAT OF SUMMER VACA-
TION. HERE'S A BIT OF A BLAST FROM THE PAST. ENJOY!

PREPARE YOUR FAMILY'S
FAVORITE ICE CREAM SAND-
WICHES WITH YOUR OWN SPE-
CIAL TWIST. USE A PREPARED
BROWNIE RECIPE, PUR-
CHASED CHOCOLATE WAFER
COOKIES, OR OVERSIZED
STORE BOUGHT CHOCOLATE
CHIP COOKIES AS A SANDWICH
BASE. ALL FLAVORS OF ICE
CREAM WILL BE FUN TO WORK
WITH. TRY COFFEE, MINT
CHIP, STRAWBERRY, OR YOUR
FAVORITE SORBET. DIP THE
SIDES OF THE SANDWICHES IN
CHOPPED NUTS, CHOPPED
MINT CANDIES, SUGAR SPRIN-
KLES OR CHOPPED CANDIED
FRUIT. YOU CAN DIP THE
SANDWICHES IN CHOCOLATE
AND PLACE THEM BACK INTO
THE FREEZER TO SET UP.

1½ cups all-purpose flour
½ cup cocoa powder
1 teaspoon baking powder
¾ cup butter, room temperature (1½ sticks)
1 cup granulated sugar
2 large eggs
1 teaspoon vanilla extract

1 pint vanilla ice cream, softened

Preheat the oven to 350°.

1. Whisk together the flour, cocoa powder and baking powder in a bowl. Set aside.

2. Use an electric mixer to combine the butter and sugar until soft and fluffy.

3. Stir in the eggs, one at a time.

4. Stir in the vanilla.

5. Stir in the flour/cocoa mixture until just combined.

6. Coat the bottom of a 13 x 17-inch rimmed baking sheet with vegetable oil spray. Line the pan with parchment paper. Allow the parchment paper to overhang both ends of the pan.

7. Pour the batter onto the parchment paper; it will be stiff. Top the batter with a sheet of plastic wrap. Use your hands to pat the plastic topped batter into the baking sheet. Remove the plastic wrap. Use a fork to poke holes in the batter to prevent it from puffing.

8. Bake for 25 to 30 minutes or until a toothpick, inserted into the center, comes out clean.

9. Cool completely in the pan. Lift the parchment paper from the pan and place it onto your work surface. Cut the cookie dough into 2 equal halves.

10. Quickly spread 1 half of the cookie dough with softened ice cream. Top with the second half. Place into the freezer for 10 minutes. Remove from the freezer and cut into squares or rectangles. Quickly wrap the ice cream sandwiches with plastic wrap and place them into the freezer.

YIELD: 10 TO 12 SANDWICHES • PREPARATION TIME: 45 MINUTES

Banana Split Bread Pudding

BAKING THE BREAD PUDDING IN A MUFFIN TIN PRODUCES INDIVIDUAL
SERVINGS, MAKING THIS A PERFECT PARTY DESSERT FOR KIDS AND US BIG-
GER KIDS.

2 cups milk
½ cup granulated sugar
3 large eggs, beaten
1 1-pound loaf cinnamon swirl bread, cut into 1-inch squares
1 cup chopped peanuts

1 pint vanilla ice cream
Chocolate Sauce (see recipe on page 343)
3 ripe bananas, sliced (about 1½ cups)
Whipped cream
Cherries

USING CINNAMON SWIRL
BREAD IN THIS RECIPE PRO-
VIDES A QUICK WAY TO SEA-
SON THE PUDDING. YOU CAN
USE PLAIN WHITE BREAD AND
ADD SPICES, CHOCOLATE, OR
DRIED FRUIT IF YOU LIKE. IF
YOU BUTTER THE BREAD,
BEFORE YOU SOAK IT IN THE
CUSTARD, THE DISH IS
CALLED BREAD AND BUTTER
PUDDING. BREAD PUDDING
CAN BE SERVED WARM OR
COLD, WITH A DESSERT
SAUCE OR CREAM.

Preheat the oven to 350°.
1. Whisk together the milk, sugar, and eggs in a bowl.
2. Toss the bread into the milk mixture, making sure that all of
the bread is submerged. Cover and place into the refrigerator,
allowing the bread to soak up all of the custard, about 15 minutes.
3. Coat a 12-cup muffin tin with vegetable oil spray. Divide the
bread mixture between the cups. Top each one with chopped
peanuts. Bake for 25 to 30 minutes or until a toothpick, inserted
into the center, comes out clean.
4. Remove from the oven and allow the bread pudding to cool.
5. Place the bread pudding into serving
dishes. Top with vanilla ice cream, chocolate
sauce, sliced bananas, whipped cream, and a
cherry on top!

SERVINGS: 12 • PREPARATION TIME: 1 HOUR

White Chocolate and Peppermint Candy

THERE IS NOTHING SIMPLER THAN THIS RECIPE FOR CHOCOLATE-MINT CANDY. YOU CAN SUBSTITUTE WITH MILK CHOCOLATE AND ADD NUTS, COCONUT OR RAISINS FOR MORE FUN!

1 small bag peppermint candies (about 2 dozen round candies)
1 11-ounce package white chocolate chips
2 tablespoons cream
¼ teaspoon peppermint extract

CHOCOLATE STARTS WITH BEANS, FERMENTED AND THEN ROASTED TO PRODUCE CHOCOLATE LIQUOR. HOW THE CHOCOLATE LIQUOR IS PROCESSED DETERMINES THE TYPE OF CHOCOLATE. WHITE CHOCOLATE, AS YOU MIGHT GUESS, CONTAINS NONE OF THE CHOCOLATE LIQUOR. IT IS A BLEND OF COCOA BUTTER, SUGAR AND MILK SOLIDS.

1. Unwrap the candies. Place them into a plastic bag. Use a rolling pin or a meat mallet to crush the candies into small crumbs.
2. Melt the white chocolate chips in the top of a double boiler over simmering water. (Alternatively, melt the chocolate in the microwave on medium heat, stirring often.) Stir in the cream.
3. Stir the peppermint extract into the melted chocolate.
4. Stir in half of the candy pieces.
5. Place a Silpat liner into a 13 x 17-inch rimmed baking sheet (or line with parchment paper).
6. Spread the melted chocolate/candy mixture into the pan, ¼-inch thick. You do not have to fill the edges of the pan.
7. Sprinkle the remaining candies over top.
8. Let the candy stand at room temperature until completely hardened, about 1 hour. Break into pieces.

YIELD: 24 1-INCH CANDY PIECES • PREPARATION TIME: 15 MINUTES

Chocolate Almond Toffee Crunch

A THERMOMETER IS A VERY USEFUL TOOL IN MONITORING THE STAGES OF
TURNING CARAMELIZED SUGAR INTO A SUBSTANCE THAT WORKS IN
CRUNCHY CANDY. WATCH YOUR THERMOMETER DO THE GUESSWORK; THIS
MIXTURE WILL BE VERY HOT AND YOU SHOULD BE CAREFUL WHEN STIRRING
AND POURING.

1 cup sliced almonds
1 cup shredded sweetened coconut
1 cup unsalted butter
1½ cups granulated sugar
½ cup water
¼ cup honey
¼ cup dark rum
2 cups semi sweet chocolate chips

WHEN IT'S TIME TO ATTEND
HOLIDAY PARTIES, HOMEMADE
CANDY MAKES AN EXCELLENT
HOSTESS GIFT! USE CHINESE
TAKE-OUT CONTAINERS, OR
SIMPLE GIFT BOXES, LINED
WITH WAXED PAPER. GOURMET
STORES SELL WAXED TISSUE
PAPER, SIMPLE GIFT BOXES,
OR BAGS. ARRANGE PIECES
OF CANDY ON CELLOPHANE
PAPER, AND TIE TOGETHER
WITH A DECORATIVE RIBBON.

Preheat the oven to 350°.

1. Place the almonds and coconut on a baking sheet and toast
until golden, about 5 minutes.

2. Melt the butter, sugar, water, honey, and rum in a saucepan
over medium high heat. Cook until the sugar is dissolved.
Continue cooking, stirring often, until the mixture reaches 300°
on a candy thermometer, about 25 to 30 minutes. Stir in the
almonds.

3. Carefully pour the toffee into a 13 x 17-inch rimmed baking
sheet, lined with a Silpat liner. Spread to about ¼-inch thickness.

4. Melt the chocolate chips in a double boiler over simmering
water (or in a microwave over medium heat).

5. Use a paper towel to wipe off any moisture, collecting on the
toffee. Spread the melted chocolate over the toffee.

6. Sprinkle the toasted coconut on top
of the chocolate. Let the candies stand
at room temperature until completely
hardened, about 1 hour. Break into
pieces.

YIELD: 24 1-INCH CANDY PIECES •
PREPARATION TIME: 45 MINUTES

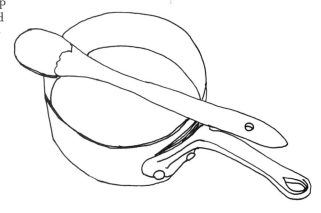

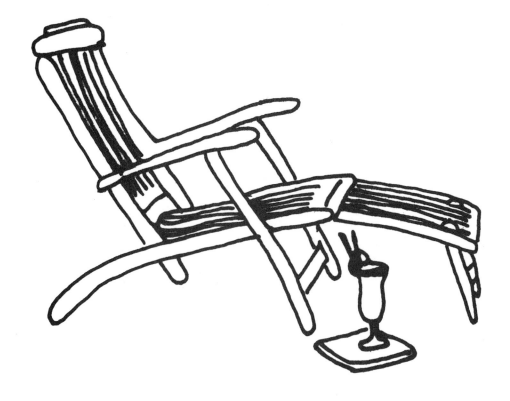

Chapter 14
Recipes for Livin' the Good Life

Celebrate Good Times
Making Every Day Special

Now that we share an enthusiasm for fresh taste, new traditions and the joy of good food, we can incorporate this passion into our busy lives. Begin with everyday meals and then reach out to family and friends. You will be surprised at just how easy it is to put everything together.

Breakfast and Brunch

MORNING HAS BROKEN
Brunch on the Back Porch

Spend time with your best friend and watch the sunrise, cherishing the beginning of a new day. Accent the menu with slices of fresh watermelon, drizzled with olive oil and splattered with fresh mint. Reserve extra muffins for weekday snacks. Good morning sunshine!

SOUTHWESTERN TORTILLA OMELET WRAP
CINNAMON SUGARED BACON
BANANA ORANGE MUFFINS

GREAT BALLS OF FIRE
Spicy Saturday Morning

Grab a pal and begin the day with a brisk walk, a summer swim or a quick trip to the gym. Follow with a peppery splurge of a breakfast. Begin with tangy Bloody Mary tomato juice, made by adding ground pepper, horseradish and a celery sprig to ordinary tomato juice.

SMOKED TROUT HASH WITH FRIED EGGS
BLUE CORNBREAD WITH RED CHILI BUTTER

HOUSE OF THE RISING SUN
Sunday Breakfast

A good night sleep is just what the doctor ordered. When you add a healthy breakfast, the rest of your day is destined to be fabulous! For an extra blast of protein, you can add Breakfast Sausage Patties made from ground turkey to the menu.

OPEN FACE EGG WHITE OMELET WITH GOAT CHEESE AND CARAMELIZED VEGGIES
GRILLED PEACH AND RED PEPPER SALSA
WHOLE WHEAT POWER MUFFINS WITH ALMOND STREUSEL TOPPING

WHAT A WONDERFUL WORLD
Lazy Weekend Brunch Splurge with Friends

Invite your long lost pals to join you for a late morning filled with good food and catch-up conversation.

EGGS BENEDICT WITH SMOKED SALMON, CAJUN HOLLANDAISE AND FRIED OYSTER GARNISH
BRAISED BABY TOMATOES, RADISHES AND CUCUMBER WITH MINT
CRISPY HASH BROWN POTATOES

THE MORNING AFTER
Relaxing Brunch

Occasionally we over-indulge, pull an all nighter studying for exams, or stay up into the wee hours watching TEVO. Whatever the reason for waking up late the next morning, nothing improves the day like a fantastic brunch. Serve the meal with sliced blood oranges, sprinkled with brown sugar, and then broiled until just bubbling. Top off the meal with a piping hot cup of Irish Coffee. (A little hair of the dog that bit ya couldn't hurt!)

PUMPKIN GRIDDLE CAKES WITH SAUTÉED APPLES
SAUTÉED CANADIAN BACON WITH MAPLE GLAZE
MANGO LEMON SNACK CAKE
IRISH COFFEE

Lunch and Snacks

LEAVIN' ON A JET PLANE
Lunchbox Special

Whether you're packing up a lunch to eat at your desk, or stuffing a paper sack to bring along on your "no frills" plane ride, this menu combination is sure to bring smiles between appointments. If you have an extra minute or two, dig out your best thermos and add ladlefuls of Easy Blender Gazpacho.

GRILLED RUM MARINATED FLANK STEAK SANDWICHES WITH CHIPOTLE LIME AIOLI
OVEN BAKED SEASONED POTATO CHIPS WITH CARAMELIZED ONION DIP
CLASSIC DATE BARS

ONE FINE DAY
Desk Top Picnic

Why not splurge during the week and create a respite for friends and coworkers? Prepare a fabulous lunch—all done in advance—and invite others to join you in the feast. Weather per-mitting, pack up your gang and your picnic, move outside to the nearest table, and inhale the sweet fresh air, while you all enjoy the fruits of your labor!

LOBSTER COBB SALAD WITH TOMATO GINGER VINAIGRETTE
CHILLED ROASTED TOMATO SOUP WITH CREAM CHEESE PESTO SWIRL AND PINE NUT GARNISH
CAROB CARROT CUPCAKES WITH TOFU "CREAM" FROSTING

I Did It My Way
Hoagie Lunch

With just a little imagination, you can vastly improve on that everyday ham and cheese with delectably satisfying results. Here is another Jon (as in turkey sub creator) invention: slice the pickles and pile them onto the sub.

JON'S TURKEY SUB WITH PESTO AND PROVOLONE
TOASTED PITA CHIPS WITH SPICY TUNA DIP
DILL PICKLES
CHOCOLATE MERINGUE COOKIES

Friday on My Mind
Luncheon with Coworkers

Since Friday commences your weekend of fun, why not move up the end of the week start date with a celebratory Friday lunch!

INSPIRED ONION AND BACON TART
MESCLUN SALAD WITH BRIE CHEESE, TOASTED ALMONDS, MANDARIN ORANGES AND SESAME DRESSING
CHOCOLATE WALNUT SHORTBREAD COOKIES

I've Got You, Babe
Share a Sammich Lunch

Is hubby working round the clock? Did Junior forget his lunch money? Don't despair! Drop what you're doing, pack up some goodies, and spend some quality time with the people you love.

THE BEST TUNA SALAD SANDWICH
SPICY POTATO SALAD
MACADAMIA NUT BUTTER COOKIES

Quarter to Three
Snack Break Treats

Make your desk a favorite stop during the workday by stashing a few of these treats in the drawer.

EASY GRANOLA AND BEST TRAIL MIX
WHITE CHOCOLATE AND PEPPERMINT CANDY
ALMOND FIG BARS
MACADAMIA AND CHOCOLATE CHIP BISCOTTI
OVER-THE-TOP POPCORN BALLS

Family Suppers

HOOKED ON A FEELING
Fish Tale Supper

Gather up the gang for a supper you can prepare in mere minutes. Swap stories round the dinner table and wait to become a legend in your own right, serving a fabulous post-dinner dessert. Prepare enough salmon to turn into salmon salad for tomorrow's lunch. Save extra squares of cake for tomorrow's after school snack.

CUMIN CRUSTED SALMON WITH TARRAGON CAPER SAUCE
CREAMY CHEESE GRITS
WILTED SPINACH SALAD WITH WARM CIDER DRESSING
GINGER APPLE CRUMB CAKE

I WANT TO HOLD YOUR HAND
Hands On Weekday Fare

Serve a meal that everyone can dig into—finger food that's fast, fabulous, and FUN.

STEAMED ARTICHOKES WITH BALSAMIC MAYONNAISE DIPPING SAUCE
QUICK FRENCH BREAD PIZZA MARGHERITA
NOT SO SLOPPY JOE HOAGIES

TAKE IT EASY
Lite and Easy Dinner

While the soup simmers, you can arrange the salad for a supper that is simple, full of veggies and pleasing to boot! Use the freshest berries available, and serve with store bought sorbet for a refreshing dessert. Garnish with fresh mint and just a dab of low fat vanilla yogurt.

GINGER LENTIL SOUP
ARRANGED GREEK SALAD WITH GRILLED CHICKEN

BORN TO BE WILD
Spiced Up Supper

Park your Harley in the garage, and settle in for a supper that's just a little bit on the wild side.

CHIPOTLE SPICED COCKTAIL MEATBALLS SIMMERED IN TOMATO SAUCE AND SERVED WITH CILANTRO CREAM
JALAPEÑO CHEESE GRIT CAKES
CHILI ROASTED CORN ON THE COBB WITH LIME CREAM
DOUBLE CHOCOLATE PHYLLO CUPS

RAINY DAYS AND MONDAYS
Blue Plate Special

The best thing about eating all of these diner favorites at home are the leftovers!

CRISP ICEBERG SALAD WITH CHIPOTLE THOUSAND ISLAND DRESSING
WARM OPEN FACE MEATLOAF SANDWICH WITH TOMATO GRAVY
CREAMED SPINACH WITH BOURSIN CHEESE
OLD-FASHIONED LEMON MERINGUE PIE

JUST CAN'T HELP MYSELF
Tummy Warming Dinner

There's no reason to feel guilty about coming back for seconds on this delicious meal. For a quick dessert, marinate sliced strawberries in a small amount of strawberry liquor while you prepare dinner. Spoon the strawberries over prepared angel food cake and top with shaved chocolate.

HOISIN AND GINGER SPICED PORK WITH VEGGIES
GINGER RISOTTO
ORANGE LACED GREEN BEANS IN WINE SAUCE

Some Kinda Wonderful
Dinners For Two

Whether you are cooking as an empty nester, newlywed or a single parent, there are many times when meals prepared and shared with your significant other are, indeed, your most cherished moments. *Fresh Traditions* has just these occasions in mind, making sure the food is leisurely prepared, designed to be eaten unhurriedly, and superlative in presentation. Since we're cooking for a mere two, we can afford to over spend on the very best ingredients. Create some space to work together in the kitchen; it's part of the FUN!

LOVE LOVE ME DO
Luscious Dinner

Take a lesson from a childhood game of tag; designate one cook to work on the appy and dessert, while the other cook assembles the ragu, grills the chops and prepares the veggies. You can always play paper-rocks-scissors for the honor of head chef!

BAKED OYSTERS ROCKEFELLER
GRILLED LAMB CHOPS WITH RAGU OF ROASTED SHALLOTS, FRESH PEAS AND MUSHROOMS
ASPARAGUS RIBBONS
CHERRIES JUBILEE

LOVE POTION NUMBER NINE
Lingering Over Dinner

Recipe for a romantic evening: Open your bottom dresser drawer. Toss in (or squeeze in!) your pager, cell phone and laptop. Repeat with your partner's electronic accessories. Now, shut the drawer. You're on you way to an excellent evening.

SILVER DOLLAR POTATO PANCAKES WITH SMOKED SALMON
ROASTED DUCK BREAST WITH POACHED CHERRY SAUCE
BABY BOK CHOY IN GINGER SOY SAUCE
PUMPKIN CRÈME CARAMEL

GOOD LOVIN'

Dinner At Dusk

Many experts suggest that dining sooner is better than later. Why not give "sooner" a try? Both you and your partner plan to leave the office a half an hour earlier than usual, and see what happens!

CLASSIC CAESAR SALAD PREPARED TABLESIDE
TEQUILA MOJO MARINATED PORK TENDERLOINS WITH BLACK BEAN SAUCE
CELERY ROOT PURÉE
TIRAMISU

SEALED WITH A KISS

Comfort Supper

Combine a few classic dishes into one lovely supper and you have a date that sparks memories while creating new ones, too!

SHRIMP AND SCALLOP MARTINIS WITH A TWIST
CHILLED GREEN SALAD WITH WARM GOAT CHEESE AND RASPBERRY VINAIGRETTE
CHICKEN CORDON BLEU
BAKED BROCCOLI WITH BROWN BUTTER BREAD CRUMBS
CLASSIC BANANA NUT BREAD

SATURDAY IN THE PARK

Supper on the Lawn

Pack your picnic basket and grab your sweetie. Spread out a blanket, pop open a bottle of wine, and dig into a meal designed to celebrate togetherness. For picnic fare, bake cupcakes instead of a layer cake. The moist cakes will last for days, even though the memory of the evening will last much longer.

CLASSIC BRUSCHETTA WITH CHOPPED TOMATOES AND BASIL
SPICY LOBSTER ROLLS WITH ORANGE SESAME MAYONNAISE
SWEET CORN CHOWDER WITH KIELBASA, PEPPERS AND CHIVES
VALENTINE'S DAY RED VELVET CAKE WITH CREAM CHEESE FROSTING

We Are Family

Fresh Traditions for Family Events

Bringing everyone together is an extraordinary accomplishment when you consider how spread apart we are as families. Not only are we separated by miles, but by careers, calendars, and time constraints. When we are, in fact, fortunate enough to share some rare free time together, why not make it a grand occasion? Plan a festive menu, prepare in advance, and be sure to accept help when offered; this recipe of protocol makes for a great party the entire family will stand up and applaud. Encore, encore!

SEE YOU IN SEPTEMBER
Graduation Party

Cover all the bases with this menu, featuring skewers of flavors from around the world. Make the skewers in advance, or simply have all the ingredients ready; invite your group to thread and grill their own. Set up a self-serve sundae bar to go with the moist cake. Freeze scoops of your favorite flavors of ice cream in a large bowl. Set out the ice cream with bowls of toppings, like crumbled cookies, whipped cream, chopped nuts, mini marshmallows, hot fudge and caramel syrups.

BEEF, ONION, PEPPER AND TOMATO KABOBS WITH CHIMICHURRI SAUCE
GRILLED MAHI MAHI SKEWERS WITH BANANA SALSA
SHERRY MARINATED SHRIMP SKEWERS WITH WARM BLACK BEAN RELISH
MEXICAN CHILI CORN AND TOMATILLO SKEWERS WITH CHIPOTLE LIME YOGURT
BARBECUED PORK TENDERLOIN SKEWERS WITH CRANBERRY, CORN AND AVOCADO RELISH
MUSTARD COATED CHICKEN SKEWERS WITH GRILLED VEGGIE SALSA
GARDEN SLAW WITH JICAMA AND GREEN APPLES
ORZO SALAD WITH SPRING VEGGIES
THREE MILKS CAKE (TRES LECHES)

TOSTADAS IN MARGARETVILLE
Birthday Party

This is a truly "hands on" party menu that both little kids and we bigger kids can enjoy. Prepare all of the ingredients and encourage your guests to build their own "TOST-Tah Dah!"

BEEF AND BEAN NACHO CASSEROLE
BEEF AND SAUTÉED ONION TOSTADAS WITH AVOCADO AND JACK CHEESE
SHREDDED BEEF TOSTADAS WITH CARAMELIZED ONIONS, SPINACH AND GOAT CHEESE
PULLED PORK TOSTADAS TOPPED WITH SPICY SLAW
SHRIMP TOSTADAS WITH TOMATILLO PURÉE AND AVOCADO SALSA
CHUTNEY SAUCED GRILLED CHICKEN AND MUSHROOM TOSTADAS
BLACK BEAN AND BUTTERNUT SQUASH TOSTADAS WITH ROASTED JALAPEÑO GARNISH
CREAMY CUCUMBER AND SWEET ONION SALAD
CLASSIC ANGEL FOOD CAKE WITH CITRUS GLAZE

AMERICAN PIE
Fourth of July Celebration

Take a shortcut or two: purchase prepared cole slaw, macaroni salad, and baked beans to round out the buffet. Better yet, ask Auntie Marge to bring her best outdoor casserole!

GRILLED GRAPE LEAF BUNDLES STUFFED WITH BRIE CHEESE
PERFECTLY GRILLED CHICKEN WITH MAPLE RUM GLAZE
GRILLED POTATO SALAD WITH SHERRY VINAIGRETTE
THREE BEAN SALAD WITH TARRAGON VINAIGRETTE
BASIL AND PARMESAN TOPPED RICOTTA BREAD
FRESH BAKED CHERRY AND APPLE PIE

NIGHTS IN WHITE SATIN
Couples Wedding Shower

A milestone occasion—your baby's getting MARRIED! Celebrate with their friends and yours. Offer two different entrées to please both sets of future family members.

SEARED TUNA NACHOS WITH WASABI CREAM SAUCE AND HOT MANGO KETCHUP
CLASSIC BEEF STROGANOFF WITH WILD MUSHROOMS
CIOPPINO SERVED OVER LINGUINI
BAKED STUFFED HEIRLOOM TOMATOES WITH GOAT CHEESE
GOLDEN STUFFED CAULIFLOWER
ORANGE BUTTER CAKE WITH MERLOT POACHED CHERRIES

TIME IN A BOTTLE
Holiday Party

Blend tradition with a fresh approach by inserting a few new recipes into your special holiday celebration.

SHERRIED CHICKEN LIVERS ON TOAST POINTS
OVEN ROASTED TURKEY WITH BRANDY SPIKED GRAVY
CARAMELIZED ONION BREAD PUDDING
MASHED SWEET POTATOES WITH MAPLE GRANOLA TOPPING
BRUSSELS SPROUTS IN HORSERADISH CREAM SAUCE
CANDY CANE TRIFLE

You've Got A Friend
Menus For Pals

Rewarding, satisfying socialization is an important part of health and happiness. Throw open your front door and invite your coworkers, new neighbors and extended family to share food and fun. Start with a great meal and you're on your way to a great time!

Reasons to Partee

SATURDAY NIGHT'S ALL RIGHT
Movie Club Supper

Assemble the gang and take in an evening movie or rent the latest DVD. Come back to your place and serve a yummy supper while everyone plays movie critic. (Don't worry about the garlic in these dishes—as long as all of you indulge, no one will notice!)

SAUSAGE AND SPINACH STUFFED MUSHROOMS
ROMAINE SALAD WITH TEN CLOVES OF GARLIC
BROILED VEAL CHOPS WITH LIME HERB BUTTER
BUTTERNUT SQUASH RISOTTO WITH WILD MUSHROOMS
FRESH BAKED GARLIC ROLLS WITH BASIL OIL DIPPING SAUCE
PUMPKIN TOFU CHEESECAKE WITH CHOCOLATE COOKIE CRUMB CRUST

Book Club Evening

Starting a book club is as easy as gathering your pals and going to the library. You choose the first selection and host the first party. From then on, everyone else takes a turn. When forming your club, think outside the box. Mother-daughter clubs, couples groups, and coworker teams are all good ways to organize.

SAUTÉED SUCCOTASH BRUSCHETTA TOPPED WITH GRILLED SHRIMP
CHICKEN CUTLETS TOPPED WITH EGGPLANT, FONTINA CHEESE AND SHERRY MUSHROOMS
SOFT GOAT CHEESE POLENTA WITH TOMATO BASIL SAUCE
SLOW SIMMERED COLLARD GREENS
SOUTHERN PECAN PIE

BRIDGE OVER TROUBLED WATER
Bridge Club Buffet

Make everything in advance and set up the buffet when your partner determines that it's your turn to be dummy. Use diamond and heart shapes to cut out the shortbread cookies. Serve the meal with iced tea and The Perfect Cup of Coffee.

CREAM OF ROASTED TOMATO SOUP WITH GRILLED CHEESE CROUTON
ASIAN INSPIRED CHICKEN SOUP
SEAFOOD SALAD IN AVOCADO BOATS
THYME ROASTED CHICKEN SALAD WITH APPLES AND ALMONDS
ORANGE COCONUT GLAZED BANANA BREAD MINI LOAVES
SHORTBREAD COOKIES
THE PERFECT CUP OF COFFEE

Ain't No Mountain High Enough
Menus for Grills and Camp Fires

ONE FINE DAY
Skillet Brunch

Pack up your cast iron skillet for a super breakfast cooked over an early morning fire. Bake the breakfast cake in advance and carry it along—just in case you forget to bring the matches!

SKILLET CORN CAKES WITH RASPBERRY BASIL JAM
GOLDEN POTATO CAKES WITH HAM
SIMPLE CHERRY BREAKFAST CAKE

BLUE MOON

Campfire Supper

To insure that you transport your food in optimum condition, remember to keep everything chilled. Form the burgers, wrap them separately and place them into your cooler. Use ice packs and frozen water bottles to surround the food, to make sure that all of the ingredients stay cold.

PRETTY PICKLES

FRESHLY GROUND BEEF BURGERS

CHEDDAR CORNBREAD

S'MORS

FIRE AND RAIN

Lunch on the Veranda

Let the weather determine whether you grill inside or out! Regardless of what Mother Nature intends to serve up, plug in your trusty panini machine and invite guests to create their own special sandwich.

CLASSIC GRILLED CHEESE SANDWICH WITH BACON AND TOMATO

GRILLED MOZZARELLA CHEESE SANDWICH WITH TUNA, RED PEPPER AND BASIL

GRILLED BRIE AND APPLE SANDWICH WITH SPICY APPLE CHUTNEY

CLASSIC CABBAGE AND CARROT COLESLAW

MAPLE PECAN BARS

LIGHT MY FIRE

Summer House Supper on the Grill

An easy way to entertain guests at your summer vacation home is to fire up the grill. For added fun, par boil the potatoes, cut them in half, drizzle with olive oil and grill them before smashing!

LEMON CHARRED CALAMARI

ROASTED PEPPERS STUFFED WITH TUNA AND OLIVE SALAD

GRILLED SWORDFISH STEAKS WITH WARM SUN-DRIED TOMATO RELISH

CREAMY SMASHED POTATOES WITH GREEN ONIONS

CHOCOLATE, BANANA AND WALNUT TRIFLE

ROLLIN' DOWN THE RIVER

Afternoon Cruise

Keep the work level down to a minimum, turn up the flavor to maximum, and get ready to entertain your sailing pals. They won't believe you can produce all of these tempting treats from one little galley.

ASPARAGUS, ROASTED PEPPER AND FONTINA CHEESE TOASTS

OPEN FACE RYE TOASTS WITH SPINACH, CANNELLINI BEANS AND WHITE CHEDDAR CHEESE

TUNA CAKES WITH AVOCADO MAYONNAISE

BANANA SPLIT BREAD PUDDINGS

Weekends with Friends

TWILIGHT TIME
Welcome Supper

When you have invited guests spending the weekend in your home, the first meal is great fun. Start the festivities with a simple yet delicious supper that sets the tone for the days that will follow.

SHRIMP SPRING ROLLS
ROASTED CHICKEN WITH HERB BUTTER
WARM BUTTERNUT SQUASH AND LENTIL SALAD
APPLE PANDOWDY

IT'S ALL IN THE GAME
Supper after Golf

Leave the scorecards at the 19th hole, and overlook your partner's toe kick out of the rough as your foursome comes together over a great meal.

EGGPLANT AND TOMATO STACKS WITH PARMIGIANO-REGGIANO
STEAK DIANE
POTATO GRATIN WITH CARAMELIZED ONIONS AND GOAT CHEESE
BRAISED BRUSSELS SPROUTS IN WINE WITH ORANGE ZEST
DARK CHOCOLATE CAKE WITH RICH CHOCOLATE ICING

REACH OUT, I'LL BE THERE
Tennis Pals Supper

Serve up a great meal to your fellow weekend warriors, after you "take no prisoners" in a friendly doubles match.

BLACK BEAN SOUP WITH DRY SHERRY FLOATER
PAN FRIED PECAN CRUSTED TROUT WITH WILTED ARUGULA SALAD
BAKED POLENTA SQUARES WITH MUSHROOM RAGU
VANILLA ICE CREAM
TOPPED WITH CHOCOLATE ALMOND TOFFEE CRUNCH PIECES

AFTER MIDNIGHT
Late Night Snack

Grab your flannel robe and mosey down to the kitchen for an oh so naughty midnight meal.

MAPLE FLAVORED FRENCH TOAST
COCONUT BATTERED APPLE RINGS

Stand By Me
Pot Luck Prizes

Use these updated classic soups and casseroles for potluck dinner with friends, at a neighborhood block party, or as a shared supper with your family meal club. The recipes can stand alone as take-along fare, but when organized, they can also provide a meal plan for busy families to follow. The idea is that each recipe can be doubled or quadrupled to feed four families of four members each. Family meal sharing groups can make use of this plan to cook once a week for all four families. Then, for the next three days, your family becomes the beneficiary of fabulous meals cooked for them—the ultimate meals on wheels!

ARE YOU LONESOME TONIGHT
Cheer Up A Friend Supper
Prepare something special for a sick pal, grieving family, or a down on his luck buddy, and you'll both feel a little bit better.

OLD WORLD CHICKEN SOUP WITH MATZO BALLS
BAKED MACARONI AND CHEESE WITH SAUSAGE CRUMBLES
JUST LIKE GRAMMY'S APPLE STRUDEL

CALIFORNIA DREAMIN'
Welcome to the Neighborhood Casserole
When the moving van rolls into the driveway next door, meet and greet your new neighbors with a tote-along meal. Remember to bring paper plates, napkins and a helping hand to unpack.

LAYERED CHOPPED VEGGIE SALAD
GREEK MOUSSAKA CASSEROLE
SAINT LOUIS GOOEY BUTTER CAKE

POPSICLES AND ICICLES
Family Supper Club Menu
Make enough to feed three other families. Pack up everything, and drop off the meal in plenty of time to drive back home and enjoy dinner with your own crew. Now, put your feet up and enjoy the rest of the week as the other families take turns bringing their dinners to you. What a fresh spin on meals on wheels!

MINESTRONE SOUP WITH ESCAROLE AND SHELLS
CHORIZO SAUSAGE AND SPICED CHICKEN CASSEROLE WITH SPANISH RICE
JULIENNE ZUCCHINI WITH SPINACH AND BASIL PESTO
NEIGHBORHOOD ICE CREAM SANDWICHES

Day by Day
Balanced Weekly Meal Plan

A successful meal plan is a healthy marriage of your family's likes and dislikes, nutritious foods, and ways around those pesky time constraints. Use this meal plan as a guideline to create one that works for you.

Sunday Brunch

THREE EGG OMELET WITH HAM AND CHEESE
GOOEY MAPLE PECAN ROLLS
SLICED TOMATOES DRIZZLED WITH BALSAMIC VINEGAR

Sunday Night Family Dinner

BRAISED LAMB WITH RED WINE TOMATO GRAVY (MAKE EXTRA)
ROASTED ROOT VEGETABLES WITH BALSAMIC GLAZE
TOSSED SALAD WITH FRESH VEGGIES
TROPICAL CARROT CAKE WITH COCONUT CREAM CHEESE FROSTING (SERVE EXTRAS DURING THE WEEK)

Monday Night Supper

GRILLED SALMON WITH MAPLE GLAZE (MAKE EXTRA)
GARLIC ROASTED CAULIFLOWER
WILTED SPINACH SALAD WITH WARM CIDER DRESSING

Tuesday's Lunch Box

SALMON SALAD MADE WITH LEFTOVERS AND THE LAST SLICE OF CARROT CAKE

Tuesday Night Supper

PASTA PUTTANESCA
BROCCOLI RABE SAUTÉED WITH GARLIC AND RED PEPPER
PARMESAN THYME BREAD
FRESH BERRIES WITH LOW FAT YOGURT

Wednesday Night Supper

MOIST AND FLUFFY TURKEY LOAF
ROASTED SPAGHETTI SQUASH WITH GARLIC BUTTER AND PARSLEY
CLASSIC DATE BARS

Thursday's Lunch Box

COLD TURKEY MEATLOAF SANDWICH ON PARMESAN THYME BREAD
ADD A CLASSIC DATE BAR FOR A SWEET SURPRISE

Thursday Night Supper

INDIVIDUAL SHEPHERD'S PIE SKILLETS (MADE WITH LEFTOVER LAMB)
OLD FASHIONED CREAMED CORN
MESCLUN SALAD

Friday Night Family Fun

MAKE YOUR OWN PANINI SANDWICHES (YOU CHOOSE YOUR FAVORITE INGREDIENTS!)
SHRIMP FAJITAS
QUESADILLA S'MORES

Saturday's on the Go Breakfast

HOMEMADE CINNAMON WAFFLES
SAUTÉED CANADIAN BACON WITH MAPLE GLAZE

Saturday's Quick Lunch

LENTIL SOUP WITH WILD MUSHROOMS (SAVE EXTRAS FOR MONDAY'S LUNCH BOX)
CALIFORNIA TURKEY CLUB WITH LEMON MAYONNAISE AND RED ONION MARMALADE

Saturday Company's Coming Dinner

CAJUN CRUSTED SCALLOPS SERVED OVER CHEDDAR GRITS WITH SPICY MARINARA SAUCE
CLASSIC CAESAR SALAD PREPARED TABLESIDE
BEEF WELLINGTON
RISOTTO PRIMAVERA
ORANGE BUTTER CAKE WITH MERLOT POACHED CHERRIES

Visit www.Jorj.com to see more weekly meal plans, menus and party plans for your *Fresh Traditions.*

Index

Almond Fig Bars, 333
anchovies
  Classic Caesar Salad Prepared Tableside, 88
  Niçoise Tuna Hoagies with Sun-Dried Tomato Vinaigrette, 127
  Olive Tapenade for Bruschetta, 148
  Pasta Puttanesca, 182
  Roasted Peppers Stuffed with Tuna and Olive Salad, 223
  Romaine Salad with Ten Cloves of Garlic Dressing, 89
  Snapper Vera Cruz, 251
apples
  Apple Pandowdy, 341
  Braised Savoy Cabbage with Apples and Cinnamon, 202
  Coconut Battered Apple Rings, 59
  Fresh Baked Cherry and Apple Pie, 340
  Garden Slaw with Jicama and Green Apples, 91
  Ginger Apple Crumb Cake, 53
  Grilled Brie and Apple Sandwich with Spicy Apple Chutney, 116
  Pumpkin Griddle Cakes with Sautéed Apples 39
  Southern Style Dressing with Sausage and Apples, 194
  Spicy Apple Chutney, 116
  Thyme-Roasted Chicken Salad with Apples and Almonds, 259
Arranged Greek Salad with Grilled Chicken, 99
artichokes
  Baby Artichoke Risotto, 184
  Braisesd Baby Artichokes in Lemon Cream Sauce, 207
  Braised Chicken Pieces with Chorizo Sausage and Baby Artichokes, 257
  Fried Baby Artichokes, 207
  Grilled Artichokes in Tarragon Sauce, 206
  Orange Roughy Oreganato, 252
  Sherry Marinated Shrimp Skewers with Warm Black Bean Relish, 132
  Steamed Artichokes with Balsamic Mayonnaise Dipping Sauce, 206
arugula
  Pan-Fried Pecan Crusted Trout with Wilted Arugula Salad, 247
  Whole Trout Stuffed with Eggplant and Arugula with Lemon Rosemary Butter Sauce 248

Asian Inspired Chicken Soup, 73
asparagus
  Asparagus and Spinach Pancakes, 161
  Asparagus Ribbons, 219
  Asparagus, Roasted Pepper, and Fontina Cheese Toasts, 105
  Grilled Radicchio, Asparagus, Roasted Pepper, and Mozzarella Panini, 120
  Orzo Salad with Spring Veggies, 189
  Risotto Primavera, 184
avocado
  Barbecued Pork Tenderloin Skewers with Cranberry, Corn and Avocado Relish, 134
  Beef and Sautéed Onion Tostadas with Avocado and Jack Cheese, 138
  Seafood Salad in Avocado Boats, 28
  Shrimp Tostadas with Tomatillo Purée and Avocado Salsa, 142
  Tuna Cakes with Avocado Mayonnaise, 238
Authentic Cuban Sandwiches, 119

B

Baby Artichoke Risotto, 184
baby back ribs, beer-basted, with Jack Daniels barbecue sauce, 294
Baby Bok Choy in Ginger Soy Sauce, 203
bacon
  Cinnamon Sugared Bacon, 25
  Classic Grilled Cheese Sandwich with Bacon and Tomato, 114
  Green Beans with Bacon, 218
  Sautéed Canadian Bacon with Maple Glaze, 25
Baked Broccoli with Brown Buttered Bread Crumbs, 200
Baked Butternut Squash Purée with Mint and Cardamom, 132
Baked Cauliflower with Cashews, 216
Baked Halibut with Julienne Vegetables and Buttery Dill Sauce, 239
Baked Macaroni and Cheese with Sausage Crumbles, 176
Baked Oysters Rockefeller, 159
Baked Polenta Squares with Mushroom Ragu, 191
Baked Stuffed Lobster in Mornay Sauce, 232
Baked Stuffed Heirloom Tomatoes with Goat Cheese, 204
Baking Tostadas, 142

bananas
  Banana Orange Muffins, 49
  Banana Split Bread Pudding, 349
  Chocolate, Banana, and Walnut Trifle, 338
  Classic Banana Nut Bread, 46
  Grilled Mahi Mahi Skewers with Banana Salsa, 131
  Mocha French Toast Waffles with Caramelized Bananas, 42
  Orange Coconut Glazed Banana Bread Mini Loaves, 47
bar cookies
  Almond Fig Bars, 333
  Classic Date Bars, 332
  Maple Pecan Bars, 319
Bar Keeper's Snack, 172
barley
  Lentil and Barley Soup, 81
  Red Bean Soup with Barley and Diced Ham, 81
Barbecued Pork Tenderloin Skewers with Cranberry, Corn and Avocado Relish, 134
barramundi
  Pan-Sautéed Barramundi with Dilled Cream and Caper Sauce, 243
  Roasted Barramundi with Banana Salsa, 243
Basil and Parmesan Topped Ricotta Bread, 68
beans
  Beef and Bean Nacho Casserole, 162
  Black Bean and Butternut Squash Tostadas with Roasted Jalapeño Garnish, 139
  Black Bean Soup with Dry Sherry Floater, 80
  Chopped Kale with Navy Beans, 197
  Jambalaya, 187
  Open Face Rye Toasts with Spinach, Cannellini Beans, and White Cheddar Cheese, 106
  Red Bean Soup with Barley and Diced Ham, 81
  Sherry Marinated Shrimp Skewers with Warm Black Bean Relish, 132
  Swiss Chard with Red Beans, 197
  Tequila Mojo-Marinated Pork Tenderloins with Black Bean Sauce, 292
  Three Bean Salad with Tarragon Vinaigrette, 102
  Turkey and White Bean Chili, 276
  White Bean Dip, 155
beef
  Beef and Bean Nacho Casserole, 162
  Beef and Sautéed Onion Tostadas with Avocado and Jack Cheese, 138
  Beef Brisket Braised in Beer, 287
  Beef Burgers with Gorgonzola, 117
  Beef, Onions, Pepper, and Tomato Kabobs with Chimichurri Sauce, 130
  Beef Short Ribs in Red Wine Sauce, 288
  Beef Wellington, 280
  Chipotle-Spiced Cocktail Meatballs Simmered in Tomato Sauce and Served with Cilantro Cream, 158
  Classick Beef Stroganoff with Wild Mushrooms, 284
  French Dip Sandwiches with Au Jus, 107
  Freshly Ground Beef Burgers, 117
  Grilled Rum Marinated Flank Steak Sandwiches with Chipotle Lime Aioli, 108
  Grilled Steak, 133
  Ground Meat and Peas, 285
  Herbed Beef Burgers, 117
  Mustard-Crusted Broiled Skirt Steak, 283
  Not So Sloppy Joe Hoagies, 118
  Pan-Seared Steaks with Bordelaisse Sauce, 281
  Roast Beef, 107
  Shredded Beef Tostadas with Caramelized Onions, Spinach, and Goat Cheese, 136
  Slow-Cooked Barbecued Beef, 289
  Steak "Diane," 282
  Warm Open Face Meatloaf Sandwich with Tomato Gravy, 112
  Yankee Pot Roast, 286
Beer-Basted Baby Back Ribs with Jack Daniels Barbecue Sauce, 294
beets
  Best Beets, 226
  Marinated Beets, 226
Best Beets, 226
Best Trail Mix, 172
beverages, see coffee
Bimini Bread, 66
biscotti, macadamia and chocolate chip, 331
Biscuits N' Gravy with Country Sausage, 26
Black Bean and Butternut Squash Tostadas with Roasted Jalapeño Garnish, 139
Black Bean Soup with Dry Sherry Floater, 80
Blanched Veggie Pickles, 199
blueberry buttermilk pancakes, double, with blueberry syrup, 38
Blue Corn Bread with Red Chile Butter, 64
bok choy
  Baby Bok Choy in Ginger Soy Sauce, 203
  Grilled Baby Bok Choy with Dijon Vinaigrette, 203
Boursin cheese, creamed spinach with, 224

Braised Baby Artichokes in Lemon Cream Sauce, 207

Braised Baby Tomatoes, Radishes, and Cucumber with Mint. 205

Braised Brussels Sprouts in Wine with Orange Zest, 215

Braised Brussels Sprouts with Herbs, 215

Braised Chicken Pieces with Chorizo Sausage and Baby Artichokes, 257

Braised Lamb Risotto, 184

Braised Lamb with Fennel, 302

Braised Lamb with Red Wine Tomato Gravy, 302

Braised Savoy Cabbage with Apples and Cinnamon, 202

bread pudding
    Banana Split Bread Pudding, 349
    Caramelized Onion Bread Pudding, 193

Breakfast Grits, 192

Breakfast Sausage Patties, 27

Brie
    Grilled Brie and Apple Sandwich with Spicy Apple Chutney, 116
    Grilled Grape Leaf Bundles Stuffed with Brie Cheese and Chutney, 171
    Mesclun Salad with Brie Cheese, Toasted Almonds, Mandarin Oranges, and Sesame Dressing, 95

broccoli
    Asian Inspired Chicken Soup, 73
    Baked Broccoli with Brown Buttered Bread Crumbs, 200
    Broccoli with Ginger Sauce, 200
    Sautéed Broccoli with Lemon, 200

broccoli rabe
    Broccoli Rabe Sautéed with Garlic and Red Pepper, 201
    Lasagna with Broccoli Rabe, 201
    Pasta with Broccoli Rabe, Sun-Dried Tomatoes, and Fresh Mozzarella, 201

Broiled Veal Chops with Lime Herb Butter, 311

Broiled Veggies, 135

bruschetta
    Classic Bruschetta with Chopped Tomatoes and Basil, 148
    Parmesan Thyme Bruschetta, 69
    Sautéed Succotash Bruschetta Topped with Grilled Shrimp, 149

Brussels sprouts
    Braised Brussels Sprouts with Herbs, 215
    Brussels Sprouts in Horseradish Cream Sauce, 214

butter cake, St. Louis gooey, 51

Buttermilk Biscuits, 26

Buttermilk Fried Chicken, 260

Butternut Squash Purée, 220

Butternut Squash Risotto with Wild Mushrooms, 185

C

cabbage
    Braised Savoy Cabbage with Apples and Cinnamon, 202
    Cabbage with Caraway Seeds, 202
    Cabbage with Pepper and Garlic, 202
    Classic Cabbage and Carrot Coleslaw, 90
    Our Grandma's Stuffed Cabbage Rolls, 274
    Pulled Pork Tostadas Topped with Spicy Slaw, 140

Caesar salad, classic, prepared tableside, 88

Cajun Crusted Scallops Served Over Cheddar Grits with Tomato Hot Sauce, 150

Cajun Spice Mix, 29

cakes
    Carob Carrot Cupcakes with Tofu Cream Frosting, 324
    Classic Angel Food Cake with Lemon Glaze, 329
    Dark Chocolate Cake with Rich Chocolate Icing, 328
    Ginger Apple Crumb Cake, 53
    Mango Lemon Snack Cake, 52
    Orange Butter Cake with Merlot Poached Cherries, 344
    Saint Louis Gooey Butter Cake, 51
    Simple Cherry Breakfast Cake, 55
    Sour Cream Coffee Cake with Pecan and Pear Filling, 54
    Three Milks Cake (Tres Leches), 325
    Tropical Carrot Cake with Coconut Cream Cheese Frosting, 322
    Valentine's Day Red Velvet Cake with Walnut Cream Cheese Frosting, 326

calamari
    Fried Calamari with Tuna Caper Dipping Sauce, 230
    Lemon Charred Calamari, 231
    Seafood Risotto, 184

California Turkey Club with Lemon Mayonnaise and Red Onion Marmalade, 109

candy
    Chocolate Almond Toffee Crunch, 351

White Chocolate and Peppermint Candy, 350
Candy Cane Trifle, 337
Caramelized Onion Bread Pudding, 193
Carob Carrot Cupcakes with Tofu Cream
  Frosting, 324
carrots
  Baked Halibut with Julienne Vegetables and
    Buttery Dill Sauce, 239
  Carob Carrot Cupcakes with Tofu Cream
    Frosting, 324
  Classic Cabbage and Carrot Coleslaw, 90
  Hoisin and Ginger Spiced Pork with Veggies,
    293
  Individual Shepherd's Pie Skillets, 301
  Moroccan Spiced Braised Veal Shanks with
    Toasted Orzo, 308
  Osso Buco with Gremolata Garnish, 306
  Poached Sole with GInger, Green Onions, and
    Carrots, 250
  Roasted Root Vegetables with Balsamic Glaze,
    221
  Sunday Night Roasted Leg of Lamb with Brown
    Veggies and Dark Gravy, 296
  Tropical Carrot Cake with Coconut Cream
    Cheese Frosting, 322
  Yankee Pot Roast, 286
casseroles
  Beef and Bean Nacho Casserole, 162
  Chorizo Sausage and Spiced Chicken Casserole
    with Spanish Rice, 188
  Greek Moussaka Casserole, 293
  Turkey La Bamba Casserole, 273
cauliflower
  Baked Cauliflower with Cashews, 216
  Garlic Roasted Cauliflower, 217
  Golden Stuffed Cauliflower, 216
Celery Root Purée, 211
char, pan-seared Arctic, with Watercress Sauce,
  246
Cheddar Corn Bread, 63
cheesecake, pumpkin tofu, with chocolate cookie
  crumb crust, 347
cherries
  Cherries Jubilee, 344
  Fresh Baked Cherry and Apple Pie, 340
  Orange Butter Cake with Merlot Poached
    Cherries, 344
  Roast Duck Breasts with Poached Cherry Sauce,
    278
  Simple Cherry Breakfast Cake, 55

chicken
  Arranged Greek Salad with Grilled Chicken,
    99
  Asian Inspired Chicken Soup, 73
  Braised Chicken Pieces with Chorizo Sausage
    and Baby Artichokes, 257
  Buttermilk Fried Chicken, 260
  Chicken a la King Served Over Pasta Rags, 180
  Chicken Cacciatore, 256
  Chicken Cordon Bleu, 267
  Chicken Cutlets Topped with Eggplant,
    Fontina Cheese, and Sherry Mushrooms, 269
  Chicken Finger Salad with Roasted Garlic
    Ranch Dressing, 262
  Chicken Liver Pâté, 167
  Chorizo Sausage and Spiced Chicken Casserole
    with Spanish Rice, 188
  Chutney Sauced Grilled Chicken and
    Mushroom Tostadas, 144
  Colombian Style Chicken Soup with Jalapeño
    Relish, 74
  Individual Chicken Pot Pies, 264
  Lemon Caper Chicken Cutlets, 266
  Lemon Ginger Chicken, 266
  Mustard-Coated Chicken Skewers with Grilled
    Veggie Salsa, 135
  Old World Chicken Soup with Matzo Balls, 72
  Pepperoni Stuffed Chicken Breasts with Red
    Bell Pepper Sauce, 268
  Open Faced Sautéed Chicken Liver and Fried
    Egg Sandwich with Red Onion, 113
  Oven-Fried Chicken, 261
  Pasta with Zucchini, Chicken, and Pesto, 225
  Perfectly Grilled Chicken with Maple Rum
    Glaze, 263
  Roasted Chicken with Herb Butter, 258
  Rumaki, 166
  Sautéed Chicken Livers on Toast Points, 167
  Thyme-Roasted Chicken Salad with Apples and
    Almonds, 259
  Traditional Chicken Francese, 265
chilean sea bass, yogurt-marinated, with coconut
  and chutney, 241
Chili Roasted Corn on the Cob with Lime
  Cream, 209
chili, turkey and white bean, 276
Chilled Green Salad with Warm Goat Cheese and
  Raspberry Vinaigrette, 97
Chilled Roasted Tomato Soup with Cream Cheese
  Pesto Swirl and Toasted Pine Nuts, 78

Chipotle Spiced Cocktail Meatballs Simmered in
    Tomato Sauce and Served with Cilantro
    Cream, 158
Chips, 254
chocolate
    Chocolate Almond Toffee Crunch, 351
    Chocolate Meringue Cookies, 321
    Chocolate Walnut Shortbread Cookies, 335
    Chocolate, Banana, and Walnut Trifle, 338
    Dark Chocolate Cake with Rich Chocolate Icing
        328
    Double Chocolate Phyllo Cups, 316
    Macadamia and Chocolate Chip Biscotti, 331
    Pumpkin Tofu Cheesecake with Chocolate
        Cookie Crumb Crust, 347
    Quesadilla S'Mores, 343
    S'Mores, 342
    Warm Chocolate Sauce, 343
    White Chocolate and Peppermint Candy, 350
Chopped Kale with Navy Beans, 197
Chorizo Sausage and Spiced Chicken Casserole
    with Spanish Rice, 188
chowder
    New England Style Clam Chowder, 82
    Sweet Corn Chowder with Kielbasa, Peppers
        and Chives, 83
chutney
    Chutney-Sauced Grilled Chicken and
        Mushroom Tostadas, 144
    Grilled Grape Leaf Bundles Stuffed with Brie
        Cheese and Chutney, 171
    Spicy Apple Chutney, 116
    Yogurt-Marinated Chilean Sea Bass with
        Coconut and Chutney, 241
Cinnamon Sugared Bacon, 25
Cioppino Served Over Linguini, 181
Citrus Pull-Apart Rolls, 62
clams
    Cioppino Served Over Linguini, 181
    New England Style Clam Chowder, 82
Classic Angel Food Cake with Lemon Glaze, 329
Classic Banana Nut Bread, 46
Classic Beef Stroganoff with Wild Mushrooms,
    284
Classic Bruschetta with Chopped Tomatoes and
    Basil, 148
Classic Cabbage and Carrot Coleslaw, 90
Classic Caesar Salad Prepared Tableside, 88
Classic Date Bars, 322
Classic Grilled Cheese Sandwich with Bacon and
    Tomato, 114

Classic Shrimp Cocktail, 151
coconut
    Coconut Battered Apple Rings, 59
    Orange Coconut Glazed Banana Bread Mini
        Loaves, 47
    Tropical Carrot Cake with Coconut Cream
        Cheese Frosting, 322
    Yogurt-Marinated Chilean Sea Bass with
        Coconut and Chutney, 241
Coddled Eggs, 88
coffee
    Irish Coffee, 45
    Mexican Coffee, 44
    Perfect Cup of Coffee, The, 44
coleslaw, classic cabbage and carrot, 90
collard greens
    Kielbasa and Collard Greens, 196
    Slow-Simmered Collard Greens, 196
Colombian Style Chicken Soup with Jalapeño
    Relish, 74
Cooked Custard Variation (Tiramisu), 336
cookies, *also see* bar cookies
    Chocolate Meringue Cookies, 321
    Chocolate Walnut Shortbread Cookies, 335
    Macadamia Nut Butter Cookies, 330
    Shortbread Cookies, 334
Coquilles St. Jacques, 234
corn bread
    Blue Corn Bread with Red Chile Butter, 64
    Cheddar Corn Bread, 63
corn
    Barbecued Pork Tenderloin Skewers with
        Cranberry, Corn and Avocado Relish, 134
    Chili Roasted Corn on the Cob with Lime
        Cream, 209
    Mexican Chili Corn and Tomatillo Skewers
        with Chipotle Lime Yogurt, 133
    Old-Fashioned Creamed Corn, 208
    Southwestern Style Creamed Corn, 208
    Sweet Potato and Toasted Corn Pancakes, 161
corn cakes, skillet, with raspberry basil jam, 40
Corned Beef Hash with Poached Eggs, 23
Cornish hens, Moroccan spiced, with forty cloves
    of garlic, 271
Cornmeal Waffles with Pecan Honey Butter, 36
crab
    Sautéed Crab Cakes with Three Sauces, 236
    Shellfish Cannelloni, 176
cranberries
    Barbecued Pork Tenderloin Skewers with
        Cranberry, Corn and Avocado Relish, 134

Simply Roasted Duck with Orange Cranberry Glaze, 277

Creamed Spinach with Boursin Cheese, 224

Cream of Roasted Tomato Soup with Grilled Cheese Croutons, 76

Creamy Cheese Grits, 192

Creamy Cucumber and Sweet Onion Salad, 101

Creamy Mustard Sauce, 127

Creamy Smashed Parmesan Potatoes with Green Onions, 210

Crisp Iceberg Salad with Chipotle Thousand Island Dressing, 96

Crispy Hash Brown Potatoes, 30

croutons
Croutons, 88
Red Onion Soup with Sun-Dried Tomato and Gruyere Crouton, 84
Three Onion and Tequila Soup with Fried Tortellini Crouton, 85

cucumbers
Braised Baby Tomatoes, Radishes, and Cucumbers with Mint, 205
Creamy Cucumber and Sweet Onion Salad, 101
Dill Pickles, 198
Orzo Salad with Spring Veggies, 189

Cumin Crusted Salmon with Tarragon Caper Sauce, 244

cupcakes, carob carot, with tofu cream frosting, 324

custard
Cooked Custard Variation, 336
Pumpkin Crème Caramel, 346

D

Dark Chocolate Cake with Rich Chocolate Icing, 328

date bars, classic, 332

Dill Pickles, 198

dip, white bean, 155

Diver Scallops with Peas, Wild Mushrooms, and Cabernet Sauce, 235

Double Blueberry Buttermilk Pancakes with Blueberry Syrup, 38

Double Chocolate Phyllo Cups, 316

doughnuts, Tuesday's cake, 58

dressing, southern style, with sausage and apples, 194

duck
Roasted Duck Breasts with Poached Cherry Sauce, 278
Simply Roasted Duck with Orange Cranberry Glaze, 277

E

Easy Blender Gazpacho Soup, 79

Easy Granola and Best Trail Mix, 172

Edamame with Lemon Pepper-Flavored Salt, 173

Edamame with Wasabi Dipping Sauce, 173

eggplant
Chicken Cutlets Topped with Eggplant, Fontina Cheese, and Sherry Mushrooms, 269
Eggplant and Tomato Stacks with Parmigiano-Reggiano, 153
Greek Moussaka Casserole, 298
Mustard-Coated Chicken Skewers with Grilled Veggie Salsa, 135
Stuffed Eggplant "Sandwiches" with Tomato Relish, 123
Whole Trout Stuffed with Eggplant and Arugula with Lemon Rosemary Butter Sauce, 248

eggs
Coddled Eggs, 88
Corned Beef Hash with Poached Eggs, 23
Eggs Benedict with Smoked Salmon, Cajun Hollandaise and Fried Oyster Garnish, 29
Incredibly Easy Eggs Benedict, 28
Open Faced Sautéed Chicken Liver and Fried Egg Sandwich with Red Onion, 113
Open Face Egg White Omelet with Goat Cheese and Caramelized Veggies, 22
Original Quiche Lorraine, 32
Sausage and Mushroom Strata, 34
Smoked Trout Hash with Fried Eggs, 24
Southwestern Tortilla Omelet Wrap, 21
Three Egg Omelet with Ham and Cheese, 20

F

fajitas, shrimp, 229

French bread pizza Margherita, quick, 104

French Dip Sandwiches with Au Jus, 107

French toast
Maple Flavored French Toast, 41
Mocha French Toast Waffles with Caramelized Bananas, 42

Fresh Baked Cherry and Apple Pie, 340

Fresh Baked Garlic Rolls with Basil Oil for Dipping, 67

Freshly Ground Beef Burgers, 117
Freshly Ground Pork, Veal and Turkey Burgers, 117
Fresh Sea Bass Provençal, 242
Fried Baby Artichokes, 207
Fried Calamari with Tuna Caper Dipping Sauce, 230
Fried Ginger, 87
Fried Oysters, 29
Fried Tilapia Fingers, 254
Fried Tortellini, 85

G

Garden Slaw with Jicama and Green Apples, 91
garlic
    Garlic Roasted Cauliflower, 217
    Romaine Salad with Ten Cloves of Garlic Dressing, 89
ginger
    Ginger and Soy Marinated Halibut, 240
    Ginger Apple Crumb Cake, 53
    Ginger Lentil Soup, 87
    Ginger Risotto, 186
    Lobster Cobb Salad with Tomato Ginger Vinaigrette, 100
goat cheese
    Baked Stuffed Heirloom Tomatoes with Goat Cheese, 204
    Chilled Green Salad with Warm Goat Cheese and Raspberry Vinaigrette, 97
    Goat Cheese and Pancetta Wontons with Oriental Dipping Sauce, 169
    Open Face Egg White Omelet with Goat Cheese and Caramelized Veggies, 22
    Potato Gratin with Caramelized Onions and Goat Cheesse, 212
    Shredded Beef Tostadas with Caramelized Onions, Spinach, and Goat Cheese, 136
    Soft Goat Cheese Polenta with Tomato Basil Sauce, 190
Golden Mashed Potatoes, 210
Golden Potato Cakes with Ham, 31
Golden Stuffed Cauliflower, 216
Gooey Maple Pecan Rolls, 60
granola, easy, and best trail mix, 172
grape leaf bundles stuffed with Brie cheese and chutney, grilled, 171
Greek Moussaka Casserole, 298
Greek salad, arranged, with grilled chicken, 99

green beans
    Green Beans with Bacon, 218
    Orange-Laced Green Beans in Wine Sauce, 218
Green Beans with Mushrooms, 218
Grilled Artichokes with Tarragon Sauce, 206
Grilled Baby Bok Choy with Dijon Vinaigrette, 203
Grilled Brie and Apple Sandwich with Spicy Apple Chutney, 116
grilled cheese sandwich, classic, with bacon and tomato, 114
Grilled Grape Leaf Bundles Stuffed with Brie Cheese and Chutney, 171
Grilled Lamb Chops with Ragu of Roasted Shallots, Fresh Peas, and Mushrooms, 300
Grilled Mahi Mahi Skewers with Banana Salsa, 131
Grilled Mozzarella Cheese Sandwich with Tuna, Red Pepper and Basil, 115
Grilled Peach and Pepper Salsa, 156
Grilled Potato Salad with Dijon Vinaigrette, 93
Grilled Radicchio, Asparagus, Roasted Pepper, and Mozzarella Panini, 120
Grilled Ratatouille Vegetable Sandwich with Fontina Cheese, 111
Grilled Rum Marinated Flank Steak Sandwiches with Chipotle Lime Aioli, 108
Grilled Salmon with Maple Orange Glaze, 245
Grilled Steak, 133
Grilled Swordfish Steaks with Warm Sun-Dried Tomato Relish, 253
grits
    Breakfast Grits, 192
    Cajun Crusted Scallops Served Over Cheddar Grits with Tomato Hot Sauce, 150
    Creamy Cheese Grits, 192
    Jalapeño Cheese Grit Cakes, 192
Ground Meat and Peas, 285
Ground Turkey Meatballs and Ground Turkey Mini-loaves, 272
Gruyere, Sun-Dried Tomato and Watercress Panini with Olive Tapenade, 121

H

halibut
    Baked Halibut with Julienne Vegetables and Buttery Dill Sauce, 239
    Ginger and Soy Marinated Halibut, 240
ham
    Authentic Cuban Sandwiches, 119

Golden Potato Cakes with Ham, 31
Monte Cristo Sandwich with Mustard Jam, 122
Red Bean Soup with Barley and Diced Ham, 81
hash
Corned Beef Hash with Poached Eggs, 23
Smoked Trout Hash with Fried Eggs, 24
Herbed Beef Burgers, 117
hoagies, not so sloppy Joes, 118
Hoisin and Ginger Spiced Pork with Veggies, 293
Hollandaise Sauce, 28
Homemade Cinnamon Waffles, 35
Hot Mango Ketchup, 165

I

ice cream sandwiches, neighborhood, 348
Incredibly Easy Eggs Benedict, 28
Individual Chicken Pot Pies, 264
Individual Shepherd's Pie Skillets, 301
Inspired Onion and Bacon Tart, 33
Irish Coffee, 45
Irish Soda Bread, 65
Italian Braised Beef Short Ribs, 288

J

Jalapeño Cheese Grit Cakes, 192
Jambalaya, 187
Jon's Turkey Sub with Pesto and Provolone, 110
Julienne Zucchini with Spinach and Basil Pesto, 225
Just Like Grammy's Apple Strudel, 314

K

kale, chopped, with navy beans, 197
keilbasa
Kielbasa with Broccoli Rabe, 201
Sweet Corn Chowder with Kielbasa, Peppers and Chives, 83
Kicked Up Spinach, 197

L

lamb
Braised Lamb Risotto, 184
Braised Lamb with Fennel, 302
Braised Lamb with Red Wine Tomato Gravy, 302
Greek Moussaka Casserole, 298

Grilled Lamb Chops with Ragu of Roasted Shallots, Fresh Peas, and Mushrooms, 300
Individual Shepherd's Pie Skillets, 301
Marinated Lamb Shoulder Chops, 303
Sage Marinated Braised Lamb, 302
Sunday Night Roasted Leg of Lamb with Brown Veggies and Dark Gravy, 296
Layered Chopped Veggie Salad, 98
lemon
California Turkey Club with Lemon Mayonnaise and Red Onion Marmalade, 109
Classic Angel Food Cake with Lemon Glaze, 329
Lemon Baked Pork Chops with Green Peppercorn Sauce, 291
Lemon Caper Chicken Cutlets, 265
Lemon Charred Calamari, 231
Lemon Ginger Chicken, 266
Mango Lemon Snack Cake, 52
Old-Fashioned Lemon Meringue Pie, 320
lentils
Ginger Lentil Soup, 87
Lentil and Barley Soup, 81
Lentil Soup with Wild Mushrooms, 86
Warm Butternut Squash and Lentil Salad, 220
lobster
Baked Stuffed Lobster in Mornay Sauce, 232
Lobster Cobb Salad with Tomato Ginger Vinaigrette, 100
Lobster in Arrabiata Sauce, 233
Lobster Ravioli with Brown Butter Sage Sauce, 170
New England Style Lobster Roll, 124
Seafood Salad in Avocado Boats, 228
Shellfish Cannelloni, 176
Spicy Lobster Rolls with Orange Sesame Mayonnaise, 125

M

Macadamia and Chocolate Chip Biscotti, 331
Macadamia Nut Butter Cookies, 330
macaroni and cheese, baked, with sausage crumbles, 176
mahi mahi
Grilled Mahi Mahi Skewers with Banana Salsa, 131
mangoes
Hot Mango Ketchup, 165
Mango Lemon Snack Cake, 52

Seared Tuna Nachos with Wasabi Cream and Hot Mango Ketchup, 164
maple
Gooey Maple Pecan Rolls, 60
Grilled Salmon with Maple Orange Glaze, 245
Maple Flavored French Toast, 41
Maple Pecan Bars, 319
Mashed Sweet Potatoes with Maple Granola Topping, 213
Perfectly Grilled Chicken with Maple Rum Glaze, 263
Sautéed Canadian Bacon with Maple Glaze, 25
marinara sauce, simple, 305
Marinated Beets, 226
Marinated Lamb Shoulder Chops, 303
Marinating Turkey, 270
Mashed Potatoes, 112
Mashed Sweet Potatoes with Maple Granola Topping, 213
Mashed Sweet Potatoes with Rum "Gravy," 213
meatballs
Chipotle-Spiced Cocktail Meatballs Simmered in Tomato Sauce and Served with Cilantro Cream, 158
Swedish Meatballs, 157
meatloaf
Warm Open Face Meatloaf Sandwich with Tomato Gravy, 112
Mesclun Salad with Brie Cheese, Toasted Almonds, Mandarin Oranges, and Sesame Dressing, 95
Mexican Chili Corn and Tomatillo Skewers with Chipotle Lime Yogurt, 133
Mexican Coffee, 44
Minestrone Soup with Escarole and Shells, 77
Mocha French Toast Waffles with Caramelized Bananas, 42
Moist and Fluffy Turkey Loaf, 272
Monte Cristo Sandwich with Mustard Jam, 122
More Ways with Roasted Veggies, 221
Moroccan Spiced Braised Veal Shanks with Toasted Orzo, 308
Moroccan Spiced Cornish Hens with Forty Cloves of Garlic, 271
muffins
Banana Orange Muffins, 49
Chutney Sauced Grilled Chicken and Mushroom Tostadas, 144
Pumpkin Pie Muffins with Walnut Topping, 48
Whole Wheat Power Muffins with Almond Streusel Topping, 50

mushrooms
Baked Polenta Squares with Mushroom Ragu, 191
Chicken Cutlets Topped with Eggplant, Fontina Cheese, and Sherry Mushrooms, 269
Classic Beef Stroganoff with Wild Mushrooms, 284
Coquilles St. Jacques, 234
Diver Scallops with Peas, Wild Mushrooms, and Cabernet Sauce, 235
Green Beans with Mushrooms, 218
Grilled Lamb Chops with Ragu of Roasted Shallots, Fresh Peas, and Mushrooms, 300
Lentil Soup with Wild Mushrooms, 86
Sausage and Mushroom Strata, 34
Sausage and Spinach Stuffed Mushrooms, 152
Veal Marsala, 304
Veal Rollatini with Mushrooms and Leeks, 305
Mustard Coated Chicken Skewers with Grilled Veggie Salsa, 135
Mustard-Crusted Broiled Skirt Steak, 283
Mustard-Glazed Tomatoes, 204

N

nachos
Beef and Bean Nacho Cassesrole, 162
Seared Tuna Nachos with Wasabi Cream and Hot Mango Ketchup, 164
Ultimate Nachos, 162
Neighborhood Ice Cream Sandwiches, 348
New England Style Clam Chowder, 82
New England Style Lobster Roll, 124
Niçoise Tuna Hoagies with Sun-Dried Tomato Vinaigrette, 127
Not So Sloppy Joe Hoagies, 118

O

Old-Fashioned Creamed Corn, 208
Old-Fashioned Lemon Meringue Pie, 320
Old-Fashioned Scottish Scones, 56
Old World Chicken Soup with Matzo Balls, 72
olives
Arranged Greek Salad with Grilled Chicken, 99
Fresh Sea Bass Provençal, 242
Grilled Swordfish Steaks with Warm Sun-Dried Tomato Relish, 253

Niçoise Tuna Hoagies with Sun-Dried Tomato Vinaigrette, 127

Olive Tapenade for Bruschetta, 148

Orange Roughy Oreganato, 252

Pasta Puttanesca, 182

Roasted Peppers Stuffed with Tuna and Olive Salad, 223

Shrimp and Scallop Martinis with a Twist, 151

Spaghetti Squash Puttanesca, 183

Tapenade, 121

omelets

Open Face Egg White Omelet with Goat Cheese and Caramelized Veggies, 22

Southwestern Tortilla Omelet Wrap, 21

Three Egg Omelet with Ham and Cheese, 20

onions

Beef and Sautéed Onion Tostadas with Avocado and Jack Cheese, 138

Beef, Onions, Pepper, and Tomato Kabobs with Chimichurri Sauce, 130

California Turkey Club with Lemon Mayonnaise and Red Onion Marmalade, 109

Caramelized Onion Bread Pudding, 193

Creamy Cucumber and Sweet Onion Salad, 101

Hoisin and Ginger Spiced Pork with Veggies, 293

Open Faced Sautéed Chicken Liver and Fried Egg Sandwich with Red Onion, 113

Oven-Baked Seasoned Potato Chips with Caramelized Onion Dip, 154

Poached Sole with Ginger, Green Onions, and Carrots, 250

Potato Gratin with Caramelized Onions and Goat Cheese, 212

Red Onion Soup with Sun-Dried Tomato and Gruyere Crouton, 84

Roasted Root Vegetables with Balsamic Glaze, 221

Shredded Beef Tostadas with Caramelized Onions, Spinach, and Goat Cheese, 136

Sunday Night Roasted Leg of Lamb with Brown Veggies and Dark Gravy, 296

Three Onion and Tequila Soup with Fried Tortellini Crouton, 85

Open Faced Sautéed Chicken Liver and Fried Egg Sandwich with Red Onion, 113

Open Face Egg White Omelet with Goat Cheese and Caramelized Veggies, 22

Open Face Rye Toasts with Spinach, Cannellini Beans, and White Cheddar Cheese, 106

Orange Roughy Oreganato, 252

oranges

Mesclun Salad with Brie Cheese, Toasted Almonds, Mandarin Oranges, and Sesame Dressing, 95

Orange Butter Cake with Merlot Poached Cherries, 344

Orange Coconut Glazed Banana Bread Mini Loaves, 47

Orange-Laced Green Beans in Wine Sauce, 218

Simply Roasted Duck with Orange Cranberry Glaze, 277

Original Quiche Lorraine, 32

orzo

Moroccan Spiced Braised Veal Shanks with Toasted Orzo, 308

Orzo Salad with Spring Veggies, 189

Osso Buco with Gremolata Garnish, 306

Our Grandma's Stuffed Cabbage Rolls, 274

Oven-Baked Seasoned Potato Chips with Caramelized Onion Dip, 154

Oven-Fried Chicken, 261

Oven-Roasted Turkey with Brandy Spiked Gravy, 270

Over-the-Top Popcorn Balls, 174

oysters

Baked Oysters Rockefeller, 159

Eggs Benedict with Smoked Salmon, Cajun Hollandaise and Fried Oyster Garnish, 29

Fried Oysters, 29

Oyster Shooters, 160

P

pancakes

Asparagus and Spinach Pancakes, 161

Double Blueberry Buttermilk Pancakes with Blueberry Syrup, 38

Pancakes to Go, 161

Pumpkin Griddle Cakes with Sautéed Apples 39

Silver Dollar Potato Pancakes with Smoked Salmon, 160

Skillet Corn Cakes with Raspberry Basil Jam, 40

Sweet Potato and Toasted Corn Pancakes, 161

pandowdy, apple, 341

Pan-Fried Pecan Crusted Trout with Wilted Arugula Salad, 247

panini
  Grilled Radicchio, Asparagus, Roasted Pepper,
    and Mozzarella Panini, 120
  Gruyere, Sun-Dried Tomato and Watercress
    Panini with Olive Tapenade, 121
Pan-Sautéed Barramundi with Dilled Cream and
  Caper Sauce, 243
Pan-Seared Arctic Char with Watercress Sauce,
  246
Pan-Seared Steaks with Bordelaise Sauce, 281
Parmesan Thyme Bread, 69
Parmesan Thyme Bruschetta, 69
Pasta for Ravioli, 170
Pasta Puttanesca, 182
Pasta with Broccoli Rabe, Sun-Dried Tomatoes
  and Fresh Mozzarella, 201
Pasta with Zucchini, Chicken and Pesto, 225
peaches
  Grilled Peach and Pepper Salsa, 156
pears
  Sour Cream Coffee Cake with Pecan and Pear
    Filling, 54
  Sour Cream Oatmeal Waffles with Grilled Pear
    Slices, 37
peas
  Chicken a la King Served Over Pasta Rags, 180
  Diver Scallops with Peas, Wild Mushrooms, and
    Cabernet Sauce, 235
  Grilled Lamb Chops with Ragu of Roasted
    Shallots, Fresh Peas, and Mushrooms, 300
  Ground Meat and Peas, 285
  Individual Chicken Pot Pies, 264
  Individual Shepherd's Pie Skillets, 301
  Orzo Salad with Spring Vegetables, 189
  Risotto Primavera, 184
pecans
  Cornmeal Waffles with Pecan Honey Butter, 36
  Easy Granola and Best Trail Mix, 172
  Gooey Maple Pecan Rolls, 60
  Maple Pecan Bars, 319
  Pan-Fried Pecan Crusted Trout with Wilted
    Arugula Salad, 247
  Sour Cream Coffee Cake with Pecan and Pear
    Filling, 54
  Southern Pecan Pie, 318
Pepperoni Stuffed Chicken Breasts with Red Bell
  Pepper Sauce, 268
peppers, roasted, stuffed with tuna and olive
  salad, 223
Perfectly Grilled Chicken with Maple Rum Glaze,
  263

pesto
  Chilled Roasted Tomato Soup with Cream
    Cheese Pesto Swirl and Toasted Pine Nuts, 78
  Grilled Radicchio, Asparagus, Roasted Pepper,
    and Mozzarella Panini, 120
  Grilled Ratatouille Vegetable Sandwich with
    Fontina Cheese, 111
  Jon's Turkey Sub with Pesto and Provolone, 110
  Julienne Zucchini with Spinach and Basil
    Pesto, 225
  Pasta with Zucchini, Chicken, and Pesto, 225
pickles
  Blanched Veggie Pickles, 199
  Dill Pickles, 198
  Pretty Pickles with Ginger, 199
  Spiced Pickles, 199
pies
  Fresh Baked Cherry and Apple Pie, 340
  Old-Fashioned Lemon Meringue Pie, 320
  Southern Pecan Pie, 318
pita chips, toasted, with spicy tuna dip, 155
Poached Sole with Ginger, Green Onions. and
  Carrots, 250
poblano peppers
  Lobster in Arrabiata Sauce, 232
  Mustard-Coated Chicken Skewers with Grilled
    Veggie Salsa, 135
  Roasted Poblano Peppers, 222
  Stuffed Poblano Peppers with Roasted Tomato
    Sauce, 222
polenta
  Baked Polenta Squares with Mushroom Ragu,
    191
  Soft Goat Cheese Polenta with Tomato Basil
    Sauce, 190
popcorn
  Over-the-Top Popcorn Balls, 174
  Popcorn Bars, 174
pork
  Authentic Cuban Sandwiches, 119
  Barbecued Pork Tenderloin Skewers with
    Cranberry, Corn and Avocado Relish, 134
  Chipotle-Spiced Cocktail Meatballs Simmered
    in Tomato Sauce and Served with Cilantro
    Cream, 158
  Freshly Ground Pork, Veal and Turkey Burgers,
    117
  Hoisin and Ginger Spiced Pork with Veggies,
    293
  Lemon Baked Pork Chops with Green
    Peppercorn Sauce, 291

Pork Spare Ribs with Sauerkraut, 295
Pulled Pork Tostadas Topped with Spicy Slaw, 140
Sausage Stuffed Pork Roast, 290
Tequila Mojo-Marinated Pork Tenderloins with Black Bean Sauce, 292
potatoes
    Creamy Smashed Parmesan Potatoes with Green Onions, 210
    Crispy Hash Brown Potatoes, 30
    Golden Potato Cakes with Ham, 31
    Grilled Potato Salad with Dijon Vinaigrette, 93
    Individual Shepherd's Pie Skillets, 301
    Mashed Potatoes, 112
    Mashed Sweet Potatoes with Maple Granola Topping, 213
    Mashed Sweet Potatoes with Rum "Gravy," 213
    Oven-Baked Seasoned Potato Chips with Caramelized Onion Dip, 154
    Potato Gratin with Caramelized Onions and Goat Cheese, 211
    Potato Gratin with Fontina Cheese and Roasted Garlic, 212
    Roasted Root Vegetables with Balsamic Glaze, 221
    Silver Dollar Potato Pancakes with Smoked Salmon, 160
    Spicy Potato Salad, 92
    Sunday Night Roasted Leg of Lamb wih Brown Veggies and Dark Gravy, 296
    Sweet Potato and Toasted Corn Pancakes, 161
    Ways with Potato Gratin for Brunch, 212
    Yankee Pot Roast, 286
pot pie, veal and veggie, 309
pot roast, Yankee, 286
Pretty Pickles with Ginger, 199
Pulled Pork Tostadas Topped with Spicy Slaw, 140
Pumpkin Crème Caramel, 346
Pumpkin Griddle Cakes with Sautéed Apples 39
Pumpkin Pie Muffins with Walnut Topping, 48
Pumpkin Tofu Cheesecake with Chocolate Cookie Crumb Crust, 347

Q

Quesadilla S'mores, 343
quiche Lorraine, original, 32
Quick French Bread Pizza Margherita, 104

R

radicchio, asparagus, roasted pepper, and mozzarella panini, grilled, 120
raspberries
    Chilled Green Salad with Warm Goat Cheese and Raspberry Vinaigrette, 97
    Skillet Corn Cakes with Raspberry Basil Jam, 40
ratatouille
    Grilled Ratatouille Vegetable Sandwich with Fontina Cheese, 111
    Ratatouille Salad, 111
ravioli
    Lobster Ravioli with Brown Butter Sage Sauce, 170
    Pasta for Ravioli, 170
    Veal and Spinach-Filled Ravioli with Sherry Cream Sauce, 177
Red Bean Soup with Barley and Diced Ham, 81
Red Bean Soup with Sausage and Orzo, 81
Red Onion Marmalade, 109
Red Onion Soup with Sun-Dried Tomato and Gruyere Crouton, 84
red velvet cake, Valentine's Day, with walnut cream cheese frosting, 326
Red Wine Sauce, 280
ribs
    Beef Short Ribs in Red Wine Sauce, 288
    Beer-Basted Baby Back Ribs with Jack Daniels Barbecue Sauce, 294
    Italian Braised Beef Short RIbs, 288
    Pork Spare Ribs with Sauerkraut, 295
rice, *also see* risotto
    Chorizo Sausage and Spiced Chicken Casserole with Spanish Rice, 188
    Jambalaya, 187
    Stuffed Poblano Peppers with Roasted Tomato Sauce, 222
ricotta bread, basil and Parmesan topped, 63
risotto
    Baby Artichoke Risotto, 184
    Braised Lamb Risotto, 184
    Butternut Squash Risotto with Wild Mushooms, 185
    Ginger Risotto, 186
    Risotto Primavera, 184
    Seafood Risotto, 184
Roast Beef, 107
Roasted Barramundi with Banana Salsa, 243
Roasted Bell Peppers, 105
Roasted Celery Root, 211

Roasted Chicken with Herb Butter, 258
Roasted Duck Breasts with Poached Cherry Sauce, 278
Roasted Peppers Stuffed with Tuna and Olive Salad, 223
Roasted Poblano Peppers, 222
Roasted Root Vegetables with Balsamic Glaze, 221
Roasted Spaghetti Squash with Cumin Oil, 183
Roasted Spaghetti Squash with Garlic Butter and Parsley, 183
rolls
    Citrus Pull-Apart Rolls, 62
    Gooey Maple Pecan Rolls, 60
    Fresh Baked Garlic Rolls with Basil Oil for Dipping, 67
Romaine Salad with Ten Cloves of Garlic Dressing, 89
rum
    Chocolate Almond Toffee Crunch, 357
    Grilled Rum Marinated Flank Steak Sandwiches with Chipotle Lime Aoli, 108
    Mashed Sweet Potatoes with Rum "Gravy," 213
    Mocha French Toast Waffles with Caramelized Bananas, 42
    Perfectly Grilled Chicken with Maple Rum Glaze, 263
    Southern Pecan Pie, 318
    Three Milks Cake (Tres Leches), 325
Rumaki, 166

S

Sage Marinated Braised Lamb, 302
Saint Louis Gooey Butter Cake, 51
salads, 88-102
    Best Tuna Salaad Sandwich, 126
    Chicken Finger Salad with Roasted Garlic Ranch Dressing, 262
    New England Style Lobster Roll, 124
    Niçoise Tuna Hoagies with Sun-Dried Tomato Vinaigrette, 127
    Orzo Salad with Spring Veggies, 189
    Pan-Fried Pecan Crusted Trout with Wilted Arugula Salad, 247
    Roast Peppers Stuffed With Tuna and Olive Salad, 223
    Seafood Salad in Avocado Boats, 228
    Shrimp and Scallop Martinis with a Twist, 151
    Spicy Lobster Rolls with Orange Sesame Mayonnaise, 125
    Thyme-Roasted Chicken Salad with Apples and Almonds, 259
    Warm Butternut Squash and Lentil Salad, 220
salmon
    Cumin Crusted Salmon with Tarragon Caper Sauce, 244
    Eggs Benedict with Smoked Salmon, Cajun Hollandaise and Fried Oyster Garnish, 29
    Grilled Salmon with Maple Orange Glaze, 245
    Silver Dollar Potato Pancakes with Smoked Salmon, 160
salsa
    Grilled Mahi Mahi Skewers with Banana Salsa, 131
    Grilled Peach and Pepper Salsa, 156
    Mustard-Coated Chicken Skewers with Grilled Veggie Salsa, 135
    Shrimp Tostadas with Tomatillo Purée and Avocado Salsa, 142
sauce
    Creamy Mustard Sauce, 127
    Hollandaise Sauce, 28
    Red Wine Sauce, 280
    Warm Chocolate Sauce, 343
sauerkraut, pork spare ribs with, 295
sausage
    Baked Macaroni and Cheese with Sausage Crumbles, 176
    Biscuits N' Gravy with Country Sausage, 26
    Braised Chicken Pieces with Chorizo Sausage and Baby Artichokes, 257
    Breakfast Sausage Patties, 27
    Chorizo Sausage and Spiced Chicken Casserole with Spanish Rice, 188
    Red Bean Soup with Sausage and Orzo, 81
    Sausage and Mushroom Strata, 34
    Sausage and Spinach Stuffed Mushrooms, 152
    Sausage Stuffed Pork Roast, 290
    Southern Style Dressing with Sausage and Apples, 194
Sautéed Broccoli with Lemon, 200
Sautéed Canadian Bacon with Maple Glaze, 25
Sautéed Crab Cakes with Three Sauces, 236
Sautéed Succotash Bruschetta Topped with Grilled Shrimp, 149
scallops
    Cajun Crusted Scallops Served Over Cheddar Grits with Tomato Hot Sauce, 150
    Cioppino Served Over Linguini, 181
    Coquilles St. Jaques, 234

Diver Scallops with Peas, Wild Mushrooms, and Cabernet Sauce, 235
Seafood Risotto, 184
Shrimp and Scallop Martinis with a Twist, 151
scones
Old-Fashioned Scottish Scones, 56
Strawberry Buttermilk Scones, 57
sea bass
Fresh Sea Bass Provençal, 242
Yogurt-Marinated Chilean Sea Bass with Coconut and Chutney, 241
Seafood Risotto, 184
Seafood Salad in Avocado Boats, 228
Seared Tuna Nachos with Wasabi Cream and Hot Mango Ketchup, 164
Shellfish Cannelloni, 176
Sherried Chicken Livers on Toast Points, 167
Sherry Marinated Shrimp Skewers with Warm Black Bean Relish, 132
Shortbread Cookies, 334
Shredded Beef Tostadas with Caramelized Onions, Spinach, and Goat Cheese, 136
shrimp
Cioppino Served Over Linguini, 181
Classic Shrimp Cocktail, 151
Jambalaya, 187
Sautéed Succotash Bruschetta Topped with Grilled Shrimp, 149
Seafood Risotto, 184
Seafood Salad in Avocado Boats, 228
Shellfish Cannelloni, 176
Sherry Marinated Shrimp Skewers with Warm Black Bean Relish, 132
Shrimp and Scallop Martinis with a Twist, 151
Shrimp Fajitas, 229
Shrimp Spring Rolls, 168
Shrimp Tostadas with Tomatillo Purée and Avocado Salsa, 142
Silver Dollar Potato Pancakes with Smoked Salmon, 160
Simple Cherry Breakfast Cake, 55
Simple Marinara Sauce, 305
Simply Roasted Duck with Orange Cranberry Glaze, 277
Skillet Corn Cakes with Raspberry Basil Jam, 40
slaw
Classic Cabbage and Carrot Coleslaw, 90
Garden Slaw with Jicama and Green Apples, 91
Pulled Pork Tostadas Topped with Spicy Slaw, 140
Slow-Cooked Barbecued Beef, 289

Slow Cooker Minestrone, 77
Slow-Roasted Cherry Tomatoes, 205
Slow Simmered Collard Greens, 196
Smoked Trout Hash with Fried Eggs, 24
S'mores, 342
Snapper Vera Cruz, 251
Soft Goat Cheese Polenta with Tomato Basil Sauce, 190
sole
Poached Sole with Ginger, Green Onions, and Carrots, 250
Sole Meuniere, 249
Sour Cream Coffee Cake with Pecan and Pear Filling, 54
Sour Cream Oatmeal Waffles with Grilled Pear Slices, 37
Southern Pecan Pie, 318
Southern Style Dressing with Sausage and Apples, 194
Southwestern Spice Grits, 192
Southwestern Style Creamed Corn, 208
Southwestern Tortilla Omelet Wrap, 21
Spaghetti Squash Puttanesca, 183
Spiced Pickles, 199
spice mix, Cajun, 29
Spicy Apple Chutney, 116
Spicy Lobster Rolls with Orange Sesame Mayonnaise, 125
Spicy Potato Salad, 92
spinach
Asparagus and Spinach Pancakes, 161
Baked Oysters Rockefeller, 159
Creamed Spinach with Boursin Cheese, 224
Julienne Zucchini with Spinach and Basil Pesto, 225
Kicked Up Spinach, 197
Open Face Rye Toasts with Spinach, Cannellini Beans, and White Cheddar Cheese, 106
Shredded Beef Tostadas with Caramelized Onions, Spinach, and Goat Cheese, 136
Veal and Spinach-Filled Ravioli with Sherry Cream Sauce, 177
Wilted Spinach Salad with Warm Cider Dressing, 94
spring rolls, shrimp, 168
squash
Baked Butternut Squash Purée with Mint and Cardamom, 132
Baked Halibut with Julienne Vegetables and Buttery Dill Sauce, 239

Black Bean and Butternut Squash Tostadas with Roasted Jalapeño Garnish, 139
Blanched Veggie Pickles, 199
Butternut Squash Purée, 220
Butternut Squash Risotto with Wild Mushrooms, 185
Grilled Ratatouille Vegetable Sandwich with Fontina Cheese, 111
Mexican Chili Corn and Tomatillo Skewers with Chipotle Lime Yogurt, 133
Moroccan Spiced Braised Veal Shanks with Toasted Orzo, 308
Moroccan Spiced Cornish Hens with Forty Cloves of Garlic, 271
Pretty Pickles with Ginger, 199
Risotto Primavera, 184
Roasted Spaghetti Squash with Cumin Oil, 183
Roasted Spaghetti Squash with Garlic Butter and Parsley, 183
Sausage and Spinach Stuffed Mushrooms, 152
Spaghetti Squash Puttanesca, 183
Warm Butternut Squash and Lentil Salad, 220
steak
   Grilled Rum Marinated Flank Steak Sandwiches with Chipotle Lime Aioli, 108
   Grilled Steak, 133
   Mustard-Crusted Broiled Skirt Steak, 283
   Pan-Seared Steaks with Bordelaise Sauce, 281
   Steak "Diane," 282
Steamed Artichokes with Balsamic Mayonnaise Dipping Sauce, 206
strata, sausage and mushroom, 34
Strawberry Buttermilk Scones, 57
Stuffed Eggplant "Sandwiches" with Tomato Relish, 123
Stuffed Poblano Peppers with Roasted Tomato Sauce, 222
Sunday Night Roasted Leg of Lamb with Brown Veggies and Dark Gravy, 296
Swedish Meatballs, 157
Sweet Corn Chowder with Kielbasa, Peppers and Chives, 83
sweet potatoes
   Mashed Sweet Potatoes with Maple Granola Topping, 213
   Mashed Sweet Potatoes with Rum "Gravy," 213
   Moroccan Spiced Braised Veal Shanks with Toasted Orzo, 308
   Roasted Root Vegetables with Balsamic Glaze, 221
   Sweet Potato and Toasted Corn Pancakes, 161

Swiss Chard with Red Beans, 197
swordfish steaks, grilled, with warm sun-dried tomato relish, 253

T

tapenades
   Olive Tapenade for Bruschetta, 148
   Tapenade, 121
tart, inspired onion and bacon, 33
Tequila Mojo-Marinated Pork Tenderloins with Black Bean Sauce, 292
The Best Tuna Salad Sandwich, 126
The Perfect Cup of Coffee, 44
Three Bean Salad with Tarragon Vinaigrette, 102
Three Egg Omelet with Ham and Cheese, 20
Three Milks Cake (Tres Leches), 325
Three Onion and Tequila Soup with Fried Tortellini Crouton, 85
Thyme-Roasted Chicken Salad with Apples and Almonds, 259
tilapia fingers, fried, 254
Tiramisu, 336
Toasted Pine Nuts, 78
Toasted Pita Chips with Spicy Tuna Dip, 155
tomatillos
   Mexican Chili Corn and Tomatillo Skewers with Chipotle Lime Yogurt, 133
   Shrimp Tostadas with Tomatillo Purée and Avocado Salsa, 142
tomatoes
   Baked Stuffed Heirloom Tomatoes with Goat Cheese, 204
   Beef, Onions, Pepper, and Tomato Kabobs with Chimichurri Sauce, 130
   Braised Baby Tomatoes, Radishes, and Cucumbers with Mint, 205
   Braised Lamb with Red Wine Tomato Gravy, 302
   Cajun Crusted Scallops Served Over Cheddar Grits with Tomato Hot Sauce, 150
   Chicken Cacciatore, 256
   Chipotle-Spiced Cocktail Meatballs Simmered in Tomato Sauce and Served with Cilantro Cream, 158
   Chilled Roasted Tomato Soup with Cream Cheese Pesto Swirl and Toasted Pine Nuts, 78
   Classic Bruschetta with Chopped Tomatoes and Basil, 148
   Classic Grilled Cheese Sandwich with Bacon and Tomato, 114

Cream of Roasted Tomato Soup with Grilled Cheese Croutons, 76
Easy Blender Gazpacho Soup, 79
Eggplant and Tomato Stacks with Parmigiano-Reggiano, 153
Grilled Swordfish Steaks with Warm Sun-Dried Tomato Relish, 253
Gruyere, Sun-Dried Tomato and Watercress Panini with Olive Tapenade, 121
Italian Braised Beef Short Ribs, 288
Lobster Cobb Salad with Tomato Ginger Vinaigrette, 100
Lobster in Arrabatia Sauce, 233
Mustard-Coated Chicken Skewers with Grilled Veggie Salsa, 135
Mustard-Glazed Tomatoes, 204
Niçoise Tuna Hoagies with Sun-Dried Tomato Vinaigrette, 127
Orzo Salad with Spring Veggies, 189
Osso Buco with Gremolata Garnish, 306
Oyster Shooters, 160
Pasta with Broccoli Rabe, Sun-Dried Tomatoes, and Fresh Mozzarella, 201
Pepperoni Stuffed Chicken Breasts with Red Bell Pepper Sauce, 268
Quick French Bread Pizza Margherita, 104
Red Onion Soup with Sun-Dried Tomato and Gruyere Crouton, 84
Simple Marinara Sauce, 305
Slow-Roasted Cherry Tomatoes, 205
Snapper Vera Cruz, 251
Soft Goat Cheese Polenta with Tomato Basil Sauce, 190
Stuffed Eggplant "Sandwiches" with Tomato Relish, 123
Stuffed Poblano Peppers with Roasted Tomato Sauce, 222
Tomato Bread Salad, 204
Warm Open Face Meatloaf Sandwich with Tomato Gravy, 112
tortellini, fried, 85
Traditional Chicken Francese, 265
trail mix, best, 172
trifle
Candy Cane Trifle, 337
Chocolate, Banana, and Walnut Trifle, 338
Tropical Carrot Cake with Coconut Cream Cheese Frosting, 322
trout
Pan-Fried Pecan Crusted Trout with Wilted Arugula Salad, 247

Whole Trout Stuffed with Eggplant and Arugula with Lemon Rosemary Butter Sauce, 248
Tuesday's Cake Doughnuts, 58
tuna
Best Tuna Salad Sandwich, The, 126
Fried Calamari with Tuna Caper Dipping Sauce, 230
Grilled Mozzarella Cheese Sandwich with Tuna, Red Pepper and Basil, 115
Niçoise Tuna Hoagies with Sun-Dried Tomato Vinaigrette, 127
Roasted Peppers Stuffed with Tuna and Olive Salad, 223
Seared Tuna Nachos with Wasabi Cream and Hot Mango Ketchup, 164
Toasted Pita Chips with Spicy Tuna Dip, 155
Tuna Cakes with Avocado Mayonnaise, 238
Tuna Melt, The, 126
turkey
California Turkey Club with Lemon Mayonnaise and Red Onion Marmalade, 109
Ground Turkey Meatballs and Ground Turkey Mini-loaves, 272
Jon's Turkey Sub with Pesto and Provolone, 110
Marinating Turkey, 270
Moist and Fluffy Turkey Loaf, 272
Monte Cristo Sandwich with Mustard Jam, 122
Oven-Roasted Turkey with Brandy Spiked Gravy, 270
Turkey and White Bean Chili, 276
Turkey La Bamba Casserole, 273

U

Ultimate Nachos, 162

V

Valentine's Day Red Velvet Cake with Walnut Cream Cheese Frosting, 326
veal
Broiled Veal Chops with Lime Herb Butter, 311
Freshly Ground Pork, Veal and Turkey Burgers, 117
Moroccan Spiced Braised Veal Shanks wih Toasted Orzo, 308
Osso Buco with Gremolata Garnish, 306
Swedish Meatballs, 157

Veal and Spinach-Filled Ravioli with Sherry Cream Sauce, 177
Veal and Veggie Pot Pie, 309
Veal Chops Milanese, 310
Veal Marsala, 304
Veal Rollatini with Mushrooms and Leeks, 305

W

waffles
  Cornmeal Waffles with Pecan Honey Butter, 36
  Homemade Cinnamon Waffles, 35
  Mocha French Toast Waffles with Caramelized Bananas, 42
  Sour Cream Oatmeal Waffles with Grilled Pear Slices, 37
Warm Butternut Squash and Lentil Salad, 220
Warm Chocolate Sauce 343
Warm Open Face Meatloaf Sandwich with Tomato Gravy, 112
watercress
  Gruyere, Sun-Dried Tomato and Watercress Panini with Olive Tapenade, 121
  Lobster Cobb Salad with Tomato Ginger Vinaigrette, 100
  Pan-Seared Arctic Char with Watercress Sauce, 246
Ways with Potato Gratin for Brunch, 212
White Bean Dip, 155
White Chocolate and Peppermint Candy, 350

Whole Trout Stuffed with Eggplant and Arugula with Lemon Rosemary Butter Sauce, 248
Whole Wheat Herb Bread, 69
Whole Wheat Power Muffins with Almond Streusel Topping, 50
Wilted Spinach Salad with Warm Cider Dressing, 94
wontons, goat cheese and pancetta, with Oriental dipping sauce, 169

Y

Yankee Pot Roast, 286
Yogurt-Marinated Chilean Sea Bass with Coconut and Chutney, 241

Z

zucchini
  Baked Halibut with Julienne Vegetables and Buttery Dill Sauce, 239
  Grilled Ratatouille Vegetable Sandwich with Fontina Cheese, 111
  Julienne Zucchini with Spinach and Basil Pesto, 225
  Mexican Chili Corn and Tomatillo Skewers with Chipotle Lime Aioli, 133
  Pasta with Zucchini, Chicken, and Pesto, 225
  Pretty Pickles with Ginger, 199
  Risotto Primavera, 184